수능 내신 1등급 대비 전국연합 학력평가

20일 완성 영어 독해

빈칸순삽입

기본

수능 모의고사 전문 출판
입시플라이

수능 내신 영어 1등급
결론은 '빈순삽'

수능과 내신에서 영어 1등급을 위한 핵심은 [빈칸 추론·글의 순서·문장 삽입] 유형입니다. **이 세 가지 유형은 8문항으로 전체 45문항 중 18% 밖에 안 되지만, [빈칸 추론·글의 순서·문장 삽입] 유형의 정답 여부로 1등급, 2등급, 3등급이 결정됩니다.**

해마다 수능에서 **영어 등급을 결정하는 대표적 '오답률 1위'는 역시 [빈칸 추론]**이며, 그 뒤로 [글의 순서, 문장 삽입]으로 이어지기 때문에 **수능과 내신 '영어 1등급을 목표'한다면 반드시 이 세 가지 유형을 정복**해야 합니다.

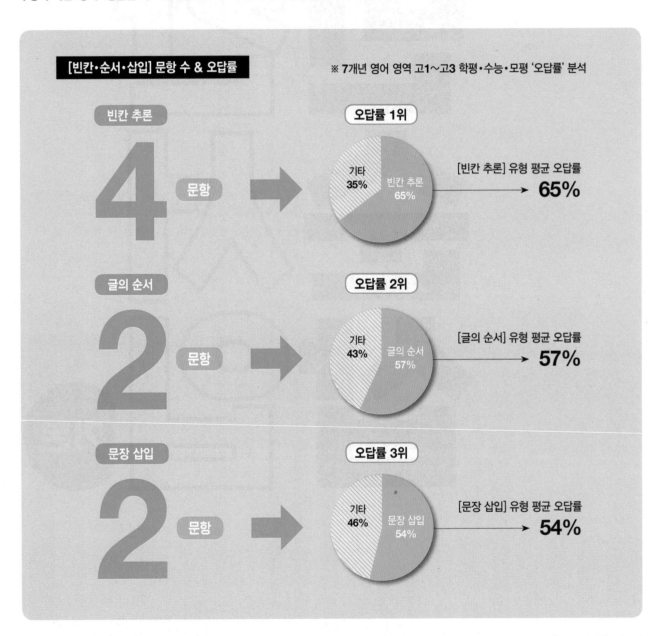

[빈칸·순서·삽입] 문항 수 & 오답률

※ 7개년 영어 영역 고1~고3 학평·수능·모평 '오답률' 분석

빈칸 추론

4 문항 →

오답률 1위

기타 35%
빈칸 추론 65%

[빈칸 추론] 유형 평균 오답률 → **65%**

글의 순서

2 문항 →

오답률 2위

기타 43%
글의 순서 57%

[글의 순서] 유형 평균 오답률 → **57%**

문장 삽입

2 문항 →

오답률 3위

기타 46%
문장 삽입 54%

[문장 삽입] 유형 평균 오답률 → **54%**

※ 오답률 **60% 이상**의 고난도 문제 중 **70%**는 [빈칸·순서·삽입] 유형이며, 최근에는 *[빈칸 추론] 문제뿐 아니라 [글의 순서]와 [문장 삽입] 문제들도 어렵게 출제*된 경우가 많았습니다.

※ 오답률 집계는 기관에 따라 오차가 있을 수 있습니다.

하루 12문제 20분 20일
영어 '1등급' 완성

[빈칸 추론·글의 순서·문장 삽입] 유형의 문제가 모두 어려운 것은 아닙니다. 하루 12문제씩, 20분 학습에는 평이한 문제부터 고난도 2점, 고난도 3점 문항까지 적절히 난이도를 분산 배치해 학습 부담은 낮추고, 효과는 최대한 올릴 수 있도록 '20일 완성'으로 구성했습니다.
[빈칸 추론·글의 순서·문장 삽입] 유형의 문제를 대비하는 가장 좋은 방법은 최근 수능에 출제되었던 기출 문제와 학력평가 문제들을 토대로 '다양한 지문의 문제를 풀어보는 것'입니다.

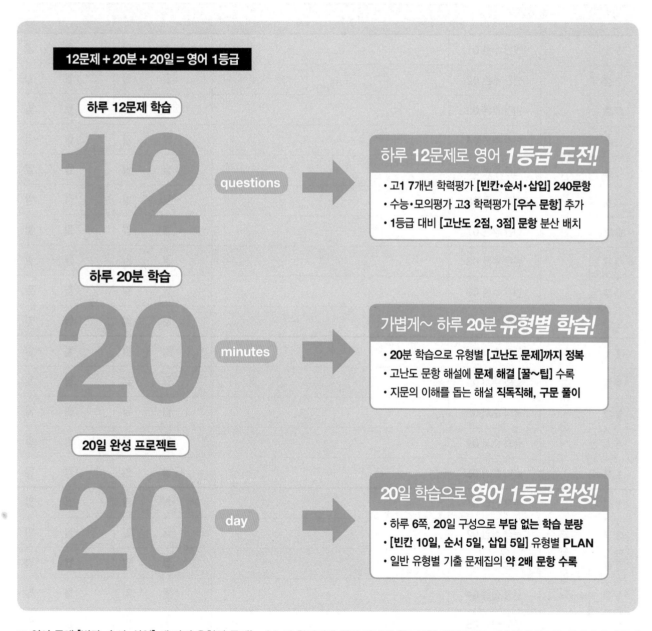

12문제 + 20분 + 20일 = 영어 1등급

하루 12문제 학습

12 questions →

하루 12문제로 영어 *1등급 도전!*
- 고1 7개년 학력평가 [빈칸·순서·삽입] 240문항
- 수능·모의평가 고3 학력평가 [우수 문항] 추가
- 1등급 대비 [고난도 2점, 3점] 문항 분산 배치

하루 20분 학습

20 minutes →

가볍게~ 하루 20분 *유형별 학습!*
- 20분 학습으로 유형별 [고난도 문제]까지 정복
- 고난도 문항 해설에 문제 해결 [꿀~팁] 수록
- 지문의 이해를 돕는 해설 직독직해, 구문 풀이

20일 완성 프로젝트

20 day →

20일 학습으로 *영어 1등급 완성!*
- 하루 6쪽, 20일 구성으로 부담 없는 학습 분량
- [빈칸 10일, 순서 5일, 삽입 5일] 유형별 PLAN
- 일반 유형별 기출 문제집의 약 2배 문항 수록

※ 영어 독해 [빈칸·순서·삽입] 세 가지 유형의 문제는 수능과 학력평가 뿐만 아니라 학교시험 내신에서도 비슷한 유형으로 출제되기 때문에 수능, 내신 모두 영어 1등급'을 위한 필수 유형입니다.

영어 독해 '빈칸·순서·삽입'

20 Day_ planner 기본

- 날짜별로 정해진 **학습 분량에 맞춰 공부**하고 학습 결과를 기록합니다.
- **planner**를 이용해 학습 일정을 계획하고 자신의 성적을 체크하면서 **20일 완성으로 목표**를 세우세요.
- 학습 분량은 하루 **12문제**로 하시되 자신의 **학습 패턴과 상황에 따라 10일 완성으로 학습**하셔도 좋습니다.

Day	구분	영어 독해 유형	틀린 문제 & 복습해야 할 문제	학습 날짜		복습 날짜	
01	빈칸 추론	빈칸 추론 01		월	일	월	일
02		빈칸 추론 02		월	일	월	일
03		빈칸 추론 03		월	일	월	일
04		빈칸 추론 04		월	일	월	일
05		빈칸 추론 05		월	일	월	일
06		빈칸 추론 06		월	일	월	일
07		빈칸 추론 07		월	일	월	일
08		빈칸 추론 08		월	일	월	일
09		빈칸 추론 09		월	일	월	일
10		빈칸 추론 10		월	일	월	일
11	글의 순서	글의 순서 01		월	일	월	일
12		글의 순서 02		월	일	월	일
13		글의 순서 03		월	일	월	일
14		글의 순서 04		월	일	월	일
15		글의 순서 05		월	일	월	일
16	문장 삽입	문장 삽입 01		월	일	월	일
17		문장 삽입 02		월	일	월	일
18		문장 삽입 03		월	일	월	일
19		문장 삽입 04		월	일	월	일
20		문장 삽입 05		월	일	월	일

영어 독해 '빈칸·순서·삽입'

Contents

빈칸 추론

영어 독해에서 가장 문항수가 많고, 배점이 높아 문항의 난이도 또한 기본으로 높은 게 특징이며, 오답률 1위에 해당할 만큼 까다로운 문제가 많이 출제되고 있습니다. 최근 수능 유형은 주어진 지문이 어려워 해석이 쉽지 않은 경우도 있지만, 선택지에 매력적인 오답이 있어 헷갈리는 1~2문제 때문에 등급이 달라지는 사례가 많았습니다.

▶ 빈칸 추론 유형

> **[31~34] 다음 빈칸에 들어갈 말로 가장 적절한 것을 고르시오.**

영어 영역 31~34번에 해당하는 빈칸 추론은 주어진 제시문을 읽고 그 내용을 이해한 후 빈칸이 포함된 문장과 절 이외의 나머지 부분을 통해 질문에 알맞은 적절한 내용을 빈칸에 완성하는 문제입니다.

중요한 것은 지문의 내용만 묻는 게 아니고 **핵심 어구와 절을 완성하는 유형도 있어 빈칸 추론 기출문제 중** 고난도 2점, 고난도 3점 문항들을 집중적으로 풀어보고, 지문을 분석하는 논리적 훈련을 통해 고난도 문항에 대한 확실한 대비를 해야 합니다.

 꿀팁! 지문 속 표현들을 통해 핵심 내용을 파악 후 선지를 빈칸에 넣고 전후 흐름이 연결 되는지, 빈칸에 들어갈 내용과 잘 통하는지 확인한다.

▶ 빈칸 추론 교재 구성

> **하루 12문항 _ 20분 학습 _ 10일 완성 = 총 120문항**

빈칸 추론은 제시문부터 선지까지 모두 영어로 읽고 답을 해야 하는 부담이 있는 유형입니다. 특히 소재가 정치, 과학, 예술, 철학 등 다양하게 출제되고 있어 **"빈칸이 [전반부, 중반부, 후반부]에 있을 때로 기출 문제를 구분"**하여 **학습의 효율성**을 높였습니다.

Day 01~02

빈칸이 '전반부'에 있을 때
글의 나머지 내용을 종합해야하는 경우가 많으니 끝까지 쭉 읽고 내용을 파악한다.

Day 03~05

빈칸이 '중반부'에 있을 때
글의 흐름이 하나가 아니고 반전이 있거나 주제를 반박하는 함정이 있으니 주의한다.

Day 06~10

빈칸이 '후반부'에 있을 때
글의 전체 내용을 종합하여 주제문에 자주 등장하는 핵심어 위주로 결론을 완성한다.

PART I
빈칸 추론

Day 01~Day 10

DAY 01

※ 점수 표기가 없는 문항은 모두 2점입니다.

빈칸이 전반부에 있을 때 **빈칸 추론 01**

● 날짜:　　월　　일　● 시작 시각:　　시　　분　　초

● 목표 시간 : 20분

01

고1·2023년 3월 31번

다음 빈칸에 들어갈 말로 가장 적절한 것을 고르시오.

People differ in how quickly they can reset their biological clocks to overcome jet lag, and the speed of recovery depends on the _____ of travel. Generally, it's easier to fly westward and lengthen your day than it is to fly eastward and shorten it. This east-west difference in jet lag is sizable enough to have an impact on the performance of sports teams. Studies have found that teams flying westward perform significantly better than teams flying eastward in professional baseball and college football. A more recent study of more than 46,000 Major League Baseball games found additional evidence that eastward travel is tougher than westward travel.

＊jet lag: 시차로 인한 피로감

① direction
② purpose
③ season
④ length
⑤ cost

02

고1·2018년 6월 31번

다음 빈칸에 들어갈 말로 가장 적절한 것을 고르시오.

One outcome of motivation is behavior that takes considerable _____. For example, if you are motivated to buy a good car, you will research vehicles online, look at ads, visit dealerships, and so on. Likewise, if you are motivated to lose weight, you will buy low-fat foods, eat smaller portions, and exercise. Motivation not only drives the final behaviors that bring a goal closer but also creates willingness to expend time and energy on preparatory behaviors. Thus, someone motivated to buy a new smartphone may earn extra money for it, drive through a storm to reach the store, and then wait in line to buy it.

＊preparatory: 준비의

① risk
② effort
③ memory
④ fortune
⑤ experience

03

다음 빈칸에 들어갈 말로 가장 적절한 것을 고르시오.

There is nothing more fundamental to the human spirit than the need to be _____. It is the intuitive force that sparks our imaginations and opens pathways to life-changing opportunities. It is the catalyst for progress and personal freedom. Public transportation has been vital to that progress and freedom for more than two centuries. The transportation industry has always done more than carry travelers from one destination to another. It connects people, places, and possibilities. It provides access to what people need, what they love, and what they aspire to become. In so doing, it grows communities, creates jobs, strengthens the economy, expands social and commercial networks, saves time and energy, and helps millions of people achieve a better life.

* catalyst: 촉매, 기폭제

① secure   ② mobile
③ exceptional   ④ competitive
⑤ independent

04

다음 빈칸에 들어갈 말로 가장 적절한 것을 고르시오.

Sometimes it is the _____ that gives a business a competitive advantage. Until recently, bicycles had to have many gears, often 15 or 20, for them to be considered high-end. But fixed-gear bikes with minimal features have become more popular, as those who buy them are happy to pay more for much less. The overall profitability of these bikes is much higher than the more complex ones because they do a single thing really well without the cost of added complexity. Companies should be careful of getting into a war over adding more features with their competitors, as this will increase cost and almost certainly reduce profitability because of competitive pressure on price.

* high-end: 최고급의

① simpler product
② affordable price
③ consumer loyalty
④ customized design
⑤ eco-friendly technology

05

다음 빈칸에 들어갈 말로 가장 적절한 것을 고르시오.

If you want the confidence that comes from achieving what you set out to do each day, then it's important to _____. Over-optimism about what can be achieved within a certain time frame is a problem. So work on it. Make a practice of estimating the amount of time needed alongside items on your 'things to do' list, and learn by experience when tasks take a greater or lesser time than expected. Give attention also to fitting the task to the available time. There are some tasks that you can only set about if you have a significant amount of time available. There is no point in trying to gear up for such a task when you only have a short period available. So schedule the time you need for the longer tasks and put the short tasks into the spare moments in between.

＊ gear up: 준비를 갖추다, 대비하다

① what benefits you can get
② how practical your tasks are
③ how long things are going to take
④ why failures are meaningful in life
⑤ why your leisure time should come first

06

다음 빈칸에 들어갈 말로 가장 적절한 것을 고르시오.

We become more successful when we _____ _____. For example, doctors put in a positive mood before making a diagnosis show almost three times more intelligence and creativity than doctors in a neutral state, and they make accurate diagnoses 19 percent faster. Salespeople who are optimistic sell more than those who are pessimistic by 56 percent. Students who are made to feel happy before taking math achievement tests perform much better than their neutral peers. It turns out that our brains are literally programmed to perform at their best not when they are negative or even neutral, but when they are positive.

① focus on a specific goal
② get along well with others
③ are the best at what we do
④ are happier and more positive
⑤ feel more inspired and creative

07

고1 · 2019년 3월 33번

다음 빈칸에 들어갈 말로 가장 적절한 것을 고르시오. [3점]

A lovely technique for helping children take the first steps towards creating their own, unique story, is to ask them to _____ _____ . One story I have done this with frequently is a tale I call Benno and the Beasts. It is based on a story called St. Benno and the Frog, found in an old book by Helen Waddell. In the original, the saint meets a frog in a marsh and tells it to be quiet in case it disturbs his prayers. Later, he regrets this, in case God was enjoying listening to the sound of the frog. I invite children to think of different animals for the saint to meet and different places for him to meet them. I then tell them the story including their own ideas. It is a most effective way of involving children in the art of creating stories and they love hearing their ideas used.

* marsh: 늪

① help you complete a story before you tell it
② choose some books they are interested in
③ read as many book reviews as possible
④ listen to a story and write a summary
⑤ draw a picture about their experience

08

고1 · 2023년 6월 34번

다음 빈칸에 들어갈 말로 가장 적절한 것을 고르시오. [3점]

_____ boosts sales. Brian Wansink, Professor of Marketing at Cornell University, investigated the effectiveness of this tactic in 1998. He persuaded three supermarkets in Sioux City, Iowa, to offer Campbell's soup at a small discount: 79 cents rather than 89 cents. The discounted soup was sold in one of three conditions: a control, where there was no limit on the volume of purchases, or two tests, where customers were limited to either four or twelve cans. In the unlimited condition shoppers bought 3.3 cans on average, whereas in the scarce condition, when there was a limit, they bought 5.3 on average. This suggests scarcity encourages sales. The findings are particularly strong because the test took place in a supermarket with genuine shoppers. It didn't rely on claimed data, nor was it held in a laboratory where consumers might behave differently.

* tactic: 전략

① Promoting products through social media
② Reducing the risk of producing poor quality items
③ Restricting the number of items customers can buy
④ Offering several options that customers find attractive
⑤ Emphasizing the safety of products with research data

09

다음 빈칸에 들어갈 말로 가장 적절한 것을 고르시오. [3점]

　　As much as we can learn by examining fossils, it is important to remember that they seldom _____ _____. Things only fossilize under certain sets of conditions. Modern insect communities are highly diverse in tropical forests, but the recent fossil record captures little of that diversity. Many creatures are consumed entirely or decompose rapidly when they die, so there may be no fossil record at all for important groups. It's a bit similar to a family photo album. Maybe when you were born your parents took lots of pictures, but over the years they took photographs occasionally, and sometimes they got busy and forgot to take pictures at all. Very few of us have a complete photo record of our life. Fossils are just like that. Sometimes you get very clear pictures of the past, while at other times there are big gaps, and you need to notice what they are.

* decompose: 부패하다

① tell the entire story
② require further study
③ teach us a wrong lesson
④ change their original traits
⑤ make room for imagination

10 1등급 대비 고난도 3점 문제

다음 빈칸에 들어갈 말로 가장 적절한 것을 고르시오. [3점]

　　We worry that the robots are taking our jobs, but just as common a problem is that the robots are taking our _____. In the large warehouses so common behind the scenes of today's economy, human 'pickers' hurry around grabbing products off shelves and moving them to where they can be packed and dispatched. In their ears are headpieces: the voice of 'Jennifer', a piece of software, tells them where to go and what to do, controlling the smallest details of their movements. Jennifer breaks down instructions into tiny chunks, to minimise error and maximise productivity — for example, rather than picking eighteen copies of a book off a shelf, the human worker would be politely instructed to pick five. Then another five. Then yet another five. Then another three. Working in such conditions reduces people to machines made of flesh. Rather than asking us to think or adapt, the Jennifer unit takes over the thought process and treats workers as an inexpensive source of some visual processing and a pair of opposable thumbs.

* dispatch: 발송하다　** chunk: 덩어리

① reliability　　　② judgment
③ endurance　　　④ sociability
⑤ cooperation

11 1등급 대비 고난도 3점 문제

다음 빈칸에 들어갈 말로 가장 적절한 것을 고르시오. [3점]

One real concern in the marketing industry today is how to _____ in the age of the remote control and mobile devices. With the growing popularity of digital video recorders, consumers can mute, fast-forward, and skip over commercials entirely. Some advertisers are trying to adapt to these technologies, by planting hidden coupons in frames of their television commercials. Others are desperately trying to make their advertisements more interesting and entertaining to discourage viewers from skipping their ads; still others are simply giving up on television advertising altogether. Some industry experts predict that cable providers and advertisers will eventually be forced to provide incentives in order to encourage consumers to watch their messages. These incentives may come in the form of coupons, or a reduction in the cable bill for each advertisement watched.

＊mute: 음소거하다

① guide people to be wise consumers
② reduce the cost of television advertising
③ keep a close eye on the quality of products
④ make it possible to deliver any goods any time
⑤ win the battle for broadcast advertising exposure

12 1등급 대비 고난도 3점 문제

다음 빈칸에 들어갈 말로 가장 적절한 것을 고르시오. [3점]

Having extremely vivid memories of past emotional experiences and only weak memories of past everyday events means we _____.
We tend to view the past as a concentrated time line of emotionally exciting events. We remember the arousing aspects of an episode and forget the boring bits. A summer vacation will be recalled for its highlights, and the less exciting parts will fade away with time, eventually to be forgotten forever. As a result, when we estimate how our next summer vacation will make us feel, we overestimate the positive. It seems as though an imprecise picture of the past is one reason for our inaccurate forecasts of the future.

① focus primarily on the future
② remember every detail of our lives
③ maintain a biased perception of the past
④ have trouble overcoming our emotional problems
⑤ share negative emotional experiences with others

학습 Check! ▶ 몰라서 틀린 문항 × 표기 ▶ 헷갈렸거나 찍은 문항 △ 표기 ▶ ×, △ 문항은 다시 풀고 ✔ 표기를 하세요.

종료 시각	시 분 초	문항 번호	01	02	03	04	05	06	07	08	09	10	11	12
소요 시간	분 초	채점 결과												
초과 시간	분 초	틀린 문항 복습												

DAY 02

※ 점수 표기가 없는 문항은 모두 **2점**입니다.

빈칸이 전반부에 있을 때 **빈칸 추론 02**

● 날짜 :　　월　　일　● 시작 시각 :　　시　　분　　초

● 목표 시간 : 20분

01

고1·2020년 3월 31번

다음 빈칸에 들어갈 말로 가장 적절한 것을 고르시오.

Remember that _____ is always of the essence. If an apology is not accepted, thank the individual for hearing you out and leave the door open for if and when he wishes to reconcile. Be conscious of the fact that just because someone accepts your apology does not mean she has fully forgiven you. It can take time, maybe a long time, before the injured party can completely let go and fully trust you again. There is little you can do to speed this process up. If the person is truly important to you, it is worthwhile to give him or her the time and space needed to heal. Do not expect the person to go right back to acting normally immediately.

＊reconcile: 화해하다

① curiosity
② independence
③ patience
④ creativity
⑤ honesty

02

고1·2019년 9월 31번

다음 빈칸에 들어갈 말로 가장 적절한 것을 고르시오.

_____ provides a change to the environment for journalists. Newspaper stories, television reports, and even early online reporting (prior to communication technology such as tablets and smartphones) required one central place to which a reporter would submit his or her news story for printing, broadcast, or posting. Now, though, a reporter can shoot video, record audio, and type directly on their smartphones or tablets and post a news story instantly. Journalists do not need to report to a central location where they all contact sources, type, or edit video. A story can be instantaneously written, shot, and made available to the entire world. The news cycle, and thus the job of the journalist, never takes a break. Thus the "24-hour" news cycle that emerged from the rise of cable TV is now a thing of the past. The news "cycle" is really a constant.

① Mobility
② Sensitivity
③ Creativity
④ Accuracy
⑤ Responsibility

03

다음 빈칸에 들어갈 말로 가장 적절한 것을 고르시오.

If you follow science news, you will have noticed that _____ among animals has become a hot topic in the mass media. For example, in late 2007 the science media widely reported a study by Claudia Rutte and Michael Taborsky suggesting that rats display what they call "generalized reciprocity." They each provided help to an unfamiliar and unrelated individual, based on their own previous experience of having been helped by an unfamiliar rat. Rutte and Taborsky trained rats in a cooperative task of pulling a stick to obtain food for a partner. Rats who had been helped previously by an unknown partner were more likely to help others. Before this research was conducted, generalized reciprocity was thought to be unique to humans.

① friction ② diversity
③ hierarchy ④ cooperation
⑤ independence

04

다음 빈칸에 들어갈 말로 가장 적절한 것을 고르시오.

All improvement in your life begins with an improvement in your _____. If you talk to unhappy people and ask them what they think about most of the time, you will find that almost without fail, they think about their problems, their bills, their negative relationships, and all the difficulties in their lives. But when you talk to successful, happy people, you find that they think and talk most of the time about the things that they want to be, do, and have. They think and talk about the specific action steps they can take to get them. They dwell continually on vivid, exciting pictures of what their goals will look like when they are realized, and what their dreams will look like when they come true.

① mental pictures
② physical competence
③ cooperative attitude
④ learning environment
⑤ academic achievements

05

다음 빈칸에 들어갈 말로 가장 적절한 것을 고르시오.

Many evolutionary biologists argue that humans _____. We needed to trade, and we needed to establish trust in order to trade. Language is very handy when you are trying to conduct business with someone. Two early humans could not only agree to trade three wooden bowls for six bunches of bananas but establish rules as well. What wood was used for the bowls? Where did you get the bananas? That business deal would have been nearly impossible using only gestures and confusing noises, and carrying it out according to terms agreed upon creates a bond of trust. Language allows us to be specific, and this is where conversation plays a key role.

① used body language to communicate
② instinctively knew who to depend on
③ often changed rules for their own needs
④ lived independently for their own survival
⑤ developed language for economic reasons

06

다음 빈칸에 들어갈 말로 가장 적절한 것을 고르시오.

A key to engagement and achievement is providing students with _____.
My scholarly work and my teaching have been deeply influenced by the work of Rosalie Fink. She interviewed twelve adults who were highly successful in their work, including a physicist, a biochemist, and a company CEO. All of them had dyslexia and had had significant problems with reading throughout their school years. While she expected to find that they had avoided reading and discovered ways to bypass it or compensate with other strategies for learning, she found the opposite. "To my surprise, I found that these dyslexics were enthusiastic readers...they rarely avoided reading. On the contrary, they sought out books." The pattern Fink discovered was that all of her subjects had been passionate in some personal interest. The areas of interest included religion, math, business, science, history, and biography. What mattered was that they read voraciously to find out more.

＊dyslexia: 난독증 ＊＊voraciously: 탐욕스럽게

① examples from official textbooks
② relevant texts they will be interested in
③ enough chances to exchange information
④ different genres for different age groups
⑤ early reading experience to develop logic skills

07

다음 빈칸에 들어갈 말로 가장 적절한 것을 고르시오. [3점]

The last two decades of research on the science of learning have shown conclusively that we remember things better, and longer, if _____. This is the teaching method practiced by physics professor Eric Mazur. He doesn't lecture in his classes at Harvard. Instead, he asks students difficult questions, based on their homework reading, that require them to pull together sources of information to solve a problem. Mazur doesn't give them the answer; instead, he asks the students to break off into small groups and discuss the problem among themselves. Eventually, nearly everyone in the class gets the answer right, and the concepts stick with them because they had to find their own way to the answer.

① they are taught repeatedly in class
② we fully focus on them without any distractions
③ equal opportunities are given to complete tasks
④ there's no right or wrong way to learn about a topic
⑤ we discover them ourselves rather than being told them

08

다음 빈칸에 들어갈 말로 가장 적절한 것을 고르시오. [3점]

There is good evidence that in organic development, perception starts with _____. For example, when two-year-old children and chimpanzees had learned that, of two boxes presented to them, the one with a triangle of a particular size and shape always contained attractive food, they had no difficulty applying their training to triangles of very different appearance. The triangles were made smaller or larger or turned upside down. A black triangle on a white background was replaced by a white triangle on a black background, or an outlined triangle by a solid one. These changes seemed not to interfere with recognition. Similar results were obtained with rats. Karl Lashley, a psychologist, has asserted that simple transpositions of this type are universal in all animals including humans.

* transposition: 치환

① interpreting different gestures
② establishing social frameworks
③ identifying the information of colors
④ separating the self from the environment
⑤ recognizing outstanding structural features

09

다음 빈칸에 들어갈 말로 가장 적절한 것을 고르시오. [3점]

The demand for freshness can _____ _____. While freshness is now being used as a term in food marketing as part of a return to nature, the demand for year-round supplies of fresh produce such as soft fruit and exotic vegetables has led to the widespread use of hot houses in cold climates and increasing reliance on total quality control — management by temperature control, use of pesticides and computer/satellite-based logistics. The demand for freshness has also contributed to concerns about food wastage. Use of 'best before', 'sell by' and 'eat by' labels has legally allowed institutional waste. Campaigners have exposed the scandal of over-production and waste. Tristram Stuart, one of the global band of anti-waste campaigners, argues that, with freshly made sandwiches, over-ordering is standard practice across the retail sector to avoid the appearance of empty shelf space, leading to high volumes of waste when supply regularly exceeds demand.

* pesticide: 살충제 ** logistics: 물류, 유통

① have hidden environmental costs
② worsen the global hunger problem
③ bring about technological advances
④ improve nutrition and quality of food
⑤ diversify the diet of a local community

10

다음 빈칸에 들어갈 말로 가장 적절한 것을 고르시오. [3점]

There is a major problem with _____ _____. To determine the number of objects by counting, such as determining how many apples there are on a table, many children would touch or point to the first apple and say "one," then move on to the second apple and say "two," and continue in this manner until all the apples are counted. If we start at 0, we would have to touch nothing and say "zero," but then we would have to start touching apples and calling out "one, two, three" and so on. This can be very confusing because there would be a need to stress when to touch and when not to touch. If a child accidentally touches an apple while saying "zero," then the total number of apples will be off by 1.

① counting from 0
② numbering in reverse order
③ adding up the numbers given
④ learning words through games
⑤ saying numbers in a loud voice

11 1등급 대비 고난도 3점 문제

다음 빈칸에 들어갈 말로 가장 적절한 것을 고르시오. [3점]

The best way in which innovation changes our lives is by _____. The main theme of human history is that we become steadily more specialized in what we produce, and steadily more diversified in what we consume: we move away from unstable self-sufficiency to safer mutual interdependence. By concentrating on serving other people's needs for forty hours a week — which we call a job — you can spend the other seventy-two hours (not counting fifty-six hours in bed) relying on the services provided to you by other people. Innovation has made it possible to work for a fraction of a second in order to be able to afford to turn on an electric lamp for an hour, providing the quantity of light that would have required a whole day's work if you had to make it yourself by collecting and refining sesame oil or lamb fat to burn in a simple lamp, as much of humanity did in the not so distant past.

*a fraction of a second: 아주 짧은 시간 **refine: 정제하다

① respecting the values of the old days
② enabling people to work for each other
③ providing opportunities to think creatively
④ satisfying customers with personalized services
⑤ introducing and commercializing unusual products

12 1등급 대비 고난도 3점 문제

다음 빈칸에 들어갈 말로 가장 적절한 것을 고르시오. [3점]

Interestingly, in nature, _____. The distinction between predator and prey offers a clarifying example of this. The key feature that distinguishes predator species from prey species isn't the presence of claws or any other feature related to biological weaponry. The key feature is *the position of their eyes*. Predators evolved with eyes facing forward — which allows for binocular vision that offers accurate depth perception when pursuing prey. Prey, on the other hand, often have eyes facing outward, maximizing peripheral vision, which allows the hunted to detect danger that may be approaching from any angle. Consistent with our place at the top of the food chain, humans have eyes that face forward. We have the ability to gauge depth and pursue our goals, but we can also miss important action on our periphery.

*depth perception: 거리 감각 **periphery: 주변

① eyes facing outward are linked with the success of hunting
② the more powerful species have a narrower field of vision
③ humans' eyes facing forward enable them to detect danger
④ eyesight is closely related to the extinction of weak species
⑤ animals use their eyesight to identify members of their species

---

학습 Check!

▶ 몰라서 틀린 문항 × 표기 ▶ 헷갈렸거나 찍은 문항 △ 표기 ▶ ×, △ 문항은 다시 풀고 ✔ 표기를 하세요.

종료 시각	시 분 초	문항 번호	01	02	03	04	05	06	07	08	09	10	11	12
소요 시간	분 초	채점 결과												
초과 시간	분 초	틀린 문항 복습												

DAY 03

※ 점수 표기가 없는 문항은 모두 2점입니다.

빈칸이 중반부에 있을 때 **빈칸 추론 03**

● 날짜 :　월　일　● 시작 시각 :　시　분　초

● 목표 시간 : 20분

01

다음 빈칸에 들어갈 말로 가장 적절한 것을 고르시오.

We don't send telegraphs to communicate anymore, but it's a great metaphor for giving advance notice. Sometimes, you must inform those close to you of upcoming change by conveying important information well in advance. There's a huge difference between saying, "From now on, we will do things differently," which doesn't give people enough time to understand and accept the change, and saying something like, "Starting next month, we're going to approach things differently." Telegraphing empowers people to _____. Telegraphing involves the art of seeing an upcoming event or circumstance and giving others enough time to process and accept the change. Telegraph anything that will take people out of what is familiar and comfortable to them. This will allow processing time for them to accept the circumstances and make the most of what's happening.

① unite
② adapt
③ object
④ compete
⑤ recover

02

다음 빈칸에 들어갈 말로 가장 적절한 것을 고르시오. [3점]

Good managers have learned to overcome the initial feelings of anxiety when assigning tasks. They are aware that no two people act in exactly the same way and so do not feel threatened if they see one employee going about a task differently than another. Instead, they focus on _____. If a job was successfully done, as long as people are working in a manner acceptable to the organization (for example, as long as salespeople are keeping to the company's ethical selling policy), then that's fine. If an acceptable final outcome wasn't achieved, then such managers respond by discussing it with the employee and analyzing the situation, to find out what training or additional skills that person will need to do the task successfully in the future.

＊assign: (일·책임 등을) 맡기다

① the end result
② the welfare policy
③ the uniform procedure
④ the informal atmosphere
⑤ the employee's personality

03

다음 빈칸에 들어갈 말로 가장 적절한 것을 고르시오. [3점]

The famous primatologist Frans de Waal, of Emory University, says humans downplay similarities between us and other animals as a way of maintaining our spot at the top of our imaginary ladder. Scientists, de Waal points out, can be some of the worst offenders — employing technical language to _____ _____. They call "kissing" in chimps "mouth-to-mouth contact"; they call "friends" between primates "favorite affiliation partners"; they interpret evidence showing that crows and chimps can make tools as being somehow qualitatively different from the kind of toolmaking said to define humanity. If an animal can beat us at a cognitive task — like how certain bird species can remember the precise locations of thousands of seeds — they write it off as instinct, not intelligence. This and so many more tricks of language are what de Waal has termed "linguistic castration." The way we use our tongues to disempower animals, the way we invent words to maintain our spot at the top.

* primatologist: 영장류학자　** affiliation: 제휴

① define human instincts
② overestimate chimps' intelligence
③ distance the other animals from us
④ identify animals' negative emotions
⑤ correct our misconceptions about nature

04

다음 빈칸에 들어갈 말로 가장 적절한 것을 고르시오. [3점]

Within a store, the wall marks the back of the store, but not the end of the marketing. Merchandisers often use the back wall as a magnet, because it means that _____. This is a good thing because distance traveled relates more directly to sales per entering customer than any other measurable consumer variable. Sometimes, the wall's attraction is simply appealing to the senses, a wall decoration that catches the eye or a sound that catches the ear. Sometimes the attraction is specific goods. In supermarkets, the dairy is often at the back, because people frequently come just for milk. At video rental shops, it's the new releases.

* merchandiser: 상품 판매업자　** variable: 변수

① the store looks larger than it is
② more products can be stored there
③ people have to walk through the whole store
④ the store provides customers with cultural events
⑤ people don't need to spend too much time in the store

05

다음 빈칸에 들어갈 말로 가장 적절한 것을 고르시오. [3점]

All mammals need to leave their parents and set up on their own at some point. But human adults generally provide a comfortable existence — enough food arrives on the table, money is given at regular intervals, the bills get paid and the electricity for the TV doesn't usually run out. If teenagers didn't build up a fairly major disrespect for and conflict with their parents or carers, they'd never want to leave. In fact, _____ _____ is probably a necessary part of growing up. Later, when you live independently, away from them, you can start to love them again because you won't need to be fighting to get away from them. And you can come back sometimes for a home-cooked meal.

① developing financial management skills
② learning from other people's experiences
③ figuring out your strengths and interests
④ managing relationship problems with your peers
⑤ falling out of love with the adults who look after you

06

다음 빈칸에 들어갈 말로 가장 적절한 것을 고르시오. [3점]

Some deep-sea organisms are known to use bioluminescence as a lure, to attract prey with a little glow imitating the movements of their favorite fish, or like fireflies, as a sexual attractant to find mates. While there are many possible evolutionary theories for the survival value of bioluminescence, one of the most fascinating is to _____. The color of almost all bioluminescent molecules is blue-green, the same color as the ocean above. By self-glowing blue-green, the creatures no longer cast a shadow or create a silhouette, especially when viewed from below against the brighter waters above. Rather, by glowing themselves, they can blend into the sparkles, reflections, and scattered blue-green glow of sunlight or moonlight. Thus, they are most likely making their own light not to see, but to be un-seen.

＊bioluminescence: 생물 발광　＊＊lure: 가짜 미끼

① send a signal for help
② threaten enemies nearby
③ lift the veil of hidden prey
④ create a cloak of invisibility
⑤ serve as a navigation system

07

다음 빈칸에 들어갈 말로 가장 적절한 것을 고르시오.

Fans feel for feeling's own sake. They make meanings beyond what seems to be on offer. They build identities and experiences, and make artistic creations of their own to share with others. A person can be an individual fan, feeling an "idealized connection with a star, strong feelings of memory and nostalgia," and engaging in activities like "collecting to develop a sense of self." But, more often, individual experiences are embedded in social contexts where other people with shared attachments socialize around the object of their affections. Much of the pleasure of fandom _____ _____. In their diaries, Bostonians of the 1800s described being part of the crowds at concerts as part of the pleasure of attendance. A compelling argument can be made that what fans love is less the object of their fandom than the attachments to (and differentiations from) one another that those affections afford.

*embed: 끼워 넣다   **compelling: 강력한

① is enhanced by collaborations between global stars
② results from frequent personal contact with a star
③ deepens as fans age together with their idols
④ comes from being connected to other fans
⑤ is heightened by stars' media appearances

08 [1등급 대비 고난도 2편 문제]

다음 빈칸에 들어갈 말로 가장 적절한 것을 고르시오.

Generalization without specific examples that humanize writing is boring to the listener and to the reader. Who wants to read platitudes all day? Who wants to hear the words great, greater, best, smartest, finest, humanitarian, on and on and on without specific examples? Instead of using these 'nothing words,' leave them out completely and just describe the _____. There is nothing worse than reading a scene in a novel in which a main character is described up front as heroic or brave or tragic or funny, while thereafter, the writer quickly moves on to something else. That's no good, no good at all. You have to use less one word descriptions and more detailed, engaging descriptions if you want to make something real.

*platitude: 상투적인 말

① similarities
② particulars
③ fantasies
④ boredom
⑤ wisdom

DAY 03

09 1등급 대비 고난도 2점 문제

다음 빈칸에 들어갈 말로 가장 적절한 것을 고르시오.

When reading another scientist's findings, think critically about the experiment. Ask yourself: Were observations recorded during or after the experiment? Do the conclusions make sense? Can the results be repeated? Are the sources of information reliable? You should also ask if the scientist or group conducting the experiment was unbiased. Being unbiased means that you have no special interest in the outcome of the experiment. For example, if a drug company pays for an experiment to test how well one of its new products works, there is a special interest involved: The drug company profits if the experiment shows that its product is effective. Therefore, the experimenters aren't _____. They might ensure the conclusion is positive and benefits the drug company. When assessing results, think about any biases that may be present!

① inventive
② objective
③ untrustworthy
④ unreliable
⑤ decisive

10 1등급 대비 고난도 3점 문제

다음 빈칸에 들어갈 말로 가장 적절한 것을 고르시오. [3점]

Why doesn't the modern American accent sound similar to a British accent? After all, didn't the British colonize the U.S.? Experts believe that British residents and the colonists who settled America all sounded the same back in the 18th century, and they probably all sounded more like modern Americans than modern Brits. The accent that we identify as British today was developed around the time of the American Revolution by people of low birth rank who had become wealthy during the Industrial Revolution. To distinguish themselves from other commoners, these people developed new ways of speaking to set themselves apart and demonstrate their new, elevated _____. In the 19th century, this distinctive accent was standardized as Received Pronunciation and taught widely by pronunciation tutors to people who wanted to learn to speak fashionably.

＊Received Pronunciation: 영국 표준 발음

① social status
② fashion sense
③ political pressures
④ colonial involvement
⑤ intellectual achievements

11 1등급 대비 고난도 3점 문제   고1·2022년 6월 34번

다음 빈칸에 들어갈 말로 가장 적절한 것을 고르시오. [3점]

Researchers are working on a project that asks coastal towns how they are preparing for rising sea levels. Some towns have risk assessments; some towns even have a plan. But it's a rare town that is actually carrying out a plan. One reason we've failed to act on climate change is the common belief that _____ _____. For decades, climate change was a prediction about the future, so scientists talked about it in the future tense. This became a habit — so that even today many scientists still use the future tense, even though we know that a climate crisis is ongoing. Scientists also often focus on regions most affected by the crisis, such as Bangladesh or the West Antarctic Ice Sheet, which for most Americans are physically remote.

① it is not related to science
② it is far away in time and space
③ energy efficiency matters the most
④ careful planning can fix the problem
⑤ it is too late to prevent it from happening

12 1등급 대비 고난도 3점 문제   고1·2023년 6월 32번

다음 빈칸에 들어갈 말로 가장 적절한 것을 고르시오. [3점]

Think of the brain as a city. If you were to look out over a city and ask "where is the economy located?" you'd see there's no good answer to the question. Instead, the economy emerges from the interaction of all the elements — from the stores and the banks to the merchants and the customers. And so it is with the brain's operation: it doesn't happen in one spot. Just as in a city, no neighborhood of the brain _____ _____. In brains and in cities, everything emerges from the interaction between residents, at all scales, locally and distantly. Just as trains bring materials and textiles into a city, which become processed into the economy, so the raw electrochemical signals from sensory organs are transported along superhighways of neurons. There the signals undergo processing and transformation into our conscious reality.

＊electrochemical: 전기화학의

① operates in isolation
② suffers from rapid changes
③ resembles economic elements
④ works in a systematic way
⑤ interacts with another

DAY 03

학습 Check!   ▶ 몰라서 틀린 문항 × 표기 ▶ 헷갈렸거나 찍은 문항 △ 표기 ▶ ×, △ 문항은 다시 풀고 ✔ 표기를 하세요.

종료 시각	시	분	초	문항 번호	01	02	03	04	05	06	07	08	09	10	11	12
소요 시간		분	초	채점 결과												
초과 시간		분	초	틀린 문항 복습												

DAY 04

※ 점수 표기가 없는 문항은 모두 2점입니다.

빈칸이 중반부에 있을 때 **빈칸 추론 04**

● 날짜 :　　　월　　　일　 ● 시작 시각 :　　　시　　　분　　　초

● 목표 시간 : 20분

01

고1 · 2017년 6월 31번

다음 빈칸에 들어갈 말로 가장 적절한 것을 고르시오.

　If we lived on a planet where nothing ever changed, there would be little to do. There would be nothing to figure out and there would be no reason for science. And if we lived in an unpredictable world, where things changed in random or very complex ways, we would not be able to figure things out. Again, there would be no such thing as science. But we live in an in-between universe, where things change, but according to _____. If I throw a stick up in the air, it always falls down. If the sun sets in the west, it always rises again the next morning in the east. And so it becomes possible to figure things out. We can do science, and with it we can improve our lives.

① age
② luck
③ belief
④ rules
⑤ interests

02

고3 · 2024학년도 6월 31번

다음 빈칸에 들어갈 말로 가장 적절한 것을 고르시오.

　People have always needed to eat, and they always will. Rising emphasis on self-expression values does not put an end to material desires. But prevailing economic orientations are gradually being reshaped. People who work in the knowledge sector continue to seek high salaries, but they place equal or greater emphasis on doing stimulating work and being able to follow their own time schedules. Consumption is becoming progressively less determined by the need for sustenance and the practical use of the goods consumed. People still eat, but a growing component of food's value is determined by its _____ aspects. People pay a premium to eat exotic cuisines that provide an interesting experience or that symbolize a distinctive life-style. The publics of postindustrial societies place growing emphasis on "political consumerism," such as boycotting goods whose production violates ecological or ethical standards. Consumption is less and less a matter of sustenance and more and more a question of life-style — and choice.

* prevail: 우세하다　** cuisine: 요리

① quantitative
② nonmaterial
③ nutritional
④ invariable
⑤ economic

03

다음 빈칸에 들어갈 말로 가장 적절한 것을 고르시오. [3점]

It's hard enough to stick with goals you want to accomplish, but sometimes we make goals we're not even thrilled about in the first place. We set resolutions based on what we're supposed to do, or what others think we're supposed to do, rather than what really matters to us. This makes it nearly impossible to stick to the goal. For example, reading more is a good habit, but if you're only doing it because you feel like that's what you're supposed to do, not because you actually want to learn more, you're going to have a hard time reaching the goal. Instead, make goals based on _____. Now, this isn't to say you should read less. The idea is to first consider what matters to you, then figure out what you need to do to get there.

① your moral duty
② a strict deadline
③ your own values
④ parental guidance
⑤ job market trends

04

다음 빈칸에 들어갈 말로 가장 적절한 것을 고르시오. [3점]

Scientists believe that the frogs' ancestors were water-dwelling, fishlike animals. The first frogs and their relatives gained the ability to come out on land and enjoy the opportunities for food and shelter there. But they _____.
A frog's lungs do not work very well, and it gets part of its oxygen by breathing through its skin. But for this kind of "breathing" to work properly, the frog's skin must stay moist. And so the frog must remain near the water where it can take a dip every now and then to keep from drying out. Frogs must also lay their eggs in water, as their fishlike ancestors did. And eggs laid in the water must develop into water creatures, if they are to survive. For frogs, metamorphosis thus provides the bridge between the water-dwelling young forms and the land-dwelling adults.

* metamorphosis: 탈바꿈

① still kept many ties to the water
② had almost all the necessary organs
③ had to develop an appetite for new foods
④ often competed with land-dwelling species
⑤ suffered from rapid changes in temperature

05

다음 빈칸에 들어갈 말로 가장 적절한 것을 고르시오.

Not only does memory underlie our ability to think at all, it defines the content of our experiences and how we preserve them for years to come. Memory _____. If I were to suffer from heart failure and depend upon an artificial heart, I would be no less myself. If I lost an arm in an accident and had it replaced with an artificial arm, I would still be essentially *me*. As long as my mind and memories remain intact, I will continue to be the same person, no matter which part of my body (other than the brain) is replaced. On the other hand, when someone suffers from advanced Alzheimer's disease and his memories fade, people often say that he "is not himself anymore," or that it is as if the person "is no longer there," though his body remains unchanged.

* intact: 손상되지 않은

① makes us who we are
② has to do with our body
③ reflects what we expect
④ lets us understand others
⑤ helps us learn from the past

06

다음 빈칸에 들어갈 말로 가장 적절한 것을 고르시오. [3점]

Someone else's body language affects our own body, which then creates an emotional echo that makes us feel accordingly. As Louis Armstrong sang, "When you're smiling, the whole world smiles with you." If copying another's smile makes us feel happy, the emotion of the smiler has been transmitted via our body. Strange as it may sound, this theory states that _____. For example, our mood can be improved by simply lifting up the corners of our mouth. If people are asked to bite down on a pencil lengthwise, taking care not to let the pencil touch their lips (thus forcing the mouth into a smile-like shape), they judge cartoons funnier than if they have been asked to frown. The primacy of the body is sometimes summarized in the phrase "I must be afraid, because I'm running."

* lengthwise: 길게 ** frown: 얼굴을 찡그리다

① language guides our actions
② emotions arise from our bodies
③ body language hides our feelings
④ what others say affects our mood
⑤ negative emotions easily disappear

07 1등급 대비 고난도 2점 문제

다음 빈칸에 들어갈 말로 가장 적절한 것을 고르시오.

In a culture where there is a belief that you can have anything you truly want, there is no problem in choosing. Many cultures, however, do not maintain this belief. In fact, many people do not believe that life is about getting what you want. Life is about doing what you are *supposed* to do. The reason they have trouble making choices is they believe that what they may want is not related to what they are supposed to do. The weight of outside considerations is greater than their _____. When this is an issue in a group, we discuss what makes for good decisions. If a person can be unburdened from their cares and duties and, just for a moment, consider what appeals to them, they get the chance to sort out what is important to them. Then they can consider and negotiate with their external pressures.

① desires   ② merits
③ abilities   ④ limitations
⑤ worries

08 1등급 대비 고난도 2점 문제

다음 빈칸에 들어갈 말로 가장 적절한 것을 고르시오.

We have to recognize that there always exists in us the strongest need to utilize *all* our attention. And this is quite evident in the great amount of displeasure we feel any time the entirety of our capacity for attention is not being put to use. When this is the case, we will seek _____. If we are playing a chess game with a weaker opponent, we will seek to supplement this activity with another: such as watching TV, or listening to music, or playing another chess game at the same time. Very often this reveals itself in unconscious movements, such as playing with something in one's hands or pacing around the room; and if such an action also serves to increase pleasure or relieve displeasure, all the better.

＊supplement: 보충하다

① to please others with what we are good at
② to pay more attention to the given task
③ to find outlets for our unused attention
④ to play with a stronger opponent
⑤ to give our brain a short break

09 1등급 대비 고난도 2점 문제

다음 빈칸에 들어갈 말로 가장 적절한 것을 고르시오.

Face-to-face interaction is a uniquely powerful — and sometimes the only — way to share many kinds of knowledge, from the simplest to the most complex. It is one of the best ways to stimulate new thinking and ideas, too. Most of us would have had difficulty learning how to tie a shoelace only from pictures, or how to do arithmetic from a book. Psychologist Mihàly Csikszentmihàlyi found, while studying high achievers, that a large number of Nobel Prize winners were the students of previous winners: they had access to the same literature as everyone else, but _____ made a crucial difference to their creativity. Within organisations this makes conversation both a crucial factor for high-level professional skills and the most important way of sharing everyday information.

＊arithmetic: 계산 ＊＊literature: (연구) 문헌

① natural talent
② regular practice
③ personal contact
④ complex knowledge
⑤ powerful motivation

10 1등급 대비 고난도 3점 문제

다음 빈칸에 들어갈 말로 가장 적절한 것을 고르시오. [3점]

What do advertising and map-making have in common? Without doubt the best answer is their shared need to communicate a limited version of the truth. An advertisement must create an image that's appealing and a map must present an image that's clear, but neither can meet its goal by _____.
Ads will cover up or play down negative aspects of the company or service they advertise. In this way, they can promote a favorable comparison with similar products or differentiate a product from its competitors. Likewise, the map must remove details that would be confusing.

① reducing the amount of information
② telling or showing everything
③ listening to people's voices
④ relying on visual images only
⑤ making itself available to everyone

11 1등급 대비 고난도 3점 문제

고1 · 2021년 11월 33번

다음 빈칸에 들어갈 말로 가장 적절한 것을 고르시오. [3점]

Over time, babies construct expectations about what sounds they will hear when. They hold in memory the sound patterns that occur on a regular basis. They make hypotheses like, "If I hear *this* sound first, it probably will be followed by *that* sound." Scientists conclude that much of babies' skill in learning language is due to their _____. For babies, this means that they appear to pay close attention to the patterns that repeat in language. They remember, in a systematic way, how often sounds occur, in what order, with what intervals, and with what changes of pitch. This memory store allows them to track, within the neural circuits of their brains, the frequency of sound patterns and to use this knowledge to make predictions about the meaning in patterns of sounds.

① lack of social pressures

② ability to calculate statistics

③ desire to interact with others

④ preference for simpler sounds

⑤ tendency to imitate caregivers

12 1등급 대비 고난도 3점 문제

고1 · 2020년 11월 34번

다음 빈칸에 들어갈 말로 가장 적절한 것을 고르시오. [3점]

Back in 1996, an American airline was faced with an interesting problem. At a time when most other airlines were losing money or going under, over 100 cities were begging the company to service their locations. However, that's not the interesting part. What's interesting is that the company turned down over 95 percent of those offers and began serving only four new locations. It turned down tremendous growth because _____. Sure, its executives wanted to grow each year, but they didn't want to grow too much. Unlike other famous companies, they wanted to set their own pace, one that could be sustained in the long term. By doing this, they established a safety margin for growth that helped them continue to thrive at a time when the other airlines were flailing.

＊ flail: 마구 흔들리다

① it was being faced with serious financial crises

② there was no specific long-term plan on marketing

③ company leadership had set an upper limit for growth

④ its executives worried about the competing airlines' future

⑤ the company had emphasized moral duties more than profits

DAY 05

※ 점수 표기가 없는 문항은 모두 **2점**입니다.

빈칸이 중반부에 있을 때 **빈칸 추론 05**

● 날짜 :   월   일 ● 시작 시각 :   시   분   초

● 목표 시간 : 20분

01

다음 빈칸에 들어갈 말로 가장 적절한 것을 고르시오.

In the post-World War II years after 1945, unparalleled economic growth fueled a building boom and a massive migration from the central cities to the new suburban areas. The suburbs were far more dependent on the automobile, signaling the shift from primary dependence on public transportation to private cars. Soon this led to the construction of better highways and freeways and the decline and even loss of public transportation. With all of these changes came a _____ of leisure. As more people owned their own homes, with more space inside and lovely yards outside, their recreation and leisure time was increasingly centered around the home or, at most, the neighborhood. One major activity of this home-based leisure was watching television. No longer did one have to ride the trolly to the theater to watch a movie; similar entertainment was available for free and more conveniently from television.

*unparalleled: 유례없는

① downfall ② uniformity
③ restoration ④ privatization
⑤ customization

02

다음 빈칸에 들어갈 말로 가장 적절한 것을 고르시오.

Here's the unpleasant truth: we are all biased. Every human being is affected by unconscious biases that lead us to make incorrect assumptions about other people. Everyone. To a certain extent, bias is a(n) _____ _____. If you're an early human, perhaps *Homo Erectus*, walking around the jungles, you may see an animal approaching. You have to make very fast assumptions about whether that animal is safe or not, based solely on its appearance. The same is true of other humans. You make split-second decisions about threats in order to have plenty of time to escape, if necessary. This could be one root of our tendency to categorize and label others based on their looks and their clothes.

① necessary survival skill
② origin of imagination
③ undesirable mental capacity
④ barrier to relationships
⑤ challenge to moral judgment

03

다음 빈칸에 들어갈 말로 가장 적절한 것을 고르시오. [3점]

Business consultant Frans Johansson describes the *Medici effect* as the emergence of new ideas and creative solutions when different backgrounds and disciplines come together. The term is derived from the 15th-century Medici family, who helped usher in the Renaissance by bringing together artists, writers, and other creatives from all over the world. Arguably, the Renaissance was a result of the exchange of ideas between these different groups in close contact with each other. Sound familiar? If you are unable to diversify your own talent and skill, then _____ might very well just do the trick. Believing that all new ideas come from combining existing notions in creative ways, Johansson recommends utilizing a mix of backgrounds, experiences, and expertise in staffing to bring about the best possible solutions, perspectives, and innovations in business.

＊usher in: ~이 시작되게 하다

① having others around you to compensate
② taking some time to reflect on yourself
③ correcting the mistakes of the past
④ maximizing your own strength
⑤ setting a specific objective

04

다음 빈칸에 들어갈 말로 가장 적절한 것을 고르시오. [3점]

When meeting someone in person, body language experts say that smiling can portray confidence and warmth. Online, however, smiley faces could be doing some serious damage to your career. In a new study, researchers found that using smiley faces _____ _____. The study says, "contrary to actual smiles, smileys do not increase perceptions of warmth and actually decrease perceptions of competence." The report also explains, "Perceptions of low competence, in turn, lessened information sharing." Chances are, if you are including a smiley face in an email for work, the last thing you want is for your co-workers to think that you are so inadequate that they chose not to share information with you.

① makes you look incompetent
② causes conflict between generations
③ clarifies the intention of the message
④ results in low scores in writing tests
⑤ helps create a casual work environment

05

다음 빈칸에 들어갈 말로 가장 적절한 것을 고르시오. [3점]

It is common to assume that creativity concerns primarily the relation between actor(creator) and artifact (creation). However, from a sociocultural standpoint, the creative act is never "complete" in the absence of a second position — that of an audience. While the actor or creator him/herself is the first audience of the artifact being produced, this kind of distantiation can only be achieved by _____. This means that, in order to be an audience to your own creation, a history of interaction with others is needed. We exist in a social world that constantly confronts us with the "view of the other." It is the view we include and blend into our own activity, including creative activity. This outside perspective is essential for creativity because it gives new meaning and value to the creative act and its product.

* artifact: 창작물

① exploring the absolute truth in existence
② following a series of precise and logical steps
③ looking outside and drawing inspiration from nature
④ internalizing the perspective of others on one's work
⑤ pushing the audience to the limits of its endurance

06

다음 빈칸에 들어갈 말로 가장 적절한 것을 고르시오. [3점]

Vision is like shooting at a moving target. Plenty of things can go wrong in the future and plenty more can change in unpredictable ways. When such things happen, you should be prepared to _____. For example, a businessman's optimistic forecast can be blown away by a cruel recession or by aggressive competition in ways he could not have foreseen. Or in another scenario, his sales can skyrocket and his numbers can get even better. In any event, he will be foolish to stick to his old vision in the face of new data. There is nothing wrong in modifying your vision or even abandoning it, as necessary.

* recession: 경기 침체

① explain your vision logically to others
② defend the wrong decisions you've made
③ build a community to share your experience
④ make your vision conform to the new reality
⑤ consult experts to predict the future economy

07 1등급 대비 고난도 2점 문제

다음 빈칸에 들어갈 말로 가장 적절한 것을 고르시오.

One of the most important aspects of providing good care is making sure that an animal's needs are being met consistently and predictably. Like humans, animals need a sense of control. So an animal who may get enough food but doesn't know when the food will appear and can see no consistent schedule may experience distress. We can provide a sense of control by ensuring that our animal's environment is _____ : there is always water available and always in the same place. There is always food when we get up in the morning and after our evening walk. There will always be a time and place to eliminate, without having to hold things in to the point of discomfort. Human companions can display consistent emotional support, rather than providing love one moment and withholding love the next. When animals know what to expect, they can feel more confident and calm.

* eliminate: 배설하다

① silent
② natural
③ isolated
④ dynamic
⑤ predictable

08 1등급 대비 고난도 2점 문제

다음 빈칸에 들어갈 말로 가장 적절한 것을 고르시오.

Research has confirmed that athletes are less likely to participate in unacceptable behavior than are non-athletes. However, moral reasoning and good sporting behavior seem to decline as athletes progress to higher competitive levels, in part because of the increased emphasis on winning. Thus winning can be _____ _____ in teaching character development. Some athletes may want to win so much that they lie, cheat, and break team rules. They may develop undesirable character traits that can enhance their ability to win in the short term. However, when athletes resist the temptation to win in a dishonest way, they can develop positive character traits that last a lifetime. Character is a learned behavior, and a sense of fair play develops only if coaches plan to teach those lessons systematically.

* trait: 특성

① a piece of cake
② a one-way street
③ a bird in the hand
④ a fish out of water
⑤ a double-edged sword

09 1등급 대비 고난도 3점 문제

다음 빈칸에 들어갈 말로 가장 적절한 것을 고르시오. [3점]

Since a great deal of day-to-day academic work is boring and repetitive, you need to be well motivated to keep doing it. A mathematician sharpens her pencils, works on a proof, tries a few approaches, gets nowhere, and finishes for the day. A writer sits down at his desk, produces a few hundred words, decides they are no good, throws them in the bin, and hopes for better inspiration tomorrow. To produce something worthwhile — if it ever happens — may require years of such _____ labor. The Nobel Prize-winning biologist Peter Medawar said that about four-fifths of his time in science was wasted, adding sadly that "nearly all scientific research leads nowhere." What kept all of these people going when things were going badly was their passion for their subject. Without such passion, they would have achieved nothing.

* proof: (수학) 증명

① cooperative ② productive
③ fruitless ④ dangerous
⑤ irregular

10 1등급 대비 고난도 3점 문제

다음 빈칸에 들어갈 말로 가장 적절한 것을 고르시오. [3점]

Questions convey interest, but sometimes the interest they convey is not closely related to what the person is trying to say. Sometimes the distraction is obvious. If you're telling a friend all the unpleasant things you experienced on your vacation, and she interrupts with a lot of questions about where you stayed, you won't feel listened to. At other times people seem to be following but can't help trying to lead. These listeners force their own narrative structures on our experience. Their questions assume that _____: "Problems should be denied or made to go away"; "Everyone should be together"; "Bullies must be confronted." By finishing our sentences, pumping us with questions, and otherwise pushing us to say what they want to hear, controlling listeners violate our right to tell our own stories.

① our stories should fit their scripts
② friends should share everything
③ people have different tastes
④ many questions are always better
⑤ their problems can be solved at once

11 [1등급 대비 고난도 3점 문제]

다음 빈칸에 들어갈 말로 가장 적절한 것을 고르시오. [3점]

It is difficult to know how to determine whether one culture is better than another. What is the cultural rank order of rock, jazz, and classical music? When it comes to public opinion polls about whether cultural changes are for the better or the worse, looking forward would lead to one answer and looking backward would lead to a very different answer. Our children would be horrified if they were told they had to go back to the culture of their grandparents. Our parents would be horrified if they were told they had to participate in the culture of their grandchildren. Humans tend to _____ _____. After a certain age, anxieties arise when sudden cultural changes are coming. Our culture is part of who we are and where we stand, and we don't like to think that who we are and where we stand are short-lived.

① seek cooperation between generations
② be forgetful of what they experienced
③ adjust quickly to the new environment
④ make efforts to remember what their ancestors did
⑤ like what they have grown up in and gotten used to

12 [1등급 대비 고난도 3점 문제]

다음 빈칸에 들어갈 말로 가장 적절한 것을 고르시오. [3점]

There is a famous Spanish proverb that says, "The belly rules the mind." This is a clinically proven fact. Food is the original mind-controlling drug. Every time we eat, we bombard our brains with a feast of chemicals, triggering an explosive hormonal chain reaction that directly influences the way we think. Countless studies have shown that the positive emotional state induced by a good meal _____. It triggers an instinctive desire to repay the provider. This is why executives regularly combine business meetings with meals, why lobbyists invite politicians to attend receptions, lunches, and dinners, and why major state occasions almost always involve an impressive banquet. Churchill called this "dining diplomacy," and sociologists have confirmed that this principle is a strong motivator across all human cultures.

* banquet: 연회

① leads us to make a fair judgement
② interferes with cooperation with others
③ does harm to serious diplomatic occasions
④ plays a critical role in improving our health
⑤ enhances our receptiveness to be persuaded

DAY 05

| 학습 Check! | ▶ 몰라서 틀린 문항 × 표기 ▶ 헷갈렸거나 찍은 문항 △ 표기 ▶ ×, △ 문항은 다시 풀고 ✔ 표기를 하세요. |

종료 시각	시 분 초	문항 번호	01	02	03	04	05	06	07	08	09	10	11	12
소요 시간	분 초	채점 결과												
초과 시간	분 초	틀린 문항 복습												

DAY 06

※ 점수 표기가 없는 문항은 모두 **2점**입니다.

빈칸이 후반부에 있을 때 **빈칸 추론 06**

● 날짜 :　　월　　일 ● 시작 시각 :　　시　　분　　초

● 목표 시간 : 20분

01

고1 • 2017년 3월 31번

다음 빈칸에 들어갈 말로 가장 적절한 것을 고르시오. [3점]

In small towns the same workman makes chairs and doors and tables, and often the same person builds houses. And it is, of course, impossible for a man of many trades to be skilled in all of them. In large cities, on the other hand, because many people make demands on each trade, one trade alone — very often even less than a whole trade — is enough to support a man. For instance, one man makes shoes for men, and another for women. And there are places even where one man earns a living by only stitching shoes, another by cutting them out, and another by sewing the uppers together. Such skilled workers may have used simple tools, but their _____ did result in more efficient and productive work.

＊trade: 직종

① specialization
② criticism
③ competition
④ diligence
⑤ imagination

02

고1 • 2022년 11월 31번

다음 빈칸에 들어갈 말로 가장 적절한 것을 고르시오.

To demonstrate how best to defeat the habit of delaying, Dan Ariely, a professor of psychology and behavioral economics, performed an experiment on students in three of his classes at MIT. He assigned all classes three reports over the course of the semester. The first class had to choose three due dates for themselves, up to and including the last day of class. The second had no deadlines — all three papers just had to be submitted by the last day of class. In his third class, he gave students three set deadlines over the course of the semester. At the end of the semester, he found that students with set deadlines received the best grades, the students with no deadlines had the worst, and those who could choose their own deadlines fell somewhere in the middle. Ariely concludes that _____ — whether by the professor or by students who recognize their own tendencies to delay things — improves self-control and performance.

① offering rewards
② removing obstacles
③ restricting freedom
④ increasing assignments
⑤ encouraging competition

03

다음 빈칸에 들어갈 말로 가장 적절한 것을 고르시오. [3점]

In 1995, a group of high school students in Miner County, South Dakota, started planning a revival. They wanted to do something that might revive their dying community. Miner County had been failing for decades. Farm and industrial jobs had slowly dried up, and nothing had replaced them. The students started investigating the situation. One finding in particular disturbed them. They discovered that half of the residents had been shopping outside the county, driving an hour to Sioux Falls to shop in larger stores. Most of the things that could improve the situation were out of the students' control. But they did uncover one thing that was very much in their control: inviting the residents to _____. They found their first slogan: Let's keep Miner dollars in Miner County.

＊resident: 주민

① work out regularly
② spend money locally
③ drive their cars safely
④ treat strangers nicely
⑤ share work equally

04

다음 빈칸에 들어갈 말로 가장 적절한 것을 고르시오.

The quest for knowledge in the material world is a never-ending pursuit, but the quest does not mean that a thoroughly schooled person is an educated person or that an educated person is a wise person. We are too often blinded by our ignorance of our ignorance, and our pursuit of knowledge is no guarantee of wisdom. Hence, we are prone to becoming the blind leading the blind because our overemphasis on competition in nearly everything makes looking good more important than being good. The resultant fear of being thought a fool and criticized therefore is one of greatest enemies of true learning. Although our ignorance is undeniably vast, it is from the vastness of this selfsame ignorance that our sense of wonder grows. But, when we do not know we are ignorant, we do not know enough to even question, let alone investigate, our ignorance. No one can teach another person anything. All one can do with and for someone else is to facilitate learning by helping the person to _____.

＊prone to: ~하기 쉬운 ＊＊selfsame: 똑같은

① find their role in teamwork
② learn from others' successes and failures
③ make the most of technology for learning
④ obtain knowledge from wonderful experts
⑤ discover the wonder of their ignorance

05

다음 빈칸에 들어갈 말로 가장 적절한 것을 고르시오. [3점]

Everything in the world around us was finished in the mind of its creator before it was started. The houses we live in, the cars we drive, and our clothing — all of these began with an idea. Each idea was then studied, refined and perfected before the first nail was driven or the first piece of cloth was cut. Long before the idea was turned into a physical reality, the mind had clearly pictured the finished product. The human being designs his or her own future through much the same process. We begin with an idea about how the future will be. Over a period of time we refine and perfect the vision. Before long, our every thought, decision and activity are all working in harmony to bring into existence what we _____.

＊refine: 다듬다

① didn't even have the potential to accomplish
② have mentally concluded about the future
③ haven't been able to picture in our mind
④ considered careless and irresponsible
⑤ have observed in some professionals

06

다음 빈칸에 들어갈 말로 가장 적절한 것을 고르시오. [3점]

The good news is, where you end up ten years from now is up to you. You are free to choose what you want to make of your life. It's called *free will* and it's your basic right. What's more, you can turn it on instantly! At any moment, you can choose to start showing more respect for yourself or stop hanging out with friends who bring you down. After all, you choose to be happy or miserable. The reality is that although you are free to choose, you can't choose the consequences of your choices. It's a package deal. As the old saying goes, "_____." Choice and consequence go together like mashed potatoes and gravy.

＊gravy: (육즙을 이용해 만든) 소스

① From saying to doing is a long step
② A good beginning makes a good ending
③ One man's trash is another man's treasure
④ If you pick up one end of the stick, you pick up the other
⑤ The best means of destroying an enemy is to make him your friend

07 1등급 대비 고난도 2점 문제

다음 빈칸에 들어갈 말로 가장 적절한 것을 고르시오.

Individuals who perform at a high level in their profession often have instant credibility with others. People admire them, they want to be like them, and they feel connected to them. When they speak, others listen — even if the area of their skill has nothing to do with the advice they give. Think about a world-famous basketball player. He has made more money from endorsements than he ever did playing basketball. Is it because of his knowledge of the products he endorses? No. It's because of what he can do with a basketball. The same can be said of an Olympic medalist swimmer. People listen to him because of what he can do in the pool. And when an actor tells us we should drive a certain car, we don't listen because of his expertise on engines. We listen because we admire his talent. _____ connects. If you possess a high level of ability in an area, others may desire to connect with you because of it.

＊endorsement: (유명인의 텔레비전 등에서의 상품) 보증 선전

① Patience
② Sacrifice
③ Honesty
④ Excellence
⑤ Creativity

08 1등급 대비 고난도 2점 문제

다음 빈칸에 들어갈 말로 가장 적절한 것을 고르시오.

As the tenth anniversary of the terrorist attacks of September 11, 2001, approached, 9/11-related media stories peaked in the days immediately surrounding the anniversary date and then dropped off rapidly in the weeks thereafter. Surveys conducted during those times asked citizens to choose two "especially important" events from the past seventy years. Two weeks prior to the anniversary, before the media blitz began, about 30 percent of respondents named 9/11. But as the anniversary drew closer, and the media treatment intensified, survey respondents started identifying 9/11 in increasing numbers — to a high of 65 percent. Two weeks later, though, after reportage had decreased to earlier levels, once again only about 30 percent of the participants placed it among their two especially important events of the past seventy years. Clearly, the _____ of news coverage can make a big difference in the *perceived* significance of an issue among observers as they are exposed to the coverage.

＊blitz: 대선전, 집중 공세

① accuracy
② tone
③ amount
④ source
⑤ type

DAY 06

09 1등급 대비 고난도 3점 문제

다음 빈칸에 들어갈 말로 가장 적절한 것을 고르시오. [3점]

The law of demand is that the demand for goods and services increases as prices fall, and the demand falls as prices increase. *Giffen goods* are special types of products for which the traditional law of demand does not apply. Instead of switching to cheaper replacements, consumers demand more of giffen goods when the price increases and less of them when the price decreases. Taking an example, rice in China is a giffen good because people tend to purchase less of it when the price falls. The reason for this is, when the price of rice falls, people have more money to spend on other types of products such as meat and dairy and, therefore, change their spending pattern. On the other hand, as rice prices increase, people _____.

① order more meat
② consume more rice
③ try to get new jobs
④ increase their savings
⑤ start to invest overseas

10 1등급 대비 고난도 3점 문제

다음 빈칸에 들어갈 말로 가장 적절한 것을 고르시오. [3점]

For many people, *ability* refers to intellectual competence, so they want everything they do to reflect how smart they are — writing a brilliant legal brief, getting the highest grade on a test, writing elegant computer code, saying something exceptionally wise or witty in a conversation. You could also define ability in terms of a particular skill or talent, such as how well one plays the piano, learns a language, or serves a tennis ball. Some people focus on their ability to be attractive, entertaining, up on the latest trends, or to have the newest gadgets. However ability may be defined, a problem occurs when _____ _____. The performance becomes the *only* measure of the person; nothing else is taken into account. An outstanding performance means an outstanding person; an average performance means an average person. Period.

① it is the sole determinant of one's self-worth
② you are distracted by others' achievements
③ there is too much competition in one field
④ you ignore feedback about a performance
⑤ it is not accompanied by effort

11 1등급 대비 고난도 3점 문제

고1 · 2019년 11월 33번

다음 빈칸에 들어갈 말로 가장 적절한 것을 고르시오. [3점]

Focusing on the differences among societies conceals a deeper reality: their similarities are greater and more profound than their dissimilarities. Imagine studying two hills while standing on a ten-thousand-foot-high plateau. Seen from your perspective, one hill appears to be three hundred feet high, and the other appears to be nine hundred feet. This difference may seem large, and you might focus your attention on what local forces, such as erosion, account for the difference in size. But this narrow perspective misses the opportunity to study the other, more significant geological forces that created what are actually two very similar mountains, one 10,300 feet high and the other 10,900 feet. And when it comes to human societies, people have been standing on a ten-thousand-foot plateau, letting the differences among societies _____.

* erosion: 침식

① prove the uniqueness of each society
② prevent cross-cultural understanding
③ mask the more overwhelming similarities
④ change their perspective on what diversity is
⑤ encourage them to step out of their mental frame

12 1등급 대비 고난도 3점 문제

고1 · 2020년 3월 34번

다음 빈칸에 들어갈 말로 가장 적절한 것을 고르시오. [3점]

Say you normally go to a park to walk or work out. Maybe today you should choose a different park. Why? Well, who knows? Maybe it's because you need the connection to the different energy in the other park. Maybe you'll run into people there that you've never met before. You could make a new best friend simply by visiting a different park. You never know what great things will happen to you until you step outside the zone where you feel comfortable. If you're staying in your comfort zone and you're not pushing yourself past that same old energy, then you're not going to move forward on your path. By forcing yourself to do something different, you're awakening yourself on a spiritual level and you're forcing yourself to do something that will benefit you in the long run. As they say, _____.

① variety is the spice of life
② fantasy is the mirror of reality
③ failure teaches more than success
④ laziness is the mother of invention
⑤ conflict strengthens the relationship

DAY 06

학습 Check!

▶ 몰라서 틀린 문항 × 표기 ▶ 헷갈렸거나 찍은 문항 △ 표기 ▶ ×, △ 문항은 다시 풀고 ✔ 표기를 하세요.

종료 시각	시 분 초	문항 번호	01	02	03	04	05	06	07	08	09	10	11	12
소요 시간	분 초	채점 결과												
초과 시간	분 초	틀린 문항 복습												

DAY 07

※ 점수 표기가 없는 문항은 모두 2점입니다.

빈칸이 후반부에 있을 때 **빈칸 추론 07**

● 날짜 :　월　일　● 시작 시각 :　시　분　초

● 목표 시간 : 20분

01

고3 • 2022학년도 수능 31번

다음 빈칸에 들어갈 말로 가장 적절한 것을 고르시오.

Humour involves not just practical disengagement but cognitive disengagement. As long as something is funny, we are for the moment not concerned with whether it is real or fictional, true or false. This is why we give considerable leeway to people telling funny stories. If they are getting extra laughs by exaggerating the silliness of a situation or even by making up a few details, we are happy to grant them comic licence, a kind of poetic licence. Indeed, someone listening to a funny story who tries to correct the teller — 'No, he didn't spill the spaghetti on the keyboard and the monitor, just on the keyboard' — will probably be told by the other listeners to stop interrupting. The creator of humour is putting ideas into people's heads for the pleasure those ideas will bring, not to provide _____ information.

＊cognitive: 인식의　＊＊leeway: 여지

① accurate
② detailed
③ useful
④ additional
⑤ alternative

02

고1 • 2019년 6월 33번

다음 빈칸에 들어갈 말로 가장 적절한 것을 고르시오.

The mind is essentially a survival machine. Attack and defense against other minds, gathering, storing, and analyzing information — this is what it is good at, but it is not at all creative. All true artists create from a place of no-mind, from inner stillness. Even great scientists have reported that their creative breakthroughs came at a time of mental quietude. The surprising result of a nationwide inquiry among America's most famous mathematicians, including Einstein, to find out their working methods, was that thinking "plays only a subordinate part in the brief, decisive phase of the creative act itself." So I would say that the simple reason why the majority of scientists are *not* creative is not because they don't know how to think, but because they don't know how to _____!

＊quietude: 정적　＊＊subordinate: 부수적인

① organize their ideas
② interact socially
③ stop thinking
④ gather information
⑤ use their imagination

03

다음 빈칸에 들어갈 말로 가장 적절한 것을 고르시오.

Motivation may come from several sources. It may be the respect I give every student, the daily greeting I give at my classroom door, the undivided attention when I listen to a student, a pat on the shoulder whether the job was done well or not, an accepting smile, or simply "I love you" when it is most needed. It may simply be asking how things are at home. For one student considering dropping out of school, it was a note from me after one of his frequent absences saying that he made my day when I saw him in school. He came to me with the note with tears in his eyes and thanked me. He will graduate this year. Whatever technique is used, the students must know that you _____. But the concern must be genuine — the students can't be fooled.

① care about them
② keep your words
③ differ from them
④ evaluate their performance
⑤ communicate with their parents

04

다음 빈칸에 들어갈 말로 가장 적절한 것을 고르시오.

More than just *having* territories, animals also *partition* them. And this insight turned out to be particularly useful for zoo husbandry. An animal's territory has an internal arrangement that Heini Hediger compared to the inside of a person's house. Most of us assign separate functions to separate rooms, but even if you look at a one-room house you will find the same internal specialization. In a cabin or a mud hut, or even a Mesolithic cave from 30,000 years ago, this part is for cooking, that part is for sleeping; this part is for making tools and weaving, that part is for waste. We keep _____. To a varying extent, other animals do the same. A part of an animal's territory is for eating, a part for sleeping, a part for swimming or wallowing, a part may be set aside for waste, depending on the species of animal.

＊husbandry: 관리

① an interest in close neighbors
② a neat functional organization
③ a stock of emergency supplies
④ a distance from potential rivals
⑤ a strictly observed daily routine

DAY 07

05

다음 빈칸에 들어갈 말로 가장 적절한 것을 고르시오. [3점]

Did you know you actually think in images and not in words? Images are simply mental pictures showing ideas and experiences. Early humans communicated their ideas and experiences to others for thousands of years by drawing pictures in the sand or on the walls of their caves. Only recently have humans created various languages and alphabets to symbolize these "picture" messages. Your mind has not yet adapted to this relatively new development. An image has a much greater impact on your brain than words; the nerves from the eye to the brain are twenty-five times larger than the nerves from the ear to the brain. You often remember a person's face but not his or her name, for example. The old saying, "_____," is true.

① Actions speak louder than words

② A bad workman blames his tools

③ You can't judge a book by its cover

④ The pen is mightier than the sword

⑤ A picture is worth a thousand words

06

다음 빈칸에 들어갈 말로 가장 적절한 것을 고르시오. [3점]

In the studies of Colin Cherry at the Massachusetts Institute for Technology back in the 1950s, his participants listened to voices in one ear at a time and then through both ears in an effort to determine whether we can listen to two people talk at the same time. One ear always contained a message that the listener had to repeat back (called "shadowing") while the other ear included people speaking. The trick was to see if you could totally focus on the main message and also hear someone talking in your other ear. Cleverly, Cherry found it was impossible for his participants to know whether the message in the other ear was spoken by a man or woman, in English or another language, or was even comprised of real words at all! In other words, people could not _____.

① decide what they should do in the moment

② remember a message with too many words

③ analyze which information was more accurate

④ speak their own ideas while listening to others

⑤ process two pieces of information at the same time

07 1등급 대비 고난도 2점 문제

다음 빈칸에 들어갈 말로 가장 적절한 것을 고르시오.

One of the big questions faced this past year was how to keep innovation rolling when people were working entirely virtually. But experts say that digital work didn't have a negative effect on innovation and creativity. Working within limits pushes us to solve problems. Overall, virtual meeting platforms put more constraints on communication and collaboration than face-to-face settings. For instance, with the press of a button, virtual meeting hosts can control the size of breakout groups and enforce time constraints; only one person can speak at a time; nonverbal signals, particularly those below the shoulders, are diminished; "seating arrangements" are assigned by the platform, not by individuals; and visual access to others may be limited by the size of each participant's screen. Such _____ are likely to stretch participants beyond their usual ways of thinking, boosting creativity.

① restrictions   ② responsibilities
③ memories   ④ coincidences
⑤ traditions

08 1등급 대비 고난도 3점 문제

다음 빈칸에 들어갈 말로 가장 적절한 것을 고르시오. [3점]

In an experiment, researchers presented participants with two photos of faces and asked participants to choose the photo that they thought was more attractive, and then handed participants that photo. Using a clever trick inspired by stage magic, when participants received the photo, it had been switched to the photo not chosen by the participant — the less attractive photo. Remarkably, most participants accepted this photo as their own choice and then proceeded to give arguments for why they had chosen that face in the first place. This revealed a striking mismatch between our choices and our ability to _____. This same finding has since been observed in various domains including taste for jam and financial decisions.

① keep focused
② solve problems
③ rationalize outcomes
④ control our emotions
⑤ attract others' attention

09 1등급 대비 고난도 3점 문제

다음 빈칸에 들어갈 말로 가장 적절한 것을 고르시오. [3점]

Most of us are suspicious of rapid cognition. We believe that the quality of the decision is directly related to the time and effort that went into making it. That's what we tell our children: "Haste makes waste." "Look before you leap." "Stop and think." "Don't judge a book by its cover." We believe that we are always better off gathering as much information as possible and spending as much time as possible in careful consideration. But there are moments, particularly in time-driven, critical situations, when _____, when our snap judgments and first impressions can offer better means of making sense of the world. Survivors have somehow learned this lesson and have developed and sharpened their skill of rapid cognition.

* cognition: 인식

① haste does not make waste
② it is never too late to learn
③ many hands make light work
④ slow and steady wins the race
⑤ you don't judge by appearances

10 1등급 대비 고난도 3점 문제

다음 빈칸에 들어갈 말로 가장 적절한 것을 고르시오. [3점]

We're often told that newborns and infants are comforted by rocking because this motion is similar to what they experienced in the womb, and that they must take comfort in this familiar feeling. This may be true; however, to date there are no convincing data that demonstrate a significant relationship between the amount of time a mother moves during pregnancy and her newborn's response to rocking. Just as likely is the idea that newborns come to associate gentle rocking with being fed. Parents understand that rocking quiets a newborn, and they very often provide gentle, repetitive movement during feeding. Since the appearance of food is a primary reinforcer, newborns may _____ _____ because they have been conditioned through a process of associative learning.

* womb: 자궁 ** reinforcer: 강화물

① acquire a fondness for motion
② want consistent feeding
③ dislike severe rocking
④ remember the tastes of food
⑤ form a bond with their mothers

11 1등급 대비 고난도 3점 문제

고1 · 2020년 6월 34번

다음 빈칸에 들어갈 말로 가장 적절한 것을 고르시오. [3점]

One of the main reasons that students may think they know the material, even when they don't, is that they mistake familiarity for understanding. Here is how it works: You read the chapter once, perhaps highlighting as you go. Then later, you read the chapter again, perhaps focusing on the highlighted material. As you read it over, the material is familiar because you remember it from before, and this familiarity might lead you to think, "Okay, I know that." The problem is that this feeling of familiarity is not necessarily equivalent to knowing the material and may be of no help when you have to come up with an answer on the exam. In fact, familiarity can often lead to errors on multiple-choice exams because you might pick a choice that looks familiar, only to find later that it was something you had read, but _____.

* equivalent: 동등한

① you couldn't recall the parts you had highlighted
② it wasn't really the best answer to the question
③ that familiarity was based on your understanding
④ repetition enabled you to pick the correct answer
⑤ it indicated that familiarity was naturally built up

12 1등급 대비 고난도 3점 문제

고1 · 2021년 3월 34번

다음 빈칸에 들어갈 말로 가장 적절한 것을 고르시오. [3점]

It is important to distinguish between being legally allowed to do something, and actually being able to go and do it. A law could be passed allowing everyone, if they so wish, to run a mile in two minutes. That would not, however, increase their *effective* freedom, because, although allowed to do so, they are physically incapable of it. Having a minimum of restrictions and a maximum of possibilities is fine. But in the real world most people will never have the opportunity either to become all that they are allowed to become, or to need to be restrained from doing everything that is possible for them to do. Their effective freedom depends on actually _____.

* restriction: 제약 ** restrain: 저지하다

① respecting others' rights to freedom
② protecting and providing for the needy
③ learning what socially acceptable behaviors are
④ determining how much they can expect from others
⑤ having the means and ability to do what they choose

DAY 07

▶ 몰라서 틀린 문항 × 표기 ▶ 헷갈렸거나 찍은 문항 △ 표기 ▶ ×, △ 문항은 다시 풀고 ✔ 표기를 하세요.

종료 시각	시 분 초	문항 번호	01	02	03	04	05	06	07	08	09	10	11	12
소요 시간	분 초	채점 결과												
초과 시간	분 초	틀린 문항 복습												

DAY 08

※ 점수 표기가 없는 문항은 모두 **2점**입니다.

빈칸이 후반부에 있을 때 **빈칸 추론 08**

● 날짜 : 　월　일 ● 시작 시각 : 　시　분　초

● 목표 시간 : 20분

01

고1 · 2023년 9월 31번

다음 빈칸에 들어갈 말로 가장 적절한 것을 고르시오.

　Many people are terrified to fly in airplanes. Often, this fear stems from a lack of control. The pilot is in control, not the passengers, and this lack of control instills fear. Many potential passengers are so afraid they choose to drive great distances to get to a destination instead of flying. But their decision to drive is based solely on emotion, not logic. Logic says that statistically, the odds of dying in a car crash are around 1 in 5,000, while the odds of dying in a plane crash are closer to 1 in 11 million. If you're going to take a risk, especially one that could possibly involve your well-being, wouldn't you want the odds in your favor? However, most people choose the option that will cause them the least amount of _____. Pay attention to the thoughts you have about taking the risk and make sure you're basing your decision on facts, not just feelings.

＊instill: 스며들게 하다

① anxiety　　　　② boredom
③ confidence　　 ④ satisfaction
⑤ responsibility

02

고1 · 2017년 3월 32번

다음 빈칸에 들어갈 말로 가장 적절한 것을 고르시오. [3점]

　About four billion years ago, molecules joined together to form cells. About two billion years later, cells joined together to form more complex cells. And then a billion years later, these more complex cells joined together to form multicellular organisms. All of these evolved because the participating individuals could, by working together, spread their genetic material in new and more effective ways. Fast-forward another billion years to our world, which is full of social animals, from ants to wolves to humans. The same principle applies. Ants and wolves in groups can do things that no single ant or wolf can do, and we humans, by _____, have become the earth's dominant species.

＊molecule: 분자

① cooperating with one another
② fighting against enemies
③ studying other species
④ inventing various machines
⑤ paying attention to differences

03

다음 빈칸에 들어갈 말로 가장 적절한 것을 고르시오.

People have always wanted to be around other people and to learn from them. Cities have long been dynamos of social possibility, foundries of art, music, and fashion. Slang, or, if you prefer, "lexical innovation," has always started in cities — an outgrowth of all those different people so frequently exposed to one another. It spreads outward, in a manner not unlike trans-missible disease, which itself typically "takes off" in cities. If, as the noted linguist Leonard Bloomfield argued, the way a person talks is a "composite result of what he has heard before," then language innovation would happen where the most people heard and talked to the most other people. Cities drive taste change because they _____, who not surprisingly are often the creative people cities seem to attract. Media, ever more global, ever more far-reaching, spread language faster to more people.

＊foundry: 주물 공장 ＊＊lexical: 어휘의

① provide rich source materials for artists
② offer the greatest exposure to other people
③ cause cultural conflicts among users of slang
④ present ideal research environments to linguists
⑤ reduce the social mobility of ambitious outsiders

04

다음 빈칸에 들어갈 말로 가장 적절한 것을 고르시오. [3점]

Just think for a moment of all the people upon whom your participation in your class depends. Clearly, the class requires a teacher to teach it and students to take it. However, it also depends on many other people and organizations. Someone had to decide when the class would be held and in what room, communicate that information to you, and enroll you in that class. Someone also had to write a textbook, and with the assistance of many other people — printers, editors, salespeople, and bookstore employees — it has arrived in your hands. Thus, a class that seems to involve just you, your fellow students, and your teacher is in fact _____.

① more interesting than playing games
② the product of the efforts of hundreds of people
③ the place where students can improve writing skills
④ most effective when combined with online learning
⑤ the race where everyone is a winner

05

다음 빈칸에 들어갈 말로 가장 적절한 것을 고르시오. [3점]

How funny are you? While some people are natural humorists, being funny is a set of skills that can be learned. Exceptionally funny people don't depend upon their memory to keep track of everything they find funny. In the olden days, great comedians carried notebooks to write down funny thoughts or observations and scrapbooks for news clippings that struck them as funny. Today, you can do that easily with your smartphone. If you have a funny thought, record it as an audio note. If you read a funny article, save the link in your bookmarks. The world is a funny place and your existence within it is probably funnier. Accepting that fact is a blessing that gives you everything you need to see humor and craft stories on a daily basis. All you have to do is _____.

① keep away from new technology
② take risks and challenge yourself
③ have friendly people close to you
④ document them and then tell someone
⑤ improve interpersonal relationship at work

06

다음 빈칸에 들어갈 말로 가장 적절한 것을 고르시오. [3점]

From an economic perspective, a short-lived event can become an innovative event if it generates goods and services that can be sold to people, in particular to those from outside the locality. The remarkable growth of art exhibitions, cultural festivals and sports competitions, for example, can be analysed in this light. They are temporary activities that can attract large numbers of outsiders to a locality, bringing in new sources of income. But even here, there is a two-way interaction between the event and the context. The existence of an infrastructure, a reputation, a history of an activity for an area may have important effects on the economic success or failure of an event. In other words, events do not take place in a vacuum. They depend on an existing context which has been in the making for a long time. The short-lived event, therefore, would _____.

* infrastructure: 기반 시설

① build a new context with other short-lived events
② take place free from this spatial and temporal limit
③ be performed in relation to this long-term context
④ interact with well-known events from another locality
⑤ evolve itself from a local event to a global one in the end

07 1등급 대비 고난도 2점 문제

다음 빈칸에 들어갈 말로 가장 적절한 것을 고르시오.

People engage in typical patterns of interaction based on the relationship between their roles and the roles of others. Employers are expected to interact with employees in a certain way, as are doctors with patients. In each case, actions are restricted by the role responsibilities and obligations associated with individuals' positions within society. For instance, parents and children are linked by certain rights, privileges, and obligations. Parents are responsible for providing their children with the basic necessities of life — food, clothing, shelter, and so forth. These expectations are so powerful that not meeting them may make the parents vulnerable to charges of negligence or abuse. Children, in turn, are expected to do as their parents say. Thus, interactions within a relationship are functions not only of the individual personalities of the people involved but also of the role requirements associated with the _____ they have.

* vulnerable: 비난받기 쉬운　** negligence: 태만

① careers　　　　② statuses
③ abilities　　　　④ motivations
⑤ perspectives

08 1등급 대비 고난도 3점 문제

다음 빈칸에 들어갈 말로 가장 적절한 것을 고르시오. [3점]

There is a very old story involving a man trying to fix his broken boiler. Despite his best efforts over many months, he can't do it. Eventually, he gives up and decides to call in an expert. The engineer arrives, gives one gentle tap on the side of the boiler, and it springs to life. The engineer gives a bill to the man, and the man argues that he should pay only a small fee as the job took the engineer only a few moments. The engineer explains that the man is not paying for the time he took to tap the boiler but rather the years of experience involved in knowing exactly where to tap. Just like the expert engineer tapping the boiler, effective change _____. In fact, it is often simply a question of knowing exactly where to tap.

① needs competition among experts
② does not have to be time-consuming
③ requires the development of equipment
④ does not come from previous experience
⑤ often takes place as a result of good luck

DAY 08

09 1등급 대비 고난도 3점 문제
고1 · 2021년 6월 33번

다음 빈칸에 들어갈 말로 가장 적절한 것을 고르시오. [3점]

Due to technological innovations, music can now be experienced by more people, for more of the time than ever before. Mass availability has given individuals unheard-of control over their own sound-environment. However, it has also confronted them with the simultaneous availability of countless genres of music, in which they have to orient themselves. People start filtering out and organizing their digital libraries like they used to do with their physical music collections. However, there is the difference that the choice lies in their own hands. Without being restricted to the limited collection of music-distributors, nor being guided by the local radio program as a 'preselector' of the latest hits, the individual actively has to _____ _____. The search for the right song is thus associated with considerable effort.

＊simultaneous: 동시의

① choose and determine his or her musical preferences
② understand the technical aspects of recording sessions
③ share unique and inspiring playlists on social media
④ interpret lyrics with background knowledge of the songs
⑤ seek the advice of a voice specialist for better performances

10 1등급 대비 고난도 3점 문제
고1 · 2023년 3월 33번

다음 빈칸에 들어갈 말로 가장 적절한 것을 고르시오. [3점]

In Lewis Carroll's *Through the Looking-Glass*, the Red Queen takes Alice on a race through the countryside. They run and they run, but then Alice discovers that they're still under the same tree that they started from. The Red Queen explains to Alice: "*here*, you see, it takes all the running you can do, to keep in the same place." Biologists sometimes use this Red Queen Effect to explain an evolutionary principle. If foxes evolve to run faster so they can catch more rabbits, then only the fastest rabbits will live long enough to make a new generation of bunnies that run even faster — in which case, of course, only the fastest foxes will catch enough rabbits to thrive and pass on their genes. Even though they might run, the two species _____.

＊thrive: 번성하다

① just stay in place
② end up walking slowly
③ never run into each other
④ won't be able to adapt to changes
⑤ cannot run faster than their parents

11 1등급 대비 고난도 3점 문제

다음 빈칸에 들어갈 말로 가장 적절한 것을 고르시오. [3점]

In a study at Princeton University in 1992, research scientists looked at two different groups of mice. One group was made intellectually superior by modifying the gene for the glutamate receptor. Glutamate is a brain chemical that is necessary in learning. The other group was genetically manipulated to be intellectually inferior, also done by modifying the gene for the glutamate receptor. The smart mice were then raised in standard cages, while the inferior mice were raised in large cages with toys and exercise wheels and with lots of social interaction. At the end of the study, although the intellectually inferior mice were genetically handicapped, they were able to perform just as well as their genetic superiors. This was a real triumph for nurture over nature. Genes are turned on or off _____ .

* glutamate: 글루타민산염 ** manipulate: 조작하다

① by themselves for survival
② free from social interaction
③ based on what is around you
④ depending on genetic superiority
⑤ so as to keep ourselves entertained

12 1등급 대비 고난도 3점 문제

다음 빈칸에 들어갈 말로 가장 적절한 것을 고르시오. [3점]

The acceleration of human migration toward the shores is a contemporary phenomenon, but the knowledge and understanding of the potential risks regarding coastal living are not. Indeed, even at a time when human-induced greenhouse-gas emissions were not exponentially altering the climate, warming the oceans, and leading to rising seas, our ancestors knew how to better listen to and respect the many movements and warnings of the seas, thus _____ .
For instance, along Japan's coast, hundreds of so-called tsunami stones, some more than six centuries old, were put in place to warn people not to build homes below a certain point. Over the world, moon and tides, winds, rains and hurricanes were naturally guiding humans' settlement choice.

* exponentially: 기하급수적으로

① ruining natural habitats
② leveling the ground evenly
③ forming primitive superstitions
④ blaming their ancestors
⑤ settling farther inland

학습 Check!

▶ 몰라서 틀린 문항 × 표기 ▶ 헷갈렸거나 찍은 문항 △ 표기 ▶ ×, △ 문항은 다시 풀고 ✔ 표기를 하세요.

종료 시각	시 분 초	문항 번호	01	02	03	04	05	06	07	08	09	10	11	12
소요 시간	분 초	채점 결과												
초과 시간	분 초	틀린 문항 복습												

DAY 09

※ 점수 표기가 없는 문항은 모두 **2점**입니다.

빈칸이 후반부에 있을 때 **빈칸 추론 09**

● 날짜 :　　월　　일　● 시작 시각 :　　시　　분　　초

● 목표 시간 : 20분

01

고3·2020학년도 6월 31번

다음 빈칸에 들어갈 말로 가장 적절한 것을 고르시오.

Some people have defined wildlife damage management as the science and management of overabundant species, but this definition is too narrow. All wildlife species act in ways that harm human interests. Thus, all species cause wildlife damage, not just overabundant ones. One interesting example of this involves endangered peregrine falcons in California, which prey on another endangered species, the California least tern. Certainly, we would not consider peregrine falcons as being overabundant, but we wish that they would not feed on an endangered species. In this case, one of the negative values associated with a peregrine falcon population is that its predation reduces the population of another endangered species. The goal of wildlife damage management in this case would be to stop the falcons from eating the terns without _____ the falcons.

＊peregrine falcon: 송골매　＊＊least tern: 작은 제비갈매기

① cloning
② harming
③ training
④ overfeeding
⑤ domesticating

02

고1·2020년 3월 32번

다음 빈칸에 들어갈 말로 가장 적절한 것을 고르시오.

Although many small businesses have excellent websites, they typically can't afford aggressive online campaigns. One way to get the word out is through an advertising exchange, in which advertisers place banners on each other's websites for free. For example, a company selling beauty products could place its banner on a site that sells women's shoes, and in turn, the shoe company could put a banner on the beauty product site. Neither company charges the other; they simply exchange ad space. Advertising exchanges are gaining in popularity, especially among marketers who do not have much money and who don't have a large sales team. By _____, advertisers find new outlets that reach their target audiences that they would not otherwise be able to afford.

＊aggressive: 매우 적극적인　＊＊outlet: 출구

① trading space
② getting funded
③ sharing reviews
④ renting factory facilities
⑤ increasing TV commercials

03

다음 빈칸에 들어갈 말로 가장 적절한 것을 고르시오.

If you've ever made a poor choice, you might be interested in learning how to break that habit. One great way to trick your brain into doing so is to sign a "Ulysses Contract." The name of this life tip comes from the Greek myth about Ulysses, a captain whose ship sailed past the island of the Sirens, a tribe of dangerous women who lured victims to their death with their irresistible songs. Knowing that he would otherwise be unable to resist, Ulysses instructed his crew to stuff their ears with cotton and tie him to the ship's mast to prevent him from turning their ship towards the Sirens. It worked for him and you can do the same thing by _____. For example, if you want to stay off your cellphone and concentrate on your work, delete the apps that distract you or ask a friend to change your password!

* lure: 유혹하다 ** mast: 돛대

① letting go of all-or-nothing mindset
② finding reasons why you want to change
③ locking yourself out of your temptations
④ building a plan and tracking your progress
⑤ focusing on breaking one bad habit at a time

04

다음 빈칸에 들어갈 말로 가장 적절한 것을 고르시오.

The prevailing view among developmental scientists is that people are active contributors to their own development. People are influenced by the physical and social contexts in which they live, but they also play a role in influencing their development by interacting with, and changing, those contexts. Even infants influence the world around them and construct their own development through their interactions. Consider an infant who smiles at each adult he sees; he influences his world because adults are likely to smile, use "baby talk," and play with him in response. The infant brings adults into close contact, making one-on-one interactions and creating opportunities for learning. By engaging the world around them, thinking, being curious, and interacting with people, objects, and the world around them, individuals of all ages are "_____."

① mirrors of their generation
② shields against social conflicts
③ explorers in their own career path
④ followers of their childhood dreams
⑤ manufacturers of their own development

05

다음 빈칸에 들어갈 말로 가장 적절한 것을 고르시오. [3점]

Houston Airport executives faced plenty of complaints regarding baggage claim time, so they increased the number of baggage handlers. Although it reduced the average wait time to eight minutes, complaints didn't stop. It took about a minute to get from the arrival gate to baggage claim, so the passengers spent seven more minutes waiting for their bags. The solution was to move the arrival gates away from the baggage claim so it took passengers about seven minutes to walk there. It resulted in complaints reducing to almost zero. Research shows occupied time feels shorter than unoccupied time. People usually exaggerate about the time they waited, and what they find most bothersome is time spent unoccupied. Thus, occupying the passengers' time by _____ gave them the idea they didn't have to wait as long.

＊baggage claim (area): 수하물 찾는 곳

① having them wait in line
② making them walk longer
③ producing more advertisements
④ bothering them with complaints
⑤ hiring more staff to handle bags

06

다음 빈칸에 들어갈 말로 가장 적절한 것을 고르시오. [3점]

In Dutch bicycle culture, it is common to have a passenger on the backseat. So as to follow the rider's movements, the person on the backseat needs to hold on tightly. Bicycles turn not just by steering but also by leaning, so the passenger needs to lean the same way as the rider. A passenger who would keep sitting up straight would literally be a pain in the behind. On motorcycles, this is even more critical. Their higher speed requires more leaning on turns, and lack of coordination can be disastrous. The passenger is a true partner in the ride, expected to _____.

① warn other people of danger
② stop the rider from speeding
③ mirror the rider's every move
④ relieve the rider's emotional anxiety
⑤ monitor the road conditions carefully

07

다음 빈칸에 들어갈 말로 가장 적절한 것을 고르시오. [3점]

The empiricist philosopher John Locke argued that when the human being was first born, the mind was simply a blank slate — a *tabula rasa* — waiting to be written on by experience. Locke believed that our experience shapes who we are and who we become — and therefore he also believed that, given different experiences, human beings would have different characters. The influence of these ideas was profound, particularly for the new colonies in America, for example, because these were conscious attempts to make a new start and to form a new society. The new society was to operate on a different basis from that of European culture, which was based on the feudal system in which people's place in society was almost entirely determined by birth, and which therefore tended to emphasize innate characteristics. Locke's emphasis on the importance of experience in forming the human being provided _____ .

* empiricist: 경험주의자 ** slate: 석판
*** feudal: 봉건 제도의

① foundations for reinforcing ties between European and colonial societies

② new opportunities for European societies to value their tradition

③ an optimistic framework for those trying to form a different society

④ an example of the role that nature plays in building character

⑤ an access to expertise in the areas of philosophy and science

08 1등급 대비 고난도 2점 문제

다음 빈칸에 들어갈 말로 가장 적절한 것을 고르시오.

Humans are champion long-distance runners. As soon as a person and a chimp start running they both get hot. Chimps quickly overheat; humans do not, because they are much better at shedding body heat. According to one leading theory, ancestral humans lost their hair over successive generations because less hair meant cooler, more effective long-distance running. That ability let our ancestors outmaneuver and outrun prey. Try wearing a couple of extra jackets — or better yet, fur coats — on a hot humid day and run a mile. Now, take those jackets off and try it again. You'll see what a difference _____ makes.

* shed: 떨어뜨리다 ** outmaneuver: ～에게 이기다

① hot weather
② a lack of fur
③ muscle strength
④ excessive exercise
⑤ a diversity of species

09 1등급 대비 고난도 3점 문제

다음 빈칸에 들어갈 말로 가장 적절한 것을 고르시오. [3점]

Creativity is a skill we usually consider uniquely human. For all of human history, we have been the most creative beings on Earth. Birds can make their nests, ants can make their hills, but no other species on Earth comes close to the level of creativity we humans display. However, just in the last decade we have acquired the ability to do amazing things with computers, like developing robots. With the artificial intelligence boom of the 2010s, computers can now recognize faces, translate languages, take calls for you, write poems, and beat players at the world's most complicated board game, to name a few things. All of a sudden, we must face the possibility that our ability to be creative is not _____.

① unrivaled
② learned
③ universal
④ ignored
⑤ challenged

10 1등급 대비 고난도 3점 문제

다음 빈칸에 들어갈 말로 가장 적절한 것을 고르시오. [3점]

If you ask a physicist how long it would take a marble to fall from the top of a ten-story building, he will likely answer the question by assuming that the marble falls in a vacuum. In reality, the building is surrounded by air, which applies friction to the falling marble and slows it down. Yet the physicist will point out that the friction on the marble is so small that its effect is negligible. Assuming the marble falls in a vacuum simplifies the problem without substantially affecting the answer. Economists make assumptions for the same reason: Assumptions can simplify the complex world and make it easier to understand. To study the effects of international trade, for example, we might assume that the world consists of only two countries and that each country produces only two goods. By doing so, we can _____. Thus, we are in a better position to understand international trade in the complex world.

＊negligible: 무시할 수 있는

① prevent violations of consumer rights
② understand the value of cultural diversity
③ guarantee the safety of experimenters in labs
④ focus our thinking on the essence of the problem
⑤ realize the differences between physics and economics

11 1등급 대비 고난도 3점 문제

다음 빈칸에 들어갈 말로 가장 적절한 것을 고르시오. [3점]

We like to make a show of how much our decisions are based on rational considerations, but the truth is that we are largely governed by our emotions, which continually influence our perceptions. What this means is that the people around you, constantly under the pull of their emotions, change their ideas by the day or by the hour, depending on their mood. You must never assume that what people say or do in a particular moment is a statement of their permanent desires. Yesterday they were in love with your idea; today they seem cold. This will confuse you and if you are not careful, you will waste valuable mental space trying to figure out their real feelings, their mood of the moment, and their fleeting motivations. It is best to _____ from their shifting emotions so that you are not caught up in the process.

＊fleeting: 빨리 지나가는

① cultivate both distance and a degree of detachment
② find out some clues or hints to their occupation
③ learn to be more empathetic for them
④ discover honesty in their character
⑤ relieve their anxiety and worries

12 1등급 대비 고난도 3점 문제

다음 빈칸에 들어갈 말로 가장 적절한 것을 고르시오. [3점]

What do rural Africans think as they pass fields of cash crops such as sunflowers, roses, or coffee, while walking five kilometers a day to collect water? Some African countries find it difficult to feed their own people or provide safe drinking water, yet precious water is used to produce export crops for European markets. But, African farmers cannot help but grow those crops because they are one of only a few sources of income for them. In a sense, African countries are exporting their water in the very crops they grow. They need water, but they also need to export water through the crops they produce. Environmental pressure groups argue that European customers who buy African coffee or flowers are _____ in Africa.

① lowering the prices of crops
② making water shortages worse
③ making farmers' incomes lower
④ producing goods with more profit
⑤ criticizing the unfair trade of water

DAY 09

학습 Check!

▶ 몰라서 틀린 문항 × 표기　▶ 헷갈렸거나 찍은 문항 △ 표기　▶ ×, △ 문항은 다시 풀고 ✔ 표기를 하세요.

종료 시각	시	분	초	문항 번호	01	02	03	04	05	06	07	08	09	10	11	12
소요 시간		분	초	채점 결과												
초과 시간		분	초	틀린 문항 복습												

DAY 10

※ 점수 표기가 없는 문항은 모두 2점입니다.

빈칸이 후반부에 있을 때 **빈칸 추론 10**

● 날짜 :   월   일 ● 시작 시각 :   시   분   초

● 목표 시간 : 20분

01

고3 · 2023년 4월 31번

다음 빈칸에 들어갈 말로 가장 적절한 것을 고르시오.

Although a balance or harmony between partners clearly develops over time in a relationship, it is also a factor in initial attraction and interest in a partner. That is, to the extent that two people share similar verbal and nonverbal habits in a first meeting, they will be more comfortable with one another. For example, fast-paced individuals talk and move quickly and are more expressive, whereas slow-paced individuals have a different tempo and are less expressive. Initial interactions between people at opposite ends of such a continuum may be more difficult than those between similar types. In the case of contrasting styles, individuals may be less interested in pursuing a relationship than if they were similar in interaction styles. Individuals with similar styles, however, are more comfortable and find that they just seem to "click" with one another. Thus, _____ may provide a selection filter for the initiation of a relationship.

① information deficit
② cultural adaptability
③ meaning negotiation
④ behavioral coordination
⑤ unconditional acceptance

02

고1 · 2021년 3월 32번

다음 빈칸에 들어갈 말로 가장 적절한 것을 고르시오.

When a child is upset, the easiest and quickest way to calm them down is to give them food. This acts as a distraction from the feelings they are having, gives them something to do with their hands and mouth and shifts their attention from whatever was upsetting them. If the food chosen is also seen as a treat such as sweets or a biscuit, then the child will feel 'treated' and happier. In the shorter term using food like this is effective. But in the longer term it can be harmful as we quickly learn that food is a good way to _____. Then as we go through life, whenever we feel annoyed, anxious or even just bored, we turn to food to make ourselves feel better.

① make friends
② learn etiquettes
③ improve memory
④ manage emotions
⑤ celebrate achievements

03

고1 • 2018년 9월 31번

다음 빈칸에 들어갈 말로 가장 적절한 것을 고르시오. [3점]

One CEO in one of Silicon Valley's most innovative companies has what would seem like a boring, creativity-killing routine. He holds a three-hour meeting that starts at 9:00 A.M. one day a week. It is never missed or rescheduled at a different time. It is mandatory — so much so that even in this global firm all the executives know never to schedule any travel that will conflict with the meeting. At first glance there is nothing particularly unique about this. But what *is* unique is the quality of ideas that come out of _____. Because the CEO has eliminated the mental cost involved in planning the meeting or thinking about who will or won't be there, people can focus on creative problem solving.

① consumer complaints
② the regular meetings
③ traveling experiences
④ flexible working hours
⑤ the financial incentives

04

고3 • 2024학년도 9월 32번

다음 빈칸에 들어갈 말로 가장 적절한 것을 고르시오.

Many people create and share pictures and videos on the Internet. The difficulty is finding what you want. Typically, people want to search using words (rather than, say, example sketches). Because most pictures don't come with words attached, it is natural to try and build tagging systems that tag images with relevant words. The underlying machinery is straightforward — we apply image classification and object detection methods and tag the image with the output words. But tags aren't _____. It matters who is doing what, and tags don't capture this. For example, tagging a picture of a cat in the street with the object categories "cat", "street", "trash can" and "fish bones" leaves out the information that the cat is pulling the fish bones out of an open trash can on the street.

① a set of words that allow users to identify an individual object
② a comprehensive description of what is happening in an image
③ a reliable resource for categorizing information by pictures
④ a primary means of organizing a sequential order of words
⑤ a useful filter for sorting similar but not identical images

05

다음 빈칸에 들어갈 말로 가장 적절한 것을 고르시오.

We are more likely to eat in a restaurant if we know that it is usually busy. Even when nobody tells us a restaurant is good, our herd behavior determines our decision-making. Let's suppose you walk toward two empty restaurants. You do not know which one to enter. However, you suddenly see a group of six people enter one of them. Which one are you more likely to enter, the empty one or the other one? Most people would go into the restaurant with people in it. Let's suppose you and a friend go into that restaurant. Now, it has eight people in it. Others see that one restaurant is empty and the other has eight people in it. So, _____ _____.

＊ herd: 무리, 떼

① both restaurants are getting busier
② you and your friend start hesitating
③ your decision has no impact on others
④ they reject what lots of other people do
⑤ they decide to do the same as the other eight

06

다음 빈칸에 들어갈 말로 가장 적절한 것을 고르시오. [3점]

Music connects people to one another not only through a shared interest or hobby, but also through emotional connections to particular songs, communities, and artists. The significance of others in the search for the self is meaningful; as Agger, a sociology professor, states, "identities are largely social products, formed in relation to others and how we think they view us." And Frith, a socio-musicologist, argues that popular music has such connections. For music fans, the genres, artists, and songs in which people find meaning, thus, function as potential "places" through which one's identity can be positioned in relation to others: they act as chains that hold at least parts of one's identity in place. The connections made through shared musical passions provide a sense of safety and security in the notion that there are groups of similar people who can provide _____.

① the foundation for social reform
② the feedback for pop culture
③ the feeling of a community
④ the access to traditional songs
⑤ the solution for copyright issues

07

다음 빈칸에 들어갈 말로 가장 적절한 것을 고르시오. [3점]

Most times a foreign language is spoken in film, subtitles are used to translate the dialogue for the viewer. However, there are occasions when foreign dialogue is left unsubtitled (and thus incomprehensible to most of the target audience). This is often done if the movie is seen mainly from the viewpoint of a particular character who does not speak the language. Such absence of subtitles allows the audience to feel a similar sense of incomprehension and alienation that the character feels. An example of this is seen in *Not Without My Daughter*. The Persian language dialogue spoken by the Iranian characters is not subtitled because the main character Betty Mahmoody does not speak Persian and the audience is _____ .

＊subtitle: 자막(을 넣다)　＊＊incomprehensible: 이해할 수 없는

＊＊＊alienation: 소외

① seeing the film from her viewpoint
② impressed by her language skills
③ attracted to her beautiful voice
④ participating in a heated debate
⑤ learning the language used in the film

08 1등급 대비 고난도 2점 문제

다음 빈칸에 들어갈 말로 가장 적절한 것을 고르시오.

One big difference between science and stage magic is that while magicians hide their mistakes from the audience, in science you make your mistakes in public. You show them off so that everybody can learn from them. This way, you get the advantage of everybody else's experience, and not just your own idiosyncratic path through the space of mistakes. This, by the way, is another reason why we humans are so much smarter than every other species. It is not that our brains are bigger or more powerful, or even that we have the ability to reflect on our own past errors, but that we _____ that our individual brains have earned from their individual histories of trial and error.

＊idiosyncratic: (개인에게) 특유한

① share the benefits
② overlook the insights
③ develop creative skills
④ exaggerate the achievements
⑤ underestimate the knowledge

09 1등급 대비 고난도 3점 문제

다음 빈칸에 들어갈 말로 가장 적절한 것을 고르시오. [3점]

People are attracted to individuals and things they cannot readily obtain. In the case with things, people are more attracted to a desired object because it is out of their reach. When the object of desire is finally gained, the attraction for the object rapidly decreases. Christmas presents provide a good example of this phenomenon. Toys children wanted all year long are thrown away several days after they are taken from gift boxes under the tree. The phenomenon also holds true for human interaction, particularly in the early stages of a developing relationship. The common dating rule has scientific merit. An individual should not always make himself or herself readily available to the person they are targeting for a longer-term relationship. A certain level of _____ will make you more of a mystery and a challenge.

① distrust
② difference
③ intelligence
④ irresponsibility
⑤ unavailability

10 1등급 대비 고난도 3점 문제

다음 빈칸에 들어갈 말로 가장 적절한 것을 고르시오. [3점]

Our homes aren't just ecosystems, they're unique ones, hosting species that are adapted to indoor environments and pushing evolution in new directions. Indoor microbes, insects, and rats have all evolved the ability to survive our chemical attacks, developing resistance to antibacterials, insecticides, and poisons. German cockroaches are known to have developed a distaste for glucose, which is commonly used as bait in roach traps. Some indoor insects, which have fewer opportunities to feed than their outdoor counterparts, seem to have developed the ability to survive when food is limited. Dunn and other ecologists have suggested that as the planet becomes more developed and more urban, more species will _____. Over a long enough time period, indoor living could drive our evolution, too. Perhaps my indoorsy self represents the future of humanity.

* glucose: 포도당 ** bait: 미끼

① produce chemicals to protect themselves
② become extinct with the destroyed habitats
③ evolve the traits they need to thrive indoors
④ compete with outside organisms to find their prey
⑤ break the boundaries between wildlife and humans

11 [1등급 대비 고난도 3점 문제]

다음 빈칸에 들어갈 말로 가장 적절한 것을 고르시오. [3점]

One dynamic that can change dramatically in sport is the concept of the home-field advantage, in which perceived demands and resources seem to play a role. Under normal circumstances, the home ground would appear to provide greater perceived resources (fans, home field, and so on). However, researchers Roy Baumeister and Andrew Steinhilber were among the first to point out that these competitive factors can change; for example, the success percentage for home teams in the final games of a playoff or World Series seems to drop. Fans can become part of the perceived demands rather than resources under those circumstances. This change in perception can also explain why a team that's struggling at the start of the year will _____ to reduce perceived demands and pressures.

＊perceive: 인식하다 ＊＊playoff: 우승 결정전

① often welcome a road trip
② avoid international matches
③ focus on increasing ticket sales
④ want to have an eco-friendly stadium
⑤ try to advertise their upcoming games

12 [1등급 대비 고난도 3점 문제]

다음 빈칸에 들어갈 말로 가장 적절한 것을 고르시오. [3점]

Recently I was with a client who had spent almost five hours with me. As we were parting for the evening, we reflected on what we had covered that day. Even though our conversation was very collegial, I noticed that my client was holding one leg at a right angle to his body, seemingly wanting to take off on its own. At that point I said, "You really do have to leave now, don't you?" "Yes," he admitted. "I am so sorry. I didn't want to be rude but I have to call London and I only have five minutes!" Here was a case where my client's language and most of his body revealed nothing but positive feelings. His feet, however, were _____ _____, and they clearly told me that as much as he wanted to stay, duty was calling.

＊collegial: 평등하게 책임을 지는

① a signal of his politeness
② the subject of the conversation
③ expressing interest in my words
④ the most honest communicators
⑤ stepping excitedly onto the ground

DAY 10

글의 순서

최근 수능에서는 **글의 순서가 빈칸 추론 못지않게 어렵고 까다롭게 출제**된 경우가 많았습니다. 실제 **수능과 내신 1~2등급을 받는 수험생들도 글의 순서 문제를 어려워하는 경향**이 있습니다. 영어 영역에서 **1등급을 목표한다면 반드시 글의 순서 2문항도 확실한 대비**를 해야 합니다.

▶ 글의 순서 유형

> **[36~37] 주어진 글 다음에 이어질 글의 순서로 가장 적절한 것을 고르시오.**

영어 영역 **36~37번에 해당하는 글의 순서는 주어진 한 문단의 글과 이어지는 나머지 (A), (B), (C) 세 문단의 연결고리를 찾아 논리적으로 순서를 정하는 문제**입니다.

글의 순서는 해석을 기본으로 하기 때문에 **어법과 구문에 대한 실력이 있어야** 하며, **A글과 B글이 연결되는 근거를 찾아서 단락들을 연결하는 것이므로 연결고리가 되는 대명사나 연결사, 지시어가 가리키는 것을 잘 파악**해야 합니다. 특히 연결고리의 단서가 주어지지 않는 고난도 문제에 대한 대응력도 키워야합니다.

> **꿀팁!** 수능에 자주 출제되는 연결사를 익히고, 순서를 연결 한 후 전체 글을 다시 읽으며 흐름이 처음부터 끝까지 잘 이어지는지 확인한다.

▶ 글의 순서 교재 구성

> **하루 12문항 _ 20분 학습 _ 5일 완성 = 총 60문항**

글의 순서는 주어진 글부터 (A), (B), (C) 문단이 순차적으로 자연스럽게 연결고리를 찾을 수 있는 문항의 경우 정답률이 높습니다. 하지만 **주어진 글 뒤에 어떤 단락이 와야 하는지 명확하지 않은 경우**가 있는데 기출문제를 통해서 단락을 연결하는 연습과 전체적인 흐름을 확인하는 훈련을 할 수 있도록 했습니다.

소재를 파악하자

주어진 글을 어떻게 연결할지 고민하지 말고, 일단 **글을 읽고 정확히 어떤 내용에 관한 글인지를 소재를 파악**한다.

단서가 핵심이다

this, that, it 등 지시어가 가리키는 것과 문장 간의 연결 고리가 되는 대명사, 연결사 및 부사구를 단서로 활용한다.

결정 NO, 임시 OK

예를 들어 **주어진 글과 (B), (C)가 순서라고 생각이 들어도 바로 결정하지 말고, 임시적으로 연결만 해 놓은 다음 글의 전체적인 흐름을 다시 한 번 확인한 후 결정하는 습관**을 길러야한다.

PART II
글의 순서

Day 11~Day 15

DAY 11

※ 점수 표기가 없는 문항은 모두 **2점**입니다.

글의 순서 01

● 날짜 :　월　일　● 시작 시각 :　시　분　초

● 목표 시간 : 20분

01

주어진 글 다음에 이어질 글의 순서로 가장 적절한 것을 고르시오.

Managers are always looking for ways to increase productivity, which is the ratio of costs to output in production. Adam Smith, writing when the manufacturing industry was new, described a way that production could be made more efficient, known as the "division of labor."

(A) Because each worker specializes in one job, he or she can work much faster without changing from one task to another. Now 10 workers can produce thousands of pins in a day — a huge increase in productivity from the 200 they would have produced before.

(B) One worker could do all these tasks, and make 20 pins in a day. But this work can be divided into its separate processes, with a number of workers each performing one task.

(C) Making most manufactured goods involves several different processes using different skills. Smith's example was the manufacture of pins: the wire is straightened, sharpened, a head is put on, and then it is polished.

* ratio: 비율

① (A) − (C) − (B)　　② (B) − (A) − (C)
③ (B) − (C) − (A)　　④ (C) − (A) − (B)
⑤ (C) − (B) − (A)

02

주어진 글 다음에 이어질 글의 순서로 가장 적절한 것을 고르시오.

With nearly a billion hungry people in the world, there is obviously no single cause.

(A) The reason people are hungry in those countries is that the products produced there can be sold on the world market for more than the local citizens can afford to pay for them. In the modern age you do not starve because you have no food, you starve because you have no money.

(B) However, far and away the biggest cause is poverty. Seventy-nine percent of the world's hungry live in nations that are net exporters of food. How can this be?

(C) So the problem really is that food is, in the grand scheme of things, too expensive and many people are too poor to buy it. The answer will be in continuing the trend of lowering the cost of food.

* net exporter: 순 수출국　** scheme: 체계, 조직

① (A) − (C) − (B)　　② (B) − (A) − (C)
③ (B) − (C) − (A)　　④ (C) − (A) − (B)
⑤ (C) − (B) − (A)

03

주어진 글 다음에 이어질 글의 순서로 가장 적절한 것을 고르시오.

> A god called Moinee was defeated by a rival god called Dromerdeener in a terrible battle up in the stars. Moinee fell out of the stars down to Tasmania to die.

(A) He took pity on the people, gave them bendable knees and cut off their inconvenient kangaroo tails so they could all sit down at last. Then they lived happily ever after.

(B) Then he died. The people hated having kangaroo tails and no knees, and they cried out to the heavens for help. Dromerdeener heard their cry and came down to Tasmania to see what the matter was.

(C) Before he died, he wanted to give a last blessing to his final resting place, so he decided to create humans. But he was in such a hurry, knowing he was dying, that he forgot to give them knees; and he absent-mindedly gave them big tails like kangaroos, which meant they couldn't sit down.

① (A) – (C) – (B) ② (B) – (A) – (C)
③ (B) – (C) – (A) ④ (C) – (A) – (B)
⑤ (C) – (B) – (A)

04

주어진 글 다음에 이어질 글의 순서로 가장 적절한 것을 고르시오.

> When you look at a map, you may conclude — as commercial airline navigators once did — that the best way to get from Amsterdam to Tokyo is to head in an easterly direction along what is known as the Mediterranean route.

(A) After you've decided on a goal, work hard to accomplish it, but keep looking for ways of achieving the goal more efficiently, perhaps from a different angle. This approach is sometimes known as *reframing*.

(B) But look at a globe instead of a map, and your perspective may change. Rather than heading east on the Mediterranean route, commercial planes going from Amsterdam to Tokyo now fly north! That's right.

(C) They take what is known as the 'polar route,' flying over the North Pole to Alaska, and then west to Tokyo — for a savings of roughly 1,500 miles! What is the lesson here?

① (A) – (C) – (B) ② (B) – (A) – (C)
③ (B) – (C) – (A) ④ (C) – (A) – (B)
⑤ (C) – (B) – (A)

05

주어진 글 다음에 이어질 글의 순서로 가장 적절한 것을 고르시오.

> The scientific study of the physical characteristics of colors can be traced back to Isaac Newton.

(A) It was only when Newton placed a second prism in the path of the spectrum that he found something new. The composite colors produced a white beam. Thus he concluded that white light can be produced by combining the spectral colors.

(B) One day, he spotted a set of prisms at a big county fair. He took them home and began to experiment with them. In a darkened room he allowed a thin ray of sunlight to fall on a triangular glass prism.

(C) As soon as the white ray hit the prism, it separated into the familiar colors of the rainbow. This finding was not new, as humans had observed the rainbow since the beginning of time.

＊composite: 합성의

① (A) − (C) − (B)
② (B) − (A) − (C)
③ (B) − (C) − (A)
④ (C) − (A) − (B)
⑤ (C) − (B) − (A)

06

주어진 글 다음에 이어질 글의 순서로 가장 적절한 것을 고르시오.

> Even though two variables seem to be related, there may not be a causal relationship.

(A) Does this mean that the size of one's feet (independent variable) causes an improvement in reading skills (dependent variable)? Certainly not. This false relationship is caused by a third factor, age, that is related to shoe size as well as reading ability.

(B) Hence, when researchers attempt to make causal claims about the relationship between an independent and a dependent variable, they must control for — or rule out — other variables that may be creating a spurious relationship.

(C) In fact, the two variables may merely seem to be associated with each other due to the effect of some third variable. Sociologists call such misleading relationships spurious. A classic example is the apparent association between children's shoe size and reading ability. It seems that as shoe size increases, reading ability improves.

＊variable: 변인 ＊＊spurious: 허위의, 가짜의

① (A) − (C) − (B)
② (B) − (A) − (C)
③ (B) − (C) − (A)
④ (C) − (A) − (B)
⑤ (C) − (B) − (A)

07

주어진 글 다음에 이어질 글의 순서로 가장 적절한 것을 고르시오. [3점]

> The next time you're out under a clear, dark sky, look up. If you've picked a good spot for stargazing, you'll see a sky full of stars, shining and twinkling like thousands of brilliant jewels.

(A) It might be easier if you describe patterns of stars. You could say something like, "See that big triangle of bright stars there?" Or, "Do you see those five stars that look like a big letter W?"

(B) But this amazing sight of stars can also be confusing. Try and point out a single star to someone. Chances are, that person will have a hard time knowing exactly which star you're looking at.

(C) When you do that, you're doing exactly what we all do when we look at the stars. We look for patterns, not just so that we can point something out to someone else, but also because that's what we humans have always done.

① (A) − (C) − (B) ② (B) − (A) − (C)
③ (B) − (C) − (A) ④ (C) − (A) − (B)
⑤ (C) − (B) − (A)

08

주어진 글 다음에 이어질 글의 순서로 가장 적절한 것을 고르시오. [3점]

> Maybe you've heard this joke: "How do you eat an elephant?" The answer is "one bite at a time."

(A) Common crystal habits include squares, triangles, and six-sided hexagons. Usually crystals form when liquids cool, such as when you create ice cubes. Many times, crystals form in ways that do not allow for perfect shapes. If conditions are too cold, too hot, or there isn't enough source material, they can form strange, twisted shapes.

(B) So, how do you "build" the Earth? That's simple, too: one atom at a time. Atoms are the basic building blocks of crystals, and since all rocks are made up of crystals, the more you know about atoms, the better. Crystals come in a variety of shapes that scientists call *habits*.

(C) But when conditions are right, we see beautiful displays. Usually, this involves a slow, steady environment where the individual atoms have plenty of time to join and fit perfectly into what's known as the *crystal lattice*. This is the basic structure of atoms that is seen time after time.

① (A) − (C) − (B) ② (B) − (A) − (C)
③ (B) − (C) − (A) ④ (C) − (A) − (B)
⑤ (C) − (B) − (A)

09

주어진 글 다음에 이어질 글의 순서로 가장 적절한 것을 고르시오.
[3점]

> Each beech tree grows in a particular location and soil conditions can vary greatly in just a few yards. The soil can have a great deal of water or almost no water. It can be full of nutrients or not.

(A) This is taking place underground through the roots. Whoever has an abundance of sugar hands some over; whoever is running short gets help. Their network acts as a system to make sure that no trees fall too far behind.

(B) However, the rate is the same. Whether they are thick or thin, all the trees of the same species are using light to produce the same amount of sugar per leaf. Some trees have plenty of sugar and some have less, but the trees equalize this difference between them by transferring sugar.

(C) Accordingly, each tree grows more quickly or more slowly and produces more or less sugar, and thus you would expect every tree to be photosynthesizing at a different rate.

＊photosynthesize: 광합성하다

① (A) − (C) − (B) 　② (B) − (A) − (C)
③ (B) − (C) − (A) 　④ (C) − (A) − (B)
⑤ (C) − (B) − (A)

10 　1등급 대비 고난도 2점 문제

주어진 글 다음에 이어질 글의 순서로 가장 적절한 것을 고르시오.

> To be successful, you need to understand the vital difference between believing you will succeed, and believing you will succeed easily.

(A) Unrealistic optimists, on the other hand, believe that success will happen to them — that the universe will reward them for all their positive thinking, or that somehow they will be transformed overnight into the kind of person for whom obstacles don't exist anymore.

(B) Put another way, it's the difference between being a realistic optimist, and an unrealistic optimist. Realistic optimists believe they will succeed, but also believe they have to make success happen — through things like careful planning and choosing the right strategies.

(C) They recognize the need for giving serious thought to how they will deal with obstacles. This preparation only increases their confidence in their own ability to get things done.

① (A) − (C) − (B) 　② (B) − (A) − (C)
③ (B) − (C) − (A) 　④ (C) − (A) − (B)
⑤ (C) − (B) − (A)

11 1등급 대비 고난도 3점 문제

주어진 글 다음에 이어질 글의 순서로 가장 적절한 것을 고르시오. [3점]

> Natural processes form minerals in many ways. For example, hot melted rock material, called magma, cools when it reaches the Earth's surface, or even if it's trapped below the surface. As magma cools, its atoms lose heat energy, move closer together, and begin to combine into compounds.

(A) Also, the size of the crystals that form depends partly on how rapidly the magma cools. When magma cools slowly, the crystals that form are generally large enough to see with the unaided eye.

(B) During this process, atoms of the different compounds arrange themselves into orderly, repeating patterns. The type and amount of elements present in a magma partly determine which minerals will form.

(C) This is because the atoms have enough time to move together and form into larger crystals. When magma cools rapidly, the crystals that form will be small. In such cases, you can't easily see individual mineral crystals.

＊compound: 화합물

① (A) − (C) − (B)　　② (B) − (A) − (C)
③ (B) − (C) − (A)　　④ (C) − (A) − (B)
⑤ (C) − (B) − (A)

12 1등급 대비 고난도 3점 문제

주어진 글 다음에 이어질 글의 순서로 가장 적절한 것을 고르시오. [3점]

> In a study, a researcher pretending to be a volunteer surveyed a California neighborhood, asking residents if they would allow a large sign reading "Drive Carefully" to be displayed on their front lawns.

(A) The reason that they agreed was this: two weeks earlier, these residents had been asked by another volunteer to make a small commitment to display a tiny sign that read "Be a Safe Driver" in their windows.

(B) Since it was such a small and simple request, nearly all of them agreed. The astonishing result was that the initial small commitment deeply influenced their willingness to accept the much larger request two weeks later.

(C) To help them understand what it would look like, the volunteer showed his participants a picture of the large sign blocking the view of a beautiful house. Naturally, most people refused, but in one particular group, an incredible 76 percent actually approved.

① (A) − (C) − (B)　　② (B) − (A) − (C)
③ (B) − (C) − (A)　　④ (C) − (A) − (B)
⑤ (C) − (B) − (A)

학습 Check! ▶ 몰라서 틀린 문항 × 표기　▶ 헷갈렸거나 찍은 문항 △ 표기　▶ ×, △ 문항은 다시 풀고 ✔ 표기를 하세요.

종료 시각	시 분 초	문항 번호	01	02	03	04	05	06	07	08	09	10	11	12
소요 시간	분 초	채점 결과												
초과 시간	분 초	틀린 문항 복습												

DAY 12

※ 점수 표기가 없는 문항은 모두 **2점**입니다.

글의 순서 02

● 날짜 : 월 일 ● 시작 시각 : 시 분 초

● 목표 시간 : 20분

01

고1·2023년 9월 37번

주어진 글 다음에 이어질 글의 순서로 가장 적절한 것을 고르시오.

> When you pluck a guitar string it moves back and forth hundreds of times every second.

(A) The vibration of the wood creates more powerful waves in the air pressure, which travel away from the guitar. When the waves reach your eardrums they flex in and out the same number of times a second as the original string.

(B) Naturally, this movement is so fast that you cannot see it — you just see the blurred outline of the moving string. Strings vibrating in this way on their own make hardly any noise because strings are very thin and don't push much air about.

(C) But if you attach a string to a big hollow box (like a guitar body), then the vibration is amplified and the note is heard loud and clear. The vibration of the string is passed on to the wooden panels of the guitar body, which vibrate back and forth at the same rate as the string.

* pluck: (현악기를) 뜯다 ** amplify: 증폭시키다

① (A) − (C) − (B) ② (B) − (A) − (C)
③ (B) − (C) − (A) ④ (C) − (A) − (B)
⑤ (C) − (B) − (A)

02

고1·2021년 3월 36번

주어진 글 다음에 이어질 글의 순서로 가장 적절한 것을 고르시오.

> Almost all major sporting activities are played with a ball.

(A) A ball might have the correct size and weight but if it is made as a hollow ball of steel it will be too stiff and if it is made from light foam rubber with a heavy center it will be too soft.

(B) The rules of the game always include rules about the type of ball that is allowed, starting with the size and weight of the ball. The ball must also have a certain stiffness.

(C) Similarly, along with stiffness, a ball needs to bounce properly. A solid rubber ball would be too bouncy for most sports, and a solid ball made of clay would not bounce at all.

* stiffness: 단단함

① (A) − (C) − (B) ② (B) − (A) − (C)
③ (B) − (C) − (A) ④ (C) − (A) − (B)
⑤ (C) − (B) − (A)

03

주어진 글 다음에 이어질 글의 순서로 가장 적절한 것을 고르시오.

When we compare human and animal desire we find many extraordinary differences. Animals tend to eat with their stomachs, and humans with their brains.

(A) It is due, also, to the knowledge that, in an insecure world, pleasure is uncertain. Therefore, the immediate pleasure of eating must be exploited to the full, even though it does violence to the digestion.

(B) This is largely due to anxiety, to the knowledge that a constant supply of food is uncertain. Therefore, they eat as much as possible while they can.

(C) When animals' stomachs are full, they stop eating, but humans are never sure when to stop. When they have eaten as much as their bellies can take, they still feel empty, they still feel an urge for further gratification.

* gratification: 만족감

① (A) − (C) − (B)　　② (B) − (A) − (C)
③ (B) − (C) − (A)　　④ (C) − (A) − (B)
⑤ (C) − (B) − (A)

04

주어진 글 다음에 이어질 글의 순서로 가장 적절한 것을 고르시오.

Use a plastic pen and rub it on your hair about ten times and then hold the pen close to small pieces of tissue paper or chalk dust.

(A) During a thunderstorm, clouds may become charged as they rub against each other. The lightning that we often see during a storm is caused by a large flow of electrical charges between charged clouds and the earth.

(B) This kind of electricity is produced by friction, and the pen becomes electrically charged. Static electricity is also found in the atmosphere.

(C) You will find that the bits of paper or chalk dust cling to the pen. What you have done there is to create a form of electricity called static electricity.

① (A) − (C) − (B)　　② (B) − (A) − (C)
③ (B) − (C) − (A)　　④ (C) − (A) − (B)
⑤ (C) − (B) − (A)

05

주어진 글 다음에 이어질 글의 순서로 가장 적절한 것을 고르시오.

Interpersonal messages combine content and relationship dimensions. That is, they refer to the real world, to something external to both speaker and listener; at the same time they also refer to the relationship between parties.

(A) You can appreciate this most clearly if you visualize the same command being made by the trainee to the supervisor. It appears awkward and out of place, because it violates the normal relationship between supervisor and trainee.

(B) It also contains a relationship message that says something about the connection between the supervisor and the trainee. Even the use of the simple command shows there is a status difference that allows the supervisor to command the trainee.

(C) For example, a supervisor may say to a trainee, "See me after the meeting." This simple message has a content message that tells the trainee to see the supervisor after the meeting.

① (A) − (C) − (B) ② (B) − (A) − (C)
③ (B) − (C) − (A) ④ (C) − (A) − (B)
⑤ (C) − (B) − (A)

06

주어진 글 다음에 이어질 글의 순서로 가장 적절한 것을 고르시오.

In early 19th century London, a young man named Charles Dickens had a strong desire to be a writer. But everything seemed to be against him.

(A) Moreover, he had so little confidence in his ability to write that he mailed his writings secretly at night to editors so that nobody would laugh at him. Story after story was refused.

(B) He had never been able to attend school for more than four years. His father had been in jail because he couldn't pay his debts, and this young man often knew the pain of hunger.

(C) But one day, one editor recognized and praised him. The praise that he received from getting one story in print changed his whole life. His works have been widely read and still enjoy great popularity.

① (A) − (C) − (B) ② (B) − (A) − (C)
③ (B) − (C) − (A) ④ (C) − (A) − (B)
⑤ (C) − (B) − (A)

07

주어진 글 다음에 이어질 글의 순서로 가장 적절한 것을 고르시오.

> Color can impact how you perceive weight. Dark colors look heavy, and bright colors look less so. Interior designers often paint darker colors below brighter colors to put the viewer at ease.

(A) In fact, black is perceived to be twice as heavy as white. Carrying the same product in a black shopping bag, versus a white one, feels heavier. So, small but expensive products like neckties and accessories are often sold in dark-colored shopping bags or cases.

(B) In contrast, shelving dark-colored products on top can create the illusion that they might fall over, which can be a source of anxiety for some shoppers. Black and white, which have a brightness of 0% and 100%, respectively, show the most dramatic difference in perceived weight.

(C) Product displays work the same way. Place bright-colored products higher and dark-colored products lower, given that they are of similar size. This will look more stable and allow customers to comfortably browse the products from top to bottom.

① (A) – (C) – (B) ② (B) – (A) – (C)
③ (B) – (C) – (A) ④ (C) – (A) – (B)
⑤ (C) – (B) – (A)

08

주어진 글 다음에 이어질 글의 순서로 가장 적절한 것을 고르시오.
[3점]

> Up until about 6,000 years ago, most people were farmers. Many lived in different places throughout the year, hunting for food or moving their livestock to areas with enough food.

(A) For example, priests wanted to know when to carry out religious ceremonies. This was when people first invented clocks — devices that show, measure, and keep track of passing time.

(B) There was no need to tell the time because life depended on natural cycles, such as the changing seasons or sunrise and sunset. Gradually more people started to live in larger settlements, and some needed to tell the time.

(C) Clocks have been important ever since. Today, clocks are used for important things such as setting busy airport timetables — if the time is incorrect, aeroplanes might crash into each other when taking off or landing!

① (A) – (C) – (B) ② (B) – (A) – (C)
③ (B) – (C) – (A) ④ (C) – (A) – (B)
⑤ (C) – (B) – (A)

09

주어진 글 다음에 이어질 글의 순서로 가장 적절한 것을 고르시오.
[3점]

Robert Schumann once said, "The laws of morals are those of art." What the great man is saying here is that there is good music and bad music.

(A) It's the same with performances: a bad performance isn't necessarily the result of incompetence. Some of the worst performances occur when the performers, no matter how accomplished, are thinking more of themselves than of the music they're playing.

(B) The greatest music, even if it's tragic in nature, takes us to a world higher than ours; somehow the beauty uplifts us. Bad music, on the other hand, degrades us.

(C) These doubtful characters aren't really listening to what the composer is saying — they're just showing off, hoping that they'll have a great 'success' with the public. The performer's basic task is to try to understand the meaning of the music, and then to communicate it honestly to others.

＊incompetence: 무능　＊＊degrade: 격하시키다

① (A) － (C) － (B)
② (B) － (A) － (C)
③ (B) － (C) － (A)
④ (C) － (A) － (B)
⑤ (C) － (B) － (A)

10 **1등급 대비 고난도 2점 문제**

주어진 글 다음에 이어질 글의 순서로 가장 적절한 것을 고르시오.

In the Old Stone Age, small bands of 20 to 60 people wandered from place to place in search of food. Once people began farming, they could settle down near their farms.

(A) While some workers grew crops, others built new houses and made tools. Village dwellers also learned to work together to do a task faster.

(B) For example, toolmakers could share the work of making stone axes and knives. By working together, they could make more tools in the same amount of time.

(C) As a result, towns and villages grew larger. Living in communities allowed people to organize themselves more efficiently. They could divide up the work of producing food and other things they needed.

＊dweller: 거주자

① (A) － (C) － (B)
② (B) － (A) － (C)
③ (B) － (C) － (A)
④ (C) － (A) － (B)
⑤ (C) － (B) － (A)

11 1등급 대비 고난도 3점 문제
고1 · 2019년 11월 37번

주어진 글 다음에 이어질 글의 순서로 가장 적절한 것을 고르시오. [3점]

Many studies have shown that people's health and subjective well-being are affected by ethnic relations. Members of minority groups in general have poorer health outcomes than the majority group.

(A) One possible answer is stress. From multiple physiological studies, we know that encounters with members of other ethnic-racial categories, even in the relatively safe environment of laboratories, trigger stress responses.

(B) But that difference remains even when obvious factors, such as social class and access to medical services are controlled for. This suggests that dominance relations have their own effect on people's health. How could that be the case?

(C) Minority individuals have many encounters with majority individuals, each of which may trigger such responses. However minimal these effects may be, their frequency may increase total stress, which would account for part of the health disadvantage of minority individuals.

① (A) – (C) – (B)　　② (B) – (A) – (C)
③ (B) – (C) – (A)　　④ (C) – (A) – (B)
⑤ (C) – (B) – (A)

12 1등급 대비 고난도 3점 문제
고1 · 2019년 3월 36번

주어진 글 다음에 이어질 글의 순서로 가장 적절한 것을 고르시오. [3점]

The basic difference between an AI robot and a normal robot is the ability of the robot and its software to make decisions, and learn and adapt to its environment based on data from its sensors.

(A) For instance, if faced with the same situation, such as running into an obstacle, then the robot will always do the same thing, such as go around the obstacle to the left. An AI robot, however, can do two things the normal robot cannot: make decisions and learn from experience.

(B) It will adapt to circumstances, and may do something different each time a situation is faced. The AI robot may try to push the obstacle out of the way, or make up a new route, or change goals.

(C) To be a bit more specific, the normal robot shows deterministic behaviors. That is, for a set of inputs, the robot will always produce the same output.

* deterministic: 결정론적인

① (A) – (C) – (B)　　② (B) – (A) – (C)
③ (B) – (C) – (A)　　④ (C) – (A) – (B)
⑤ (C) – (B) – (A)

학습 Check!

▶ 몰라서 틀린 문항 × 표기　▶ 헷갈렸거나 찍은 문항 △ 표기　▶ ×, △ 문항은 다시 풀고 ✔ 표기를 하세요.

종료 시각	시 분 초	문항 번호	01	02	03	04	05	06	07	08	09	10	11	12
소요 시간	분 초	채점 결과												
초과 시간	분 초	틀린 문항 복습												

[Day 12] 글의 순서 02　081

DAY 13

글의 순서 03

※ 점수 표기가 없는 문항은 모두 **2점**입니다.

● 날짜 :　　월　　일　● 시작 시각 :　　시　　분　　초

● 목표 시간 : 20분

01

고1 • 2022년 11월 36번

주어진 글 다음에 이어질 글의 순서로 가장 적절한 것을 고르시오.

Things are changing. It has been reported that 42 percent of jobs in Canada are at risk, and 62 percent of jobs in America will be in danger due to advances in automation.

(A) However, what's difficult to automate is the ability to creatively solve problems. Whereas workers in "doing" roles can be replaced by robots, the role of creatively solving problems is more dependent on an irreplaceable individual.

(B) You might say that the numbers seem a bit unrealistic, but the threat is real. One fast food franchise has a robot that can flip a burger in ten seconds. It is just a simple task but the robot could replace an entire crew.

(C) Highly skilled jobs are also at risk. A supercomputer, for instance, can suggest available treatments for specific illnesses in an automated way, drawing on the body of medical research and data on diseases.

① (A) − (C) − (B)
② (B) − (A) − (C)
③ (B) − (C) − (A)
④ (C) − (A) − (B)
⑤ (C) − (B) − (A)

02

고1 • 2021년 6월 36번

주어진 글 다음에 이어질 글의 순서로 가장 적절한 것을 고르시오.

Starting from birth, babies are immediately attracted to faces. Scientists were able to show this by having babies look at two simple images, one that looks more like a face than the other.

(A) These changes help the organisms to survive, making them alert to enemies. By being able to recognize faces from afar or in the dark, humans were able to know someone was coming and protect themselves from possible danger.

(B) One reason babies might like faces is because of something called evolution. Evolution involves changes to the structures of an organism(such as the brain) that occur over many generations.

(C) By measuring where the babies looked, scientists found that the babies looked at the face-like image more than they looked at the non-face image. Even though babies have poor eyesight, they prefer to look at faces. But why?

① (A) − (C) − (B)
② (B) − (A) − (C)
③ (B) − (C) − (A)
④ (C) − (A) − (B)
⑤ (C) − (B) − (A)

03

주어진 글 다음에 이어질 글의 순서로 가장 적절한 것을 고르시오.

> In 1824, Peru won its freedom from Spain. Soon after, Simón Bolívar, the general who had led the liberating forces, called a meeting to write the first version of the constitution for the new country.

(A) "Then," said Bolívar, "I'll add whatever is necessary to this million pesos you have given me and I will buy all the slaves in Peru and set them free. It makes no sense to free a nation, unless all its citizens enjoy freedom as well."

(B) Bolívar accepted the gift and then asked, "How many slaves are there in Peru?" He was told there were about three thousand. "And how much does a slave sell for?" he wanted to know. "About 350 pesos for a man," was the answer.

(C) After the meeting, the people wanted to do something special for Bolívar to show their appreciation for all he had done for them, so they offered him a gift of one million pesos, a very large amount of money in those days.

* constitution: 헌법

① (A) – (C) – (B)   ② (B) – (A) – (C)
③ (B) – (C) – (A)   ④ (C) – (A) – (B)
⑤ (C) – (B) – (A)

04

주어진 글 다음에 이어질 글의 순서로 가장 적절한 것을 고르시오.

> Collaboration is the basis for most of the foundational arts and sciences.

(A) For example, his sketches of human anatomy were a collaboration with Marcantonio della Torre, an anatomist from the University of Pavia. Their collaboration is important because it marries the artist with the scientist.

(B) It is often believed that Shakespeare, like most playwrights of his period, did not always write alone, and many of his plays are considered collaborative or were rewritten after their original composition. Leonardo Da Vinci made his sketches individually, but he collaborated with other people to add the finer details.

(C) Similarly, Marie Curie's husband stopped his original research and joined Marie in hers. They went on to collaboratively discover radium, which overturned old ideas in physics and chemistry.

* anatomy: 해부학적 구조

① (A) – (C) – (B)   ② (B) – (A) – (C)
③ (B) – (C) – (A)   ④ (C) – (A) – (B)
⑤ (C) – (B) – (A)

DAY 13

05

주어진 글 다음에 이어질 글의 순서로 가장 적절한 것을 고르시오.

No one likes to think they're average, least of all below average.

(A) Over the days and weeks from our resolution to change, we start to notice it popping up again and again. The old habit's well-practiced performance is beating our conscious desire for change into submission.

(B) This over-confidence in self-control can lead people to assume they'll be able to control themselves in situations in which, it turns out, they can't. This is why trying to stop an unwanted habit can be an extremely frustrating task.

(C) When asked by psychologists, most people rate themselves above average on all manner of measures including intelligence, looks, health, and so on. Self-control is no different: people consistently overestimate their ability to control themselves.

① (A) – (C) – (B)　　② (B) – (A) – (C)
③ (B) – (C) – (A)　　④ (C) – (A) – (B)
⑤ (C) – (B) – (A)

06

주어진 글 다음에 이어질 글의 순서로 가장 적절한 것을 고르시오.

Students work to get good grades even when they have no interest in their studies. People seek job advancement even when they are happy with the jobs they already have.

(A) It's like being in a crowded football stadium, watching the crucial play. A spectator several rows in front stands up to get a better view, and a chain reaction follows.

(B) And if someone refuses to stand, he might just as well not be at the game at all. When people pursue goods that are positional, they can't help being in the rat race. To choose not to run is to lose.

(C) Soon everyone is standing, just to be able to see as well as before. Everyone is on their feet rather than sitting, but no one's position has improved.

＊ rat race: 치열하고 무의미한 경쟁

① (A) – (C) – (B)　　② (B) – (A) – (C)
③ (B) – (C) – (A)　　④ (C) – (A) – (B)
⑤ (C) – (B) – (A)

07

주어진 글 다음에 이어질 글의 순서로 가장 적절한 것을 고르시오.

Making a small request that people will accept will naturally increase the chances of their accepting a bigger request afterwards.

(A) After this, the salesperson asks you if you are interested in buying any cruelty-free cosmetics from their store. Given the fact that most people agree to the prior request to sign the petition, they will be more likely to purchase the cosmetics.

(B) For instance, a salesperson might request you to sign a petition to prevent cruelty against animals. This is a very small request, and most people will do what the salesperson asks.

(C) They make such purchases because the salesperson takes advantage of a human tendency to be consistent in their words and actions. People want to be consistent and will keep saying yes if they have already said it once.

＊petition: 청원서

① (A) − (C) − (B) ② (B) − (A) − (C)
③ (B) − (C) − (A) ④ (C) − (A) − (B)
⑤ (C) − (B) − (A)

08

주어진 글 다음에 이어질 글의 순서로 가장 적절한 것을 고르시오.
[3점]

Ethical and moral systems are different for every culture. According to cultural relativism, all of these systems are equally valid, and no system is better than another.

(A) There exists an inherent logical inconsistency in cultural relativism, however. If one accepts the idea that there is no right or wrong, then there exists no way to make judgments in the first place. To deal with this inconsistency, cultural relativism creates "tolerance."

(B) The basis of cultural relativism is the notion that no true standards of good and evil actually exist. Therefore, judging whether something is right or wrong is based on individual societies' beliefs, and any moral or ethical opinions are affected by an individual's cultural perspective.

(C) However, with tolerance comes intolerance, which means that tolerance must imply some sort of ultimate good. Thus, tolerance also goes against the very notion of cultural relativism, and the boundaries of logic make cultural relativism impossible.

＊tolerance: 관용

① (A) − (C) − (B) ② (B) − (A) − (C)
③ (B) − (C) − (A) ④ (C) − (A) − (B)
⑤ (C) − (B) − (A)

09

주어진 글 다음에 이어질 글의 순서로 가장 적절한 것을 고르시오.
[3점]

According to legend, once a vampire bites a person, that person turns into a vampire who seeks the blood of others. A researcher came up with some simple math, which proves that these highly popular creatures can't exist.

(A) In just two-and-a-half years, the original human population would all have become vampires with no humans left. But look around you. Have vampires taken over the world? No, because there's no such thing.

(B) If the first vampire came into existence that day and bit one person a month, there would have been two vampires by February 1st, 1600. A month later there would have been four, the next month eight, then sixteen, and so on.

(C) University of Central Florida physics professor Costas Efthimiou's work breaks down the myth. Suppose that on January 1st, 1600, the human population was just over five hundred million.

① (A) − (C) − (B)　　② (B) − (A) − (C)
③ (B) − (C) − (A)　　④ (C) − (A) − (B)
⑤ (C) − (B) − (A)

10

주어진 글 다음에 이어질 글의 순서로 가장 적절한 것을 고르시오.

The growing complexity of computer software has direct implications for our global safety and security, particularly as the physical objects upon which we depend — things like cars, airplanes, bridges, tunnels, and implantable medical devices — transform themselves into computer code.

(A) As all this code grows in size and complexity, so too do the number of errors and software bugs. According to a study by Carnegie Mellon University, commercial software typically has twenty to thirty bugs for every thousand lines of code — 50 million lines of code means 1 million to 1.5 million potential errors to be exploited.

(B) This is the basis for all malware attacks that take advantage of these computer bugs to get the code to do something it was not originally intended to do. As computer code grows more elaborate, software bugs flourish and security suffers, with increasing consequences for society at large.

(C) Physical things are increasingly becoming information technologies. Cars are "computers we ride in," and airplanes are nothing more than "flying Solaris boxes attached to bucketfuls of industrial control systems."

＊exploit: 활용하다

① (A) − (C) − (B)　　② (B) − (A) − (C)
③ (B) − (C) − (A)　　④ (C) − (A) − (B)
⑤ (C) − (B) − (A)

11 1등급 대비 고난도 2번 문제

주어진 글 다음에 이어질 글의 순서로 가장 적절한 것을 고르시오.

Mirrors and other smooth, shiny surfaces reflect light. We see reflections from such surfaces because the rays of light form an image on the retina of our eyes.

(A) Keep your eyes on the reflected image while you are writing and not on your paper. After a little practice, it will be easier to write "backwards." When your friend receives such a message he will be able to read it by holding the paper up to a mirror.

(B) Stand a mirror upright on the table, so that a piece of paper on the table can be clearly seen in the mirror. Now write a message that looks right when you look in the mirror.

(C) Such images are always reversed. Look at yourself in a mirror, wink your right eye and your left eye seems to wink back at you. You can use a mirror to send a coded message to a friend.

* retina: (눈의) 망막

① (A) − (C) − (B) ② (B) − (A) − (C)
③ (B) − (C) − (A) ④ (C) − (A) − (B)
⑤ (C) − (B) − (A)

12 1등급 대비 고난도 3번 문제

주어진 글 다음에 이어질 글의 순서로 가장 적절한 것을 고르시오.
[3점]

Most people have a perfect time of day when they feel they are at their best, whether in the morning, evening, or afternoon.

(A) When your mind and body are less alert than at your "peak" hours, the muse of creativity awakens and is allowed to roam more freely. In other words, when your mental machinery is loose rather than standing at attention, the creativity flows.

(B) However, if the task you face demands creativity and novel ideas, it's best to tackle it at your "worst" time of day! So if you are an early bird, make sure to attack your creative task in the evening, and vice versa for night owls.

(C) Some of us are night owls, some early birds, and others in between may feel most active during the afternoon hours. If you are able to organize your day and divide your work, make it a point to deal with tasks that demand attention at your best time of the day.

* roam: (어슬렁어슬렁) 거닐다

① (A) − (C) − (B) ② (B) − (A) − (C)
③ (B) − (C) − (A) ④ (C) − (A) − (B)
⑤ (C) − (B) − (A)

학습 Check!

▶ 몰라서 틀린 문항 × 표기 ▶ 헷갈렸거나 찍은 문항 △ 표기 ▶ ×, △ 문항은 다시 풀고 ✔ 표기를 하세요.

종료 시각	시	분	초	문항 번호	01	02	03	04	05	06	07	08	09	10	11	12
소요 시간		분	초	채점 결과												
초과 시간		분	초	틀린 문항 복습												

DAY 14

※ 점수 표기가 없는 문항은 모두 **2점**입니다.

글의 순서 **04**

● 날짜 : 　월　일　● 시작 시각 :　시　분　초

● 목표 시간 : 20분

01

고1 • 2022년 3월 36번

주어진 글 다음에 이어질 글의 순서로 가장 적절한 것을 고르시오.

Toward the end of the 19th century, a new architectural attitude emerged. Industrial architecture, the argument went, was ugly and inhuman; past styles had more to do with pretension than what people needed in their homes.

(A) But they supplied people's needs perfectly and, at their best, had a beauty that came from the craftsman's skill and the rootedness of the house in its locality.

(B) Instead of these approaches, why not look at the way ordinary country builders worked in the past? They developed their craft skills over generations, demonstrating mastery of both tools and materials.

(C) Those materials were local, and used with simplicity — houses built this way had plain wooden floors and whitewashed walls inside.

　＊pretension: 허세, 가식

① (A) − (C) − (B)　　② (B) − (A) − (C)
③ (B) − (C) − (A)　　④ (C) − (A) − (B)
⑤ (C) − (B) − (A)

02

고1 • 2021년 6월 37번

주어진 글 다음에 이어질 글의 순서로 가장 적절한 것을 고르시오.

People spend much of their time interacting with media, but that does not mean that people have the critical skills to analyze and understand it.

(A) Research from New York University found that people over 65 shared seven times as much misinformation as their younger counterparts. All of this raises a question: What's the solution to the misinformation problem?

(B) One well-known study from Stanford University in 2016 demonstrated that youth are easily fooled by misinformation, especially when it comes through social media channels. This weakness is not found only in youth, however.

(C) Governments and tech platforms certainly have a role to play in blocking misinformation. However, every individual needs to take responsibility for combating this threat by becoming more information literate.

　＊counterpart: 상대방

① (A) − (C) − (B)　　② (B) − (A) − (C)
③ (B) − (C) − (A)　　④ (C) − (A) − (B)
⑤ (C) − (B) − (A)

03

고1 · 2018년 3월 35번

주어진 글 다음에 이어질 글의 순서로 가장 적절한 것을 고르시오.

Suppose that you are busy working on a project one day and you have no time to buy lunch. All of a sudden your best friend shows up with your favorite sandwich.

(A) The key difference between these two cases is the level of trust. You trust your best friend so much that you won't worry about him knowing you too well, but you certainly would not give the same level of trust to a stranger.

(B) He tells you that he knows you are busy and he wants to help you out by buying you the sandwich. In this case, you are very likely to appreciate your friend's help.

(C) However, if a stranger shows up with the same sandwich and offers it to you, you won't appreciate it. Instead, you would be confused. You would likely think "Who are you, and how do you know what kind of sandwich I like to eat?"

① (A) − (C) − (B)　　② (B) − (A) − (C)
③ (B) − (C) − (A)　　④ (C) − (A) − (B)
⑤ (C) − (B) − (A)

04

고1 · 2020년 9월 36번

주어진 글 다음에 이어질 글의 순서로 가장 적절한 것을 고르시오.

We make decisions based on what we *think* we know. It wasn't too long ago that the majority of people believed the world was flat.

(A) It wasn't until that minor detail was revealed — the world is round — that behaviors changed on a massive scale. Upon this discovery, societies began to travel across the planet. Trade routes were established; spices were traded.

(B) This perceived truth impacted behavior. During this period, there was very little exploration. People feared that if they traveled too far they might fall off the edge of the earth. So for the most part they didn't dare to travel.

(C) New ideas, like mathematics, were shared between societies which allowed for all kinds of innovations and advancements. The correction of a simple false assumption moved the human race forward.

① (A) − (C) − (B)　　② (B) − (A) − (C)
③ (B) − (C) − (A)　　④ (C) − (A) − (B)
⑤ (C) − (B) − (A)

DAY 14

05

고1·2018년 9월 37번

주어진 글 다음에 이어질 글의 순서로 가장 적절한 것을 고르시오.

Trade will not occur unless both parties want what the other party has to offer.

(A) However, if the farmer is enterprising and utilizes his network of village friends, he might discover that the baker is in need of some new cast-iron trivets for cooling his bread, and it just so happens that the blacksmith needs a new lamb's wool sweater.

(B) This is referred to as the double coincidence of wants. Suppose a farmer wants to trade eggs with a baker for a loaf of bread. If the baker has no need or desire for eggs, then the farmer is out of luck and does not get any bread.

(C) Upon further investigation, the farmer discovers that the weaver has been wanting an omelet for the past week. The farmer will then trade the eggs for the sweater, the sweater for the trivets, and the trivets for his fresh-baked loaf of bread.

＊trivet: 삼각 거치대

① (A) − (C) − (B) 　　② (B) − (A) − (C)
③ (B) − (C) − (A) 　　④ (C) − (A) − (B)
⑤ (C) − (B) − (A)

06

고1·2020년 3월 35번

주어진 글 다음에 이어질 글의 순서로 가장 적절한 것을 고르시오.
[3점]

Ideas about how much disclosure is appropriate vary among cultures.

(A) On the other hand, Japanese tend to do little disclosing about themselves to others except to the few people with whom they are very close. In general, Asians do not reach out to strangers.

(B) Those born in the United States tend to be high disclosers, even showing a willingness to disclose information about themselves to strangers. This may explain why Americans seem particularly easy to meet and are good at cocktail-party conversation.

(C) They do, however, show great care for each other, since they view harmony as essential to relationship improvement. They work hard to prevent those they view as outsiders from getting information they believe to be unfavorable.

＊disclosure: (정보의) 공개

① (A) − (C) − (B) 　　② (B) − (A) − (C)
③ (B) − (C) − (A) 　　④ (C) − (A) − (B)
⑤ (C) − (B) − (A)

07

주어진 글 다음에 이어질 글의 순서로 가장 적절한 것을 고르시오.

> For its time, ancient Greek civilization was remarkably advanced. The Greeks figured out mathematics, geometry, and calculus long before calculators were available. Centuries before telescopes were invented, they proposed that the earth might rotate on an axis or revolve around the sun.

(A) But they were still a primitive people. There were many aspects of the world around them that they didn't understand very well. They had big questions, like *Why are we here?* and *Why is smoke coming out of that nearby volcano?*

(B) Myths provided answers to those questions. They were educational tools, passing knowledge from one generation to the next. They also taught morality and conveyed truth about the complexity of life. In this way, the Greeks were able to understand right and wrong in their lives.

(C) Along with these mathematical, scientific advances, the Greeks produced some of the early dramatic plays and poetry. In a world ruled by powerful kings and bloodthirsty warriors, the Greeks even developed the idea of democracy.

* geometry: 기하학

① (A) − (C) − (B) ② (B) − (A) − (C)
③ (B) − (C) − (A) ④ (C) − (A) − (B)
⑤ (C) − (B) − (A)

08

주어진 글 다음에 이어질 글의 순서로 가장 적절한 것을 고르시오.
[3점]

> One of the most essential decisions any of us can make is how we invest our time.

(A) During this period, people worked for more than eighty hours a week in factories. But there were some who spent their few precious free hours reading books or getting involved in politics instead of following the majority into the pubs.

(B) Of course, how we invest time is not our decision alone to make. Many factors determine what we should do either because we are members of the human race, or because we belong to a certain culture and society.

(C) Nevertheless, there is room for personal choice, and control over time is to a certain extent in our hands. Even in the most oppressive decades of the Industrial Revolution, people didn't give up their free will when it came to time.

* oppressive: 억압적인

① (A) − (C) − (B) ② (B) − (A) − (C)
③ (B) − (C) − (A) ④ (C) − (A) − (B)
⑤ (C) − (B) − (A)

09

주어진 글 다음에 이어질 글의 순서로 가장 적절한 것을 고르시오.

A fascinating species of water flea exhibits a kind of flexibility that evolutionary biologists call *adaptive plasticity*.

(A) That's a clever trick, because producing spines and a helmet is costly, in terms of energy, and conserving energy is essential for an organism's ability to survive and reproduce. The water flea only expends the energy needed to produce spines and a helmet when it needs to.

(B) If the baby water flea is developing into an adult in water that includes the chemical signatures of creatures that prey on water fleas, it develops a helmet and spines to defend itself against predators. If the water around it doesn't include the chemical signatures of predators, the water flea doesn't develop these protective devices.

(C) So it may well be that this plasticity is an adaptation: a trait that came to exist in a species because it contributed to reproductive fitness. There are many cases, across many species, of adaptive plasticity. Plasticity is conducive to fitness if there is sufficient variation in the environment.

＊spine: 가시 돌기 ＊＊conducive: 도움되는

① (A) − (C) − (B) ② (B) − (A) − (C)
③ (B) − (C) − (A) ④ (C) − (A) − (B)
⑤ (C) − (B) − (A)

10

주어진 글 다음에 이어질 글의 순서로 가장 적절한 것을 고르시오.

When two natural bodies of water stand at different levels, building a canal between them presents a complicated engineering problem.

(A) Then the upper gates open and the ship passes through. For downstream passage, the process works the opposite way. The ship enters the lock from the upper level, and water is pumped from the lock until the ship is in line with the lower level.

(B) When a vessel is going upstream, the upper gates stay closed as the ship enters the lock at the lower water level. The downstream gates are then closed and more water is pumped into the basin. The rising water lifts the vessel to the level of the upper body of water.

(C) To make up for the difference in level, engineers build one or more water "steps," called locks, that carry ships or boats up or down between the two levels. A lock is an artificial water basin. It has a long rectangular shape with concrete walls and a pair of gates at each end.

＊rectangular: 직사각형의

① (A) − (C) − (B) ② (B) − (A) − (C)
③ (B) − (C) − (A) ④ (C) − (A) − (B)
⑤ (C) − (B) − (A)

11 1등급 대비 고난도 2점 문제

주어진 글 다음에 이어질 글의 순서로 가장 적절한 것을 고르시오.

> Roughly twenty years ago, brick-and-mortar stores began to give way to electronic commerce. For good or bad, the shift fundamentally changed consumers' perception of the shopping experience.

(A) Before long, the e-commerce book market naturally expanded to include additional categories, like CDs and DVDs. E-commerce soon snowballed into the enormous industry it is today, where you can buy everything from toilet paper to cars online.

(B) Nowhere was the shift more obvious than with book sales, which is how online bookstores got their start. Physical bookstores simply could not stock as many titles as a virtual bookstore could. There is only so much space available on a shelf.

(C) In addition to greater variety, online bookstores were also able to offer aggressive discounts thanks to their lower operating costs. The combination of lower prices and greater selection led to the slow, steady rise of online bookstores.

* brick-and-mortar: 오프라인 거래의

① (A) − (C) − (B)   ② (B) − (A) − (C)
③ (B) − (C) − (A)   ④ (C) − (A) − (B)
⑤ (C) − (B) − (A)

12 1등급 대비 고난도 3점 문제

주어진 글 다음에 이어질 글의 순서로 가장 적절한 것을 고르시오. [3점]

> In negotiation, there often will be issues that you do not care about — but that the other side cares about very much! It is important to identify these issues.

(A) Now you are in a position to give her something that she values (at no cost to you) and get something of value in return. For example, you might start a month earlier and receive a larger bonus for doing so.

(B) Similarly, when purchasing my home, I discovered that the seller was very interested in closing the deal as soon as possible. So I agreed to close one month earlier than originally offered, and the seller agreed to a lower price.

(C) For example, you may not care about whether you start your new job in June or July. But if your potential boss strongly prefers that you start as soon as possible, that's a valuable piece of information.

① (A) − (C) − (B)   ② (B) − (A) − (C)
③ (B) − (C) − (A)   ④ (C) − (A) − (B)
⑤ (C) − (B) − (A)

DAY 14

학습 Check!

▶ 몰라서 틀린 문항 × 표기 ▶ 헷갈렸거나 찍은 문항 △ 표기 ▶ ×, △ 문항은 다시 풀고 ✔ 표기를 하세요.

종료 시각	시 분 초	문항 번호	01	02	03	04	05	06	07	08	09	10	11	12
소요 시간	분 초	채점 결과												
초과 시간	분 초	틀린 문항 복습												

DAY 15

※ 점수 표기가 없는 문항은 모두 **2점**입니다.

글의 순서 05

● 날짜 :　　월　　일　● 시작 시각 :　　시　　분　　초

● 목표 시간 : 20분

01

주어진 글 다음에 이어질 글의 순서로 가장 적절한 것을 고르시오.

> Mrs. Klein told her first graders to draw a picture of something to be thankful for. She thought that most of the class would draw turkeys or Thanksgiving tables. But Douglas drew something different.

(A) The class was so responsive that Mrs. Klein had almost forgotten about Douglas. After she had the others at work on another project, she asked Douglas whose hand it was. He answered softly, "It's yours. Thank you, Mrs. Klein."

(B) Douglas was a boy who usually spent time alone and stayed around her while his classmates went outside together during break time. What the boy drew was a hand. But whose hand? His image immediately attracted the other students' interest.

(C) So, everyone rushed to talk about whose hand it was. "It must be the hand of God that brings us food," said one student. "A farmer's," said a second student, "because they raise the turkeys." "It looks more like a police officer's," added another, "they protect us."

① (A) − (C) − (B)　　② (B) − (A) − (C)
③ (B) − (C) − (A)　　④ (C) − (A) − (B)
⑤ (C) − (B) − (A)

02

주어진 글 다음에 이어질 글의 순서로 가장 적절한 것을 고르시오.

> Imagine yourself at a party. It is dark and a group of friends ask you to take a picture of them. You grab your camera, point, and shoot your friends.

(A) This is a common problem called the *red-eye effect*. It is caused because the light from the flash penetrates the eyes through the pupils, and then gets reflected to the camera from the back of the eyes where a large amount of blood is present.

(B) The camera automatically turns on the flash as there is not enough light available to produce a correct exposure. The result is half of your friends appear in the picture with two bright red circles instead of their eyes.

(C) This blood is the reason why the eyes look red in the photograph. This effect is more noticeable when there is not much light in the environment. This is because pupils dilate when it is dark, allowing more light to get inside the eye and producing a larger red-eye effect.

* penetrate: 통과하다　** pupil: 동공
*** dilate: 확장(팽창)하다

① (A) − (C) − (B)　　② (B) − (A) − (C)
③ (B) − (C) − (A)　　④ (C) − (A) − (B)
⑤ (C) − (B) − (A)

03

고1 · 2017년 3월 36번

주어진 글 다음에 이어질 글의 순서로 가장 적절한 것을 고르시오.

Andrew Carnegie, the great early-twentieth-century businessman, once heard his sister complain about her two sons.

(A) Within days he received warm grateful letters from both boys, who noted at the letters' end that he had unfortunately forgotten to include the check. If the check had been enclosed, would they have responded so quickly?

(B) They were away at college and rarely responded to her letters. Carnegie told her that if he wrote them he would get an immediate response.

(C) He sent off two warm letters to the boys, and told them that he was happy to send each of them a check for a hundred dollars (a large sum in those days). Then he mailed the letters, but didn't enclose the checks.

＊enclose: 동봉하다

① (A) – (C) – (B)　　② (B) – (A) – (C)
③ (B) – (C) – (A)　　④ (C) – (A) – (B)
⑤ (C) – (B) – (A)

04

고1 · 2019년 9월 36번

주어진 글 다음에 이어질 글의 순서로 가장 적절한 것을 고르시오.

We always have a lot of bacteria around us, as they live almost everywhere — in air, soil, in different parts of our bodies, and even in some of the foods we eat. But do not worry!

(A) But unfortunately, a few of these wonderful creatures can sometimes make us sick. This is when we need to see a doctor, who may prescribe medicines to control the infection.

(B) Most bacteria are good for us. Some live in our digestive systems and help us digest our food, and some live in the environment and produce oxygen so that we can breathe and live on Earth.

(C) But what exactly are these medicines and how do they fight with bacteria? These medicines are called "antibiotics," which means "against the life of bacteria." Antibiotics either kill bacteria or stop them from growing.

① (A) – (C) – (B)　　② (B) – (A) – (C)
③ (B) – (C) – (A)　　④ (C) – (A) – (B)
⑤ (C) – (B) – (A)

05

주어진 글 다음에 이어질 글의 순서로 가장 적절한 것을 고르시오.

Memory has two types — implicit and explicit memory. When you learn things without really thinking about it, it's implicit memory or body memory. Knowing how to breathe when you were born is an implicit memory.

(A) Explicit memories, on the other hand, are the memories or the specific things that you consciously try to recall. You use explicit memory every day on a conscious level.

(B) No one taught this to you. Some of the things you've learned since childhood also become implicit memories. Implicit memories are imprinted in the brain's autonomic portion; that is why even after years of not riding a bike you still know how to ride.

(C) Trying to find the keys, trying to remember when an event is supposed to take place, where it's going to be held, and with whom you are going. Explicit memories are the tasks you have written down on your calendar or planner.

① (A) − (C) − (B)
② (B) − (A) − (C)
③ (B) − (C) − (A)
④ (C) − (A) − (B)
⑤ (C) − (B) − (A)

06

주어진 글 다음에 이어질 글의 순서로 가장 적절한 것을 고르시오.
[3점]

Understanding how to develop respect for and a knowledge of other cultures begins with reexamining the golden rule: "I treat others in the way I want to be treated."

(A) It can also create a frustrating situation where we believe we are doing what is right, but what we are doing is not being interpreted in the way in which it was meant. This miscommunication can lead to problems.

(B) In a multicultural setting, however, where words, gestures, beliefs, and views may have different meanings, this rule has an unintended result; it can send a message that my culture is better than yours.

(C) This rule makes sense on some level; if we treat others as well as we want to be treated, we will be treated well in return. This rule works well in a monocultural setting, where everyone is working within the same cultural framework.

① (A) − (C) − (B)
② (B) − (A) − (C)
③ (B) − (C) − (A)
④ (C) − (A) − (B)
⑤ (C) − (B) − (A)

07

주어진 글 다음에 이어질 글의 순서로 가장 적절한 것을 고르시오.
[3점]

> Why does garbage exist in the human system but not more broadly in nature?

(A) The output of the microbes — rich humus and soil — is in turn the very material from which a new oak tree may grow. Even the carbon dioxide that the squirrel breathes out is what that tree may breathe in.

(B) Nature is a beautiful harmony of systems whereby every system's output is a useful input for other systems. An acorn that falls from a tree is an important input for a squirrel that eats it. The by-product of that delicious meal — the squirrel's poop — is an important input for the microbes that consume it.

(C) This cycle is the fundamental reason why life has thrived on our planet for millions of years. It's like the Ouroboros — the ancient symbol depicting a snake or dragon eating its own tail; in a way, nature truly is a constant cycle of consuming itself.

*microbe: 미생물

① (A) − (C) − (B) 　② (B) − (A) − (C)
③ (B) − (C) − (A) 　④ (C) − (A) − (B)
⑤ (C) − (B) − (A)

08

주어진 글 다음에 이어질 글의 순서로 가장 적절한 것을 고르시오.
[3점]

> If you start collecting and analyzing data without first clarifying the question you are trying to answer, you're probably doing yourself more harm than good.

(A) In the design plan, you clarify the issues you are trying to solve, state your hypotheses, and list what is required to prove those hypotheses. Developing this plan before you start researching will greatly increase your problem-solving productivity.

(B) You'll end up drowning in a flood of information and realize only later that most of that research was a waste of time. To avoid this problem, you should develop a problem-solving design plan before you start collecting information.

(C) In addition, putting your plan down on paper will not only clarify your thoughts. If you're working in a group, this plan will also help your team focus on what to do and provide the starting point for your group brainstorming.

*hypothesis: 가설

① (A) − (C) − (B) 　② (B) − (A) − (C)
③ (B) − (C) − (A) 　④ (C) − (A) − (B)
⑤ (C) − (B) − (A)

09

주어진 글 다음에 이어질 글의 순서로 가장 적절한 것을 고르시오. [3점]

If you had to write a math equation, you probably wouldn't write, "Twenty-eight plus fourteen equals forty-two." It would take too long to write and it would be hard to read quickly.

(A) For example, the chemical formula for water is H2O. That tells us that a water molecule is made up of two hydrogen ("H" and "2") atoms and one oxygen ("O") atom.

(B) You would write, "28 + 14 = 42." Chemistry is the same way. Chemists have to write chemical equations all the time, and it would take too long to write and read if they had to spell everything out.

(C) So chemists use symbols, just like we do in math. A chemical formula lists all the elements that form each molecule and uses a small number to the bottom right of an element's symbol to stand for the number of atoms of that element.

＊chemical formula: 화학식 ＊＊molecule: 분자

① (A) － (C) － (B) ② (B) － (A) － (C)
③ (B) － (C) － (A) ④ (C) － (A) － (B)
⑤ (C) － (B) － (A)

10

주어진 글 다음에 이어질 글의 순서로 가장 적절한 것을 고르시오.

In the fifth century *B.C.E.*, the Greek philosopher Protagoras pronounced, "Man is the measure of all things." In other words, we feel entitled to ask the world, "What good are you?"

(A) Abilities said to "make us human" — empathy, communication, grief, toolmaking, and so on — all exist to varying degrees among other minds sharing the world with us. Animals with backbones (fishes, amphibians, reptiles, birds, and mammals) all share the same basic skeleton, organs, nervous systems, hormones, and behaviors.

(B) We assume that we are the world's standard, that all things should be compared to us. Such an assumption makes us overlook a lot.

(C) Just as different models of automobiles each have an engine, drive train, four wheels, doors, and seats, we differ mainly in terms of our outside contours and a few internal tweaks. But like naive car buyers, most people see only animals' varied exteriors.

＊contour: 윤곽, 외형 ＊＊tweak: 조정, 개조

① (A) － (C) － (B) ② (B) － (A) － (C)
③ (B) － (C) － (A) ④ (C) － (A) － (B)
⑤ (C) － (B) － (A)

11 1등급 대비 고난도 3점 문제

주어진 글 다음에 이어질 글의 순서로 가장 적절한 것을 고르시오.
[3점]

Literary works, by their nature, suggest rather than explain; they imply rather than state their claims boldly and directly.

(A) What a text implies is often of great interest to us. And our work of figuring out a text's implications tests our analytical powers. In considering what a text suggests, we gain practice in making sense of texts.

(B) But whatever the proportion of a work's showing to telling, there is always something for readers to interpret. Thus we ask the question "What does the text suggest?" as a way to approach literary interpretation, as a way to begin thinking about a text's implications.

(C) This broad generalization, however, does not mean that works of literature do not include direct statements. Depending on when they were written and by whom, literary works may contain large amounts of direct telling and lesser amounts of suggestion and implication.

① (A) – (C) – (B) ② (B) – (A) – (C)
③ (B) – (C) – (A) ④ (C) – (A) – (B)
⑤ (C) – (B) – (A)

12 1등급 대비 고난도 3점 문제

주어진 글 다음에 이어질 글의 순서로 가장 적절한 것을 고르시오.
[3점]

From a correlational observation, we conclude that one variable is related to a second variable. But neither behavior could be directly causing the other even though there is a relationship.

(A) They found the best predictor to be the number of tattoos the rider had. It would be a ridiculous error to conclude that tattoos cause motorcycle accidents or that motorcycle accidents cause tattoos.

(B) The following example will illustrate why it is difficult to make causal statements on the basis of correlational observation. The researchers at the U.S. Army conducted a study of motorcycle accidents, attempting to correlate the number of accidents with other variables such as socioeconomic level and age.

(C) Obviously, a third variable is related to both — perhaps preference for risk. A person who is willing to take risks likes to be tattooed and also takes more chances on a motorcycle.

＊ variable: 변인

① (A) – (C) – (B) ② (B) – (A) – (C)
③ (B) – (C) – (A) ④ (C) – (A) – (B)
⑤ (C) – (B) – (A)

학습 Check!

▶ 몰라서 틀린 문항 × 표기 ▶ 헷갈렸거나 찍은 문항 △ 표기 ▶ ×, △ 문항은 다시 풀고 ✔ 표기를 하세요.

종료 시각	시 분 초	문항 번호	01	02	03	04	05	06	07	08	09	10	11	12
소요 시간	분 초	채점 결과												
초과 시간	분 초	틀린 문항 복습												

문장 삽입

수능 영어 **문장 삽입**에서 무엇보다 중요한 것은 연결사를 정확히 알고 이해를 하는 것입니다. 단순히 **뜻**만 알고 있는 것이 아니고, **연결사 앞 문장과 뒤에 나오는 문장이 어떤 관계에 있는지를 추론**할 수 있어야합니다.

영어 영역 1등급을 위한 '오답 3대장' 중 마지막 관문인 '문장 삽입'을 반드시 정복해 목표를 이루시기를 바랍니다.

▶ 문장 삽입 유형

> **[38~39]** 글의 흐름으로 보아 주어진 문장이 들어가기에 가장 적절한 곳을 고르시오.

영어 영역 38~39번에 해당하는 문장 삽입은 연결어 등의 단서를 이용해 주어진 한 문장을 끼워 넣어 논리적인 흐름에 맞게 만드는 문제입니다.

글을 쭉 읽으며 문장 사이의 대비가 자연스럽지 않거나 연결이 어색한 문장들 사이에 주어진 문장을 그 사이에 넣어 흐름이 매끄러운지 확인하는 훈련을 해야 하며, 충분한 연습이 가능하도록 기출문제를 수록했습니다.

 꿀팁! 갑자기 흐름이 끊겨서 어색한 곳을 찾아내 주어진 문장을 알맞은 위치에 넣고, 전 후 흐름이 자연스럽게 이어졌는지 확인한다.

▶ 문장 삽입 교재 구성

> **하루 12문항 _ 20분 학습 _ 5일 완성 = 총 60문항**

문장 삽입은 앞 문장에는 등장하지 않았던 어구가 갑자기 나오거나 문맥상 원인이 주어지지 않았는데 결과가 갑자기 등장한다면, 또는 글의 흐름이 아무 연결어 없이 완전히 전환되거나 화재가 넘어가는 부분이 정답일 수 있습니다. 일관성을 유지하는 주제를 파악하여 **'주어진 문장의 위치를 찾는 연습'**이 영어 **'1등급으로 향하는 실력'**이 됩니다.

단서에 유의하자

한정사(such, both…), 대명사, 지시어, 정관사, 대동사, 연결어, 시간 흐름 등의 단서에 유의해서 해석한다.

흐름을 파악하자

글의 전반부가 부정이고 후반으로 갈수록 긍정이라면 삽입 문장은 역접이 시작하는 부분일 가능성이 높다.

논리의 비약을 찾자

주어진 문장에서 논리적 흐름이 이상한 곳과 글에서 내용상의 단절되는 부분을 찾으면 쉽게 답을 찾을 수 있다.

2020

PART III
문장 삽입

Day 16~Day 20

DAY 16

※ 점수 표기가 없는 문항은 모두 2점입니다.

문장 삽입 01

● 날짜 :   월   일 ● 시작 시각 :   시   분   초

● 목표 시간 : 20분

01

고1 · 2023년 3월 38번

글의 흐름으로 보아, 주어진 문장이 들어가기에 가장 적절한 곳을 고르시오.

> Bad carbohydrates, on the other hand, are simple sugars.

All carbohydrates are basically sugars. (①) Complex carbohydrates are the good carbohydrates for your body. (②) These complex sugar compounds are very difficult to break down and can trap other nutrients like vitamins and minerals in their chains. (③) As they slowly break down, the other nutrients are also released into your body, and can provide you with fuel for a number of hours. (④) Because their structure is not complex, they are easy to break down and hold few nutrients for your body other than the sugars from which they are made. (⑤) Your body breaks down these carbohydrates rather quickly and what it cannot use is converted to fat and stored in the body.

＊carbohydrate: 탄수화물 ＊＊convert: 바꾸다

02

고1 · 2021년 6월 38번

글의 흐름으로 보아, 주어진 문장이 들어가기에 가장 적절한 곳을 고르시오.

> As the sticks approach each other, the air immediately in front of them is compressed and energy builds up.

Sound and light travel in waves. An analogy often given for sound is that of throwing a small stone onto the surface of a still pond. Waves radiate outwards from the point of impact, just as sound waves radiate from the sound source. (①) This is due to a disturbance in the air around us. (②) If you bang two sticks together, you will get a sound. (③) When the point of impact occurs, this energy is released as sound waves. (④) If you try the same experiment with two heavy stones, exactly the same thing occurs, but you get a different sound due to the density and surface of the stones, and as they have likely displaced more air, a louder sound. (⑤) And so, a physical disturbance in the atmosphere around us will produce a sound.

＊analogy: 비유 ＊＊radiate: 사방으로 퍼지다

03

글의 흐름으로 보아, 주어진 문장이 들어가기에 가장 적절한 곳을 고르시오.

> However, we live in a society where gender roles and boundaries are not as strict as in prior generations.

Gender research shows a complex relationship between gender and conflict styles. (①) Some research suggests that women from Western cultures tend to be more caring than men. (②) This tendency may result from socialization processes in which women are encouraged to care for their families and men are encouraged to be successful in competitive work environments. (③) There is significant variability in assertiveness and cooperation among women, as well as among men. (④) Although conflict resolution experts should be able to recognize cultural and gender differences, they should also be aware of within-group variations and the risks of stereotyping. (⑤) Culture and gender may affect the way people perceive, interpret, and respond to conflict; however, we must be careful to avoid overgeneralizations and to consider individual differences.

04

글의 흐름으로 보아, 주어진 문장이 들어가기에 가장 적절한 곳을 고르시오.

> However, when you start putting the plan into practice to achieve your goal, the happiness, excitement, and a lot of fuel suddenly disappear.

When we set a plan, we are very excited about it. (①) In this stage, we can even imagine ourselves victoriously dancing on the top of that mountain, feeling successful and ultimately happy. (②) That is because the road to your goal, the implementation of the plan is not as appealing as the plan. (③) You can easily lose motivation when you face the plain reality of the road to success. (④) The road is paved with grey stones and offers less intense emotions than those imagined at the beginning. (⑤) When you reach the end and look back at the road, however, you'll realize how much more valuable, colorful, and meaningful it was than you anticipated it to be in the moment.

05

글의 흐름으로 보아, 주어진 문장이 들어가기에 가장 적절한 곳을 고르시오. [3점]

> Instead of that, say to them, 'I can't deal with that now but what I can do is I can ask Brian to give you a hand and he should be able to explain them.'

Whenever you say what you can't do, say what you can do. This ends a sentence on a positive note and has a much lower tendency to cause someone to challenge it. (①) Consider this situation — a colleague comes up to you and asks you to look over some figures with them before a meeting they are having tomorrow. (②) You simply say, 'No, I can't deal with this now.' (③) This may then lead to them insisting how important your input is, increasing the pressure on you to give in. (④) Or, 'I can't deal with that now but I can find you in about half an hour when I have finished.' (⑤) Either of these types of responses are better than ending it with a negative.

06

글의 흐름으로 보아, 주어진 문장이 들어가기에 가장 적절한 곳을 고르시오.

> Instead, much like the young child learning how to play 'nicely', the apprentice scientist gains his or her understanding of the moral values inherent in the role by absorption from their colleagues — socialization.

As particular practices are repeated over time and become more widely shared, the values that they embody are reinforced and reproduced and we speak of them as becoming 'institutionalized'. (①) In some cases, this institutionalization has a formal face to it, with rules and protocols written down, and specialized roles created to ensure that procedures are followed correctly. (②) The main institutions of state — parliament, courts, police and so on — along with certain of the professions, exhibit this formal character. (③) Other social institutions, perhaps the majority, are not like this; science is an example. (④) Although scientists are trained in the substantive content of their discipline, they are not formally instructed in 'how to be a good scientist'. (⑤) We think that these values, along with the values that inform many of the professions, are under threat, just as the value of the professions themselves is under threat.

* apprentice: 도제, 견습 ** inherent: 내재된

07 1등급 대비 고난도 2편 문제 　　　고1 · 2023년 6월 38번

글의 흐름으로 보아, 주어진 문장이 들어가기에 가장 적절한 곳을 고르시오.

> Yet we know that the face that stares back at us from the glass is not the same, cannot be the same, as it was 10 minutes ago.

Sometimes the pace of change is far slower. (①) The face you saw reflected in your mirror this morning probably appeared no different from the face you saw the day before — or a week or a month ago. (②) The proof is in your photo album: Look at a photograph taken of yourself 5 or 10 years ago and you see clear differences between the face in the snapshot and the face in your mirror. (③) If you lived in a world without mirrors for a year and then saw your reflection, you might be surprised by the change. (④) After an interval of 10 years without seeing yourself, you might not at first recognize the person peering from the mirror. (⑤) Even something as basic as our own face changes from moment to moment.

* peer: 응시하다

08 1등급 대비 고난도 2편 문제 　　　고1 · 2020년 11월 38번

글의 흐름으로 보아, 주어진 문장이 들어가기에 가장 적절한 곳을 고르시오.

> It is the reason that individuals with certain forms of blindness do not entirely lose their circadian rhythm.

Daylight isn't the only signal that the brain can use for the purpose of biological clock resetting, though it is the principal and preferential signal, when present. (①) So long as they are reliably repeating, the brain can also use other external cues, such as food, exercise, and even regularly timed social interaction. (②) All of these events have the ability to reset the biological clock, allowing it to strike a precise twenty-four-hour note. (③) Despite not receiving light cues due to their blindness, other phenomena act as their resetting triggers. (④) Any signal that the brain uses for the purpose of clock resetting is termed a zeitgeber, from the German "time giver" or "synchronizer." (⑤) Thus, while light is the most reliable and thus the primary zeitgeber, there are many factors that can be used in addition to, or in the absence of, daylight.

* circadian rhythm: 24시간 주기 리듬

09 1등급 대비 고난도 2편 문제 〔고1 · 2021년 3월 38번〕

글의 흐름으로 보아, 주어진 문장이 들어가기에 가장 적절한 곳을 고르시오.

> Meanwhile, improving by 1 percent isn't particularly notable, but it can be far more meaningful in the long run.

It is so easy to overestimate the importance of one defining moment and underestimate the value of making small improvements on a daily basis. Too often, we convince ourselves that massive success requires massive action. (①) Whether it is losing weight, winning a championship, or achieving any other goal, we put pressure on ourselves to make some earthshaking improvement that everyone will talk about. (②) The difference this tiny improvement can make over time is surprising. (③) Here's how the math works out: if you can get 1 percent better each day for one year, you'll end up thirty-seven times better by the time you're done. (④) Conversely, if you get 1 percent worse each day for one year, you'll decline nearly down to zero. (⑤) What starts as a small win or a minor failure adds up to something much more.

10 1등급 대비 고난도 2편 문제 〔고1 · 2016년 11월 37번〕

글의 흐름으로 보아, 주어진 문장이 들어가기에 가장 적절한 곳을 고르시오.

> They are more likely to benefit from the assistance of a formal teaching environment.

Your personality and sense of responsibility affect not only your relationships with others, your job, and your hobbies, but also your learning abilities and style. (①) Some people are very self-driven. (②) They are more likely to be lifelong learners. (③) Many tend to be independent learners and do not require structured classes with instructors to guide them. (④) Other individuals are peer-oriented and often follow the lead of another in unfamiliar situations. (⑤) They may be less likely to pursue learning throughout life without direct access to formal learning scenarios or the influence of a friend or spouse.

11 1등급 대비 고난도 3점 문제

글의 흐름으로 보아, 주어진 문장이 들어가기에 가장 적절한 곳을 고르시오. [3점]

> But after this brief moment of rest, the pendulum swings back again and therefore part of the total energy is then given in the form of kinetic energy.

In general, kinetic energy is the energy associated with motion, while potential energy represents the energy which is "stored" in a physical system. Moreover, the total energy is always conserved. (①) But while the total energy remains unchanged, the kinetic and potential parts of the total energy can change all the time. (②) Imagine, for example, a pendulum which swings back and forth. (③) When it swings, it sweeps out an arc and then slows down as it comes closer to its highest point, where the pendulum does not move at all. (④) So at this point, the energy is completely given in terms of potential energy. (⑤) So as the pendulum swings, kinetic and potential energy constantly change into each other.

* pendulum: 추(錘) ** arc: 호(弧)

12 1등급 대비 고난도 3점 문제

글의 흐름으로 보아, 주어진 문장이 들어가기에 가장 적절한 곳을 고르시오. [3점]

> However, thinking about it this way overlooks debt among people in low-income brackets who have no other way than debt to acquire basic necessities of life.

Have you heard someone say, "He has no one to blame but himself" for some problem? In everyday life we often blame people for "creating" their own problems. (①) Although individual behavior can contribute to social problems, our individual experiences are often largely beyond our own control. (②) They are determined by society as a whole — by its historical development and its organization. (③) If a person sinks into debt because of overspending or credit card abuse, other people often consider the problem to be the result of the individual's personal failings. (④) By contrast, at middle- and upper-income levels, overspending takes on a variety of meanings typically influenced by what people think of as essential for their well-being and associated with the so-called "good life" that is so heavily marketed. (⑤) But across income and wealth levels, larger-scale economic and social problems may affect the person's ability to pay for consumer goods and services.

DAY 16

학습 Check!

▶ 몰라서 틀린 문항 × 표기 ▶ 헷갈렸거나 찍은 문항 △ 표기 ▶ ×, △ 문항은 다시 풀고 ✔ 표기를 하세요.

종료 시각	시	분	초	문항 번호	01	02	03	04	05	06	07	08	09	10	11	12
소요 시간		분	초	채점 결과												
초과 시간		분	초	틀린 문항 복습												

DAY 17

※ 점수 표기가 없는 문항은 모두 **2점**입니다.

문장 삽입 02

● 날짜 :　월　일 ● 시작 시각 :　시　분　초

● 목표 시간 : 20분

01

글의 흐름으로 보아, 주어진 문장이 들어가기에 가장 적절한 곳을 고르시오.

> However, do not assume that a product is perfectly complementary, as customers may not be completely locked in to the product.

A "complementary good" is a product that is often consumed alongside another product. (①) For example, popcorn is a complementary good to a movie, while a travel pillow is a complementary good for a long plane journey. (②) When the popularity of one product increases, the sales of its complementary good also increase. (③) By producing goods that complement other products that are already (or about to be) popular, you can ensure a steady stream of demand for your product. (④) Some products enjoy perfect complementary status — they *have* to be consumed together, such as a lamp and a lightbulb. (⑤) For example, although motorists may seem required to purchase gasoline to run their cars, they can switch to electric cars.

02

글의 흐름으로 보아, 주어진 문장이 들어가기에 가장 적절한 곳을 고르시오.

> The stage director must gain the audience's attention and direct their eyes to a particular spot or actor.

Achieving focus in a movie is easy. Directors can simply point the camera at whatever they want the audience to look at. (①) Close-ups and slow camera shots can emphasize a killer's hand or a character's brief glance of guilt. (②) On stage, focus is much more difficult because the audience is free to look wherever they like. (③) This can be done through lighting, costumes, scenery, voice, and movements. (④) Focus can be gained by simply putting a spotlight on one actor, by having one actor in red and everyone else in gray, or by having one actor move while the others remain still. (⑤) All these techniques will quickly draw the audience's attention to the actor whom the director wants to be in focus.

03

고1 · 2021년 9월 39번

글의 흐름으로 보아, 주어진 문장이 들어가기에 가장 적절한 곳을 고르시오.

> The sales director kept an air horn outside his office and would come out and blow the horn every time a salesperson settled a deal.

Rewarding business success doesn't always have to be done in a material way. (①) A software company I once worked for had a great way of recognizing sales success. (②) The noise, of course, interrupted anything and everything happening in the office because it was unbelievably loud. (③) However, it had an amazingly positive impact on everyone. (④) Sometimes rewarding success can be as easy as that, especially when peer recognition is important. (⑤) You should have seen the way the rest of the sales team wanted the air horn blown for them.

* air horn: (압축 공기로 작동하는) 경적

04

고1 · 2016년 11월 38번

글의 흐름으로 보아, 주어진 문장이 들어가기에 가장 적절한 곳을 고르시오.

> As they passed the ball, a man in a gorilla suit walked into the middle of the group, thumped his chest a bit and then walked off.

George Orwell wrote: "To see what is in front of your nose needs constant struggle." We are surrounded by opportunities, but often we do not even see them. (①) Professor Richard Wiseman did a dramatic and extreme test of this. (②) He asked a group of volunteers to count the number of times a basketball team passed the ball. (③) Quite a few volunteers counted correctly, but only 5 out of over 20 volunteers noticed the gorilla. (④) The same applies to our professional lives. (⑤) We are so focused on keeping score and managing day to day that we do not notice the endless opportunities that are in front of our noses.

05

글의 흐름으로 보아, 주어진 문장이 들어가기에 가장 적절한 곳을 고르시오. [3점]

> Grown-ups rarely explain the meaning of new words to children, let alone how grammatical rules work.

Our brains are constantly solving problems. (①) Every time we learn, or remember, or make sense of something, we solve a problem. (②) Some psychologists have characterized all infant language-learning as problem-solving, extending to children such scientific procedures as "learning by experiment," or "hypothesis-testing." (③) Instead they use the words or the rules in conversation and leave it to children to figure out what is going on. (④) In order to learn language, an infant must make sense of the contexts in which language occurs; problems must be solved. (⑤) We have all been solving problems of this kind since childhood, usually without awareness of what we are doing.

06

글의 흐름으로 보아, 주어진 문장이 들어가기에 가장 적절한 곳을 고르시오.

> It was not until relatively recent times that scientists came to understand the relationships between the structural elements of materials and their properties.

The earliest humans had access to only a very limited number of materials, those that occur naturally: stone, wood, clay, skins, and so on. (①) With time, they discovered techniques for producing materials that had properties superior to those of the natural ones; these new materials included pottery and various metals. (②) Furthermore, it was discovered that the properties of a material could be altered by heat treatments and by the addition of other substances. (③) At this point, materials utilization was totally a selection process that involved deciding from a given, rather limited set of materials, the one best suited for an application based on its characteristics. (④) This knowledge, acquired over approximately the past 100 years, has empowered them to fashion, to a large degree, the characteristics of materials. (⑤) Thus, tens of thousands of different materials have evolved with rather specialized characteristics that meet the needs of our modern and complex society, including metals, plastics, glasses, and fibers.

07 1등급 대비 고난도 2점 문제

글의 흐름으로 보아, 주어진 문장이 들어가기에 가장 적절한 곳을 고르시오.

> Since the dawn of civilization, our ancestors created myths and told legendary stories about the night sky.

We are connected to the night sky in many ways. (①) It has always inspired people to wonder and to imagine. (②) Elements of those narratives became embedded in the social and cultural identities of many generations. (③) On a practical level, the night sky helped past generations to keep track of time and create calendars — essential to developing societies as aids to farming and seasonal gathering. (④) For many centuries, it also provided a useful navigation tool, vital for commerce and for exploring new worlds. (⑤) Even in modern times, many people in remote areas of the planet observe the night sky for such practical purposes.

＊embed: 깊이 새겨 두다 ＊＊commerce: 무역

08 1등급 대비 고난도 2점 문제

글의 흐름으로 보아, 주어진 문장이 들어가기에 가장 적절한 곳을 고르시오.

> In return, the guest had duties to his host.

Geography influenced human relationships in Greece. Because the land made travel so difficult, the guest-host relationship was valued. (①) If a stranger, even a poor man, appeared at your door, it was your duty to be a good host, to give him a shelter and share your food with him. (②) "We do not sit at a table only to eat, but to eat together," said the Greek author Plutarch. (③) Dining was a sign of the human community and differentiated men from beasts. (④) These included not abusing his host's hospitality by staying too long, usually not more than three days. (⑤) A violation of this relationship by either side brought human and divine anger.

＊hospitality: 환대 ＊＊divine: 신(神)의

DAY 17

09 1등급 대비 고난도 2점 문제

글의 흐름으로 보아, 주어진 문장이 들어가기에 가장 적절한 곳을 고르시오.

> But as soon as he puts skis on his feet, it is as though he had to learn to walk all over again.

Reading is like skiing. When done well, when done by an expert, both reading and skiing are graceful, harmonious activities. When done by a beginner, both are awkward, frustrating, and slow. (①) Learning to ski is one of the most embarrassing experiences an adult can undergo. (②) After all, an adult has been walking for a long time; he knows where his feet are; he knows how to put one foot in front of the other in order to get somewhere. (③) He slips and slides, falls down, has trouble getting up, and generally looks — and feels — like a fool. (④) It is the same with reading. (⑤) Probably you have been reading for a long time, too, and starting to learn all over again would be humiliating.

10 1등급 대비 고난도 2점 문제

글의 흐름으로 보아, 주어진 문장이 들어가기에 가장 적절한 곳을 고르시오.

> By contrast, many present-day stories have a less definitive ending.

In the classical fairy tale the conflict is often permanently resolved. Without exception, the hero and heroine live happily ever after. (①) Often the conflict in those stories is only partly resolved, or a new conflict appears making the audience think further. (②) This is particularly true of thriller and horror genres, where audiences are kept on the edge of their seats throughout. (③) Consider Henrik Ibsen's play, *A Doll's House*, where, in the end, Nora leaves her family and marriage. (④) Nora disappears out of the front door and we are left with many unanswered questions such as "Where did Nora go?" and "What will happen to her?" (⑤) An open ending is a powerful tool, providing food for thought that forces the audience to think about what might happen next.

＊definitive: 확정적인

11 1등급 대비 고난도 3점 문제
고1·2023년 6월 39번

글의 흐름으로 보아, 주어진 문장이 들어가기에 가장 적절한 곳을 고르시오. [3점]

As children absorb more evidence from the world around them, certain possibilities become much more likely and more useful and harden into knowledge or beliefs.

According to educational psychologist Susan Engel, curiosity begins to decrease as young as four years old. By the time we are adults, we have fewer questions and more default settings. As Henry James put it, "Disinterested curiosity is past, the mental grooves and channels set." (①) The decline in curiosity can be traced in the development of the brain through childhood. (②) Though smaller than the adult brain, the infant brain contains millions more neural connections. (③) The wiring, however, is a mess; the lines of communication between infant neurons are far less efficient than between those in the adult brain. (④) The baby's perception of the world is consequently both intensely rich and wildly disordered. (⑤) The neural pathways that enable those beliefs become faster and more automatic, while the ones that the child doesn't use regularly are pruned away.

* default setting: 기본값 ** groove: 고랑
*** prune: 가지치기하다

12 1등급 대비 고난도 3점 문제
고1·2020년 9월 38번

글의 흐름으로 보아, 주어진 문장이 들어가기에 가장 적절한 곳을 고르시오. [3점]

The few times that they do occur, it is the possessor who tries to make someone leave the circle.

Reciprocity can be explored in captivity by handing one chimpanzee a large amount of food, such as a watermelon or leafy branch, and then observing what follows. (①) The owner will be center stage, with a group of others around him or her, soon to be followed by newly formed groups around those who obtained a sizable share, until all food has been distributed. (②) Beggars may complain and cry, but aggressive conflicts are rare. (③) She will hit them over their head with her branch or bark at them in a high-pitched voice until they leave her alone. (④) Whatever their rank, possessors control the food flow. (⑤) Once chimpanzees enter reciprocity mode, their social rank no longer matters.

* reciprocity: 호혜주의, 상호의 이익

DAY 17

학습 Check!

▶ 몰라서 틀린 문항 × 표기 ▶ 헷갈렸거나 찍은 문항 △ 표기 ▶ ×, △ 문항은 다시 풀고 ✔ 표기를 하세요.

종료 시각	시 분 초	문항 번호	01	02	03	04	05	06	07	08	09	10	11	12
소요 시간	분 초	채점 결과												
초과 시간	분 초	틀린 문항 복습												

DAY 18

※ 점수 표기가 없는 문항은 모두 2점입니다.

문장 삽입 03

● 날짜 : 월   일 ● 시작 시각 : 시   분   초

● 목표 시간 : 20분

01

글의 흐름으로 보아, 주어진 문장이 들어가기에 가장 적절한 곳을 고르시오.

> If we could magically remove the glasses, we would find the two water bodies would not mix well.

Take two glasses of water. Put a little bit of orange juice into one and a little bit of lemon juice into the other. (①)What you have are essentially two glasses of water but with a completely different chemical makeup. (②) If we take the glass containing orange juice and heat it, we will still have two different glasses of water with different chemical makeups, but now they will also have different temperatures. (③) Perhaps they would mix a little where they met; however, they would remain separate because of their different chemical makeups and temperatures. (④) The warmer water would float on the surface of the cold water because of its lighter weight. (⑤) In the ocean we have bodies of water that differ in temperature and salt content; for this reason, they do not mix.

02

글의 흐름으로 보아, 주어진 문장이 들어가기에 가장 적절한 곳을 고르시오.

> Because of these obstacles, most research missions in space are accomplished through the use of spacecraft without crews aboard.

Currently, we cannot send humans to other planets. One obstacle is that such a trip would take years. (①) A spacecraft would need to carry enough air, water, and other supplies needed for survival on the long journey. (②) Another obstacle is the harsh conditions on other planets, such as extreme heat and cold. (③) Some planets do not even have surfaces to land on. (④) These explorations pose no risk to human life and are less expensive than ones involving astronauts. (⑤) The spacecraft carry instruments that test the compositions and characteristics of planets.

＊composition: 구성 성분

03

글의 흐름으로 보아, 주어진 문장이 들어가기에 가장 적절한 곳을 고르시오.

In addition to positive comments, the director and manager will undoubtedly have comments about what still needs work.

After the technical rehearsal, the theater company will meet with the director, technical managers, and stage manager to review the rehearsal. Usually there will be comments about all the good things about the performance. (①) Individuals should make mental and written notes on the positive comments about their own personal contributions as well as those directed toward the crew and the entire company. (②) Building on positive accomplishments can reduce nervousness. (③) Sometimes, these negative comments can seem overwhelming and stressful. (④) Time pressures to make these last-minute changes can be a source of stress. (⑤) Take each suggestion with good humor and enthusiasm and tackle each task one by one.

04

글의 흐름으로 보아, 주어진 문장이 들어가기에 가장 적절한 곳을 고르시오.

In contrast, Europe has never come close to political unification.

China's frequent times of unity and Europe's constant disunity both have a long history. (①) The most productive areas of modern China were politically joined for the first time in 221 BC, and have remained so for most of the time since then. (②) It has had only a single writing system from the beginning, a single principal language for a long time, and solid cultural unity for two thousand years. (③) It was divided into 500 states in AD 1500, got down to a minimum of 25 states in the 1980s, and is now up again to over 40. (④) It still has 45 languages, and even greater cultural diversity. (⑤) The current disagreements about the issue of unifying Europe are typical of Europe's disunity.

05

글의 흐름으로 보아, 주어진 문장이 들어가기에 가장 적절한 곳을 고르시오. [3점]

> But, when there is biodiversity, the effects of a sudden change are not so dramatic.

When an ecosystem is biodiverse, wildlife have more opportunities to obtain food and shelter. Different species react and respond to changes in their environment differently. (①) For example, imagine a forest with only one type of plant in it, which is the only source of food and habitat for the entire forest food web. (②) Now, there is a sudden dry season and this plant dies. (③) Plant-eating animals completely lose their food source and die out, and so do the animals that prey upon them. (④) Different species of plants respond to the drought differently, and many can survive a dry season. (⑤) Many animals have a variety of food sources and don't just rely on one plant; now our forest ecosystem is no longer at the death!

* biodiversity: (생물학적) 종 다양성   ** habitat: 서식지

06

글의 흐름으로 보아, 주어진 문장이 들어가기에 가장 적절한 곳을 고르시오.

> When Kaldi reported his observation to the local monastery, the abbot became the first person to brew a pot of coffee and note its flavor and alerting effect when he drank it.

Although humans have been drinking coffee for centuries, it is not clear just where coffee originated or who first discovered it. (①) However, the predominant legend has it that a goatherd discovered coffee in the Ethiopian highlands. (②) Various dates for this legend include 900 BC, 300 AD, and 800 AD. (③) Regardless of the actual date, it is said that Kaldi, the goatherd, noticed that his goats did not sleep at night after eating berries from what would later be known as a coffee tree. (④) Word of the awakening effects and the pleasant taste of this new beverage soon spread beyond the monastery. (⑤) The story of Kaldi might be more fable than fact, but at least some historical evidence indicates that coffee did originate in the Ethiopian highlands.

* abbot: 수도원장

07 1등급 대비 고난도 2점 문제

글의 흐름으로 보아, 주어진 문장이 들어가기에 가장 적절한 곳을 고르시오.

> But, a blind person will associate the same friend with a unique combination of experiences from their non-visual senses that act to represent that friend.

Humans born without sight are not able to collect visual experiences, so they understand the world entirely through their other senses. (①) As a result, people with blindness at birth develop an amazing ability to understand the world through the collection of experiences and memories that come from these non-visual senses. (②) The dreams of a person who has been without sight since birth can be just as vivid and imaginative as those of someone with normal vision. (③) They are unique, however, because their dreams are constructed from the non-visual experiences and memories they have collected. (④) A person with normal vision will dream about a familiar friend using visual memories of shape, lighting, and colour. (⑤) In other words, people blind at birth have similar overall dreaming experiences even though they do not dream in pictures.

08 1등급 대비 고난도 2점 문제

글의 흐름으로 보아, 주어진 문장이 들어가기에 가장 적절한 곳을 고르시오.

> This may have worked in the past, but today, with interconnected team processes, we don't want all people who are the same.

Most of us have hired many people based on human resources criteria along with some technical and personal information that the boss thought was important. (①) I have found that most people like to hire people just like themselves. (②) In a team, some need to be leaders, some need to be doers, some need to provide creative strengths, some need to be inspirers, some need to provide imagination, and so on. (③) In other words, we are looking for a diversified team where members complement one another. (④) When putting together a new team or hiring team members, we need to look at each individual and how he or she fits into the whole of our team objective. (⑤) The bigger the team, the more possibilities exist for diversity.

* criteria: 기준

09 1등급 대비 고난도 2편 문제   고1·2018년 9월 39번

글의 흐름으로 보아, 주어진 문장이 들어가기에 가장 적절한 곳을 고르시오. 기본

> So a patient whose heart has stopped can no longer be regarded as dead.

Traditionally, people were declared dead when their hearts stopped beating, their blood stopped circulating and they stopped breathing. (①) So doctors would listen for a heartbeat, or occasionally conduct the famous mirror test to see if there were any signs of moisture from the potential deceased's breath. (②) It is commonly known that when people's hearts stop and they breathe their last, they are dead. (③) But in the last half-century, doctors have proved time and time again that they can revive many patients whose hearts have stopped beating by various techniques such as cardiopulmonary resuscitation. (④) Instead, the patient is said to be 'clinically dead'. (⑤) Someone who is only clinically dead can often be brought back to life.

* cardiopulmonary resuscitation: 심폐소생술(CPR)

10 1등급 대비 고난도 2편 문제   고1·2018년 3월 37번

글의 흐름으로 보아, 주어진 문장이 들어가기에 가장 적절한 곳을 고르시오.

> A camping trip where each person attempted to gain the maximum rewards from the other campers in exchange for the use of his or her talents would quickly end in disaster and unhappiness.

The philosopher G. A. Cohen provides an example of a camping trip as a metaphor for the ideal society. (①) On a camping trip, he argues, it is unimaginable that someone would say something like, "I cooked the dinner and therefore you can't eat it unless you pay me for my superior cooking skills." (②) Rather, one person cooks dinner, another sets up the tent, another purifies the water, and so on, each in accordance with his or her abilities. (③) All these goods are shared and a spirit of community makes all participants happier. (④) Moreover, the experience would be ruined if people were to behave in such a way. (⑤) So, we would have a better life in a more equal and cooperative society.

* metaphor: 비유

11 1등급 대비 고난도 3점 문제

고1 · 2023년 9월 38번

글의 흐름으로 보아, 주어진 문장이 들어가기에 가장 적절한 곳을 고르시오. [3점]

> Other individuals prefer integrating work and family roles all day long.

Boundaries between work and home are blurring as portable digital technology makes it increasingly possible to work anywhere, anytime. Individuals differ in how they like to manage their time to meet work and outside responsibilities. (①) Some people prefer to separate or segment roles so that boundary crossings are minimized. (②) For example, these people might keep separate email accounts for work and family and try to conduct work at the workplace and take care of family matters only during breaks and non-work time. (③) We've even noticed more of these "segmenters" carrying two phones — one for work and one for personal use. (④) Flexible schedules work well for these individuals because they enable greater distinction between time at work and time in other roles. (⑤) This might entail constantly trading text messsages with children from the office, or monitoring emails at home and on vacation, rather than returning to work to find hundreds of messages in their inbox.

* entail: 수반하다

12 1등급 대비 고난도 3점 문제

고1 · 2020년 11월 39번

글의 흐름으로 보아, 주어진 문장이 들어가기에 가장 적절한 곳을 고르시오. [3점]

> More recently, agriculture has in many places lost its local character, and has become incorporated into the global economy.

Earlier agricultural systems were integrated with and co-evolved with technologies, beliefs, myths and traditions as part of an integrated social system. (①) Generally, people planted a variety of crops in different areas, in the hope of obtaining a reasonably stable food supply. (②) These systems could only be maintained at low population levels, and were relatively non-destructive (but not always). (③) This has led to increased pressure on agricultural land for exchange commodities and export goods. (④) More land is being diverted from local food production to "cash crops" for export and exchange; fewer types of crops are raised, and each crop is raised in much greater quantities than before. (⑤) Thus, ever more land is converted from forest (and other natural systems) for agriculture for export, rather than using land for subsistence crops.

* subsistence crop: 자급자족용 작물

학습 Check!

▶ 몰라서 틀린 문항 × 표기 ▶ 헷갈렸거나 찍은 문항 △ 표기 ▶ ×, △ 문항은 다시 풀고 ✔ 표기를 하세요.

종료 시각	시 분 초	문항 번호	01	02	03	04	05	06	07	08	09	10	11	12
소요 시간	분 초	채점 결과												
초과 시간	분 초	틀린 문항 복습												

DAY 19

※ 점수 표기가 없는 문항은 모두 2점입니다.

문장 삽입 04

● 날짜 :　월　일　● 시작 시각 :　시　분　초

● 목표 시간 : 20분

01

글의 흐름으로 보아, 주어진 문장이 들어가기에 가장 적절한 곳을 고르시오.

> For example, if you rub your hands together quickly, they will get warmer.

Friction is a force between two surfaces that are sliding, or trying to slide, across each other. For example, when you try to push a book along the floor, friction makes this difficult. Friction always works in the direction opposite to the direction in which the object is moving, or trying to move. So, friction always slows a moving object down. (①) The amount of friction depends on the surface materials. (②) The rougher the surface is, the more friction is produced. (③) Friction also produces heat. (④) Friction can be a useful force because it prevents our shoes slipping on the floor when we walk and stops car tires skidding on the road. (⑤) When you walk, friction is caused between the tread on your shoes and the ground, acting to grip the ground and prevent sliding.

＊skid: 미끄러지다　＊＊tread: 접지면, 바닥

02

글의 흐름으로 보아, 주어진 문장이 들어가기에 가장 적절한 곳을 고르시오.

> In this way, quick judgements are not only relevant in employment matters; they are equally applicable in love and relationship matters too.

You've probably heard the expression, "first impressions matter a lot". (①) Life really doesn't give many people a second chance to make a good first impression. (②) It has been determined that it takes only a few seconds for anyone to assess another individual. (③) This is very noticeable in recruitment processes, where top recruiters can predict the direction of their eventual decision on any candidate within a few seconds of introducing themselves. (④) So, a candidate's CV may 'speak' knowledge and competence, but their appearance and introduction may tell of a lack of coordination, fear, and poor interpersonal skills. (⑤) On a date with a wonderful somebody who you've painstakingly tracked down for months, subtle things like bad breath or wrinkled clothes may spoil your noble efforts.

＊CV: 이력서(curriculum vitae)

03

고1 · 2021년 9월 38번

글의 흐름으로 보아, 주어진 문장이 들어가기에 가장 적절한 곳을 고르시오.

> However, using caffeine to improve alertness and mental performance doesn't replace getting a good night's sleep.

Studies have consistently shown caffeine to be effective when used together with a pain reliever to treat headaches. (①) The positive correlation between caffeine intake and staying alert throughout the day has also been well established. (②) As little as 60mg (the amount typically in one cup of tea) can lead to a faster reaction time. (③) One study from 2018 showed that coffee improved reaction times in those with or without poor sleep, but caffeine seemed to increase errors in the group with little sleep. (④) Additionally, this study showed that even with caffeine, the group with little sleep did not score as well as those with adequate sleep. (⑤) It suggests that caffeine does not fully make up for inadequate sleep.

04

고1 · 2018년 6월 37번

글의 흐름으로 보아, 주어진 문장이 들어가기에 가장 적절한 곳을 고르시오.

> Dinosaurs, however, did once live.

When I was very young, I had a difficulty telling the difference between dinosaurs and dragons. (①) But there is a significant difference between them. (②) Dragons appear in Greek myths, legends about England's King Arthur, Chinese New Year parades, and in many tales throughout human history. (③) But even if they feature in stories created today, they have always been the products of the human imagination and never existed. (④) They walked the earth for a very long time, even if human beings never saw them. (⑤) They existed around 200 million years ago, and we know about them because their bones have been preserved as fossils.

05

글의 흐름으로 보아, 주어진 문장이 들어가기에 가장 적절한 곳을 고르시오. [3점]

> It was also found that those students who expected the lecturer to be warm tended to interact with him more.

People commonly make the mistaken assumption that because a person has one type of characteristic, then they automatically have other characteristics which go with it. (①) In one study, university students were given descriptions of a guest lecturer before he spoke to the group. (②) Half the students received a description containing the word 'warm', the other half were told the speaker was 'cold'. (③) The guest lecturer then led a discussion, after which the students were asked to give their impressions of him. (④) As expected, there were large differences between the impressions formed by the students, depending upon their original information of the lecturer. (⑤) This shows that different expectations not only affect the impressions we form but also our behaviour and the relationship which is formed.

06

글의 흐름으로 보아, 주어진 문장이 들어가기에 가장 적절한 곳을 고르시오. [3점]

> Such critics are usually unaware of the real nature of social science and of its special problems and basic limitations.

Some people believe that the social sciences are falling behind the natural sciences. (①) They maintain that not only does social science have no exact laws, but it also has failed to eliminate great social evils such as racial discrimination, crime, poverty, and war. (②) They suggest that social scientists have failed to accomplish what might reasonably have been expected of them. (③) For example, they forget that the solution to a social problem requires not only knowledge but also the ability to influence people. (④) Even if social scientists discover the procedures that could reasonably be followed to achieve social improvement, they are seldom in a position to control social action. (⑤) For that matter, even dictators find that there are limits to their power to change society.

07

글의 흐름으로 보아, 주어진 문장이 들어가기에 가장 적절한 곳을 고르시오.

There's a reason for that: traditionally, park designers attempted to create such a feeling by planting tall trees at park boundaries, building stone walls, and constructing other means of partition.

Parks take the shape demanded by the cultural concerns of their time. Once parks are in place, they are no inert stage — their purposes and meanings are made and remade by planners and by park users. Moments of park creation are particularly telling, however, for they reveal and actualize ideas about nature and its relationship to urban society. (①) Indeed, what distinguishes a park from the broader category of public space is the representation of nature that parks are meant to embody. (②) Public spaces include parks, concrete plazas, sidewalks, even indoor atriums. (③) Parks typically have trees, grass, and other plants as their central features. (④) When entering a city park, people often imagine a sharp separation from streets, cars, and buildings. (⑤) What's behind this idea is not only landscape architects' desire to design aesthetically suggestive park spaces, but a much longer history of Western thought that envisions cities and nature as antithetical spaces and oppositional forces.

＊aesthetically: 미적으로 ＊＊antithetical: 대조적인

08 1등급 대비 고난도 2개 문제

글의 흐름으로 보아, 주어진 문장이 들어가기에 가장 적절한 곳을 고르시오.

Unfortunately, it is also likely to "crowd out" other activities that produce more sustainable social contributions to our social well-being.

Television is the number one leisure activity in the United States and Europe, consuming more than half of our free time. (①) We generally think of television as a way to relax, tune out, and escape from our troubles for a bit each day. (②) While this is true, there is increasing evidence that we are more motivated to tune in to our favorite shows and characters when we are feeling lonely or have a greater need for social connection. (③) Television watching does satisfy these social needs to some extent, at least in the short run. (④) The more television we watch, the less likely we are to volunteer our time or to spend time with people in our social networks. (⑤) In other words, the more time we make for *Friends*, the less time we have for friends in real life.

＊*Friends*: 프렌즈(미국의 한 방송국에서 방영된 시트콤)

DAY 19

[해설편 p.120]

09 1등급 대비 고난도 2점 문제
고1 · 2019년 6월 38번

글의 흐름으로 보아, 주어진 문장이 들어가기에 가장 적절한 곳을 고르시오.

> When the boy learned that he had misspelled the word, he went to the judges and told them.

Some years ago at the national spelling bee in Washington, D.C., a thirteen-year-old boy was asked to spell *echolalia*, a word that means a tendency to repeat whatever one hears. (①) Although he misspelled the word, the judges misheard him, told him he had spelled the word right, and allowed him to advance. (②) So he was eliminated from the competition after all. (③) Newspaper headlines the next day called the honest young man a "spelling bee hero," and his photo appeared in *The New York Times*. (④) "The judges said I had a lot of honesty," the boy told reporters. (⑤) He added that part of his motive was, "I didn't want to feel like a liar."

＊spelling bee: 단어 철자 맞히기 대회

10 1등급 대비 고난도 2점 문제
고1 · 2017년 3월 37번

글의 흐름으로 보아, 주어진 문장이 들어가기에 가장 적절한 곳을 고르시오.

> When you hit puberty, however, sometimes these forever-friendships go through growing pains.

Childhood friends — friends you've known forever — are really special. (①) They know everything about you, and you've shared lots of firsts. (②) You find that you have less in common than you used to. (③) Maybe you're into rap and she's into pop, or you go to different schools and have different groups of friends. (④) Change can be scary, but remember: Friends, even best friends, don't have to be exactly alike. (⑤) Having friends with other interests keeps life interesting — just think of what you can learn from each other.

＊puberty: 사춘기

11 1등급 대비 고난도 3점 문제

고1 · 2022년 11월 38번

글의 흐름으로 보아, 주어진 문장이 들어가기에 가장 적절한 곳을 고르시오. [3점]

> Nevertheless, language is enormously important in human life and contributes largely to our ability to cooperate with each other in dealing with the world.

Should we use language to understand mind or mind to understand language? (①) Analytic philosophy historically assumes that language is basic and that mind would make sense if proper use of language was appreciated. (②) Modern cognitive science, however, rightly judges that language is just one aspect of mind of great importance in human beings but not fundamental to all kinds of thinking. (③) Countless species of animals manage to navigate the world, solve problems, and learn without using language, through brain mechanisms that are largely preserved in the minds of humans. (④) There is no reason to assume that language is fundamental to mental operations. (⑤) Our species *homo sapiens* has been astonishingly successful, which depended in part on language, first as an effective contributor to collaborative problem solving and much later, as collective memory through written records.

＊appreciate: (제대로) 인식하다

12 1등급 대비 고난도 3점 문제

고1 · 2020년 3월 37번

글의 흐름으로 보아, 주어진 문장이 들어가기에 가장 적절한 곳을 고르시오. [3점]

> In the U.S. we have so many metaphors for time and its passing that we think of time as "a thing," that is "the weekend is almost gone," or "I haven't got the time."

There are some cultures that can be referred to as "people who live outside of time." The Amondawa tribe, living in Brazil, does not have a concept of time that can be measured or counted. (①) Rather they live in a world of serial events, rather than seeing events as being rooted in time. (②) Researchers also found that no one had an age. (③) Instead, they change their names to reflect their stage of life and position within their society, so a little child will give up their name to a newborn sibling and take on a new one. (④) We think such statements are objective, but they aren't. (⑤) We create these metaphors, but the Amondawa don't talk or think in metaphors for time.

＊metaphor: 은유 ＊＊sibling: 형제자매

DAY 19

▶ 몰라서 틀린 문항 × 표기   ▶ 헷갈렸거나 찍은 문항 △ 표기   ▶ ×, △ 문항은 다시 풀고 ✔ 표기를 하세요.

종료 시각	시	분	초	문항 번호	01	02	03	04	05	06	07	08	09	10	11	12
소요 시간		분	초	채점 결과												
초과 시간		분	초	틀린 문항 복습												

DAY 20

※ 점수 표기가 없는 문항은 모두 2점입니다.

문장 삽입 05

● 날짜 :　　월　　일　● 시작 시각 :　　시　　분　　초

● 목표 시간 : 20분

01

고1 · 2021년 11월 38번

글의 흐름으로 보아, 주어진 문장이 들어가기에 가장 적절한 곳을 고르시오.

> Worse, some are contaminated with other substances and contain ingredients not listed on the label.

According to top nutrition experts, most nutrients are better absorbed and used by the body when consumed from a whole food instead of a supplement. (①) However, many people feel the need to take pills, powders, and supplements in an attempt to obtain nutrients and fill the gaps in their diets. (②) We hope these will give us more energy, prevent us from catching a cold in the winter, or improve our skin and hair. (③) But in reality, the large majority of supplements are artificial and may not even be completely absorbed by your body. (④) For example, a recent investigative report found heavy metals in 40 percent of 134 brands of protein powders on the market. (⑤) With little control and regulation, taking supplements is a gamble and often costly.

＊contaminate: 오염시키다　＊＊supplement: 보충제

02

고1 · 2019년 9월 38번

글의 흐름으로 보아, 주어진 문장이 들어가기에 가장 적절한 곳을 고르시오.

> The other main clue you might use to tell what a friend is feeling would be to look at his or her facial expression.

Have you ever thought about how you can tell what somebody else is feeling? (①) Sometimes, friends might tell you that they are feeling happy or sad but, even if they do not tell you, I am sure that you would be able to make a good guess about what kind of mood they are in. (②) You might get a clue from the tone of voice that they use. (③) For example, they may raise their voice if they are angry or talk in a shaky way if they are scared. (④) We have lots of muscles in our faces which enable us to move our face into lots of different positions. (⑤) This happens spontaneously when we feel a particular emotion.

03

글의 흐름으로 보아, 주어진 문장이 들어가기에 가장 적절한 곳을 고르시오.

> Yet libraries must still provide quietness for study and reading, because many of our students want a quiet study environment.

Acoustic concerns in school libraries are much more important and complex today than they were in the past. (①) Years ago, before electronic resources were such a vital part of the library environment, we had only to deal with noise produced by people. (②) Today, the widespread use of computers, printers, and other equipment has added machine noise. (③) People noise has also increased, because group work and instruction are essential parts of the learning process. (④) So, the modern school library is no longer the quiet zone it once was. (⑤) Considering this need for library surroundings, it is important to design spaces where unwanted noise can be eliminated or at least kept to a minimum.

＊acoustic: 소리의

04

글의 흐름으로 보아, 주어진 문장이 들어가기에 가장 적절한 곳을 고르시오.

> So skin cells, hair cells, and nail cells no longer produce new cells.

Do hair and fingernails continue to grow after a person dies? The short answer is no, though it may not seem that way to the casual observer. (①) That's because after death, the human body dehydrates, causing the skin to shrink, or become smaller. (②) This shrinking exposes the parts of the nails and hair that were once under the skin, causing them to appear longer than before. (③) Typically, fingernails grow about 0.1 millimeters a day, but in order to grow, they need glucose — a simple sugar that helps to power the body. (④) Once the body dies, there's no more glucose. (⑤) Moreover, a complex hormonal regulation directs the growth of hair and nails, none of which is possible once a person dies.

＊dehydrate: 수분이 빠지다

DAY **20**

05

글의 흐름으로 보아, 주어진 문장이 들어가기에 가장 적절한 곳을 고르시오. [3점]

> However, if you tried to copy the original rather than your imaginary drawing, you might find your drawing now was a little better.

Imagine in your mind one of your favorite paintings, drawings, cartoon characters or something equally complex. (①) Now, with that picture in your mind, try to draw what your mind sees. (②) Unless you are unusually gifted, your drawing will look completely different from what you are seeing with your mind's eye. (③) Furthermore, if you copied the picture many times, you would find that each time your drawing would get a little better, a little more accurate. (④) Practice makes perfect. (⑤) This is because you are developing the skills of coordinating what your mind perceives with the movement of your body parts.

＊coordinate ~ with ...: ~와 …을 조화시키다

06

글의 흐름으로 보아, 주어진 문장이 들어가기에 가장 적절한 곳을 고르시오. [3점]

> It has been observed that at each level of transfer, a large proportion, 80 − 90 percent, of the potential energy is lost as heat.

Food chain means the transfer of food energy from the source in plants through a series of organisms with the repeated process of eating and being eaten. (①) In a grassland, grass is eaten by rabbits while rabbits in turn are eaten by foxes. (②) This is an example of a simple food chain. (③) This food chain implies the sequence in which food energy is transferred from producer to consumer or higher trophic level. (④) Hence the number of steps or links in a sequence is restricted, usually to four or five. (⑤) The shorter the food chain or the nearer the organism is to the beginning of the chain, the greater the available energy intake is.

＊trophic: 영양의

07

글의 흐름으로 보아, 주어진 문장이 들어가기에 가장 적절한 곳을 고르시오.

> When the team painted fireflies' light organs dark, a new set of bats took twice as long to learn to avoid them.

Fireflies don't just light up their behinds to attract mates, they also glow to tell bats not to eat them. This twist in the tale of the trait that gives fireflies their name was discovered by Jesse Barber and his colleagues. The glow's warning role benefits both fireflies and bats, because these insects taste disgusting to the mammals. (①) When swallowed, chemicals released by fireflies cause bats to throw them back up. (②) The team placed eight bats in a dark room with three or four fireflies plus three times as many tasty insects, including beetles and moths, for four days. (③) During the first night, all the bats captured at least one firefly. (④) But by the fourth night, most bats had learned to avoid fireflies and catch all the other prey instead. (⑤) It had long been thought that firefly bioluminescence mainly acted as a mating signal, but the new finding explains why firefly larvae also glow despite being immature for mating.

* bioluminescence: 생물 발광(發光)

** larvae: larva(애벌레)의 복수형

08 1등급 대비 고난도 2類 문제

글의 흐름으로 보아, 주어진 문장이 들어가기에 가장 적절한 곳을 고르시오.

> However, as society becomes more diverse, the likelihood that people share assumptions and values diminishes.

The way we communicate influences our ability to build strong and healthy communities. Traditional ways of building communities have emphasized debate and argument. (①) For example, the United States has a strong tradition of using town hall meetings to deliberate important issues within communities. (②) In these settings, advocates for each side of the issue present arguments for their positions, and public issues have been discussed in such public forums. (③) Yet for debate and argument to work well, people need to come to such forums with similar assumptions and values. (④) The shared assumptions and values serve as a foundation for the discussion. (⑤) As a result, forms of communication such as argument and debate become polarized, which may drive communities apart as opposed to bringing them together.

09 1등급 대비 고난도 2점 문제

고1 · 2017년 6월 38번

글의 흐름으로 보아, 주어진 문장이 들어가기에 가장 적절한 곳을 고르시오.

> Throw away your own hesitation and forget all your concerns about whether you are musically talented or whether you can sing or play an instrument.

Music appeals powerfully to young children. (①) Watch preschoolers' faces and bodies when they hear rhythm and sound — they light up and move eagerly and enthusiastically. (②) They communicate comfortably, express themselves creatively, and let out all sorts of thoughts and emotions as they interact with music. (③) In a word, young children think music is a lot of fun, so do all you can to make the most of the situation. (④) They don't matter when you are enjoying music with your child. (⑤) Just follow his or her lead, have fun, sing songs together, listen to different kinds of music, move, dance, and enjoy.

10 1등급 대비 고난도 2점 문제

고1 · 2020년 3월 38번

글의 흐름으로 보아, 주어진 문장이 들어가기에 가장 적절한 곳을 고르시오.

> Of course, within cultures individual attitudes can vary dramatically.

The natural world provides a rich source of symbols used in art and literature. (①) Plants and animals are central to mythology, dance, song, poetry, rituals, festivals, and holidays around the world. (②) Different cultures can exhibit opposite attitudes toward a given species. (③) Snakes, for example, are honored by some cultures and hated by others. (④) Rats are considered pests in much of Europe and North America and greatly respected in some parts of India. (⑤) For instance, in Britain many people dislike rodents, and yet there are several associations devoted to breeding them, including the National Mouse Club and the National Fancy Rat Club.

* pest: 유해 동물 ** rodent: (쥐, 다람쥐 등이 속한) 설치류

11 1등급 대비 고난도 3점 문제

글의 흐름으로 보아, 주어진 문장이 들어가기에 가장 적절한 곳을 고르시오. [3점]

> What we need is a reliable and reproducible method for measuring the relative hotness or coldness of objects rather than the rate of energy transfer.

We often associate the concept of temperature with how hot or cold an object feels when we touch it. In this way, our senses provide us with a qualitative indication of temperature. (①) Our senses, however, are unreliable and often mislead us. (②) For example, if you stand in bare feet with one foot on carpet and the other on a tile floor, the tile feels colder than the carpet *even though both are at the same temperature.* (③) The two objects feel different because tile transfers energy by heat at a higher rate than carpet does. (④) Your skin "measures" the rate of energy transfer by heat rather than the actual temperature. (⑤) Scientists have developed a variety of thermometers for making such quantitative measurements.

＊thermometer: 온도계

12 1등급 대비 고난도 3점 문제

글의 흐름으로 보아, 주어진 문장이 들어가기에 가장 적절한 곳을 고르시오. [3점]

> Before a trip, research how the native inhabitants dress, work, and eat.

The continued survival of the human race can be explained by our ability to adapt to our environment. (①) While we may have lost some of our ancient ancestors' survival skills, we have learned new skills as they have become necessary. (②) Today, the gap between the skills we once had and the skills we now have grows ever wider as we rely more heavily on modern technology. (③) Therefore, when you head off into the wilderness, it is important to fully prepare for the environment. (④) How they have adapted to their way of life will help you to understand the environment and allow you to select the best gear and learn the correct skills. (⑤) This is crucial because most survival situations arise as a result of a series of events that could have been avoided.

＊inhabitant: 주민

학습 Check!

▶ 몰라서 틀린 문항 × 표기 ▶ 헷갈렸거나 찍은 문항 △ 표기 ▶ ×, △ 문항은 다시 풀고 ✔ 표기를 하세요.

종료 시각	시 분 초	문항 번호	01	02	03	04	05	06	07	08	09	10	11	12
소요 시간	분 초	채점 결과												
초과 시간	분 초	틀린 문항 복습												

MEMO

PART I · 빈칸 추론 [Day 01~Day 10]

Day 01 빈칸 추론 01

01 ① 02 ② 03 ② 04 ① 05 ③ 06 ④ 07 ① 08 ③ 09 ① 10 ②
11 ⑤ 12 ③

Day 02 빈칸 추론 02

01 ③ 02 ① 03 ④ 04 ① 05 ⑤ 06 ② 07 ⑤ 08 ⑤ 09 ① 10 ①
11 ② 12 ②

Day 03 빈칸 추론 03

01 ② 02 ① 03 ③ 04 ③ 05 ⑤ 06 ④ 07 ④ 08 ② 09 ② 10 ①
11 ② 12 ①

Day 04 빈칸 추론 04

01 ④ 02 ② 03 ③ 04 ① 05 ① 06 ② 07 ① 08 ③ 09 ③ 10 ②
11 ② 12 ③

Day 05 빈칸 추론 05

01 ④ 02 ① 03 ① 04 ① 05 ④ 06 ④ 07 ⑤ 08 ⑤ 09 ③ 10 ①
11 ⑤ 12 ⑤

Day 06 빈칸 추론 06

01 ① 02 ③ 03 ② 04 ⑤ 05 ② 06 ④ 07 ④ 08 ③ 09 ② 10 ①
11 ③ 12 ①

Day 07 빈칸 추론 07

01 ① 02 ③ 03 ① 04 ② 05 ⑤ 06 ⑤ 07 ① 08 ③ 09 ① 10 ①
11 ② 12 ⑤

Day 08 빈칸 추론 08

01 ① 02 ① 03 ② 04 ② 05 ④ 06 ③ 07 ② 08 ② 09 ① 10 ①
11 ③ 12 ⑤

Day 09 빈칸 추론 09

01 ② 02 ① 03 ③ 04 ⑤ 05 ② 06 ③ 07 ③ 08 ② 09 ① 10 ④
11 ① 12 ②

Day 10 빈칸 추론 10

01 ④ 02 ④ 03 ② 04 ② 05 ⑤ 06 ③ 07 ① 08 ① 09 ⑤ 10 ③
11 ① 12 ④

PART II · 글의 순서 [Day 11~Day 15]

Day 11 글의 순서 01

01 ⑤ 02 ② 03 ⑤ 04 ③ 05 ③ 06 ④ 07 ② 08 ② 09 ⑤ 10 ③
11 ② 12 ④

Day 12 글의 순서 02

01 ③ 02 ② 03 ⑤ 04 ⑤ 05 ⑤ 06 ② 07 ⑤ 08 ② 09 ② 10 ④
11 ② 12 ④

Day 13 글의 순서 03

01 ③ 02 ⑤ 03 ⑤ 04 ② 05 ⑤ 06 ① 07 ② 08 ② 09 ⑤ 10 ④
11 ⑤ 12 ⑤

Day 14 글의 순서 04

01 ③ 02 ② 03 ③ 04 ② 05 ② 06 ② 07 ④ 08 ③ 09 ② 10 ⑤
11 ③ 12 ④

Day 15 글의 순서 05

01 ③ 02 ② 03 ③ 04 ② 05 ② 06 ⑤ 07 ② 08 ② 09 ③ 10 ②
11 ⑤ 12 ②

PART III · 문장 삽입 [Day 16~Day 20]

Day 16 문장 삽입 01

01 ④ 02 ② 03 ③ 04 ② 05 ④ 06 ⑤ 07 ② 08 ③ 09 ② 10 ⑤
11 ⑤ 12 ④

Day 17 문장 삽입 02

01 ⑤ 02 ③ 03 ② 04 ③ 05 ③ 06 ④ 07 ② 08 ④ 09 ③ 10 ①
11 ⑤ 12 ③

Day 18 문장 삽입 03

01 ③ 02 ④ 03 ③ 04 ③ 05 ④ 06 ④ 07 ⑤ 08 ② 09 ④ 10 ④
11 ⑤ 12 ③

Day 19 문장 삽입 04

01 ④ 02 ⑤ 03 ③ 04 ④ 05 ⑤ 06 ③ 07 ⑤ 08 ④ 09 ② 10 ②
11 ⑤ 12 ④

Day 20 문장 삽입 05

01 ④ 02 ④ 03 ⑤ 04 ⑤ 05 ③ 06 ④ 07 ⑤ 08 ⑤ 09 ④ 10 ⑤
11 ⑤ 12 ④

수능기출 베스트셀러
리얼 오리지널

수능 내신 1등급 대비 전국연합 학력평가

20일 완성 영어 독해

빈칸순서삽입

20 Days completed

2020

하루 20분   20일 완성

기본
해설편

- 고1 최근 7개년 전국연합학력평가 기출 [빈칸·순서·삽입] 총 240문항 수록
- 하루 12문제를 20분씩 학습하는 [20일 완성] 영어 1등급 PLAN
- 평이한 2점, 3점 문항과 [고난도 2점, 3점] 문항을 매회 체계적으로 배치
- 지문의 이해를 돕는 [직독직해, 구문풀이] 해설 및 고난도 문제 해결 꿀팁

수능 모의고사 전문 출판
 입시플라이

PART Ⅰ · 빈칸 추론 [Day 01~Day 10]

Day 01　빈칸 추론 01

01 ① 02 ② 03 ② 04 ① 05 ③ 06 ④ 07 ① 08 ③ 09 ① 10 ②
11 ⑤ 12 ③

Day 02　빈칸 추론 02

01 ③ 02 ① 03 ④ 04 ① 05 ⑤ 06 ② 07 ⑤ 08 ⑤ 09 ① 10 ①
11 ② 12 ②

Day 03　빈칸 추론 03

01 ② 02 ① 03 ③ 04 ③ 05 ⑤ 06 ④ 07 ④ 08 ② 09 ② 10 ①
11 ② 12 ①

Day 04　빈칸 추론 04

01 ④ 02 ② 03 ③ 04 ① 05 ① 06 ② 07 ① 08 ③ 09 ③ 10 ②
11 ② 12 ③

Day 05　빈칸 추론 05

01 ④ 02 ① 03 ① 04 ① 05 ④ 06 ④ 07 ⑤ 08 ⑤ 09 ③ 10 ①
11 ⑤ 12 ⑤

Day 06　빈칸 추론 06

01 ① 02 ③ 03 ② 04 ⑤ 05 ② 06 ④ 07 ④ 08 ③ 09 ② 10 ①
11 ③ 12 ①

Day 07　빈칸 추론 07

01 ① 02 ③ 03 ① 04 ② 05 ⑤ 06 ⑤ 07 ① 08 ③ 09 ① 10 ①
11 ② 12 ⑤

Day 08　빈칸 추론 08

01 ① 02 ① 03 ② 04 ⑤ 05 ④ 06 ③ 07 ② 08 ② 09 ① 10 ①
11 ③ 12 ⑤

Day 09　빈칸 추론 09

01 ② 02 ① 03 ③ 04 ⑤ 05 ② 06 ③ 07 ③ 08 ② 09 ① 10 ④
11 ① 12 ②

Day 10　빈칸 추론 10

01 ④ 02 ④ 03 ② 04 ② 05 ⑤ 06 ③ 07 ① 08 ① 09 ⑤ 10 ③
11 ① 12 ④

PART Ⅱ · 글의 순서 [Day 11~Day 15]

Day 11　글의 순서 01

01 ⑤ 02 ② 03 ⑤ 04 ③ 05 ③ 06 ④ 07 ② 08 ② 09 ⑤ 10 ③
11 ② 12 ④

Day 12　글의 순서 02

01 ③ 02 ② 03 ⑤ 04 ⑤ 05 ⑤ 06 ② 07 ⑤ 08 ② 09 ② 10 ④
11 ② 12 ④

Day 13　글의 순서 03

01 ③ 02 ⑤ 03 ⑤ 04 ② 05 ⑤ 06 ① 07 ② 08 ② 09 ⑤ 10 ④
11 ⑤ 12 ⑤

Day 14　글의 순서 04

01 ③ 02 ② 03 ③ 04 ② 05 ② 06 ② 07 ④ 08 ③ 09 ② 10 ⑤
11 ③ 12 ④

Day 15　글의 순서 05

01 ③ 02 ② 03 ③ 04 ② 05 ② 06 ⑤ 07 ② 08 ② 09 ③ 10 ④
11 ⑤ 12 ②

PART Ⅲ · 문장 삽입 [Day 16~Day 20]

Day 16　문장 삽입 01

01 ④ 02 ③ 03 ③ 04 ② 05 ④ 06 ⑤ 07 ② 08 ③ 09 ② 10 ⑤
11 ⑤ 12 ④

Day 17　문장 삽입 02

01 ⑤ 02 ③ 03 ② 04 ③ 05 ③ 06 ④ 07 ② 08 ④ 09 ③ 10 ①
11 ⑤ 12 ③

Day 18　문장 삽입 03

01 ③ 02 ④ 03 ④ 04 ③ 05 ④ 06 ④ 07 ⑤ 08 ② 09 ④ 10 ④
11 ⑤ 12 ③

Day 19　문장 삽입 04

01 ④ 02 ⑤ 03 ③ 04 ③ 05 ⑤ 06 ③ 07 ⑤ 08 ④ 09 ② 10 ②
11 ⑤ 12 ④

Day 20　문장 삽입 05

01 ④ 02 ④ 03 ⑤ 04 ⑤ 05 ③ 06 ④ 07 ⑤ 08 ⑤ 09 ④ 10 ⑤
11 ⑤ 12 ④

20일 완성 영어독해
빈칸 순서 삽입 기본

해설편

Contents

PART I 빈칸 추론

PART II 글의 순서

PART III 문장 삽입

수록된 정답률은 실제와 차이가 있을 수 있습니다. 문제 난도를 파악하는데 참고용으로 활용하시기 바랍니다.

DAY 01 | 빈칸 추론 01

01 ①	02 ②	03 ②	04 ①	05 ③
06 ④	07 ①	08 ③	09 ①	10 ②
11 ⑤	12 ③			

---

01   비행 방향에 따른 시차 피로 차이   정답률 55% | 정답 ①

다음 빈칸에 들어갈 말로 가장 적절한 것을 고르시오.

✔ direction - 방향
② purpose - 목적
③ season - 계절
④ length - 길이
⑤ cost - 비용

People differ / in how quickly they can reset their biological clocks / to overcome jet lag, / and the speed of recovery depends on the direction of travel.
사람마다 서로 다르며, / 체내 시계를 얼마나 빨리 재설정할 수 있는지에 있어서 / 시차로 인한 피로감을 극복하기 위해서 / 그 회복 속도는 이동의 방향에 달려 있다.

Generally, / it's easier / to fly westward and lengthen your day / than it is to fly eastward and shorten it.
일반적으로, / 더 쉽다. / 서쪽으로 비행해 여러분의 하루를 연장하는 것이 / 동쪽으로 비행하여 하루를 단축하는 것보다

This east-west difference in jet lag / is sizable enough / to have an impact on the performance of sports teams.
시차로 인한 피로감에 있어 이러한 동서의 차이는 / 충분히 크다. / 스포츠 팀의 경기력에 영향을 미칠 만큼

Studies have found / that teams flying westward perform significantly better / than teams flying eastward / in professional baseball and college football.
연구는 밝혔다. / 서쪽으로 비행하는 팀이 상당히 더 잘한다고 / 동쪽으로 비행하는 팀보다 / 프로 야구와 대학 미식 축구에서

A more recent study of more than 46,000 Major League Baseball games / found additional evidence / that eastward travel is tougher than westward travel.
46,000건 이상의 메이저 리그 야구 경기에 관한 더 최근의 연구에서는 / 추가적인 증거를 발견했다. / 동쪽으로 이동하는 것이 서쪽으로 이동하는 것보다 더 힘들다는

시차로 인한 피로감을 극복하기 위해서 체내 시계를 얼마나 빨리 재설정할 수 있는지는 사람마다 서로 다르며, 그 회복 속도는 이동의 방향에 달려 있다. 일반적으로 동쪽으로 비행하여 하루를 단축하는 것보다 서쪽으로 비행해 하루를 연장하는 것이 더 쉽다. 시차로 인한 피로감에서 이러한 동서의 차이는 스포츠 팀의 경기력에 영향을 미칠 만큼 충분히 크다. 연구에 따르면 서쪽으로 비행하는 팀이 동쪽으로 비행하는 팀보다 프로 야구와 대학 미식 축구에서 상당히 더 잘한다. 46,000건 이상의 메이저 리그 야구 경기에 관한 더 최근의 연구에서는 동쪽으로 이동하는 것이 서쪽으로 이동하는 것보다 더 힘들다는 추가적인 증거를 발견했다.

Why? 왜 정답일까?

빈칸 뒤에서 동쪽으로 이동해 하루를 줄이게 되는 경우보다 서쪽으로 이동해 하루를 연장하게 되는 경우 시차 회복이 더 쉽다고 한다(Generally, it's easier to fly westward and lengthen your day than it is to fly eastward and shorten it.). 즉, 이동의 '방향'이 중요하다는 글이므로, 빈칸에 들어갈 말로 가장 적절한 것은 ① '방향'이다.

- differ in ~에 관해 다르다
- biological clock 체내 시계
- jet lag 시차로 인한 피로감
- depend on ~에 좌우되다
- lengthen ⓥ 연장하다
- shorten ⓥ 단축하다
- have an impact on ~에 영향을 주다
- significantly ⓐⓓ 상당히, 현저히
- tough ⓐ 어려운, 힘든
- reset ⓥ 재설정하다
- overcome ⓥ 극복하다
- recovery ⓝ 회복
- westward ⓐⓓ 서쪽으로
- eastward ⓐⓓ 동쪽으로
- sizable ⓐ 꽤 큰, 상당한
- performance ⓝ 경기력, 수행, 성과
- additional ⓐ 추가적인

구문 풀이

5행 This east-west difference in jet lag is sizable enough to have
「형/부 + enough + to부정사 : ~할 만큼 충분히 …한」
an impact on the performance of sports teams.

---

02   동기 부여의 효과   정답률 62% | 정답 ②

다음 빈칸에 들어갈 말로 가장 적절한 것을 고르시오.

① risk - 위험
✔ effort - 노력
③ memory - 기억
④ fortune - 행운
⑤ experience - 경험

One outcome of motivation is behavior / that takes considerable effort.
동기 부여의 한 가지 결과는 행동이다. / 상당한 노력을 필요로 하는

For example, if you are motivated to buy a good car, / you will research vehicles online, / look at ads, / visit dealerships, and so on.
예를 들어, 만약 좋은 차를 사고자 하는 동기가 있다면, / 당신은 온라인으로 차들을 검색하고, / 광고를 자세히 보며, / 자동차 대리점들을 방문하는 일 등을 할 것이다.

Likewise, if you are motivated to lose weight, / you will buy low-fat foods, / eat smaller portions, / and exercise.
마찬가지로, 살을 빼려는 동기가 있다면, / 당신은 저지방 식품을 사고, / 더 적게 먹으며, / 운동을 할 것이다.

Motivation not only drives the final behaviors / that bring a goal closer / but also creates willingness / to expend time and energy on preparatory behaviors.
동기 부여는 최종적인 행동을 이끌 뿐만 아니라, / 목표를 더 가까이 가져 오는 / 의지를 만들기도 한다. / 준비 행동에 시간과 에너지를 쓸

Thus, someone motivated to buy a new smartphone / may earn extra money for it, / drive through a storm to reach the store, / and then wait in line to buy it.
따라서 새 스마트폰을 사고자 하는 동기가 있는 사람은 / 그것을 위해 추가적인 돈을 벌고, / 가게에 가기 위해 폭풍 속을 운전하며, / 그것을 사려고 줄을 서서 기다릴지도 모른다.

동기 부여의 한 가지 결과는 상당한 노력을 필요로 하는 행동이다. 예를 들어, 만약 좋은 차를 사고자 하는 동기가 있다면, 당신은 온라인으로 차들을 검색하고, 광고를 자세히 보며, 자동차 대리점들을 방문하는 일 등을 할 것이다. 마찬가지로, 살을 빼려는 동기가 있다면, 당신은 저지방 식품을 사고, 더 적게 먹으며, 운동을 할 것이다. 동기 부여는 목표를 더 가까이 가져 오는 최종적인 행동을 이끌 뿐만 아니라, 준비 행동에 시간과 에너지를 쓸 의지를 만들기도 한다. 따라서 새 스마트폰을 사고자 하는 동기가 있는 사람은 그것을 위해 추가적인 돈을 벌고, 가게에 가기 위해 폭풍 속을 운전하며, 그것을 사려고 줄을 서서 기다릴지도 모른다.

Why? 왜 정답일까?

'Motivation not only drives the final behaviors that bring a goal closer but also creates willingness to expend time and energy on preparatory behaviors.'에서 동기 부여는 목표가 가까워지게 만들 행동을 이끌어낼 뿐 아니라 준비 행동에 시간과 에너지를 들일 의지를 만들어내기도 한다고 이야기하는데, 이는 결국 목표를 위해 '노력'을 기울이도록 유도한다는 말이므로, 빈칸에 들어갈 말로 가장 적절한 것은 ② '노력'이다.

- outcome ⓝ 결과
- considerable ⓐ 상당한
- lose weight 살을 빼다
- drive ⓥ 이끌다, 유도하다
- willingness ⓝ 기꺼이 ~하려는 마음, 의지
- motivation ⓝ 동기 부여, 동기
- dealership ⓝ 대리점
- portion ⓝ (음식의) 1인분
- behavior ⓝ 행동
- expend ⓥ (시간·노력·비용을) 들이다, 쓰다

구문 풀이

7행 Motivation not only drives the final behaviors [that bring a
「not only + A +
goal closer] but also creates willingness [to expend time and energy
but also + B : A뿐 아니라 B도」
on preparatory behaviors].

---

03   이동을 통한 인간의 진보와 자유 실현   정답률 45% | 정답 ②

다음 빈칸에 들어갈 말로 가장 적절한 것을 고르시오.

① secure - 안정되려는
✔ mobile - 이동하려는
③ exceptional - 특출나려는
④ competitive - 경쟁하려는
⑤ independent - 독립하려는

There is nothing more fundamental to the human spirit / than the need to be mobile.
인간의 정신에는 더 근본적인 것은 없다. / 이동하려는 욕구보다

It is the intuitive force / that sparks our imaginations / and opens pathways to life-changing opportunities.
그것은 직관적인 힘이다. / 우리의 상상력을 자극하고 / 삶을 변화시킬 기회로 가는 길을 열어주는

It is the catalyst for progress and personal freedom.
그것은 진보와 개인의 자유의 촉매이다.

Public transportation has been vital / to that progress and freedom / for more than two centuries.
대중교통은 없어서는 안 될 것이었다. / 그 진보와 자유에 / 2세기 넘게

The transportation industry / has always done more / than carry travelers from one destination to another.
운송 산업은 / 항상 더 많은 일을 해 왔다. / 한 목적지에서 다른 목적지로 이동하는 사람들을 실어나르는 것보다

It connects people, places, and possibilities.
그것은 사람, 장소 그리고 가능성을 연결해 준다.

It provides access / to what people need, / what they love, / and what they aspire to become.
그것은 접근성을 제공해 준다. / 사람들이 필요로 하는 것과 / 그들이 좋아하는 것과 / 그들이 되고자 열망하는 것에 대한

In so doing, / it grows communities, / creates jobs, / strengthens the economy, / expands social and commercial networks, / saves time and energy, / and helps millions of people achieve a better life.
그렇게 하면서 / 그것은 공동체를 성장시키고, / 일자리를 창출하고, / 경제를 강화하고, / 사회와 상업 네트워크를 확장하고, / 시간과 에너지를 절약해 주며 / 수백만 명의 사람들이 더 나은 삶을 누릴 수 있도록 돕는다.

인간의 정신에는 이동하려는 욕구보다 더 근본적인 것은 없다. 그것은 우리의 상상력을 자극하고 삶을 변화시킬 기회로 가는 길을 열어주는 직관적인 힘이다. 그것은 진보와 개인의 자유의 촉매이다. 대중교통은 2세기 넘게 그 진보와 자유에 없어서는 안 될 것이었다. 운송 산업은 항상 한 목적지에서 다른 목적지로 이동하는 사람들을 실어 나르는 것 이상의 일을 해 왔다. 그것은 사람, 장소 그리고 가능성을 연결해 준다. 그것은 사람들이 필요로 하는 것과 좋아하는 것과 되고자 열망하는 것에 대한 접근성을 제공해 준다. 그렇게 하면서 그것은 공동체를 성장시키고, 일자리를 창출하고, 경제를 강화하고, 사회와 상업 네트워크를 확장하고, 시간과 에너지를 절약해 주며 수백만 명의 사람들이 더 나은 삶을 누릴 수 있도록 돕는다.

Why? 왜 정답일까?

'Public transportation has been vital ~' 이하로 인간의 이동을 가능케 하는 수단인 대중교통이 인간의 진보와 자유에 없어서는 안 될 것이었다는 설명이 제시되고 있다. 이를 근거로 볼 때, 빈칸이 포함된 문장 또한 인간의 '이동'이 매우 근본적이고 중요하다는 의미를 나타내야 한다. 따라서 빈칸에 들어갈 말로 가장 적절한 것은 ② '이동하려는'이다.

- **fundamental** ⓐ 근본적인
- **spark** ⓥ 자극하다, 유발하다
- **public transportation** 대중교통
- **aspire** ⓥ 열망하다
- **secure** ⓐ 안정된
- **exceptional** ⓐ 특출난, 이례적인
- **intuitive** ⓐ 직관적인
- **progress** ⓝ 진보, 진전
- **vital** ⓐ 없어서는 안 되는, 필수적인
- **strengthen** ⓥ 강화하다
- **mobile** ⓐ 이동하는, 기동성 있는

구문 풀이

2행 It is the intuitive force [that sparks our imaginations and
대명사 / 선행사 / 주격 관·대 / 동사1
opens pathways to life-changing opportunities].
동사2

---

04 더 단순한 제품의 이점 　정답률 53% | 정답 ①

다음 빈칸에 들어갈 말로 가장 적절한 것을 고르시오.
✔ simpler product - 더 단순한 제품
② affordable price - 적당한 가격
③ consumer loyalty - 고객 충성도
④ customized design - 맞춤화된 디자인
⑤ eco-friendly technology - 친환경 기술

Sometimes it is the simpler product / that gives a business a competitive advantage.
때때로 더 단순한 제품이다. / 기업에게 경쟁 우위를 주는 것은

Until recently, / bicycles had to have many gears, / often 15 or 20, / for them to be considered high-end.
최근까지, / 자전거는 많은 기어가 있어야 했다. / 흔히 15개 혹은 20개의 / 최고급이라고 여겨지기 위해서는

But fixed-gear bikes with minimal features / have become more popular, / as those who buy them / are happy to pay more for much less.
그러나 최소한의 기능을 가지고 있는 고정식 기어 자전거들은 / 점점 더 인기를 얻게 되었다. / 이를 사는 사람들이 / 훨씬 적은 것에 기꺼이 더 지불함에 따라

The overall profitability of these bikes / is much higher than the more complex ones / because they do a single thing really well / without the cost of added complexity.
이런 자전거들의 전반적인 수익성은 / 더 복잡한 것들보다 훨씬 더 큰데 / 그것들이 한 가지를 정말 잘하기 때문이다. / 추가되는 복잡성에 대한 비용 없이

Companies should be careful of getting into a war / over adding more features with their competitors, / as this will increase cost / and almost certainly reduce profitability / because of competitive pressure on price.
기업들은 전쟁을 하는 것을 조심해야 하는데, / 경쟁 업체와 더 많은 기능을 추가하는 것에 관한 / 이것이 비용을 증가시키고 / 수익성을 거의 확실히 감소시킬 것이기 때문이다. / 가격에 대한 경쟁적인 압박 때문에

때때로 기업에게 경쟁 우위를 주는 것은 더 단순한 제품이다. 최근까지, 자전거는 최고급이라고 여겨지기 위해서는 흔히 15개 혹은 20개의 많은 기어가 있어야 했다. 그러나 최소한의 기능을 가지고 있는 고정식 기어 자전거들은 이를 사는 사람들이 훨씬 적은 것에 기꺼이 더 지불함에 따라 점점 더 인기를 얻게 되었다. 이런 자전거들의 전반적인 수익성은 더 복잡한 것들보다 훨씬 더 큰데 그것들이 추가되는 복잡성에 대한 비용 없이 한 가지를 정말 잘하기 때문이다. 기업들은 경쟁 업체와 더 많은 기능들을 추가하는 전쟁을 하는 것을 조심해야 하는데, 이것이 가격에 대한 경쟁적인 압박 때문에 비용을 증가시키고 수익성을 거의 확실히 감소시킬 것이기 때문이다.

Why? 왜 정답일까?

글 중반 이후 단순한 제품은 생산 비용의 증가 없이 확실한 강점을 가져 전반적으로 수익성이 더 높다(The overall profitability of these bikes is much higher than the more complex ones ~)는 내용이 제시되므로, 빈칸에 들어갈 말로 가장 적절한 것은 ① '더 단순한 제품'이다.

- **competitive advantage** 경쟁 우위
- **feature** ⓝ (제품의) 기능, 특징
- **profitability** ⓝ 수익성
- **reduce** ⓥ 줄이다, 감소시키다
- **loyalty** ⓝ 충성도
- **minimal** ⓐ 최소의
- **overall** ⓐ 전반적인
- **complexity** ⓝ 복잡성
- **affordable** ⓐ (가격이) 적당한, 감당 가능한
- **customized** ⓐ 맞춤 제작된

구문 풀이

2행 Until recently, bicycles had to have many gears, (often 15 or
( ): 삽입구(many gears 부연)
20), for them to be considered high-end.
의미상 주어 　부사적 용법(목적)

---

05 일 처리에 걸리는 시간 제대로 파악하기 　정답률 54% | 정답 ③

다음 빈칸에 들어갈 말로 가장 적절한 것을 고르시오.
① what benefits you can get
여러분이 어떤 이득을 얻을 수 있는지
② how practical your tasks are
여러분의 과업이 얼마나 현실성 있는지
✔ how long things are going to take
일에 시간이 얼마나 오래 걸릴지
④ why failures are meaningful in life
실패가 왜 인생에서 의미가 있는지
⑤ why your leisure time should come first
왜 여러분의 여가 시간이 가장 우선이어야 하는지

If you want the confidence / that comes from achieving / what you set out to do each day, / then it's important / to understand how long things are going to take.
만약 여러분이 자신감을 원한다면 / 성취해 얻어지는 / 매일 여러분이 하고자 착수하는 일을 / 그러면 중요하다. / 일에 시간이 얼마나 오래 걸리는지 아는 것이

Over-optimism about what can be achieved / within a certain time frame / is a problem.
성취될 수 있는 것에 대한 지나친 낙관주의 / 어떤 특정 기간 내에 / 문제다.

So work on it. // Make a practice of estimating the amount of time needed / alongside items on your 'things to do' list, / and learn by experience / when tasks take a greater or lesser time than expected.
그러므로 그것을 개선하려고 노력하라. // 필요한 시간의 양을 추산하는 것을 습관화하고, / '해야 할 일' 목록에 있는 항목과 함께, / 경험을 통해 배우라. / 언제 과제가 예상보다 더 많은 시간 또는 더 적은 시간을 필요로 하는지

Give attention / also to fitting the task to the available time.
주의를 기울여라. / 그 이용 가능한 시간에 과제를 맞추는 것에도 또한

There are some tasks / that you can only set about / if you have a significant amount of time available.
몇몇 과제가 있다. / 여러분이 비로소 시작할 수 있는 / 여러분이 이용할 시간이 상당히 많아야만

There is no point / in trying to gear up for such a task / when you only have a short period available.
무의미하다. / 그런 과제를 위해 준비하려 애쓰는 것은 / 여러분에게 이용 가능한 시간이 얼마 없을 때

So schedule the time / you need for the longer tasks / and put the short tasks into the spare moments in between.
그러므로 시간을 계획하라, / 여러분이 시간이 더 오래 걸리는 과제에 필요로 하는 / 그리고 그 사이 남는 시간에 시간이 짧게 걸리는 과제를 배치하라.

만약 매일 하고자 착수하는 일을 성취해 얻어지는 자신감을 원한다면 일에 시간이 얼마나 오래 걸릴지 아는 것이 중요하다. 어떤 특정 기간 내에 성취될 수 있는 것에 대한 지나친 낙관주의는 문제다. 그러므로 그것을 개선하려고 노력하라. '해야 할 일' 목록에 있는 항목과 함께, 필요한 시간의 양을 추산하는 것을 습관화하고, 언제 과제에 예상보다 더 많고 또 더 적은 시간이 걸리는지 경험을 통해 배우라. 그 이용 가능한 시간에 과제를 맞추는 것에도 또한 주의를 기울이라. 이용할 시간이 상당히 많아야만 시작할 수 있는 몇몇 과제가 있다. 여러분에게 이용 가능한 시간이 얼마 없을 때 그런 과제를 위해 준비하려 애쓰는 것은 무의미하다. 그러므로 시간이 더 오래 걸리는 과제에 필요한 시간을 계획하고, 그 사이 남는 시간에 시간이 짧게 걸리는 과제를 배치하라.

Why? 왜 정답일까?

과업을 끝내는 데 걸리는 시간을 정확히 추산하고 계획할 줄 알아야 한다(Make a practice of estimating the amount of time needed ~)는 내용의 글이므로, 빈칸에 들어갈 말로 가장 적절한 것은 ③ '일에 시간이 얼마나 오래 걸릴지'이다.

- confidence ⓝ 자신감
- time frame (어떤 일에 쓸 수 있는) 시간(대)
- make a practice of ~을 습관으로 하다
- learn by experience 경험을 통해 배우다
- set about ~을 시작하다
- there is no point in ~하는 것은 의미가 없다
- gear up 준비를 갖추다, 대비하다
- set out 착수하다
- work on ~에 공을 들이다
- estimate ⓥ 추산하다
- fit ⓥ ~에 맞추다
- practical ⓐ 현실성 있는, 타당한

구문 풀이

11행 There is no point in trying to gear up for such a task when
「there is no point in + 동명사 : ~해봐야 의미가 없다」
you only have a short period available.

---

06 긍정성의 가치
정답률 77% | 정답 ④

다음 빈칸에 들어갈 말로 가장 적절한 것을 고르시오.

① focus on a specific goal – 구체적인 목표에 집중할
② get along well with others – 다른 이들과 잘 지낼
③ are the best at what we do – 우리가 하는 것에 최고일
✓④ are happier and more positive – 더 행복하고 더 긍정적일
⑤ feel more inspired and creative – 좀 더 영감을 느끼고 창의성을 느낄

We become more successful / when we are happier and more positive.
우리는 더 성공적이게 된다. / 우리가 더 행복하고 더 긍정적일 때

For example, / doctors put in a positive mood / before making a diagnosis / show almost three times more intelligence and creativity / than doctors in a neutral state, / and they make accurate diagnoses 19 percent faster.
예를 들어, / 긍정적인 기분이 된 의사는 / 진단을 내리기 전 / 거의 세 배 더 높은 사고력과 창의력을 보이고, / 중립적인 상태의 의사보다 / 정확한 진단을 19퍼센트 더 빠르게 내린다.

Salespeople who are optimistic / sell more than those who are pessimistic / by 56 percent.
낙관적인 판매원이 / 비관적인 판매원보다 더 많이 판매한다. / 56퍼센트만큼

Students who are made to feel happy / before taking math achievement tests / perform much better than their neutral peers.
기분이 좋아진 학생들은 / 수학 성취 평가를 보기 전 / 중립적인 또래들보다 훨씬 더 잘한다.

It turns out / that our brains are literally programmed / to perform at their best / not when they are negative or even neutral, / but when they are positive.
~함이 드러난다. / 우리의 두뇌는 말 그대로 프로그램되어 있음이 / 최상의 상태에서 기능하도록 / 그것이 부정적이거나 심지어 중립적일 때가 아니라 / 그것이 긍정적일 때

우리는 더 행복하고 더 긍정적일 때 더 성공적이게 된다. 예를 들어, 진단을 내리기 전 긍정적인 기분이 된 의사는 중립적인 상태의 의사보다 거의 세 배 더 높은 사고력과 창의력을 보이고, 정확한 진단을 19퍼센트 더 빠르게 내린다. 낙관적인 판매원이 비관적인 판매원보다 56퍼센트 더 많이 판매한다. 수학 성취 평가를 보기 전 기분이 좋아진 학생들은 중립적인 (기분의) 또래들보다 훨씬 더 잘한다. 우리의 두뇌는 부정적이거나 심지어 중립적일 때가 아니라 긍정적일 때 최상의 상태에서 기능하도록 말 그대로 프로그램화되어 있음이 드러난다.

Why? 왜 정답일까?

빈칸 뒤의 예시에서 긍정적인 의사가 더 높은 사고력과 창의력을 보이고 낙관적인 판매원이 비관적인 판매원보다 더 많이 판매하며 기분이 좋은 학생들이 훨씬 더 잘한다고 설명하고, 마지막 문장에서 주제문을 다시 정리해서 언급하고 있다(It turns out that

our brains ~ perform at their best ~ when they are positive.). 따라서, 빈칸에 들어갈 말로 가장 적절한 것은 ④ '더 행복하고 더 긍정적일'이다.

- diagnosis ⓝ 진단
- neutral ⓐ 중립적인
- pessimistic ⓐ 비관적인
- intelligence ⓝ 사고력
- optimistic ⓐ 낙천적인
- literally ⓐⓓ 말 그대로

구문 풀이

2행 For example, doctors [put in a positive mood before making a diagnosis] show almost three times more intelligence and creativity / than doctors in a neutral state, / and they make accurate diagnoses 19 percent faster.
주어 / 과거분사 / 전치사+동명사 / 동사

---

07 아이들을 이야기 창작에 참여시키기
정답률 43% | 정답 ①

다음 빈칸에 들어갈 말로 가장 적절한 것을 고르시오. [3점]

✓① help you complete a story before you tell it
여러분이 이야기를 들려주기 전에 그것을 완성하는 것을 도와 달라고
② choose some books they are interested in
자신이 관심 있는 책을 골라 보라고
③ read as many book reviews as possible
가능한 한 많은 서평을 읽어 보라고
④ listen to a story and write a summary
이야기를 듣고 요약해서 써 보라고
⑤ draw a picture about their experience
자신의 경험에 대한 그림을 그려 보라고

A lovely technique / for helping children take the first steps / towards creating their own, unique story, / is to ask them / to help you complete a story / before you tell it.
멋진 기법은 / 아이들로 하여금 첫 걸음을 내딛게 하는 데 도움이 되는 / 자신만의 독특한 이야기를 창작하도록 / 그들에게 요청하는 것이다. / 그것을 완성하는 것을 도와 달라고 / 여러분이 이야기를 들려주기 전에

One story / I have done this with frequently / is a tale / I call Benno and the Beasts.
이야기는 / 내가 흔히 이 기법을 사용해 본 / 이야기이다. / 내가 Benno and the Beasts라고 부르는

It is based on a story / called St. Benno and the Frog, / found in an old book by Helen Waddell.
그것은 이야기를 기반으로 한다. / St. Benno and the Frog이라는 / Helen Waddell이 쓴 오래된 책에 들어 있는

In the original, / the saint meets a frog in a marsh / and tells it to be quiet / in case it disturbs his prayers.
원작에서는 / 그 성자가 늪에 사는 개구리 한 마리를 만나서 / 개구리에게 조용히 하라고 말한다. / 자신의 기도를 방해할 수 있으니

Later, / he regrets this, / in case God was enjoying / listening to the sound of the frog.
나중에 / 그는 이렇게 말한 것을 후회한다. / 신이 즐기고 있었을 수도 있었으니 / 그 개구리의 소리를 듣는 것을

I invite children / to think of / different animals for the saint to meet / and different places for him to meet them.
나는 아이들로 하여금 권한다. / 생각해 보라고 / 그 성자가 만날 여러 다른 동물과 / 그가 그 동물들을 만날 여러 다른 장소를

I then tell them the story / including their own ideas.
그러고 나서 나는 그들에게 그 이야기를 들려준다. / 그들 자신의 생각을 포함하고 있는

It is a most effective way / of involving children in the art of creating stories / and they love hearing their ideas used.
그것은 매우 효과적인 방법이고, / 아이들을 이야기를 창작하는 기술에 참여시키는 / 그들은 자신의 생각이 사용된 것을 듣는 것을 아주 좋아한다.

아이들이 자신만의 독특한 이야기를 창작하도록 첫 걸음을 내딛게 하는 데 도움이 되는 멋진 기법은 그들에게 여러분이 이야기를 들려주기 전에 그것을 완성하는 것을 도와 달라고 요청하는 것이다. 내가 자주 이 기법을 사용해 본 이야기는 내가 Benno and the Beasts라는 이야기이다. 그것은 Helen Waddell이 쓴 오래된 책에 들어 있는 St. Benno and the Frog이라는 이야기를 바탕으로 한다. 원작에서는 그 성자가 늪에 사는 개구리 한 마리를 만나서 자신의 기도를 방해할 수 있으니 개구리에게 조용히 하라고 말한다. 나중에 그는 신이 그 개구리의 소리를 듣는 것을 즐기고 있었을까봐 이를 후회한다. 나는 아이들로 하여금 그 성자가 만날 여러 다른 동물과 그가 그 동물들을 만날 여러 다른 장소를 생각해 보라고 권한다. 그러고 나서 나는 그들에게 그들 자신의 생각을 포함하고 있는 이야기를 들려준다. 그것은 이야기를 창작하는 기술에 아이들을 참여시키는 매우 효과적인 방법이고, 그들은 자신의 생각이 사용된 이야기를 듣는 것을 아주 좋아한다.

Why? 왜 정답일까?

첫 문장에 빈칸이 나오므로 주제문을 완성하는 문제이다. 빈칸 뒤에 전개되는 예시의 핵

심 부분인 'I invite children to think of different animals for the saint to meet and different places for him to meet them. I then tell them the story including their own ideas.'에서, 필자는 아이들에게 이야기를 마저 들려주기 전에 아이들로 하여금 먼저 내용을 직접 상상해보게 하고 후에 아이들의 생각을 넣은 이야기를 다시 들려준다고 하였고, 이어서 결론인 마지막 문장에서는 이 기법이 아이들을 이야기 창작에 참여시키는 데 도움이 된다고 하였다. 즉 아이들이 자신만의 이야기를 만들어보도록 유도하기 위해서는 이야기 중간에 아이들이 직접 상상력을 발휘해볼 기회를 주어야 한다는 것이 글의 요지이므로, 빈칸에 들어갈 말로 가장 적절한 것은 ① '여러분이 이야기를 들려주기 전에 그것을 완성하는 것을 도와 달라고'이다.

- unique ⓐ 독특한
- tale ⓝ 이야기
- original ⓐ 원작의, 원본의
- disturb ⓥ 방해하다, 건드리다
- regret ⓥ 후회하다, 유감으로 생각하다
- effective ⓐ 효과적인
- frequently ⓐⓓ 자주, 흔히, 빈번하게
- be based on ~에 기반을 두다
- saint ⓝ 성자 같은 사람
- prayer ⓝ 기도
- invite ⓥ 권하다, 유도하다, 청하다
- involve ⓥ 참여시키다, 연관시키다

구문 풀이

1행 A lovely technique [for helping children take the first steps
주어 / 준사역동사 / 원형부정사
towards creating their own, unique story], is to ask them to help you
전치사 동명사 / 동사 주격 보어 「ask + 목적어 + to부정사 : ~에게 …하도록 요청하다」
complete a story before you tell it.

---

08 구매를 이끄는 희소성
정답률 59% | 정답 ③

다음 빈칸에 들어갈 말로 가장 적절한 것을 고르시오. [3점]

① Promoting products through social media
소셜 미디어를 통해 제품을 홍보하는 것
② Reducing the risk of producing poor quality items
질이 좋지 않은 제품을 생산할 위험을 낮추는 것
✔③ Restricting the number of items customers can buy
고객이 구입할 수 있는 품목의 개수를 제한하는 것
④ Offering several options that customers find attractive
고객들이 매력적이라고 생각하는 몇 가지 선택 사항을 제시하는 것
⑤ Emphasizing the safety of products with research data
연구 데이터로 제품의 안전성을 강조하는 것

Restricting the number of items customers can buy / boosts sales.
고객이 구입할 수 있는 품목의 개수를 제한하는 것은 / 매출을 증가시킨다.
Brian Wansink, / Professor of Marketing at Cornell University, / investigated the effectiveness of this tactic in 1998.
Brian Wansink는 / Cornell University의 마케팅 교수인 / 1998년에 이 전략의 효과를 조사했다.
He persuaded three supermarkets in Sioux City, Iowa, / to offer Campbell's soup at a small discount: / 79 cents rather than 89 cents.
그는 Iowa 주 Sioux City에 있는 세 개의 슈퍼마켓을 설득했다. / Campbell의 수프를 약간 할인하여 제공하도록 / 즉 89센트가 아닌 79센트로
The discounted soup was sold in one of three conditions: / a control, / where there was no limit on the volume of purchases, / or two tests, / where customers were limited to either four or twelve cans.
할인된 수프는 세 가지 조건 중 하나의 조건으로 판매되었다. / 즉 하나의 통제 집단, / 구매량에 제한이 없는 / 또는 두 개의 실험 집단 / 고객이 4개 아니면 12개의 캔으로 제한되는
In the unlimited condition / shoppers bought 3.3 cans on average, / whereas in the scarce condition, / when there was a limit, / they bought 5.3 on average.
무제한 조건에서 / 구매자들은 평균 3.3캔을 구입했고, / 반면 희소 조건에서는 / 제한이 있던 / 그들은 평균 5.3캔을 구입했다.
This suggests / scarcity encourages sales.
이것은 보여준다. / 희소성이 판매를 장려한다는 것을
The findings are particularly strong / because the test took place / in a supermarket with genuine shoppers.
그 결과는 특히 타당하다. / 이 실험이 진행되었기 때문에 / 진짜 구매자들이 있는 슈퍼마켓에서
It didn't rely on claimed data, / nor was it held in a laboratory / where consumers might behave differently.
그것은 주장된 데이터에 의존하지 않았고, / 그것은 실험실에서 이루어진 것도 아니었다. / 소비자들이 다르게 행동할지도 모르는

고객이 구입할 수 있는 품목의 개수를 제한하는 것은 매출을 증가시킨다. Cornell University의 마케팅 교수인 Brian Wansink는 1998년에 이 전략의 효과를 조사했다. 그는 Iowa 주 Sioux City에 있는 세 개의 슈퍼마켓이 Campbell의 수프를 약간 할인하여 89센트가 아닌 79센트로 제공하도록 설득했다. 할인된 수프는 세 가지 조건 중 하나의 조건으로 판매되었다. 구매량에 제한이 없는 하나의 통제 집단, 또는 고객이 4개 아니면 12개의 캔으로 제한되는 두 개의 실험 집단이 그것이었다. 무제한 조건에서 구매자들은 평균 3.3캔을 구입했던 반면, 제한이 있던 희소 조건에서는 평균 5.3캔을 구입했다. 이것은 희소성

이 판매를 장려한다는 것을 보여준다. 이 실험은 진짜 구매자들이 있는 슈퍼마켓에서 진행되었기 때문에 그 결과는 특히 타당하다. 그것은 주장된 데이터에 의존하지 않았고, 소비자들이 다르게 행동할지도 모르는 실험실에서 이루어진 것도 아니었다.

Why? 왜 정답일까?

빈칸 뒤로 소개된 연구에서, 구매 개수에 제한이 있었던 실험군이 제품을 가장 많이 구입했다고 설명하며, 희소성이 판매를 장려한다는 결론을 정리하고 있다(~ scarcity encourages sales.). 따라서 빈칸에 들어갈 말로 가장 적절한 것은 ③ '고객이 구입할 수 있는 품목의 개수를 제한하는 것'이다.

- investigate ⓥ 조사하다
- tactic ⓝ 전략
- rather than ~ 대신에
- control ⓝ 통제 집단
- scarcity ⓝ 희소성
- rely on ~에 의존하다
- behave ⓥ 행동하다
- attractive ⓐ 매력적인
- effectiveness ⓝ 유효성, 효과 있음
- persuade ⓥ 설득하다
- condition ⓝ 조건
- unlimited ⓐ 제한되지 않은, 무제한의
- genuine ⓐ 진짜의
- laboratory ⓝ 실험실
- differently ⓐⓓ 다르게
- emphasize ⓥ 강조하다

구문 풀이

15행 It didn't rely on claimed data, nor was it held in a laboratory
부정문 「부정어 + be + 주어 + p.p. : 도치 구문(~도 않다)」
where consumers might behave differently.

---

09 화석으로 얻는 정보의 불완전성
정답률 49% | 정답 ①

다음 빈칸에 들어갈 말로 가장 적절한 것을 고르시오. [3점]

✔① tell the entire story – 완전한 이야기를 전달하지
② require further study – 더 깊은 연구를 필요로 하지
③ teach us a wrong lesson – 우리에게 잘못된 교훈을 가르쳐주지
④ change their original traits – 그것의 원래 특성을 바꾸지
⑤ make room for imagination – 상상의 여지를 남기지

As much as we can learn by examining fossils, / it is important to remember / that they seldom tell the entire story.
우리가 화석을 조사하며 많은 것을 배울 수 있기는 하지만, / 기억하는 것이 중요하다. / 그것들이 좀처럼 완전한 이야기를 전달하지 않는다는 것을
Things only fossilize under certain sets of conditions.
생물들은 일련의 특정 조건 하에서만 화석화된다.
Modern insect communities are highly diverse in tropical forests, / but the recent fossil record captures little of that diversity.
현대 곤충 군집들은 열대 우림 지역에서 매우 다양하지만, / 최근 화석 기록은 그 다양성을 거의 담아내지 않는다.
Many creatures are consumed entirely or decompose rapidly / when they die, / so there may be no fossil record at all / for important groups.
많은 생명체는 완전히 먹히거나 급속히 부패해서 / 그들이 죽을 때 / 화석 기록이 전혀 존재하지 않을 수도 있다. / 중요한 집단에 관한
It's a bit similar to a family photo album.
그것은 가족 사진첩과도 약간 비슷하다.
Maybe when you were born / your parents took lots of pictures, / but over the years / they took photographs occasionally, / and sometimes they got busy / and forgot to take pictures at all.
아마도 여러분이 태어났을 때 / 여러분의 부모님은 사진을 많이 찍었겠지만, / 시간이 흐르면서 / 그들은 가끔 사진을 찍었고, / 때로는 그들은 바빠져서 / 사진 찍는 것을 아예 잊어버렸을지도 모른다.
Very few of us have a complete photo record of our life.
우리 중 인생의 완전한 사진 기록을 가진 사람은 거의 없다.
Fossils are just like that.
화석이 바로 그것과 같다.
Sometimes you get very clear pictures of the past, / while at other times there are big gaps, / and you need to notice what they are.
때때로 여러분은 과거에 대한 매우 명확한 그림을 가지지만 / 다른 때에는 큰 공백들이 존재하고, / 여러분은 그것들이 무엇인지를 인지할 필요가 있다.

우리가 화석을 조사하며 많은 것을 배울 수 있기는 하지만, 그것들이 좀처럼 완전한 이야기를 전달하지 않는다는 것을 기억하는 것이 중요하다. 생물들은 일련의 특정 조건 하에서만 화석화된다. 현대 곤충 군집들은 열대 우림 지역에서 매우 다양하지만, 최근 화석 기록은 그 다양성을 거의 담아내지 않는다. 많은 생명체는 죽을 때 완전히 먹히거나 급속히 부패해서 중요한 집단에 관한 화석 기록이 전혀 존재하지 않을 수도 있다. 그것은 가족 사진첩과도 약간 비슷하다. 아마도 여러분이 태어났을 때 여러분의 부모님은 사진을 많이 찍었겠지만, 시간이 흐르면서 그들은 가끔 사진을 찍었고, 때로는 바빠져서 사진 찍는 것을 아예 잊어버렸을지도 모른다. 우리 중 인생의 완전한 사진 기록을 가진

사람은 거의 없다. 화석이 바로 그것과 같다. 때때로 여러분은 과거에 대한 매우 명확한 그림을 가지지만 다른 때에는 큰 공백들이 존재하고, 여러분은 그것들이 무엇인지를 인지할 필요가 있다.

Why? 왜 정답일까?

마지막 두 문장인 'Fossils are just like that. Sometimes you get very clear pictures of the past, while at other times there are big gaps, ~'에서 화석을 통해 과거에 대해 명확한 그림을 얻는 경우도 있지만 다른 경우 공백도 있을 수 있다고 언급하는 것으로 보아, 빈칸이 포함된 문장은 화석을 통해 '온전한 이야기를 얻지' 못할 수도 있다는 의미가 되어야 한다. 따라서 빈칸에 들어갈 말로 가장 적절한 것은 ① '완전한 이야기를 전달하지'이다.

- **examine** ⓥ 조사하다
- **fossilize** ⓥ 화석화하다
- **consume** ⓥ 먹다, 소비하다
- **entirely** ⓐⓓ 완전히
- **occasionally** ⓐⓓ 가끔, 때때로
- **trait** ⓝ 특성
- **make room for** ~의 여지를 남기다, ~을 위해 (자리를) 양보하다

구문 풀이

1행 ┌→ 〈문장 맨 앞의〉 as + 원급 + as : ~하기는 하지만, ~한 만큼이나
As much as we can learn by examining fossils, it is important
　　　　　　　　　　　　　~함으로써　　　　　가주어
to remember that they seldom tell the entire story.
진주어　접속사(~것)　준부정어(좀처럼 ~않다)

★★★ 1등급 대비 고난도 3점 문제

10 우리의 판단력을 앗아가는 로봇　　정답률 46% | 정답 ②

다음 빈칸에 들어갈 말로 가장 적절한 것을 고르시오. [3점]

① reliability – 신뢰성　　　✓ judgment – 판단력
③ endurance – 인내　　　④ sociability – 사교성
⑤ cooperation – 협력

We worry that the robots are taking our jobs, / but just as common a problem is / that the robots are taking our judgment.
우리는 로봇이 우리의 직업을 빼앗고 있다고 걱정하지만, / 그만큼 흔한 문제는 ~이다. / 로봇이 우리의 판단력을 빼앗고 있다는 것

In the large warehouses / so common behind the scenes of today's economy, / human 'pickers' hurry around / grabbing products off shelves / and moving them to where they can be packed and dispatched.
거대한 창고에서, / 오늘날의 경제 배후에 있는 아주 흔한 / 인간 '집게'는 서둘러서 / 선반에서 상품을 집어내고, / 그것들이 포장되고 발송될 수 있는 곳으로 이동시킨다.

In their ears are headpieces: / the voice of 'Jennifer', / a piece of software, / tells them where to go and what to do, / controlling the smallest details of their movements.
그들의 귀에는 헤드폰이 있는데, / 'Jennifer'의 목소리가 / 한 소프트웨어 프로그램인 / 이들에게 어디로 가고 무엇을 할지 말해준다. / 이들 움직임의 가장 작은 세부 사항들을 조종하면서

Jennifer breaks down instructions into tiny chunks, / to minimise error and maximise productivity / — for example, / rather than picking eighteen copies of a book off a shelf, / the human worker would be politely instructed to pick five.
Jennifer는 지시 사항을 아주 작은 덩어리로 쪼개는데, / 실수를 줄이고 생산성을 최대화하기 위해 / 가령 / 선반에서 책 18권을 집어내기보다는, / 인간 작업자는 5권을 집어내라고 정중하게 지시받을 것이다.

Then another five. // Then yet another five. // Then another three.
그다음 또 5권. // 그다음 또 5권. // 그다음 또 3권.

Working in such conditions / reduces people to machines / made of flesh.
그러한 조건에서 일하는 것은 / 사람을 기계로 격하시킨다. / 살로 만들어진

Rather than asking us to think or adapt, / the Jennifer unit takes over the thought process / and treats workers as an inexpensive source / of some visual processing and a pair of opposable thumbs.
우리에게 생각하거나 적응하라고 요구하기보다는, / Jennifer라는 장치는 사고 과정을 지배하고, / 작업자들을 값싼 자원으로 다룬다. / 약간의 시각적 처리 과정과 마주 볼 수 있는 엄지 한 쌍이 있는

우리는 로봇이 우리의 직업을 빼앗고 있다고 걱정하지만, 그만큼 흔한 문제는 로봇이 우리의 판단력을 빼앗고 있다는 것이다. 오늘날의 경제 배후에 있는 아주 흔한 거대한 창고에서, 인간 '집게'는 서둘러서 선반에서 상품을 집어내고, 그것들이 포장되고 발송될 수 있는 곳으로 이동시킨다. 그들의 귀에는 헤드폰이 있는데, 한 소프트웨어 프로그램인 'Jennifer'의 목소리가 이들 움직임의 가장 작은 세부 사항들을 조종하면서, 이들에게 어디로 가고 무엇을 할지 말해준다. Jennifer는 실수를 줄이고 생산성을 최대화하기 위해 지시 사항을 아주 작은 덩어리로 쪼개는데, 가령 인간 작업자는 선반에서 책 18권을 집어내기보다는, 5권을 집어내라고 정중하게 지시받을 것이다. 그다음 또 5권. 그다음 또 5권. 그다음 또 3권을 집으라는 지시를 받을 것이다. 그러한 조건에서 일하는

것은 사람을 살로 만들어진 기계로 격하시킨다. Jennifer라는 장치는 우리에게 생각하거나 적응하라고 요구하기보다는, 사고 과정을 지배하고, 작업자들을 약간의 시각적 처리 과정과 마주 볼 수 있는 엄지 한 쌍이 있는 값싼 자원으로 다룬다.

Why? 왜 정답일까?

창고 노동자들이 기계에게 아주 작은 행동까지 지시받으며 일한다(~ tells them where to go and what to do, controlling the smallest details of their movements.)는 예시를 통해, 인간이 기계로 격하되고 사고 과정을 박탈당하는 상황에 놓여 있음을 설명하는 글이다. 따라서 빈칸에 들어갈 말로 가장 적절한 것은 로봇에 지배당한 사고 과정(thought process)을 다르게 표현한 말인 ② '판단력'이다.

- **warehouse** ⓝ 창고
- **grab** ⓥ 집어내다
- **headpiece** ⓝ 헤드폰, 지성, 판단력
- **break down** 쪼개다
- **flesh** ⓝ (사람, 동물의) 살
- **take over** 지배하다, 장악하다
- **opposable** ⓐ 마주볼 수 있는
- **endurance** ⓝ 인내

구문 풀이

15행 Working in such conditions reduces people to machines
　　　동명사구 주어　　　　　　　　　　　동사(단수)
made of flesh.
과거분사구

★★ 문제 해결 꿀~팁 ★★

▶ 많이 틀린 이유는?
로봇 때문에 인간의 신뢰성이나 사교성이 떨어진다는 내용은 아니므로 ①이나 ④는 답으로 적절하지 않다.

▶ 문제 해결 방법은?
예시의 결론을 정리하는 'Rather than asking us to think or adapt, the Jennifer unit takes over the thought process ~'가 핵심이다. 이 thought process와 통하는 단어를 골라야 한다.

★★★ 1등급 대비 고난도 3점 문제

11 오늘날 마케팅 산업의 과제　　정답률 45% | 정답 ⑤

다음 빈칸에 들어갈 말로 가장 적절한 것을 고르시오. [3점]

① guide people to be wise consumers
사람들이 현명한 소비자가 되도록 인도하는가
② reduce the cost of television advertising
텔레비전 광고의 비용을 줄이는가
③ keep a close eye on the quality of products
제품의 질에 대해 주시하는가
④ make it possible to deliver any goods any time
언제든 어떤 재화를 배달하는 것을 가능하게 하는가
✓ win the battle for broadcast advertising exposure
방송 광고 노출 전쟁에서 승리하는가

One real concern in the marketing industry today is / how to win the battle for broadcast advertising exposure / in the age of the remote control and mobile devices.
오늘날 마케팅 산업에서 한 가지 실질적인 관심사는 / 어떻게 방송 광고 노출 전쟁에서 승리하는가이다. / 리모컨과 휴대 장비의 시대에

With the growing popularity of digital video recorders, / consumers can mute, / fast-forward, / and skip over commercials entirely.
디지털 영상 녹화기의 인기가 증가하면서 / 소비자들은 광고의 소리를 줄이거나, / 광고를 빨리 감거나, / 아예 건너뛰어 버릴 수 있다.

Some advertisers are trying to adapt to these technologies, / by planting hidden coupons / in frames of their television commercials.
일부 광고주들은 이러한 기술에 적응하려고 노력 중이다. / 숨겨진 쿠폰을 심어두어 / 텔레비전 광고 프레임 속에

Others are desperately trying / to make their advertisements more interesting and entertaining / to discourage viewers from skipping their ads; / still others are simply giving up on television advertising altogether.
다른 광고주들은 절박하게 노력 중이고, / 광고를 더 흥미롭고 재미있게 만들기 위해 / 시청자들이 광고를 건너뛰지 못하게 하기 위해 / 또 다른 광고주들은 완전히 텔레비전 광고를 포기해 버린다.

Some industry experts predict / that cable providers and advertisers / will eventually be forced to provide incentives / in order to encourage consumers to watch their messages.
몇몇 산업 전문가들은 예측한다. / 케이블 공급자와 광고주들이 / 결국에는 어쩔 수 없이 인센티브를 제공하게 될 것이라고 / 그들의 메시지를 소비자들이 보게 하기 위해서

These incentives may come / in the form of coupons, / or a reduction in the cable bill / for each advertisement watched.
이러한 인센티브는 나타날 것이다. / 쿠폰의 형태로 / 또는 케이블 요금의 절감 형태로 / 시청되는 매 광고마다

오늘날 마케팅 산업에서 한 가지 실질적인 관심사는 리모컨과 휴대 장비의 시대에 어떻게 **방송 광고 노출 전쟁에서 승리하는가**이다. 디지털 영상 녹화기의 인기가 증가하면서 소비자들은 광고의 소리를 줄이거나, 광고를 빨리 감거나, 아예 건너뛰어 버릴 수 있다. 일부 광고주들은 텔레비전 광고 프레임 속에 숨겨진 쿠폰을 심어두어 이러한 기술에 적응하려고 노력 중이다. 다른 광고주들은 시청자들이 광고를 건너뛰지 못하게 하기 위해 광고를 더 흥미롭고 재미있게 만들기 위해 절박하게 노력 중이고, 또 다른 광고주들은 완전히 텔레비전 광고를 포기해 버린다. 몇몇 산업 전문가들은 케이블 공급자와 광고주들이 결국에는 그들의 메시지를 소비자들이 보게 하기 위해서 어쩔 수 없이 인센티브를 제공하게 될 것이라 예측한다. 이러한 인센티브는 쿠폰, 또는 광고를 한 번 볼 때마다 케이블 요금을 절감해주는 형태로 나타날 것이다.

Why? 왜 정답일까?

빈칸 뒤의 문장에 따르면 오늘날 디지털 영상 녹화기의 인기가 증가하면서 사람들은 원하는 대로 광고의 소리를 줄이거나, 광고를 빨리 감거나, 아예 건너뛸 수 있게 되었는데, 이 때문에 광고주들은 쿠폰을 심어두거나 광고를 더 재미있게 만드는 등의 노력을 기울여 소비자들로 하여금 광고를 보게 하려고 한다(Some advertisers are trying to adapt to these technologies, by planting hidden coupons in frames of their television commercials. Others are desperately trying to make their advertisements more interesting and entertaining to discourage viewers from skipping their ads;). 따라서 빈칸에 들어갈 말로 가장 적절한 것은 이러한 노력의 목적을 적절히 요약한 ⑤ '방송 광고 노출 전쟁에서 승리하는가'이다.

- concern ⓝ 관심사, 걱정
- remote ⓐ 원격의
- mute ⓥ ~의 소리를 줄이다
- commercial ⓝ 광고 ⓐ 상업의
- advertiser ⓝ 광고주
- plant ⓥ 놓다, 두다
- entertaining ⓐ 재미있는, 즐거움을 주는
- altogether ⓐⓓ 아예, 완전히
- eventually ⓐⓓ 결국
- in the form of ~의 형태로
- industry ⓝ 산업
- popularity ⓝ 인기
- skip over ~을 건너뛰다, ~을 묵과하다
- entirely ⓐⓓ 아예, 전부, 전적으로
- adapt to ~에 적응하다
- desperately ⓐⓓ 절박하게, 간절하게
- give up on ~을 포기하다
- predict ⓥ 예측하다
- incentive ⓝ 장려책

구문 풀이

> 12행 Some industry experts predict that cable providers and
> 　　　　　　　　　　　　　　　　　　　　　(접속사)
> advertisers will eventually be forced to provide incentives /
> 　　　　　　　　(어쩔 수 없이 ~하다)
> in order to encourage consumers to watch their messages.
> (부사적 용법(~하기 위해))　　　(to encourage의 목적격 보어(to부정사))

★★ 문제 해결 꿀~팁 ★★

▶ 많이 틀린 이유는?
본문 중 그대로 빈칸에 대응될 말이 없고, 예시를 읽고 요약해야 한다는 점에서 어려운 문제였다. 최다 오답인 ②는 '광고주의 비용 절감'을 언급하는데, 이는 지문 마지막 부분에서 광고주들이 소비자들로 하여금 광고를 계속 보게 하기 위해서 '케이블 비용을 깎아준다는' 내용을 잘못 이해한 것이다. 이는 광고주 입장에서의 비용 절감이라기보다는 소비자 입장에서 누리는 혜택이라고 볼 수 있다.

▶ 문제 해결 방법은?
흔히 예시는 주제문을 잘 이해한 경우라면 건너뛰어도 무방할 때가 많지만 이 문제는 유일한 주제문이 빈칸이고 나머지가 예시이기 때문에 예문들을 잘 읽어야 한다. 본격적으로 광고주에 대한 세부 내용을 말하는 'Some advisers ~. Others ~' 부분을 읽어 적절히 요약한 말을 빈칸에 넣도록 한다.

★★★ 1등급 대비 고난도 3점 문제

12 우리가 과거를 바라보는 방식　　　정답률 45% | 정답 ③

다음 빈칸에 들어갈 말로 가장 적절한 것을 고르시오. [3점]

① focus primarily on the future
　주로 미래에 집중한다
② remember every detail of our lives
　삶의 모든 세부사항을 기억한다
✓③ maintain a biased perception of the past
　과거에 대한 편향된 인식을 유지한다
④ have trouble overcoming our emotional problems
　정서적 문제를 극복하는 데 어려움을 겪는다
⑤ share negative emotional experiences with others
　부정적인 정서적 경험을 타인과 공유한다

Having extremely vivid memories of past emotional experiences / and only weak memories of past everyday events / means / we <u>maintain a biased perception of the past</u>.
과거의 정서적 경험을 지극히 생생하게 기억하는 것은 / 그리고 과거의 일상적인 사건을 희미하게 / 의미한다 / 우리가 과거에 대한 편향된 인식을 유지한다는 것을

We tend to view the past / as a concentrated time line of emotionally exciting events.
우리는 과거를 바라보는 경향이 있다. / 정서적으로 흥미진진한 사건들의 집약된 시간 선상으로

We remember the arousing aspects of an episode / and forget the boring bits.
우리는 일화의 자극적인 측면을 기억하고 / 지루한 부분은 잊어버린다.

A summer vacation will be recalled for its highlights, / and the less exciting parts will fade away with time, / eventually to be forgotten forever.
여름휴가는 가장 흥미로운 부분이 기억에 남고, / 덜 흥미로운 부분은 시간이 지나면서 희미해지다가 / 결국 영원히 잊힐 것이다.

As a result, / when we estimate / how our next summer vacation will make us feel, / we overestimate the positive.
그 결과, / 우리가 추정할 때 / 우리의 다음 여름휴가가 어떤 느낌이 들게 하는지를 / 우리는 긍정적인 면을 과대평가한다.

It seems / as though an imprecise picture of the past is one reason / for our inaccurate forecasts of the future.
~처럼 보인다. / 과거에 대한 부정확한 기억이 하나의 이유인 것처럼 / 미래에 대해 부정확한 예측의

과거의 정서적 경험을 지극히 생생하게 기억하는 것과 과거의 일상적인 사건을 희미하게 기억하는 것은 우리가 과거에 대한 편향된 인식을 유지한다는 것을 의미한다. 우리는 과거를 정서적으로 흥미진진한 사건들의 집약된 시간 선상으로 바라보는 경향이 있다. 일화의 자극적인 측면을 기억하고 지루한 부분은 잊어버린다. 여름휴가는 가장 흥미로운 부분이 기억에 남고, 덜 흥미로운 부분은 시간이 지나면서 희미해지다가 결국 영원히 잊힐 것이다. 그 결과, 우리의 다음 여름휴가가 어떤 느낌이 들게 하는지를 추정할 때, 우리는 긍정적인 면을 과대평가한다. 과거에 대한 부정확한 기억이 미래에 대해 부정확한 예측을 낳는 하나의 이유인 것처럼 보인다.

Why? 왜 정답일까?

'We tend to view the past as a concentrated time line of emotionally exciting events.'에서 우리는 과거를 '정서적으로 흥미진진한' 사건의 연속으로서 기억하는 경향이 있다고 말한 데 이어, 'As a result, when we estimate how our next summer vacation will make us feel, we overestimate the positive.'에서는 그리하여 우리가 과거에 갔던 여름휴가 등을 떠올릴 때 좋은 측면을 과장해서 기억하게 된다는 내용을 제시한다. 따라서 빈칸에 들어갈 말로 가장 적절한 것은 ③ '과거에 대한 편향된 인식을 유지한다'이다.

- extremely ⓐⓓ 지극히, 극도로, 매우
- emotional ⓐ 정서적인
- arousing ⓐ 자극적인, 흥분시키는
- estimate ⓥ 추정하다, 평가하다
- imprecise ⓐ 부정확한
- vivid ⓐ 생생한
- concentrated ⓐ 집약된, 집중적인, 농축된
- fade away 희미해지다, (빛이) 바래다
- overestimate ⓥ 과대평가하다
- inaccurate ⓐ 부정확한

구문 풀이

> 6행 A summer vacation will be recalled for its highlights, / and
> 　　　(주어1)　　　　　　　(동사1(미래시제 수동태))
> the less exciting parts will fade away with time, eventually
> 　　　　(주어2)　　　　　(동사2(희미해지다))　(시간이 지나며)
> to be forgotten forever.
> (부사적 용법(결과))

★★ 문제 해결 꿀~팁 ★★

▶ 많이 틀린 이유는?
과거 인식에 관한 추상적인 내용을 다루어 읽기 어려운 지문이었다. 오답으로 ①이 많이 나왔는데 마지막 문장에 '미래를 예측하는' 것과 관련된 말이 나와 혼란이 야기된 것으로 보인다.

▶ 문제 해결 방법은?
빈칸 뒤에 예문 및 부연 문장이 나오므로 '결과'를 말한 'As a result' 뒤를 읽어 답을 추론하도록 한다. 과거 경험에 대해 긍정적인 면을 크게 평가하여 기억한다는 것은 결국 과거를 '부정확하게' 인식한다는 것을 나타낸다.

DAY 02 　　빈칸 추론 02

01 ③	02 ①	03 ④	04 ①	05 ⑤
06 ②	07 ⑤	08 ⑤	09 ①	10 ①
11 ②	12 ②			

01 　 상처 받은 상대방에게 시간을 주며 기다려주기 　 정답률 56% | 정답 ③

다음 빈칸에 들어갈 말로 가장 적절한 것을 고르시오.

① curiosity – 호기심　　　② independence – 자립
✓ patience – 인내　　　　④ creativity – 창의성
⑤ honesty – 정직

Remember that patience is always of the essence.
인내가 항상 가장 중요하다는 것을 기억해라.

If an apology is not accepted, / thank the individual for hearing you out / and leave the door open / for if and when he wishes to reconcile.
사과가 받아들여지지 않으면, / 그 사람이 여러분의 말을 끝까지 들어줬다는 것에 감사하고, / 문(가능성)을 열어 두어라. / 그 사람이 화해하고 싶을 경우와 시기를 위해

Be conscious of the fact / that just because someone accepts your apology / does not mean she has fully forgiven you.
사실을 알고 있어라. / 단지 누군가가 여러분의 사과를 받아들인다고 해서 / 그 사람이 여러분을 온전히 용서했다는 뜻이 아니라는

It can take time, maybe a long time, / before the injured party can completely let go / and fully trust you again.
시간이 걸릴 수 있고, 어쩌면 오래 걸릴 수 있다. / 상처받은 당사자가 완전히 떨쳐 버리기까지 / 그리고 여러분을 온전히 다시 믿기까지

There is little you can do / to speed this process up.
여러분이 할 수 있는 것은 거의 없다. / 이 과정을 빠르게 하기 위해

If the person is truly important to you, / it is worthwhile / to give him or her the time and space needed to heal.
그 사람이 여러분에게 진정으로 중요하다면, / 가치가 있다. / 그에게 치유되는 데 필요한 시간과 공간을 주는 것이

Do not expect the person / to go right back to acting normally immediately.
그 사람에게 기대하지 마라. / 즉시 평상시처럼 행동하는 것으로 바로 돌아갈 것이라고

인내가 항상 가장 중요하다는 것을 기억해라. 사과가 받아들여지지 않으면, 그 사람이 여러분의 말을 끝까지 들어줬다는 것에 감사하고, 그 사람이 화해하고 싶을 경우와 시기를 위해 문(가능성)을 열어 두어라. 단지 누군가가 여러분의 사과를 받아들인다고 해서 그 사람이 여러분을 온전히 용서했다는 뜻이 아니라는 사실을 알고 있어라. 상처받은 당사자가 완전히 떨쳐 버리고 여러분을 온전히 다시 믿기까지 시간이 걸릴 수 있고, 어쩌면 오래 걸릴 수 있다. 이 과정을 빠르게 하기 위해 여러분이 할 수 있는 것은 거의 없다. 그 사람이 여러분에게 진정으로 중요하다면, 그 사람에게 치유되는 데 필요한 시간과 공간을 주는 것이 가치가 있다. 그 사람이 즉시 평상시의 행동으로 바로 돌아갈 것이라고 기대하지 마라.

Why? 왜 정답일까?

마지막 세 문장에서 용서의 과정을 빠르게 할 방법은 없고, 상대방에게 시간을 줄 필요가 있으므로 상대방이 곧바로 평상시대로 돌아갈 것이라는 기대를 하지 말라(~ it is worthwhile to give him or her the time and space needed to heal. Do not expect the person to go right back to acting normally immediately.)고 조언하고 있다. 이는 상대방을 기다려주며 인내심을 발휘하라는 내용으로 요약할 수 있으므로, 빈칸에 들어갈 말로 가장 적절한 것은 ③ '인내'이다.

● be of the essence 가장 중요하다
● accept ⓥ 받아들이다
● conscious ⓐ 알고 있는, 의식하는
● injured ⓐ 상처받은, 부상 당한
● speed up 빨라지게 하다
● immediately ⓐⓓ 즉시, 곧
● independence ⓝ 자립, 독립
● apology ⓝ 사과
● hear ~ out ~의 말을 끝까지 들어주다
● take time 시간이 걸리다
● let go (걱정·근심 등을) 떨쳐 버리다
● normally ⓐⓓ 정상적으로
● curiosity ⓝ 호기심
● patience ⓝ 인내

구문 풀이

4행 Be conscious of the fact that just because someone accepts
　　　　　　　　　　　　　　　　동격 접속사 ↲　주어(부사절이 명사절처럼 쓰임)
your apology does not mean she has fully forgiven you.
　　　　　　　　　동사　　　　　　목적어

02 　 오늘날의 뉴스 순환 　 정답률 63% | 정답 ①

다음 빈칸에 들어갈 말로 가장 적절한 것을 고르시오.

✓ Mobility – 기동성　　　　② Sensitivity – 민감성
③ Creativity – 창의성　　　④ Accuracy – 정확성
⑤ Responsibility – 책임감

Mobility provides a change / to the environment for journalists.
기동성은 변화를 제공한다. / 저널리스트들의 환경에 대한

Newspaper stories, television reports, and even early online reporting / (prior to communication technology / such as tablets and smartphones) / required one central place / to which a reporter would submit his or her news story / for printing, broadcast, or posting.
신문 기사, 텔레비전 보도, 그리고 심지어 초기 온라인 보도는 / (통신 기술 이전의 / 태블릿과 스마트폰과 같은) / 하나의 중심적인 장소를 필요로 했다. / 기자가 자신의 뉴스 기사를 제출할 / 인쇄, 방송, 또는 게시를 위해

Now, though, / a reporter can shoot video, / record audio, / and type directly on their smartphones or tablets / and post a news story instantly.
그러나 이제 / 기자는 비디오를 촬영하고, / 오디오를 녹음하며, / 자신의 스마트폰이나 태블릿에 직접 타이핑해서 / 즉시 뉴스 기사를 게시할 수 있다.

Journalists do not need to report to a central location / where they all contact sources, type, or edit video.
저널리스트들은 중심 장소에 보고할 필요가 없다. / 모두가 정보의 원천과 접촉하거나, 타이핑하거나, 또는 비디오를 편집하는

A story can be instantaneously written, / shot, / and made available to the entire world.
기사는 즉석에서 작성되고, / 촬영되고, / 전 세계에서 보는 것이 가능해질 수 있다.

The news cycle, and thus the job of the journalist, / never takes a break.
뉴스의 순환과 결국 저널리스트의 일은 / 결코 멈추지 않는다.

Thus the "24-hour" news cycle / that emerged from the rise of cable TV / is now a thing of the past.
그러므로 '24시간'의 뉴스 순환은 / 케이블 TV의 성장으로 나타난 / 이제 과거의 것이다.

The news "cycle" is really a constant.
뉴스 '순환'은 정말로 끊임없이 계속되는 것이다.

기동성은 저널리스트들의 환경에 대한 변화를 제공한다. 신문 기사, 텔레비전 보도, 그리고 심지어 (태블릿과 스마트폰과 같은 통신 기술 이전의) 초기 온라인 보도는 기자가 인쇄, 방송, 또는 게시를 위해 자신의 뉴스 기사를 제출할 하나의 중심적인 장소를 필요로 했다. 그러나 이제 기자는 비디오를 촬영하고, 오디오를 녹음하며, 자신의 스마트폰이나 태블릿에 직접 타이핑해서 즉시 뉴스 기사를 게시할 수 있다. 저널리스트들은 모두가 정보의 원천과 접촉하거나, 타이핑하거나, 또는 비디오를 편집하는 중심 장소에 보고할 필요가 없다. 기사는 즉석에서 작성되고, 촬영되고, 전 세계에서 보는 것이 가능해질 수 있다. 뉴스의 순환과 결국 저널리스트의 일은 결코 멈추지 않는다. 그러므로 케이블 TV의 성장으로 나타난 '24시간'의 뉴스 순환은 이제 과거의 것이다. 뉴스 '순환'은 정말로 끊임없이 계속되는 것이다.

Why? 왜 정답일까?

글 중간의 'Now, though, ~' 앞뒤로 글의 흐름이 반전되는 글이다. 예전에는 기자들이 기사를 제출할 중심적인 장소가 필요했지만 이제는 스마트폰이나 태블릿을 활용하여 언제 어디서든 기사 작성이 이루어질 수 있기 때문에 멈추지 않는 뉴스의 순환이 가능해졌다(The news cycle, and thus the job of the journalist, never takes a break.)는 내용이 언급되고 있다. 따라서 빈칸에 들어갈 말로 가장 적절한 것은 장소에 구애받지 않고 이어질 수 있는 기자 업무의 특성을 설명하기에 적합한 ① '기동성'이다.

● prior to ~의 이전에
● central ⓐ 중심적인
● printing ⓝ 인쇄
● posting ⓝ 게시
● directly ⓐⓓ 곧장
● instantly ⓐⓓ 즉시
● source ⓝ 원천, 근원
● instantaneously ⓐⓓ 즉석에서
● emerge ⓥ 나타나다
● cable TV 유선방송
● require ⓥ 필요로 하다
● submit ⓥ 제출하다
● broadcast ⓝ 방송
● shoot ⓥ 촬영하다
● post ⓥ 게시하다
● location ⓝ 장소, 위치
● edit ⓥ 편집하다
● take a break 멈추다
● rise ⓝ 성장, 상승, 증가
● constant ⓝ 일정불변의 것

구문 풀이

2행 Newspaper stories, television reports, and even early online
　　　　　　　　　　주어(A, B, and C)
reporting (prior to communication technology such as tablets and
　　　　　　　　　~ 이전에
smartphones) required one central place [to which a reporter would
　　　　　　　　　동사　　목적어(선행사)　= where
submit his or her news story for printing, broadcast, or posting].

---

03 일반화된 호혜성에 기반한 동물의 협동
정답률 69% | 정답 ④

다음 빈칸에 들어갈 말로 가장 적절한 것을 고르시오.

① friction – 마찰
② diversity – 다양성
③ hierarchy – 계층
✔ cooperation – 협동
⑤ independence – 독립성

If you follow science news, / you will have noticed / that <u>cooperation</u> among animals has become a hot topic / in the mass media.
만약 여러분이 과학 뉴스에 관심을 가진다면, / 여러분은 알아차리게 될 것이다. / 동물들 사이의 협동이 뜨거운 화제가 되어 왔다는 것을 / 대중 매체에서

For example, / in late 2007 / the science media widely reported a study / by Claudia Rutte and Michael Taborsky / suggesting that rats display / what they call "generalized reciprocity."
예를 들어, / 2007년 후반에 / 과학 매체는 연구를 널리 보도했다. / Claudia Rutte와 Michael Taborsky가 / 쥐들이 보여 준다고 시사하는 / 그들에 의한 '일반화된 호혜성'이라고 부르는 것을

They each provided help / to an unfamiliar and unrelated individual, / based on their own previous experience / of having been helped by an unfamiliar rat.
그들 각각이 도움을 제공했다. / 낯설고 무관한 개체에게 / 자신의 이전 경험에 근거하여 / 낯선 쥐에 의해 도움을 받았던

Rutte and Taborsky trained rats / in a cooperative task of pulling a stick / to obtain food for a partner.
Rutte와 Taborsky는 쥐들에게 훈련시켰다. / 막대기를 잡아당기는 협동적 과업을 / 파트너를 위한 음식을 얻기 위해

Rats / who had been helped previously by an unknown partner / were more likely to help others.
쥐는 / 이전에 모르는 파트너에게 도움을 받은 적이 있는 / 다른 쥐들을 돕는 경향이 더 높았다.

Before this research was conducted, / generalized reciprocity was thought / to be unique to humans.
이 연구가 수행되기 전에는, / 일반화된 호혜성은 여겨졌다. / 인간들에게 고유한 것으로

만약 여러분이 과학 뉴스에 관심을 가진다면, 여러분은 동물들 사이의 협동이 대중 매체에서 뜨거운 화제가 되어 왔다는 것을 알아차리게 될 것이다. 예를 들어, 2007년 후반에 과학 매체는 Claudia Rutte와 Michael Taborsky가 '일반화된 호혜성'이라고 부르는 것을 쥐들이 보여 준다고 시사하는, 그들에 의한 연구를 널리 보도했다. 쥐들 각각이 낯선 쥐에 의해 도움을 받았던 자신의 이전 경험에 근거하여 낯설고 무관한 개체에게 도움을 제공했다. Rutte와 Taborsky는 쥐들에게 파트너를 위한 음식을 얻기 위해 막대기를 잡아당기는 협동적 과업을 훈련시켰다. 이전에 모르는 파트너에게 도움을 받은 적이 있는 쥐는 다른 쥐들을 돕는 경향이 더 컸다. 이 연구가 수행되기 전에는, 일반화된 호혜성은 인간들에게 고유한 것으로 여겨졌다.

Why? 왜 정답일까?

인간뿐 아니라 동물 또한 일반화된 호혜성(generalized reciprocity)에 근거하여 협력한다는 내용을 설명한 글로, For example 이하에서 쥐들이 낯설고 무관한 개체끼리도 서로 돕는다는 결론을 밝혀낸 실험을 소개하고 있다. 따라서 빈칸에 들어갈 말로 가장 적절한 것은 ④ '협동'이다.

● **generalize** ⓥ 일반화하다
● **unfamiliar** ⓐ 낯선, 익숙하지 않은
● **cooperative** ⓐ 협동적인
● **previously** ⓐⓓ 이전에, 사전에, 미리
● **reciprocity** ⓝ 호혜성, 이익 교환
● **unrelated** ⓐ 무관한, 관계없는, 친족이 아닌
● **obtain** ⓥ 얻다
● **conduct** ⓥ 수행하다

구문 풀이

6행 They each provided help to an unfamiliar and unrelated individual, based on their own previous experience of having been [분사구문(~에 기반을 두어)] [전치사] helped by an unfamiliar rat.
완료 수동 동명사 : 주절보다 먼저 일어남

04 삶의 향상을 부르는 긍정적인 상상
정답률 55% | 정답 ①

다음 빈칸에 들어갈 말로 가장 적절한 것을 고르시오.

✔ mental pictures – 머릿속 그림
② physical competence – 신체적 능력
③ cooperative attitude – 협동적 태도
④ learning environment – 학습 환경
⑤ academic achievements – 학업적 성취

All improvement in your life / begins with an improvement / in your <u>mental pictures</u>.
당신 삶에서의 모든 향상은 / 향상으로 시작된다. / 당신의 머릿속 그림에서의

If you talk to unhappy people / and ask them what they think about most of the time, / you will find / that almost without fail, they think / about their

당신 삶에서의 모든 향상은 / 향상으로 시작된다. / 당신의 머릿속 그림에서의

problems, their bills, their negative relationships, / and all the difficulties in their lives.
만약 당신이 불행한 사람들과 이야기하면서 / 그들에게 대부분의 시간에 무슨 생각을 하는지 물어본다면, / 당신은 발견할 것이다. / 거의 틀림없이 그들이 생각한다는 것을 / 자신의 문제, 고지서, 부정적인 관계, / 그리고 그들의 삶에서의 모든 어려움에 대해

But when you talk to successful, happy people, / you find / that they think and talk most of the time / about the things that they want to be, do, and have.
그러나 당신이 성공적이고 행복한 사람들과 이야기할 때는, / 당신은 알게 된다. / 그들이 대부분의 시간 동안 생각하고 이야기한다는 것을 / 그들이 되고 싶고, 하고 싶고, 가지고 싶은 것들에 대해

They think and talk about the specific action steps / they can take to get them.
그들은 구체적인 행동 단계에 대해 생각하고 이야기한다. / 그것들을 얻기 위해서 취할 수 있는

They dwell continually on vivid, exciting pictures / of what their goals will look like / when they are realized, / and what their dreams will look like / when they come true.
그들은 생생하고 흥미로운 그림들에 대해 끊임없이 깊이 생각한다. / 그들의 목표가 어떻게 보일지, / 그것들이 실현되었을 때 / 그리고 그들의 꿈이 어떻게 보일지에 대한 / 그것들이 실현되었을 때

당신 삶에서의 모든 향상은 당신의 머릿속 그림에서의 향상으로 시작된다. 만약 당신이 불행한 사람들과 이야기하면서 그들에게 대부분의 시간에 무슨 생각을 하는지 물어본다면, 거의 틀림없이 그들이 자신의 문제, 고지서, 부정적인 관계, 그리고 그들의 삶에서의 모든 어려움에 대해 생각한다는 것을 발견할 것이다. 그러나 당신이 성공적이고 행복한 사람들과 이야기할 때는, 그들이 대부분의 시간 동안 그들이 되고 싶고, 하고 싶고, 가지고 싶은 것들에 대해 생각하고 이야기한다는 것을 알게 된다. 그들은 그것들을 얻기 위해서 취할 수 있는 구체적인 행동 단계에 대해 생각하고 이야기한다. 그들은 그들의 목표가 실현되었을 때 어떻게 보일지, 그리고 그들의 꿈이 실현되었을 때 어떻게 보일지에 대한 생생하고 흥미로운 그림들에 대해 끊임없이 깊이 생각한다.

Why? 왜 정답일까?

주제문인 첫 문장의 빈칸을 완성하는 문제이다. 글 중간의 But 앞에서 불행한 사람들은 어려움에 대해 주로 생각한다는 내용이 언급된 후, 뒤에서는 성공하고 행복한 사람들의 경우 자신이 되고 싶은 모습, 하고 싶거나 가지고 싶은 것들에 대해 생각한다는 내용이 이어진다. 특히 마지막 문장에서 성공한 이들이 꿈이 실현되었을 때에 관한 생생하고 흥미로운 그림을 머릿속에 그린다(~ exciting pictures of what their goals will look like when they are realized, and what their dreams will look like when they come true.)는 표현이 나온다. 따라서 빈칸에 들어갈 말로 가장 적절한 것은 ① '머릿속 그림'이다.

● **improvement** ⓝ 향상
● **without fail** 틀림없이, 반드시
● **specific** ⓐ 구체적인
● **continually** ⓐⓓ 끊임없이
● **come true** 실현되다
● **achievement** ⓝ 성취
● **unhappy** ⓐ 행복하지 않은
● **bill** ⓝ 고지서, 청구서
● **dwell on** ~에 대해 깊이 생각하다
● **vivid** ⓐ 생생한
● **competence** ⓝ 능력, 역량

구문 풀이

11행 They dwell continually on vivid, exciting pictures of what
[동사구] [목적어] [의문사1]
their goals will look like when they are realized, and what their
dreams will look like when they come true.
[의문사2]

05 언어 발달의 이유
정답률 63% | 정답 ⑤

다음 빈칸에 들어길 말로 가장 직절한 깃을 고르시오.

① used body language to communicate – 의사소통하기 위해 몸짓 언어를 사용했다
② instinctively knew who to depend on – 누구에게 의지할지 본능적으로 알았다
③ often changed rules for their own needs – 자신의 필요를 위해 종종 규칙을 바꾸었다
④ lived independently for their own survival – 생존을 위해 독립적으로 살았다
✔ developed language for economic reasons – 경제적인 이유로 언어를 발달시켰다

Many evolutionary biologists argue / that humans <u>developed language for economic reasons</u>.
많은 진화 생물학자들은 주장한다. / 인간이 경제적인 이유로 언어를 발달시켰다고

We needed to trade, / and we needed to establish trust / in order to trade.
우리는 거래해야 했고, / 우리는 신뢰를 확립해야 했다. / 거래하기 위해서는

Language is very handy / when you are trying to conduct business with someone.
언어는 매우 편리하다. / 당신이 누군가와 거래할 때

Two early humans could not only agree / to trade three wooden bowls for six bunches of bananas / but establish rules as well.
초창기의 두 인간은 동의할 수 있었을 뿐만 아니라 / 3개의 나무 그릇을 6다발의 바나나와 거래하기로 / 규칙을 정할 수도 있었다.

What wood was used for the bowls?
그 그릇들을 만드는 데 무슨 나무를 사용했나?
Where did you get the bananas?
어디서 그 바나나를 얻게 되었나?
That business deal would have been nearly impossible / using only gestures and confusing noises, / and carrying it out / according to terms agreed upon / creates a bond of trust.
그 상업 거래는 거의 불가능했을 것이고, / 단지 제스처와 혼란스런 소음만을 사용해서는 / 그것을 실행하는 것이 / 합의된 조항에 따라서 / 신뢰라는 결속을 만든다.
Language allows us to be specific, / and this is where conversation plays a key role.
언어는 우리가 구체적이도록 해주고, / 여기서 대화가 중요한 역할을 한다.

───

많은 진화 생물학자들은 인간이 경제적인 이유로 언어를 발달시켰다고 주장한다. 우리는 거래해야 했고, 거래하기 위해서는 신뢰를 확립해야 했다. 언어는 당신이 누군가와 거래할 때 매우 편리하다. 초창기의 두 인간은 3개의 나무 그릇을 6다발의 바나나와 거래하기로 동의할 수 있었을 뿐만 아니라 규칙을 정할 수도 있었다. 그 그릇들을 만드는 데 무슨 나무를 사용했나? 어디서 그 바나나를 얻게 되었나? 단지 제스처와 혼란스런 소음만을 사용해서는 그 상업 거래는 거의 불가능했을 것이고, 합의된 조항에 따라서 그것을 실행하는 것이 신뢰라는 결속을 만든다. 언어는 우리가 구체적이도록 해주고, 여기서 대화가 중요한 역할을 한다.

Why? 왜 정답일까?

예시를 마무리하는 마지막 두 문장에서 초기 인간은 제스처와 소음만을 사용해서 상업 거래를 수행할 수 없었을 것이므로 언어를 발달시켜 대화를 수행했을 것이라고 한다. 따라서 빈칸에 들어갈 말로 가장 적절한 것은 ⑤ '경제적인 이유로 언어를 발달시켰다'이다.

- evolutionary ⓐ 진화의
- conduct ⓥ 수행하다
- carry out 수행하다
- bond ⓝ 유대 (관계)
- instinctively [ad] 본능적으로
- establish ⓥ 확립하다, 구축하다
- as well (문미에서) 또한
- terms ⓝ (합의, 계약 등의) 조건
- specific ⓐ 구체적인

구문 풀이

9행 That business deal would have been nearly impossible using
　　　주어1　　　　　　　동사1(과거에 대한 추측)　　　　　　　분사구문(~하면서)
only gestures and confusing noises, and carrying it out according
　　　　　　　　　　　　　　　　　　　　　　주어2(동명사구)
to terms agreed upon creates a bond of trust.
　　　과거분사구　　　동사2(단수)

06 학습자의 관심사에 맞는 읽기 자료 제공 　정답률 56% | 정답 ②

다음 빈칸에 들어갈 말로 가장 적절한 것을 고르시오.

① examples from official textbooks
　공식 교과서에서 뽑은 예시
✓ relevant texts they will be interested in
　학생들이 관심 있어 할 적절한 글
③ enough chances to exchange information
　정보를 교환할 충분한 기회
④ different genres for different age groups
　각 연령마다 다른 장르
⑤ early reading experience to develop logic skills
　논리력을 키우기 위한 조기 읽기 경험

A key to engagement and achievement / is providing students with relevant texts / they will be interested in.
참여와 성취의 핵심은 / 적절한 글을 학생들에게 제공하는 것이다. / 그들이 관심 있어 할
My scholarly work and my teaching / have been deeply influenced / by the work of Rosalie Fink.
내 학문적인 연구와 수업은 / 깊이 영향을 받아왔다. / Rosalie Fink의 연구에 의해
She interviewed twelve adults / who were highly successful in their work, / including a physicist, a biochemist, and a company CEO.
그녀는 열두 명의 성인들과 면담했다. / 자기 직업에서 매우 성공한 / 물리학자, 생화학자, 회사의 최고 경영자를 포함해
All of them had dyslexia / and had had significant problems with reading / throughout their school years.
그들 모두가 난독증이 있었고, / 읽기에 상당한 문제를 겪었다. / 학령기 내내
While she expected to find / that they had avoided reading / and discovered ways / to bypass it or compensate with other strategies for learning, / she found the opposite.
그녀는 알게 되리라고 예상했다 / 그들이 학습할 때 읽기를 피하고, / 방법을 찾아냈다는 것을 / 그것을 우회하거나 다른 전략들로 학습을 보완할 / 하지만 그녀는 정반대를 알아냈다.
"To my surprise, / I found / that these dyslexics were enthusiastic readers... / they rarely avoided reading. / On the contrary, / they sought out books."

"놀랍게도, / 나는 알아냈다. / 난독증이 있는 이런 사람들이 열정적인 독자인 것을… / 이들이 좀처럼 읽기를 피하지 않는 것을 / 거꾸로, 그들은 책을 찾았다."
The pattern Fink discovered / was / that all of her subjects had been passionate / in some personal interest.
Fink가 발견한 패턴은 / ~이었다. / 그녀의 실험 대상자 모두가 열정적이었다는 것 / 어떤 개인적인 관심사에
The areas of interest included / religion, math, business, science, history, and biography.
관심 분야는 포함했다. / 종교, 수학, 상업, 과학, 역사 그리고 생물학을
What mattered was / that they read voraciously to find out more.
중요한 것은 ~이었다. / 그들이 더 많이 알아내기 위해 탐욕스럽게 읽었다는 것

참여와 성취의 핵심은 학생들이 관심 있어 할 적절한 글을 그들에게 제공하는 것이다. 내 학문적인 연구와 수업은 Rosalie Fink의 연구에 깊이 영향을 받아왔다. 그녀는 물리학자, 생화학자, 회사의 최고 경영자를 포함해 자기 직업에서 매우 성공한 열두 명의 성인들과 면담했다. 그들 모두가 난독증이 있었고, 학령기 내내 읽기에 상당한 문제를 겪었다. 그녀는 그들이 학습할 때 읽기를 피하고, 그것을 우회하거나 다른 전략들로 학습을 보완할 방법을 찾아냈다는 것을 알게 되리라고 예상했으나, 정반대를 알아냈다. "놀랍게도, 나는 난독증이 있는 이런 사람들이 열정적인 독자인 것을… 이들이 좀처럼 읽기를 피하지 않는 것을 알아냈다. 거꾸로, 그들은 책을 찾았다." Fink가 발견한 패턴은 그녀의 실험 대상자 모두가 어떤 개인적인 관심사에 열정적이었다는 것이었다. 관심 분야는 종교, 수학, 상업, 과학, 역사 그리고 생물학을 포함했다. 중요한 것은 그들이 더 많이 알아내기 위해 탐욕스럽게 읽었다는 것이었다.

Why? 왜 정답일까?

마지막 두 문장에서 어린 시절 난독증을 겪었으나 성공한 사람들을 연구한 결과, 자신이 관심을 두었던 분야에 대해 열정을 갖고 있었으며(passionate in some personal interest) 더 많은 것을 알기 위해 닥치는 대로 글을 읽었다는 것을 알아냈다고 한다. 이를 통해 결국 학생을 좋은 학습자로 만들려면 '흥미를 가질 만한 글'을 제시하라는 결론을 도출할 수 있다. 따라서 빈칸에 들어갈 말로 가장 적절한 것은 ② '학생들이 관심 있어 할 적절한 글'이다.

- engagement ⓝ 참여, 몰입
- provide A with B A에게 B를 제공하다
- biochemist ⓝ 생화학자
- significant ⓐ 상당한, 심각한
- bypass ⓥ 우회하다
- opposite ⓝ 정반대
- seek out ~을 찾아내다
- personal ⓐ 개인적인
- biography ⓝ (인물의) 전기
- official ⓐ 공식적인
- achievement ⓝ 성취
- physicist ⓝ 물리학자
- dyslexia ⓝ 난독증
- discover ⓥ 찾아내다, 발견하다
- compensate for ~을 보완하다, 보상하다
- enthusiastic ⓐ 열정적인, 열성적인
- subject ⓝ 실험 대상자
- religion ⓝ 종교
- voraciously [ad] 탐욕스럽게
- relevant ⓐ 적절한

구문 풀이

9행 While she expected to find [that they had avoided reading
　　　　　　「expect + to부정사: ~하기를 기대하다」　　동사1
and discovered ways to bypass it or compensate with other strategies
　　동사2　　　　　　　　　　　　　　　　수식(형용사적 용법)
for learning], she found the opposite.

07 직접 찾아내면 더 오래 남는 지식 　정답률 52% | 정답 ⑤

다음 빈칸에 들어갈 말로 가장 적절한 것을 고르시오. [3점]

① they are taught repeatedly in class
　그들이 수업에서 반복해서 배운다면
② we fully focus on them without any distractions
　우리가 어떤 방해도 받지 않고 그들에게 완전히 집중한다면
③ equal opportunities are given to complete tasks
　과업을 완수할 기회가 똑같이 부여된다면
④ there's no right or wrong way to learn about a topic
　어떤 주제에 대해 배우는 옳은 방식도 틀린 방식도 없다면
✓ we discover them ourselves rather than being told them
　우리가 무언가에 관해서 듣기보다 스스로 발견한다면

The last two decades of research / on the science of learning / have shown conclusively / that we remember things better, and longer, / if we discover them ourselves rather than being told them.
지난 20년간의 연구는 / 학습과학에 관한 / 결론적으로 보여주었다. / 우리는 무언가를 더 잘 기억하고, 더 오래 기억한다는 것을 / 만약 우리가 그것들을 스스로 발견한다면
This is the teaching method / practiced by physics professor Eric Mazur.
이것은 실천된 교수법이다. / 물리학 교수 Eric Mazur에 의해
He doesn't lecture in his classes at Harvard.
그는 하버드 수업에서 강의를 하지 않는다.
Instead, he asks students difficult questions, / based on their homework reading, / that require them to pull together sources of information / to solve a problem.

대신에, 그는 학생들에게 어려운 질문을 던진다. / 독서 활동 과제에 기반하여 / 그들이 정보 자료를 모으도록 요구하는 / 문제를 해결하기 위해

Mazur doesn't give them the answer; / instead, he asks the students / to break off into small groups / and discuss the problem among themselves.
Mazur는 그들에게 답을 주지 않는다. / 대신에, 그는 학생들에게 요구한다. / 소그룹으로 나누어 / 그들 스스로 문제를 토론하도록

Eventually, / nearly everyone in the class gets the answer right, / and the concepts stick with them / because they had to find their own way to the answer.
결국, / 강좌의 거의 모든 사람들이 정답을 맞히고, / 이러한 개념들은 그들에게 오래 남는다 / 그들이 정답으로 가는 길을 스스로 찾았기 때문에

학습과학에 관한 지난 20년간의 연구는 만약 우리가 무언가에 관해서 듣기보다 스스로 발견한다면 우리는 그것들을 더 잘 기억하고, 더 오래 기억한다는 것을 결론적으로 보여주었다. 이것은 물리학 교수 Eric Mazur에 의해 실천되는 교수법이다. 그는 하버드 수업에서 (설명식) 강의를 하지 않는다. 대신에, 그는 독서 활동 과제에 기반하여 학생들에게 문제를 해결하기 위해 정보 자료를 모으도록 요구하는 어려운 질문을 던진다. Mazur는 그들에게 답을 주지 않는다. 대신에, 그는 학생들을 소그룹으로 나누어 그들 스스로 문제를 토론하도록 요구한다. 결국, 강좌의 거의 모든 사람들이 정답을 맞히고, 그들이 정답으로 가는 길을 스스로 찾았기 때문에 이러한 개념들은 그들에게 오래 남는다.

Why? 왜 정답일까?

마지막 두 문장에서 Eric Mazur 교수는 학생들에게 질문을 던진 후 직접 토론해 답을 도출하게 하여 머릿속에 더 오래 남을 지식을 알려준다는 내용을 제시한다. 따라서 빈칸에 들어갈 말로 가장 적절한 것은 우리가 어떤 것을 더 오래 기억하려면 직접 알아내는 것이 낫다는 의미를 완성하는 ⑤ '우리가 무언가에 관해서 듣기보다 스스로 발견한다면' 이다.

- **conclusively** [ad] 결론적으로
- **break off** ~을 분리시키다
- **stick with** ~와 함께 머물다
- **distraction** [n] 정신을 산만하게 하는 것, 주의를 흩뜨리는 것
- **complete** [v] 완수하다
- **physics** [n] 물리학
- **eventually** [ad] 결국
- **repeatedly** [ad] 반복해서

구문 풀이

6행 **Instead, he asks students difficult questions, (based on their homework reading), [that require them to pull together sources of information to solve a problem].**
4형식 동사 / 간접목적어 / 직접목적어 / ( ): 삽입구 / 주격 관·대 / [ ]: 직접목적어 수식

---

08 특징 중심으로 대상을 파악하는 인간과 동물 　정답률 44% | 정답 ⑤

다음 빈칸에 들어갈 말로 가장 적절한 것을 고르시오. [3점]
① interpreting different gestures – 다양한 몸짓을 해석하는 것
② establishing social frameworks – 사회적인 구조를 세우는 것
③ identifying the information of colors – 색깔 정보를 확인하는 것
④ separating the self from the environment – 환경에서 자신을 분리하는 것
✔ recognizing outstanding structural features – 두드러진 구조적 특징을 파악하는 것

There is good evidence / that in organic development, / perception starts with recognizing outstanding structural features.
충분한 증거가 있다. / 유기적 발달에서, / 지각은 두드러진 구조적 특징을 파악하는 것에서 시작된다

For example, / when two-year-old children and chimpanzees had learned / that, of two boxes presented to them, / the one with a triangle of a particular size and shape / always contained attractive food, / they had no difficulty applying their training / to triangles of very different appearance.
예를 들어, / 2살 어린이와 침팬지가 알았을 때, / 그들에게 주어지는 2개의 상자 중 / 특정 크기와 모양의 삼각형이 있는 상자에 / 항상 맛있어 보이는 음식이 있다는 것을 / 그들은 그들의 훈련을 적용하는 것에 어려움이 없었다. / 다른 모양의 삼각형에도

The triangles were made smaller or larger / or turned upside down.
삼각형은 더 작아지거나 커지거나 / 뒤집혔다.

A black triangle on a white background / was replaced by a white triangle on a black background, / or an outlined triangle by a solid one.
흰색 바탕의 검은 삼각형은 검은 바탕의 흰색 삼각형으로 대체되었다. / 또는 외곽선이 있는 삼각형은 단색의 것으로

These changes seemed not to interfere with recognition.
이런 변화는 인식을 저해하지 않는 것으로 보였다.

Similar results were obtained with rats.
유사한 결과가 쥐에서도 얻어졌다.

Karl Lashley, a psychologist, has asserted / that simple transpositions of this type are universal / in all animals including humans.
심리학자인 Karl Lashley는 주장했다. / 이런 유형의 단순한 치환이 보편적이라고 / 인간을 포함하여 모든 동물에게

유기적 발달에서, 지각은 두드러진 구조적 특징을 파악하는 것에서 시작된다는 충분한 증거가 있다. 예를 들어, 2살 어린이와 침팬지가 그들에게 주어지는 2개의 상자 중 특정 크기와 모양의 삼각형이 있는 상자에 항상 맛있어 보이는 음식이 있다는 것을 알았을 때, 다른 모양의 삼각형에도 그들의 훈련을 적용하는 것에 어려움이 없었다. 삼각형은 더 작아지거나 커지거나 뒤집혔다. 흰색 바탕의 검은 삼각형은 검은 바탕의 흰색 삼각형으로, 또는 외곽선이 있는 삼각형은 단색의 것으로 대체되었다. 이런 변화는 인식을 저해하지 않는 것으로 보였다. 유사한 결과가 쥐에서도 언급되었다. 심리학자인 Karl Lashley는 이런 유형의 단순한 치환이 인간을 포함하여 모든 동물에게 보편적이라고 주장했다.

Why? 왜 정답일까?

삼각형의 모양이나 색을 조금씩 달리하더라도 그 도형이 맛있는 음식과 연관되어 있다는 의미를 동물이나 사람이 인식하기에는 충분하다(**These changes seemed not to interfere with recognition.**)는 내용을 통해, 인간을 포함한 동물들은 어떤 형태를 인식할 때 두드러진 특징을 중심으로 대략적인 파악을 해 나간다는 것을 유추할 수 있다. 따라서 빈칸에 들어갈 말로 가장 적절한 것은 ⑤ '두드러진 구조적 특징을 파악하는 것'이다.

- **evidence** [n] 증거
- **perception** [n] 지각, 인식
- **particular** [a] 특정한, 특별한
- **appearance** [n] 모양, 외모
- **interfere with** ~을 저해하다, 방해하다
- **assert** [v] 주장하다
- **establish** [v] 세우다, 설립하다
- **organic** [a] 유기적인
- **present** [v] 주다, 제시하다
- **contain** [v] ~이 들어있다
- **replace** [v] 대체하다, 대신하다
- **recognition** [n] 인식, 알아봄
- **interpret** [v] 해석하다, 이해하다
- **separate** [v] 분리하다, 나누다

구문 풀이

2행 **For example, when two-year-old children and chimpanzees had learned {that, of two boxes [presented to them], the one with a triangle of a particular size and shape always contained attractive food}, / they had no difficulty applying their training to triangles of very different appearance.**
시간 접속사 / 접속사 / 과거분사 / 주어 / 동사 / { }: learned의 목적어 / ~하는 데 어려움이 없다

---

09 신선함의 환경적 대가 　정답률 48% | 정답 ①

다음 빈칸에 들어갈 말로 가장 적절한 것을 고르시오. [3점]
✔ have hidden environmental costs – 숨겨진 환경적인 대가를 지니고 있을
② worsen the global hunger problem – 세계 기아 문제를 악화시킬
③ bring about technological advances – 기술 진보를 가져올
④ improve nutrition and quality of food – 영양과 음식 품질을 개선할
⑤ diversify the diet of a local community – 지역 사회의 식단을 다양화할

The demand for freshness / can have hidden environmental costs.
신선함에 대한 요구는 / 숨겨진 환경적인 대가를 지니고 있을 수 있다.

While freshness is now being used / as a term in food marketing / as part of a return to nature, / the demand for year-round supplies of fresh produce / such as soft fruit and exotic vegetables / has led to / the widespread use of hot houses in cold climates / and increasing reliance on total quality control / — management by temperature control, use of pesticides and computer/ satellite-based logistics.
현재 신선함이 사용되고 있는 한편, / 식품 마케팅에서 하나의 용어로 / 자연으로 돌아가는 것의 일환으로 / 신선한 식품의 연중 공급에 대한 요구는 / 부드러운 과일이나 외국산 채소와 같은 / ~로 이어져 왔다. / 추운 기후에서의 광범위한 온실 사용과 / 총체적인 품질 관리에 대한 의존성의 증가로 / 즉 온도 조절에 의한 관리, 살충제 사용, 그리고 컴퓨터/위성 기반물류

The demand for freshness / has also contributed to concerns about food wastage.
신선함에 대한 요구는 / 또한 식량 낭비에 대한 우려의 원인이 되었다.

Use of 'best before', 'sell by' and 'eat by' labels / has legally allowed institutional waste.
'유통 기한', '판매 시한', '섭취 시한' 등의 라벨 사용은 / 제도적인 폐기물 생산을 법적으로 허용해 왔다.

Campaigners have exposed the scandal of over-production and waste.
운동가들은 과잉 생산이나 폐기물에 대한 추문을 폭로해 왔다.

Tristram Stuart, / one of the global band of anti-waste campaigners, / argues / that, with freshly made sandwiches, / over-ordering is standard practice across the retail sector / to avoid the appearance of empty shelf space, / leading to high volumes of waste / when supply regularly exceeds demand.
Tristram Stuart는 / 폐기물 반대 세계 연대 소속 운동가 중 한 명인 / 주장한다. / 신선하게 만들어진 샌드위치

와 함께, / 초과 주문이 소매 산업 분야 전반에서 이루어지는 일반적인 행태이며, / 판매대가 비어 보이는 것을 막기 위한 / 이것은 엄청난 양의 폐기물로 이어진다고 / 공급이 정기적으로 수요를 초과하면

신선함에 대한 요구는 숨겨진 환경적인 대가를 지니고 있을 수 있다. 자연으로 돌아가는 것의 일환으로 현재 신선함이 식품 마케팅에서 하나의 용어로 사용되고 있는 한편, 부드러운 과일이나 외국산 채소와 같은 신선한 식품의 연중 공급에 대한 요구는 추운 기후에서의 광범위한 온실 사용과 총체적인 품질 관리 — 온도 조절에 의한 관리, 살충제 사용, 그리고 컴퓨터/위성 기반 물류 — 에 대한 의존성의 증가로 이어져 왔다. 신선함에 대한 요구는 또한 식량 낭비에 대한 우려의 원인이 되었다. '유통 기한', '판매 시한', '섭취 시한' 등의 라벨 사용은 제도적인 폐기물 생산을 법적으로 허용해 왔다. (환경) 운동가들은 과잉 생산이나 폐기물에 대한 추문을 폭로해 왔다. 폐기물 반대 세계 연대 소속 운동가 중 한 명인 Tristram Stuart는 신선하게 만들어진 샌드위치와 함께, 판매대가 비어 보이는 것을 막기 위한 초과 주문이 소매 산업 분야 전반에서 이루어지는 일반적인 행태이며, 이것은 공급이 정기적으로 수요를 초과하면 엄청난 양의 폐기물로 이어진다고 주장한다.

Why? 왜 정답일까?

빈칸 뒤에서 '신선한' 식품 공급에 대한 요구가 커지면서 환경적 비용을 많이 야기하는 온실 또는 품질 관리 기법에 대한 의존성이 증가했으며, 폐기물 또한 더 많이 용인되는 사태가 일어났다고 한다. 따라서 빈칸에 들어갈 말로 가장 적절한 것은 ① '숨겨진 환경적인 대가를 지니고 있을'이다.

- year-round ⓐ 연중 계속되는
- reliance ⓝ 의존
- institutional ⓐ 제도적인, 기관의
- diversify ⓥ 다양화하다
- exotic ⓐ 외국의, 이국적인
- satellite ⓝ 위성
- bring about ~을 가져오다, 야기하다

구문 풀이

2행 While freshness is now being used as a term in food marketing
접속사(~인 한편)
as part of a return to nature, the demand (for year-round supplies of
주어
fresh produce) (such as soft fruit and exotic vegetables) has led to
동사(단수)
the widespread use of hot houses in cold climates and increasing
reliance on total quality control — {management by temperature
control, use of pesticides and computer/satellite-based logistics}.
{ } : total quality control 보충 설명

---

10 0부터 숫자 세기의 문제점　　정답률 73% | 정답 ①

다음 빈칸에 들어갈 말로 가장 적절한 것을 고르시오. [3점]

✓ counting from 0 – 0부터 숫자를 세는 것
② numbering in reverse order – 수를 거꾸로 매기는 것
③ adding up the numbers given – 주어진 수를 더하는 것
④ learning words through games – 게임을 통해 단어를 익히는 것
⑤ saying numbers in a loud voice – 큰 소리로 수를 말하는 것

There is a major problem / with counting from 0.
중대한 문제가 있다. / 0부터 숫자를 세는 것에는
To determine the number of objects by counting, / such as determining how many apples there are on a table, / many children would touch or point to the first apple / and say "one," / then move on to the second apple and say "two," / and continue in this manner / until all the apples are counted.
수를 세어 대상의 수를 판단하기 위해, / 탁자에 몇 개의 사과가 있는지를 판단하는 것처럼, / 많은 아이들은 첫 번째 사과를 만지거나 가리킨 후 / "하나"라고 말하고, / 그리고 나서 두 번째 사과로 옮겨가서 "둘"이라고 말하며, / 이런 방식으로 계속할 것이다. / 모든 사과를 셀 때까지
If we start at 0, / we would have to touch nothing / and say "zero," / but then we would have to start touching apples / and calling out "one, two, three" and so on.
만약 우리가 0부터 시작하면 / 우리는 아무것도 만지지 않고 / "영"이라고 말해야 하지만, / 그 이후로는 사과를 만지기 시작하며 / "하나, 둘, 셋" 등으로 말해야 할 것이다.
This can be very confusing / because there would be a need to stress / when to touch and when not to touch.
이것은 매우 혼란스러울 수 있는데 / 그 이유는 강조할 필요가 있을 것이기 때문이다. / 언제 만지고 언제 만지지 않아야 하는지를
If a child accidentally touches an apple / while saying "zero," / then the total number of apples will be off by 1.
만약 한 아이가 실수로 사과 하나를 만진다면, / "영"이라고 말하며 / 사과의 총 개수는 한 개만큼 부족할 것이다.

0부터 숫자를 세는 것에는 중대한 문제가 있다. 탁자에 몇 개의 사과가 있는지

를 판단하는 것처럼, 수를 세어 대상의 수를 판단하기 위해, 많은 아이들은 첫 번째 사과를 만지거나 가리킨 후 "하나"라고 말하고, 그러고 나서 두 번째 사과로 옮겨가서 "둘"이라고 말하며, 모든 사과를 셀 때까지 이런 방식으로 계속할 것이다. 만약 우리가 0부터 시작하면 아무것도 만지지 않고 "영"이라고 말해야 하지만, 그 이후로는 사과를 만지기 시작하며 "하나, 둘, 셋" 등으로 말해야 할 것이다. 이것은 매우 혼란스러울 수 있는데 그 이유는 언제 만지고 언제 만지지 않아야 하는지를 강조할 필요가 있을 것이기 때문이다. 만약 한 아이가 실수로 "영"이라고 말하며 사과 하나를 만진다면, 사과의 총 개수는 한 개만큼 부족할 것이다.

Why? 왜 정답일까?

첫 문장에 빈칸이 있으므로 주제문을 완성하는 문제이며, 두 번째 문장부터 사과를 직접 만지며 수를 세는 경우를 예로 들고 있다. 특히 'This can be very confusing ~' 이후로 0부터 사과를 세어가는 방식이 수를 세고 있는 아이들로 하여금 혼동을 유발할 수 있음이 지적되고 있다. 0부터 수를 세면 언제 사과를 만지고 만지지 말아야 하는지를 따로 가르쳐야 할 수도 있기에 헷갈린다는 것이다(~ there would be a need to stress when to touch and when not to touch.). 따라서 빈칸에 들어갈 말로 가장 적절한 것은 ① '0부터 숫자를 세는 것'이다.

- determine ⓥ 알아내다
- move on to ~로 넘어가다
- call out ~을 부르다, 호출하다
- stress ⓥ 강조하다
- reverse ⓐ 거꾸로의
- point to ~을 가리키다
- manner ⓝ 방식
- confusing ⓐ 혼란을 유발하는
- accidentally ⓐⓓ 실수로, 우연히

구문 풀이

10행 This can be very confusing / because there would be a need
이유 접속사　　동사　　주어
to stress {when to touch} and {when not to touch}.
형용사적 용법　　{ } : 목적어(의문사 + to부정사)

★★★ 1등급 대비 고난도 3점 문제

11 혁신이 우리 삶을 바꾸는 방식　　정답률 37% | 정답 ②

다음 빈칸에 들어갈 말로 가장 적절한 것을 고르시오. [3점]

① respecting the values of the old days
과거의 가치관을 존중하는 것
✓ enabling people to work for each other
사람들이 서로를 위해 일할 수 있게 하는 것
③ providing opportunities to think creatively
창의적으로 사고할 기회를 주는 것
④ satisfying customers with personalized services
개인에 맞춰진 서비스로 고객을 만족시키는 것
⑤ introducing and commercializing unusual products
특이한 제품을 도입하고 상업화하는 것

The best way in which innovation changes our lives / is by enabling people to work for each other.
혁신이 우리의 삶을 바꾸는 최고의 방법은 / 사람들이 서로를 위해 일할 수 있게 하는 것이다.
The main theme of human history / is that we become steadily more specialized / in what we produce, / and steadily more diversified / in what we consume: / we move away / from unstable self-sufficiency / to safer mutual interdependence.
인류 역사의 주요한 주제는 / 우리가 꾸준히 더 전문화되고 우리가 생산하는 것에 있어 / 꾸준히 더 다양화되는 것이다. / 우리가 소비하는 것에 있어 / 즉, 우리는 옮겨간다는 것이다. / 불안정한 자급자족에서 / 더 안전한 서로 간의 상호의존으로
By concentrating on serving other people's needs / for forty hours a week / — which we call a job — / you can spend the other seventy-two hours / (not counting fifty-six hours in bed) / relying on the services / provided to you by other people.
다른 사람들의 필요를 충족시키는 것에 집중하여 / 일주일에 40시간 동안 / 즉 우리가 직업이라고 부르는 것에 / 여러분은 나머지 72시간을 보낼 수 있다. / (잠자는 56시간은 빼고) / 서비스에 의지해 / 다른 사람들에 의해 여러분에게 제공되는
Innovation has made it possible / to work for a fraction of a second / in order to be able to afford to turn on an electric lamp for an hour, / providing the quantity of light / that would have required a whole day's work / if you had to make it yourself / by collecting and refining sesame oil or lamb fat / to burn in a simple lamp, / as much of humanity did / in the not so distant past.
혁신은 가능하게 해주었는데 / 아주 짧은 시간 일하는 것을 / 전등을 한 시간 켤 수 있는 여유를 갖기 위해 / 이는 ~한 만큼의 빛을 제공해 준다. / 하루 종일의 노고가 들었을 / 여러분이 그 등을 스스로 만들어야 했다면 / 참기름이나 양의 지방을 모으고 정제해 / 그저 등 하나를 켜기 위해 / 많은 인류가 했던 것처럼 / 그리 멀지 않은 과거에

혁신이 우리의 삶을 바꾸는 최고의 방법은 사람들이 서로를 위해 일할 수 있게

하는 것이다. 인류 역사의 주요한 주제는 우리가 생산에 있어 꾸준히 더 전문화되고 소비에 있어 꾸준히 더 다양화되는 것이다. 즉, 우리는 불안정한 자급자족에서 더 안전한 서로 간의 상호의존으로 옮겨간다는 것이다. 일주일에 40시간 동안 다른 사람들의 필요를 충족시키는 것, 즉 우리가 직업이라고 부르는 것에 집중하여, 여러분은 (잠자는 56시간은 빼고) 나머지 72시간을 다른 사람들이 제공하는 서비스에 의지해 보낼 수 있다. 혁신은 아주 짧은 시간 일하고도 전등을 한 시간 켤 수 있는 여유를 갖게 해주었는데, 이는 그리 멀지 않은 과거에 많은 인류가 했던 것처럼 여러분이 그저 등 하나를 켜기 위해 참기름이나 양의 지방을 모으고 정제해 그 등을 스스로 만들어야 했다면 하루 종일의 노고가 들었을 만큼의 빛을 제공해 준다.

Why? 왜 정답일까?

생산이 꾸준히 전문화되고 소비가 꾸준히 다양해지는 과정에서 인간은 각자 맡은 일에 집중하는 동시에 타인의 서비스에도 의존해 살게 된다(By concentrating on serving other people's needs for forty hours a week ~ you can spend ~ relying on the services provided to you by other people.)고 한다. 즉 각자 세분화된 역할을 수행하는 사람들이 '서로 의존해가며' 삶이 변화되는 과정이 곧 혁신이라는 것이다. 따라서 빈칸에 들어갈 말로 가장 적절한 것은 ② '사람들이 서로를 위해 일할 수 있게 하는 것'이다.

- innovation ⑪ 혁신
- specialize ⓥ 전문화하다
- unstable ⓐ 불안정한
- mutual ⓐ 상호의
- concentrate on ~에 집중하다
- rely on ~에 의존하다
- afford ⓥ ~할 여유가 있다
- refine ⓥ 정제하다
- burn up 태우다
- commercialize ⓥ 상업화하다
- steadily ⓐⓓ 꾸준히
- diversify ⓥ 다양화하다
- self-sufficiency ⑪ 자급자족
- interdependence ⑪ 상호 의존성
- serve one's needs ~의 필요를 충족하다
- a fraction of a second 아주 짧은 시간
- quantity ⑪ 양
- lamb ⑪ (어린) 양
- personalize ⓥ 개인의 필요에 맞추다

구문 풀이

11행 Innovation has made it possible to work for a fraction of a
　　　　　　　　　　　가목적어　　　진목적어
second in order to be able to afford to turn on an electric lamp for
an hour, providing the quantity of light [that would have required a
　　　　　분사구문　　　　　　선행사　　　　　~했을 것이다
whole day's work if you had to make it yourself by collecting and
refining sesame oil or lamb fat to burn in a simple lamp, as much of
humanity did in the not so distant past].　[ ]: 형용사절
대동사(= made it by themselves by collecting and refining ~)

★★ 문제 해결 꿀~팁 ★★

▶ 많이 틀린 이유는?
Innovation을 보고 creatively가 포함된 ③을 고른다거나, more specialized를 보고 personalized가 포함된 ④를 고를 수 있지만, 모두 글의 핵심 내용과 관련이 없다. 이 글의 주제는 사람들이 모든 일을 혼자 해결하던 시대에 비해 점점 각자 전문된 일을 맡으며 각자 자기 분야가 아닌 일에 대해서는 '서로 의존할' 수밖에 없게 된다는 것이다.

▶ 문제 해결 방법은?
빈칸 뒤의 핵심어인 mutual interdependence를 재진술한 표현이 정답이다.

★★★ 1등급 대비 고난도 3점 문제

12 포식자와 피식자의 눈 구조　　　　정답률 32% | 정답 ②

다음 빈칸에 들어갈 말로 가장 적절한 것을 고르시오. [3점]

① eyes facing outward are linked with the success of hunting
바깥쪽을 향하는 눈은 사냥의 성공과 연관되어 있다
✔ the more powerful species have a narrower field of vision
더 강한 종은 더 좁은 시야를 가지고 있다
③ humans' eyes facing forward enable them to detect danger
앞쪽을 향하고 있는 인간의 눈은 인간으로 하여금 위험을 감지할 수 있게 한다
④ eyesight is closely related to the extinction of weak species
시야는 약한 종의 멸종과 밀접하게 관련되어 있다
⑤ animals use their eyesight to identify members of their species
동물들은 자기 종에 속한 개체를 알아보기 위해 시력을 쓴다

Interestingly, in nature, / the more powerful species have a narrower field of vision.
흥미롭게도 자연에서 / 더 강한 종은 더 좁은 시야를 가지고 있다.
The distinction between predator and prey / offers a clarifying example of this.
포식자와 피식자의 대비는 / 이에 대한 분명한 예를 제공한다.

The key feature / that distinguishes predator species from prey species / isn't the presence of claws or any other feature / related to biological weaponry.
주요 특징은 / 포식자 종과 피식자 종을 구별하는 / 발톱이나, 다른 특징의 존재가 아니다. / 생물학적 무기와 관련된 어떤
The key feature is *the position of their eyes.*
중요한 특징은 *눈의 위치*이다.
Predators evolved with eyes facing forward / — which allows for binocular vision / that offers accurate depth perception / when pursuing prey.
포식자는 앞쪽을 향하고 있는 눈을 가지도록 진화하였고, / 이것은 양안시(兩眼視)를 허용한다. / 정확한 거리 감각을 제공하는 / 사냥감을 쫓을 때
Prey, / on the other hand, / often have eyes facing outward, / maximizing peripheral vision, / which allows the hunted to detect danger / that may be approaching from any angle.
피식자는 / 반면에 / 대체로 바깥쪽을 향하는 눈을 가지고 있으며, / 주변 시야를 최대화하는, / 이로 인해 사냥의 대상은 위험을 감지할 수 있다. / 어떤 각도에서든 접근하고 있을지 모르는
Consistent with our place / at the top of the food chain, / humans have eyes / that face forward.
우리의 위치와 일치하게도, / 먹이 사슬의 꼭대기에 있는 / 인간은 눈을 가지고 있다. / 앞쪽을 향하는
We have the ability / to gauge depth and pursue our goals, / but we can also miss important action on our periphery.
우리는 능력을 갖추고 있지만, / 거리를 측정하고 목표물들을 추적할 수 있는 / 또한 우리 주변의 중요한 행동을 놓칠 수도 있다.

흥미롭게도 자연에서 더 강한 종은 더 좁은 시야를 가지고 있다. 포식자와 피식자의 대비는 이에 대한 분명한 예를 제공한다. 포식자 종과 피식자 종을 구별하는 주요 특징은 발톱이나, 생물학적 무기와 관련된 어떤 다른 특징의 존재가 아니다. 중요한 특징은 눈의 위치이다. 포식자는 앞쪽을 향하고 있는 눈을 가지도록 진화하였고, 이것은 사냥감을 쫓을 때 정확한 거리 감각을 제공하는 양안시(兩眼視)를 허용한다. 반면에 피식자는 대체로 주변 시야를 최대화하는, 바깥쪽을 향하는 눈을 가지고 있으며, 이로 인해 사냥의 대상은 어떤 각도에서든 접근하고 있을지 모르는 위험을 감지할 수 있다. 먹이 사슬의 꼭대기에 있는 우리의 위치와 일치하듯, 인간은 앞쪽을 향하는 눈을 가지고 있다. 우리는 거리를 측정하고 목표물들을 추격할 수 있는 능력을 갖추고 있지만, 또한 우리 주변의 중요한 행동을 놓칠 수도 있다.

Why? 왜 정답일까?

포식자와 피식자를 구별짓는 주요한 차이점으로 눈의 위치(*the position of their eyes*)를 지적한 글이다. 포식자는 사냥할 때 거리 파악에 유리하도록 눈이 앞쪽을 향해 있지만, 피식자는 위험을 감지하는 데 유리하도록 눈이 바깥쪽을 향해 있다고 설명하고 있으므로, 빈칸에 들어갈 말로 가장 적절한 것은 ② '더 강한 종은 더 좁은 시야를 가지고 있다'이다.

- distinction ⑪ 차이, 대조, 구별
- clarify ⓥ 분명하게 하다, 명확히 하다
- presence ⑪ 존재
- weaponry ⑪ 무기, 무기류
- accurate ⓐ 정확한
- pursue ⓥ (붙잡기 위해) 뒤쫓다, 추적하다
- approach ⓥ 다가가다, 접근하다
- extinction ⑪ 멸종
- predator ⑪ 포식자, 천적
- species ⑪ (생물의) 종
- claw ⑪ 발톱, 집게발
- binocular ⓐ 두 눈으로 보는
- perception ⑪ 지각, 감지, 인지
- detect ⓥ 감지하다
- consistent with ~에 일치하는

구문 풀이

3행 The key feature [that distinguishes predator species from
　　　　　　주어　　　　주격 관계대명사
prey species] isn't the presence of claws or any other feature [(that is)
　　　　　　　동사(단수)　　　　　　　　　선행사　　　생략
related to biological weaponry].
~와 관련된

★★ 문제 해결 꿀~팁 ★★

▶ 많이 틀린 이유는?
빈칸 뒤에서 포식자와 피식자의 시야 구조상 차이를 다양한 예로 설명하고 있지만, 눈 구조를 사냥의 성공 여부와 연결시키고 있지는 않으므로 ①은 정답이 아니다. 또한 본문에서 인간은 가장 강력한 종으로서 포식자 특유의 전방 시야 구조를 발달시켜 왔으며 주변의 행동은 놓치기도 한다고 설명하는 것으로 볼 때 ③ 또한 답으로 부적절하다.

▶ 문제 해결 방법은?
예시가 여러 개 나올 때에는 가장 이해하기 쉬운 예시부터 읽어 내용의 흐름을 파악한다. 이 글의 경우 인간의 예를 언급하는 마지막 두 문장이 비교적 쉬우므로, 여기서 '시야 구조'와 '먹이 사슬 상 위치'를 키워드로 삼은 후 다시 처음부터 글을 이해해보도록 한다.

DAY 03 빈칸 추론 03

01 ②	02 ①	03 ③	04 ③	05 ⑤
06 ④	07 ④	08 ②	09 ②	10 ①
11 ②	12 ①			

01 사전 통보로 변화에 적응할 시간을 주기
정답률 61% | 정답 ②

다음 빈칸에 들어갈 말로 가장 적절한 것을 고르시오.

① unite - 연합할
✔ adapt - 적응할
③ object - 반대할
④ compete - 경쟁할
⑤ recover - 회복할

We don't send telegraphs to communicate anymore, / but it's a great metaphor for giving advance notice.
우리는 소통하기 위해 더 이상 전보를 보내지 않지만 / 이것은 사전 통보를 하는 것에 대한 훌륭한 비유이다.

Sometimes, / you must inform those close to you / of upcoming change / by conveying important information well in advance.
때때로, / 여러분은 자신에게 가까운 사람들에게 알려야 한다. / 다가오는 변화를 / 중요한 정보를 미리 잘 전달함으로써

There's a huge difference / between saying, "From now on, we will do things differently," / which doesn't give people enough time / to understand and accept the change, / and saying something like, "Starting next month, we're going to approach things differently."
큰 차이가 있다. / "지금부터 우리는 일을 다르게 할 겁니다."라고 말하는 것과 / 사람들에게 충분한 시간을 주지 않는 / 그 변화를 이해하고 받아들일 / "다음 달부터 우리는 일에 다르게 접근할 겁니다." 같은 말을 하는 것 사이에는

Telegraphing empowers people to adapt.
전보를 보내는 것은 사람들이 적응할 수 있도록 해 준다.

Telegraphing involves the art / of seeing an upcoming event or circumstance / and giving others enough time / to process and accept the change.
전보를 보내는 것은 기술을 포함한다. / 다가오는 사건이나 상황을 보고 / 다른 사람들에게 충분한 시간을 주는 / 그 변화를 처리하고 받아들일

Telegraph anything / that will take people out of / what is familiar and comfortable to them.
무엇이든 전보로 보내라. / 사람들을 ~에서 벗어나게 할 / 그들에게 익숙하고 편안한 것

This will allow processing time / for them to accept the circumstances / and make the most of what's happening.
이것은 처리 시간을 허락할 것이다. / 그들이 그 상황을 받아들이고 / 일어나고 있는 일을 최대한으로 활용할 수 있는

우리는 소통하기 위해 더 이상 전보를 보내지 않지만 이것은 사전 통보를 하는 것에 대한 훌륭한 비유이다. 때때로 여러분은 중요한 정보를 미리 잘 전달함으로써 다가오는 변화를 자신에게 가까운 사람들에게 알려야 한다. 사람들에게 그 변화를 이해하고 받아들일 충분한 시간을 주지 않고 "지금부터 우리는 일을 다르게 할 겁니다."라고 말하는 것과 "다음 달부터 우리는 일에 다르게 접근할 겁니다." 같은 말을 하는 것 사이에는 큰 차이가 있다. 전보를 보내는 것은 사람들이 적응할 수 있도록 해 준다. 전보를 보내는 것은 다가오는 사건이나 상황을 보고 다른 사람들에게 그 변화를 처리하고 받아들일 충분한 시간을 주는 기술을 포함한다. 사람들을 익숙하고 편안한 것에서 벗어나게 할 무엇이든 전보로 보내라. 이것은 그들이 그 상황을 받아들이고 일어나고 있는 일을 최대한으로 활용할 수 있는 처리 시간을 허락할 것이다.

Why? 왜 정답일까?

빈칸이 포함된 문장 뒤에서 비유적 의미의 전보는 사람들이 다가오는 변화를 처리하고 받아들일 시간을 충분히 준다(Telegraphing involves the art of seeing an upcoming event or circumstance and giving others enough time to process and accept the change. / This will allow processing time for them to accept the circumstances and make the most of what's happening.)고 설명하므로, 빈칸에 들어갈 말로 가장 적절한 것은 ② '적응할'이다.

- telegraph ⓝ 전보
- metaphor ⓝ 은유
- notice ⓝ 통지, 통보
- convey ⓥ 전달하다
- accept ⓥ 받아들이다
- circumstance ⓝ 상황
- comfortable ⓐ 편안한
- anymore ⓐⓓ 더 이상
- advance ⓐ 사전의
- upcoming ⓐ 다가오는
- from now on 이제부터, 지금부터
- involve ⓥ 포함하다
- familiar ⓐ 익숙한
- make the most of ~을 최대한 활용하다

구문 풀이

3행 Sometimes, you must inform those close to you of upcoming
「inform + A of B : A에게 B를 알리다」
change by conveying important information well in advance.
「by + 동명사 : ~함으로써」

02 업무의 결과를 보고 상황을 파악하는 관리자들
정답률 42% | 정답 ①

다음 빈칸에 들어갈 말로 가장 적절한 것을 고르시오. [3점]

✔ the end result - 최종 결과
② the welfare policy - 복지 정책
③ the uniform procedure - 획일적인 절차
④ the informal atmosphere - 격식에 얽매이지 않는 분위기
⑤ the employee's personality - 직원의 성격

Good managers / have learned to overcome the initial feelings of anxiety / when assigning tasks.
좋은 관리자들은 / 초기 불안감을 극복하는 것을 배워왔다. / 업무를 맡길 때의

They are aware / that no two people act in exactly the same way / and so do not feel threatened / if they see one employee going about a task / differently than another.
그들은 알고 있고, / 어떤 두 사람도 정확히 똑같은 방식으로 행동하지 않는다는 것을 / 그래서 두려움을 느끼지 않는다. / 한 직원이 업무를 시작하는 것을 보더라도 / 다른 사람과 다르게

Instead, they focus on the end result.
대신에, 그들은 최종 결과에 초점을 맞춘다.

If a job was successfully done, / as long as people are working in a manner / acceptable to the organization / (for example, / as long as salespeople are keeping to the company's ethical selling policy), / then that's fine.
만약 어떤 업무가 성공적으로 처리되었다면, / 사람들이 방식으로 일을 하는 한 / 조직에 수용될 만한 / (예컨대, / 판매원들이 회사의 윤리적 판매 정책을 준수하는 한) / 그것은 괜찮다.

If an acceptable final outcome wasn't achieved, / then such managers respond / by discussing it with the employee / and analyzing the situation, / to find out what training or additional skills that person will need / to do the task successfully in the future.
만약 수용할 만한 최종 결과가 성취되지 않았다면, / 그러한 관리자들은 대응하여, / 그 직원과 논의하고 / 상황을 분석하는 것으로 / 어떤 훈련이나 추가적인 기술을 필요로 하는지를 알아낸다. / 그 사람이 미래에 그 업무를 성공적으로 수행하기 위해

좋은 관리자들은 업무를 맡길 때의 초기 불안감을 극복하는 것을 배워왔다. 그들은 어떤 두 사람도 정확히 똑같은 방식으로 행동하지 않는다는 것을 알고 있고, 그래서 한 직원이 다른 사람과 다르게 업무를 시작하는 것을 보더라도 두려움을 느끼지 않는다. 대신에, 그들은 최종 결과에 초점을 맞춘다. 만약 어떤 업무가 성공적으로 처리되었다면, 사람들이 조직에 수용될 만한 방식으로 일을 하는 한(예컨대, 판매원들이 회사의 윤리적 판매 정책을 준수하는 한) 그것은 괜찮다. 만약 수용할 만한 최종 결과가 성취되지 않았다면, 그러한 관리자들은 그 직원과 논의하고 상황을 분석하는 것으로 대응하여, 그 사람이 미래에 그 업무를 성공적으로 수행하기 위해 어떤 훈련이나 추가적인 기술을 필요로 하는지를 알아낸다.

Why? 왜 정답일까?

빈칸 뒤의 예문에서 관리자들은 업무의 결과, 즉 일이 결국 잘 처리되었는지 혹은 그렇지 않았는지를 보고 직원과 상황에 대한 판단을 내린다고 이야기하므로, 빈칸에 들어갈 말로 가장 적절한 것은 ① '최종 결과'이다.

- initial ⓐ 초기의, 처음의
- threatened ⓐ 위협감을 느끼는
- successfully ⓐⓓ 성공적으로
- acceptable ⓐ 수용될만한, 용인되는
- respond ⓥ 대응하다, 응답하다
- additional ⓐ 추가적인, 추가의
- uniform ⓐ 획일적인, 균일한, 한결같은
- personality ⓝ 성격
- anxiety ⓝ 불안, 걱정, 염려
- focus on ~에 집중하다
- manner ⓝ 방식
- ethical ⓐ 윤리적인, 도덕적인
- analyze ⓥ 분석하다
- welfare ⓝ 복지
- informal ⓐ 격식에 얽매이지 않은

구문 풀이

2행 They are aware {that no two people act in exactly the same
동사1   접속사   { }: 명사절
way} and so do not feel threatened if they see one employee
동사2   지각동사
going about a task differently than another.
현재분사(시작하다)   ~와는 달리, 다르게

03 언어적 수법으로 다른 동물과 거리를 두는 인간　정답률 43% | 정답 ③

다음 빈칸에 들어갈 말로 가장 적절한 것을 고르시오. [3점]

① define human instincts – 인간의 본능을 정의하는
② overestimate chimps' intelligence – 침팬지의 지능을 과대평가하는
✔ distance the other animals from us – 우리와 다른 동물들 사이에 거리를 두는
④ identify animals' negative emotions – 동물의 부정적 감정을 식별하는
⑤ correct our misconceptions about nature – 자연에 대한 우리의 오해를 정정하는

The famous primatologist Frans de Waal, of Emory University, / says / humans downplay similarities / between us and other animals / as a way of maintaining our spot / at the top of our imaginary ladder.
Emory 대학의 유명한 영장류학자 Frans de Waal은 / 말한다. / 인간은 유사성을 경시한다고 / 우리와 다른 동물들 사이의 / 우리 위치를 유지할 방법으로 / 상상 속 사다리의 꼭대기에 있는

Scientists, / de Waal points out, / can be some of the worst offenders / — employing technical language / to distance the other animals from us.
과학자들은 / de Waal은 지적한다. / 최악의 죄를 범하는 자들 중 일부일 수 있다고 / 전문 언어를 사용하는 / 우리와 다른 동물들 사이에 거리를 두기 위해

They call "kissing" in chimps "mouth-to-mouth contact"; / they call "friends" between primates "favorite affiliation partners"; / they interpret evidence / showing that crows and chimps can make tools / as being somehow qualitatively different / from the kind of toolmaking said to define humanity.
그들은 침팬지의 '키스'를 '입과 입의 접촉'이라고 부르고, / 그들은 영장류 사이의 '친구'를 '좋아하는 제휴 파트너'라고 부르며, / 그들은 증거를 해석한다. / 까마귀와 침팬지가 도구를 만들 수 있다는 것을 보여주는 / 아무래도 질적으로 다르다고 / 인류를 정의한다고 하는 종류의 도구 제작과는

If an animal can beat us at a cognitive task / — like how certain bird species can remember the precise locations of thousands of seeds — / they write it off as instinct, / not intelligence.
만약 동물이 인지적인 과업에서 우리를 이길 수 있다면, / 특정 종의 새들이 수천 개의 씨앗의 정확한 위치를 기억할 수 있듯이, / 그들은 그것을 본능으로 치부한다. / 지능이 아니라

This and so many more tricks of language / are what de Waal has termed "linguistic castration."
이것과 더 많은 언어적 수법은 / de Waal이 '언어적 거세'라고 명명한 것이다.

The way we use our tongues / to disempower animals, / the way we invent words / to maintain our spot at the top.
우리의 언어를 사용하는 방식이며, / 우리가 동물로부터 힘을 빼앗기 위해 / 우리가 단어들을 만들어내는 방식이다. / 우리의 꼭대기 위치를 지키려고

Emory 대학의 유명한 영장류학자 Frans de Waal은 인간은 상상 속 사다리의 꼭대기에 있는 우리 위치를 유지할 방법으로 우리와 다른 동물들 사이의 유사성을 경시한다고 말한다. de Waal은 과학자들이 전문 언어를 사용해 우리와 다른 동물들 사이에 거리를 두는 최악의 죄를 범하는 자들 중 일부일 수 있다고 지적한다. 그들은 침팬지의 '키스'를 '입과 입의 접촉'이라고 부르고, 영장류 사이의 '친구'를 '좋아하는 제휴 파트너'라고 부르며, 그들은 까마귀와 침팬지가 도구를 만들 수 있다는 것을 보여주는 증거가 인류를 정의한다고 하는 종류의 도구 제작과는 아무래도 질적으로 다르다고 해석한다. 만약 특정 종의 새들이 수천 개의 씨앗의 정확한 위치를 기억할 수 있는 경우처럼, 동물이 인지적인 과업에서 우리를 이길 수 있다면, 그들은 그것을 지능이 아니라 본능으로 치부한다. 이것과 더 많은 언어적 수법은 de Waal이 '언어적 거세'라고 명명한 것이다. 우리가 동물로부터 힘을 빼앗기 위해 우리의 언어를 사용하는 방식이며, 우리의 꼭대기 위치를 지키려고 단어들을 만들어내는 방식이다.

Why? 왜 정답일까?

우리가 인간과 동물이 서로 다름을 강조하는(humans downplay similarities between us and other animals) 언어 사용으로 교묘하게 우월한 입지를 지키려고 한다는 것을 지적하는 내용이므로, 빈칸에 들어갈 말로 가장 적절한 것은 ③ '우리와 다른 동물들 사이에 거리를 두는'이다.

- primatologist ⓝ 영장류학자
- similarity ⓝ 유사성
- imaginary ⓐ 상상의
- offender ⓝ 범죄자, 나쁜 짓을 하는 사람
- technical ⓐ 전문적인
- chimp ⓝ 침팬지
- affiliation ⓝ 제휴
- crow ⓝ 까마귀
- toolmaking ⓝ 도구 제작
- humanity ⓝ 인류
- cognitive ⓐ 인지적인
- write off as ~라고 치부하다
- intelligence ⓝ 지능

- downplay ⓥ 경시하다
- spot ⓝ 위치 ⓥ 파악하다
- ladder ⓝ 사다리
- employ ⓥ 이용하다, 고용하다
- language ⓝ 언어
- primate ⓝ 영장류
- interpret A as B A를 B로 해석하다
- qualitatively ⓐ𝖽 질적으로
- define ⓥ 정의하다
- beat ⓥ 이기다
- precise ⓐ 정확한
- instinct ⓝ 본능
- trick ⓝ 수법, 트릭

- term ⓥ (특정 용어로) 칭하다 ⓝ 용어
- overestimate ⓥ 과대평가하다
- distance A from B A와 B 사이에 거리를 두다
- identify ⓥ 식별하다, 알아보다, 확인하다
- disempower ⓥ ~로부터 힘을 빼앗다
- misconception ⓝ 오해

구문 풀이

9행 ~ they interpret evidence (showing that crows and chimps
　　interpret + A +
can make tools) as being somehow qualitatively different from the
　　as + B : A를 B로 해석하다
kind of toolmaking [(that is) said to define humanity].
　　생략

04 매장 뒷벽을 활용한 판매 증대 전략　정답률 43% | 정답 ③

다음 빈칸에 들어갈 말로 가장 적절한 것을 고르시오. [3점]

① the store looks larger than it is
　그 매장이 실제보다 더 커 보인다
② more products can be stored there
　더 많은 제품이 그곳에 보관될 수 있다
✔ people have to walk through the whole store
　사람들이 매장 전체를 걸어야 한다
④ the store provides customers with cultural events
　상점이 고객에게 문화 행사를 제공한다
⑤ people don't need to spend too much time in the store
　사람들이 상점에서 너무 많은 시간을 보낼 필요가 없다

Within a store, / the wall marks the back of the store, / but not the end of the marketing.
상점 안에서, / 벽은 매장의 뒤쪽을 나타내지만, / 마케팅의 끝을 나타내지는 않는다.

Merchandisers often use the back wall as a magnet, / because it means / that people have to walk through the whole store.
상품 판매업자는 종종 뒷벽을 자석처럼 사용하는데, / 이것은 의미하기 때문이다. / 사람들이 매장 전체를 걸어야 한다는 것을

This is a good thing / because distance traveled relates more directly / to sales per entering customer / than any other measurable consumer variable.
이것은 좋은 일인데, / 이동 거리가 더 직접적으로 관련되어 있기 때문이다. / 방문 고객당 판매량과 / 측정 가능한 다른 어떤 소비자 변수보다

Sometimes, the wall's attraction is simply appealing to the senses, / a wall decoration that catches the eye / or a sound that catches the ear.
때로는 벽이 사람의 관심을 끄는 것은 정말로 감각에 호소하는 것이다. / 시선을 끄는 벽의 장식물이나 / 귀를 기울이게 하는 소리가 (그것에 해당한다.)

Sometimes the attraction is specific goods.
때로는 사람의 관심을 끄는 것이 특정 상품이기도 하다.

In supermarkets, the dairy is often at the back, / because people frequently come just for milk.
슈퍼마켓에서 유제품은 흔히 뒤편에 위치하는데, / 사람들이 자주 우유만 사러 오기 때문이다.

At video rental shops, it's the new releases.
비디오 대여점에서는 그것이 새로 출시된 비디오이다.

상점 안에서, 벽은 매장의 뒤쪽을 나타내지만, 마케팅의 끝을 나타내지는 않는다. 상품 판매업자는 종종 뒷벽을 자석처럼 사용하는데, 이것은 사람들이 매장 전체를 걸어야 한다는 것을 의미하기 때문이다. 이것은 좋은 일인데, 측정 가능한 다른 어떤 소비자 변수보다 이동 거리가 방문 고객당 판매량과 더 직접적으로 관련되어 있기 때문이다. 때로는 벽이 사람의 관심을 끄는 것은 정말로 감각에 호소하는 것인데, 시선을 끄는 벽의 장식물이나 귀를 기울이게 하는 소리가 그것에 해당한다. 때로는 사람의 관심을 끄는 것이 특정 상품이기도 하다. 슈퍼마켓에서 유제품은 흔히 뒤편에 위치하는데, 사람들이 자주 우유만 사러 오기 때문이다. 비디오 대여점에서는 그것이 새로 출시된 비디오이다.

Why? 왜 정답일까?

빈칸 뒤의 '~ distance traveled relates more directly to sales ~'에서 이동 거리가 매출과 관련이 높은 요인임이 언급되므로, 빈칸 앞에서 '뒷벽이 자석처럼 쓰인다'고 말한 것은 사람들을 상점 뒤편까지 오게 하여 고객의 이동거리를 늘리고 이를 통해 판매를 증대하려는 전략을 설명한 것으로 볼 수 있다. 따라서 빈칸에 들어갈 말로 가장 적절한 것은 ③ '사람들이 매장 전체를 걸어야 한다'이다.

- mark ⓥ 나타내다, 표시하다
- distance ⓝ 거리
- customer ⓝ 고객
- attraction ⓝ 사람의 관심을 끄는 것
- specific ⓐ 특정한
- frequently ⓐ𝖽 자주, 흔히
- cultural event 문화 행사

- magnet ⓝ 자석[사람을 끄는 것]
- relate to ~에 관련되다
- measurable ⓐ 측정 가능한
- appealing to ~에 호소하는
- dairy ⓝ 유제품
- release ⓝ 출시, 발매(물)

DAY 03

구문 풀이

4행 This is a good thing / because distance traveled relates more
이유 접속사(~ 때문에)　　　　　　~에 관련되다
directly to sales per entering customer than any other measurable
　　　　　　　　　　　　　　　「than any other+단수명사(다른 어떤 ~보다)」
consumer variable.

05　성장 과정의 일부인 자립
정답률 45% | 정답 ⑤

다음 빈칸에 들어갈 말로 가장 적절한 것을 고르시오. [3점]

① developing financial management skills
금전 관리 기술을 발달시키는 것
② learning from other people's experiences
다른 사람의 경험에서 배우는 것
③ figuring out your strengths and interests
여러분의 강점과 흥미를 알아내는 것
④ managing relationship problems with your peers
동료와의 인간관계 문제를 관리하는 것
✓ falling out of love with the adults who look after you
자신을 보살펴 주는 어른과 정을 떼는 것

All mammals need to leave their parents / and set up on their own / at some point.
모든 포유동물은 부모를 떠나서 / 스스로 자립해야 한다. / 어느 시점에서는
But human adults generally provide a comfortable existence / — enough
food arrives on the table, / money is given at regular intervals, / the bills get
paid / and the electricity for the TV doesn't usually run out.
하지만 성인 인간은 대개 안락한 생활을 제공하는데, / 충분한 음식이 식탁 위에 차려지고, / 일정한 기간마다 돈
이 지급되며, / 청구서가 지불되고, / TV 전기가 대개 끊기지 않는다.
If teenagers didn't build up / a fairly major disrespect for and conflict with /
their parents or carers, / they'd never want to leave.
십 대 아이가 키우지 않는다면, / 매우 심각한 불손과 갈등을 / 부모나 보호자에 대한 / 그들은 결코 떠나고 싶어
하지 않을 것이다.
In fact, / falling out of love with the adults / who look after you / is probably
a necessary part of growing up.
사실, / 어른과의 정을 떼는 것은 / 보살펴 주는 / 아마도 성장의 필수적인 부분일 것이다.
Later, / when you live independently, away from them, / you can start to love
them again / because you won't need to be fighting / to get away from them.
나중에, / 여러분이 그들과 떨어져서 독립적으로 생활하게 되면, / 그들을 다시 사랑하기 시작할 수 있을 것이다.
/ 싸울 필요가 없을 것이기 때문에 / 그들에게서 벗어나기 위해서
And you can come back sometimes / for a home-cooked meal.
그리고 여러분은 돌아올 수 있다. / 가끔 집 밥을 먹기 위해

모든 포유동물은 어느 시점에서는 부모를 떠나서 자립해야 한다. 하지만 성인
인간은 대개 안락한 생활을 제공하여, 충분한 음식이 식탁 위에 차려지고, 일
정한 기간마다 돈이 지급되며, 청구서가 지불되고, TV 전기가 대개 끊기지 않
는다. 십 대 아이가 부모나 보호자에 대한 매우 심각한 불손과 갈등을 키우지
않는다면, 그들은 결코 떠나고 싶어 하지 않을 것이다. 사실, 자신을 보살펴 주
는 어른과 정을 떼는 것은 아마도 성장의 필수적인 부분일 것이다. 나중에, 여
러분이 그들과 떨어져서 독립적으로 생활하게 되면, 그들에게서 벗어나기 위해
서 싸울 필요가 없을 것이기 때문에 그들을 다시 사랑하기 시작할 수 있을
것이다. 그리고 여러분은 가끔 집 밥을 먹기 위해 돌아올 수 있다.

Why?　왜 정답일까?

첫 문장에서 모든 포유류는 어느 시점이 되면 부모를 떠나 자립해야 한다(All
mammals need to leave their parents and set up on their own at
some point.)는 핵심 내용이 나오므로, 강조의 연결어인 In fact 뒤의 빈칸 또한 '자립'
에 관련된 내용을 언급할 것임을 유추할 수 있다. 따라서 빈칸에 들어갈 말로 가장 적절
한 것은 ⑤ '자신을 보살펴 주는 어른과 정을 떼는 것'이다.

- **mammal** ⓝ 포유동물
- **run out** (공급품 등이) 다 떨어지다
- **disrespect** ⓝ 불손, 무례, 결례
- **independently** ⓐⓓ 독립하여
- **financial** ⓐ 재정적인, 금전적인
- **peer** ⓝ 동료, 친구
- **fall out of love with** ~와 정을 떼다
- **existence** ⓝ 생활, 생계, 존재, 현존
- **fairly** ⓐⓓ 상당히, 꽤
- **conflict** ⓝ 갈등, 충돌
- **home-cooked** 가정에서 만든
- **strength** ⓝ 강점, 힘
- **manage** ⓥ 살아 나가다, 지내다

구문 풀이

2행 But human adults generally provide a comfortable existence /

{ — enough food arrives on the table, money is given at regular
　　　주어1　　　동사1(자동사)　　　주어2　　동사2(수동태)
intervals, the bills get paid and the electricity for the TV doesn't
　　주어3　　동사3(수동태)　　　　　주어4　　　동사4(자동사)
usually run out}.　{ }: a comfortable existence의 내용 설명

06　심해 생물이 자체 발광하는 이유
정답률 55% | 정답 ④

다음 빈칸에 들어갈 말로 가장 적절한 것을 고르시오. [3점]

① send a signal for help – 도움 요청의 신호를 보내는
② threaten enemies nearby – 주위의 적을 위협하는
③ lift the veil of hidden prey – 숨어 있는 먹이의 베일을 벗기는
✓ create a cloak of invisibility – 보이지 않는 망토를 만드는
⑤ serve as a navigation system – 네비게이션 시스템의 역할을 하는

Some deep-sea organisms / are known to use bioluminescence as a lure, / to
attract prey with a little glow / imitating the movements of their favorite fish,
/ or like fireflies, / as a sexual attractant to find mates.
일부 심해 생물은 / 가짜 미끼로 생물 발광을 활용한다고 알려져 있다. / 작은 빛으로 먹이를 유혹하기 위해 / 그
들이 좋아하는 물고기의 움직임을 모방하는 / 혹은 반딧불이처럼 / 짝을 찾기 위한 성적 유인 물질로
While there are many possible evolutionary theories / for the survival value
of bioluminescence, / one of the most fascinating is / to create a cloak of
invisibility.
많은 가능한 진화 이론이 있지만 / 생물 발광의 생존가에 대한 / 가장 흥미로운 것 중 하나는 ~이다. / 보이지 않
는 망토를 만드는 것
The color of almost all bioluminescent molecules / is blue-green, / the same
color as the ocean above.
거의 모든 생물 발광 분자의 색깔은 / 청록색이다. / 바다 위층과 같은 색인
By self-glowing blue-green, / the creatures no longer cast a shadow or create
a silhouette, / especially when viewed from below / against the brighter
waters above.
청록색으로 자체 발광함으로써 / 생물은 더 이상 그림자를 드리우거나 실루엣을 만들어 내지 않는다. / 특히 아
래에서 보여질 때 / 위쪽의 더 밝은 물을 배경으로
Rather, / by glowing themselves, / they can blend into the sparkles,
reflections, and scattered blue-green glow / of sunlight or moonlight.
오히려 / 스스로 발광함으로써 / 그들은 반짝임, 반사 그리고 분산된 청록색 빛에 섞일 수 있다. / 햇빛 혹은 달빛의
Thus, / they are most likely making their own light / not to see, but to be
un-seen.
따라서 / 그들은 자신만의 빛을 분명 만들어 내고 있을 것이다. / 보기 위해서가 아니라 보이지 않기 위해서

일부 심해 생물은 그들이 좋아하는 물고기의 움직임을 모방하는 작은 빛으로
먹이를 유혹하기 위해 가짜 미끼로, 혹은 반딧불이처럼 짝을 찾기 위한 성적
유인 물질로 생물 발광을 활용한다고 알려져 있다. 생물 발광의 생존가에 대한
많은 가능한 진화 이론이 있지만, 가장 흥미로운 것 중 하나는 보이지 않는 망
토를 만드는 것이다. 거의 모든 생물 발광 분자의 색깔은 바다 위층과 같은 색
인 청록색이다. 청록색으로 자체 발광함으로써 생물은 특히 위쪽의 더 밝은 물
을 배경으로 아래에서 볼 때 더 이상 그림자를 드리우거나 실루엣을 만들어 내
지 않는다. 오히려 스스로 발광함으로써 그들은 햇빛 혹은 달빛의 반짝임, 반
사 그리고 분산된 청록색 빛에 섞일 수 있다. 따라서 그들은 보기 위해서가 아
니라 보이지 않기 위해서 분명 자신만의 빛을 만들어 내고 있을 것이다.

Why?　왜 정답일까?

마지막 두 문장에서 심해 생물들이 자체 발광하는 이유를 설명하는데, 이들은 바다 위층
과 똑같은 색인 청록색으로 빛을 냄으로써 오히려 그 빛에 섞이고(~ by glowing
themselves, they can blend into ~), 눈에 더 띄지 않게 될 수 있다(~ most
likely making their own light not to see, but to be un-seen.)는 것이다. 따
라서 빈칸에 들어갈 말로 가장 적절한 것은 '눈에 보이지 않으려' 한다는 목적을 비유적으
로 설명한 ④ '보이지 않는 망토를 만드는'이다.

- **attractant** ⓝ 유인 물질
- **cast** ⓥ 드리우다, 던지다
- **scatter** ⓥ 흩뜨리다, 분산하다
- **cloak** ⓝ 망토
- **fascinating** ⓐ 매력적인, 흥미로운
- **blend into** ~에 섞이다
- **threaten** ⓥ 위협하다
- **invisibility** ⓝ 보이지 않음

구문 풀이

1행 Some deep-sea organisms are known to use bioluminescence
　전치사1(~로서)　　　　　　　「be known +to부정사: ~한다고 알려지다」
as a lure, to attract prey with a little glow imitating the movements
　　　　부사적 용법(~하기 위해)
of their favorite fish, or like fireflies, as a sexual attractant to find mates.
　　　　　　　　　　전치사2(~로서)　　　　　　　형용사적 용법

07　팬덤의 대상보다도 더 중요한 팬들 간의 교류
정답률 58% | 정답 ④

다음 빈칸에 들어갈 말로 가장 적절한 것을 고르시오.

① is enhanced by collaborations between global stars
세계적인 스타 간의 협업으로 고양된다

② results from frequent personal contact with a star
스타와 자주 개인적인 연락을 나누는 데서 기인한다
③ deepens as fans age together with their idols
팬이 그들의 우상과 함께 나이 들수록 깊어진다
✓ comes from being connected to other fans
다른 팬들과 관계를 맺는 데서 온다
⑤ is heightened by stars' media appearances
스타가 미디어에 등장함으로써 고양된다

Fans feel for feeling's own sake.
팬은 감정 그 자체를 느낀다.

They make meanings / beyond what seems to be on offer.
그들은 의미를 만든다. / 제공된다고 보이는 것을 넘어서는

They build identities and experiences, / and make artistic creations of their own / to share with others.
그들은 정체성과 경험을 만들고, 자신의 예술적 창작물을 만들어 / 다른 사람들과 공유하려고

A person can be an individual fan, / feeling an "idealized connection with a star, / strong feelings of memory and nostalgia," / and engaging in activities / like "collecting to develop a sense of self."
한 사람은 개인적인 팬이 되어, / '어떤 스타와 이상적인 관계'를 느끼며, 즉 '기억과 향수의 강한 감정' / 활동을 할 수 있다. / '자아감 형성을 위해 수집하기'와 같은

But, more often, / individual experiences are embedded in social contexts / where other people with shared attachments / socialize around the object of their affections.
그러나 더 흔히 / 개인적인 경험은 사회적인 상황에 끼워 넣어져 있다. / 애착을 공유하는 다른 사람들이 / 애정의 대상을 중심으로 교제하는

Much of the pleasure of fandom / comes from being connected to other fans.
팬덤의 많은 즐거움은 / 다른 팬들과 관계를 맺는 데서 온다.

In their diaries, / Bostonians of the 1800s / described being part of the crowds at concerts / as part of the pleasure of attendance.
그들의 일기에 / 1800년대의 보스턴 사람들은 / 콘서트에 모인 군중의 일부가 되는 것을 묘사했다. / 참석하는 즐거움의 일부라고

A compelling argument can be made / that what fans love is less the object of their fandom / than the attachments to (and differentiations from) one another / that those affections afford.
강력한 주장이 제기될 수 있다. / 팬이 사랑하는 것은 팬덤의 대상이라기보다 / 서로에 대한 애착(그리고 서로 간의 차이)이라는 / 그 애정이 제공하는

팬은 감정 그 자체를 느낀다. 그들은 제공된다고 보이는 것을 넘어서는 의미를 만든다. 그들은 정체성과 경험을 만들고, 자신의 예술적 창작물을 만들어 다른 사람들과 공유한다. 한 사람은 개인적인 팬이 되어, '어떤 스타와 이상적인 관계, 기억과 향수의 강한 감정'을 느끼며, '자아감 형성을 위해 수집하기' 등의 활동을 할 수 있다. 그러나 더 흔히 개인적인 경험은 애착을 공유하는 다른 사람들이 애정의 대상을 중심으로 교제하는 사회적인 상황에 끼워 넣어져 있다. 팬덤의 많은 즐거움은 다른 팬들과 관계를 맺는 데서 온다. 1800년대의 보스턴 사람들은 콘서트에 모인 군중의 일부가 되는 것이 참석하는 즐거움의 일부라고 일기에 묘사했다. 팬이 사랑하는 것은 팬덤의 대상이라기보다 그 애정이 제공하는 서로에 대한 애착(그리고 서로 간의 차이)이라는 강력한 주장이 제기될 수 있다.

Why? 왜 정답일까?

팬으로서의 개인적 경험은 팬덤을 공유하는 다른 사람들과의 사회적 상황과 맞물려 있다(~ individual experiences are embedded in social contexts where other people with shared attachments socialize ~)는 빈칸 앞의 내용으로 보아, 빈칸에 들어갈 말로 가장 적절한 것은 ④ '다른 팬들과 관계를 맺는 데서 온다'이다.

- for one's own sake 그 자체로
- artistic ⓐ 예술적인
- nostalgia ⓝ 향수
- sense of self 자아 관념
- attachment ⓝ 애착
- affection ⓝ 애정
- describe ⓥ 기술하다, 묘사하다
- attendance ⓝ 참석
- argument ⓝ 주장, 논거
- afford ⓥ (격식) 주다, 제공하다
- collaboration ⓝ 협업, 협력
- heighten ⓥ 고양시키다

- identity ⓝ 정체성
- idealize ⓥ 이상화하다
- collect ⓥ 모으다, 수집하다
- embed ⓥ 끼워 넣다
- socialize ⓥ 교제하다, 사회화하다
- fandom ⓝ 팬덤
- part of ~의 일부
- compelling ⓐ 강력한
- differentiation ⓝ 차이
- enhance ⓥ 고양시키다, 강화하다
- conflict ⓝ 갈등

구문 풀이

15행 A compelling argument can be made [that what fans love is
　　　　　주어　　　　　　동사(수동태)　　　[ ]: 주어 동격
less the object of their fandom than the attachments to (and
「less+A+than+B : A라기보다 B인」
differentiations from) one another that those affections afford].

08　세밀한 묘사의 필요성　　정답률 46% | 정답 ②

다음 빈칸에 들어갈 말로 가장 적절한 것을 고르시오.

① similarities – 유사점　　✓ particulars – 세부 사항
③ fantasies – 환상　　④ boredom – 지루함
⑤ wisdom – 지혜

Generalization without specific examples / that humanize writing / is boring to the listener and to the reader.
구체적인 사례가 없는 일반화는 / 글을 인간미 있게 하는 / 듣는 사람과 읽는 사람에게 지루하다.

Who wants to read platitudes all day?
누가 상투적인 말을 온종일 읽고 싶어 하겠는가?

Who wants to hear the words / great, greater, best, smartest, finest, humanitarian, on and on and on / without specific examples?
누가 듣고 싶어 하겠는가? / 위대한, 더 위대한, 최고의, 제일 똑똑한, 가장 훌륭한, 인도주의적인, 이런 말들을 계속해서 끊임없이 / 구체적인 사례가 없이

Instead of using these 'nothing words,' / leave them out completely / and just describe the particulars.
이런 '공허한 말들'을 사용하는 대신에, / 그것들을 완전히 빼고 / 세부 사항만을 서술하라.

There is nothing worse than reading a scene in a novel / in which a main character is described up front / as heroic or brave or tragic or funny, / while thereafter, the writer quickly moves on to something else.
소설 속 장면을 읽는 것보다 더 끔찍한 것은 없다. / 주인공이 대놓고 묘사되는 / 영웅적이다, 용감하다, 비극적이다, 혹은 웃긴다고 / 한편 그 후 작가가 다른 것으로 빠르게 넘어가는

That's no good, no good at all.
그건 좋지 않으며, 전혀 좋지 않다.

You have to use less one word descriptions / and more detailed, engaging descriptions / if you want to make something real.
여러분은 한 단어 묘사는 덜 사용하고, / 세밀하고 마음을 끄는 묘사를 더 많이 사용해야 한다. / 여러분이 어떤 것을 실감 나는 것으로 만들고 싶다면

글을 인간미 있게 하는 구체적인 사례가 없는 일반화는 듣는 사람에게도 읽는 사람에게도 지루하다. 누가 상투적인 말을 온종일 읽고 싶어 하겠는가? 구체적인 사례가 없이 위대한, 더 위대한, 최고의, 제일 똑똑한, 가장 훌륭한, 인도주의적인, 이런 말들을 누가 계속해서 끊임없이 듣고 싶어 하겠는가? 이런 '공허한 말들'을 사용하는 대신에, 그것들을 완전히 빼고 세부 사항만을 서술하라. 주인공을 대놓고 영웅적이다, 용감하다, 비극적이다, 혹은 웃긴다고 묘사한 후 작가가 다른 것으로 빠르게 넘어가는 소설 속 장면을 읽는 것보다 더 끔찍한 것은 없다. 그건 좋지 않으며, 전혀 좋지 않다. 어떤 것을 실감 나는 것으로 만들고 싶다면, 한 단어 짜리 묘사는 덜 사용하고, 세밀하고 마음을 끄는 묘사를 더 많이 사용해야 한다.

Why? 왜 정답일까?

마지막 문장에서 장면을 실감 나게 만들려면 세밀하고 마음을 끄는 묘사를 사용해야 한다(You have to use less one word descriptions and more detailed, engaging descriptions if you want to make something real.)고 언급하는 것으로 보아, 빈칸에 들어갈 말로 가장 적절한 것은 ② '세부 사항'이다. 이는 빈칸 앞의 specific examples을 재진술한 말이기도 하다.

- specific ⓐ 구체적인
- humanitarian ⓐ 인도주의적인
- engaging ⓐ 마음을 끄는, 몰입시키는
- humanize ⓥ 인간적으로 만들다
- leave out ~을 빼다

구문 풀이

7행　There is nothing worse than reading a scene in a novel
　　　　　　　　　　　　　　　　　　　　　　　선행사
「nothing+비교급+than : ~보다 더 …한 것은 없다(최상급 의미)」
[in which a main character is described up front as heroic or brave
= where
or tragic or funny, while thereafter, the writer quickly moves on to
something else].

★★ 문제 해결 꿀~팁 ★★

▶ 많이 틀린 이유는?
첫 문장의 Generalization만 보고 ①을 고르면 안 된다. '특별한' 사례의 공통점을 찾아 '일반화'하라는 내용은 글 어디에도 없기 때문이다.
▶ 문제 해결 방법은?
빈칸이 주제문인 명령문에 있으므로, 마찬가지로 '~해야 한다'라는 당위의 의미를 나타내는 마지막 문장을 잘 읽어야 한다. more detailed, engaging와 같은 의미의 단어를 빈칸에 넣으면 된다.

★★★ 1등급 대비 고난도 2점 문제

09 실험을 비판적으로 바라보기   정답률 39% | 정답 ②

다음 빈칸에 들어갈 말로 가장 적절한 것을 고르시오.

① inventive – 독창적이지
✓ objective – 객관적이지
③ untrustworthy – 믿을 수 없는지
④ unreliable – 신뢰성이 없는지
⑤ decisive – 결정적이지

When reading another scientist's findings, / think critically about the experiment.
다른 과학자의 실험 결과물을 읽을 때, / 그 실험에 대해 비판적으로 생각하라.

Ask yourself: / Were observations recorded / during or after the experiment?
당신 자신에게 물어라. / 관찰들이 기록되었나? / 실험 도중에 혹은 후에

Do the conclusions make sense?
결론이 합리적인가?

Can the results be repeated?
그 결과들은 반복될 수 있는가?

Are the sources of information reliable?
정보의 출처는 신뢰할만한가?

You should also ask / if the scientist or group conducting the experiment / was unbiased.
당신은 또한 물어야 한다. / 실험을 수행한 그 과학자나 그룹이 / 한쪽으로 치우치지 않았는지

Being unbiased means / that you have no special interest / in the outcome of the experiment.
한쪽으로 치우치지 않음을 의미한다. / 당신이 특별한 이익을 얻지 않는다는 것을 / 실험의 결과로

For example, if a drug company pays for an experiment / to test how well one of its new products works, / there is a special interest involved:
예를 들면, 만약 한 제약 회사가 실험 비용을 지불한다면, / 그 회사의 새로운 제품 중 하나가 얼마나 잘 작용하는지 시험해보기 위한 / 특별한 이익이 관련된 것이다.

The drug company profits / if the experiment shows that its product is effective.
그 제약 회사는 이익을 본다. / 만약 실험이 그 제품이 효과 있음을 보여준다면

Therefore, the experimenters aren't objective.
따라서, 그 실험자들은 객관적이지 않다.

They might ensure / the conclusion is positive and benefits the drug company.
그들은 보장할지도 모른다. / 결론이 긍정적이며 제약 회사에 이익을 주도록

When assessing results, / think about any biases that may be present!
결과들을 평가할 때, / 있을 수 있는 어떤 치우침에 대해 생각하라!

다른 과학자의 실험 결과물을 읽을 때, 그 실험에 대해 비판적으로 생각하라. 당신 자신에게 물어라. 관찰들이 실험 도중에 혹은 후에 기록되었나? 결론이 합리적인가? 그 결과들은 반복될 수 있는가? 정보의 출처는 신뢰할만한가? 당신은 실험을 수행한 그 과학자나 그룹이 한쪽으로 치우치지 않았는지도 물어야 한다. 한쪽으로 치우치지 않음은 당신이 실험의 결과로 특별한 이익을 얻지 않는다는 것을 의미한다. 예를 들면, 만약 한 제약 회사가 그 회사의 새로운 제품 중 하나가 얼마나 잘 작용하는지 시험해보기 위한 실험 비용을 지불한다면, 특별한 이익이 관련된 것이다. 즉 만약 실험이 그 제품이 효과 있음을 보여준다면, 그 제약 회사는 이익을 본다. 따라서, 그 실험자들은 객관적이지 않다. 그들은 결론이 긍정적이며 제약 회사에 이익을 주도록 보장할지도 모른다. 결과들을 평가할 때, 있을 수 있는 어떤 치우침에 대해 생각하라!

Why? 왜 정답일까?

첫 문장에서 실험을 비판적으로 바라보라고 조언한 후 'You should also ask if the scientist or group conducting the experiment was unbiased.', 'When assessing results, think about any biases that may be present!'에서 특히 실험이 어느 한쪽으로 편향되지는 않는지 확인해야 한다는 조언을 보태고 있다. 따라서 빈칸에 들어갈 말로 가장 적절한 것은 실험이 '객관적이지' 않을 수 있으므로 주의가 필요함을 상기시키는 ② '객관적이지'이다.

- critically ⓐd 비판적으로
- make sense ⓥ 합리적이다
- conduct ⓥ 수행하다
- interest ⓝ 이익
- profit ⓥ 이득을 보다 ⓝ 이득
- ensure ⓥ 보장하다
- inventive ⓐ 독창적인
- untrustworthy ⓐ 믿을 만하지 않은
- observation ⓝ 관찰
- reliable ⓐ 신뢰성 있는, 믿을 만한
- unbiased ⓐ 편파적이지 않은
- outcome ⓝ 결과
- experimenter ⓝ 실험자
- assess ⓥ 평가하다
- objective ⓐ 객관적인
- decisive ⓐ 결정적인

구문 풀이

5행 You should also ask if the scientist or group conducting the
접속사(~인지 아닌지)↲   주어   현재분사구
experiment was unbiased.
동사

★★ 문제 해결 꿀~팁 ★★

▶ 많이 틀린 이유는?
빈칸 앞에 aren't라는 부정 표현이 나오므로 빈칸에 주제와 반대되는 말이 들어가야 하는데, ③의 untrustworthy와 ④의 unreliable은 모두 '신뢰성이 없다'는 의미로 그 자체로 주제를 나타낸다.

▶ 문제 해결 방법은?
앞 문장의 내용을 충실히 이해하면 쉽게 답을 고를 수 있다. 앞에서 제약 회사가 연구에 돈을 대는 경우 '특별한 이익이 관련된다'고 언급하는데, 이는 바꾸어 말하면 연구의 '객관성'이 떨어진다는 뜻이다.

★★★ 1등급 대비 고난도 3점 문제

10 영국 악센트와 미국 악센트의 차이 발생 과정   정답률 43% | 정답 ①

다음 빈칸에 들어갈 말로 가장 적절한 것을 고르시오. [3점]

✓ social status – 사회적 지위
② fashion sense – 패션 감각
③ political pressures – 정치적 압력
④ colonial involvement – 식민적 포섭
⑤ intellectual achievements – 지적 성취

Why doesn't the modern American accent / sound similar to a British accent?
왜 현대 미국의 악센트는 / 영국의 악센트와 비슷하게 들리지 않는가?

After all, didn't the British colonize the U.S.?
결국에는 영국이 미국을 식민지로 만들지 않았는가?

Experts believe / that British residents / and the colonists who settled America / all sounded the same back in the 18th century, / and they probably all sounded more like modern Americans / than modern Brits.
전문가들은 믿는다. / 영국 주민들과 / 미국에 정착한 식민지 개척자들은 / 모두 18세기 무렵에는 발음이 똑같았으며, / 아마 모두 현대 미국 발음에 더 가까웠다고 / 현대 영국 발음보다는

The accent that we identify as British today / was developed around the time of the American Revolution / by people of low birth rank / who had become wealthy during the Industrial Revolution.
우리가 오늘날 영국 악센트라고 인식하는 악센트는 / 미국 독립혁명 무렵 만들어졌다. / 하층계급으로 태어났지만 / 산업혁명 기간에 부유해진 사람들에 의해

To distinguish themselves from other commoners, / these people developed new ways of speaking / to set themselves apart / and demonstrate their new, elevated social status.
자신들과 다른 평민들을 구분하기 위하여 / 그들은 새로운 말하기 방식을 개발해 냈는데, / 그들 스스로를 구별시키고 / 새로이 높아진 사회적 지위를 드러내기 위함이었다.

In the 19th century, / this distinctive accent / was standardized as Received Pronunciation / and taught widely by pronunciation tutors to people / who wanted to learn to speak fashionably.
19세기에, / 이 독특한 악센트는 / 영국 표준 발음으로 표준화되었고 / 발음 지도 강사들에 의해 사람들에게 널리 가르쳐졌다. / 세련되게 말하는 법을 배우고 싶어 하는

왜 현대 미국의 악센트는 영국의 악센트와 비슷하게 들리지 않는가? 결국에는 영국이 미국을 식민지로 만들지 않았는가? 전문가들은 영국 주민들과 미국에 정착한 식민지 개척자들 모두 18세기 무렵에는 발음이 똑같았으며, 아마 모두 현대 영국 발음보다는 현대 미국 발음에 더 가까웠다고 믿는다. 우리가 오늘날 영국 악센트라고 인식하는 악센트는 하층계급으로 태어났지만 산업혁명 기간에 부유해진 사람들에 의해 미국 독립혁명 무렵 만들어졌다. 자신들과 다른 평민들을 구분하기 위하여 그들은 새로운 말하기 방식을 개발해 냈는데, 이는 그들 스스로를 구별시키고 새로이 높아진 사회적 지위를 드러내기 위함이었다. 19세기에, 이 독특한 악센트는 영국 표준 발음으로 표준화되었고 세련되게 말하는 법을 배우고 싶어 하는 사람들을 가르치는 발음 지도 강사들에 의해 널리 가르쳐졌다.

Why? 왜 정답일까?

'The accent that we identify as British today was developed around the time of the American Revolution by people of low birth rank who had become wealthy during the Industrial Revolution.'에서 오늘날 우리가

영국 악센트라고 인식하는 것은 산업혁명 기간 중 본래는 가난한 하층민이었다가 부를 거머쥐게 된 사람들에 의해 만들어졌다고 하는데, 이는 부의 축적과 함께 자신은 다른 평민과 다르다는 것을 드러내고 싶었던 사람들이 현대 영국 악센트를 만들어낸 것이라는 내용을 시사한다. 따라서 빈칸에 들어갈 말로 가장 적절한 것은 ① '사회적 지위'이다.

- **accent** ⓝ 악센트, 억양
- **settle** ⓥ 정착하다
- **wealthy** ⓐ 부유한
- **commoner** ⓝ 평민
- **elevated** ⓐ (지위가) 높은
- **pronunciation** ⓝ 발음
- **colonize** ⓥ 식민지로 만들다
- **identify** ⓥ 인식하다, 식별하다
- **distinguish** ⓥ 구별하다, 구분하다
- **set apart** ~와 구별시키다
- **standardize** ⓥ 표준화시키다

구문 풀이

7행 The accent [that we identify as British today] was developed
주어 / 주격 관계대명사 / →~라고 인식하다 / 동사(과거 수동)
around the time of the American Revolution by people of low birth
선행사
rank [who had become wealthy during the Industrial Revolution].
동사(과거완료) / 전치사(~하는 동안)
→주격 관계대명사

★★ 문제 해결 꿀~팁 ★★

▶ 많이 틀린 이유는?
빈칸의 근거가 될 말이 그대로 지문에 등장하지 않아 유추 및 일반화의 과정을 거쳐야 한다는 점에서 어려운 문제였다. 오답률은 대동소이한 가운데 ④에 다소 선택이 편중되었는데, 지문에 나온 **colonize, colonists** 등의 단어가 혼동을 유발한 것으로 보인다.

▶ 문제 해결 방법은?
핵심은 부유층이 '자신을 평민과 분리시키고 싶은' 욕구 때문에 현대 영국 악센트를 만들었다는 것이다. 여기서 분리는 당연히 돈에 따라온 '우월적인 지위'를 과시하는 행위로 이해할 수 있다.

★★★ 1등급 대비 고난도 3점 문제

11 기후 변화 대처가 '현재' 이루어지지 않는 이유   정답률 45% | 정답 ②

다음 빈칸에 들어갈 말로 가장 적절한 것을 고르시오. [3점]

① it is not related to science
그것이 과학과 관련이 없다
✓ it is far away in time and space
그것이 시공간적으로 멀리 떨어져 있다
③ energy efficiency matters the most
에너지 효율이 가장 중요하다
④ careful planning can fix the problem
신중한 계획이 문제를 해결할 수 있다
⑤ it is too late to prevent it from happening
그것이 일어나지 않도록 막기에는 너무 늦었다

Researchers are working on a project / that asks coastal towns / how they are preparing for rising sea levels.
연구원들은 프로젝트를 진행하고 있다. / 해안가 마을들에게 묻는 / 해수면 상승에 어떻게 대비하고 있는지

Some towns have risk assessments; / some towns even have a plan.
어떤 마을은 위험 평가를 하고 / 어떤 마을들은 심지어 계획을 가지고 있다.

But it's a rare town / that is actually carrying out a plan.
하지만 마을은 드물다 / 실제로 계획을 실행하고 있는

One reason we've failed to act on climate change / is the common belief / that it is far away in time and space.
우리가 기후 변화에 대처하는 데 실패한 한 가지 이유 / 일반적인 믿음 때문이다. / 그것이 시공간적으로 멀리 떨어져 있다는

For decades, / climate change was a prediction about the future, / so scientists talked about it in the future tense.
수십 년 동안, / 기후 변화는 미래에 대한 예측이었기 때문에 / 과학자들은 미래 시제로 기후 변화에 대해 이야기했다.

This became a habit — / so that even today / many scientists still use the future tense, / even though we know / that a climate crisis is ongoing.
이것이 습관이 되어 / 그 결과 오늘날에도 / 많은 과학자들이 여전히 미래 시제를 사용하고 있다. / 우리가 알고 있음에도, / 기후 위기가 진행중이라는 것을

Scientists also often focus on regions / most affected by the crisis, / such as Bangladesh or the West Antarctic Ice Sheet, / which for most Americans are physically remote.
과학자들은 또한 지역에 초점을 맞추고 있으며, / 위기의 영향을 가장 많이 받는 / 방글라데시나 서남극 빙상처럼 / 그 지역은 대부분의 미국인들에게는 물리적으로 멀리 떨어져 있다.

연구원들은 해안가 마을들이 해수면 상승에 어떻게 대비하고 있는지 묻는 프로젝트를 진행하고 있다. 어떤 마을들은 위험 평가를 하고 어떤 마을들은 심지

어 계획을 가지고 있다. 하지만 실제로 계획을 실행하고 있는 마을은 드물다. 우리가 기후 변화에 대처하는 데 실패한 한 가지 이유는 그것이 시공간적으로 멀리 떨어져 있다는 일반적인 믿음 때문이다. 수십 년 동안, 기후 변화는 미래에 대한 예측이었기 때문에 과학자들은 미래 시제로 기후 변화에 대해 이야기했다. 이것이 습관이 되어, 비록 우리가 기후 위기가 진행중이라는 것을 알고 있음에도, 많은 과학자들이 오늘날에도 여전히 미래 시제를 사용하고 있다. 과학자들은 또한 방글라데시나 서남극 빙상처럼 위기의 영향을 가장 많이 받는 지역에 초점을 맞추고 있으며, 그 지역은 대부분의 미국인들에게는 물리적으로 멀리 떨어져 있다.

Why? 왜 정답일까?

빈칸 뒤에 따르면, 기후 변화는 현재가 아닌 미래의 사건으로 여겨져 늘 미래 시제로 묘사되며(use the future tense), 기후 위기에 취약한 지역 또한 과학자들에게는 물리적으로 멀리 떨어진(physically remote) 곳이다. 다시 말해 기후 변화와 그로 인한 여파는 늘 '지금 여기와는 동떨어진' 사건으로 취급되고 있다는 것이 글의 핵심 내용이므로, 빈칸에 들어갈 말로 가장 적절한 것은 ② '그것이 시공간적으로 멀리 떨어져 있다'이다.

- **sea level** 해수면
- **prediction** ⓝ 예측
- **crisis** ⓝ 위기
- **Antarctic** ⓐ 남극의
- **remote** ⓐ 멀리 떨어진
- **assessment** ⓝ 평가
- **tense** ⓝ (문법) 시제
- **ongoing** ⓐ 진행 중인
- **physically** ⓐⓓ 물리적으로, 신체적으로

구문 풀이

5행 One reason [we've failed to act on climate change] is
주어 / [ ] : 관계부사절 / 동사(단수)
the common belief {that it is far away in time and space}.
주격 보어 / { } : 동격절(= the common belief)

★★ 문제 해결 꿀~팁 ★★

▶ 많이 틀린 이유는?
⑤는 일반적으로 많이 언급되는 내용이지만 글에서 보면 기후 변화를 막기에 '시간적으로 너무 늦었다'는 내용은 글에서 다뤄지지 않았다.

▶ 문제 해결 방법은?
빈칸이 글 중간에 있으면 주로 뒤에 답에 대한 힌트가 있다. 여기서도 빈칸 뒤를 보면, 과학자들은 기후 변화에 관해 아직도 미래 시제로 말하며, 지리적으로도 멀리 떨어진 곳을 연구하는 데 집중한다는 점을 지적하고 있다. 이는 기후 변화를 '시간·공간적으로 동떨어진' 일로 여기는 경향을 비판하는 것이다.

★★★ 1등급 대비 고난도 3점 문제

12 도시처럼 상호작용으로 작동하는 뇌   정답률 43% | 정답 ①

다음 빈칸에 들어갈 말로 가장 적절한 것을 고르시오. [3점]

✓ operates in isolation – 독립적으로 작동하지
② suffers from rapid changes – 급속한 변화로 고생하지
③ resembles economic elements – 경제적 요소를 닮지
④ works in a systematic way – 체계적으로 작동하지
⑤ interacts with another – 서로 상호 작용하지

Think of the brain as a city.
뇌를 도시라고 생각해보라.

If you were to look out over a city / and ask "where is the economy located?" / you'd see / there's no good answer to the question.
만약 당신이 도시를 내다보며 / "경제는 어디에 위치해 있나요?"라고 묻는다면 / 당신은 알게 될 것이다. / 그 질문에 좋은 답이 없다는 것을

Instead, / the economy emerges / from the interaction of all the elements / — from the stores and the banks / to the merchants and the customers.
대신, / 경제는 나타난다. / 모든 요소의 상호 작용으로부터 / 상점과 은행에서 / 상인과 고객에 이르기까지

And so it is with the brain's operation: / it doesn't happen in one spot.
뇌의 작용도 그렇다. / 즉 그것은 한 곳에서 일어나지 않는다.

Just as in a city, / no neighborhood of the brain / operates in isolation.
도시에서처럼, / 뇌의 어떤 지역도 ~않는다. / 독립적으로 작동하지

In brains and in cities, / everything emerges / from the interaction between residents, / at all scales, / locally and distantly.
뇌와 도시 안에서, / 모든 것은 나타난다. / 거주자들 간의 상호 작용으로부터 / 모든 규모로, / 근거리든 원거리든

Just as trains bring materials and textiles into a city, / which become processed into the economy, / so the raw electrochemical signals from sensory organs / are transported along superhighways of neurons.

기차가 자재와 직물을 도시로 들여오고, / 그것이 경제 속으로 처리되는 것처럼, / 감각 기관으로부터의 가공되지 않은 전기화학적 신호는 / 뉴런의 초고속도로를 따라서 전해진다.

There / the signals undergo processing / and transformation into our conscious reality.
거기서 / 신호는 처리를 겪는다. / 그리고 우리의 의식적인 현실로의 변형을

뇌를 도시라고 생각해보라. 만약 당신이 도시를 내다보며 "경제는 어디에 위치해 있나요?"라고 묻는다면 그 질문에 좋은 답이 없다는 것을 알게 될 것이다. 대신, 경제는 상점과 은행에서 상인과 고객에 이르기까지 모든 요소의 상호 작용으로부터 나타난다. 뇌의 작용도 그렇다. 즉 그것은 한 곳에서 일어나지 않는다. 도시에서처럼, 뇌의 어떤 지역도 독립적으로 작동하지 않는다. 뇌와 도시 안에서, 모든 것은 모든 규모로, 근거리든 원거리든, 거주자들 간의 상호 작용으로부터 나타난다. 기차가 자재와 직물을 도시로 들여오고, 그것이 경제 속으로 처리되는 것처럼, 감각 기관으로부터의 가공되지 않은 전기화학적 신호는 뉴런의 초고속도로를 따라서 전해진다. 거기서 신호는 처리와 우리의 의식적인 현실로의 변형을 겪는다.

Why? 왜 정답일까?

경제가 모든 요소의 상호 작용으로 작동하는 것처럼 뇌 또한 그렇다(**And so it is with the brain's operation: it doesn't happen in one spot.** / ~ **everything emerges from the interaction ~**)는 내용이므로, 빈칸에 들어갈 말로 가장 적절한 것은 ① '독립적으로 작동하지'이다.

- **think of A as B** A를 B로 여기다
- **element** ⓝ 요소
- **operation** ⓝ 작동, 작용
- **distantly** ⓐd 멀리, 원거리로
- **process** ⓥ 가공하다, 처리하다
- **electrochemical** ⓐ 전기화학의
- **transport** ⓥ 수송하다, 실어 나르다
- **transformation** ⓝ 변화, 변모
- **in isolation** 고립되어
- **emerge** ⓥ 나타나다, 생겨나다
- **merchant** ⓝ 상인
- **locally** ⓐd 국지적으로
- **textile** ⓝ 직물
- **raw** ⓐ 원재료의, 날것의
- **sensory organ** 감각 기관
- **undergo** ⓥ 거치다, 겪다
- **conscious** ⓐ 의식적인

구문 풀이

1행 If you were to look out over a city and ask "where is the
「if + 주어 + were to + 동사원형1 + ~   동사원형2 ~
economy located?" you'd see there's no good answer to the question.
주어 + 조동사 과거형 + 동사원형 : 가정법 미래(거의 불가능한 상황에 대한 가정)」

★★ 문제 해결 꿀~팁 ★★

▶ **많이 틀린 이유는?**
도시가 많은 경제 주체의 상호 작용을 통해 돌아가듯이 뇌 또한 수많은 요소의 상호 작용으로 돌아간다는 내용이다. 주어가 「no + 명사」 형태이므로, 빈칸에는 주제와 반대되는 말을 넣어야 문장 전체가 주제를 나타내게 된다. 하지만 ③은 '경제 주체와 비슷하다'는 주제를 직접 제시하므로, 이를 빈칸에 넣어 읽으면 '뇌의 그 어느 구역도 경제 주체와 비슷하지 않다'는 의미가 되어버린다. 즉 ③은 주제와 정반대되는 의미를 완성한다.

▶ **문제 해결 방법은?**
'뇌 = 도시'라는 비유를 확인하고, 둘의 공통점이 무엇인지 파악한 후, 선택지를 하나씩 대입하며 빈칸 문장의 의미를 주의 깊게 이해해 보자.

DAY 04 | 빈칸 추론 04

01 ④	02 ②	03 ③	04 ①	05 ①
06 ②	07 ①	08 ③	09 ③	10 ②
11 ②	12 ③			

01 우리 세계에서 과학이 가능한 이유   정답률 67% | 정답 ④

다음 빈칸에 들어갈 말로 가장 적절한 것을 고르시오.
① age - 나이
② luck - 행운
③ belief - 믿음
✔ rules - 법칙
⑤ interests - 흥미

If we lived on a planet where nothing ever changed, / there would be little to do.
우리가 만일 그 어떤 것도 변한 적이 없는 행성 위에 살았더라면, / 할 일이 거의 없었을 것이다.
There would be nothing to figure out / and there would be no reason for science.
알아내야 할 것도 없고 / 과학이 있을 이유도 없었을 것이다.
And if we lived in an unpredictable world, / where things changed in random or very complex ways, / we would not be able to figure things out.
그리고 만일 우리가 예측 불가한 세계에 살았더라면, / 만물이 무작위로 혹은 아주 복잡하게 변하는 / 우리는 상황을 알 수 없었을 것이다.
Again, there would be no such thing as science.
다시 한 번, 과학 같은 것은 없었을 것이다.
But we live in an in-between universe, / where things change, / but according to rules.
하지만 우리는 중간 세계에 살고 있다. / 만물이 변하기는 하되 / 법칙에 따라 변하는
If I throw a stick up in the air, / it always falls down.
내가 만일 막대를 공중에 던지면 / 이는 항상 떨어진다.
If the sun sets in the west, / it always rises again the next morning in the east.
태양은 서쪽으로 지면 / 항상 다음날 아침 동쪽에서 뜬다.
And so it becomes possible / to figure things out.
그래서 가능해진다. / 상황을 예측하는 것이
We can do science, / and with it we can improve our lives.
우리는 과학을 할 수 있고, / 과학을 가지고 삶을 개선해 나갈 수 있다.

우리가 만일 그 어떤 것도 변한 적이 없는 행성 위에 살았더라면, 할 일이 거의 없었을 것이다. 알아내야 할 것도 없고 과학이 있을 이유도 없었을 것이다. 그리고 만일 우리가 만물이 무작위로 혹은 아주 복잡하게 변하는 예측 불가한 세계에 살았더라면, 우리는 상황을 알 수 없었을 것이다. 다시 한 번, 과학 같은 것은 없었을 것이다. 하지만 우리는 만물이 변하기는 하되 법칙에 따라 변하는 중간 세계에 살고 있다. 내가 만일 막대를 공중에 던지면 이는 항상 떨어진다. 태양은 서쪽으로 지면 항상 다음날 아침 동쪽에서 뜬다. 그래서 상황을 예측하는 것이 가능해진다. 우리는 과학을 할 수 있고, 과학을 가지고 삶을 개선해 나갈 수 있다.

Why? 왜 정답일까?

빈칸 앞의 문장에서 현재의 반대를 상상하는 가정법 과거 구문을 통해 만일 우리가 무작위로 혹은 매우 복잡한 방식으로 만물이 변하는 세계에 살았더라면 과학 같은 것은 없었을 것(**And if we lived in an unpredictable world, where things changed in random or very complex ways, we would not be able to figure things out.**)이라고 말하는데, 빈칸 문장은 현실은 다행히도 그렇지 않고 만물이 변하기는 하되 일정한 '법칙'에 따라 변한다는 내용을 피력하고 있다. 따라서 빈칸에 들어갈 말로 가장 적절한 것은 법칙'이다. 빈칸 뒤에 나오는 막대 및 태양의 예에서 변화에는 반드시 정해진 패턴이나 결과가 있어 예측이 가능하다는 점을 부연하고 있다.

- **planet** ⓝ 행성
- **unpredictable** ⓐ 예측할 수 없는
- **complex** ⓐ 복잡한
- **universe** ⓝ 우주
- **set** ⓥ (해 또는 달이) 지다
- **figure out** 알아내다
- **random** ⓐ 무작위의
- **in-between** 중간의
- **according to** ~에 따라
- **improve** ⓥ 개선하다, 향상시키다

구문 풀이

4행 And if we lived in an unpredictable world, [where things
「if + 주어 + 과거 동사   관계부사
changed / in random or very complex ways], we would not be able
주어 + would + 동사원형 : 가정법 과거」
to figure things out.

02 소비의 목적 변화
정답률 44% | 정답 ②

다음 빈칸에 들어갈 말로 가장 적절한 것을 고르시오.

① quantitative – 양적인　　✔ nonmaterial – 비물질적인
③ nutritional – 영양의　　④ invariable – 불변의
⑤ economic – 경제적인

People have always needed to eat, / and they always will.
사람들은 항상 먹을 것이 필요했으며, / 또 항상 그럴 것이다.

Rising emphasis on self-expression values / does not put an end to material desires.
자기표현 가치에 관한 늘어나는 강조가 / 물질적 욕구를 끝내지는 않는다.

But / prevailing economic orientations are gradually being reshaped.
하지만 / 우세한 경제적 방향성이 서서히 재형성되고 있다.

People who work in the knowledge sector / continue to seek high salaries, / but they place equal or greater emphasis / on doing stimulating work / and being able to follow their own time schedules.
지식 부문에서 일하는 사람들은 / 계속 높은 급료를 추구하지만, / 그들은 그 이상의 중점을 둔다. / 아주 즐거운 일을 하고 / 자기 시간 계획을 따를 수 있는 것에

Consumption is becoming progressively less determined / by the need for sustenance / and the practical use of the goods consumed.
소비는 점진적으로 결정되는 경우가 덜해진다. / 생존에 대한 필요와 / 소비되는 재화의 실용적 사용으로

People still eat, / but a growing component of food's value / is determined by its nonmaterial aspects.
사람들은 여전히 먹지만, / 음식 가치의 점점 더 많은 구성 요소는 / 그것의 비물질적인 측면에 의해 결정된다.

People pay a premium / to eat exotic cuisines / that provide an interesting experience / or that symbolize a distinctive life-style.
사람들은 추가 금액을 낸다. / 이국적인 요리를 먹으려고 / 흥미로운 경험을 제공하거나 / 독특한 생활 방식을 상징하는

The publics of postindustrial societies / place growing emphasis on "political consumerism," / such as boycotting goods / whose production violates ecological or ethical standards.
탈공업화 사회의 대중은 / '정치적 소비주의'에 점점 더 많은 중점을 둔다. / 상품을 구매하기를 거부하는 것 같은 / 그것의 생산이 생태적 또는 윤리적 기준을 위반하는

Consumption is less and less a matter of sustenance / and more and more a question of life-style / — and choice.
소비는 생존의 문제로는 점점 덜 여겨지고, / 점점 더 생활 양식의 문제가 되고 있다. / 즉 선택

사람들은 항상 먹을 것이 필요했으며, 또 항상 그럴 것이다. 자기표현 가치에 관한 늘어나는 강조가 물질적 욕구를 끝내지는 않는다. 하지만 우세한 경제적 방향성이 서서히 재형성되고 있다. 지식 부문에서 일하는 사람들은 계속 높은 급료를 추구하지만, 그들은 아주 즐거운 일을 하고 자기 시간 계획을 따를 수 있는 것에 그 이상의 중점을 둔다. 소비는 점진적으로 생존에 대한 필요와 소비되는 재화의 실용적 사용으로 결정되는 경우가 덜해진다. 사람들은 여전히 먹지만, 음식 가치의 구성 요소는 점점 더 그것의 비물질적인 측면에 의해 결정된다. 사람들은 흥미로운 경험을 제공하거나 독특한 생활 방식을 상징하는 이국적인 요리를 먹으려고 추가 금액을 낸다. 탈공업화 사회의 대중은 '정치적 소비주의'에 점점 더 많은 중점을 두며, 생산이 생태적 또는 윤리적 기준을 위반하는 상품 구매를 거부하는 등의 행위를 한다. 소비는 생존의 문제로는 점점 덜 여겨지고, 점점 더 생활 양식, 즉 선택의 문제가 되고 있다.

Why? 왜 정답일까?

탈산업화 사회에서 소비는 생존의 문제보다는 생활 양식과 선택의 문제로 여겨지고 있다(Consumption is less and less a matter of sustenance and more and more a question of life-style — and choice.)는 내용이다. 빈칸 뒤에서 사람들이 이국적인 요리를 '경험'하는 것을 중시하고, 생태 또는 윤리적 가치를 위해 특정 물품 구매를 반대하는 등 '물질적이지 않은', 생활 양식적 측면에 의해 소비 행동을 결정하는 사례를 든다. 따라서 빈칸에 들어갈 말로 가장 적절한 것은 ② '비물질적인'이다.

● emphasis ⓝ 강조, 역점
● put an end to ~을 끝내다
● prevail ⓥ 우세하다
● gradually ⓐⓓ 점차
● seek ⓥ 추구하다
● place ⓥ 두다, 놓다
● stimulating ⓐ 아주 즐거운, 자극이 되는
● progressively ⓐⓓ 계속해서
● component ⓝ 구성 요소
● exotic ⓐ 이국적인
● symbolize ⓥ 상징하다
● postindustrial ⓐ 탈공업화의
● violate ⓥ 위반하다

● self-expression 자기 표현
● desire ⓝ 욕구, 욕망
● orientation ⓝ 방향, 지향
● reshape ⓥ 재형성하다
● salary ⓝ 급료
● equal ⓐ 똑같은
● consumption ⓝ 소비
● sustenance ⓝ 생명 유지, 지속
● premium ⓝ 추가 금액, 할증금
● cuisine ⓝ 요리
● distinctive ⓐ 독특한
● consumerism ⓝ 소비주의
● ecological ⓐ 생태적인

구문 풀이

5행 People [who work in the knowledge sector] continue to seek
　　　　주어　주격 관계대명사　　　　　　　동사(복수)
high salaries, but they place equal or greater emphasis on doing
　　　　　　　　　　　　　　　전치사↲　동명사1
stimulating work and being able to follow their own time schedules.
동명사2

---

03 자신만의 가치 기준에 근거한 목표 수립의 필요성
정답률 71% | 정답 ③

다음 빈칸에 들어갈 말로 가장 적절한 것을 고르시오. [3점]

① your moral duty – 자신의 도덕적 의무　　② a strict deadline – 엄격한 기한
✔ your own values – 자신만의 가치 기준　　④ parental guidance – 부모의 지도
⑤ job market trends – 직업 시장의 추세

It's hard enough to stick with goals / you want to accomplish, / but sometimes we make goals / we're not even thrilled about in the first place.
목표를 고수하는 것은 매우 어렵지만, / 당신이 이루고 싶은 / 때때로 우리는 목표를 세우기도 한다. / 심지어 애초부터 우리가 감동받지 못할

We set resolutions / based on what we're supposed to do, / or what others think we're supposed to do, / rather than what really matters to us.
우리는 다짐을 한다. / 우리가 해야만 하는 것에 기초하여 / 또는 다른 사람들이 생각하기에 우리가 해야만 하는 것 / 우리에게 진짜 중요한 것이라기보다

This makes it nearly impossible / to stick to the goal.
이는 거의 불가능하게 만든다. / 목표를 고수하는 것

For example, reading more is a good habit, / but if you're only doing it / because you feel like / that's what you're supposed to do, / not because you actually want to learn more, / you're going to have a hard time / reaching the goal.
예를 들어, 독서를 더 하는 것은 좋은 습관이지만, / 당신이 오로지 그렇게 하고 있다면, / 당신이 ~처럼 느껴서 / 그것이 당신이 해야만 하는 것처럼 / 당신이 실제로 더 배우기를 원해서가 아니라 / 당신은 어려움을 겪을 것이다. / 목표에 도달하는 데

Instead, make goals / based on your own values.
대신에, 목표를 세워라. / 자신만의 가치 기준에 기초하여

Now, this isn't to say / you should read less.
이제, 말하려는 것이 아니다. / 당신이 독서를 더 적게 해야 한다는 것을

The idea is to first consider what matters to you, / then figure out what you need to do / to get there.
핵심은 우선 자신에게 무엇이 중요한지 생각하는 것이고, / 그 다음 당신이 할 필요가 있는 일을 알아내는 것이다. / 목표에 도달하기 위해

당신이 이루고 싶은 목표를 고수하는 것은 매우 어렵지만, 때때로 우리는 심지어 애초부터 우리가 감동받지 못할 목표를 세우기도 한다. 우리는 우리에게 진짜 중요한 것이라기보다 우리가 해야만 하는 것, 또는 다른 사람들이 생각하기에 우리가 해야만 하는 것에 기초하여 다짐을 한다. 이는 목표를 고수하는 것을 거의 불가능하게 만든다. 예를 들어, 독서를 더 하는 것은 좋은 습관이지만, 실제로 더 배우기를 원해서가 아니라 해야만 하는 것처럼 느껴서 그렇게 하고 있다면, 당신은 목표에 도달하는 데 어려움을 겪을 것이다. 대신에, 자신만의 가치 기준에 기초하여 목표를 세워라. 이제 독서를 더 적게 해야 한다는 것을 말하려는 것이 아니다. 핵심은 우선 자신에게 무엇이 중요한지 생각한 다음, 목표에 도달하기 위해 할 필요가 있는 일을 알아내는 것이다.

Why? 왜 정답일까?

'The idea is to first consider what matters to you, then figure out what you need to do to get there.'에서 스스로에게 뭐가 중요한지를 먼저 고민하고 목표에 도달하려면 무엇을 해야 하는지 파악하라고 이야기하는데, 여기서 핵심은 남들이 해야 한다고 말하는 것에 근거하여 결심을 하기보다는 자기 자신에게 필요한 것을 파악하라는 데 있다. 따라서 빈칸에 들어갈 말로 가장 적절한 것은 ③ '자신만의 가치 기준'이다.

● stick with ~을 고수하다
● resolution ⓝ 다짐, 결심
● actually ⓐⓓ 실제로

● accomplish ⓥ 성취하다, 달성하다
● impossible ⓐ 불가능한
● figure out 알아내다, 이해하다

구문 풀이

3행 We set resolutions based on [what we're supposed to do], or
　　　　　　　　　　　　　관계대명사(~것)
[what (others think) we're supposed to do], rather than [what really matters to us].
관계대명사(~것) 삽입절(~가 생각하기로는)　~라기보다는, ~ 대신에 관계대명사(~것)

04 수생 생물의 특성을 유지하며 발달한 개구리 정답률 60% | 정답 ①

다음 빈칸에 들어갈 말로 가장 적절한 것을 고르시오. [3점]

☑ still kept many ties to the water
여전히 물과의 여러 인연을 유지했다
② had almost all the necessary organs
필요한 신체 기관을 거의 모두 갖추고 있었다
③ had to develop an appetite for new foods
새로운 음식에 대한 식욕을 발달시켜야 했다
④ often competed with land-dwelling species
땅에 사는 생물 종들과 종종 경쟁했다
⑤ suffered from rapid changes in temperature
기온의 급격한 변화로 고생했다

Scientists believe / that the frogs' ancestors were water-dwelling, fishlike animals.
과학자들은 믿는다. / 개구리의 조상이 물에 사는, 물고기 같은 동물이었다고

The first frogs and their relatives / gained the ability / to come out on land / and enjoy the opportunities for food and shelter there.
최초의 개구리와 그들의 친척은 / 능력을 얻었다. / 육지로 나와 / 그곳에서 먹을 것과 살 곳에 대한 기회를 누릴 수 있는

But they still kept many ties to the water.
하지만 개구리는 여전히 물과의 여러 인연을 유지했다.

A frog's lungs do not work very well, / and it gets part of its oxygen / by breathing through its skin.
개구리의 폐는 그다지 기능을 잘하지 않고, / 개구리는 산소를 일부 얻는다. / 피부를 통해 호흡함으로써

But for this kind of "breathing" to work properly, / the frog's skin must stay moist.
하지만 이런 종류의 '호흡'이 제대로 이뤄지기 위해서는, / 개구리의 피부가 촉촉하게 유지되어야 한다.

And so the frog must remain near the water / where it can take a dip every now and then / to keep from drying out.
그래서 개구리는 물의 근처에 있어야 한다. / 이따금 몸을 잠깐 담글 수 있는 / 건조해지는 것을 막기 위해

Frogs must also lay their eggs in water, / as their fishlike ancestors did.
개구리 역시 물속에 알을 낳아야 한다. / 물고기 같은 조상들이 그랬던 것처럼.

And eggs laid in the water / must develop into water creatures, / if they are to survive.
그리고 물속에 낳은 알은 / 물에 사는 생물로 발달해야 한다. / 그것들이 살아남으려면

For frogs, / metamorphosis thus provides the bridge / between the water-dwelling young forms and the land-dwelling adults.
개구리에게 있어서 / 따라서 탈바꿈은 다리를 제공한다. / 물에 사는 어린 형체와 육지에 사는 성체를 이어주는

과학자들은 개구리의 조상이 물에 사는, 물고기 같은 동물이었다고 믿는다. 최초의 개구리와 그들의 친척은 육지로 나와 그곳에서 먹을 것과 살 곳에 대한 기회를 누릴 수 있는 능력을 얻었다. 하지만 개구리는 여전히 물과의 여러 인연을 유지했다. 개구리의 폐는 그다지 기능을 잘하지 않고, 개구리는 피부를 통해 호흡함으로써 산소를 일부 얻는다. 하지만 이런 종류의 '호흡'이 제대로 이뤄지기 위해서는, 개구리의 피부가 촉촉하게 유지되어야 한다. 그래서 개구리는 건조해지는 것을 막기 위해 이따금 몸을 잠깐 담글 수 있는 물의 근처에 있어야 한다. 물고기 같은 조상들이 그랬던 것처럼, 개구리 역시 물속에 알을 낳아야 한다. 그리고 물속에 낳은 알이 살아남으려면, 물에 사는 생물로 발달해야 한다. 따라서, 개구리에게 있어서 탈바꿈은 물에 사는 어린 형체와 육지에 사는 성체를 이어주는 다리를 제공한다.

Why? 왜 정답일까?

개구리는 당초 물고기 같은 동물로 기원하여 육지에서 생활하도록 진화했지만 여전히 '물에 사는' 생물로서의 특징을 지니고 있다는 내용의 글이다. 빈칸 뒤에서 개구리는 폐가 그다지 발달해 있지 않아 피부를 이용해 호흡하는데, 호흡이 원활하기 위해서는 피부가 늘 젖어 있어야 하고, 따라서 물을 가까이 해야 하며, 알 또한 물속에 낳아 번식해야 하기에 '물에 살기 적합한' 생물로 발달할 수밖에 없는 운명임을 설명하고 있다. 이러한 흐름을 근거로 볼 때, 빈칸에 들어갈 말로 가장 적절한 것은 개구리가 '물고기다운' 특성을 완전히 포기하지 않았다는 의미의 ① '여전히 물과의 여러 인연을 유지했다'이다.

● ancestor ⓝ 조상
● relative ⓝ 친척
● moist ⓐ 촉촉한
● dry out 건조하다, 바짝 마르다
● tie ⓝ 관계, 연결
● appetite ⓝ 식욕
● dwell ⓥ 거주하다, 살다
● properly [ad] 적절히
● take a dip 잠깐 수영을 하다
● lay ⓥ (알을) 낳다
● organ ⓝ (신체) 기관
● compete with ~와 경쟁하다

구문 풀이

7행 But for this kind of "breathing" to work properly, the frog's
　　　　　　　　의미상 주어　　　　　　　부사적 용법(~하려면)
skin must stay moist.
　2형식 동사　보어

---

05 우리의 존재를 규정하는 기억 정답률 62% | 정답 ①

다음 빈칸에 들어갈 말로 가장 적절한 것을 고르시오.

☑ makes us who we are – 우리를 우리 모습으로 만들어 준다
② has to do with our body – 우리 신체와 관련이 있다
③ reflects what we expect – 우리의 예상을 반영한다
④ lets us understand others – 우리가 남을 이해하게 해준다
⑤ helps us learn from the past – 우리가 과거로부터 배우도록 도와준다

Not only does memory / underlie our ability to think at all, / it defines the content of our experiences / and how we preserve them for years to come.
기억은 ~할 뿐만 아니라 / 어쨌든 우리의 사고력의 기반이 될 / 그것은 우리의 경험의 내용을 규정한다. / 그리고 다가올 수년 간 우리가 그것을 보존하는 방식을

Memory makes us who we are.
기억은 우리를 우리 모습으로 만들어 준다.

If I were to suffer from heart failure / and depend upon an artificial heart, / I would be no less myself.
만약 내가 심부전을 앓고 / 인공 심장에 의존한다 해도 / 나는 역시 여느 때의 나일 것이다.

If I lost an arm in an accident / and had it replaced with an artificial arm, / I would still be essentially *me*.
만약 내가 사고로 한 팔을 잃고 / 그것을 인공 팔로 교체한다 해도 / 나는 여전히 본질적으로 나일 것이다.

As long as my mind and memories remain intact, / I will continue to be the same person, / no matter which part of my body (other than the brain) is replaced.
나의 정신과 기억이 손상되지 않은 한, / 나는 계속 같은 사람일 것이다. / (뇌를 제외하고) 내 신체의 어떤 부분이 교체될지라도

On the other hand, / when someone suffers from advanced Alzheimer's disease / and his memories fade, / people often say / that he "is not himself anymore," / or that it is as if the person "is no longer there," / though his body remains unchanged.
반면 / 누군가 후기 알츠하이머병을 앓고 / 그의 기억이 흐려진다면, / 사람들은 종종 말한다. / 그는 '더 이상 여느 때의 그가 아니'라거나 / 마치 그 사람이 '더 이상 그곳에 없다'는 것 같다고 / 비록 그의 신체는 변하지 않은 채로 남아 있음에도 불구하고

기억은 어쨌든 우리의 사고력의 기반이 될 뿐만 아니라 우리의 경험의 내용과 다가올 수년 간 우리가 그것을 보존하는 방식을 규정한다. 기억은 우리를 우리 모습으로 만들어 준다. 만약 내가 심부전을 앓고 인공 심장에 의존한다 해도 나는 역시 여느 때의 나일 것이다. 만약 내가 사고로 한 팔을 잃고 인공 팔로 교체한다 해도 나는 여전히 본질적으로 나일 것이다. 나의 정신과 기억이 손상되지 않은 한, (뇌를 제외하고) 내 신체의 어떤 부분이 교체될지라도 나는 계속 같은 사람일 것이다. 반면 누군가 후기 알츠하이머병을 앓고 그의 기억이 흐려진다면, 비록 그의 신체는 변하지 않은 채로 남아 있음에도 불구하고 사람들은 종종 '더 이상 여느 때의 그가 아니'라거나 마치 그 사람이 '더 이상 그곳에 없'는 것 같다고 말한다.

Why? 왜 정답일까?

빈칸 뒤에서 예시를 통해 우리는 기억을 보존하는 한 같은 사람으로 여겨지지만 (As long as my mind and memories remain intact, I will continue to be the same person, ~) 기억을 잃는 경우에는 그렇지 않다는 내용을 제시하고 있다. 따라서 예시 내용을 요약하는 빈칸에 들어갈 말로 가장 적절한 것은 기억이 곧 우리 존재의 본질을 결정짓는다는 의미의 ① '우리를 우리 모습으로 만들어 준다'이다.

● underlie ⓥ (~의) 기반을 이루다
● fade ⓥ 흐려지다, (빛이) 바래다
● essentially [ad] 본질적으로

구문 풀이

4행 If I were to suffer from heart failure and depend upon an
　　　├───→「if + 주어 + were to + 동사원형 ~」───┤
artificial heart, I would be no less myself.
　　　주어 + 조동사 과거형 + 동사원형 : 가정법 미래(가능성이 희박한 일)

---

06 신체로부터 발생하는 감정 정답률 57% | 정답 ②

다음 빈칸에 들어갈 말로 가장 적절한 것을 고르시오. [3점]

① language guides our actions – 언어가 우리 행동을 이끈다
☑ emotions arise from our bodies – 감정이 우리 신체에서 발생한다
③ body language hides our feelings – 신체 언어는 우리 감정을 숨긴다
④ what others say affects our mood – 다른 사람들의 말이 우리 감정에 영향을 미친다
⑤ negative emotions easily disappear – 부정적 감정은 쉽게 사라진다

Someone else's body language affects our own body, / which then creates an emotional echo / that makes us feel accordingly.
다른 사람의 신체 언어는 우리 자신의 신체에 영향을 미치며, / 그것은 그 후 감정적인 메아리를 만들어낸다. / 우리가 그에 맞춰 느끼게 하는

As Louis Armstrong sang, / "When you're smiling, / the whole world smiles with you."
Louis Armstrong이 노래했듯이, / "당신이 미소 지을 때, / 전 세계가 당신과 함께 미소 짓는다."

If copying another's smile / makes us feel happy, / the emotion of the smiler / has been transmitted via our body.
만약 다른 사람의 미소를 따라 하는 것이 / 우리를 행복하게 한다면, / 그 미소 짓는 사람의 감정은 / 우리의 신체를 통해 전달된 것이다.

Strange as it may sound, / this theory states / that emotions arise from our bodies.
이상하게 들릴지 모르지만, / 이 이론은 말한다. / 감정이 우리 신체에서 발생한다고

For example, / our mood can be improved / by simply lifting up the corners of our mouth.
예를 들어, / 우리의 기분은 좋아질 수 있다. / 단순히 입꼬리를 올리는 것으로

If people are asked / to bite down on a pencil lengthwise, / taking care not to let the pencil touch their lips / (thus forcing the mouth into a smile-like shape), / they judge cartoons funnier / than if they have been asked to frown.
만약 사람들이 요구받으면, / 연필을 긴 방향으로 꽉 물라고 / 연필이 입술에 닿지 않도록 조심하면서 / (그래서 억지로 입을 미소 짓는 것과 같은 모양이 되도록), / 그들은 만화를 더 재미있다고 판단한다. / 그들이 인상을 찌푸리라고 요구받은 경우보다

The primacy of the body / is sometimes summarized in the phrase / "I must be afraid, / because I'm running."
신체가 우선한다는 것은 / 때때로 구절로 요약된다. / "나는 분명 두려운가보다, / 왜냐하면 나는 도망치고 있기 때문이다."라는

다른 사람의 신체 언어는 우리 자신의 신체에 영향을 미치며, 그것은 그 후 우리가 그에 맞춰 (감정을) 느끼게 하는 감정적인 메아리를 만들어낸다. Louis Armstrong이 노래했듯이, "당신이 미소 지을 때, 전 세계가 당신과 함께 미소 짓는다." 만약 다른 사람의 미소를 따라 하는 것이 우리를 행복하게 한다면, 그 미소 짓는 사람의 감정은 우리의 신체를 통해 전달된 것이다. 이상하게 들릴지 모르지만, 이 이론은 감정이 우리 신체에서 발생한다고 말한다. 예를 들어, 우리의 기분은 단순히 입꼬리를 올리는 것으로 좋아질 수 있다. 만약 사람들이 연필을 긴 방향으로 꽉 물라고 요구받으면, 연필이 입술에 닿지 않도록 조심하면서 (그래서 억지로 입을 미소 짓는 것과 같은 모양이 되도록), 그들은 인상을 찌푸리라고 요구받은 경우보다 만화를 더 재미있다고 판단한다. 신체가 (감정에) 우선한다는 것은 "나는 분명 두려운가보다, 왜냐하면 나는 도망치고 있기 때문이다."라는 구절로 때때로 요약된다.

Why? 왜 정답일까?

빈칸 뒤의 실험에서 우리가 입꼬리를 올리고 있다 보면 더 기분이 좋아질 수 있다(~ our mood can be improved by simply lifting up the corners of our mouth.)고 설명하고, 이를 마지막 문장에서는 '(감정에 대한) 신체의 우선(The primacy of the body)'이라고 요약했다. 따라서 빈칸에 들어갈 말로 가장 적절한 것은 ② '감정이 우리 신체에서 발생한다'이다.

- emotional ⓐ 정서적인
- transmit ⓥ 전달하다
- theory ⓝ 이론
- lift up ~을 들어올리다
- bite down on ~을 깨물다
- frown ⓥ 얼굴을 찡그리다
- summarize ⓥ 요약하다
- hide ⓥ 숨기다
- accordingly ⓐ 그에 따라
- via prep ~을 통해서
- state ⓥ 진술하다
- be asked to ~하도록 요청받다
- lengthwise ⓐ 길게
- primacy ⓝ 우선함
- arise from ~에서 생겨나다

구문 풀이

7행 Strange as it may sound, this theory states that emotions
「보어+as+주어+동사 : 비록 ~일지라도(양보 구문)」
arise from our bodies.

★★★ 1등급 대비 고난도 2절 문제

07 원하는 것과 해야 할 것   정답률 41% | 정답 ①

다음 빈칸에 들어갈 말로 가장 적절한 것을 고르시오.

✔ desires – 욕망   ② merits – 장점
③ abilities – 능력   ④ limitations – 한계
⑤ worries – 걱정

In a culture / where there is a belief / that you can have anything you truly want, / there is no problem in choosing.

문화에서는 / 믿음이 있는 / 당신이 진정으로 원하는 것은 무엇이든지 가질 수 있다는 / 선택이 문제가 안 된다.

Many cultures, however, / do not maintain this belief.
그러나 많은 문화들은 / 이러한 믿음을 유지하지 못한다.

In fact, / many people do not believe / that life is about getting what you want.
사실, / 많은 사람들은 믿지 않는다. / 삶이란 당신이 원하는 것을 얻는 것이라고

Life is about doing what you are *supposed* to do.
인생은 당신이 *해야* 할 것을 하는 것이다.

The reason they have trouble making choices / is / they believe / that what they may want is not related / to what they are supposed to do.
그들이 선택을 하는 데 있어 어려움을 겪는 이유는 / ~이다. / 그들이 믿기 때문에 / 그들이 원하는 것이 관련이 없다고 / 그들이 해야 할 일과

The weight of outside considerations / is greater than their desires.
외적으로 고려할 문제의 비중이 / 그들의 욕망보다 더 크다.

When this is an issue in a group, / we discuss what makes for good decisions.
이것이 어떤 집단에서 논의 대상이 될 때, / 우리는 어떤 것이 좋은 결정인지 의논을 한다.

If a person can be unburdened from their cares and duties / and, just for a moment, / consider what appeals to them, / they get the chance / to sort out what is important to them.
만약 어떤 사람이 걱정과 의무로부터 벗어나 / 잠시 동안 / 자신에게 호소하는 것이 무엇인지를 생각해 볼 수 있다면, / 그들은 기회를 얻게 된다. / 자신에게 무엇이 중요한지를 가려낼

Then they can consider and negotiate / with their external pressures.
그러고 나서 그들은 고려하고 협상할 수 있다. / 외적인 부담에 대해

당신이 진정으로 원하는 것은 무엇이든지 가질 수 있다고 믿는 문화에서는 선택이 문제가 안 된다. 그러나 많은 문화들은 이러한 믿음을 유지하지 못한다. 사실, 많은 사람들은 삶이란 당신이 원하는 것을 얻는 것이라고 믿지 않는다. 인생은 당신이 *해야* 할 것을 하는 것이다. 그들이 선택을 하는 데 있어 어려움을 겪는 이유는 그들이 원하는 것이 그들이 해야 할 일과 관련이 없다고 믿기 때문이다. 외적으로 고려할 문제의 비중이 그들의 욕망보다 더 크다. 이것이 어떤 집단에서 논의 대상이 될 때, 우리는 어떤 것이 좋은 결정인지 의논을 한다. 만약 어떤 사람이 걱정과 의무로부터 벗어나 자신에게 호소하는 것이 무엇인지를 잠시 동안 생각해 볼 수 있다면, 그들은 자신에게 무엇이 중요한지를 가려낼 기회를 얻게 된다. 그러고 나서 그들은 외적인 부담에 대해 고려하고 협상할 수 있다.

Why? 왜 정답일까?

첫 두 문장에 따르면 많은 문화권에서 원하는 것을 다 가질 수 있다는 믿음이 유지되지 못한다고 한다. 이를 근거로 할 때, 빈칸이 포함된 문장은 '원하는 것' 이외에 고려할 문제가 더 많다는 의미여야 한다. 따라서 빈칸에 들어갈 말로 가장 적절한 것은 ① '욕망'이다.

- maintain ⓥ 유지하다
- weight ⓝ 비중, 무게
- negotiate ⓥ 협상하다
- desire ⓝ 욕망
- limitation ⓝ 한계
- have trouble ~ing ~하는 데 어려움을 겪다
- consideration ⓝ 고려 사항
- external ⓐ 외부적인
- merit ⓝ 장점

구문 풀이

1행 In a culture [where there is a belief {that you can have anything
            선행사   관계부사   { } : 동격(= a belief)
you truly want}], there is no problem in choosing.
                동사   주어

★★ 문제 해결 꿀~팁 ★★

▶ 많이 틀린 이유는?
이 글은 우리가 원하는 바를 모두 성취하지 못하고 해야 하는 일 등 외부적 요소를 고려하여 선택을 하는 경우가 대부분이라는 내용을 다루고 있다. '능력'에 관해서는 중요하게 언급되지 않으므로 ③은 빈칸에 부적절하다.

▶ 문제 해결 방법은?
'what you want'와 'what you are *supposed* to do'가 두 가지 핵심 소재인데, 빈칸 문장의 outside consideration은 이중 'what you are *supposed* to do'와 같은 말이다. 따라서 빈칸에는 'what you want'를 달리 표현하는 말이 들어가야 한다.

★★★ 1등급 대비 고난도 2절 문제

08 모든 주의력을 활용하려는 인간의 욕구   정답률 39% | 정답 ③

다음 빈칸에 들어갈 말로 가장 적절한 것을 고르시오.

① to please others with what we are good at
우리가 잘하는 것으로 남들을 기쁘게 하려

② to pay more attention to the given task
주어진 과업에 더 많은 주의를 기울이려고
✓ to find outlets for our unused attention
사용되지 않은 주의력의 배출구를 찾으려고
④ to play with a stronger opponent
더 강한 상대와 경기하려고
⑤ to give our brain a short break
우리 뇌에 짧은 휴식을 주려고

We have to recognize / that there always exists in us / the strongest need to utilize *all* our attention.
우리는 인정해야 한다. / 우리 안에 항상 존재한다는 것을 / 우리의 모든 주의력을 활용하려는 매우 강력한 욕구가

And this is quite evident / in the great amount of displeasure we feel / any time the entirety of our capacity for attention is not being put to use.
그리고 이것은 꽤 명백해진다. / 우리가 느끼는 엄청난 양의 불쾌감에서 / 우리의 주의력 전체가 사용되지 않고 있을 때마다

When this is the case, / we will seek to find outlets / for our unused attention.
이런 경우가 되면, / 우리는 배출구를 찾으려고 할 것이다. / 사용되지 않은 주의력의

If we are playing a chess game with a weaker opponent, / we will seek to supplement this activity with another: / such as watching TV, / or listening to music, / or playing another chess game at the same time.
만약 우리가 더 약한 상대와 체스 게임을 하고 있다면, / 우리는 이 활동을 또 다른 것으로 보충하려고 할 것이다. / 즉 TV 시청이나 / 음악 감상, / 또는 동시에 다른 체스 게임 하기와 같은 것

Very often this reveals itself in unconscious movements, / such as playing with something in one's hands / or pacing around the room; / and if such an action also serves to increase pleasure or relieve displeasure, / all the better.
이것은 무의식적인 움직임들로 매우 자주 나타나며, / 자기 손 안의 무언가를 가지고 놀거나 방을 돌아다니는 것과 같은 / 만약 그런 행동이 기쁨을 증가시키거나 불쾌감을 덜어주는 데에도 또한 도움이 된다면 / 더할 나위 없이 좋을 것이다.

우리는 우리의 모든 주의력을 활용하려는 매우 강력한 욕구가 우리 안에 항상 존재한다는 것을 인정해야 한다. 그리고 이것은 우리의 주의력 전체가 사용되지 않고 있을 때마다 우리가 느끼는 엄청난 양의 불쾌감에서 꽤 명백해진다. 이런 경우가 되면, 우리는 사용되지 않은 주의력의 배출구를 찾으려고 할 것이다. 만약 우리가 더 약한 상대와 체스 게임을 하고 있다면, 우리는 이 활동을 또 다른 것, 즉 TV 시청이나 음악 감상, 또는 동시에 다른 체스 게임을 하는 것 등으로 보충하려고 할 것이다. 이것은 자기 손 안의 무언가를 가지고 놀거나 방을 돌아다니는 것과 같은 무의식적인 움직임들로 매우 자주 나타나며, 만약 그런 행동이 기쁨을 증가시키거나 불쾌감을 덜어주는 데에도 또한 도움이 된다면 더할 나위 없이 좋을 것이다.

Why? 왜 정답일까?

'We have to recognize that there always exists in us the strongest need to utilize *all* our attention.'에서 우리는 주의력을 모두 활용하려는 욕구를 지니고 있다는 내용이 제시된 데 이어, 빈칸 뒤의 문장에서는 주의력이 남는 경우 동시에 다른 활동을 하며 주의력을 더 활용하려 한다는 구체적인 예시를 든다. 따라서 빈칸에 들어갈 말로 가장 적절한 것은 ③ '사용되지 않은 주의력의 배출구를 찾으려고'이다.

- **utilize** ⓥ 활용하다, 이용하다
- **displeasure** ⓝ 불쾌감
- **capacity** ⓝ 용량
- **seek** ⓥ 추구하다
- **reveal** ⓥ 드러내다
- **pace around** 돌아다니다
- **outlet** ⓝ (감정·생각·에너지의 바람직한) 배출구, 발산 수단
- **evident** ⓐ 명백한
- **entirety** ⓝ 전체, 전부
- **this is the case** 이것이 사실이다
- **opponent** ⓝ (게임·경기 등의) 상대, 반대자
- **unconscious** ⓐ 무의식적인, 무심결의
- **relieve** ⓥ 덜다, 완화하다

구문 풀이

2행 And this is quite evident in the great amount of displeasure [we feel / any time (when) the entirety of our capacity for attention is not being put to use].
~선행사
~할 때는 언제든지 ~ 주어
현재진행 수동태(~되고 있지 않다)

★★ 문제 해결 꿀~팁 ★★

▶ 많이 틀린 이유는?
주제문을 완성하는 빈칸 문제로, 앞에는 배경 설명이, 뒤에는 예시가 나온다. ④의 경우 예시로 언급된 체스 게임과 관련되어 있으나 더 강한 상대와 겨룬다는 내용이 글과 무관하다.

▶ 문제 해결 방법은?
빈칸 앞의 배경 설명보다는 빈칸의 내용을 더 쉽게 풀이해주는 예시 부분을 중점적으로 읽어 답을 찾도록 한다. 예시 문장의 '~ we will seek to supplement this activity with another ~'를 재진술한 것이 ③이다.

★★★ 1등급 대비 고난도 2점 문제

09 정보 공유에 있어 대면 상호작용의 중요성 정답률 49% | 정답 ③

다음 빈칸에 들어갈 말로 가장 적절한 것을 고르시오.
① natural talent – 천부적 재능
② regular practice – 규칙적인 연습
✓ personal contact – 개인적인 접촉
④ complex knowledge – 복잡한 지식
⑤ powerful motivation – 강력한 동기

Face-to-face interaction / is a uniquely powerful — and sometimes the only — way / to share many kinds of knowledge, / from the simplest to the most complex.
대면 상호 작용은 / 유례 없이 강력한 — 때로는 유일한 — 방법이다. / 많은 종류의 지식을 공유하는 / 가장 간단한 것부터 가장 복잡한 것까지

It is one of the best ways / to stimulate new thinking and ideas, / too.
그것은 가장 좋은 방법의 한 가지이다. / 새로운 생각과 아이디어를 자극하는 / 또한

Most of us would have had difficulty learning / how to tie a shoelace only from pictures, / or how to do arithmetic from a book.
우리 대부분이 배웠다면 어려움을 겪었을 것이다. / 그림만으로 신발 끈 묶는 법 / 또는 책으로부터 계산하는 방법을

Psychologist Mihàly Csikszentmihàlyi found, / while studying high achievers, / that a large number of Nobel Prize winners / were the students of previous winners: / they had access to the same literature as everyone else, / but personal contact made a crucial difference / to their creativity.
심리학자 Mihàly Csikszentmihàlyi는 발견했다. / 높은 성취도를 보이는 사람들을 연구하면서 / 다수의 노벨상 수상자가 / 이전 수상자들의 학생이라는 것을 / 그들은 다른 모든 사람들과 똑같은 문헌에 접근할 수 있었지만, / 개인적인 접촉이 결정적인 차이를 만들었다. / 이들의 창의성에

Within organisations / this makes conversation / both a crucial factor for high-level professional skills / and the most important way of sharing everyday information.
조직 내에서 / 이것은 대화를 만든다. / 고급 전문 기술을 위한 매우 중요한 요소이자 / 일상 정보를 공유하는 가장 중요한 방식으로

대면 상호 작용은 가장 간단한 것부터 가장 복잡한 것까지 많은 종류의 지식을 공유하는 유례 없이 강력한 — 때로는 유일한 — 방법이다. 그것은 새로운 생각과 아이디어를 자극하는 최고의 방법 중 하나이기도 하다. 우리 대부분이 그림으로만 신발 끈 묶는 법을 배웠거나, 책으로 셈법을 배웠다면 어려움을 겪었을 것이다. 심리학자 Mihàly Csikszentmihàlyi는 높은 성취도를 보이는 사람들을 연구하면서 다수의 노벨상 수상자가 이전 (노벨상) 수상자들의 학생들이라는 것을 발견했다. 그들은 다른 모든 사람들과 똑같은 (연구) 문헌에 접근할 수 있었지만, 개인적인 접촉이 이들의 창의성에 결정적인 차이를 만들었다. 이로 인해 조직 내에서 대화는 고급 전문 기술을 위한 매우 중요한 요소이자 일상 정보를 공유하는 가장 중요한 방식이 된다.

Why? 왜 정답일까?

첫 문장과 마지막 문장에서 정보를 공유하는 가장 중요한 방법으로 대면 상호 작용(Face-to-face interaction) 또는 대화(conversation)를 언급하고 있다. 따라서 빈칸에 들어갈 말로 가장 적절한 것은 ③ '개인적인 접촉'이다.

- **interaction** ⓝ 상호 작용
- **simplest** ⓐ 가장 간단한
- **stimulate** ⓥ 자극하다
- **achiever** ⓝ 성취도를 보이는 사람
- **conversation** ⓝ 대화
- **uniquely** ⓐⅾ 유례없이
- **complex** ⓐ 복잡한
- **arithmetic** ⓝ 산수
- **crucial** ⓐ 아주 중요한, 중대한
- **factor** ⓝ 요소

구문 풀이

5행 Most of us would have had difficulty learning {how to tie a
「have difficulty + 동명사」: ~하는 데 어려움을 겪다
shoelace} only from pictures, or {how to do arithmetic} from a book.
{ }: 명사구(how + to부정사: ~하는 방법)

★★ 문제 해결 꿀~팁 ★★

▶ 많이 틀린 이유는?
글 처음과 마지막에 many kinds of knowledge, from the simplest to the most complex 또는 high-level professional skills와 같은 표현이 등장하므로 얼핏 보면 ④가 적절해 보인다. 하지만 빈칸은 이러한 정보 공유나 전문 능력 개발에 '무엇이 영향을 미치는지' 그 요인을 밝히는 것이므로 ④를 빈칸에 넣기는 부적절하다.

▶ 문제 해결 방법은?
첫 문장의 Face-to-face interaction과 마지막 문장의 conversation이 키워드이다. 이 둘을 일반화할 수 있는 표현이 바로 '빈칸'이다.

★★★ 1등급 대비 고난도 3점 문제

10 광고와 지도 제작의 공통된 특성   정답률 39% | 정답 ②

다음 빈칸에 들어갈 말로 가장 적절한 것을 고르시오. [3점]

① reducing the amount of information – 정보의 양을 줄여서
✔ telling or showing everything – 모든 것을 말하거나 보여줌
③ listening to people's voices – 사람들의 목소리에 귀 기울여서
④ relying on visual images only – 시각 이미지에만 의존해서
⑤ making itself available to everyone – 자체로 모두가 이용 가능하게 만들어서

What do advertising and map-making have in common?
광고와 지도 제작은 무슨 공통점이 있을까?

Without doubt / the best answer is their shared need / to communicate a limited version of the truth.
의심할 여지없이 / 최고의 대답은 공통된 필요성에 있다. / 제한된 형태의 사실을 전달하는

An advertisement must create an image / that's appealing / and a map must present an image that's clear, / but neither can meet its goal / by telling or showing everything.
광고는 이미지를 만들어내야 하고 / 매력적인 / 지도는 명백한 이미지를 제시해야 하지만, / 둘 다 목표를 달성할 수는 없다. / 모든 것을 말하거나 보여줌으로써

Ads will cover up or play down / negative aspects of the company or service / they advertise.
광고는 가리거나 약화시킬 것이다. / 회사나 서비스의 부정적인 측면을 / 그들이 광고하는

In this way, / they can promote a favorable comparison with similar products / or differentiate a product from its competitors.
이런 식으로, / 그들은 유사 상품과의 유리한 비교를 홍보하거나 / 제품을 그 경쟁 제품과 차별화할 수 있다.

Likewise, the map must remove details / that would be confusing.
마찬가지로, 지도는 세부사항을 지워야 한다. / 혼란을 줄 수 있는

광고와 지도 제작은 무슨 공통점이 있을까? 의심할 여지없이 최고의 대답은 제한된 형태의 사실을 전달하는 공통된 필요성에 있다. 광고는 매력적인 이미지를 만들어내야 하고 지도는 명백한 이미지를 제시해야 하지만, 둘 다 모든 것을 말하거나 보여줌으로써 목표를 달성할 수는 없다. 광고는 그들이 광고하는 회사나 서비스의 부정적인 측면을 가리거나 약화시킬 것이다. 이런 식으로, 그들은 유사 상품과의 유리한 비교를 홍보하거나 제품을 그 경쟁 제품과 차별화할 수 있다. 마찬가지로, 지도는 혼란을 줄 수 있는 세부사항을 지워야 한다.

Why? 왜 정답일까?

광고와 지도는 서로 제한된 형태의 사실만을 전달하여 목적을 달성한다(**Without doubt the best answer is their shared need to communicate a limited version of the truth.**)는 내용이다. 광고가 제품의 약점을 숨기거나 축소하여 말하듯이, 지도 또한 혼란을 줄 수 있는 세부사항을 나타내지 않는다는 것을 말하고 있다. 이를 통해 오히려 '모든 것을 말하면' 광고든 지도든 목적을 달성할 수 없으리라는 내용을 유추할 수 있어, 빈칸에 들어갈 말로 가장 적절한 것은 ② '모든 것을 말하거나 보여줌'이다.

● advertising ⓝ 광고
● have in common 공통적으로 지니다
● appealing ⓐ 매력적인
● meet ⓥ (목표나 기한 등을) 달성하다, 맞추다
● aspect ⓝ 측면
● favorable ⓐ 호의적인
● differentiate ⓥ 차별화하다
● confusing ⓐ 혼란을 주는, 혼란스러운

● map-making 지도 제작, 지도 만들기
● communicate ⓥ 전달하다
● present ⓥ 제시하다
● play down 약화시키다, 낮추다
● promote ⓥ 홍보하다, 촉진하다
● comparison ⓝ 비교
● competitor ⓝ 경쟁자, 경쟁 상대

구문 풀이

2행 Without doubt / the best answer is their shared need
의심할 여지없이
to communicate a limited version of the truth.
형용사적 용법

★★ 문제 해결 꿀~팁 ★★

▶ 많이 틀린 이유는?
빈칸 문제이니만큼 주제문을 찾으면 쉽게 답에 접근할 수 있으나, 빈칸 문장에 **neither**라는 부정어가 있으므로 주제를 거꾸로 뒤집은 내용이 답이 된다는 점에서 어려운 문제였다.

▶ 문제 해결 방법은?
글의 주제는 광고와 지도가 공통적으로 제한된 진실만을 담는다는, 즉 '다 말하지 않는' 특성이 있다는 것이다. 이를 빈칸 문장의 맥락에 맞게 뒤집어 생각하면 '다 말하면 광고나 지도가 제 기능을 못한다'는 내용을 유추할 수 있다. 최다 오답인 ①은 '정보

'양의 제한'이라는 핵심 내용을 그대로 담고 있기에, 빈칸에 넣으면 오히려 '정보를 제한할 때 광고나 지도 제작의 목적이 달성되지 않는다'는, 주제와 정반대되는 내용을 나타내게 된다.

★★★ 1등급 대비 고난도 3점 문제

11 아기의 언어 습득에 바탕이 되는 통계 분석 능력   정답률 41% | 정답 ②

다음 빈칸에 들어갈 말로 가장 적절한 것을 고르시오. [3점]

① lack of social pressures – 사회적 압력의 부족
✔ ability to calculate statistics – 통계를 계산하는 능력
③ desire to interact with others – 타인과 상호작용하려는 욕구
④ preference for simpler sounds – 더 간단한 소리에 대한 선호
⑤ tendency to imitate caregivers – 양육자를 모방하려는 경향

Over time, / babies construct expectations / about what sounds they will hear when.
시간이 지나면서 / 아기는 기대를 형성한다. / 자신이 어떤 소리를 언제 들을지에 대한

They hold in memory the sound patterns / that occur on a regular basis.
그들은 소리 패턴을 기억한다. / 규칙적으로 발생하는

They make hypotheses / like, "If I hear *this* sound first, / it probably will be followed by *that* sound."
그들은 가설을 세운다. / '내가 이 소리를 먼저 들으면 / 그것에 아마도 저 소리가 따라올 것이다'와 같은

Scientists conclude / that much of babies' skill in learning language / is due to their ability to calculate statistics.
과학자들은 결론짓는다. / 아기의 언어 학습 능력의 상당 부분이 / 통계를 계산하는 능력 때문이라고

For babies, / this means / that they appear to pay close attention / to the patterns that repeat in language.
아기에게 있어 / 이것은 의미한다. / 그들이 세심한 주의를 기울이는 것처럼 보인다는 것을 / 언어에서 반복되는 패턴에

They remember, in a systematic way, / how often sounds occur, / in what order, / with what intervals, / and with what changes of pitch.
그들은 체계적인 방식으로 기억한다. / 소리가 얼마나 자주 발생하는지를 / 어떤 순서로, / 어떤 간격으로, / 그리고 어떤 음조의 변화로

This memory store allows them to track, / within the neural circuits of their brains, / the frequency of sound patterns / and to use this knowledge / to make predictions about the meaning in patterns of sounds.
이 기억 저장소는 그들이 추적하게 해 주고, / 자신의 뇌의 신경 회로 내에서 / 소리 패턴의 빈도를 / 이 지식을 사용하도록 해 준다. / 소리 패턴의 의미에 대한 예측을 하기 위해

시간이 지나면서 아기는 자신이 어떤 소리를 언제 들을지에 대한 기대를 형성한다. 그들은 규칙적으로 발생하는 소리 패턴을 기억한다. 그들은 '내가 이 소리를 먼저 들으면 아마도 저 소리가 따라올 것이다'와 같은 가설을 세운다. 과학자들은 아기의 언어 학습 능력의 상당 부분이 통계를 계산하는 능력 때문이라고 결론짓는다. 아기에게 있어 이것은 그들이 언어에서 반복되는 패턴에 세심한 주의를 기울이는 것처럼 보인다는 것을 의미한다. 그들은 소리가 얼마나 자주, 어떤 순서로, 어떤 간격으로, 어떤 음조의 변화로 발생하는지를 체계적인 방식으로 기억한다. 이 기억 저장소는 그들이 뇌의 신경 회로 내에서 소리 패턴의 빈도를 추적하고, 이 지식을 사용해 소리 패턴의 의미에 대해 예측하게 해준다.

Why? 왜 정답일까?

마지막 두 문장에서 아기들은 패턴이 어떻게 반복되는지에 관한 세부 사항을 기억하고, 패턴의 빈도를 추적하여 후에 의미를 예측할 때 그러한 정보를 사용한다고 설명하고 있다. 빈칸에는 이러한 일련의 인지 작용을 일반화하는 말이 필요하므로, 빈칸에 들어갈 말로 가장 적절한 것은 ② '통계를 계산하는 능력'이다.

● construct ⓥ 형성하다, 구성하다
● hypothesis ⓝ 가설
● interval ⓝ 간격
● calculate ⓥ 계산하다

● on a regular basis 규칙적으로
● systematic ⓐ 체계적인
● make a prediction 예측하다
● statistics ⓝ 통계

구문 풀이

12행 This memory store allows them to track, (within the neural
                  5형식 동사   목적어   목적격 보어1
circuits of their brains), the frequency of sound patterns and to use
( ) : 삽입구   to track 목적어   목적격 보어2
this knowledge to make predictions about the meaning in patterns
                  부사적 용법(목적)
of sounds.

★★ 문제 해결 꿀~팁 ★★

▶ **많이 틀린 이유는?**

아기들의 언어 소리 습득에 관한 글이다. 빈칸 뒤로, 아기들이 언어에서 반복되는 소리에 주의를 기울이고, 소리의 빈도나 순서, 고저를 분석하여 언어 패턴을 익혀 나간다는 설명이 이어지고 있다. '더 간단한' 소리를 선호한다는 내용은 언급되지 않기에 ④는 답으로 적절하지 않다.

▶ **문제 해결 방법은?**

아기들이 주변에서 들은 소리 데이터를 바탕으로 그 패턴을 분석하여 추후 예측에 활용한다는 설명을 '통계 자료 계산(calculate statistics)'이라는 비유적 표현으로 일반화할 수 있어야 한다.

★★★ 1등급 대비 고난도 3점 문제

12 한 항공사의 어려운 시기 성장 비결   정답률 34% | 정답 ③

다음 빈칸에 들어갈 말로 가장 적절한 것을 고르시오. [3점]

① it was being faced with serious financial crises
그것이 심각한 재정 위기에 직면해 있었기

② there was no specific long-term plan on marketing
마케팅에 관한 구체적인 장기 계획이 없었기

✓③ company leadership had set an upper limit for growth
회사 지도부가 성장의 상한치를 설정했기

④ its executives worried about the competing airlines' future
회사 경영진이 경쟁 항공사의 미래를 걱정했기

⑤ the company had emphasized moral duties more than profits
회사가 이익보다도 도덕적 의무를 강조했기

Back in 1996, / an American airline was faced with an interesting problem.
1996년에 / 한 미국 항공사가 흥미로운 문제에 직면했다.

At a time / when most other airlines were losing money or going under, / over 100 cities were begging the company to service their locations.
시기에, / 대부분의 다른 항공사들이 손해를 보거나 파산하던 / 100개가 넘는 도시가 그 회사에 그들의 지역에 취항할 것을 부탁하고 있었다.

However, that's not the interesting part.
하지만, 그것이 흥미로운 부분은 아니다.

What's interesting is / that the company turned down over 95 percent of those offers / and began serving only four new locations.
흥미로운 것은 / 회사는 그 제안 중 95퍼센트 넘게 거절했고 / 네 개의 새로운 지역만 취항을 시작했다는 점이다.

It turned down tremendous growth / because <u>company leadership had set an upper limit for growth.</u>
회사는 엄청난 성장을 거절했는데 / 회사 지도부가 성장의 상한치를 설정했기 때문이다.

Sure, its executives wanted to grow each year, / but they didn't want to grow too much.
물론, 그 경영진들은 매년 성장하기를 원했지만, / 그들은 너무 많이 성장하는 것을 원하지는 않았다.

Unlike other famous companies, / they wanted to set their own pace, / one that could be sustained in the long term.
다른 유명한 회사들과는 달리, / 그들은 자신만의 속도를 정하기를 원했다. / 즉 장기간 지속될 수 있는 것

By doing this, / they established a safety margin for growth / that helped them continue to thrive / at a time / when the other airlines were flailing.
이렇게 함으로써 / 그들은 성장의 안전이 보장되는 여유를 설정했다. / 그들이 계속 번창하는 데 도움이 됐던 / 시기에 / 다른 항공사들이 마구 흔들리던

1996년에 한 미국 항공사가 흥미로운 문제에 직면했다. 대부분의 다른 항공사들이 손해를 보거나 파산하던 시기에, 100개가 넘는 도시가 그 회사에 그들의 지역에 취항할 것을 부탁하고 있었다. 하지만, 그것이 흥미로운 부분은 아니다. 흥미로운 것은 회사는 그 제안 중 95퍼센트 넘게 거절했고 네 개의 새로운 지역만 취항을 시작했다는 점이다. 회사는 엄청난 성장을 거절했는데 회사 지<u>도부가 성장의 상한치를 설정했기</u> 때문이다. 물론, 그 경영진들은 매년 성장하기를 원했지만, 너무 많이 성장하는 것을 원하지는 않았다. 다른 유명한 회사들과는 달리, 그들은 장기간 지속될 수 있는 것, 즉 자신만의 속도를 정하기를 원했다. 이렇게 함으로써 그들은 다른 항공사들이 마구 흔들리던 시기에 그들이 계속 번창하는 데 도움이 됐던, 성장의 안전이 보장되는 여유를 설정했다.

Why? 왜 정답일까?

'Sure, its executives wanted to grow each year, but they didn't want to grow too much. Unlike other famous companies, they wanted to set their own pace, ~'에 따르면 경쟁사가 고전하는 가운데 홀로 취항요청을 받았던 항공사의 경영진들은 과한 성장보다는 회사 나름의 속도대로 오래 지속되는 성장을 바랐다고 한다. 이를 근거로 할 때, 회사의 성장이 과해지지 않도록 조절하는 '상한치'가 있었을 것임을 추론할 수 있다. 따라서 빈칸에 들어갈 말로 가장 적절한 것은 ③ '회사 지도부가 성장의 상한치를 설정했기'이다.

- **go under** 파산하다
- **tremendous** ⓐ 엄청난
- **establish** ⓥ 설정하다, 확립하다
- **thrive** ⓥ 번창하다
- **emphasize** ⓥ 강조하다
- **turn down** ~을 거절하다
- **executive** ⓝ 경영진, 운영진, 간부
- **margin** ⓝ 여유, 여지
- **crisis** ⓝ 위기

구문 풀이

11행 Unlike other famous companies, they wanted to set
전치사(~와는 달리)   ▸부정대명사(= pace)   주어   동사구
their own pace, one [that could be sustained in the long term].
목적어   주격 관·대   조동사 수동태

★★ 문제 해결 꿀~팁 ★★

▶ **많이 틀린 이유는?**

글에 따르면 미국의 한 항공사는 100개가 넘는 지역으로부터 취항 제의를 받았음에도 '회사 나름의 속도에 맞게' 성장하려는 원칙을 고수하고자 네 군데에서만 새로 취항을 시작했다. 경쟁 항공사를 신경 썼다는 내용은 언급되지 않으므로 ④는 답으로 적절하지 않다.

▶ **문제 해결 방법은?**

'didn't want to grow too much', 'set their own pace' 등 핵심 표현을 재진술한 말이 빈칸에 들어가야 한다.

DAY 05 　　　빈칸 추론 05

01 ④	02 ①	03 ①	04 ①	05 ④
06 ④	07 ⑤	08 ⑤	09 ③	10 ①
11 ⑤	12 ⑤			

01 　2차 세계 대전 후 여가의 양상　　　정답률 51% | 정답 ④

다음 빈칸에 들어갈 말로 가장 적절한 것을 고르시오.

① downfall – 몰락　　　　② uniformity – 획일성
③ restoration – 회복　　✔ privatization – 사유화
⑤ customization – 맞춤화

In the post-World War II years after 1945, / unparalleled economic growth / fueled a building boom and a massive migration / from the central cities to the new suburban areas.
1945년 이후 제2차 세계대전 이후 시절에 / 유례없는 경제 성장은 / 건축 붐과 대규모 이주를 부추겼다. / 중심 도시에서 새로운 교외 지역으로의

The suburbs were far more dependent on the automobile, / signaling the shift / from primary dependence on public transportation / to private cars.
교외 지역은 자동차에 훨씬 더 많이 의존했고, / 전환을 알렸다. / 대중교통에 대한 주된 의존으로부터 / 자가용으로의

Soon this led to the construction of better highways and freeways / and the decline and even loss of public transportation.
이것은 곧 더 나은 고속도로와 초고속도로의 건설로 이어졌다. / 그리고 대중교통의 감소, 심지어 쇠퇴로

With all of these changes / came a privatization of leisure.
이러한 모든 변화와 함께 / 여가의 사유화가 이루어졌다.

As more people owned their own homes, / with more space inside and lovely yards outside, / their recreation and leisure time / was increasingly centered around the home / or, at most, the neighborhood.
더 많은 사람이 자기 집을 갖게 되면서 / 내부 공간은 더 넓어지고 외부 정원은 더 아름다운 / 그들의 휴양과 여가 시간은 / 점점 더 집에 집중되었다. / 기껏해야 이웃에

One major activity of this home-based leisure / was watching television.
가정에 기반을 둔 이런 여가의 한 가지 주요 활동은 / TV를 보는 것이었다.

No longer / did one have to ride the trolly to the theater / to watch a movie; / similar entertainment was available / for free and more conveniently / from television.
더 이상 없었다 / 전차를 타고 극장까지 갈 필요 / 영화를 보려고 / 유사한 오락(물)이 이용 가능해졌다. / 무료로 더 편리하게 / 텔레비전을 통해

1945년 이후 제2차 세계대전 이후 시절에 유례없는 경제 성장은 건축 붐과 중심 도시에서 새로운 교외 지역으로의 대규모 이주를 부추겼다. 교외 지역은 자동차에 훨씬 더 많이 의존했고, 대중교통에 주로 의존하던 것에서 자가용으로의 전환을 알렸다. 이것은 곧 더 나은 고속도로와 초고속도로의 건설과 대중교통의 감소, 심지어 쇠퇴로 이어졌다. 이러한 모든 변화와 함께 여가의 사유화가 이루어졌다. 더 많은 사람이 내부 공간은 더 넓어지고 외부 정원은 더 아름다운 자기 집을 갖게 되면서 그들의 휴양과 여가 시간은 점점 더 집, 기껏해야 이웃에 집중되었다. 가정에 기반을 둔 이런 여가의 한 가지 주요 활동은 TV를 보는 것이었다. 더 이상 전차를 타고 극장까지 영화를 보러 갈 필요가 없었고, 유사한 오락(물)이 텔레비전을 통해 무료로 더 편리하게 이용 가능해졌다.

Why? 왜 정답일까?

3차 대전 이후의 엄청난 경제 성장과 함께 집 안에서 즐기는 여가 시간(home-based leisure)이 늘어났다는 내용이므로, 빈칸에 들어갈 말로 가장 적절한 것은 ④ '사유화'이다.

- fuel ⓥ 부추기다
- suburban ⓐ 교외의
- shift ⓝ 전환
- decline ⓝ 감소
- trolly ⓝ 전차, 카트
- downfall ⓝ 몰락
- restoration ⓝ 회복, 복구
- massive ⓐ 대규모의
- automobile ⓝ 자동차
- public transportation 대중교통
- home-based ⓐ 집에 기반을 둔
- conveniently ⓐⓓ 편하게
- uniformity ⓝ 획일성
- privatization ⓝ 사유화, 민영화

구문 풀이

14행 No longer did one have to ride the trolly to the theater to
「도치 구문 : 부정어구 + did + 주어 + 동사원형」
watch a movie; similar entertainment was available for free and more conveniently from television.

02 　생존 기술의 일종인 편향　　　정답률 65% | 정답 ①

다음 빈칸에 들어갈 말로 가장 적절한 것을 고르시오.

✔ necessary survival skill – 필수적인 생존 기술
② origin of imagination – 상상력의 근원
③ undesirable mental capacity – 바람직하지 않은 정신적 능력
④ barrier to relationships – 관계에 대한 장애물
⑤ challenge to moral judgment – 도덕적 판단에 대한 도전 과제

Here's the unpleasant truth: / we are all biased.
여기 불편한 진실이 있다. / 우리는 모두 편향되어 있다.

Every human being is affected by unconscious biases / that lead us to make incorrect assumptions about other people.
모든 인간은 무의식적인 편견에 영향을 받는다. / 우리가 다른 사람들에 대해 부정확한 추측을 하도록 이끄는
Everyone.
모두가 그렇다.

To a certain extent, / bias is an necessary survival skill.
어느 정도, / 편견은 필수적인 생존 기술이다.

If you're an early human, perhaps *Homo Erectus*, / walking around the jungles, / you may see an animal approaching.
만약에 당신이, 가령 호모 에렉투스처럼, 초기 인류라면, / 정글을 돌아다니는 / 당신은 어떤 동물이 다가오는 것을 볼지 모른다.

You have to make very fast assumptions / about whether that animal is safe or not, / based solely on its appearance.
당신은 매우 빨리 추측해야 한다. / 그 동물이 안전한지 아닌지에 대해서 / 그 동물의 외양에만 기초하여
The same is true of other humans.
이것은 다른 인류에게도 똑같이 적용된다.

You make split-second decisions about threats / in order to have plenty of time to escape, / if necessary.
당신은 위협에 대해서 순간적인 결정을 내려야 한다. / 도망갈 시간이 충분하도록 / 만약 필요하다면

This could be one root of our tendency / to categorize and label others / based on their looks and their clothes.
이것은 우리의 성향의 한 근간일 수도 있다. / 타인을 범주화하고 분류하려는 / 그들의 외모와 옷으로

여기 불편한 진실이 있는데, 우리는 모두 편향되어 있다. 모든 인간은 다른 사람들에 대해 부정확한 추측을 하도록 이끄는 무의식적인 편견에 영향을 받는다. 모두가 그렇다. 어느 정도, 편견은 필수적인 생존 기술이다. 만약에 당신이, 가령 호모 에렉투스처럼, 정글을 돌아다니는 초기 인류라면, 당신은 어떤 동물이 다가오는 것을 볼지 모른다. 당신은 그 동물의 외양에만 기초하여 그 동물이 안전한지 아닌지에 대해서 매우 빨리 추측해야 한다. 이것은 다른 인류에게도 똑같이 적용된다. 당신은 만약 필요하다면 도망갈 시간이 충분하도록 위협에 대해서 순간적인 결정을 내려야 한다. 이것은 타인의 외모와 옷으로 그들을 범주화하고 분류하려는 성향의 한 근간일 수도 있다.

Why? 왜 정답일까?

빈칸 뒤를 통해 우리는 초기 인류 시절 동물을 보고 위험한지 아닌지를 빨리 판단해야 도망갈 시간을 벌 수 있었기에 편향을 발달시켜 왔고, 이것을 오늘날까지 유지해온 것임을 알 수 있다. 따라서 빈칸에 들어갈 말로 가장 적절한 것은 편향이 우리의 '생존'을 위해 발달되어 온 것이라는 의미를 완성하는 ① '필수적인 생존 기술'이다.

- unpleasant ⓐ 불쾌한
- unconscious ⓐ 무의식적인
- assumption ⓝ 가정
- approach ⓥ 다가오다, 접근하다
- The same is true of ~에도 해당하다
- categorize ⓥ 범주화하다
- bias ⓥ 편견을 갖게 하다 ⓝ 편견, 편향
- incorrect ⓐ 부정확한
- to a certain extent 어느 정도
- solely ⓐⓓ 단지, 오로지
- split-second ⓐ 찰나의, 순간적인
- undesirable ⓐ 바람직하지 않은

구문 풀이

10행 You make split-second decisions about threats in order to
have plenty of time to escape, if (it is) necessary.
형용사적 용법　접속사　생략　보어(형용사)　~하기 위해

03 　현대 기업 상황에 맞는 메디치 효과의 의미　　　정답률 48% | 정답 ①

다음 빈칸에 들어갈 말로 가장 적절한 것을 고르시오. [3점]

✔ having others around you to compensate
　여러분 주위에 보완할 다른 사람들을 두는 것
② taking some time to reflect on yourself
　자신을 돌아볼 시간을 좀 갖는 것
③ correcting the mistakes of the past
　과거의 실수를 고치는 것

④ maximizing your own strength
자신만의 강점을 극대화하는 것
⑤ setting a specific objective
구체적인 목표를 세우는 것

Business consultant Frans Johansson / describes the *Medici effect* / as the emergence of new ideas and creative solutions / when different backgrounds and disciplines come together.
기업 자문가인 Frans Johansson은 / *메디치* 효과를 기술한다. / 새로운 아이디어와 창의적인 해결책의 출현으로 / 다양한 배경과 학문 분야가 합쳐질 때

The term is derived from the 15th-century Medici family, / who helped usher in the Renaissance / by bringing together artists, writers, and other creatives / from all over the world.
그 용어는 15세기 메디치 가문에서 유래하는데, / 그들은 르네상스 시대가 시작되도록 도왔다. / 예술가, 작가 그리고 다른 창작자들을 함께 모아 / 전 세계로부터

Arguably, the Renaissance was a result of the exchange of ideas / between these different groups / in close contact with each other.
거의 틀림없이, / 르네상스 시대는 아이디어가 교환된 결과였다. / 이 다양한 집단들 사이에서 / 서로 근접한

Sound familiar?
익숙하게 들리는가?

If you are unable to diversify your own talent and skill, / then having others around you to compensate / might very well just do the trick.
만약 여러분이 자신의 재능과 기술을 다양화할 수 없다면, / 그때는 여러분 주위에 보완할 다른 사람들을 두는 것이 / 효과가 있을 수 있다.

Believing / that all new ideas come from combining existing notions in creative ways, / Johansson recommends / utilizing a mix of backgrounds, experiences, and expertise in staffing / to bring about the best possible solutions, perspectives, and innovations in business.
믿으면서, / 모든 새로운 아이디어는 기존 개념들을 창의적인 방식으로 합치는 것에서 나온다고 / Johansson은 추천한다. / 인력 배치에서 배경과 경험과 전문 지식을 혼합하여 활용할 것을 / 기업에서 가능한 최고의 해결책, 전망 그리고 혁신을 유발하기 위해

기업 자문가인 Frans Johansson은 *메디치 효과*를 다양한 배경과 학문 분야가 합쳐질 때 새로운 아이디어와 창의적인 해결책이 출현하는 것이라고 기술한다. 그 용어는 15세기 메디치 가문에서 유래하는데, 그들은 전 세계의 예술가, 작가 그리고 다른 창작자들을 함께 모아 르네상스 시대가 시작되도록 도왔다. 거의 틀림없이, 르네상스 시대는 서로 근접한 이 다양한 집단들 사이에서 아이디어가 교환된 결과였다. 익숙하게 들리는가? 만약 여러분이 자신의 재능과 기술을 다양화할 수 없다면, 그때는 여러분 주위에 보완할 다른 사람들을 두는 것이 효과가 있을 수 있다. 모든 새로운 아이디어는 기존 개념들을 창의적인 방식으로 합치는 것에서 나온다고 믿으면서, Johansson은 기업에서 가능한 최고의 해결책, 전망 그리고 혁신을 유발하기 위해 인력 배치에서 배경과 경험과 전문 지식을 혼합하여 활용할 것을 추천한다.

Why? 왜 정답일까?

'메디치 효과'의 의미를 설명하는 '~ by bringing together artists, writers, and other creatives from all over the world. Arguably, the Renaissance was a result of the exchange of ideas between these different groups in close contact with each other.'에 따르면 르네상스 시대는 메디치 가문이 전 세계의 예술가, 작가 등 다양한 집단을 한데 모아 아이디어의 교환을 촉진했던 것에서 기원했다고 한다. 이를 오늘날의 기업 상황에 적용하면, '각기 다른 재능, 기술, 경험을 지닌 사람들이 함께할 때' 혁신이 이루어질 것이라는 결론을 도출할 수 있다. 따라서 빈칸에 들어갈 말로 가장 적절한 것은 ① '여러분 주위에 보완할 다른 사람들을 두는 것'이다.

- **emergence** ⓝ 출현, 등장
- **derive A from B** A를 B로부터 끌어내다
- **in contact with** ~와 접촉하는
- **do the trick** 성공하다, 효과가 있다
- **compensate** ⓥ 보완하다, 보상하다
- **specific** ⓐ 구체적인
- **discipline** ⓝ 분야
- **arguably** [ad] 거의 틀림없이
- **diversify** ⓥ 다양화하다
- **expertise** ⓝ 전문 지식
- **reflect on** ~을 돌아보다, 성찰하다
- **objective** ⓝ 목표

구문 풀이

10행 If you are unable to diversify your own talent and skill, then
「be unable + to부정사: ~할 수 없다」
having others around you to compensate might very well just
동명사구 주어   아마 ~일 것이다
do the trick.
성공하다, 효과가 있다

---

04 업무 상황 속 웃음 이모티콘의 부작용 정답률 65% | 정답 ①

다음 빈칸에 들어갈 말로 가장 적절한 것을 고르시오. [3점]

✔ makes you look incompetent – 당신을 무능력하게 보이게 만든다

---

② causes conflict between generations – 세대 갈등을 유발한다
③ clarifies the intention of the message – 메시지의 의도를 분명히 한다
④ results in low scores in writing tests – 쓰기 시험에서의 낮은 점수로 이어진다
⑤ helps create a casual work environment – 편안한 근무 환경을 만들도록 돕는다

When meeting someone in person, / body language experts say / that smiling can portray confidence and warmth.
누군가를 직접 만났을 때, / 신체 언어 전문가들은 말한다. / 미소를 짓는 것이 자신감과 친밀감을 드러낼 수 있다고

Online, however, / smiley faces could be doing some serious damage / to your career.
그러나 온라인에서 / 웃음 이모티콘은 상당한 손상을 입힐 수 있다. / 당신의 경력에

In a new study, researchers found / that using smiley faces makes you look incompetent.
새로운 연구에서, 연구자들은 알아냈다. / 웃음 이모티콘을 사용하는 것이 당신을 무능력하게 보이게 만든다는 것을

The study says, / "contrary to actual smiles, / smileys do not increase perceptions of warmth / and actually decrease perceptions of competence."
그 연구는 말한다. / "실제 미소와 달리, / 웃음 이모티콘은 친밀감에 대한 인식을 증진시키지 않고, / 실제로 능력에 대한 인식을 감소시킨다."라고

The report also explains, / "Perceptions of low competence, / in turn, / lessened information sharing."
그 보고서는 또한 설명한다. / "능력이 낮다고 인식되는 것이 / 그 결과 / 정보 공유를 감소시켰다."라고

Chances are, / if you are including a smiley face in an email for work, / the last thing you want is / for your co-workers to think / that you are so inadequate / that they chose not to share information with you.
~일 것이다. / 만약에 당신이 업무상의 이메일에 웃음 이모티콘을 포함시키고 있다면, / 당신이 가장 바라지 않을 만한 일은 / 동료들이 생각을 하는 상황(일 것이다.) / 당신이 너무 무능하여 / 정보 공유를 하지 않기로 선택했다는

누군가를 직접 만났을 때, 신체 언어 전문가들은 미소를 짓는 것이 자신감과 친밀감을 드러낼 수 있다고 말한다. 그러나 온라인에서 웃음 이모티콘은 당신의 경력에 상당한 손상을 입힐 수 있다. 새로운 연구에서, 연구자들은 웃음 이모티콘을 사용하는 것이 당신을 무능력하게 보이게 만든다는 것을 알아냈다. 그 연구는 "실제 미소와 달리, 웃음 이모티콘은 친밀감에 대한 인식을 증진시키지 않고, 실제로 능력에 대한 인식을 감소시킨다."라고 한다. 그 보고서는 또한 "능력이 낮다고 인식되는 것이 그 결과 정보 공유를 감소시켰다."라고 설명한다. 만약에 당신이 업무상의 이메일에 웃음 이모티콘을 포함시키고 있다면, 당신이 가장 바라지 않을 만한 일은 동료들이 당신이 너무 무능하여 정보 공유를 하지 않기로 선택했다는 생각을 하는 상황일 것이다.

Why? 왜 정답일까?

연구의 예를 들어 웃음 이모티콘 사용의 부작용을 설명한 글로, 결과 부분에 주제가 있다. 'The study says' 이하에서 웃음 이모티콘은 능력에 대한 인식을 감소시킨다(smileys ~ actually decrease perceptions of competence.)고 이야기하므로, 빈칸에 들어갈 말로 가장 적절한 것은 ① '당신을 무능력하게 보이게 만든다'이다.

- **in person** 직접, 몸소
- **contrary to** ~와는 반대로
- **competence** ⓝ 능력, 역량
- **lessen** ⓥ 감소시키다, 줄이다
- **clarify** ⓥ 분명히 하다, 명확하게 하다
- **confidence** ⓝ 자신감, 신뢰
- **perception** ⓝ 인식, 지각
- **in turn** 결국, 그 결과
- **inadequate** ⓐ 무능한, 부족한

구문 풀이

10행 Chances are (that), (if you are including a smiley face in an
~할 가능성이 있다
email for work), the last thing you want is for your co-workers
( ): 조건 부사절   주어   동사   의미상 주어
to think {that you are so inadequate that they chose not to share
주격 보어   「so ~ that … : 너무 ~해서 …하다」
information with you}.

---

05 관객과의 상호 작용을 요하는 창작 행위 정답률 49% | 정답 ④

다음 빈칸에 들어갈 말로 가장 적절한 것을 고르시오. [3점]

① exploring the absolute truth in existence
현존하는 절대적 진리를 탐구하는 것
② following a series of precise and logical steps
정확하고 논리적인 일련의 단계를 따르는 것
③ looking outside and drawing inspiration from nature
밖을 보고 자연으로부터 영감을 얻는 것
✔ internalizing the perspective of others on one's work
다른 사람의 관점을 자신의 작품 속에 내면화하는 것
⑤ pushing the audience to the limits of its endurance
관객을 인내심의 한계까지 밀어붙이는 것

It is common to assume / that creativity concerns primarily the relation / between actor(creator) and artifact(creation).
가정하는 것이 일반적이다. / 창조성은 주로 관계와 연관되어 있다고 / 행위자(창작자)와 창작물(창작) 간의

However, from a sociocultural standpoint, / the creative act is never "complete" / in the absence of a second position / — that of an audience.
그러나 사회 문화적 관점에서 볼 때, / 창작 행위는 결코 '완전'하지 않다. / 제2의 입장이 부재한 상황에서는 / 다시 말해 관객의 부재

While the actor or creator him/herself / is the first audience of the artifact being produced, / this kind of distantiation can only be achieved / by internalizing the perspective of others on one's work.
행위자나 창작자 자신은 / 만들어지고 있는 창작물의 첫 번째 관객이지만, / 이런 거리두기는 오로지 이루어진다. / 다른 사람의 관점을 자신의 작품 속에 내면화하는 것으로서만

This means / that, in order to be an audience to your own creation, / a history of interaction with others is needed.
이것은 의미한다. / 자신의 창작 활동에 관객이 되기 위해서는 / 다른 사람들과 상호 작용하는 역사가 필요하다는 것

We exist in a social world / that constantly confronts us with the "view of the other."
우리는 사회적인 세상에 살고 있다. / 끊임없이 '상대방의 관점'에 마주하는

It is the view / we include and blend into our own activity, / including creative activity.
그것은 관점이다. / 우리가 우리 자신의 활동에 통합시키고 뒤섞게 되는 / 창조적인 행위를 포함해서

This outside perspective is essential for creativity / because it gives new meaning and value / to the creative act and its product.
이러한 외부 관점은 창조성에는 필수적이다. / 그것이 새로운 의미와 가치를 부여하기 때문에 / 창작 행위와 그 결과물에

창조성은 주로 행위자(창작자)와 창작물(창작) 간의 관계와 연관되어 있다고 가정하는 것이 일반적이다. 그러나 사회 문화적 관점에서 볼 때, 창작 행위는 관객의 부재, 다시 말해 제2의 입장이 부재한 상황에서는 결코 '완전'하지 않다. 행위자나 창작자 자신은 만들어지고 있는 창작물의 첫 번째 관객이지만, 이런 거리두기는 다른 사람의 관점을 자신의 작품 속에 내면화하는 것으로서만 이루어진다. 이것은 자신의 창작 활동에 관객이 되기 위해서는 다른 사람들과 상호 작용하는 역사가 필요하다는 것을 의미한다. 우리는 끊임없이 '상대방의 관점'에 마주하는 사회적인 세상에 살고 있다. 그것은 창조적인 행위를 포함해서 우리가 우리 자신의 활동에 통합시키고 뒤섞게 되는 관점이다. 이러한 외부 관점은 창작 행위와 그 결과물에 새로운 의미와 가치를 부여하기 때문에 창조성에는 필수적이다.

Why? 왜 정답일까?

두 번째 문장에서 사회 문화적 관점에 따르면 창작 행위는 제2의 관점, 즉 관객의 시각이 빠진 상태에서는 결코 완전할 수 없다고 한다. 이어서 'This means that, ~' 이하로 창작 활동에는 다른 사람과 상호 작용하는, 즉 '상대방의 관점'이 창조적 활동에 통합되는 과정이 꼭 필요하다는 내용이 이어진다. 따라서 빈칸에 들어갈 말로 가장 적절한 것은 ④ '다른 사람의 관점을 자신의 작품 속에 내면화하는 것'이다.

- **primarily** [ad] 주로
- **in the absence of** ~이 없을 때에
- **constantly** [ad] 지속적으로
- **essential** @ 필수적인, 본질적인
- **in existence** 현존하는
- **internalize** ⓥ 내면화하다
- **standpoint** ⓝ 관점
- **distantiation** ⓝ 거리두기
- **blend into** ~에 뒤섞다
- **absolute** @ 절대적인
- **precise** @ 정확한
- **endurance** ⓝ 인내심, 참을성

구문 풀이

9행 This means that, in order to be an audience to your own
접속사(~것) 부사적 용법(~하기 위해)
creation, a history of interaction with others is needed.
주어   동사(단수)

---

06 상황의 변화에 따라 비전을 조정할 필요성 정답률 61% | 정답 ④

다음 빈칸에 들어갈 말로 가장 적절한 것을 고르시오. [3점]

① explain your vision logically to others
타인에게 당신의 비전을 논리적으로 설명할
② defend the wrong decisions you've made
당신이 내린 잘못된 결정을 방어할
③ build a community to share your experience
당신의 경험을 공유할 공동체를 구축할
✓④ make your vision conform to the new reality
새로운 현실에 당신의 비전을 맞출
⑤ consult experts to predict the future economy
미래 경제를 예측하기 위해 전문가와 상담할

Vision is like shooting at a moving target.
비전은 움직이는 목표물을 쏘아 맞히는 것과 같다.

Plenty of things can go wrong in the future / and plenty more can change in unpredictable ways.
많은 것들이 미래에 잘못될 수 있고, / 더 많은 것들이 예측할 수 없는 방식으로 변할 수 있다.

When such things happen, / you should be prepared / to make your vision conform to the new reality.
그러한 일들이 일어날 때, / 당신은 준비가 되어 있어야 한다. / 새로운 현실에 당신의 비전을 맞출

For example, / a businessman's optimistic forecast / can be blown away by a cruel recession / or by aggressive competition / in ways he could not have foreseen.
예를 들어, / 한 사업가의 낙관적인 예측은 / 잔혹한 경기 침체에 의해 날아갈 수 있다. / 혹은 공격적인 경쟁에 의해 / 그가 예견할 수 없었던 방식으로

Or in another scenario, / his sales can skyrocket / and his numbers can get even better.
혹은 또 다른 시나리오에서는 / 그의 매출이 급등하거나 / 그의 수익이 훨씬 더 나아질 수 있다.

In any event, / he will be foolish to stick to his old vision / in the face of new data.
어떤 상황에서든, / 그가 그의 기존의 비전을 고수하는 것은 어리석은 일이 될 것이다. / 새로운 데이터에 직면했을 때

There is nothing wrong / in modifying your vision or even abandoning it, / as necessary.
잘못된 것이 아니다. / 당신의 비전을 수정하거나 심지어 그것을 버리는 것은 / 필요에 따라

비전은 움직이는 목표물을 쏘아 맞히는 것과 같다. 많은 것들이 미래에 잘못될 수 있고, 더 많은 것들이 예측할 수 없는 방식들로 변할 수 있다. 그러한 일들이 일어날 때, 당신은 새로운 현실에 당신의 비전을 맞출 준비가 되어 있어야 한다. 예를 들어, 한 사업가의 낙관적인 예측은 그가 예견할 수 없었던 방식으로 잔혹한 경기 침체나 공격적인 경쟁에 의해 날아갈 수 있다. 혹은 또 다른 시나리오에서는 그의 매출이 급등하거나 그의 수익이 훨씬 더 나아질 수 있다. 어떤 상황에서든, 그가 새로운 데이터에 직면했을 때 그의 기존의 비전을 고수하는 것은 어리석은 일이 될 것이다. 필요에 따라 당신의 비전을 수정하거나 심지어 그것을 버리는 것은 잘못된 것이 아니다.

Why? 왜 정답일까?

마지막 문장인 'There is nothing wrong in modifying your vision or even abandoning it, as necessary.'에서 필요에 따라 비전을 수정하거나 심지어 버리는 것은 잘못된 일이 아니라고 언급하며 상황에 따라 유연하게 비전을 조정할 필요성이 있음을 시사하므로, 빈칸에 들어갈 말로 가장 적절한 것은 ④ '새로운 현실에 당신의 비전을 맞출'이다.

- **shoot at** ~을 쏘아 맞히다
- **unpredictable** @ 예측할 수 없는
- **forecast** ⓝ 예측
- **aggressive** @ 공격적인
- **skyrocket** ⓥ 급등하다
- **in the face of** ~에 직면하여
- **abandon** ⓥ 버리다
- **conform to** ~에 맞추다, 순응하다
- **plenty** ⓝ 많음 [ad] 많이
- **optimistic** @ 낙관적인
- **cruel** @ 잔혹한, 고통스러운
- **foresee** ⓥ 예견하다
- **stick to** ~을 고수하다
- **modify** ⓥ 수정하다
- **defend** ⓥ 방어하다

구문 풀이

5행 For example, a businessman's optimistic forecast can be
조동사 수동태
blown away by a cruel recession or by aggressive competition in
전명구1   전명구2
ways [he could not have foreseen].
「could not have + 과거분사 : ~할 수 없었을 것이다」

★★★ 1등급 대비 고난도 2점 문제

07 동물을 잘 보살피기 위한 환경의 조건 정답률 51% | 정답 ⑤

다음 빈칸에 들어갈 말로 가장 적절한 것을 고르시오.

① silent - 고요하도록
② natural - 자연스럽도록
③ isolated - 고립되도록
④ dynamic - 역동적이도록
✓⑤ predictable - 예측 가능하도록

One of the most important aspects of providing good care / is making sure / that an animal's needs are being met consistently and predictably.
좋은 보살핌을 제공하는 것의 가장 중요한 측면 중 한 가지는 / 반드시 ~하는 것이다. / 동물의 욕구가 일관되고도 예측 가능하게 충족되도록

Like humans, / animals need a sense of control.
사람과 마찬가지로, / 동물은 통제감이 필요하다.

So an animal / who may get enough food / but doesn't know when the food will appear / and can see no consistent schedule / may experience distress.

그러므로 동물은 / 충분한 음식을 제공받고 있을지라도 / 음식이 언제 눈에 보일지 모르고 / 일관된 일정을 알 수 없는 / 괴로움을 겪을지도 모른다.

We can provide a sense of control / by ensuring that our animal's environment is predictable: / there is always water available / and always in the same place.
우리는 통제감을 줄 수 있다. / 우리 동물의 환경이 예측 가능하도록 보장함으로써 / 즉, 마실 수 있는 물이 늘 있고, / 늘 같은 곳에 있다.

There is always food / when we get up in the morning / and after our evening walk.
늘 음식이 있다. / 우리가 아침에 일어날 때 / 그리고 저녁 산책을 한 후에

There will always be a time and place to eliminate, / without having to hold things in to the point of discomfort.
변을 배설할 수 있는 시간과 장소가 늘 있을 것이다. / 불편할 정도로 참을 필요 없이

Human companions can display consistent emotional support, / rather than providing love one moment / and withholding love the next.
사람 친구는 일관된 정서적 지지를 보이는 것이 좋다. / 한순간에는 애정을 주다가 / 그다음에는 애정을 주지 않기보다는

When animals know what to expect, / they can feel more confident and calm.
동물이 기대할 수 있는 것이 무엇인지 알고 있을 때, / 그들은 자신감과 차분함을 더 많이 느낄 수 있다.

좋은 보살핌을 제공하는 것의 가장 중요한 측면 중에 한 가지는 반드시 동물의 욕구가 일관되고도 예측 가능하게 충족되도록 하는 것이다. 사람과 마찬가지로, 동물은 통제감이 필요하다. 그러므로 충분한 음식을 제공받고 있을지라도 음식이 언제 눈에 보일지 모르고 일관된 일정을 알 수 없는 동물은 괴로움을 겪을지도 모른다. 우리 동물의 환경이 예측 가능하도록 보장함으로써 우리는 통제감을 줄 수 있다. 즉, 마실 수 있는 물이 늘 있고, 늘 같은 곳에 있다. 아침에 일어날 때 그리고 저녁 산책을 한 후에 늘 음식이 있다. 불편할 정도로 참을 필요 없이 변을 배설할 수 있는 시간과 장소가 늘 있을 것이다. 사람 친구는 한순간에는 애정을 주다가 그다음에는 애정을 주지 않기보다는 일관된 정서적 지지를 보이는 것이 좋다. 기대할 수 있는 것이 무엇인지 알고 있을 때, 동물은 자신감과 차분함을 더 많이 느낄 수 있다.

Why? 왜 정답일까?

첫 문장인 'One of the most important aspects of providing good care is making sure that an animal's needs are being met consistently and predictably.'에서 동물을 잘 보살피기 위해서는 동물의 욕구가 일관적이고도 예측 가능한 방식으로 충족되게 해줄 필요가 있다고 언급하고 있다. 따라서 빈칸에 들어갈 말로 가장 적절한 것은 동물의 환경을 '예측 가능하게' 만들어 주어야 한다는 의미를 완성하는 ⑤ '예측 가능하도록'이다.

- aspect ⓝ 측면
- consistently ⓐd 일관적으로
- sense of control 통제감
- ensure ⓥ 반드시 ~하다, 보장하다
- discomfort ⓝ 불편함
- confident ⓐ 자신감 있는
- make sure 반드시 ~하다
- predictably ⓐd 예측 가능하게
- distress ⓝ 괴로움
- to the point of ~할 수 있을 정도로
- withhold ⓥ 주지 않다
- isolated ⓐ 고립된

구문 풀이

4행 So an animal [who may get enough food but doesn't know
　　　　　　주어(선행사) 주격 관·대 동사구1　　　　동사구2
when the food will appear and can see no consistent schedule]
의문사(언제 ~할지)　　　　　동사구3
may experience distress.
동사

★★ 문제 해결 꿀~팁 ★★

▶ **많이 틀린 이유는?**
빈칸 뒤에서 반려동물에게 정해진 장소와 시간에 따라 어떤 것을 기대할 수 있는 안정적인 환경을 제공할 필요가 있다는 내용이 주를 이루고 있다. 이 안정된 환경이 꼭 '자연스러운' 것이라고 볼 수는 없으므로 ②는 답으로 부적절하다.

▶ **문제 해결 방법은?**
첫 문장에서 '일관되고 예측 가능한' 환경의 중요성을 언급한 데 이어, 마지막 문장에서도 동물에게 '무엇을 기대할 수 있는지'가 분명한 환경을 주는 것이 좋다는 내용을 제시하고 있으므로 ⑤가 답으로 가장 적절하다.

★★★ 1등급 대비 고난도 2점 문제

08 선수의 인성과 도덕성에 양면적으로 작용하는 승리　정답률 43% | 정답 ⑤

다음 빈칸에 들어갈 말로 가장 적절한 것을 고르시오.
① a piece of cake – 식은 죽 먹기(아주 쉬운 일)
② a one-way street – 일방통행로

---

③ a bird in the hand – 수중에 든 새(확실한 일)
④ a fish out of water – 물 밖에 나온 고기(낯선 환경에서 불편해하는 사람)
☑ a double-edged sword – 양날의 검(양면성을 가진 상황)

Research has confirmed / that athletes are less likely to participate in unacceptable behavior / than are non-athletes.
연구는 확인해준다. / 운동선수는 받아들여지지 않는 행동을 덜 할 것이라고 / 선수가 아닌 사람들보다

However, / moral reasoning and good sporting behavior / seem to decline / as athletes progress to higher competitive levels, / in part because of the increased emphasis on winning.
그러나 / 도덕적 분별력과 바람직한 스포츠 행위가 / 감소하는 것 같다. / 운동선수가 더 높은 경쟁적 수준까지 올라감에 따라 / 부분적으로 승리에 대한 강조가 커지기 때문에

Thus winning can be a double-edged sword / in teaching character development.
그래서 승리라는 것은 양날의 검이 될 수 있다. / 인성 함양을 가르치는 데 있어서

Some athletes may want to win so much / that they lie, cheat, and break team rules.
어떤 선수는 너무나 이기려고 하다 보니 / 그 결과 거짓말하고 속이고 팀 규칙을 위반한다.

They may develop undesirable character traits / that can enhance their ability to win in the short term.
그들은 바람직하지 못한 인격 특성을 계발할지 모른다. / 단시간에 이길 수 있는 자신의 능력을 강화할 수 있는

However, / when athletes resist the temptation / to win in a dishonest way, / they can develop positive character traits / that last a lifetime.
그러나 / 선수가 유혹에 저항할 때 / 부정직한 방법으로 이기고자 하는 / 그들은 긍정적인 인격 특성을 계발할 수 있다. / 일생동안 지속되는

Character is a learned behavior, / and a sense of fair play develops / only if coaches plan to teach those lessons systematically.
인성이라는 것은 학습되는 행동이며 / 페어플레이 정신이 발달한다. / 코치가 그러한 교훈을 체계적으로 가르치고자 계획할 때 비로소

연구에 따르면 운동선수는 선수가 아닌 사람들보다 (사회적으로) 받아들여지지 않는 행동을 덜 할 것이라고 한다. 그러나 운동선수가 더 높은 경쟁적 수준까지 올라감에 따라 부분적으로 승리에 대한 강조가 커지기 때문에 도덕적 분별력과 바람직한 스포츠 행위가 감소하는 것 같다. 그래서 승리라는 것은 인성 함양을 가르치는 데 있어서 양날의 검이 될 수 있다. 어떤 선수는 너무나 이기려고 하다 보니 그 결과 거짓말하고 속이고 팀 규칙을 위반한다. 그들은 단시간에 이길 수 있는 자신의 능력을 강화할 수 있는 바람직하지 못한 인격 특성을 계발할지 모른다. 그러나 선수가 부정직한 방법으로 이기고자 하는 유혹에 저항할 때 그들은 일생동안 지속되는 긍정적인 인격 특성을 계발할 수 있다. 인성이라는 것은 학습되는 행동이며 코치가 그러한 교훈을 체계적으로 가르치고자 계획할 때 비로소 페어플레이 정신이 발달한다.

Why? 왜 정답일까?

첫 두 문장에 따르면 운동선수는 선수가 아닌 사람들에 비할 때 사회적으로 용인되지 않는 행동을 덜 하는 경향이 있지만, 승리가 강조되는 환경에 살기 때문에 경쟁이 심해질수록 도덕적 분별력이 떨어질 수 있다고 한다(~ athletes are less likely to participate in unacceptable behavior ~. However, moral reasoning and good sporting behavior seem to decline ~.). 따라서 빈칸에 들어갈 말로 가장 적절한 것은 승리라는 것이 선수의 인격 또는 도덕성 함양에 양면적으로 작용할 수 있다는 의미의 ⑤ '양날의 검'이다.

- confirm ⓥ (맞다고) 확인하다
- reasoning ⓝ 추론 (능력)
- competitive ⓐ 경쟁하는, 경쟁력 있는
- undesirable ⓐ 바람직하지 않은
- resist ⓥ 저항하다
- dishonest ⓐ 부정직한
- systematically ⓐd 체계적으로
- unacceptable ⓐ 받아들여지지 않는
- decline ⓥ 감소하다
- emphasis ⓝ 강조
- enhance ⓥ 강화하다
- temptation ⓝ 유혹
- learned ⓐ 학습된, 후천적인

구문 풀이

1행 Research has confirmed that athletes are less likely
　　　　　　　　　　　　接속사(~것)　　　「be less likely +
to participate in unacceptable behavior than are non-athletes.
to부정사: 덜 ~하는 경향이 있다　　　「than + 동사 + 주어 : 도치 구문」

★★ 문제 해결 꿀~팁 ★★

▶ **많이 틀린 이유는?**
빈칸 뒤에 따르면 선수들은 승리를 위해 부도덕한 행동을 저지르면서 바람직하지 못한 인격 특성을 키우게 될 수 있지만, 한편으로 부정직한 승리의 유혹에 저항하는 과정에서 좋은 인격 특성을 함양하게 될 수도 있다고 한다. 이는 결국 승리가 선수에게 좋은 쪽과 나쁜 쪽 둘 다로 작용할 수 있다는 의미이므로, ② 'a one-way street

(일방통행로)은 빈칸에 적합하지 않다. 또한 ① 'a piece of cake(식은 죽 먹기)'는 글의 내용과 전혀 관련이 없다.

▶ 문제 해결 방법은?
빈칸 뒤의 세부 진술을 읽고 일반적인 결론을 도출한 뒤, 이를 다시 비유적으로 잘 나타낸 선택지를 찾아야 하는 문제이다. 핵심은 승리의 '양면성'에 있음을 염두에 둔다.

8행 To produce something worthwhile / — if it ever happens — /
　　to부정사구 주어　　　　　　　　　　　　　　「if ever : 설령 ~한다 할지라도」
may require years of such fruitless labor.
　동사

★★ 문제 해결 꿀~팁 ★★

▶ 많이 틀린 이유는?
비록 평소의 과업이 '성과가 없고 지루한' 일일지라도 열정과 동기를 다해 노력할 필요가 있다는 내용이 글의 주제이므로 ③이 답으로 가장 적절하다. 특히 글 후반부의 인용구 "nearly all scientific research leads nowhere."에서 nowhere가 빈칸에 들어갈 말과 같은 의미를 나타낸다는 점을 기억해 둔다. 최다 오답인 ②는 '생산적인'이라는 뜻으로 정답인 ③과 의미가 상반된다.

▶ 문제 해결 방법은?
주제문과 더불어 예시도 꼼꼼히 읽어야 답을 알 수 있는 문제이므로, 시간을 들여 글을 통독하도록 한다.

★★★ 1등급 대비 고난도 3점 문제

09 지속적인 노력의 중요성　　　　　　　정답률 30% | 정답 ③

다음 빈칸에 들어갈 말로 가장 적절한 것을 고르시오. [3점]

① cooperative – 협동하는　　　② productive – 생산적인
✔ fruitless – 결실 없는　　　　④ dangerous – 위험한
⑤ irregular – 불규칙한

Since a great deal of day-to-day academic work / is boring and repetitive, / you need to be well motivated / to keep doing it.
날마다 해야 하는 많은 학업이 / 지루하고 반복적이기 때문에, / 동기부여가 잘 되어야 한다. / 그것을 계속하기 위해서는

A mathematician sharpens her pencils, / works on a proof, / tries a few approaches, / gets nowhere, / and finishes for the day.
어느 수학자는 연필을 깎고, / 어떤 증명을 해내려고 애쓰며, / 몇 가지 접근법을 시도하고, / 아무런 성과를 내지 못하고, / 하루를 끝낸다.

A writer sits down at his desk, / produces a few hundred words, / decides they are no good, / throws them in the bin, / and hopes for better inspiration tomorrow.
어느 작가는 책상에 앉아 / 몇 백 단어의 글을 창작하고, / 그것이 별로라고 판단하며, / 쓰레기통에 그것을 던져 버리고, / 내일 더 나은 영감을 기대한다.

To produce something worthwhile / — if it ever happens — / may require years of such fruitless labor.
가치 있는 것을 만들어 내는 것은, / 행여나 그런 일이 일어난다면, / 여러 해 동안의 그런 결실 없는 노동을 필요로 할지도 모른다.

The Nobel Prize-winning biologist Peter Medawar said / that about four-fifths of his time in science was wasted, / adding sadly that "nearly all scientific research leads nowhere."
노벨상을 수상한 생물학자 Peter Medawar는 말하면서, / 그가 과학에 들인 시간 중 5분의 4 정도가 헛되었다고 / "거의 모든 과학적 연구가 성과를 내지 못한다."라고 애석해하며 덧붙였다.

What kept all of these people going / when things were going badly / was their passion for their subject.
이 모든 사람들을 계속하게 했던 것은 / 상황이 악화되고 있을 때 / 자신들의 주제에 대한 열정이었다.

Without such passion, / they would have achieved nothing.
그러한 열정이 없었더라면, / 그들은 아무것도 이루지 못했을 것이다.

날마다 해야 하는 많은 학업이 지루하고 반복적이기 때문에, 그것을 계속하기 위해서는 동기부여가 잘 되어야 한다. 어느 수학자는 연필을 깎고, 어떤 증명을 해내려고 애쓰며, 몇 가지 접근법을 시도하고, 아무런 성과를 내지 못하고, 하루를 끝낸다. 어느 작가는 책상에 앉아 몇 백 단어의 글을 창작하고, 그것이 별로라고 판단하며, 쓰레기통에 그것을 던져 버리고, 내일 더 나은 영감을 기대한다. 가치 있는 것을 만들어 내는 것은, 행여나 그런 일이 일어난다면, 여러 해 동안의 그런 결실 없는 노동을 필요로 할지도 모른다. 노벨상을 수상한 생물학자 Peter Medawar는 그가 과학에 들인 시간 중 5분의 4 정도가 헛되었다고 말하면서, "거의 모든 과학적 연구가 성과를 내지 못한다."라고 애석해하며 덧붙였다. 상황이 악화되고 있을 때 이 모든 사람들을 계속하게 했던 것은 자신들의 주제에 대한 열정이었다. 그러한 열정이 없었더라면, 그들은 아무것도 이루지 못했을 것이다.

Why? 왜 정답일까?

'Since a great deal of day-to-day academic work is boring and repetitive, you need to be well motivated to keep doing it.'에서 매일의 과업이 지루하고 반복적일지라도 동기를 갖고 지속하는 것이 중요하다고 말한 데 이어, 마지막 세 문장에서는 실제로 많은 연구가 성과가 없음에도 불구하고("nearly all scientific research leads nowhere.") 주제에 대한 열정을 갖고 연구를 지속하여 성과를 거둔 과학자들에 관해 이야기한다. 따라서 빈칸에 들어갈 말로 가장 적절한 것은 ③ '결실 없는'이다.

● repetitive ⓐ 반복적인
● sharpen ⓥ 날카롭게 하다, 뾰족하게 하다
● approach ⓝ 접근법
● bin ⓝ 쓰레기통
● worthwhile ⓐ 가치 있는
● biologist ⓝ 생물학자
● mathematician ⓝ 수학자
● work on ~을 연구하다, 작업하다
● get nowhere 아무런 성과를 내지 못하다
● inspiration ⓝ 영감
● require ⓥ 필요하다
● passion ⓝ 열정

★★★ 1등급 대비 고난도 3점 문제

10 질문의 양면성　　　　　　　정답률 44% | 정답 ①

다음 빈칸에 들어갈 말로 가장 적절한 것을 고르시오. [3점]

✔ our stories should fit their scripts – 우리의 이야기가 그들의 대본에 들어맞아야 한다.
② friends should share everything – 친구들은 모든 것을 공유해야 한다
③ people have different tastes – 사람들은 취향이 다르다
④ many questions are always better – 질문이 많으면 항상 더 좋다
⑤ their problems can be solved at once – 그들의 문제는 즉시 해결될 수 있다

Questions convey interest, / but sometimes the interest they convey / is not closely related / to what the person is trying to say.
질문은 관심을 전달하지만, / 때때로 그것이 전달하는 그 관심은 / 밀접한 관련이 없다. / 그 사람이 말하려고 하는 것과는

Sometimes the distraction is obvious.
때때로 주의가 분산되는 것이 분명하다.

If you're telling a friend / all the unpleasant things / you experienced on your vacation, / and she interrupts with a lot of questions / about where you stayed, / you won't feel listened to.
만약 여러분이 친구에게 말하고 있는데 / 모든 불쾌한 것들을 / 여러분이 휴가 중에 경험했던 / 친구가 질문을 많이 하면서 방해한다면 / 여러분이 어디에 머물렀는지에 대해 / 여러분은 경청되고 있다고 느끼지 않을 것이다.

At other times / people seem to be following / but can't help trying to lead.
다른 때에는 / 사람들이 잘 듣고 있는 것처럼 보이지만 / (대화를) 주도하려고 하지 않고는 못 배긴다.

These listeners / force their own narrative structures on our experience.
이런 청자들은 / 우리의 경험에 자신들의 이야기 구조를 강요한다.

Their questions assume / that our stories should fit their scripts: / "Problems should be denied or made to go away"; / "Everyone should be together"; / "Bullies must be confronted."
그들의 질문은 가정한다. / 우리의 이야기가 그들의 대본에 들어맞아야 한다고 / "문제들은 부인되거나 사라지게 만들어져야 해.", / "모든 사람은 함께 있어야 해.", / "사람들을 못살게 구는 사람들에게는 맞서야 해."

By finishing our sentences, / pumping us with questions, / and otherwise pushing us to say what they want to hear, / controlling listeners violate our right / to tell our own stories.
우리의 문장을 끝내고, / 우리에게 질문을 퍼붓고, / 그렇지 않으면 그들이 듣고 싶은 것을 말하도록 우리에게 강요함으로써, / 통제하려는 청자들은 우리의 권리를 침해한다. / 우리 자신의 이야기를 할

질문은 관심을 전달하지만, 때때로 그것이 전달하는 그 관심은 그 사람이 말하려고 하는 것과는 밀접한 관련이 없다. 때때로 주의가 분산되는 것이 분명하다. 만약 여러분이 휴가 중에 경험했던 모든 불쾌한 것들을 친구에게 말하고 있는데 친구가 여러분이 어디에 머물렀는지에 대해 질문을 많이 하면서 방해한다면 여러분은 (친구가) 경청하고 있다고 느끼지 않을 것이다. 어떤 때에는 사람들이 잘 듣고 있는 것처럼 보이지만 (대화를) 주도하려고 하지 않고는 못 배긴다. 이런 청자들은 우리의 경험에 자신들의 이야기 구조를 강요한다. 그들의 질문은 우리의 이야기가 그들의 대본에 들어맞아야 한다고 가정한다. "문제들을 부인하거나 사라지게 해야 해.", "모든 사람은 함께 있어야 해.", "사람들을 못살게 구는 사람들에게는 맞서야 해." 우리의 문장을 끝내고, 우리에게 질문을 퍼붓고, 그렇지 않으면 그들이 듣고 싶은 것을 말하도록 우리에게 강요함으로써, 통제하려는 청자들은 우리 자신의 이야기를 할 우리의 권리를 침해한다.

Why? 왜 정답일까?

빈칸 앞에서 질문이 많은 청자들은 우리의 경험에 자기 자신들의 이야기 구조를 강요한

DAY 05

다(These listeners force their own narrative structures on our experience.)라고 말한 데 이어 빈칸 뒤에는 이들이 우리에게 질문을 퍼붓고 그렇지 않으면 그들이 듣고 싶은 것을 말하도록 우리에게 강요한다(~ pushing us to say what they want to hear, ~.)고 한다. 따라서 빈칸에 들어갈 말로 가장 적절한 것은 ① '우리의 이야기가 그들의 대본에 들어맞아야 한다.'이다.

- ● be related to ~에 관계가 있다
- ● obvious ⓐ 명백한, 분명한
- ● structure ⓝ 구조
- ● confront ⓥ 직면하다
- ● violate ⓥ 침해하다
- ● distraction ⓝ 주의가 분산되는 것
- ● narrative ⓐ 이야기의
- ● assume ⓥ 가정하다
- ● pump 퍼붓다

구문 풀이

4행 If you're telling a friend all the unpleasant things [you
접속사(만약 ~라면) (목적격 관계대명사 생략)
experienced on your vacation], and she interrupts with a lot of
questions about [where you stayed], / you won't feel listened to.
간접의문문(명사절) 과거분사

★★ 문제 해결 꿀~팁 ★★

▶ 많이 틀린 이유는?
선택지에 비유가 등장하여 이 의미를 파악하지 못했다면 어렵게 느껴졌을 문제이다. 오답 선택지 중 ④는 주제와 반대되고 나머지는 글의 내용과 관련이 없다.

▶ 문제 해결 방법은?
정답 선택지의 '대본'은 '청자가 이미 정해놓은 이야기'라는 뜻을 나타내는 비유이다. 영어 실력뿐 아니라 논리적 추론 능력을 묻는 빈칸 문제에서는 비유나 함축적인 표현이 자주 등장하므로 기출을 많이 보며 추론하는 연습을 해 두도록 한다.

★★★ 1등급 대비 고난도 3점 문제

11 문화적 변화에 대한 인간의 태도 　　　　정답률 36% | 정답 ⑤

다음 빈칸에 들어갈 말로 가장 적절한 것을 고르시오. [3점]

① seek cooperation between generations
세대 간 협력을 추구하는
② be forgetful of what they experienced
그들이 경험한 것을 잘 잊어버리는
③ adjust quickly to the new environment
새로운 환경에 빠르게 적응하는
④ make efforts to remember what their ancestors did
자신의 조상이 했던 것을 기억하려고 노력하는
✔ like what they have grown up in and gotten used to
자신이 자라고 익숙해진 것을 좋아하는

It is difficult to know how to determine / whether one culture is better than another.
방법을 알기는 어렵다. / 한 문화가 다른 문화보다 나은지를 결정하는

What is the cultural rank order / of rock, jazz, and classical music?
문화적인 순위는 어떻게 될까? / 록, 재즈, 고전 음악의

When it comes to public opinion polls / about whether cultural changes are for the better or the worse, / looking forward would lead to one answer / and looking backward would lead to a very different answer.
여론 조사에 관한 한, / 문화적 변화가 더 나아지는 것인지 더 나빠지는 것인지에 관한 / 앞을 내다보는 것과 / 뒤돌아보는 것은 아주 다른 대답으로 이어진다.

Our children would be horrified / if they were told / they had to go back to the culture of their grandparents.
우리 아이들은 겁이 날 것이다. / 말을 들으면 / 조부모의 문화로 되돌아가야 한다는

Our parents would be horrified / if they were told / they had to participate in the culture of their grandchildren.
우리 부모님은 겁이 날 것이다. / 들으면 / 손주의 문화에 참여해야 한다고

Humans tend to like / what they have grown up in / and gotten used to.
인간은 좋아하는 경향이 있다. / 자신이 자라고 / 익숙해진 것을

After a certain age, / anxieties arise / when sudden cultural changes are coming.
특정한 나이 이후에는 / 불안감이 생긴다. / 갑작스러운 문화적 변화가 다가오고 있을 때

Our culture is part of / who we are and where we stand, / and we don't like to think / that who we are and where we stand / are short-lived.
우리 문화는 일부이고, / 우리의 정체성과 우리의 입지의 / 우리는 생각하고 싶어 하지 않는다. / 우리의 정체성과 우리의 입지가 / 오래가지 못한다고

한 문화가 다른 문화보다 더 나은지를 결정하는 방법을 알기는 어렵다. 록, 재즈, 고전 음악의 문화적인 순위는 어떻게 될까? 문화적 변화가 더 나아지는 것인지 더 나빠지는 것인지에 관한 여론 조사에 관한 한, 앞을 내다보는 것과 뒤를 돌아보는 것은 아주 다른 대답으로 이어진다. 우리 아이들은 조부모의 문화

로 되돌아가야 한다는 말을 들으면 겁이 날 것이다. 우리 부모님은 손주의 문화에 참여해야 한다고 들으면 겁이 날 것이다. 인간은 자신이 자라고 익숙해진 것을 좋아하는 경향이 있다. 특정한 나이 이후에는 갑작스러운 문화적 변화가 다가오고 있을 때 불안감이 생긴다. 우리 문화는 우리의 정체성과 우리의 입지의 일부이고, 우리는 우리의 정체성과 우리의 입지가 오래가지 못한다고 생각하고 싶어 하지 않는다.

Why? 왜 정답일까?

인간은 특정한 나이가 지나면 갑작스러운 문화의 변화에 불안감을 느끼는데 이는 우리의 문화가 우리 정체성과 입지의 일부로 여겨지기 때문이라는(Our culture is part of who we are and where we stand, ~) 내용을 다룬 글이다. 우리는 우리 자신의 문화가 오래가지 못한다고 여기고 싶어 하지 않는다는 내용의 마지막 문장을 근거로 볼 때, 빈칸 앞의 두 문장에서 언급하듯이 우리가 다른 세대의 문화에 참여해야 한다고 생각하면 겁을 내는 이유는 우리가 우리 자신의 문화를 가장 편하게 여기고 좋아하기 때문임을 유추할 수 있으므로, 빈칸에 들어갈 말로 가장 적절한 것은 ⑤ '자신이 자라고 익숙해진 것을 좋아하는'이다.

- ● determine ⓥ 결정하다, 정하다
- ● public opinion poll 여론 조사
- ● participate in ~에 참여하다
- ● certain ⓐ 특정한, 일정한
- ● arise ⓥ 생기다, 발생하다
- ● seek ⓥ 찾다
- ● adjust ⓥ 적응하다
- ● culture ⓝ 문화
- ● horrified ⓐ 겁에 질린, 무서워하는
- ● grandchildren ⓝ 손자
- ● anxiety ⓝ 불안, 걱정
- ● short-lived 오래 가지 못하는, 단기적인
- ● cooperation ⓝ 협력
- ● ancestor ⓝ 조상

구문 풀이

3행 When it comes to public opinion polls about {whether cultural
~에 관한 한 명사구 ~인지 아닌지
changes are for the better or the worse}, looking forward would lead
{ }: 명사절(about의 목적어) 동명사구 주어1 동사1
to one answer and looking backward would lead to a very different
동명사구 주어2 동사2
answer.

★★ 문제 해결 꿀~팁 ★★

▶ 많이 틀린 이유는?
인간은 자신이 익숙하게 느끼는 문화를 좋아한다는 내용의 글로, 빈칸 앞의 예시와 뒤의 결론 내용을 종합하면 답을 고를 수 있다. 최다 오답인 ④는 사람들이 조상의 행동을 기억하려고 애쓴다는 뜻인데 이는 본문의 내용과 관계가 없다. 새로운 환경에 대한 적응력을 언급하는 ③은 우리가 새로운 문화에 잘 적응한다는 뜻으로 이해될 수 있으므로 주제와 상반된다.

▶ 문제 해결 방법은?
결론이 다소 추상적이므로 예시를 통해 글을 이해하면 쉽다. 아이이든 노인이든 서로 다른 세대의 문화에 참여해야 한다면 겁부터 날 것이라는 언급을 통해, 익숙한 것을 좋게 여기는 인간의 특성을 유추하도록 한다.

★★★ 1등급 대비 고난도 3점 문제

12 음식이 마음에 미치는 영향 　　　　정답률 37% | 정답 ⑤

다음 빈칸에 들어갈 말로 가장 적절한 것을 고르시오. [3점]

① leads us to make a fair judgement
우리가 공정한 판단을 내리게 유도한다
② interferes with cooperation with others
타인과의 협력을 방해한다
③ does harm to serious diplomatic occasions
심각한 외교 상황에 해를 끼친다
④ plays a critical role in improving our health
우리의 건강을 증진하는 데 중요한 역할을 한다
✔ enhances our receptiveness to be persuaded
설득되는 데 대한 우리의 수용성을 높인다

There is a famous Spanish proverb / that says, "The belly rules the mind."
유명한 스페인 속담이 있다. / '배가 마음을 다스린다'라고 하는

This is a clinically proven fact.
이것은 임상적으로 증명된 사실이다.

Food is the original mind-controlling drug.
음식은 원래 마음을 지배하는 약이다.

Every time we eat, / we bombard our brains with a feast of chemicals, / triggering an explosive hormonal chain reaction / that directly influences the way we think.
우리가 먹을 때마다 / 우리는 자신의 두뇌에 화학 물질의 향연을 퍼부어 / 폭발적인 호르몬 연쇄 반응을 유발한다. / 우리가 생각하는 방식에 직접적으로 영향을 미치는

Countless studies have shown / that the positive emotional state / induced by a good meal / enhances our receptiveness to be persuaded.
수많은 연구는 보여주었다. / 긍정적인 감정 상태가 / 근사한 식사로 유도된 / 설득되는 데 대한 우리의 수용성을 높인다는 것을

It triggers an instinctive desire / to repay the provider.
그것은 본능적인 욕구를 유발한다. / 그 제공자에게 보답하려는

This is why executives regularly combine business meetings with meals, / why lobbyists invite politicians / to attend receptions, lunches, and dinners, / and why major state occasions / almost always involve an impressive banquet.
이것이 경영진이 정기적으로 업무 회의와 식사를 결합하는 이유이고, / 로비스트들이 정치인들을 초대하는 이유이고, / 환영회, 점심 식사, 저녁 식사에 참석하도록 / 주요 국가 행사가 / 거의 항상 인상적인 연회를 포함하는 이유이다.

Churchill called this "dining diplomacy," / and sociologists have confirmed / that this principle is a strong motivator / across all human cultures.
Churchill은 이것을 '식사 외교'라고 불렀고, / 사회학자들은 확인해 왔다. / 이 원리가 강력한 동기 부여물이라는 것을 / 모든 인류 문화에 걸쳐

'배가 마음을 다스린다'라고 하는 유명한 스페인 속담이 있다. 이것은 임상적으로 증명된 사실이다. 음식은 원래 마음을 지배하는 약이다. 우리가 먹을 때마다 우리는 자신의 두뇌에 화학 물질의 향연을 퍼부어 우리가 생각하는 방식에 직접적으로 영향을 미치는 폭발적인 호르몬 연쇄 반응을 유발한다. 수많은 연구는 근사한 식사로 유도된 긍정적인 감정 상태가 설득되는 데 대한 우리의 수용성을 높인다는 것을 보여주었다. 그것은 그 제공자에게 보답하려는 본능적인 욕구를 유발한다. 이것이 경영진이 정기적으로 업무 회의와 식사를 결합하는 이유이고, 로비스트들이 정치인들을 환영회, 점심 식사, 저녁 식사에 참석하도록 초대하는 이유이고, 주요 국가 행사가 거의 항상 인상적인 연회를 포함하는 이유이다. Churchill은 이것을 '식사 외교'라고 불렀고, 사회학자들은 이 원리가 모든 인류 문화에 걸쳐 강력한 동기 부여물이라는 것을 확인해 왔다.

Why? 왜 정답일까?

첫 세 문장에서 스페인 속담을 예로 들며 음식이 마음을 지배한다(Food is the original mind-controlling drug.)는 것이 사실이라는 점을 언급하고, 빈칸 뒤에서는 이러한 이유로 각종 업무 상황에 연회와 식사가 포함된다고 설명한다. 따라서 빈칸에 들어갈 말로 가장 적절한 것은 근사한 식사로 긍정적인 감정 상태에 이르렀을 때의 결과를 적절히 유추한 ⑤ '설득되는 데 대한 우리의 수용성을 높인다'이다.

- clinically ad 임상적으로
- feast n 향연
- explosive a 폭발적인
- instinctive a 본능적인
- reception n 환영회
- diplomacy n 외교
- interfere with ~을 방해하다
- enhance v 높이다, 향상시키다
- bombard A with B v A에 B를 퍼붓다
- trigger v 유발하다
- induce v 유도하다
- executive n 경영진
- impressive a 인상적인
- principle n 원리
- do harm to v ~에 해를 끼치다
- receptiveness n 수용성, 감수성

구문 풀이

3행 Every time we eat, we bombard our brains with a feast of
~할 때마다 「bombard +A + with + B : A에 B를 퍼붓다」
chemicals, triggering an explosive hormonal chain reaction [that
분사구문(그리고 ~하다) 선행사 주격 관계대명사
directly influences the way we think].

★★ 문제 해결 꿀~팁 ★★

▶ 많이 틀린 이유는?
'배가 마음을 지배한다' 말이 있듯이 사람은 특히 근사한 식사를 하면 감정과 사고 과정에 영향을 받아 '설득되기 쉬운' 상태가 되고, 이 때문에 '식사 외교'라는 말이 등장할 만큼 다양한 사회적 상황에 식사가 수반된다는 내용을 다룬 글이다. ②는 근사한 식사가 도리어 '사람들 간 협력을 방해한다'는 의미를 나타내므로 주제와 상반된다.

▶ 문제 해결 방법은?
빈칸 바로 뒤의 문장에서 a good meal을 It으로 받아 근사한 식사는 식사를 제공해준 사람에게 보답하려는 본능을 일깨운다고 언급하고 있다. 이를 근거로 볼 때, 좋은 식사를 대접받으면 '(상대방의) 부탁에 설득될 가능성이 높아진다'는 내용이 빈칸에 들어가야 한다.

DAY 06 — 빈칸 추론 06

01 ①	02 ③	03 ②	04 ⑤	05 ②
06 ④	07 ④	08 ③	09 ②	10 ①
11 ③	12 ①			

01 대도시의 분업 정답률 48% | 전답 ①

다음 빈칸에 들어갈 말로 가장 적절한 것을 고르시오. [3점]

✔ ① specialization - 전문화
② criticism - 비판
③ competition - 경쟁
④ diligence - 근면
⑤ imagination - 상상

In small towns / the same workman makes chairs and doors and tables, / and often the same person builds houses.
작은 마을에서는 / 똑같은 일꾼이 의자와 문, 탁자를 만들고, / 바로 같은 사람이 종종 집도 짓는다.

And it is, of course, impossible / for a man of many trades / to be skilled in all of them.
그리고 물론 불가능하다. / 많은 직업을 가진 한 사람이 / 그 모든 데 능하기는

In large cities, on the other hand, / because many people make demands on each trade, / one trade alone / — very often even less than a whole trade — / is enough to support a man.
반면에 대도시에서는, / 많은 사람들이 각 직종을 필요로 하기에, / 한 가지 직종만으로도, / 아주 흔하게 전체 직종에 훨씬 못 미치는 / 한 사람이 먹고 사는 데 충분하다.

For instance, / one man makes shoes for men, / and another for women.
예를 들어, / 한 사람은 남자 신발을 만들고, / 다른 사람은 여자 신발을 만든다.

And there are places / even where one man earns a living / by only stitching shoes, / another by cutting them out, / and another by sewing the uppers together.
그리고 경우까지도 있다. / 어떤 사람은 생계를 꾸려가는 / 신발을 깁기만 하여 / 다른 사람은 자르기만 하고, / 또 다른 사람은 신발 윗창을 꿰매기만 하여

Such skilled workers may have used simple tools, / but their specialization / did result in more efficient and productive work.
그런 숙련된 노동자들은 간단한 도구만을 썼을지도 모르지만, / 그들의 전문화는 / 정말로 더 효율적이고 생산적인 작업으로 이어졌다.

작은 마을에서는 똑같은 일꾼이 의자와 문, 탁자를 만들고, 바로 같은 사람이 종종 집도 짓는다. 그리고 물론 많은 직업을 가진 한 사람이 그 모든 데 능하기는 불가능하다. 반면에 대도시에서는, 많은 사람들이 각 직종을 필요로 하기에, 아주 흔하게 전체 직종에 훨씬 못 미치는 한 가지 직종만으로도, 한 사람이 먹고 사는 데 충분하다. 예를 들어, 한 사람은 남자 신발을 만들고, 다른 사람은 여자 신발을 만든다. 그리고 어떤 사람은 신발을 깁기만 하고, 다른 사람은 자르기만 하고, 또 다른 사람은 신발 윗창을 꿰매기만 하여 생계를 꾸려가는 경우까지도 있다. 그런 숙련된 노동자들은 간단한 도구만을 썼을지도 모르지만, 그들의 전문화는 정말로 더 효율적이고 생산적인 작업으로 이어졌다.

Why? 왜 정답일까?

작은 마을과 대도시의 업무 방식을 대조한 글이다. 작은 마을에서는 한 사람이 여러 가지 일을 하게 되지만, 대도시에서는 한 사람이 한 가지 직종만 갖고서도 먹고 사는 데 충분하여 분업이 이루어진다(In large cities, ~, because many people make demands on each trade, one trade alone—very often even less than a whole trade—is enough to support a man.)고 이야기하므로, 빈칸에 들어갈 말로 적절한 것은 '분업'과 대응될 수 있는 ① '전문화'이다.

- workman n 일꾼, 노동자, 직공
- skilled a 숙련된
- stitch v 깁다, 꿰매다, 바느질하다
- result in ~로 이어지다, ~을 초래하다
- productive a 생산적인
- diligence n 근면
- impossible a 불가능한
- place n 경우
- sew v 꿰매다, 깁다
- efficient a 효율적인
- criticism n 비판

구문 풀이

12행 Such skilled workers may have used simple tools, / but their
「may have + 과거분사 : ~했을지도 모른다」
specialization did result in more efficient and productive work.
동사 강조(과거) 원형

02 정해진 마감일이 과업 성과에 미치는 영향   정답률 56% | 정답 ③

다음 빈칸에 들어갈 말로 가장 적절한 것을 고르시오.

① offering rewards – 보상을 제공하는 것
② removing obstacles – 장애물을 제거하는 것
✔ restricting freedom – 자유를 제한하는 것
④ increasing assignments – 과제를 늘리는 것
⑤ encouraging competition – 경쟁을 부추기는 것

To demonstrate how best to defeat the habit of delaying, / Dan Ariely, a professor of psychology and behavioral economics, / performed an experiment on students / in three of his classes at MIT.
미루는 습관을 가장 잘 무너뜨리는 방법을 설명하기 위해, / 심리학 및 행동경제학 교수인 Dan Ariely는 / 학생들을 대상으로 실험을 수행했다. / MIT에서의 수업 중 세 반에서

He assigned all classes three reports / over the course of the semester.
그는 모든 수업에 보고서 세 개를 과제로 부여했다. / 학기 과정 동안

The first class had to choose three due dates for themselves, / up to and including the last day of class.
첫 번째 수업의 학생들은 마감일 세 개를 스스로 선택해야 했다. / 종강일까지 포함해서

The second had no deadlines / — all three papers just had to be submitted / by the last day of class.
두 번째는 마감일이 없었고, / 세 개의 보고서 모두 제출되기만 하면 되었다. / 종강일까지

In his third class, / he gave students three set deadlines / over the course of the semester.
세 번째 수업에서, / 그는 학생들에게 세 개의 정해진 마감일을 주었다. / 학기 과정 동안

At the end of the semester, / he found / that students with set deadlines / received the best grades, / the students with no deadlines / had the worst, / and those who could choose their own deadlines / fell somewhere in the middle.
학기 말에, / 그는 알아냈다. / 마감일이 정해진 학생들이 / 최고의 성적을 받았고, / 마감일이 없는 학생들은 / 최하의 성적을 받았으며, / 마감일을 선택할 수 있었던 학생들은 / 그 중간 어딘가의 위치에 있었다는 것을

Ariely concludes / that restricting freedom — whether by the professor / or by students who recognize their own tendencies to delay things — / improves self-control and performance.
Ariely는 결론짓는다. / 자유를 제한하는 것은 / 교수에 의해서든 / 혹은 일을 미루는 자기 성향을 인식한 학생들에 의해서든, / 자기 통제와 성과를 향상시킨다고

미루는 습관을 가장 잘 무너뜨리는 방법을 설명하기 위해, 심리학 및 행동경제학 교수인 Dan Ariely는 MIT에서의 수업 중 세 반에서 학생들을 대상으로 실험을 수행했다. 그는 학기 과정 동안 모든 수업에 보고서 세 개를 과제로 부여했다. 첫 번째 수업의 학생들은 종강일까지 포함해서 마감일 세 개를 스스로 선택해야 했다. 두 번째는 마감일이 없었고, 세 개의 보고서 모두 종강일까지 제출되기만 하면 되었다. 세 번째 수업에서, 그는 학기 과정 동안 학생들에게 세 개의 정해진 마감일을 주었다. 학기 말에, 그는 마감일이 정해진 학생들이 최고의 성적을 받았고, 마감일이 없는 학생들은 최하의 성적을 받았으며, 마감일을 선택할 수 있었던 학생들은 그 중간 어딘가의 위치에 있었다는 것을 알아냈다. Ariely가 결론짓기로, 교수에 의해서든 혹은 일을 미루는 자기 성향을 인식한 학생들에 의해서든, 자유를 제한하는 것은 자기 통제와 성과를 향상시킨다.

Why? 왜 정답일까?

연구를 소개하는 글이므로 결과 부분인 '~ he found that students with set deadlines received the best grades, ~'이 중요하다. 이 내용에 따르면, 마감일이 '정해져' 있었던 학생들이 다른 두 집단에 비해 성적이 가장 높았다고 한다. 마감을 정해둔다는 것은 결국 일정 부분 '자유를 제한한다'는 의미와 같으므로, 빈칸에 들어갈 말로 가장 적절한 것은 ③ '자유를 제한하는 것'이다.

- demonstrate ⓥ 입증하다
- behavioral ⓐ 행동의
- assign ⓥ 할당하다
- for oneself 스스로
- set ⓐ 정해진
- tendency ⓝ 경향, 성향
- obstacle ⓝ 장애물
- defeat ⓥ 무너뜨리다, 패배시키다
- experiment ⓝ 실험 ⓥ 실험하다
- due date 마감일
- up to and including ~까지 포함해서
- receive ⓥ 받다
- self-control ⓝ 자기 통제
- restrict ⓥ 제한하다

구문 풀이

15행 Ariely concludes that restricting freedom — whether by the
                              주어(명사)
professor or by students who recognize their own tendencies to
「whether+A+or+B : A이든 B이든(부사절)」
delay things — improves self-control and performance.
            동사(단수)

---

03 Minor County의 소비 지역화 운동   정답률 69% | 정답 ②

다음 빈칸에 들어갈 말로 가장 적절한 것을 고르시오. [3점]

① work out regularly – 규칙적으로 운동하도록
✔ spend money locally – 그 지역에서 돈을 쓰도록
③ drive their cars safely – 차를 안전하게 운전하도록
④ treat strangers nicely – 낯선 사람을 친절하게 대하도록
⑤ share work equally – 일을 똑같이 나누도록

In 1995, / a group of high school students in Miner County, South Dakota, / started planning a revival.
1995년, / South Dakota 주 Miner County에 사는 한 무리의 고교생들이 / 부흥을 계획하기 시작했다.

They wanted to do something / that might revive their dying community.
그들은 무언가를 하고 싶었다. / 죽어가는 자기네 지역 사회를 되살릴 수 있는

Miner County had been failing for decades.
Miner County는 몇 십 년 간 침체되고 있었다.

Farm and industrial jobs had slowly dried up, / and nothing had replaced them.
농장 및 산업 일자리가 천천히 줄어들었고 / 이를 대체하는 것은 없었다.

The students started investigating the situation.
학생들은 상황을 조사하기 시작했다.

One finding in particular disturbed them.
특히 한 가지 결과가 그들의 마음을 불편하게 했다.

They discovered / that half of the residents had been shopping outside the county, / driving an hour to Sioux Falls / to shop in larger stores.
그들은 알아냈다. / 주민의 절반이 자기들 지역 바깥에서 쇼핑을 해 오고 있었다는 것을 / Sioux Falls로 한 시간을 운전해 가서, / 더 큰 가게에서 장을 보려고

Most of the things / that could improve the situation / were out of the students' control.
대부분의 일들이 / 상황을 나아지게 할 수 있는 / 학생들의 통제력을 벗어나 있었다.

But they did uncover one thing / that was very much in their control: / inviting the residents to spend money locally.
하지만 그들은 한 가지 것을 진정 알아냈는데, / 자신들이 아주 많이 통제할 수 있는 / 주민들이 그 지역에서 돈을 쓰도록 요청하는 것이었다.

They found their first slogan: / Let's keep Miner dollars in Miner County.
그들은 첫 번째 표어를 찾았다. / Miner의 돈은 Miner County 안에 두자.

1995년, South Dakota 주 Miner County에 사는 한 무리의 고교생들이 부흥을 계획하기 시작했다. 그들은 죽어가는 자기네 지역 사회를 되살릴 수 있는 무언가를 하고 싶었다. Miner County는 몇 십 년 간 침체되고 있었다. 농장 및 산업 일자리가 천천히 줄어들었고 이를 대체하는 것은 없었다. 학생들은 상황을 조사하기 시작했다. 특히 한 가지 결과가 그들의 마음을 불편하게 했다. 그들은 주민의 절반이 더 큰 가게에서 장을 보려고 Sioux Falls로 한 시간을 운전해 가서, 자기들 지역 바깥에서 쇼핑을 해 오고 있었다는 것을 알아냈다. 상황을 나아지게 할 수 있는 대부분의 일들이 학생들의 통제력을 벗어나 있었다. 하지만 그들은 자신들이 통제할 수 있는 한 가지 것을 진정 알아냈는데, 주민들이 그 지역에서 돈을 쓰도록 요청하는 것이었다. 그들은 첫 번째 표어를 찾았다. (그것은) Miner의 돈은 Miner County 안에 두자(였다).

Why? 왜 정답일까?

글 중간에서 마을의 침체 이유를 조사한 결과 학생들은 주민들이 외부 지역에서 쇼핑을 하는 것이 문제임을 파악했다고 하는데, 이를 해결하기 위한 대책은 마지막 문장의 표어 내용대로 사람들이 지역 내부에서 돈을 쓰도록 하는 것(Let's keep Miner dollars in Miner County.)이었다. 따라서 빈칸에 들어갈 말로 가장 적절한 것은 ② '그 지역에서 돈을 쓰도록'이다.

- revival ⓝ 부흥, 부활, 회복
- industrial ⓐ 산업의
- replace ⓥ 대체하다
- in particular 특히
- out of control 통제력을 벗어난
- invite ⓥ 부탁하다, 요청하다
- dying ⓐ 죽어가는
- dry up 줄어들다, 고갈되다, 말라붙다
- investigate ⓥ 조사하다, 수사하다
- disturb ⓥ (마음을) 불편하게 하다, 방해하다
- uncover ⓥ 알아내다, 적발하다
- slogan ⓝ 표어, 슬로건

구문 풀이

8행 They discovered that half of the residents had been shopping
             접속사   동사(과거완료 진행)
outside the county, / driving an hour to Sioux Falls to shop in larger
                    분사구문(~하면서)
stores.

04 우리 자신의 무지 인식하기
정답률 60% | 정답 ⑤

다음 빈칸에 들어갈 말로 가장 적절한 것을 고르시오.

① find their role in teamwork – 팀워크에서 자기 역할을 찾도록
② learn from others' successes and failures – 다른 사람의 성공과 실패로부터 배우도록
③ make the most of technology for learning – 학습을 위해 기술을 최대한 활용하도록
④ obtain knowledge from wonderful experts – 멋진 전문가들로부터 지식을 얻도록
✔ discover the wonder of their ignorance – 자신의 무지함의 경이로움을 알게 되도록

The quest for knowledge in the material world / is a never-ending pursuit, / but the quest does not mean / that a thoroughly schooled person is an educated person / or that an educated person is a wise person.
물질적인 세계에서 지식 탐구는 / 끝없는 추구이지만, / 그 탐구는 의미하지는 않는다. / 온전하게 학교 교육을 받은 사람이 배운 사람이라거나 / 배운 사람이 현명한 사람이라는 것을

We are too often blinded / by our ignorance of our ignorance, / and our pursuit of knowledge is no guarantee of wisdom.
우리는 너무 자주 눈 멀며, / 우리의 무지함에 대한 우리의 무지로 / 우리의 지식 추구가 현명함을 보장하는 것은 아니다.

Hence, / we are prone to / becoming the blind leading the blind / because our overemphasis on competition in nearly everything / makes looking good more important / than being good.
그래서 / 우리는 ~하기 쉽다. / 앞 못 보는 사람들을 이끄는 앞 못 보는 사람이 되기 / 왜냐하면 거의 모든 것에서 경쟁에 대한 우리의 과도한 강조는 / 훌륭해 보이는 것을 더 중요하게 만들기 때문에 / 훌륭한 것보다

The resultant fear / of being thought a fool and criticized / therefore is one of greatest enemies of true learning.
그 결과로 생기는 두려움은 / 바보라고 여겨져 비판받는 것에 대한 / 그렇기 때문에 진정한 배움의 가장 큰 적 중 하나이다.

Although our ignorance is undeniably vast, / it is from the vastness of this selfsame ignorance / that our sense of wonder grows.
우리의 무지함은 부인할 수 없을 정도로 크지만, / 다름 아닌 이 똑같은 무지함의 광대함으로부터이다. / 우리의 경이감이 자라는 것은

But, / when we do not know we are ignorant, / we do not know enough to even question, / let alone investigate, / our ignorance.
하지만, / 우리가 무지하다는 것을 우리가 모를 때, / 우리는 심지어 의문을 품을 만큼도 알지 못한다. / 조사하기는커녕 / 우리의 무지를

No one can teach another person anything.
그 누구도 타인에게 아무것도 가르쳐주지 못한다.

All one can do with and for someone else / is to facilitate learning / by helping the person to discover the wonder of their ignorance.
우리가 다른 누군가와 함께, 그리고 그 사람을 위해 해줄 수 있는 것이라고는 / 배움을 촉진하는 것뿐이다. / 그 사람이 자신의 무지함의 경이로움을 알게 되도록 도와서

물질적인 세계에서 지식 탐구는 끝없는 추구이지만, 그 탐구는 온전하게 학교 교육을 받은 사람이 배운 사람이라거나 배운 사람이 현명한 사람이라는 뜻은 아니다. 우리의 무지함에 대한 무지로 우리는 너무 자주 눈 멀며, 우리의 지식 추구가 현명함을 보장하는 것은 아니다. 그래서 거의 모든 것에서 경쟁에 대한 우리의 과도한 강조는 훌륭해 보이는 것을 (실제) 훌륭한 것보다 더 중요하게 만들기 때문에, 우리는 앞 못 보는 사람들을 이끄는 (마찬가지로) 앞 못 보는 사람이 되기 쉽다. 그 결과로 생기는, 바보라고 여겨져 비판받는 것에 대한 두려움은 그렇기 때문에 진정한 배움의 가장 큰 적 중 하나이다. 우리의 무지함은 부인할 수 없을 정도로 크지만, 우리의 경이감이 자라는 것은 다름 아닌 이 똑같은 무지함의 광대함으로부터이다. 하지만, 우리가 무지하다는 것을 우리가 모를 때, 우리는 우리의 무지를 조사하기는커녕 심지어 의문을 품을 만큼도 알지 못한다. 그 누구도 타인에게 아무것도 가르쳐주지 못한다. 우리가 다른 누군가와 함께, 그리고 그 사람을 위해 해줄 수 있는 것이라고는 그 사람이 <u>자신의 무지함의 경이로움을 알게 되도록</u> 도와서 배움을 촉진하는 것뿐이다.

Why? 왜 정답일까?

글 중반부에서 진정한 배움의 적은 자신이 모르고 있다는 그 사실을 모르는 것이며, 우리는 놀랍도록 무지하지만 바로 이 무지로부터 경이로움이 이룩된다(~ **it is from the vastness of this selfsame ignorance that our sense of wonder grows.**)고 한다. 이는 무지에 대한 깨달음이 즉 진정한 배움으로 나아갈 수 있는 '경이로운' 출발점이 된다는 의미이다. 이때 빈칸 앞의 두 문장에서는 다시 우리가 스스로의 무지를 모른다는 점을 언급한다. 우리는 우리 자신의 무지도 의심하고 조사할 만큼 제대로 알고 있지 못하며, 따라서 남을 '가르칠' 상황도 안 된다는 설명이 나온다. 이를 근거로 할 때, 우리가 타인이 진정한 배움으로 나가게 도와주기 위해 해줄 수 있는 일이라고는 그 사람이 '직접 자신의 무지를 깨닫게' 도와주는 것이라는 결론을 내릴 수 있다. 따라서 빈칸에 들어갈 말로 가장 적절한 것은 ⑤ '자신의 무지함의 경이로움을 알게 되도록(**discover the wonder of their ignorance**)'이다.

● thoroughly ad 철저히
● ignorance n 무지

● prone to ~하기 쉬운
● resultant a 그 결과로 생기는
● vast a 광대한, 큰
● let alone ~하기는커녕
● make the most of ~을 최대한 활용하다
● overemphasis n 과도한 강조
● undeniably ad 부인할 수 없을 정도로
● selfsame a 똑같은
● facilitate v 촉진하다

구문 풀이

7행 Hence, we are prone to becoming the blind leading the blind
　　　　　 ~하기 쉽다　 동명사(전치사 to의 목적어)
because our overemphasis (on competition in nearly everything)
접속사　　　　주어
makes looking good more important than being good.
동사　　목적어　　　목적격 보어

05 머릿속 아이디어일 때 이미 완성된 미래
정답률 53% | 정답 ②

다음 빈칸에 들어갈 말로 가장 적절한 것을 고르시오. [3점]

① didn't even have the potential to accomplish
성취할 잠재력조차 지니고 있지 않았던
✔ have mentally concluded about the future
미래에 대해 머릿속에서 완성한
③ haven't been able to picture in our mind
(전에는) 머릿속에 그릴 수 없었던
④ considered careless and irresponsible
조심성 없고 무책임하다고 여겼던
⑤ have observed in some professionals
몇몇 전문가에게서 관찰해 낸

Everything in the world around us / was finished in the mind of its creator / before it was started.
우리 주변 세상의 모든 것은 / 그것을 만들어 낸 사람의 마음속에서 완성되었다. / 그것이 시작되기 전에

The houses we live in, / the cars we drive, / and our clothing / — all of these began with an idea.
우리가 사는 집, / 우리가 운전하는 자동차, / 우리 옷, / 이 모든 것이 아이디어에서 시작했다.

Each idea was then studied, refined and perfected / before the first nail was driven / or the first piece of cloth was cut.
각각의 아이디어는 그런 다음 연구되고, 다듬어지고, 완성되었다. / 첫 번째 못이 박히거나 / 첫 번째 천 조각이 재단되기에 앞서

Long before the idea was turned into a physical reality, / the mind had clearly pictured the finished product.
그 아이디어가 물리적 실체로 바뀌기 훨씬 전에 / 마음은 완제품을 분명하게 그렸다.

The human being designs his or her own future / through much the same process.
인간은 자신의 미래를 설계한다. / 거의 똑같은 과정을 통해

We begin with an idea / about how the future will be.
우리는 아이디어로 시작한다. / 미래가 어떨지에 대한

Over a period of time / we refine and perfect the vision.
일정 기간에 걸쳐서 / 우리는 그 비전을 다듬어 완성한다.

Before long, / our every thought, decision and activity / are all working in harmony / to bring into existence / what we have mentally concluded about the future.
머지않아, / 우리의 모든 생각, 결정, 활동은 / 모두 조화롭게 작용하게 된다. / 생겨나게 하려고 / 우리가 미래에 대해 머릿속에서 완성한 것을

우리 주변 세상의 모든 것은 시작되기 전에 그것을 만들어 낸 사람의 마음속에서 완성되었다. 우리가 사는 집, 우리가 운전하는 자동차, 우리 옷, 이 모든 것이 아이디어에서 시작했다. 각각의 아이디어는 그런 다음 첫 번째 못이 박히거나 첫 번째 천 조각이 재단되기에 앞서 연구되고, 다듬어지고, 완성되었다. 그 아이디어가 물리적 실체로 바뀌기 훨씬 전에 마음은 완제품을 분명하게 그렸다. 인간은 거의 똑같은 과정을 통해 자신의 미래를 설계한다. 우리는 미래가 어떨지에 대한 아이디어로 시작한다. 일정 기간에 걸쳐서 우리는 그 비전을 다듬어 완성한다. 머지않아, 우리의 모든 생각, 결정, 활동은 우리가 미래에 대해 머릿속에서 완성한 것을 생겨나게 하려고 모두 조화롭게 작용하게 된다.

Why? 왜 정답일까?

첫 문장에서 세상 모든 것은 실체가 있기 이전에 머릿속에서 이미 완성된 아이디어(**finished in the mind of its creator**)였다고 설명하는데, 글 중반부에서 우리 미래 역시 같은 식으로 설계된다고 말한다. 즉, 처음에 '이미 머릿속에서 만들어진' 아이디어가 다듬어지고 구현되는 과정이 똑같이 진행된다는 의미로, 빈칸에 들어갈 말로 가장 적절한 것은 ② '미래에 대해 머릿속에서 완성한'이다.

● clothing n 옷, 의복
● perfect v 완성하다, 완벽하게 하다
● turn A into B A를 B로 바꾸다
● refine v 다듬다
● nail n 못
● picture v 상상하다, 그리다

[문제편 p.040]

- process ⓝ 과정
- before long 머지않아
- bring into existence ~을 생겨나게 하다
- careless ⓐ 조심성 없는
- professional ⓝ 전문가 ⓐ 전문적인
- over a period of time 일정 기간에 걸쳐서
- in harmony 조화롭게
- mentally ⓐ 머릿속에, 마음속으로
- irresponsible ⓐ 무책임한

구문 풀이

1행 Everything in the world around us **was finished** in the mind
주어(every-)   동사(단수)
of its creator before it was started.

---

06   선택과 결과의 연관성   정답률 45% | 정답 ④

다음 빈칸에 들어갈 말로 가장 적절한 것을 고르시오. [3점]

① From saying to doing is a long step
말에서 행동까지의 거리는 멀다
② A good beginning makes a good ending
시작이 좋으면 끝도 좋다
③ One man's trash is another man's treasure
어떤 사람의 쓰레기는 다른 사람의 보물이다
✔ If you pick up one end of the stick, you pick up the other
막대기의 한쪽 끝을 집으면 다른 쪽 끝도 집어 드는 것이다
⑤ The best means of destroying an enemy is to make him your friend
적을 멸망시키는 최선의 방법은 그를 친구로 만드는 것이다

The good news is, / where you end up ten years from now / is up to you.
좋은 소식은, / 결국 10년 후에 여러분이 있게 될 곳이 / 여러분에게 달려 있다는 것이다.

You are free to choose / what you want to make of your life.
여러분은 자유롭게 선택할 수 있다. / 여러분의 삶을 어떻게 만들어 가고 싶은지

It's called *free will* / and it's your basic right.
그것은 *자유 의지*라고 불리며, / 여러분의 기본적인 권리이다.

What's more, you can turn it on instantly!
게다가 여러분은 그것을 즉시 실행할 수도 있다!

At any moment, / you can choose to start showing more respect for yourself / or stop hanging out with friends / who bring you down.
언제든지 / 여러분은 자신을 더 존중하기 시작하기로 선택할 수 있다. / 혹은 친구들과 어울리는 것을 멈추기로 / 여러분을 힘들게 하는

After all, you choose to be happy or miserable.
결국 여러분은 행복해지기로 선택하거나, 비참해지기로 선택한다.

The reality is / that although you are free to choose, / you can't choose the consequences of your choices.
현실은, / 여러분이 선택할 자유가 있지만, / 여러분이 한 선택의 결과를 선택할 수는 없다는 것이다.

It's a package deal.
그것은 세트로 판매되는 상품이다.

As the old saying goes, / "If you pick up one end of the stick, / you pick up the other."
속담에서 말하듯이, / "여러분이 막대기의 한쪽 끝을 집으면 / 다른 쪽 끝도 집어 드는 것이다."

Choice and consequence go together / like mashed potatoes and gravy.
선택과 결과는 함께한다. / 으깬 감자와 소스처럼

좋은 소식은, 결국 10년 후에 여러분이 있게 될 곳이 여러분에게 달려 있다는 것이다. 여러분은 여러분의 삶을 어떻게 만들어 가고 싶은지 자유롭게 선택할 수 있다. 그것은 *자유 의지*라고 불리며, 여러분의 기본적인 권리이다. 게다가 여러분은 그것을 즉시 실행할 수도 있다! 언제든지 여러분은 자신을 더 존중하기 시작하거나 혹은 여러분을 힘들게 하는 친구들과 어울리는 것을 멈추기로 선택할 수 있다. 결국 여러분은 행복해지기로 선택하거나, 비참해지기로 선택한다. 현실은, 여러분이 선택할 자유가 있지만, 여러분이 한 선택의 결과를 선택할 수는 없다는 것이다. 그것은 세트로 판매되는 상품이다. 속담에서 말하듯이, "막대기의 한쪽 끝을 집으면 다른 쪽 끝도 집어 드는 것이다." 으깬 감자와 소스처럼 선택과 결과는 함께한다.

Why? 왜 정답일까?

'The reality is that ~, you can't choose the consequences of your choices. It's a package deal.'와 'Choice and consequence go together ~'에서 선택과 결과는 서로 분리된 것이 아니라 선택에 결과가 뒤따르는 형태로 함께 연관되어 있음을 이야기하므로, 빈칸에 들어갈 말로 가장 적절한 것은 ④ '막대기의 한쪽 끝을 집으면 다른 쪽 끝도 집어 드는 것이다'이다.

- end up (결국) ~하게 되다
- free will 자유 의지
- instantly ⓐ 즉시
- bring down ~을 힘들게 하다
- consequence ⓝ 결과
- saying ⓝ 속담, 격언
- treasure ⓝ 보물
- up to ~에 달린
- turn on ~을 실행[작동]시키다
- hang out with ~와 어울리다
- miserable ⓐ 비참한
- package deal 세트 상품
- mashed potato 으깬 감자

구문 풀이

8행   The reality is {that (although you are free to choose), you
접속사(~것)   양보 접속사(비록 ~일지라도)   주어
can't choose the consequences of your choices}.   { } : 보어 역할의 명사절
동사

★★★ 1등급 대비 고난도 2점 문제

07   탁월함과 타인의 신뢰   정답률 50% | 정답 ④

다음 빈칸에 들어갈 말로 가장 적절한 것을 고르시오.

① Patience - 인내심   ② Sacrifice - 희생
③ Honesty - 정직함   ✔ Excellence - 탁월함
⑤ Creativity - 창의력

Individuals / who perform at a high level in their profession / often have instant credibility with others.
사람들은 / 자기 직업에서 높은 수준으로 수행하는 / 흔히 다른 사람들에게 즉각적인 신뢰를 얻는다.

People admire them, / they want to be like them, / and they feel connected to them.
사람들은 그들을 존경하고, / 그들처럼 되고 싶어 하고, / 그들과 연결되어 있다고 느낀다.

When they speak, / others listen / — even if the area of their skill / has nothing to do with the advice they give.
그들이 말할 때, / 다른 사람들은 경청한다. / 비록 그들의 기술 분야가 / 그들이 주는 조언과 전혀 관련이 없을지라도

Think about a world-famous basketball player.
세계적으로 유명한 농구 선수에 대해 생각해 보라.

He has made more money from endorsements / than he ever did playing basketball.
그는 광고로부터 더 많은 돈을 벌었다. / 그가 농구를 하면서 그간 벌었던 것보다

Is it because of / his knowledge of the products he endorses?
그것이 ~ 때문일까? / 그가 광고하는 제품에 대한 그의 지식

No.
아니다.

It's because of / what he can do with a basketball.
그것은 ~ 때문이다. / 그가 농구로 할 수 있는 것

The same can be said of an Olympic medalist swimmer.
올림픽 메달리스트 수영 선수도 마찬가지이다.

People listen to him / because of what he can do in the pool.
사람들은 그의 말을 경청한다. / 그가 수영장에서 할 수 있는 것 때문에

And when an actor tells us / we should drive a certain car, / we don't listen / because of his expertise on engines.
그리고 어떤 배우가 우리에게 말할 때, / 우리가 특정 자동차를 운전해야 한다고 / 우리는 경청하는 것은 아니다. / 엔진에 대한 그의 전문 지식 때문에

We listen / because we admire his talent.
우리는 경청한다. / 그의 재능을 존경하기 때문에

Excellence connects.
탁월함이 연결된다.

If you possess a high level of ability in an area, / others may desire to connect with you / because of it.
만약 당신이 어떤 분야에서 높은 수준의 능력을 갖고 있다면, / 다른 사람들은 당신과 연결되기를 원할 수도 있다. / 그것 때문에

자기 직업에서 높은 수준으로 수행하는 사람들은 흔히 다른 사람들에게 즉각적인 신뢰를 얻는다. 사람들은 그들을 존경하고, 그들처럼 되고 싶어 하고, 그들과 연결되어 있다고 느낀다. 그들이 말할 때, 다른 사람들은 비록 그들의 기술 분야가 그들이 주는 조언과 전혀 관련이 없을지라도 경청한다. 세계적으로 유명한 농구 선수에 대해 생각해 보라. 그는 그가 농구를 하면서 그간 벌었던 것보다 광고로부터 더 많은 돈을 벌었다. 그것이 그가 광고하는 제품에 대한 그의 지식 때문일까? 아니다. 그것은 그가 농구로 할 수 있는 것 때문이다. 올림픽 메달리스트 수영 선수도 마찬가지이다. 사람들은 그가 수영장에서 할 수 있는 것 때문에 그의 말을 경청한다. 그리고 어떤 배우가 우리에게 특정 자동차를 운전해야 한다고 말할 때, 우리는 엔진에 대한 그의 전문 지식 때문에 경청하는 것은 아니다. 우리는 그의 재능을 존경하기 때문에 경청한다. 탁월함이 연결된다. 만약 당신이 어떤 분야에서 높은 수준의 능력을 갖고 있다면, 다른 사람들은 그것 때문에 당신과 연결되기를 원할 수도 있다.

Why? 왜 정답일까?

처음(Individuals who perform at a high level in their profession often have instant credibility with others.)과 마지막(If you possess a high level of ability in an area, others may desire to connect with you because of it.)에서 자기 분야에서 '높은 수준의 능력'을 가진 사람들은 다른 이들의 신뢰를 사기 쉽다고 언급하는 것으로 보아, 빈칸에 들어갈 말로 가장 적절한 것은 ④ '탁월함'이다.

- profession ⓝ 직업
- credibility ⓝ 신뢰
- have nothing to do with ~와 관련이 없다
- world-famous ⓐ 세계적으로 유명한
- endorsement ⓝ (유명인의 텔레비전 등에서의 상품) 보증 선전
- endorse ⓥ (유명인이 광고에 나와 특정 상품을) 보증하다, 홍보하다
- medalist ⓝ 메달리스트
- patience ⓝ 인내심
- instant ⓐ 즉각적인
- admire ⓥ 존경하다
- expertise ⓝ 전문 지식
- sacrifice ⓝ 희생

구문 풀이

7행 He has made more money from endorsements than he ever did playing basketball.
대동사(= made money)

★★ 문제 해결 꿀~팁 ★★

▶ 많이 틀린 이유는?
빈칸 바로 앞에서 '전문 지식' 때문이 아니라 '재능' 때문에 유명인들의 말을 듣게 된다고 하는데, 이것을 ② '희생'이나 ③ '정직함'의 사례로 볼 수는 없다.

▶ 문제 해결 방법은?
글 처음과 마지막에 요지가 반복 제시된다. 즉 주제문인 첫 문장을 보고 빈칸을 완성하면 간단하다.

★★★ 1등급 대비 고난도 2점 문제

08 사건의 중요성 인식에 영향을 주는 뉴스 보도의 양 정답률 44% | 정답 ③

다음 빈칸에 들어갈 말로 가장 적절한 것을 고르시오.

① accuracy - 정확성
② tone - 어조
✔ amount - 양
④ source - 근원
⑤ type - 유형

As the tenth anniversary of the terrorist attacks of September 11, 2001, approached, / 9/11-related media stories peaked / in the days immediately surrounding the anniversary date / and then dropped off rapidly in the weeks thereafter.
2001년 9월 11일 테러리스트 공격의 10주년 추모일이 다가오면서, / 9/11 관련 언론 기사(의 양)가 정점에 이르렀고, / 추모일 바로 전후로 / 그 후 몇 주 동안 급격히 줄어들었다.

Surveys conducted during those times / asked citizens to choose two "especially important" events / from the past seventy years.
그 시기 동안 실시된 조사는 / 시민들에게 '특히 중요한' 두 가지 사건을 선택하도록 요청했다. / 지난 70년 동안 있었던

Two weeks prior to the anniversary, / before the media blitz began, / about 30 percent of respondents named 9/11.
추모일 2주 전, / 미디어 대선전이 시작되기 전인 / 응답자의 약 30퍼센트가 9/11을 언급했다.

But as the anniversary drew closer, / and the media treatment intensified, / survey respondents started identifying 9/11 in increasing numbers / — to a high of 65 percent.
그러나 추모일이 더 가까워지고, / 미디어 보도가 증가함에 따라, / 더 많은 응답자들이 9/11을 선택하기 시작했고, / 그 수가 65퍼센트까지 올랐다.

Two weeks later, though, / after reportage had decreased to earlier levels, / once again only about 30 percent of the participants / placed it among their two especially important events / of the past seventy years.
그러나 2주 후에 / 보도가 이전 수준으로 줄어들자, / 다시 한 번 참가자의 약 30퍼센트만이 / 그것을 특히 중요한 두 가지 사건으로 선택했다. / 지난 70년 동안의

Clearly, / the amount of news coverage can make a big difference / in the perceived significance of an issue among observers / as they are exposed to the coverage.
명백하게, / 뉴스 보도의 양은 큰 차이를 만들 수 있다. / 관찰자들 사이에서 인지된 문제의 중요성에 있어 / 그들이 그 보도에 노출될 때

2001년 9월 11일 테러리스트 공격의 10주년 추모일이 다가오면서, 9/11 관련 언론 기사(의 양)가 추모일 바로 전후로 정점에 이르렀고, 그 후 몇 주 동안 급격히 줄어들었다. 그 시기 동안 실시된 조사는 시민들에게 지난 70년 동안 있었던 '특히 중요한' 두 가지 사건을 선택하도록 요청했다. 미디어 대선전이 시작되기 전인 추모일 2주 전, 응답자의 약 30퍼센트가 9/11을 언급했다. 그러나 추모일이 더 가까워지고, 미디어 보도가 증가함에 따라, 더 많은 응답자들이 9/11을 선택하기 시작했고, 그 수가 65퍼센트까지 올랐다. 그러나 보도가 2주

후에 이전 수준으로 줄어들자, 다시 한 번 참가자의 약 30퍼센트만이 그것을 지난 70년 동안의 특히 중요한 두 가지 사건으로 선택했다. 명백하게, 뉴스 보도의 양은 관찰자들이 그 보도에 노출될 때 그들 사이에서 인지된 문제의 중요성에 있어 큰 차이를 만들 수 있다.

Why? 왜 정답일까?

빈칸 앞의 두 문장에서 9/11 추모일이 가까워지면서 미디어 보도가 증가하자 사람들은 9/11을 '특히 중요한' 사건으로 더 많이 언급했지만, 미디어 보도가 다시 이전 수준으로 감소하자 9/11 보도를 중요한 사건으로 꼽는 사람들이 줄어들었다고 설명한다. 즉 어떤 사건에 대해 뉴스 보도가 '얼마나 많이' 이루어지는가에 따라 사건에 대한 사람들의 인식이 달라질 수 있다는 내용의 글이므로, 빈칸에 들어갈 말로 가장 적절한 것은 ③ '양'이다.

- immediately ⓐⓓ 바로 옆에
- drop off ⓥ 줄다
- intensify ⓥ (정도, 빈도, 강도가) 심해지다
- perceive ⓥ 인지하다
- accuracy ⓝ 정확성
- anniversary ⓝ 기념일
- prior to ~에 앞서
- reportage ⓝ 보도
- significance ⓝ 중요성

구문 풀이

12행 Two weeks later, though, after reportage had decreased to
부사(하지만) 시간 접속사(~한 후에) 과거완료
earlier levels, once again only about 30 percent of the participants
주어
placed it among their two especially important events of the past
동사
seventy years.

★★ 문제 해결 꿀~팁 ★★

▶ 많이 틀린 이유는?
예시 내용을 일반화하여 빈칸에 들어갈 말을 찾아야 하는데, 글에서 9/11 테러 사건이 '얼마나 많이' 보도되었는지만 언급하고 있을 뿐, 보도의 구체적인 유형을 나누고 있지는 않으므로 ⑤는 답으로 부적합하다.

▶ 문제 해결 방법은?
'the media treatment intensified ~', 'after reportage had decreased to earlier levels ~' 등을 참고하면 보도의 '양'이 곧 사건에 대한 사람들의 인식에 영향을 주는 요인임을 알 수 있다.

★★★ 1등급 대비 고난도 3점 문제

09 전통적 수요 법칙의 예외인 기펜재 정답률 56% | 정답 ②

다음 빈칸에 들어갈 말로 가장 적절한 것을 고르시오. [3점]

① order more meat - 더 많은 고기를 주문한다
✔ consume more rice - 더 많은 쌀을 소비한다
③ try to get new jobs - 새로운 일자리를 구하려 한다
④ increase their savings - 저축액을 늘린다
⑤ start to invest overseas - 해외에 투자하기 시작한다

The law of demand is / that the demand for goods and services increases / as prices fall, / and the demand falls / as prices increase.
수요의 법칙은 ~이다. / 상품과 서비스에 대한 수요가 증가하고, / 가격이 하락할수록 / 수요가 감소하는 것 / 가격이 상승할수록

Giffen goods are special types of products / for which the traditional law of demand does not apply.
기펜재는 특별한 유형의 상품이다. / 전통적인 수요 법칙이 적용되지 않는

Instead of switching to cheaper replacements, / consumers demand more of giffen goods / when the price increases / and less of them when the price decreases.
저렴한 대체품으로 바꾸는 대신 / 소비자들은 기펜재를 더 많이 필요로 한다. / 가격이 상승할 때 / 그리고 가격이 하락할 때 덜

Taking an example, / rice in China is a giffen good / because people tend to purchase less of it / when the price falls.
예를 들어, / 중국의 쌀은 기펜재이다. / 사람들이 그것을 덜 구매하는 경향이 있기 때문에 / 가격이 하락할 때

The reason for this is, / when the price of rice falls, / people have more money / to spend on other types of products / such as meat and dairy / and, therefore, change their spending pattern.
그 이유는 ~이다. / 쌀값이 하락하면, / 사람들이 돈이 많아지고, / 다른 종류의 상품에 쓸 / 고기나 유제품 같은 / 그 결과 소비 패턴을 바꾸기 때문에

On the other hand, / as rice prices increase, / people consume more rice.
반면에, / 쌀값이 상승하면, / 사람들은 더 많은 쌀을 소비한다.

수요의 법칙은 가격이 하락할수록 상품과 서비스에 대한 수요가 증가하고, 가

DAY 06

[문제편 p.042]

격이 상승할수록 수요가 감소하는 것이다. *기펜재*는 전통적인 수요 법칙이 적용되지 않는 특별한 유형의 상품이다. 저렴한 대체품으로 바꾸는 대신 소비자들은 가격이 상승할 때 기펜재를 더 많이, 가격이 하락할 때 덜 필요로 한다. 예를 들어, 중국의 쌀은 가격이 하락할 때 사람들이 덜 구매하는 경향이 있기 때문에 기펜재이다. 그 이유는, 쌀값이 하락하면, 사람들이 고기나 유제품 같은 다른 종류의 상품에 쓸 돈이 많아지고, 그 결과 소비 패턴을 바꾸기 때문이다. 반면에, 쌀값이 상승하면, 사람들은 **더 많은 쌀을 소비한다**.

Why? **왜 정답일까?**

전통적인 수요 법칙에 따르면 가격과 수요는 반비례하지만, 이 법칙의 예외에 있는 기펜재는 가격과 상승 및 하락 흐름을 같이한다(Instead of switching to cheaper replacements, consumers demand more of giffen goods when the price increases and less of them when the price decreases.)는 내용의 글이다. 중반부 이후로 중국의 쌀이 기펜재의 예시로 언급되므로, 쌀 가격이 오를 때 오히려 사람들은 '쌀을 더 산다'는 내용이 결론이어야 한다. 따라서 빈칸에 들어갈 말로 가장 적절한 것은 ② '더 많은 쌀을 소비한다'이다.

- demand ⓝ 수요 ⓥ 필요로 하다, 요구하다
- apply for ~에 적용되다
- switch to ~로 바꾸다
- replacement ⓝ 대체(품)
- dairy ⓝ 유제품
- overseas ⓐⓓ 해외에

구문 풀이

3행 *Giffen goods* are special types of products [for which the
(선행사) 「전치사+관계대명사」
traditional law of demand does not apply].

★★ 문제 해결 꿀~팁 ★★

▶ **많이 틀린 이유는?**
기펜재의 개념을 잘 이해하고 사례에 적용해야 하는 빈칸 문제이다. 최다 오답 ④는 '저축액을 늘린다'는 의미인데, 글에서 기펜재와 저축액을 연결짓는 내용은 언급되지 않았다.

▶ **문제 해결 방법은?**
글에 따르면 기펜재는 일반적 재화와 달리 가격이 오를 때 수요도 오르고, 가격이 떨어질 때 수요도 떨어지는 재화이다. 빈칸 문장에서는 '쌀 가격이 오르는' 상황을 상정하고 있으므로, '쌀에 대한 수요도 덩달아 오른다'는 결과를 예측할 수 있다.

★★★ 1등급 대비 고난도 3점 문제

10 수행으로 자기 자신의 가치를 매길 때 정답률 37% | 정답 ①

다음 빈칸에 들어갈 말로 가장 적절한 것을 고르시오. [3점]

✔ it is the sole determinant of one's self-worth
그것이 자신의 가치를 결정하는 유일한 요소일
② you are distracted by others' achievements
다른 사람의 성취에 의해 주의가 분산될
③ there is too much competition in one field
한 분야의 경쟁이 너무 심할
④ you ignore feedback about a performance
수행에 관한 피드백을 무시할
⑤ it is not accompanied by effort
그것에 노력이 따르지 않을

For many people, / *ability* refers to intellectual competence, / so they want everything they do / to reflect how smart they are / — writing a brilliant legal brief, / getting the highest grade on a test, / writing elegant computer code, / saying something exceptionally wise or witty in a conversation.
많은 사람들에게 / 능력은 지적 능력을 의미하기 때문에, / 그들은 자신이 하는 모든 것이 ~하기를 원한다. / 자신이 얼마나 똑똑한지를 보여주기를 / 훌륭한 소송 의견서를 작성하는 것, / 시험에서 최고의 성적을 받는 것, / 명쾌한 컴퓨터 코드를 작성하는 것, / 대화 도중 탁월하게 현명하거나 재치 있는 말을 하는 것

You could also define ability / in terms of a particular skill or talent, / such as how well one plays the piano, / learns a language, / or serves a tennis ball.
여러분은 또한 능력을 정의할 수도 있다. / 특정한 기술이나 재능의 관점에서 / 피아노를 얼마나 잘 치는지, / 언어를 얼마나 잘 배우는지, / 테니스공을 얼마나 잘 서브하는지와 같은

Some people focus on their ability / to be attractive, entertaining, up on the latest trends, / or to have the newest gadgets.
어떤 사람들은 능력에 초점을 맞춘다. / 매력적이고, 재미있고, 최신 유행에 맞출 수 있는 / 혹은 최신 기기를 가질 수 있는

However ability may be defined, / a problem occurs / when it is the sole determinant of one's self-worth.
능력이 어떻게 정의되든지, / 문제가 발생한다. / 그것이 자신의 가치를 결정하는 유일한 요소일 때

The performance becomes the *only* measure of the person; / nothing else is taken into account.
수행이 그 사람의 유일한 척도가 되며, / 다른 것은 고려되지 않는다.

An outstanding performance means an outstanding person; / an average performance means an average person. // Period.
뛰어난 수행은 뛰어난 사람을 의미하고, / 평범한 수행은 평범한 사람을 의미한다. // 끝.

많은 사람들에게 능력은 지적 능력을 의미하기 때문에, 그들은 자신이 하는 모든 것이 자신이 얼마나 똑똑한지를 보여주기를 원한다. 예컨대, 훌륭한 소송 의견서를 작성하는 것, 시험에서 최고의 성적을 받는 것, 명쾌한 컴퓨터 코드를 작성하는 것, 대화 도중 탁월하게 현명하거나 재치 있는 말을 하는 것이다. 여러분은 또한 피아노를 얼마나 잘 치는지, 언어를 얼마나 잘 배우는지, 테니스공을 얼마나 잘 서브하는지와 같은 특정한 기술이나 재능의 관점에서 능력을 정의할 수도 있다. 어떤 사람들은 매력적이고, 재미있고, 최신 유행에 맞추거나, 최신 기기를 가질 수 있는 능력에 초점을 맞춘다. 능력이 어떻게 정의되든지, 그것이 자신의 가치를 결정하는 유일한 요소일 때 문제가 발생한다. 수행이 그 사람의 유일한 척도가 되며, 다른 것은 고려되지 않는다. 뛰어난 수행은 뛰어난 사람을 의미하고, 평범한 수행은 평범한 사람을 의미한다. 끝.

Why? **왜 정답일까?**

빈칸 뒤에서 수행을 자신의 가치에 대한 유일한 평가 척도로 삼는 경우(The performance becomes the *only* measure of the person; nothing else is taken into account.)의 부작용을 언급하는 것으로 보아, 빈칸에 들어갈 말로 가장 적절한 것은 ① '그것이 자신의 가치를 결정하는 유일한 요소일'이다.

- competence ⓝ 능력, 역량
- reflect ⓥ 반영하다
- brilliant ⓐ 뛰어난
- brief ⓝ (법률) 취지서, 의견서, 보고서
- elegant ⓐ 명쾌한, 멋들어진
- exceptionally ⓐⓓ 탁월하게
- witty ⓐ 재치 있는
- in terms of ~의 면에서
- serve a ball 서브를 넣다
- attractive ⓐ 매력적인
- entertaining ⓐ 재미있는, 즐거움을 주는
- gadget ⓝ 장비, 기기
- measure ⓝ 척도
- take into account ~을 고려하다
- outstanding ⓐ 뛰어난
- sole ⓐ 유일한
- determinant ⓝ 결정 요소
- self-worth ⓝ 자존감, 자부심
- distracted ⓐ 정신이 팔린

구문 풀이

11행 However ability may be defined, a problem occurs when it
복합관계부사(어떻게 ~하든 간에 = no matter how)
is the sole determinant of one's self-worth.

★★ 문제 해결 꿀~팁 ★★

▶ **많이 틀린 이유는?**
특정 분야의 재능이나 역량을 보여주려 한다는 내용 때문에, 빈칸 뒤를 제대로 읽지 않으면 남과의 비교를 언급하는 ②나 수행에 대한 피드백을 언급하는 ④가 빈칸에 적절해 보인다. 하지만 빈칸 문제를 풀 때는 해당 지문 자체의 내용에 충실해야 한다.

▶ **문제 해결 방법은?**
빈칸 뒤에서 수행이 '한 사람을 평가하는 유일한 척도(the *only* measure of the person)'가 될 때를 언급하는데, 이 표현이 거의 그대로 ①에서 재진술되었다(the sole determinant of one's self-worth).

★★★ 1등급 대비 고난도 3점 문제

11 차이점에 집중할 때 가려지는 유사점 정답률 32% | 정답 ③

다음 빈칸에 들어갈 말로 가장 적절한 것을 고르시오. [3점]

① prove the uniqueness of each society
각 사회의 고유함을 입증하게
② prevent cross-cultural understanding
다문화적 이해를 막게
✔ mask the more overwhelming similarities
더 압도적인 유사점을 가리게
④ change their perspective on what diversity is
다양성이 무엇인가에 대한 그들의 견해를 바꾸게
⑤ encourage them to step out of their mental frame
그들이 정신적 틀을 벗어나도록 장려하게

Focusing on the differences among societies / conceals a deeper reality: / their similarities are greater and more profound / than their dissimilarities.
사회들 사이의 차이점에 집중하는 것은 / 더 깊은 실체를 숨기는데, / 그것들의 유사점은 더 크고 더 심오하다. / 차이점보다

Imagine studying two hills / while standing on a ten-thousand-foot-high plateau.
두 개의 언덕을 유심히 본다고 상상해 보라. / 1만 피트 높이의 고원에 서서

Seen from your perspective, / one hill appears to be three hundred feet high, / and the other appears to be nine hundred feet.
여러분의 관점에서 보면, / 한 언덕이 300피트 높이인 것처럼 보이고 / 다른 언덕이 900피트 높이인 것처럼 보인다.

This difference may seem large, / and you might focus your attention / on what local forces, such as erosion, / account for the difference in size.
이 차이가 커 보일 수 있고 / 여러분은 자신의 관심을 집중시킬지도 모른다. / 침식과 같은 어떤 국부적인 힘이 / 크기의 차이를 설명하는지에
But this narrow perspective misses the opportunity / to study the other, / more significant geological forces / that created what are actually two very similar mountains, / one 10,300 feet high and the other 10,900 feet.
그러나 이 좁은 관점은 기회를 놓치고 있다. / 다른 관점을 연구할 / 더 중대한 지질학적 힘 / 사실상 아주 비슷한 두 개의 산을 만들어 낸 / 하나는 10,300피트 높이이고 다른 하나는 10,900피트 높이로
And when it comes to human societies, / people have been standing on a ten-thousand-foot plateau, / letting the differences among societies / mask the more overwhelming similarities.
그리고 인간 사회에 관한 한, / 사람들은 1만 피트의 고원에 서서 / 사회들 사이의 차이점으로 하여금 허락하고 있다. / 더 압도적인 유사점을 가리게

사회들 사이의 차이점에 집중하는 것은 더 깊은 실체를 숨기는데, 그것들의 유사점은 차이점보다 더 크고 더 심오하다. 1만 피트 높이의 고원에 서서 두 개의 언덕을 유심히 본다고 상상해 보라. 여러분의 관점에서 보면, 한 언덕이 300피트 높이인 것처럼 보이고 다른 언덕이 900피트 높이인 것처럼 보인다. 이 차이가 커 보일 수 있고 여러분은 침식과 같은 어떤 국부적인 힘이 크기의 차이를 설명하는지에 관심을 집중할지도 모른다. 그러나 이 좁은 관점은 다른 관점, 즉 하나는 10,300피트 높이이고 다른 하나는 10,900피트 높이로 사실상 아주 비슷한 두 개의 산을 만들어 낸 더 중대한 지질학적 힘을 연구할 기회를 놓치고 있다. 그리고 인간 사회에 관한 한, 사람들은 1만 피트의 고원에 서서 사회들 사이의 차이점이 더 압도적인 유사점을 가리게 두고 있다.

Why? 왜 정답일까?

첫 문장에서 사회들 사이의 차이점에 주목하면 그들간의 유사점이라는 더 깊은 실체를 놓치게 된다(Focusing on the differences among societies conceals a deeper reality: their similarities are greater and more profound than their dissimilarities.)고 언급하고 있다. 따라서 빈칸에 들어갈 말로 가장 적절한 것은 ③ '더 압도적인 유사점을 가리게'이다.

- conceal ⓥ 숨기다
- dissimilarity ⓝ 차이점
- account for ⓥ ~을 설명하다
- significant ⓐ 중대한, 유의미한
- when it comes to ~에 관한 한
- overwhelming ⓐ 압도적인
- profound ⓐ 심오한
- plateau ⓝ 고원
- narrow ⓐ 좁은
- geological ⓐ 지질학적인
- uniqueness ⓝ 고유성
- step out of ⓥ ~에서 나오다

구문 풀이

7행 This difference may seem large, and you might focus your attention on what local forces, such as erosion, account for the difference in size.
의문형용사(어떤) / 2형식 동사 / 형용사 보어 / 「focus+A+on+B : A를 B에 집중시키다」 / 명사(주어) / 삽입구 / 동사

★★ 문제 해결 꿀~팁 ★★

▶ 많이 틀린 이유는?
첫 문장에서 제시하듯 이 글의 주제는 차이점에 집중하다보면 훨씬 더 두드러지는 유사성을 놓치기 쉽다는 것이다. ④에서 언급하는 '다양성에 관한 시각'은 주제와 무관한 소재이다.

▶ 문제 해결 방법은?
첫 문장과 마지막 문장이 결국 같은 내용을 말하는 일관된 흐름의 글이다. 예시 부분은 가볍게 넘어가고 'conceals a deeper reality: ~'을 'mask ~'로 재진술한 ③을 바로 답으로 고를 수 있도록 한다.

★★★ 1등급 대비 고난도 3점 문제

12 삶에 다양함을 주기 정답률 54% | 정답 ①

다음 빈칸에 들어갈 말로 가장 적절한 것을 고르시오. [3점]
✔ variety is the spice of life – 다양성은 인생의 묘미이다
② fantasy is the mirror of reality – 공상은 현실의 거울이다
③ failure teaches more than success – 실패는 성공보다 더 많은 것을 가르쳐준다
④ laziness is the mother of invention – 게으름은 발명의 어머니이다
⑤ conflict strengthens the relationship – 갈등은 관계를 강화한다

Say you normally go to a park to walk or work out.
여러분이 보통 어떤 공원에 산책이나 운동을 하러 간다고 하자.

Maybe today you should choose a different park.
어쩌면 오늘 여러분은 다른 공원을 선택해야겠다.
Why?
왜?
Well, who knows?
글쎄, 누가 알겠는가?
Maybe it's because you need the connection to the different energy / in the other park.
어쩌면 여러분이 다른 기운과 연결되는 것이 필요하기 때문일 것이다. / 다른 공원에서
Maybe you'll run into people there / that you've never met before.
어쩌면 여러분은 거기서 사람들을 만나게 될 것이다. / 여러분이 전에 만난 적이 없는
You could make a new best friend / simply by visiting a different park.
여러분은 새로운 가장 친한 친구를 사귈 수 있다. / 그저 다른 공원을 방문함으로써
You never know what great things will happen to you / until you step outside the zone where you feel comfortable.
여러분은 결코 자신에게 어떤 대단한 일이 일어날지 알지 못한다. / 여러분이 편안함을 느끼는 지대 밖으로 나가기 전까지
If you're staying in your comfort zone / and you're not pushing yourself past that same old energy, / then you're not going to move forward on your path.
여러분이 안락 지대에 머무르고 있다면, / 그리고 자신을 밀어붙여 늘 똑같은 기운에서 벗어나도록 하지 않는다면, / 그러면 여러분은 자신의 진로에서 앞으로 나아가지 못할 것이다.
By forcing yourself to do something different, / you're awakening yourself on a spiritual level / and you're forcing yourself to do something / that will benefit you in the long run.
자신에게 다른 어떤 것을 하게 만듦으로써, / 여러분은 영적인 차원에서 자신을 깨우치고, / 여러분은 스스로가 어떤 일을 하게 만들고 있다. / 결국에는 자신을 이롭게 할
As they say, variety is the spice of life.
사람들이 말하듯이, 다양성은 인생의 묘미이다.

보통 어떤 공원에 산책이나 운동을 하러 간다고 하자. 어쩌면 오늘 여러분은 다른 공원을 선택해야겠다. 왜? 글쎄, 누가 알겠는가? 어쩌면 여러분이 다른 공원에서 다른 기운과 연결되는 것이 필요하기 때문일 것이다. 어쩌면 여러분은 거기서 전에 만난 적이 없는 사람들을 만나게 될 것이다. 여러분은 그저 다른 공원을 방문함으로써 새로운 가장 친한 친구를 사귈 수 있다. 여러분은 편안함을 느끼는 지대 밖으로 나가고 나서야 비로소 자신에게 어떤 대단한 일이 일어날지 안다. 여러분이 안락 지대에 머무르고 있고, 자신을 밀어붙여 늘 똑같은 기운에서 벗어나도록 하지 않는다면, 자신의 진로에서 앞으로 나아가지 못할 것이다. 자신에게 다른 어떤 것을 하게 만듦으로써, 여러분은 영적인 차원에서 자신을 깨우치고, 결국에는 자신을 이롭게 할 어떤 일을 하게 만들 수 밖에 없다. 사람들이 말하듯이, 다양성은 인생의 묘미이다.

Why? 왜 정답일까?

항상 익숙하고 편안한 안락 지대를 벗어나 새로운 무언가를 시도할 때 깨달음이 일어나고 스스로를 이롭게 할 수 있다(By forcing yourself to do something different, you're awakening yourself on a spiritual level and you're forcing yourself to do something that will benefit you in the long run.)는 내용의 글이다. 따라서 빈칸에 들어갈 말로 가장 적절한 것은 '새롭고 다양한 것을 시도해보면 좋다'는 의미를 담은 ① '다양성은 인생의 묘미이다'이다.

- run into ⓥ ~을 우연히 만나다
- spiritual ⓐ 영적인, 정신적인
- spice ⓝ 묘미, 향신료
- invention ⓝ 발명
- strengthen ⓥ 강화하다
- force ⓥ (어쩔 수 없이) ~하게 하다
- in the long run 결국에는, 장기적으로
- laziness ⓝ 게으름
- conflict ⓝ 갈등

구문 풀이

7행 You never know what great things will happen to you until
「not[never] + A + until + B : B하고 나서야 비로소 A하다」
you step outside the zone [where you feel comfortable].
선행사 / 관계부사

★★ 문제 해결 꿀~팁 ★★

▶ 많이 틀린 이유는?
글 마지막 문장에 빈칸이 나오면 보통 주제를 요약하므로, 글에서 언급되지 않은 내용은 답으로 고르지 않도록 주의한다. ②의 fantasy와 reality는 본문에서 언급된 바 없고, ③의 failure과 success 또한 글의 중심 소재가 아니다.

▶ 문제 해결 방법은?
이 글에서는 different라는 형용사가 곳곳에 등장하며 '다양한 것'을 시도하라는 주장을 펼치고 있으므로 이 형용사를 variety라는 명사로 바꾼 ①이 답으로 적절하다.

DAY 07 빈칸 추론 07

01 ①	02 ③	03 ①	04 ②	05 ⑤
06 ⑤	07 ①	08 ③	09 ①	10 ①
11 ②	12 ⑤			

01 인식의 이탈을 허용하는 유머
정답률 58% | 정답 ①

다음 빈칸에 들어갈 말로 가장 적절한 것을 고르시오.

✔ accurate - 정확한
② detailed - 상세한
③ useful - 유용한
④ additional - 부가적인
⑤ alternative - 대안적인

Humour involves / not just practical disengagement / but cognitive disengagement.
유머는 포함한다. / 실제적인 이탈뿐만 아니라 / 인식의 이탈

As long as something is funny, / we are for the moment not concerned / with whether it is real or fictional, true or false.
어떤 것이 재미있다면, / 우리는 잠깐 관심을 두지 않는다. / 그것이 진짜인지 허구인지, 진실인지 거짓인지에 관해

This is why we give considerable leeway / to people telling funny stories.
이것이 우리가 상당한 여지를 주는 이유이다. / 재미있는 이야기를 하는 사람들에게

If they are getting extra laughs / by exaggerating the silliness of a situation / or even by making up a few details, / we are happy to grant them comic licence, a kind of poetic licence.
만약 그들이 추가 웃음을 얻고 있다면, / 상황의 어리석음을 과장하거나 / 심지어 몇 가지 세부 사항을 꾸며서라도 / 우리는 그들에게 기꺼이 희극적 파격, 일종의 시적 파격을 허락한다.

Indeed, / someone listening to a funny story / who tries to correct the teller / — 'No, he didn't spill the spaghetti on the keyboard and the monitor, / just on the keyboard' — / will probably be told by the other listeners / to stop interrupting.
실제로, / 재미있는 이야기를 듣고 있는 누군가가 / 말하는 사람을 바로잡으려고 하면 / '아니야, 그는 스파게티를 키보드와 모니터에 쏟은 것이 아니라 / 키보드에만 쏟았어.'라며 / 그는 아마 듣고 있는 다른 사람들에게서 말을 들을 것이다. / 방해하지 말라는

The creator of humour is putting ideas into people's heads / for the pleasure those ideas will bring, / not to provide accurate information.
유머를 만드는 사람은 사람들의 머릿속에 생각을 집어넣고 있는데, / 그 생각이 가져올 재미를 위해서이지 / 정확한 정보를 제공하기 위해서가 아니다.

유머는 실제적인 이탈뿐만 아니라 인식의 이탈을 포함한다. 어떤 것이 재미있다면, 우리는 잠깐 그것이 진짜인지 허구인지, 진실인지 거짓인지에 관해 관심을 두지 않는다. 이것이 우리가 재미있는 이야기를 하는 사람들에게 상당한 여지를 주는 이유이다. 만약 그들이 상황의 어리석음을 과장하거나 심지어 몇 가지 세부 사항을 꾸며서라도 추가 웃음을 얻고 있다면, 우리는 그들에게 기꺼이 희극적 파격, 일종의 시적 파격을 허락한다. 실제로, 재미있는 이야기를 듣고 있는 누군가가 '아니야, 그는 스파게티를 키보드와 모니터에 쏟은 것이 아니라 키보드에만 쏟았어.'라며 말하는 사람을 바로잡으려고 하면 그는 아마 듣고 있는 다른 사람들에게서 방해하지 말라는 말을 들을 것이다. 유머를 만드는 사람은 사람들의 머릿속에 생각을 집어넣고 있는데, 그 생각이 가져올 재미를 위해서이지 정확한 정보를 제공하기 위해서가 아니다.

Why? 왜 정답일까?

첫 두 문장에서 유머는 인식의 이탈을 허용하므로 우리가 어떤 대상을 재미있다고 느낀다면 그 대상이 진실인지 거짓인지는 잠시나마 관심에서 벗어난다고 언급한다. 이어서 예시를 드는 'Indeed, someone listening to a funny story ~'에 따르면 재미있는 이야기를 듣던 중 사실과 다른 부분을 바로잡으려는 사람은 다른 사람들로부터 방해하지 말라는 말을 들을 가능성이 크다고 한다. 이를 근거로 보아, 유머에서 중요한 부분은 '사실적인' 정보 전달이 아니라는 것을 유추할 수 있으므로, 빈칸에 들어갈 말로 가장 적절한 것은 ① '정확한'이다.

- **disengagement** ⓝ 이탈, 해방
- **considerable** ⓐ 상당한
- **make up** 만들어내다, 꾸며내다
- **interrupt** ⓥ 방해하다, 끼어들다
- **alternative** ⓐ 대안의
- **fictional** ⓐ 허구의
- **exaggerate** ⓥ 과장하다
- **grant** ⓥ 주다, 부여하다
- **accurate** ⓐ 정확한

구문 풀이

2행 As long as something is funny, we are (for the moment)
접속사(~하는 한) 동사2 ( ): 삽입구
not concerned with whether it is real or fictional, true or false.
~에 관심을 갖지 않는 접속사(A이든 B이든)

02 고요와 정적에서 비롯되는 창작
정답률 49% | 정답 ③

다음 빈칸에 들어갈 말로 가장 적절한 것을 고르시오.

① organize their ideas - 생각을 정리하는
② interact socially - 사회적으로 상호 작용하는
✔ stop thinking - 생각을 멈추는
④ gather information - 정보를 모으는
⑤ use their imagination - 상상력을 활용하는

The mind is essentially a survival machine.
생각은 본질적으로 생존 기계이다.

Attack and defense against other minds, / gathering, storing, and analyzing information / — this is what it is good at, / but it is not at all creative.
다른 생각에 대해 공격하고 수비하는 것 / 정보를 수집하고 저장하고 분석하며 / 이것은 생각이 잘 하는 것이지만, / 전혀 창의적이지는 않다.

All true artists create / from a place of no-mind, / from inner stillness.
모든 진정한 예술가들은 창작을 한다. / 생각이 없는 상태, 즉 내적인 고요함 속에서

Even great scientists have reported / that their creative breakthroughs / came at a time of mental quietude.
심지어 위대한 과학자들조차도 말했다. / 그들의 창의적인 돌파구는 / 정신적 정적의 시간에서 생겨났다고

The surprising result of a nationwide inquiry / among America's most famous mathematicians, including Einstein, / to find out their working methods, / was that thinking "plays only a subordinate part / in the brief, decisive phase of the creative act itself."
전국적인 조사의 놀라운 결과는 / 아인슈타인을 포함한 미국의 가장 유명한 수학자들 대상의 / 그들의 작업 방식을 알아내기 위한 / "생각이 단지 부수적인 역할만 할 뿐이다."라는 것이었다. / "창의적인 행동의 짧고 결정적인 단계에서"

So I would say / that the simple reason / why the majority of scientists are *not* creative / is not because they don't know how to think, / but because they don't know how to stop thinking!
그래서 나는 말하고 싶다. / 단순한 이유는 / 대다수의 과학자들이 창의적이지 *않은* / 그들이 생각하는 방법을 몰라서가 아니라 / 생각을 멈추는 방법을 모르기 때문이라고

생각은 본질적으로 생존 기계이다. 정보를 수집하고 저장하고 분석하며 다른 생각에 대해 공격하고 수비하는 것 — 이것은 생각이 잘 하는 것이지만, 전혀 창의적이지는 않다. 모든 진정한 예술가들은 생각이 없는 상태, 즉 내적인 고요함 속에서 창작을 한다. 심지어 위대한 과학자들조차도 그들의 창의적인 돌파구는 정신적 정적의 시간에서 생겨났다고 말했다. 아인슈타인을 포함한 미국의 가장 유명한 수학자들을 대상으로 그들의 작업 방식을 알아내기 위한 전국적인 조사의 놀라운 결과는 생각이 "창의적인 행동의 짧고 결정적인 단계에서 단지 부수적인 역할만 할 뿐이다."라는 것이었다. 그래서 나는 대다수의 과학자들이 창의적이지 *않은* 단순한 이유는 그들이 생각하는 방법을 몰라서가 아니라 생각을 멈추는 방법을 모르기 때문이라고 말하고 싶다.

Why? 왜 정답일까?

'All true artists create from a place of no-mind, from inner stillness. Even great scientists have reported that their creative breakthroughs came at a time of mental quietude.'에서 예술가와 과학자 모두 내적인 고요함 또는 마음의 정적 속에서 창작을 하고 창의적인 돌파구를 찾는다고 이야기하므로, 빈칸 또한 '고요, 정적'과 같은 의미를 나타내야 한다. 따라서 빈칸에 들어갈 말로 가장 적절한 것은 ③ '생각을 멈추는'이다.

- **essentially** ⓐⓓ 본질적으로
- **gather** ⓥ 모으다, 수집하다
- **analyze** ⓥ 분석하다
- **breakthrough** ⓝ 돌파구
- **inquiry** ⓝ 조사, 연구
- **brief** ⓐ 짧은
- **majority** ⓝ 다수, 대부분
- **socially** ⓐⓓ 사회적으로
- **defense** ⓝ 방어
- **storing** ⓝ 저장
- **stillness** ⓝ 고요함
- **nationwide** ⓐ 전국적인
- **method** ⓝ 방법
- **decisive** ⓐ 결정적인
- **organize** ⓥ 정리하다, 체계화하다
- **imagination** ⓝ 상상력

구문 풀이

12행 So I would say that the simple reason [why the majority of
접속사 주어
scientists are *not* creative] is not because they don't know how to
동사 「not＋A＋but＋B : A가 아니라 B」
think, but because they don't know how to stop thinking.

03 관심의 표현을 통한 동기 부여
정답률 59% | 정답 ①

다음 빈칸에 들어갈 말로 가장 적절한 것을 고르시오.

✔ care about them - 그들에 대해 신경 쓴다

② keep your words – 약속을 지킨다
③ differ from them – 그들과 다르다
④ evaluate their performance – 그들의 수행을 평가한다
⑤ communicate with their parents – 그들의 부모와 소통한다

Motivation may come from several sources.
동기 부여는 여러 원천에서 올 수 있다.

It may be the respect / I give every student, / the daily greeting I give at my classroom door, / the undivided attention when I listen to a student, / a pat on the shoulder whether the job was done well or not, / an accepting smile, / or simply "I love you" when it is most needed.
그것은 존중일 수 있다. / 내가 모든 학생에게 하는 / 내가 우리반 교실 문에서 매일 하는 인사, / 내가 학생의 말을 들을 때의 완전한 집중, / 일을 잘했든 못했던 어깨를 토닥여주는 것, / 포용적인 미소, / 혹은 "사랑해"라는 말이 가장 필요할 때 그저 그 말을 해주는 것일 수도 있다.)

It may simply be asking how things are at home.
그것은 그저 집에 별일이 없는지를 물어보는 것일지도 모른다.

For one student considering dropping out of school, / it was a note from me after one of his frequent absences / saying that he made my day when I saw him in school.
학교를 중퇴하는 것을 고려하던 학생에게, / 그것은 그 학생의 잦은 결석 중 어느 한 결석 후에 쓴 나의 짧은 편지였다. / 내가 그 학생을 학교에서 보았을 때 그가 나를 매우 기쁘게 해주었다는 내용의

He came to me with the note with tears in his eyes / and thanked me.
그 학생은 눈물을 글썽이며 그 편지를 들고 내게 와서 / 고맙다고 했다.

He will graduate this year.
그 학생은 올해 졸업할 것이다.

Whatever technique is used, / the students must know that you care about them.
어떤 기법이 사용되든, / 학생들은 여러분이 그들에 대해 신경 쓴다는 것을 틀림없이 알 것이다.

But the concern must be genuine / — the students can't be fooled.
그런데 그 관심은 진심이어야 하는데 / 학생들이 속을 리가 없기 때문이다.

동기 부여는 여러 원천에서 올 수 있다. 그것은 내가 모든 학생에게 하는 존중, 교실 문에서 매일 하는 인사, 학생의 말을 들을 때의 완전한 집중, 일을 잘했든 못했든 어깨를 토닥여주는 것, 포용적인 미소, 혹은 "사랑해"라는 말이 가장 필요할 때 그저 그 말을 해주는 것일 수도 있다. 그것은 그저 집에 별일이 없는지를 물어보는 것일지도 모른다. 학교를 중퇴하는 것을 고려하던 한 학생에게, 그것은 그 학생의 잦은 결석 중 어느 한 결석 후에 그 학생을 학교에서 보니 매우 기뻤다고 쓴 나의 짧은 편지였다. 그 학생은 눈물을 글썽이며 그 편지를 들고 내게 와서 고맙다고 했다. 그 학생은 올해 졸업할 것이다. 어떤 기법이 사용되든, 학생들은 여러분이 그들에 대해 신경 쓴다는 것을 틀림없이 알 것이다. 그런데 그 관심은 진심이어야 하는데 학생들이 속을 리가 없기 때문이다.

Why? 왜 정답일까?

학생들에게 동기를 부여하는 방식은 여러 가지가 있으며, 어떤 행위이든 학생에 대한 관심(concern)을 진실로 보여줄 수 있어야 한다는 내용을 다룬 글이다. 따라서 빈칸에 들어갈 말로 가장 적절한 것은 '관심'의 의미를 담은 ① '그들에 대해 신경 쓴다'이다.

- undivided ⓐ 완전한, 전적인
- attention ⓝ 집중, 주의
- a pat on the shoulder ⓝ (격려의 의미로) 어깨를 토닥임
- accepting ⓐ 포용적인, 수용적인
- drop out of school ⓥ 학교를 중퇴하다
- frequent ⓐ 잦은, 빈번한
- make one's day ⓥ ~을 행복하게 만들다
- concern ⓝ 관심, 걱정
- genuine ⓐ 진실한, 진짜의
- fool ⓥ 속이다
- keep one's words ⓥ 약속을 지키다
- evaluate ⓥ 평가하다

구문 풀이

1행 It may be the respect [I give every student], the daily greeting [I give at my classroom door], the undivided attention when I listen to a student, a pat on the shoulder whether the job was done well or not, an accepting smile, or simply "I love you" when it is most needed.
보어1 / 보어2 / 보어3 / 보어4 / ~이든 아니든 / 보어5 / 보어6

---

04 공간을 기능별로 분화하는 동물의 특성   정답률 65% | 정답 ②

다음 빈칸에 들어갈 말로 가장 적절한 것을 고르시오.

① an interest in close neighbors – 가까운 이웃에 대한 관심
✓ a neat functional organization – 정돈된 기능적 체계
③ a stock of emergency supplies – 비상 용품의 비축량

---

④ a distance from potential rivals – 잠재적 경쟁자로부터의 거리
⑤ a strictly observed daily routine – 엄격하게 지켜지는 일상

More than just *having* territories, / animals also *partition* them.
그저 영역을 갖는 것을 넘어서 / 동물은 영역을 *분할하기도* 한다.

And this insight turned out / to be particularly useful for zoo husbandry.
그리고 이러한 통찰은 밝혀졌다. / 동물원 관리에 특히 유용한 것으로

An animal's territory has an internal arrangement / that Heini Hediger compared to the inside of a person's house.
동물의 영역에는 내부 배치가 있다. / Heini Hediger가 사람의 집 내부에 비유한

Most of us assign separate functions to separate rooms, / but even if you look at a one-room house / you will find the same internal specialization.
우리 대부분은 방마다 별도의 기능을 할당하지만, / 여러분이 원룸 주택을 살펴봐도 / 여러분은 내부의 동일한 분화를 발견할 것이다.

In a cabin or a mud hut, / or even a Mesolithic cave from 30,000 years ago, / this part is for cooking, / that part is for sleeping; / this part is for making tools and weaving, / that part is for waste.
오두막이나 진흙 오두막 안에, / 혹은 심지어 3만년 전의 중석기 시대의 동굴 안에도, / 이 부분은 요리를 위한 곳이고, / 저 부분은 잠을 자기 위한 곳이며, / 이 부분은 도구 제작과 직조를 위한 곳이고, / 저 부분은 폐기물을 위한 곳이다.

We keep a neat functional organization.
우리는 정돈된 기능적 체계를 유지한다.

To a varying extent, / other animals do the same.
다양한 정도로, / 다른 동물들도 같은 행동을 한다.

A part of an animal's territory is for eating, / a part for sleeping, / a part for swimming or wallowing, / a part may be set aside for waste, / depending on the species of animal.
동물의 영역 중 일부는 먹기 위한 곳이고, / 일부는 잠을 자기 위한 곳이며, / 일부는 헤엄치거나 뒹굴기 위한 곳이고, / 일부는 폐기물을 위해 남겨두는 부분이 있을 수 있다. / 동물의 종에 따라

동물은 그저 영역을 갖는 것을 넘어서 영역을 *분할하기도* 한다. 그리고 이러한 통찰은 동물원 관리에 특히 유용한 것으로 밝혀졌다. 동물의 영역에는 Heini Hediger가 사람의 집 내부에 비유한 내부 배치가 있다. 우리 대부분은 방마다 별도의 기능을 할당하지만, 원룸 주택을 살펴봐도 (집) 내부의 동일한 분화를 발견할 것이다. 오두막이나 진흙 오두막, 혹은 심지어 3만년 전의 중석기 시대의 동굴 안에도, 이 부분은 요리를 위한 곳이고, 저 부분은 잠을 자기 위한 곳이며, 이 부분은 도구 제작과 직조를 위한 곳이고, 저 부분은 폐기물을 위한 곳이라는 구분이 있다. 우리는 정돈된 기능적 체계를 유지한다. 다양한 정도로, 다른 동물들도 같은 행동을 한다. 동물의 종에 따라, 동물의 영역 중 일부는 먹기 위한 곳이고, 일부는 잠을 자기 위한 곳이며, 일부는 헤엄치거나 뒹굴기 위한 곳이고, 일부는 폐기물을 위해 남겨두는 부분이 있을 수 있다.

Why? 왜 정답일까?

첫 문장에서 동물은 영역을 분화하는(*partition*) 습성이 있다고 언급한 뒤, 사람이 사는 공간과 동물의 거주 공간을 예로 들어 영역별로 특정한 기능이 부여되어 있음을 설명하고 있다. 따라서 빈칸에 들어갈 말로 가장 적절한 것은 이 기능별로 '분화'된 체계를 다른 말로 표현한 ② '정돈된 기능적 체계'이다.

- territory ⓝ 영역, 영토
- partition ⓥ 분할하다
- insight ⓝ 통찰력
- husbandry ⓝ 관리
- internal ⓐ 내부의
- arrangement ⓝ 배치
- compare ⓥ 비유하다, 비교하다
- separate ⓐ 별개의 ⓥ 분리하다
- function ⓝ 기능
- specialization ⓝ 분화, 전문화
- hut ⓝ 오두막
- Mesolithic ⓐ 중석기의
- weave ⓥ (직물을) 짜다
- waste ⓝ 폐기물, 쓰레기
- wallow ⓥ 뒹굴다
- set aside ~을 떼어두다, 따로 마련하다
- depending on ~에 따라
- neat ⓐ 정돈된, 단정한
- strictly ⓐⓓ 엄격하게
- daily routine 일상

구문 풀이

12행 A part of an animal's territory is for eating, a part (is) for sleeping, a part (is) for swimming or wallowing, a part may be set aside for waste, depending on the species of animal.
생략(중복) / ~에 따라

---

05 말이 아닌 이미지에 기반하여 사고하는 인간   정답률 66% | 정답 ⑤

다음 빈칸에 들어갈 말로 가장 적절한 것을 고르시오. [3점]

① Actions speak louder than words – 말보다 행동이 중요하다
② A bad workman blames his tools – 서툰 직공이 연장을 탓한다
③ You can't judge a book by its cover – 겉보기로 판단해서는 안 된다

④ The pen is mightier than the sword – 펜은 칼보다 강하다

✔ A picture is worth a thousand words – 그림 하나가 천 마디 말의 가치가 있다

Did you know you actually think in images / and not in words?
사실 우리는 이미지로 생각한다는 것을 알고 있었는가? / 말이 아닌

Images are simply mental pictures / showing ideas and experiences.
이미지는 그저 심상이다. / 생각과 경험을 보여주는

Early humans communicated their ideas and experiences to others / for thousands of years / by drawing pictures in the sand or on the walls of their caves.
초기 인류는 타인에게 자기 생각과 경험을 전달했다. / 몇 천 년 동안 / 모래 또는 동굴 벽에 그림을 그려서

Only recently have humans created / various languages and alphabets / to symbolize these "picture" messages.
오로지 최근에야 인간은 만들어 냈다. / 다양한 언어와 알파벳을 / 이런 "그림" 메시지를 상징하기 위해

Your mind has not yet adapted / to this relatively new development.
마음은 아직 적응하지 못했다. / 상대적으로 새로운 이러한 발전에

An image has a much greater impact on your brain than words; / the nerves from the eye to the brain / are twenty-five times larger / than the nerves from the ear to the brain.
이미지는 말보다 뇌에 훨씬 더 큰 영향을 미친다. / 눈부터 뇌에 이르는 신경은 / 25배 더 크다. / 귀부터 뇌에 이르는 신경보다

You often remember a person's face / but not his or her name, / for example.
당신은 종종 사람의 얼굴은 기억하지만 / 그 사람의 이름은 기억 못 한다. / 예를 들어

The old saying, / "A picture is worth a thousand words," / is true.
오래된 격언은 / "그림 하나가 천 마디 말의 가치가 있다."라는 / 맞다.

사실 우리는 말이 아닌 이미지로 생각한다는 것을 알고 있었는가? 이미지는 그저 생각과 경험을 보여주는 심상이다. 초기 인류는 몇 천 년 동안 모래 또는 동굴 벽에 그림을 그려서 타인에게 자기 생각과 경험을 전달했다. 오로지 최근에야 인간은 이런 "그림" 메시지를 상징하기 위해 다양한 언어와 알파벳을 만들어 냈다. 마음은 상대적으로 새로운 이러한 발전에 아직 적응하지 못했다. 이미지는 말보다 뇌에 훨씬 더 큰 영향을 미친다. 눈부터 뇌에 이르는 신경은 귀부터 뇌에 이르는 신경보다 25배 더 크다. 예를 들어 종종 사람의 얼굴은 기억하지만 그 사람의 이름은 기억 못 한다. "그림 하나가 천 마디 말의 가치가 있다."라는 오래된 격언은 맞다.

Why? 왜 정답일까?

인간은 말보다는 이미지에 기반하여 생각한다는 주제를 첫 문장에서 물음 형태로 제시하고 뒤에서 이를 뒷받침하는 다양한 예를 든 글이다. 글 중간의 문장에서도 말보다는 이미지가 뇌에 훨씬 큰 영향을 미친다는 내용(**An image has a much greater impact on your brain than words;**)이 반복적으로 서술되어 있어, 빈칸에 들어갈 말로 가장 적절한 것은 ⑤ '그림 하나가 천 마디 말의 가치가 있다(천 마디 말보다 이미지로 한 번 보는 게 더 낫다)'이다.

- **actually** [ad] 실제로
- **various** ⓐ 다양한
- **adapt to** ~에 적응하다
- **development** ⓝ 발전, 개발품
- **saying** ⓝ 격언, 속담
- **worth** ⓐ 가치 있는 ⓝ 재산, 중요성
- **mental** ⓐ 정신의
- **symbolize** ⓥ 상징하다
- **relatively** [ad] 상대적으로
- **nerve** ⓝ 신경
- **blame** ⓥ 비난하다, 탓하다 ⓝ 책임

구문 풀이

3행 Early humans communicated their ideas and experiences to
[전달하다(타동사)]
others / for thousands of years / by drawing pictures in the sand or
[for+숫자 기간 : ~동안] [by+동명사 : ~함으로써] 부사구1
on the walls of their caves.
부사구2

06 두 가지 다른 정보를 동시에 처리할 수 없는 인간 정답률 51% | 정답 ⑤

다음 빈칸에 들어갈 말로 가장 적절한 것을 고르시오. [3점]

① decide what they should do in the moment
그들이 그 순간 뭘 해야 하는지를 판단할

② remember a message with too many words
너무 긴 메시지를 기억할

③ analyze which information was more accurate
어떤 정보가 더 정확한지 분석할

④ speak their own ideas while listening to others
다른 사람들의 말을 들으면서 자기 생각을 말할

✔ process two pieces of information at the same time
두 개의 정보를 동시에 처리할

In the studies of Colin Cherry / at the Massachusetts Institute for Technology / back in the 1950s, / his participants listened to voices in one ear at a time /

---

and then through both ears / in an effort to determine / whether we can listen to two people talk at the same time.
Colin Cherry의 연구에서, / 메사추세츠 공과대학 소속이었던 / 1950년대 / 참가자들은 한 번은 한쪽 귀로만 목소리를 듣고, / 그다음에는 양쪽 귀로 들었다. / 판단하기 위해 / 우리가 두 사람이 이야기하는 것을 동시에 들을 수 있는지

One ear always contained a message / that the listener had to repeat back / (called "shadowing") / while the other ear included people speaking.
한쪽 귀로는 메시지를 계속 들려주었고 / 듣는 사람이 다시 반복해야 하는 / ('섀도잉'이라 불림) / 다른 한쪽 귀로는 사람들이 말하는 것을 들려주었다.

The trick was to see / if you could totally focus on the main message / and also hear someone talking in your other ear.
속임수는 알아보기 위한 것이었다. / 사람들이 주된 메시지에 완전히 집중하면서 / 다른 귀로는 다른 사람이 말하는 것 또한 들을 수 있는지를

Cleverly, / Cherry found / it was impossible / for his participants to know / whether the message in the other ear / was spoken by a man or woman, / in English or another language, / or was even comprised of real words at all!
영리하게도, / Cherry는 발견했다! / 불가능했다는 것을 / 참가자들이 알아차리는 것이 / 다른 한쪽 귀로 들리는 / 메시지가 / 남자가 말한 것인지 혹은 여자가 말한 것인지, / 영어인지 다른 외국어인지, / 심지어 실제 단어로 구성된 것인지조차 전혀

In other words, / people could not process two pieces of information at the same time.
다시 말해서, / 사람들은 두 개의 정보를 동시에 처리할 수 없었다.

1950년대 메사추세츠 공과대학 소속이었던 Colin Cherry의 연구에서, 우리가 두 사람이 이야기하는 것을 동시에 들을 수 있는지 판단하기 위해 참가자들은 한 번은 한쪽 귀로만 목소리를 듣고, 그다음에는 양쪽 귀로 들었다. 한쪽 귀로는 듣는 사람이 다시 반복해야 하는('섀도잉'이라 불림) 메시지를 계속 들려주었고 다른 한쪽 귀로는 사람들이 말하는 것을 들려주었다. 속임수는 사람들이 주된 메시지에 완전히 집중하면서 다른 귀로는 다른 사람이 말하는 것 또한 들을 수 있는지를 알아보기 위한 것이었다. 영리하게도, Cherry는 참가자들이 다른 한쪽 귀로 들리는 메시지가 남자가 말한 것인지 혹은 여자가 말한 것인지, 영어인지 다른 외국어인지, 심지어 실제 단어로 구성된 것인지조차 전혀 알아차리지 못했다는 것을 발견했다! 다시 말해서, 사람들은 두 개의 정보를 동시에 처리할 수 없었다.

Why? 왜 정답일까?

실험 결과를 제시하는 '~ it was impossible for his participants to know whether the message in the other ear was spoken by a man or woman, in English or another language, or was even comprised of real words at all!'에서 사람들은 양쪽 귀에서 각기 다른 정보가 들어올 때 이를 동시에 처리하지 못하여, 화자가 남자였는지 여자였는지, 사용된 언어가 영어였는지 다른 언어였는지 등등을 제대로 판별하지 못했다고 한다. 따라서 빈칸에 들어갈 말로 가장 적절한 것은 ⑤ '두 개의 정보를 동시에 처리할'이다.

- **at a time** 한 번에
- **contain** ⓥ 수용하다, 담다
- **shadowing** ⓝ 섀도잉(남의 말을 듣는 동시에 따라서 하는 것)
- **trick** ⓝ 속임수, 요령
- **accurate** ⓐ 정확한
- **in an effort to** ~하기 위해서
- **comprise** ⓥ ~을 구성하다

구문 풀이

8행 The trick was to see if you could totally focus on the main
주격 보어(~것) 접속사(~인지 아닌지)
message and also hear someone talking in your other ear.
지각동사 목적어 목적격 보어

★★★ 1등급 대비 고난도 2점 문제

07 혁신 지속에 도움이 되는 가상 환경의 특징 정답률 49% | 정답 ①

다음 빈칸에 들어갈 말로 가장 적절한 것을 고르시오.

✔ restrictions – 제한점
② responsibilities – 책임감
③ memories – 기억
④ coincidences – 우연의 일치
⑤ traditions – 전통

One of the big questions faced this past year / was how to keep innovation rolling / when people were working entirely virtually.
작년에 직면한 가장 큰 질문 중 하나는 / 어떻게 혁신을 지속할 것인가 하는 것이었다. / 사람들이 완전히 가상 공간에서 작업할 때

But experts say / that digital work didn't have a negative effect / on innovation and creativity.
그러나 전문가들은 말한다. / 디지털 작업이 부정적인 영향을 미치지 않았다고 / 혁신과 창의성에

Working within limits / pushes us to solve problems.

한계 내에서 일하는 것은 / 우리에게 문제를 해결하도록 독려한다.
Overall, / virtual meeting platforms put more constraints / on communication and collaboration / than face-to-face settings.
전반적으로, / 가상 미팅 플랫폼은 더 많은 제약을 가한다. / 의사소통과 협업에 / 대면 설정보다
For instance, / with the press of a button, / virtual meeting hosts can control the size of breakout groups / and enforce time constraints; / only one person can speak at a time; / nonverbal signals, / particularly those below the shoulders, / are diminished; / "seating arrangements" are assigned by the platform, / not by individuals; / and visual access to others be limited / by the size of each participant's screen.
예를 들어, / 버튼을 누르면, / 가상 회의 진행자는 소모임 그룹의 크기를 제어하고 / 시간 제한을 시행할 수 있다. / 한 번에 한 사람만이 말할 수 있다. / 비언어적 신호, / 특히 이깨 이래의 신호는 / 줄어든다. / '좌석 배치'는 플랫폼에 의해 할당된다. / 개인이 아닌 / 그리고 다른 사람에 대한 시각적 접근은 제한될 수 있다. / 각 참가자의 화면 크기에 따라
Such restrictions are likely to stretch participants / beyond their usual ways of thinking, / boosting creativity.
이러한 제한점은 참가자들을 확장시킬 가능성이 높다. / 일반적인 사고방식 너머까지 / 그리고 창의력을 증진시킬

작년에 직면한 가장 큰 질문 중 하나는 사람들이 완전히 가상 공간에서 작업할 때 어떻게 혁신을 지속할 것인가 하는 것이었다. 그러나 전문가들은 디지털 작업이 혁신과 창의성에 부정적인 영향을 미치지 않았다고 말한다. 한계 내에서 일하는 것은 우리에게 문제를 해결하도록 독려한다. 전반적으로, 가상 미팅 플랫폼은 대면 환경보다 의사소통과 협업에 더 많은 제약들을 가한다. 예를 들어, 버튼을 누르면, 가상 회의 진행자는 소모임 그룹의 크기를 제어하고 시간 제한을 시행할 수 있다. 한 번에 한 사람만이 말할 수 있다. 비언어적 신호, 특히 어깨 아래의 신호는 줄어든다. '좌석 배치'는 개인이 아닌 플랫폼에 의해 할당된다. 그리고 다른 사람에 대한 시각적 접근은 각 참가자의 화면 크기에 따라 제한될 수 있다. 이러한 제한점은 참가자들을 일반적인 사고방식 너머까지 확장시켜 창의력을 증진시킬 가능성이 높다.

Why? 왜 정답일까?

'Working within limits pushes us to solve problems.'에서 한계 내에서 작업하는 것이 문제 해결을 독려한다고 언급하는 것으로 보아, 빈칸에 들어갈 말로 가장 적절한 것은 ① '제한점'이다.

- virtually [ad] (컴퓨터를 이용해) 가상으로
- have a negative effect on ~에 부정적 영향을 미치다
- constraint [n] 제한, 한계
- breakout group 소집단
- enforce [v] 시행하다
- diminish [v] 줄이다
- seating arrangement 좌석 배치
- assign [v] 배정하다, 할당하다
- stretch [v] 늘이다, 확장하다
- coincidence [n] 우연의 일치, 동시 발생

구문 풀이

1행 One of the big questions faced this past year was {how to
주어(one of the + 복수명사) 과거분사 동사(단수)
keep innovation rolling when people were working entirely virtually}.
{ } : 주격 보어(how + to부정사 : ~하는 방법)

★★ 문제 해결 꿀~팁 ★★

▶ 많이 틀린 이유는?
Working within limits가 핵심 표현으로, 제약이나 제한이 혁신과 업무 수행에 도움이 된다는 것이 글의 주제이다. 최다 오답인 ②의 responsibilities는 '책임, (맡은) 책무'라는 뜻이므로 글 내용과 관련이 없다.

▶ 문제 해결 방법은?
핵심어인 limits, constraints와 동의어를 찾으면 된다. 빈칸 앞에 not 등 부정어도 없어, 복잡하게 사고할 필요가 없는 비교적 단순한 빈칸 문제이다.

★★★ 1등급 대비 고난도 3점 문제

08 인간의 합리화 능력 ··· 정답률 30% | 정답 ③

다음 빈칸에 들어갈 말로 가장 적절한 것을 고르시오. [3점]

① keep focused – 집중을 유지하는
② solve problems – 문제를 해결하는
✔ rationalize outcomes – 결과를 합리화하는
④ control our emotions – 우리의 감정을 조절하는
⑤ attract others' attention – 다른 사람들의 주의를 끄는

In an experiment, / researchers presented participants / with two photos of faces / and asked participants to choose the photo / that they thought was more attractive, / and then handed participants that photo.

한 실험에서, / 연구자들은 참가자들에게 제시하고 / 두 장의 얼굴 사진을 / 참가자들에게 사진을 고르라고 요청한 후에, / 더 매력적이라고 생각하는 / 그 사진을 참가자들에게 건네주었다.
Using a clever trick inspired by stage magic, / when participants received the photo, / it had been switched to the photo / not chosen by the participant / — the less attractive photo.
무대 마술에서 영감을 얻은 교묘한 속임수를 사용해, / 참가자들이 사진을 받았을 때, / 그 사진은 사진으로 교체되어 있었다. / 참가자가 선택하지 않은 / 즉 덜 매력적인 사진
Remarkably, most participants accepted this photo / as their own choice / and then proceeded to give arguments / for why they had chosen that face in the first place.
놀랍게도, 대부분의 참가자들은 이 사진을 받아들였고, / 그들 자신의 선택으로 / 그리고 나서 논거를 제시했다. / 왜 애초에 그들이 그 얼굴을 선택했는지에 대한
This revealed a striking mismatch / between our choices and our ability to rationalize outcomes.
이것은 놀라운 불일치를 드러냈다. / 우리의 선택들과 결과를 합리화하는 우리의 능력 사이의
This same finding / has since been observed in various domains / including taste for jam and financial decisions.
이와 똑같은 결과가 / 그 이후로 다양한 분야에서 관찰되었다. / 잼의 맛과 금전적 결정을 포함한

한 실험에서, 연구자들은 참가자들에게 두 장의 얼굴 사진을 제시하고 더 매력적이라고 생각하는 사진을 고르라고 요청한 후에, 그 사진을 참가자들에게 건네주었다. 무대 마술에서 영감을 얻은 교묘한 속임수를 사용해, 참가자들이 사진을 받았을 때, 그 사진은 참가자가 선택하지 않은, 즉 덜 매력적인 사진으로 교체되어 있었다. 놀랍게도, 대부분의 참가자들은 이 사진을 그들 자신의 선택으로 받아들였고, 그리고 나서 왜 애초에 그들이 그 얼굴을 선택했는지에 대한 논거를 제시했다. 이것은 우리의 선택들과 결과를 합리화하는 우리의 능력 사이의 놀라운 불일치를 드러냈다. 이와 똑같은 결과가 그 이후로 잼의 맛과 금전적 결정을 포함한 다양한 분야에서 관찰되었다.

Why? 왜 정답일까?

실험을 소개한 글로 결과가 나오는 빈칸 앞의 문장을 주의 깊게 독해하면, 참가자 대부분은 자신이 선택했던 사진이 다른 사진으로 교체되어 있었을 때 이를 자신의 선택으로 받아들이고 왜 그 사진을 선택했는지에 대한 논거까지 제시했다는 내용이 나온다(~ most participants accepted this photo as their own choice and then proceeded to give arguments for why they had chosen that face in the first place.). 이는 자신이 선택하지 않은 사진이 나왔다는 결과를 합리화하는 능력을 보여주는 사례로 볼 수 있으므로, 빈칸에 들어갈 말로 가장 적절한 것은 ③ '결과를 합리화하는'이다.

- inspire [v] 영감을 얻다
- switch [v] 바꾸다
- remarkably [ad] 놀랍게도
- proceed [v] 진행하다
- argument [n] 논거, 주장
- mismatch [n] 불일치
- domain [n] 분야
- rationalize [v] 합리화하다
- outcome [n] 결과

구문 풀이

1행 In an experiment, researchers presented participants
동사1「present + A +
with two photos of faces and asked participants to choose the photo
with + B」 : A에게 B를 제시하다   동사2「ask + 목적어 + to부정사 : ~에게 …하도록 요청하다」
[that (they thought) was more attractive], and then handed participants
주격 관계대명사 ( ) : 삽입절   동사3
that photo.

★★ 문제 해결 꿀~팁 ★★

▶ 많이 틀린 이유는?
연구의 결론을 제시하는 주제문을 완성하는 문제로, 연구 내용을 통독한 뒤 핵심 내용을 요약해 빈칸에 넣어야 한다. 글에서 참여자들의 집중력에 관해서는 언급하고 있지 않으므로 ①은 답으로 부적절하며, 타인의 관심과 주의를 끄는 방법 또한 언급되지 않았으므로 ⑤ 또한 답으로 적합하지 않다.

▶ 문제 해결 방법은?
빈칸 앞의 문장에서 부사 Remarkably는 '놀라운' 결론이 제시될 것임을 알리는 신호이다. 이 문장을 근거로 빈칸의 답을 찾도록 한다.

★★★ 1등급 대비 고난도 3점 문제

09 의사결정에 도움을 주는 신속한 인식 ··· 정답률 40% | 정답 ①

다음 빈칸에 들어갈 말로 가장 적절한 것을 고르시오. [3점]
✔ haste does not make waste – 서두르는데도 일을 망치지 않는

② it is never too late to learn – 배움이 결코 늦지 않는
③ many hands make light work – 일손이 많아지면 일거리를 더는
④ slow and steady wins the race – 더디고 꾸준하면 경주에서 이기는
⑤ you don't judge by appearances – 외모로 판단하지 않는

Most of us are suspicious of rapid cognition.
우리 대부분은 신속하게 하는 인식을 의심한다.

We believe / that the quality of the decision is directly related / to the time and effort / that went into making it.
우리는 생각한다. / 결정의 질이 직접적인 관계가 있다고 / 시간과 노력과 / 결정을 내리는 데 들어간

That's what we tell our children: / "Haste makes waste." / "Look before you leap." / "Stop and think." / "Don't judge a book by its cover."
그게 우리가 자녀들에게 말하는 것인데, / "서두르면 일을 망친다." / "돌다리도 두드려 보고 건너라." / "멈춰서 생각하라." / "겉만 보고 판단하지 마라."이다.

We believe / that we are always better off / gathering as much information as possible / and spending as much time as possible / in careful consideration.
우리는 생각한다. / 우리가 늘 더 나을 것이라고 / 최대한 많은 정보를 모아서 / 최대한 많은 시간을 시간을 보내면 / 주의 깊게 숙고하는 데

But there are moments, / particularly in time-driven, critical situations, / when haste does not make waste, / when our snap judgments and first impressions can offer better means / of making sense of the world.
하지만 순간이 있다. / 특히 시간에 쫓기는 중대한 상황 속에서는 / 서두르는데도 일을 망치지 않는, / 즉 우리의 순식간에 내리는 판단과 첫인상이 더 나은 수단을 제공할 수 있는 / 세상을 파악하는

Survivors have somehow learned this lesson / and have developed and sharpened / their skill of rapid cognition.
생존자들은 어쨌든 이 교훈을 배웠고, / 발전시켜서 연마했다. / 신속하게 인식하는 능력을

우리 대부분은 신속하게 인식한 것을 의심한다. 우리는 결정의 질이 결정을 내리는 데 들어간 시간과 노력과 직접적인 관계가 있다고 생각한다. 그게 우리가 자녀들에게 말하는 것인데, "서두르면 일을 망친다." "돌다리도 두드려 보고 건너라." "멈춰서 생각해라." "겉만 보고 판단하지 마라."이다. 우리는 최대한 많은 정보를 모아서 최대한 많은 시간을 신중히 숙고하는 데 시간을 보내면 우리가 늘 더 나을 것이라고 생각한다. 하지만 특히 시간에 쫓기는 중대한 상황 속에서는 서두르는데도 일을 망치지 않는, 즉 순식간에 내리는 우리의 판단과 첫인상이 세상을 파악하는 더 나은 수단을 제공할 수 있는 순간이 있다. 생존자들은 어쨌든 이 교훈을 배웠고, 신속하게 인식하는 능력을 키우고 연마했다.

Why? 왜 정답일까?

빈칸 뒤의 '~ when our snap judgments and first impressions can offer better means of making sense of the world.'에서 결정을 내리는 데 시간이 필요하다는 우리의 믿음과 달리 순식간의 판단과 첫인상이 세상을 파악하는 데 더 도움을 주는 순간들이 있다고 이야기하므로, 빈칸에 들어갈 말로 가장 적절한 것은 ① '서두르는데도 일을 망치지 않는'이다.

- suspicious ⓐ 의심하는
- leap ⓥ 서둘러 ~하다, 뛰어오르다
- consideration ⓝ 숙고, 고려
- time-driven 시간에 쫓기는
- make sense of ~을 이해하다
- sharpen ⓥ (기술 등을) 연마하다, 갈고닦다
- Many hands make light work. 일손이 많으면 일이 가벼워진다(백지장도 맞들면 낫다).
- steady ⓐ 꾸준한

- haste ⓝ 서두름, 급함
- well off 잘 사는
- moment ⓝ 순간, 때
- snap ⓐ 성급한, 불시의
- survivor ⓝ 생존자

- appearance ⓝ 외모

구문 풀이

8행 But there are moments, (particularly in time-driven, critical
　　　　　　　　　　　선행사　　　　　　　　　　　　( ): 삽입구
situations), [when haste does not make waste], [when our snap
　　　　　　관계부사1　　　　　　　　　　　　관계부사2
judgments and first impressions can offer better means of making
　　　　　　　　　　　　　　　　　　　　　　　전치사
sense of the world].
　　　　　　　　동명사구(~을 이해하는 것)

★★ 문제 해결 꿀~팁 ★★

▶ 많이 틀린 이유는?
빈칸 뒤의 문장을 주의 깊게 해석해야 한다. '~ when our snap judgments and first impressions can offer better means of making sense of the world.'에서 빠른 판단과 첫인상은 인식의 속도와 관련된 표현이므로, 여기서 첫인상을 외모와 연관된 말로 보아 ⑤를 고르지 않도록 주의한다.

▶ 문제 해결 방법은?
빈칸이 But으로 시작하는 문장에 있으므로, 빈칸 앞보다는 뒤에 근거가 있을 것임을 예상한 뒤 지문을 읽도록 한다.

★★★ 1등급 대비 고난도 3점 문제

10 신생아가 부드러운 흔들림을 좋아하는 이유　　정답률 27% | 정답 ①

다음 빈칸에 들어갈 말로 가장 적절한 것을 고르시오. [3점]

✔ acquire a fondness for motion – 움직임을 좋아하게 되고
② want consistent feeding – 계속 젖을 먹고 싶어 하고
③ dislike severe rocking – 너무 심한 흔들림을 싫어하고
④ remember the tastes of food – 음식의 맛을 기억하고
⑤ form a bond with their mothers – 엄마와 유대감을 형성하고

We're often told / that newborns and infants are comforted by rocking / because this motion is similar / to what they experienced in the womb, / and that they must take comfort in this familiar feeling.
우리는 ~라는 말을 자주 듣는다. / 신생아와 유아가 흔들림에 의해 편안해지는데, / 이것은 이런 움직임이 유사하기 때문이고, / 자궁 안에서 그들이 경험했던 것과 / 그들이 이런 친숙한 느낌에서 편안해지는 것이 틀림없다는

This may be true; / however, to date there are no convincing data / that demonstrate a significant relationship / between the amount of time a mother moves during pregnancy / and her newborn's response to rocking.
이것은 사실일 수 있다. / 하지만, 현재까지 설득력 있는 데이터는 없다. / 상당한 관계가 있음을 입증하는 / 임신 기간에 엄마가 움직이는 시간의 양과 / 흔들림에 대한 신생아의 반응 사이에

Just as likely is the idea / that newborns come to associate gentle rocking with being fed.
~라는 생각도 그만큼 가능할 법하다. / 신생아가 부드러운 흔들림을 젖을 먹는 것과 연관시키게 된다는

Parents understand that rocking quiets a newborn, / and they very often provide gentle, repetitive movement during feeding.
부모는 흔들어 주는 것이 신생아를 달래 준다는 것을 알고 있어서, / 그들은 젖을 주는 동안 부드럽고, 반복적인 움직임을 매우 자주 제공한다.

Since the appearance of food is a primary reinforcer, / newborns may acquire a fondness for motion / because they have been conditioned / through a process of associative learning.
음식의 등장은 일차 강화물이기 때문에, / 신생아는 움직임을 좋아하게 되었을지 모른다. / 그들이 조건화되어 왔기 때문에 / 연관 학습의 과정을 통해

신생아와 유아는 흔들림에 의해 편안해지는데, 이것은 이런 움직임이 자궁 안에서 그들이 경험했던 것과 유사하기 때문이고, 그들이 이런 친숙한 느낌에서 편안해지는 것이 틀림없다는 말을 자주 듣는다. 이것은 사실일 수 있지만, 현재까지 임신 기간에 엄마가 움직이는 시간의 양과 흔들림에 대한 신생아의 반응 사이에 상당한 관계가 있음을 입증하는 설득력 있는 데이터는 없다. 신생아가 부드러운 흔들림을 젖을 먹는 것과 연관시키게 된다는 생각도 그만큼 가능할 법하다. 부모는 흔들어 주는 것이 신생아를 달래 준다는 것을 알고 있어서, 그들은 젖을 주는 동안 부드럽고 반복적인 움직임을 매우 자주 제공한다. 음식의 등장은 일차 강화물이기 때문에, 신생아는 움직임을 좋아하게 되고, 그 이유는 그들이 연관 학습의 과정을 통해 조건화되어 왔기 때문이다.

Why? 왜 정답일까?

신생아가 부드러운 흔들림을 좋아하는 이유에 관해 다룬 글로, 'Just as likely is the idea ~'에서 아이들은 흔들림을 젖 먹는 것과 연관 짓게 되면서 흔들림을 좋아하게 될 수도 있다는 견해를 제시한다. 이어서 엄마가 아이에게 젖을 먹이는 동안 보통 아이를 편안하게 해주기 위해서 아이를 흔들어 주는 과정에서 젖, 즉 음식이 흔들림을 '좋아하게' 되는 강화물로 기능하게 된다는 설명이 나온다. 따라서 빈칸에 들어갈 말로 가장 적절한 것은 ① '움직임을 좋아하게 되고'이다.

- infant ⓝ 유아
- to date 지금까지
- demonstrate ⓥ 입증하다
- pregnancy ⓝ 임신 (기간)
- appearance ⓝ 등장
- acquire ⓥ 얻다, 습득하다
- consistent ⓐ 계속되는

- rock ⓥ 흔들다
- convincing ⓐ 설득력 있는
- significant ⓐ 상당한, 유의미한
- associate A with B ⓥ A와 B를 연관시키다
- condition ⓥ 조건화하다
- fondness ⓝ 좋아함
- severe ⓐ 심한, 가혹한

구문 풀이

1행 We're often told {that newborns and infants are comforted
　　　　　동사구(~을 듣다) 접속사　　　주어　　　　　동사(수동태)
by rocking because this motion is similar to what they experienced
　接속사(~ 때문에)　　　　　　　~와 비슷한 관계대명사(~것)
in the womb}, and {that they must take comfort in this familiar feeling}.
　　　　　　　접속사2　　　주어　　동사　　　　　　　{ }: 문장의 목적어

★★ 문제 해결 꿀~팁 ★★

▶ 많이 틀린 이유는?
첫 문장에서 'newborns and infants are comforted by rocking'을 통해

신생아나 유아는 흔들림을 좋아한다는 전제를 제시했다. 이후 'because this motion is similar to ~'와 '~ associate gentle rocking with being fed.'에서 신생아가 흔들림을 좋아하는 이유를 밝히고 있다. 따라서 결론에 해당하는 빈칸에는 전제이자 요지인 ①이 들어가야 한다. ②와 ④는 둘 다 '움직임을 좋아하는' 특성에 관한 언급 없이 '먹는 것'과 관련된 내용만을 제시하므로 오답이다.

▶ 문제 해결 방법은?
더 자세히 살펴보면, 이 글은 신생아들이 흔들림을 좋아하는 이유에 관한 통념을 반박하고 새로운 견해를 제시하는 글로, however가 흐름의 전환을 이끈다. 글을 꼼꼼히 읽기 전에 이런 연결사 중심으로 구조를 파악해 두면 핵심 내용을 쉽게 이해하는 데 도움이 된다.

★★★ 1등급 대비 고난도 3점 문제

11 친숙함이 빚는 오해   정답률 41% | 정답 ②

다음 빈칸에 들어갈 말로 가장 적절한 것을 고르시오. [3점]

① you couldn't recall the parts you had highlighted
당신은 강조 표시한 부분을 기억하지 못했다
✔ it wasn't really the best answer to the question
사실 그 질문에 대한 가장 좋은 해답은 아니었다
③ that familiarity was based on your understanding
익숙함은 이해에 기초를 둔 것이다
④ repetition enabled you to pick the correct answer
반복은 당신이 정답을 고를 수 있게 해주었다
⑤ it indicated that familiarity was naturally built up
그것은 친숙함이 자연스럽게 쌓이는 것임을 나타냈다

One of the main reasons / that students may think they know the material, / even when they don't, / is that they mistake familiarity for understanding.
주된 이유 중 하나는 / 학생들이 자료의 내용을 알고 있다고 생각할 수도 있는 / 그들이 알지 못할 때조차도, / 친숙함을 이해로 착각하기 때문이다.

Here is how it works:
그것이 작동하는 방식이 여기 있다.

You read the chapter once, / perhaps highlighting as you go.
당신은 그 장을 한 번 읽는다. / 읽을 때 아마도 강조 표시를 하면서

Then later, you read the chapter again, / perhaps focusing on the highlighted material.
그러고 나서 나중에, 당신은 그 장을 다시 읽는다. / 아마도 강조 표시된 자료에 집중하면서

As you read it over, / the material is familiar / because you remember it from before, / and this familiarity might lead you to think, / "Okay, I know that."
당신은 그것을 거듭 읽어서, / 자료가 친숙하고, / 이전에 읽은 것으로부터 그것을 기억하기 때문에 / 이러한 친숙함은 당신이 생각하게 할지도 모른다. / "좋아, 그것을 알겠어."라고

The problem is / that this feeling of familiarity / is not necessarily equivalent to knowing the material / and may be of no help / when you have to come up with an answer on the exam.
문제는 / 이런 친숙한 느낌이 / 반드시 자료를 아는 것과 같은 것은 아니며 / 아무런 도움이 되지 않을 수도 있다는 점이다. / 시험에서 답을 생각해내야 할 때

In fact, familiarity can often lead to errors on multiple-choice exams / because you might pick a choice that looks familiar, / only to find later / that it was something you had read, / but it wasn't really the best answer to the question.
사실, 친숙함은 종종 선다형 시험에서 오류를 일으킬 수 있는데, / 당신이 익숙해 보이는 선택지를 선택할 수 있기 때문에 / 결국 나중에 알게 되는 것은 / 그것은 당신이 읽었던 것인데, / 하지만 사실 그 질문에 대한 가장 좋은 해답은 아니었다는 것이다.

자료의 내용을 일지 못할 때조차도 학생들이 일고 있다고 생각할 수도 있는 주된 이유 중 하나는 친숙함을 이해로 착각하기 때문이다. 그것이 작동하는 방식이 여기 있다. 당신은 읽을 때 아마도 강조 표시를 하면서, 그 장을 한 번 읽는다. 그리고 나서 나중에, 아마도 강조 표시된 자료에 집중하면서, 그 장을 다시 읽는다. 그것을 거듭 읽어서, 이전에 읽은 것으로부터 그것을 기억하기 때문에 자료가 친숙하고, 이러한 친숙함으로 인해 "좋아, 그것을 알겠어."라고 생각하게 될지도 모른다. 문제는 이런 친숙한 느낌이 반드시 자료를 아는 것과 같은 것은 아니며 시험에서 답을 생각해야 할 때 아무런 도움이 되지 않을 수도 있다는 점이다. 사실, 당신이 익숙해 보이는 선택지를 선택할 수 있기 때문에 친숙함은 종종 선다형 시험에서 오류를 일으킬 수 있는데, 결국 나중에 알게 되는 것은 그 선택지가 당신이 읽었던 것이지만 사실 그 질문에 대한 가장 좋은 해답은 아니었다는 것이다.

Why? 왜 정답일까?

첫 문장인 'One of the main reasons that students may think they know the material, even when they don't, is that they mistake familiarity for understanding.'에서 학생들은 종종 어떤 것이 친숙할 때 그것을 알고 있다고 착각한

다는 주제를 제시한다. 이어서 빈칸 문장은 학생들이 시험에서 익숙해 보이는 선택지를 답으로 골라서 오류를 빚는다고 하므로, 익숙한 것이 '답은 아니기' 때문이라는 설명이 빈칸에 들어가야 할 것이다. 따라서 답으로 가장 적절한 것은 ② '사실 그 질문에 대한 가장 좋은 해답은 아니었다'이다.

- familiarity ⓝ 친숙함
- not necessarily 반드시 ~한 것은 아니다
- multiple-choice ⓐ 선다형의, 객관식의
- highlight ⓥ 강조 표시를 하다
- come up with ⓥ ~을 떠올리다
- recall ⓥ 기억하다, 회상하다

구문 풀이

12행 In fact, familiarity can often lead to errors on multiple-choice
                    ~로 이어지다
exams because you might pick a choice [that looks familiar], only to
      이유 접속사   선행사 ← 주격 관·대 2형식 동사
find later that it was something [you had read], but it wasn't really
        접속사(~것)   부사적 용법(결국 ~하다)
the best answer to the question.

★★ 문제 해결 꿀~팁 ★★

▶ 많이 틀린 이유는?
첫 문장에서 사람들은 익숙한 것을 아는 것으로 착각한다는 핵심 내용을 제시하는데, ③은 '익숙함은 이해에 기초를 둔다'는 뜻으로 주제와 정반대되는 의미를 나타낸다.

▶ 문제 해결 방법은?
'어떤 내용이 익숙하다고 해서 그 내용을 이해하고 있는 것은 아니'라는 것이 글의 주된 내용임을 고려할 때, 시험에서 익숙해보이는 선택지를 골랐어도 그것이 '정답은 아닐 수 있다'는 결론이 빈칸에 들어가야 한다.

★★★ 1등급 대비 고난도 3점 문제

12 실질적 자유에 영향을 주는 요소   정답률 34% | 정답 ⑤

다음 빈칸에 들어갈 말로 가장 적절한 것을 고르시오. [3점]

① respecting others' rights to freedom
다른 사람들의 자유권을 존중하는가
② protecting and providing for the needy
궁핍한 사람들을 보호하고 돕는가
③ learning what socially acceptable behaviors are
사회적으로 수용 가능한 행동이 무엇인지 아는가
④ determining how much they can expect from others
다른 사람들에게 얼마나 많은 것을 기대할 수 있는지를 정하는가
✔ having the means and ability to do what they choose
그들이 선택하는 것을 할 수 있는 수단과 능력을 갖추고 있는가

It is important / to distinguish between being legally allowed to do something, / and actually being able to go and do it.
중요하다. / 어떤 일을 할 수 있도록 법적으로 허용되는 것을 구별하는 것은 / 실제로 그것을 해 버릴 수 있는 것과

A law could be passed / allowing everyone, / if they so wish, / to run a mile in two minutes.
법이 통과될 수도 있다. / 모든 사람에게 허용하는 / 그들이 그러기를 원한다면, / 2분 안에 1마일을 달릴 수 있도록

That would not, however, increase their effective freedom, / because, although allowed to do so, / they are physically incapable of it.
그러나 그것이 그들의 실질적 자유를 증가시키지는 않을 것이다. / 그렇게 하는 것이 허용되더라도, / 그들이 물리적으로 그렇게 할 수 없기 때문에

Having a minimum of restrictions and a maximum of possibilities / is fine.
최소한의 제약과 최대한의 가능성을 두는 것은 / 괜찮다.

But in the real world / most people will never have the opportunity / either to become all that they are allowed to become, / or to need to be restrained from doing everything / that is possible for them to do.
하지만 현실 세계에서, / 대부분의 사람에게는 가능성이 없다. / 그들이 되어도 된다는 모든 것이 될 / 혹은 모든 것을 하지 못하게 저지당해야 할 / 그들이 하는 것이 가능한

Their effective freedom depends on / actually having the means and ability / to do what they choose.
그들의 실질적 자유는 달려 있다. / 실제로 수단과 능력을 갖추고 있는가에 / 그들이 선택하는 것을 할 수 있는

어떤 일을 할 수 있도록 법적으로 허용되는 것과 실제로 그것을 해 버릴 수 있는 것을 구별하는 것은 중요하다. 원한다면, 모든 사람이 2분 안에 1마일을 달릴 수 있도록 허용하는 법이 통과될 수도 있다. 그러나 그렇게 하는 것이 허용되더라도, 물리적으로 그렇게 할 수 없기 때문에, 그것이 그들의 실질적 자유를 증가시키지는 않을 것이다. 최소한의 제약과 최대한의 가능성을 두는 것은 괜찮다. 하지만 현실 세계에서, 대부분의 사람에게는 그들이 되어도 된다는 모든 것이 될 가능성이 없고, 할 수 있는 모든 것을 하지 못하게 저지당해야 할 가능성도 없을 것이다. 그들의 실질적 자유는 실제로 그들이 선택하는 것을 할 수 있는 수단과 능력을 갖추고 있는가에 달려 있다.

DAY 07

Why? 왜 정답일까?

첫 문장에서 어떤 것을 법적으로 해도 되는 상태와 실제로 그것을 행할 수 있는지를 구별하는 것이 중요하다고 언급한 데 이어, 2분 안에 1마일을 달리도록 허용하는 법이 통과되는 경우가 예시로 나온다. 예시에 따르면 2분 안에 1마일을 뛰는 것이 법적으로 가능해질지라도 '실제로 그렇게 할 수 있는' 사람들이 없기에 사람들의 실질적 자유가 증가되지 않는다고 한다. 이를 근거로 볼 때, 사람들의 '실질적' 자유란 '법으로 허용되는 행위를 실제 행할 능력이 있는지'에 따라 좌우된다는 결론을 도출할 수 있다. 따라서 빈칸에 들어갈 말로 가장 적절한 것은 ⑤ '그들이 선택하는 것을 할 수 있는 수단과 능력을 갖추고 있는가'이다.

- distinguish ⓥ 구별하다
- allowed ⓐ 허가받은, 허용된
- be incapable of ~을 할 수 없다
- physically ⓐ 신체적으로, 물리적으로
- needy ⓐ (경제적으로) 어려운, 궁핍한
- means ⓝ 수단
- legally ⓐ 법적으로
- effective ⓐ 실질적인, 효과적인
- restrain ⓥ 저지[제지]하다
- depend on ~에 좌우되다
- acceptable ⓐ 허용 가능한, 수용 가능한

구문 풀이

4행 That would not, however, increase their *effective* freedom,
주어(=앞 문장) 조동사   동사원형
because, (although (they are) allowed to do so), they are physically
접속사(~ 때문에)   생략   ( ): 삽입구 주어 동사구(~할 수 없다)
incapable of it.

★★ 문제 해결 꿀~팁 ★★

▶ **많이 틀린 이유는?**
실제로 행할 수 있는 행동이 법적으로 허용될 때 실질적 자유가 커질 수 있다는 내용의 글이다. 타인의 자유권을 존중하는 것에 관한 내용은 언급되지 않으므로 ①은 답으로 부적절하다.

▶ **문제 해결 방법은?**
첫 문장에서 어떤 일이 법적으로 허용되는 것과 그 일을 실제 할 수 있는가는 다른 개념이라고 언급한다. 이어서 법적으로 허용되더라도 실제로는 할 수 없는 일일 때 사람들의 실질적 자유는 증가하지 않는다는 것을 뒷받침하는 예시가 나온다. 이를 토대로 볼 때, 자유에 있어 중요한 것은 어떤 일이 법적으로 허용되는 것을 넘어서 '그 일을 실제로 할 수 있는지' 여부임을 알 수 있다.

DAY 08 빈칸 추론 08

01 ①	02 ①	03 ②	04 ②	05 ④
06 ③	07 ②	08 ②	09 ①	10 ①
11 ③	12 ⑤			

01 사실보다 감정에 기반한 우리의 선택   정답률 54% | 정답 ①

다음 빈칸에 들어갈 말로 가장 적절한 것을 고르시오.

✓ anxiety – 불안감
② boredom – 지루함
③ confidence – 자신감
④ satisfaction – 만족감
⑤ responsibility – 책임감

Many people are terrified to fly in airplanes.
많은 사람들은 비행기를 타는 것을 두려워한다.

Often, / this fear stems from a lack of control.
종종, / 이 두려움은 통제력의 부족에서 비롯된다.

The pilot is in control, / not the passengers, / and this lack of control instills fear.
조종사는 통제를 하지만 / 승객은 그렇지 않으며, / 이러한 통제력의 부족은 두려움을 스며들게 한다.

Many potential passengers are so afraid / they choose to drive great distances / to get to a destination / instead of flying.
많은 잠재적인 승객들은 너무 두려운 나머지 / 그들은 먼 거리를 운전하는 것을 선택한다. / 목적지에 도착하기 위해 / 비행기를 타는 대신

But / their decision to drive / is based solely on emotion, / not logic.
그러나 / 운전을 하기로 한 그들의 결정은 / 오직 감정에 근거한다. / 논리가 아닌

Logic says / that statistically, / the odds of dying in a car crash / are around 1 in 5,000, / while the odds of dying in a plane crash / are closer to 1 in 11 million.
논리에 따르면, / 통계적으로 / 자동차 사고로 사망할 확률은 / 약 5,000분의 1이다. / 비행기 사고로 사망할 확률은 / 1,100만분의 1에 가까운 반면

If you're going to take a risk, / especially one that could possibly involve your well-being, / wouldn't you want the odds in your favor?
만약 여러분이 위험을 감수할 것이라면, / 특히 여러분의 안녕을 혹시 포함할 수 있는 위험을 / 여러분에게 유리한 확률을 원하지 않겠는가?

However, / most people choose the option / that will cause them the least amount of anxiety.
그러나 / 사람들 대부분은 선택을 한다. / 그들에게 최소한의 불안감을 야기할

Pay attention to the thoughts / you have about taking the risk / and make sure you're basing your decision on facts, / not just feelings.
생각에 주의를 기울여보고 / 여러분이 위험을 감수하는 데 관해 하고 있는 / 여러분이 사실에 기반하여 결정을 내리고 있는지 확인하라. / 단지 감정이 아니고

많은 사람들은 비행기를 타는 것을 두려워한다. 종종, 이 두려움은 통제력의 부족에서 비롯된다. 조종사는 통제를 하지만 승객은 그렇지 않으며, 이러한 통제력의 부족은 두려움을 스며들게 한다. 많은 잠재적인 승객들은 너무 두려운 나머지 비행기를 타는 대신 먼 거리를 운전해 목적지에 도착하기를 선택한다. 그러나 운전을 하기로 한 그들의 결정은 논리가 아닌 오직 감정에 근거한다. 논리에 따르면, 통계적으로 자동차 사고로 사망할 확률은 약 5,000분의 1인 반면, 비행기 사고로 사망할 확률은 1,100만분의 1에 가깝다고 한다. 만약 여러분이 위험을 감수할 것이라면, 특히 여러분의 안녕을 혹시 포함할 수 있는 위험을 감수할 것이라면, 여러분에게 유리한 확률을 원하지 않겠는가? 그러나 사람들 대부분은 그들에게 최소한의 불안감을 야기할 선택을 한다. 여러분이 위험을 감수하는 데 관해 하고 있는 생각에 주의를 기울여보고, 단지 감정이 아니고 사실에 기반하여 결정을 내리고 있는지 확인하라.

Why? 왜 정답일까?

글에서 사람들이 비행기를 타는 대신 장거리 운전을 하기로 결심하는 것은 사실상 사고의 실질적 확률을 고려하지 않은, 감정 중심의 선택(their decision to drive is based solely on emotion)이라고 지적하고 있다. 즉, 사람들은 실제 통계적으로 교통사고 확률이 비행기 사고 확률보다 높은데도 오로지 '불안'을 피하려고 운전을 선택한다는 것이므로, 빈칸에 들어갈 말로 가장 적절한 것은 ① '불안감'이다.

- terrified ⓐ 겁에 질린
- lack ⓝ 부족, 결여
- potential ⓐ 잠재적인
- solely ⓐ 오로지
- statistically ⓐ 통계적으로
- stem from ~에서 기원하다
- instill ⓥ 스며들게 하다, 주입하다
- destination ⓝ 목적지
- logic ⓝ 논리
- odds ⓝ 공산, 가능성

- in one's favor ~에 유리한
- well-being ⓝ 안녕, 행복
- base ⓥ ~에 근거를 두다, 기반으로 하다
- boredom ⓝ 지루함
- crash ⓝ (차나 비행기의) 사고, 충돌
- make sure 반드시 ~하다
- anxiety ⓝ 불안

구문 풀이

4행 Many potential passengers are so afraid (that) they choose
「so ~ that : 너무 ~해서 …하다」
to drive great distances to get to a destination instead of flying.
목적어(~것)   부사적 용법(~하기 위해)

02 협력의 중요성 정답률 66% | 정답 ①

다음 빈칸에 들어갈 말로 가장 적절한 것을 고르시오. [3점]

✓① cooperating with one another – 서로 협력함
② fighting against enemies – 적에 대항하여 싸움
③ studying other species – 다른 종에 대해 공부함
④ inventing various machines – 다양한 기계를 발명함
⑤ paying attention to differences – 차이에 주의를 기울임

About four billion years ago, / molecules joined together to form cells.
대략 40억 년 전에, / 분자들은 결합하여 세포를 형성했다.

About two billion years later, / cells joined together to form more complex cells.
그리고 20억 년 뒤에, / 세포들은 결합해서 더 복합적인 세포를 형성했다.

And then a billion years later, / these more complex cells joined together / to form multicellular organisms.
그리고 그다음 10억 년 뒤에, / 이 복합적인 세포들은 결합하여 / 다세포 생물을 형성했다.

All of these evolved, / because the participating individuals could, / by working together, / spread their genetic material / in new and more effective ways.
이 모든 것들이 진화하게 되었다. / 참여한 각 개체가 / 서로 협력하여 / 자신들의 유전 물질을 퍼뜨릴 수 있었기 때문에, / 새롭고 더 효과적인 방식으로

Fast-forward another billion years to our world, / which is full of social animals, / from ants to wolves to humans.
또 다른 10억 년을 빨리감기하여 우리 세상으로 오면, / 이 곳은 사회적 동물로 가득 차 있다. / 개미부터 늑대까지

The same principle applies.
똑같은 원리가 적용된다.

Ants and wolves in groups can do things / that no single ant or wolf can do, / and we humans, by cooperating with one another, / have become the earth's dominant species.
무리를 지은 개미와 늑대는 일들을 할 수 있고, / 그 어떤 한 마리의 개미나 늑대도 할 수 없는 / 우리 인간들은 서로 협력함으로써 / 지구의 지배적인 종이 되었다.

대략 40억 년 전에, 분자들은 결합하여 세포를 형성했다. 그리고 20억 년 뒤에, 세포들은 결합해서 더 복합적인 세포를 형성했다. 그리고 그다음 10억 년 뒤에, 이 복합적인 세포들은 결합하여 다세포 생물을 형성했다. 참여한 각 개체가 서로 협력하여 자신들의 유전 물질을 새롭고 더 효과적인 방식으로 퍼뜨릴 수 있었기 때문에, 이 모든 것들이 진화하게 되었다. 또 다른 10억 년을 빨리감기하여 우리가 사는 세상으로 오면, 이 곳은 개미부터 늑대까지 사회적 동물로 가득 차 있다. 똑같은 원리가 적용된다. 무리를 지은 개미와 늑대는 그 어떤 한 마리의 개미나 늑대도 할 수 없는 일들을 할 수 있고, 우리 인간들은 서로 협력함으로써 지구의 지배적인 종이 되었다.

Why? 왜 정답일까?

첫 세 문장에서 분자, 세포, 복합적 세포는 각기 서로 결합하여 다세포 생물까지의 진화를 이루어냈다고 말하는데, 이는 결국 개체간의 협력이 진화를 이끌어내었다(All of these evolved because the participating individuals could, by working together, spread their genetic material in new and more effective ways.)는 주제를 나타낸다. 마지막 문장에서도 무리를 지은 개미나 늑대가 한 마리의 개미나 늑대보다 더 많은 일들을 해내기 마련이며 인간은 서로 '협력'하여 지구의 지배적인 종의 위치까지 올랐다고 이야기하므로, 빈칸에 들어갈 말로 가장 적절한 것은 ① '서로 협력함'이다.

- form ⓥ 형성하다, 만들다 ⓝ 형태
- multicellular ⓐ 다세포의
- evolve into ~로 진화하다
- genetic material 유전 물질
- principle ⓝ 원리, 원칙
- in groups 무리를 지어
- cooperate ⓥ 협력하다
- complex ⓐ 복잡한
- organism ⓝ 생물, 유기체
- spread 퍼뜨리다, 퍼지다
- fast-forward 빨리감기하다, 앞으로 감다
- apply 적용되다
- dominant ⓐ 지배적인
- species ⓝ (생물의) 종

구문 풀이

5행 All of these evolved / because the participating individuals
주어   동사   접속사(~ 때문에)   현재분사   주어
could, (by working together), spread their genetic material in new
조동사   「by+동명사」:~함으로써」   동사원형
and more effective ways.

03 도시에서 어휘 혁신이 일어날 수 있는 이유 정답률 62% | 정답 ②

다음 빈칸에 들어갈 말로 가장 적절한 것을 고르시오.

① provide rich source materials for artists
예술가들에게 풍부한 원재료를 공급하기
✓② offer the greatest exposure to other people
다른 사람들과의 가장 많은 접촉을 제공하기
③ cause cultural conflicts among users of slang
속어 사용자들 사이에서 문화 갈등을 초래하기
④ present ideal research environments to linguists
언어학자들에게 이상적인 연구 환경을 제공하기
⑤ reduce the social mobility of ambitious outsiders
야심에 찬 외부인의 사회 이동을 줄이기

People have always wanted / to be around other people / and to learn from them.
사람들은 항상 원해 왔다. / 다른 사람을 주위에 머무르며 / 그들로부터 배우기를

Cities have long been dynamos of social possibility, / foundries of art, music, and fashion.
도시는 오랫동안 사회적 가능성의 발전기였다. / 즉 예술, 음악, 패션의 주물 공장

Slang, or, if you prefer, "lexical innovation," / has always started in cities / — an outgrowth of all those different people / so frequently exposed to one another.
속어, 또는 여러분이 선호한다면 '어휘의 혁신'은 / 늘 도시에서 시작되었는데, / 그 모든 별의별 사람의 결과물이다. / 그렇게도 빈번히 서로에게 접촉한

It spreads outward, / in a manner not unlike transmissible disease, / which itself typically "takes off" in cities.
그것은 외부로 퍼져나가는데, / 전염성 질병과 다르지 않은 방식으로 / 그 전염성 질병 자체도 보통 도시에서 '이륙한다.'

If, as the noted linguist Leonard Bloomfield argued, / the way a person talks / is a "composite result of what he has heard before," / then language innovation would happen / where the most people heard and talked to the most other people.
만일, 저명한 언어학자 Leonard Bloomfield가 주장하듯이, / 사람이 말하는 방식이 / '전에 들었던 것을 합성한 결과물'이라면, / 언어 혁신은 일어날 것이다. / 가장 많은 사람이 가장 많은 다른 사람의 말을 듣고 가장 많은 다른 사람에게 말한 곳에서

Cities drive taste change / because they offer the greatest exposure to other people, / who not surprisingly are often the creative people / cities seem to attract.
도시는 취향 변화를 이끄는데, / 다른 사람들과의 가장 많은 접촉을 제공한다는 점에서 / 그들은 놀랄 것도 없이 흔히 창의적인 사람들이다. / 도시가 끌어들이는 듯 보이는

Media, / ever more global, ever more far-reaching, / spread language faster to more people.
미디어는 / 그 어느 때보다 더 전방위적이고, 그 어느 때보다 더 멀리까지 미치는 / 언어를 더 빨리 더 많은 사람에게 퍼뜨린다.

사람들은 항상 다른 사람들 주위에 머무르며 그들로부터 배우기를 원해 왔다. 도시는 오랫동안 사회적 가능성의 발전기, 즉 예술, 음악, 패션의 주물 공장이었다. 속어, 또는 여러분이 선호한다면 '어휘의 혁신'은 늘 도시에서 시작되었는데, 그 모든 별의별 사람이 그렇게도 빈번히 서로에게 접촉한 결과물이다. 그것은 전염성 질병과 다르지 않은 방식으로 외부로 퍼져나가는데, 그 전염성 질병 자체도 보통 도시에서 '이륙한다.' 저명한 언어학자 Leonard Bloomfield가 주장하듯이, 사람이 말하는 방식이 '전에 들었던 것을 합성한 결과물'이라면, 언어 혁신은 가장 많은 사람이 가장 많은 다른 사람의 말을 듣고 가장 많은 다른 사람에게 말한 곳에서 일어날 것이다. 도시는 다른 사람들과의 가장 많은 접촉을 제공한다는 점에서 취향 변화를 이끄는데, 그들은 놀랄 것도 없이 흔히 도시가 끌어들이는 듯 보이는 창의적인 사람들이다. 그 어느 때보다 더 전방위적이고, 그 어느 때보다 더 멀리까지 미치는 미디어는 언어를 더 빨리 더 많은 사람에게 퍼뜨린다.

Why? 왜 정답일까?

빈칸 문장 앞에서 언어 혁신은 가장 많은 사람들이 가장 많은 타인과 소통할 수 있는 (~ the most people heard and talked to the most other people.) 공간에서 일어날 것이라고 한다. 이를 근거로 볼 때, 빈칸에도 도시에 '사람들이 많기 때문에' 변화가 일어날 수 있다는 내용이 들어가야 한다. 따라서 빈칸에 들어갈 말로 가장 적절한 것은 ② '다른 사람들과의 가장 많은 접촉을 제공한다(offer the greatest exposure to other people)'이다.

DAY 08

- **learn from** ~로부터 배우다
- **foundry** ⓝ 주물 공장
- **lexical** ⓐ 어휘의
- **be exposed to** ~에 노출되다
- **one another** 서로
- **outward** [ad] 밖으로
- **take off** 이륙하다
- **drive** ⓥ 이끌다, 추진하다
- **mobility** ⓝ 이동(성)
- **dynamo** ⓝ 발전기
- **slang** ⓝ 속어
- **outgrowth** ⓝ 결과물
- **frequently** [ad] 자주, 빈번히
- **spread** ⓥ 퍼지다
- **transmissible** ⓐ 전염되는
- **composite** ⓐ 합성의 ⓝ 합성물
- **far-reaching** ⓐ 광범위한
- **ambitious** ⓐ 야심에 찬

구문 풀이

8행 If, (as the noted linguist Leonard Bloomfield argued), the way
접속사(조건) ( ):삽입절 주어
a person talks is a "composite result of what he has heard before,"
관계부사절(how 생략) 동사
then language innovation would happen where the most people
~한 곳에서
heard and talked to the most other people.

---

04 수업에 관여하는 수많은 주체   정답률 53% | 정답 ②

다음 빈칸에 들어갈 말로 가장 적절한 것을 고르시오. [3점]

① more interesting than playing games
  게임을 하는 것보다 흥미로운
✔ the product of the efforts of hundreds of people
  수백 명의 사람들의 노력의 산물
③ the place where students can improve writing skills
  학생들이 쓰기 능력을 향상시킬 수 있는 곳
④ most effective when combined with online learning
  온라인 학습과 결합될 때 가장 효과적인
⑤ the race where everyone is a winner
  모든 사람이 승자인 경주

Just think for a moment of all the people / upon whom your participation in your class depends.
모든 사람들을 잠시만 생각해 보라. / 여러분의 수업 참여를 좌우하는

Clearly, / the class requires a teacher to teach it / and students to take it.
분명히 / 그 수업은 가르칠 교사를 필요로 한다. / 그리고 들을 학생을

However, it also depends / on many other people and organizations.
하지만 그것은 또한 좌우된다. / 많은 다른 사람과 기관에

Someone had to decide / when the class would be held and in what room, / communicate that information to you, / and enroll you in that class.
누군가가 결정하고, / 언제 그리고 어떤 방에서 그 수업이 열릴지 / 그 정보를 여러분에게 전달하고, / 그 수업에 여러분을 등록해 주어야 했다.

Someone also had to write a textbook, / and with the assistance of many other people / — printers, editors, salespeople, and bookstore employees — / it has arrived in your hands.
또한 누군가가 교과서를 집필해야 했고, / 많은 다른 사람들의 도움으로 / 즉 인쇄업자, 편집자, 판매원, 서점 직원들 / 그것이 여러분의 손에 들어왔다.

Thus, a class / that seems to involve just you, your fellow students, and your teacher / is in fact the product / of the efforts of hundreds of people.
따라서 수업은 / 여러분과 학우들, 선생님만 포함하는 것처럼 보이는 / 사실 산물이다. / 수백 명의 사람들의 노력의

여러분의 수업 참여를 좌우하는 모든 사람들을 잠시만 생각해 보라. 분명히 그 수업은 가르칠 교사와 들을 학생을 필요로 한다. 하지만 그것은 또한 많은 다른 사람과 기관에 좌우된다. 누군가가 언제 그리고 어떤 방에서 그 수업이 열릴지 결정하고, 그 정보를 여러분에게 전달하고, 그 수업에 여러분을 등록해 주어야 했다. 또한 누군가가 교과서를 집필해야 했고, 많은 다른 사람들, 즉 인쇄업자, 편집자, 판매원, 서점 직원들의 도움으로 그것이 여러분의 손에 들어왔다. 따라서 여러분과 학우들, 선생님만 포함하는 것처럼 보이는 수업은 사실 수백 명의 사람들의 노력의 산물이다.

Why? 왜 정답일까?

보통 '수업'을 떠올리면 학생과 교사라는 두 주체만 생각하기 쉽지만 사실은 더 많은 존재들이 수업에 영향을 미친다(**However, it also depends on many other people and organizations.**)는 내용의 글이므로, 빈칸에 들어갈 말로 가장 적절한 것은 ② '수백 명의 사람들의 노력의 산물'이다.

- **require** ⓥ 필요로 하다, 요구하다
- **organization** ⓝ 기관
- **enroll** ⓥ 등록하다
- **editor** ⓝ 편집자
- **improve** ⓥ 향상시키다
- **combine** ⓥ 결합하다
- **participation** ⓝ 참여
- **communicate** ⓥ (정보 등을) 전달하다
- **assistance** ⓝ 도움
- **fellow** ⓝ 친구, 동료
- **effective** ⓐ 효과적인

구문 풀이

11행 Thus, / a class [that seems to involve just you, your fellow
주어 ↳주격 관계대명사
students, and your teacher] is in fact the product of the efforts of
동사 주격 보어
hundreds of people.
수백의

---

05 유머를 기록해두기   정답률 50% | 정답 ④

다음 빈칸에 들어갈 말로 가장 적절한 것을 고르시오. [3점]

① keep away from new technology
  새로운 기술을 멀리하는
② take risks and challenge yourself
  위험을 감수하고 스스로에게 도전하는
③ have friendly people close to you
  다정한 사람들을 가까이 두는
✔ document them and then tell someone
  그것들을 기록하고 그 다음 누군가에게 말하는
⑤ improve interpersonal relationship at work
  직장에서의 대인관계를 개선하는

How funny are you?
당신은 얼마나 재미있는가?

While some people are natural humorists, / being funny is a set of skills / that can be learned.
어떤 사람들은 타고난 익살꾼이지만, / 재미있다는 것은 일련의 기술들이다. / 학습할 수 있는

Exceptionally funny people don't depend upon their memory / to keep track of everything they find funny.
유난히 웃긴 사람들은 그들의 기억력에 의존하지 않는다. / 그들이 재미있다고 생각하는 모든 것을 잊어버리지 않기 위해

In the olden days, / great comedians carried notebooks / to write down funny thoughts or observations / and scrapbooks for news clippings / that struck them as funny.
예전에는, / 위대한 코미디언들은 공책들을 가지고 다녔다. / 재미있는 생각이나 관찰들을 적기 위한 / 그리고 오래된 뉴스 기사들을 위한 스크랩북을 / 그들에게 재미있다는 인상을 주는

Today, you can do that easily with your smartphone.
오늘날 당신은 스마트폰으로 그것을 쉽게 할 수 있다.

If you have a funny thought, / record it as an audio note.
만약 당신이 재미있는 생각이 있다면, / 음성 기록으로 그것을 녹음해라.

If you read a funny article, / save the link in your bookmarks.
만약 당신이 재미있는 기사를 읽는다면, / 그 링크를 당신의 북마크에 저장해라.

The world is a funny place / and your existence within it is probably funnier.
세상은 재미있는 장소이고, / 그 속에서 당신의 존재는 아마도 더 재미있을 것이다.

Accepting that fact is a blessing / that gives you everything you need / to see humor and craft stories on a daily basis.
그 사실을 받아들이는 것은 축복이다. / 필요한 모든 것을 당신에게 주는 / 매일 당신이 유머를 발견하고 이야기를 지어내는 데

All you have to do is / document them and then tell someone.
당신이 해야 하는 모든 것은 / 그것들을 기록하고 그 다음 누군가에게 말하는 것이다.

당신은 얼마나 재미있는가? 어떤 사람들은 타고난 익살꾼이지만, 재미있다는 것은 학습할 수 있는 일련의 기술들이다. 유난히 웃긴 사람들은 그들이 재미있다고 생각하는 모든 것을 잊어버리지 않기 위해 그들의 기억력에 의존하지 않는다. 예전에는, 위대한 코미디언들은 재미있는 생각이나 관찰들을 적기 위한 공책들과, 재미있다는 인상을 주는 오래된 뉴스 기사들을 위한 스크랩북을 가지고 다녔다. 오늘날 당신은 스마트폰으로 그것을 쉽게 할 수 있다. 만약 당신이 재미있는 생각이 있다면, 음성 기록으로 그것을 녹음해라. 만약 당신이 재미있는 기사를 읽는다면, 그 링크를 당신의 북마크에 저장해라. 세상은 재미있는 장소이고, 그 속에서 당신의 존재는 아마도 더 재미있을 것이다. 그 사실을 받아들이는 것은 매일 당신이 유머를 발견하고 이야기를 지어내는 데 필요한 모든 것을 당신에게 주는 축복이다. 당신이 해야 하는 모든 것은 그것들을 기록하고 그 다음 누군가에게 말하는 것이다.

Why? 왜 정답일까?

재미있는 생각이나 유머를 접할 때 적절한 방법을 활용하여 기록해두라(**If you have a funny thought, record it as an audio note. If you read a funny article, save the link in your bookmarks.**)는 내용의 글이므로, 빈칸에 들어갈 말로 가장 적절한 것은 ④ '그것들을 기록하고 그 다음 누군가에게 말하는'이다.

- **humorist** ⓝ 유머가 넘치는 사람, 유머 작가
- **keep track of** ~을 기록하다
- **clipping** ⓝ 조각
- **craft** ⓥ (공들여) 만들다, 지어내다
- **take a risk** 위험을 감수하다
- **exceptionally** [ad] 유난히, 특별히
- **observation** ⓝ 관찰
- **strike A as B** A에게 B라는 인상을 주다
- **keep away from** ~을 멀리하다
- **document** ⓥ 기록하다, 문서화하다

- improve ⓥ 개선하다, 나아지게 하다
- interpersonal ⓐ 대인관계의

- vacuum ⓝ 진공, 공백
- spatial ⓐ 공간의, 공간적인
- in relation to ~와 관련하여
- free from ~에서 벗어나, ~의 염려가 없는
- temporal ⓐ 시간의, 시간의 제약을 받는

구문 풀이

12행 Accepting that fact is a blessing [that gives you everything
　　　　동명사구 주어　　　　　　동사　주격 보어　　　　　선행사
{you need / to see humor and craft stories on a daily basis}].
　　동사원형1　　　　동사원형2　　　　매일, 날마다

구문 풀이

1행 From an economic perspective, a short-lived event
　　　　　　　　　　　　　　　　　　　　주어
can become an innovative event / if it generates goods and services
　　동사　　　　　　　　　　조건 접속사　　　　　　선행사
[that can be sold to people, in particular to those from outside the
　주격 관계대명사　　　　　　　　　　　~한 사람들
locality].

06　행사와 맥락의 연관성　정답률 41% | 정답 ③

다음 빈칸에 들어갈 말로 가장 적절한 것을 고르시오. [3점]

① build a new context with other short-lived events
　다른 단기간 행사로 새로운 맥락을 구축할
② take place free from this spatial and temporal limit
　공간과 시간의 한계를 벗어나서 발생할
✓③ be performed in relation to this long-term context
　이러한 장기간의 맥락과 관련하여 시행될
④ interact with well-known events from another locality
　다른 곳의 유명한 행사와 상호 작용할
⑤ evolve itself from a local event to a global one in the end
　결국에는 국지적 행사에서 세계적인 것으로 발전할

From an economic perspective, / a short-lived event can become an
innovative event / if it generates goods and services / that can be sold to
people, / in particular to those from outside the locality.
경제적인 관점에서 볼 때, / 단기간 행사가 혁신적인 행사가 될 수 있다. / 상품과 서비스를 만들어 낸다면 / 사람
들에게 판매될 수 있는 / 특히 외부 사람들에게

The remarkable growth / of art exhibitions, cultural festivals and sports
competitions, / for example, / can be analysed in this light.
눈에 띄는 성장은 / 예술 전시회, 문화 축제 그리고 스포츠 경기의 / 예를 들어, / 이러한 관점에서 분석될 수
있다.

They are temporary activities / that can attract large numbers of outsiders to
a locality, / bringing in new sources of income.
그것들은 일시적 활동들이다. / 많은 외부인들을 그 지역으로 끌어들여 / 새로운 수입원을 가져올 수 있는

But even here, / there is a two-way interaction / between the event and the
context.
그러나 심지어 여기에서도, / 쌍방향 상호 작용이 있다. / 행사와 맥락 간에

The existence / of an infrastructure, a reputation, a history of an activity / for
an area / may have important effects / on the economic success or failure of
an event.
존재는 / 기반 시설, 명성, 활동의 연혁의 / 한 지역의 / 중요한 영향을 미칠 수 있다. / 행사의 경제적 성공 또는
실패에

In other words, / events do not take place in a vacuum.
다시 말해서, / 행사들은 진공 상태에서 발생하지 않는다.

They depend on an existing context / which has been in the making for a
long time.
그것들은 기존의 맥락에 의존한다. / 오랜 시간 동안 만들어져 왔던

The short-lived event, / therefore, / would be performed / in relation to this
long-term context.
단기간 행사는 / 그러므로 / 시행될 것이다. / 이러한 장기간의 맥락과 관련하여

People engage in typical patterns of interaction / based on the relationship /
between their roles and the roles of others.
사람들은 전형적인 양식의 상호 작용에 참여한다. / 관계에 근거하여 / 자신의 역할과 다른 사람의 역할 사이의

Employers are expected / to interact with employees in a certain way, / as are
doctors with patients.
고용주들은 기대된다. / 직원들과 특정한 방식으로 상호 작용하도록 / 의사들이 환자들과 그러한 것처럼

In each case, actions are restricted / by the role responsibilities and
obligations / associated with individuals' positions within society.
각각의 경우에 행동은 제한된다. / 역할 책임과 의무에 의해 / 개인의 사회 내 지위와 관련된

For instance, parents and children are linked / by certain rights, privileges,
and obligations.
예를 들어 부모와 자식은 연결된다. / 특정한 권리, 특권, 의무에 의해

Parents are responsible / for providing their children with the basic
necessities of life / — food, clothing, shelter, and so forth.
부모는 책임이 있다. / 자기 자녀에게 기본적인 생필품을 제공할 / 의식주 등

These expectations are so powerful / that not meeting them may make the
parents vulnerable / to charges of negligence or abuse.
이러한 기대가 너무 강해서 / 그것을 충족시키지 못하는 것은 부모를 비난받기 쉽게 할지도 모른다. / 태만이나
학대 혐의로

Children, in turn, are expected / to do as their parents say.
역으로 아이들은 기대된다. / 자신의 부모가 말하는 대로 하도록

Thus, interactions within a relationship are functions / not only of the
individual personalities of the people involved / but also of the role
requirements associated with the statuses they have.
그러므로 관계 내의 상호 작용은 작용이다. / 연관된 사람들 개개의 성격뿐만 아니라 / 그들이 지닌 지위와 관련
된 역할 요구의

★★★ 1등급 대비 고난도 2점 문제

07　역할의 상호 작용과 관계 내 상호 작용　정답률 32% | 정답 ②

다음 빈칸에 들어갈 말로 가장 적절한 것을 고르시오.

① careers - 직업
✓② statuses - 지위
③ abilities - 능력
④ motivations - 동기
⑤ perspectives - 관점

경제적인 관점에서 볼 때, 단기간 행사는 사람들, 특히 외부 사람들에게 판매
될 수 있는 상품과 서비스를 만들어 낸다면 혁신적인 행사가 될 수 있다. 예를
들어, 예술 전시회, 문화 축제 그리고 스포츠 경기의 눈에 띄는 성장은 이러한
관점에서 분석될 수 있다. 그것들은 많은 외부인들을 그 지역으로 끌어들여 새
로운 수입원을 가져올 수 있는 일시적 활동들이다. 그러나 심지어 여기에서도,
행사와 맥락 간에 쌍방향 상호 작용이 있다. 한 지역의 기반 시설, 명성, 활동
의 연혁의 존재는 행사의 경제적 성공 또는 실패에 중요한 영향을 미칠 수 있
다. 다시 말해서, 행사들은 진공 상태에서 발생하지 않는다. 그것들은 오랜 시
간 동안 만들어져 왔던 기존의 맥락에 의존한다. 그러므로 단기간 행사는 이러
한 장기간의 맥락과 관련하여 시행될 것이다.

사람들은 자신의 역할과 다른 사람의 역할 사이의 관계에 근거하여 전형적인
양식의 상호 작용에 참여한다. 의사들이 환자들과 그러한 것처럼 고용주들은
직원들과 특정한 방식으로 상호 작용하도록 기대된다. 각각의 경우에 행동은
개인의 사회 내 지위와 관련된 역할 책임과 의무에 의해 제한된다. 예를 들어
부모와 자식은 특정한 권리, 특권, 의무에 의해 연결된다. 부모는 자기 자녀에
게 의식주 등 기본적인 생필품을 제공할 책임이 있다. 이러한 기대가 너무 강
해서 그것을 충족시키지 못하는 것은 부모를 태만이나 학대 혐의로 비난받기
쉽게 할지도 모른다. 역으로 아이들은 자신의 부모가 말하는 대로 하도록 기대
된다. 그러므로 관계 내의 상호 작용은 연관된 사람들 개개의 성격의 작용일
뿐만 아니라 그들이 지닌 지위와 관련된 역할 요구의 작용이다.

Why? 왜 정답일까?

'But even here, there is a two-way interaction between the event and
the context.'에서 단기 행사와 맥락 간에는 쌍방향의 상호 작용이 있다고 말한 데 이어,
'In other words, events do not take place in a vacuum. They depend
on an existing context which has been in the making for a long time.'
에서는 행사가 독립적으로 발생하지 않고 오랜 시간에 걸쳐 구축된 맥락에 의존하는 특
성이 있음을 이야기한다. 따라서 빈칸에 들어갈 말로 가장 적절한 것은 ③ '이러한 장기
간의 맥락과 관련하여 시행될'이다.

Why? 왜 정답일까?

첫 문장에서 사람들은 역할 간의 관계에 근거한 전형적인 상호 작용에 참여하게 된다고
언급한 후, 다양한 예시가 이어지고 있다. 특히 '~ actions are restricted by the
role responsibilities and obligations associated with individuals'
positions within society.'에서 개인의 행동은 사회 내에서의 '지위'와 연관된 책임
과 의무로 인해 제한을 받게 된다고 설명하는 것을 근거로 볼 때, 빈칸에 들어갈 말로 가
장 적절한 것은 ② '지위'이다.

- perspective ⓝ 관점, 시각
- locality ⓝ (~이 존재하는) 곳
- in this light 이러한 관점에서
- attract ⓥ 끌다, 매혹시키다
- short-lived 단기의
- remarkable ⓐ 눈에 띄는, 주목할 만한
- temporary ⓐ 일시적인
- existence ⓝ 존재, 있음

- engage in ⓥ ~에 참여하다, 관여하다
- obligation ⓝ 의무
- privilege ⓝ 특권
- charge ⓝ 혐의, 비난
- status ⓝ 지위
- restrict ⓥ 제한하다
- associated with ~와 관련된
- necessity ⓝ 필수품
- abuse ⓝ 학대, 남용
- perspective ⓝ 관점

DAY 08

구문 풀이

11행 These expectations are so powerful that not meeting them
「so ~ that … : 너무 ~해서 …하다」　　동명사구 주어
may make the parents vulnerable to charges of negligence or abuse.
5형식 동사　　목적어　　형용사 보어

★★ 문제 해결 꿀~팁 ★★

▶ 많이 틀린 이유는?
글은 상호작용의 주체가 각자의 '지위'에 따라 역할이나 책임을 부여받는다는 내용을 다루고 있다. ③의 '능력'은 언급되지 않았다.

▶ 문제 해결 방법은?
예시 앞에는 대체로 주제가 나오므로, 여기서도 For instance 앞의 'In each case ~'에 답의 근거가 있음을 예상할 수 있다.

★★★ 1등급 대비 고난도 3점 문제

08 어디가 문제인지 정확히 알고 고치기　　정답률 38% | 정답 ②

다음 빈칸에 들어갈 말로 가장 적절한 것을 고르시오. [3점]
① needs competition among experts – 전문가들 사이의 경쟁을 필요로 한다
✔ does not have to be time-consuming – 많은 시간이 걸릴 필요는 없다
③ requires the development of equipment – 장비의 발달을 요구한다
④ does not come from previous experience – 이전의 경험에서 나오지 않는다
⑤ often takes place as a result of good luck – 종종 행운의 결과로 발생한다

There is a very old story involving a man / trying to fix his broken boiler.
한 남자와 관련된 매우 오래된 이야기가 있다. / 고장 난 보일러를 고치기 위해 애쓰는
Despite his best efforts over many months, / he can't do it.
수개월에 걸친 최선의 노력에도 불구하고, / 그는 고칠 수 없다.
Eventually, he gives up / and decides to call in an expert.
결국, 그는 포기하고 / 전문가를 부르기로 결심한다.
The engineer arrives, / gives one gentle tap on the side of the boiler, / and it springs to life.
기사가 도착하여 / 보일러의 옆을 한 번 가볍게 두드리자 / 보일러가 작동하기 시작한다.
The engineer gives a bill to the man, / and the man argues / that he should pay only a small fee / as the job took the engineer only a few moments.
기사는 남자에게 청구서를 주고, / 남자는 주장한다. / 자신이 적은 요금 지불해야 한다고 / 기사가 그 일을 하는 데 조금밖에 안 걸렸기 때문에
The engineer explains / that the man is not paying for the time / he took to tap the boiler / but rather the years of experience / involved in knowing exactly where to tap.
기사는 설명한다. / 시간에 돈을 지불하는 것이 아니라 / 그가 보일러를 두드리는 데 걸린 / 수년의 경험에 대해 돈을 지불하는 것이라고 / 정확히 어디를 두드려야 할지를 아는 것과 관련된
Just like the expert engineer tapping the boiler, / effective change does not have to be time-consuming.
전문 기사가 보일러를 두드리는 것과 마찬가지로, / 효과적인 변화는 많은 시간이 걸릴 필요는 없다.
In fact, it is often simply a question / of knowing exactly where to tap.
사실, 그것은 종종 단지 문제이다. / 정확히 어디를 두드려야 할지를 아는 것의

고장 난 보일러를 고치기 위해 애쓰는 한 남자와 관련된 매우 오래된 이야기가 있다. 수개월에 걸친 최선의 노력에도 불구하고, 그는 고칠 수 없다. 결국, 그는 포기하고 전문가를 부르기로 결심한다. 기사가 도착하여 보일러의 옆을 한 번 가볍게 두드리자 보일러가 작동하기 시작한다. 기사는 남자에게 청구서를 주고, 남자는 기사가 그 일을 하는 데 조금밖에 안 걸렸기 때문에 적은 요금만 지불해야 한다고 주장한다. 기사는 보일러를 두드리는 데 걸린 시간이 아니라, 정확히 어디를 두드려야 할지를 아는 것과 관련된 수년의 경험에 대해 돈을 지불하는 것이라고 설명한다. 전문 기사가 보일러를 두드리는 것과 마찬가지로, 효과적인 변화는 많은 시간이 걸릴 필요는 없다. 사실, 그것은 종종 단지 정확히 어디를 두드려야 할지를 아는 것의 문제이다.

Why? 왜 정답일까?

예시를 먼저 소개하고 뒤에서 결론을 제시하는 미괄식의 글이다. 오랜 시간 보일러를 고치려 노력했어도 전문 보일러 기사와는 달리 보일러를 고칠 수 없었던 남자의 이야기를 통해, 효과적인 변화를 이끌어내기 위해서는 많은 시간이나 노력을 들이기보다 무엇을 어떻게 해야 할지를 정확히 알고서 행동하는 것이 중요하다는 내용을 유추할 수 있다. 따라서 빈칸에 들어갈 말로 가장 적절한 것은 ② '많은 시간이 걸릴 필요는 없다'이다.

● despite [prep] ~에도 불구하고
● call in (의사·경찰 등을) 부르다
● eventually [ad] 결국, 마침내
● gentle @ 조심스러운, 부드러운

● spring to life 갑자기 활발해지다
● argue ⓥ 주장하다, 언쟁하다
● competition ⓝ 경쟁
● equipment ⓝ 장비
● bill ⓝ 고지서
● exactly [ad] 정확히
● time-consuming 시간이 많이 걸리는
● previous @ 이전의, 사전의, 앞선

구문 풀이

8행 The engineer explains {that the man is not paying for
「not +
the time [he took to tap the boiler] / but rather the years of experience
A +　　　　　　　　　　　　　　but + B : A 아니라 B」
[involved in knowing exactly where to tap]}.
과거분사　　　　　「의문사 + to부정사(어디를 ~할지)」

★★ 문제 해결 꿀~팁 ★★

▶ 많이 틀린 이유는?
핵심 내용은 '전문가는 비전문가에 비해 경험이 있어 훨씬 덜한 시간과 노력을 들이고도 문제를 해결할 수 있다'는 것인데, 최다 오답인 ③은 장비의 발달만을 언급하고 있어 글의 내용과 관계가 없다.

▶ 문제 해결 방법은?
빈칸 문제에서 빈칸은 주제 또는 주제와 반대되는 부분에 주로 나오는데, 이 문제의 경우에는 주제와 반대되는 말이 빈칸이다. 문제를 풀기 전 빈칸 문장을 먼저 읽고, 필요한 말이 주제인지 주제와 반대되는 내용인지를 확인하도록 한다.

★★★ 1등급 대비 고난도 3점 문제

09 개인에게 넘어간 음악 선택권　　정답률 38% | 정답 ①

다음 빈칸에 들어갈 말로 가장 적절한 것을 고르시오. [3점]
✔ choose and determine his or her musical preferences
자신이 선호하는 음악을 선택하고 결정해야
② understand the technical aspects of recording sessions
녹음 세션의 기술적 측면을 이해해야
③ share unique and inspiring playlists on social media
독특하고 영감을 주는 재생 목록을 소셜 미디어에 공유해야
④ interpret lyrics with background knowledge of the songs
노래에 대한 배경지식으로 가사를 해석해야
⑤ seek the advice of a voice specialist for better performances
더 나은 공연을 위해 음성 전문가의 조언을 구해야

Due to technological innovations, / music can now be experienced by more people, / for more of the time than ever before.
기술 혁신으로 인해, / 음악은 이제 더 많은 사람에 의해 경험될 수 있다. / 이전보다 더 많은 시간 동안
Mass availability has given individuals unheard-of control / over their own sound-environment.
대중 이용 가능성은 개인들에게 전례 없는 통제권을 주었다. / 각자의 음향 환경에 대한
However, / it has also confronted them / with the simultaneous availability of countless genres of music, / in which they have to orient themselves.
하지만 / 그것은 그들을 맞닥뜨리게 했고 / 무수한 장르의 음악을 동시에 이용할 수 있는 상황에 / 그들은 그 상황에 적응해야만 한다.
People start filtering out and organizing their digital libraries / like they used to do with their physical music collections.
사람들은 자신들의 디지털 라이브러리를 걸러 내고 정리하기 시작한다. / 이전에 그들이 물리적 형태를 지닌 음악을 수집했던 것처럼
However, / there is the difference / that the choice lies in their own hands.
하지만 / 차이가 있다. / 선택권은 자신이 가진다는
Without being restricted to the limited collection of music-distributors, / nor being guided by the local radio program / as a 'preselector' of the latest hits, / the individual actively has to choose and determine his or her musical preferences.
음악 배급자의 제한된 컬렉션에 국한되지 않고, / 또한 지역 라디오 프로그램의 안내를 받지 않고, / 최신 히트곡의 '사전 선택자'인 / 개인은 적극적으로 자신이 선호하는 음악을 선택하고 결정해야 한다.
The search for the right song / is thus associated with considerable effort.
적절한 노래를 찾는 것은 / 따라서 상당한 노력과 관련이 있다.

기술 혁신으로 인해, 음악은 이제 이전보다 더 많은 시간 동안 더 많은 사람에 의해 경험될 수 있다. 대중 이용 가능성은 개인들에게 각자의 음향 환경에 대한 전례 없는 통제권을 주었다. 하지만 그들은 무수한 장르의 음악을 동시에 이용할 수 있는 상황에 맞닥뜨리게 되었고 그 상황에 적응해야만 한다. 사람은 이전에 물리적 형태를 지닌 음악을 수집했던 것처럼 자신들의 디지털 라이브러리를 걸러 내고 정리하기 시작한다. 하지만 선택권은 자신이 가진다는 차이가 있다. 음악 배급자의 제한된 컬렉션에 국한되지 않고, 또한 최신 히트곡의 '사전 선택자'인 지역 라디오 프로그램의 안내를 받지 않고, 개인은 적극적으로 자신이 선호하는 음악을 선택하고 결정해야 한다. 따라서 적절한 노래를 찾는 것은 상당한 노력과 관련이 있다.

DAY 08

Why? 왜 정답일까?

첫 두 문장에서 기술 혁신으로 인해 개인이 자신의 음향 환경을 통제할 수 있는 권한을 갖게 되었다고 한다. 특히 'However, there is the difference that the choice lies in their own hands.'에서는 무수한 장르의 음악 속에서 자신의 디지털 라이브러리를 어떻게 구성할 것인지에 대한 선택권이 개인 자신에게 있다고 언급한다. 따라서 빈칸에 들어갈 말로 가장 적절한 것은 ① '자신이 선호하는 음악을 선택하고 결정해야'이다.

- availability ⓝ 이용 가능성
- confront A with B A를 B와 대면시키다
- restrict ⓥ 국한시키다, 제한하다
- considerable ⓐ 상당한
- unheard-of ⓐ 전례 없는
- orient ⓥ 적응하다, 익숙해지다
- distributor ⓝ 배급 업자
- interpret ⓥ 해석하다

구문 풀이

5행 However, it has also confronted them with the simultaneous
「confront + A + with + B : A를 B와 대면시키다」
availability of countless genres of music, in which they have to orient
계속적 용법(= where)
themselves.

★★ 문제 해결 꿀~팁 ★★

▶ 많이 틀린 이유는?
기술 혁신으로 개인이 음악 선택권을 갖게 되었다는 내용의 글이다. 최다 오답인 ③은 개인이 소셜 미디어에 플레이리스트를 공유해야 한다는 의미인데, 개인이 직접 만든 플레이리스트를 공유해야 하는지는 글에서 언급되지 않았다. 특히 '소셜 미디어'라는 소재 자체가 글에서 아예 언급되지 않았다.

▶ 문제 해결 방법은?
주제가 드러나는 'However ~.' 문장을 잘 읽으면 쉽다. 'the choice lies in their own hands'가 문제 해결에 핵심적인 표현이다.

★★★ 1등급 대비 고난도 3점 문제

10 진화가 거듭되어도 상황이 변하지 않는 까닭 | 정답률 47% | 정답 ①

다음 빈칸에 들어갈 말로 가장 적절한 것을 고르시오. [3점]

✓ just stay in place – 제자리에 머무를 뿐이다
② end up walking slowly – 결국 느리게 걷게 된다
③ never run into each other – 결코 서로 마주치지 않는다
④ won't be able to adapt to changes – 변화에 적응할 수 없을 것이다
⑤ cannot run faster than their parents – 자기 부모보다 더 빨리 달릴 수 없다

In Lewis Carroll's *Through the Looking-Glass*, / the Red Queen takes Alice / on a race through the countryside.
Lewis Carroll의 *Through the Looking-Glass*에서 / 붉은 여왕은 Alice를 데리고 간다. / 시골을 통과하는 한 경주에

They run and they run, / but then Alice discovers / that they're still under the same tree / that they started from.
그들은 달리고 또 달리는데, / 그러다 Alice는 발견한다. / 그들이 나무 아래에 여전히 있음을 / 자신들이 출발했던

The Red Queen explains to Alice: / "*here*, you see, / it takes all the running you can do, / to keep in the same place."
붉은 여왕은 Alice에게 설명한다. / "*여기서는* 네가 보다시피 / 네가 할 수 있는 모든 뜀박질을 해야 한단다. / 같은 장소에 머물러 있으려면"이라고

Biologists sometimes use this Red Queen Effect / to explain an evolutionary principle.
생물학자들은 때때로 이 '붉은 여왕 효과'를 사용한다 / 진화의 원리를 설명하기 위해.

If foxes evolve to run faster / so they can catch more rabbits, / then only the fastest rabbits will live long enough / to make a new generation of bunnies / that run even faster / — in which case, of course, / only the fastest foxes will catch enough rabbits / to thrive and pass on their genes.
만약 여우가 더 빨리 달리게 진화한다면 / 그들이 더 많은 토끼를 잡기 위해 / 그러면 가장 빠른 토끼만이 충분히 오래 살아 / 새로운 세대의 토끼를 낳을 텐데 / 훨씬 더 빨리 달리는 / 이 경우 당연히도 / 가장 빠른 여우만이 충분한 토끼를 잡을 것이다 / 번성하여 자신들의 유전자를 물려줄 만큼.

Even though they might run, / the two species just stay in place.
그들이 달린다 해도 / 그 두 종은 제자리에 머무를 뿐이다.

Lewis Carroll의 *Through the Looking-Glass*에서, 붉은 여왕은 Alice를 데리고 시골을 통과하는 한 경주에 간다. 그들은 달리고 또 달리는데, 그러다 Alice는 자신들이 출발했던 나무 아래에 여전히 있음을 발견한다. 붉은 여왕은 Alice에게 "*여기서는* 보다시피 같은 장소에 머물러 있으려면 네가 할 수 있는 모든 뜀박질을 해야 한단다."라고 설명한다. 생물학자들은 때때로 이 '붉은 여왕 효과'를 사용해 진화의 원리를 설명한다. 만약 여우가 더 많은 토끼를 잡기 위해 더

빨리 달리게 진화한다면, 가장 빠른 토끼만이 충분히 오래 살아 훨씬 더 빨리 달리는 새로운 세대의 토끼를 낳을 텐데, 이 경우 당연히도 가장 빠른 여우만이 충분한 토끼를 잡아 번성하여 자신들의 유전자를 물려줄 것이다. 그 두 종은 달린다 해도 제자리에 머무를 뿐이다.

Why? 왜 정답일까?

원래 있던 자리를 유지하기 위해 전력 질주해야 하는(~ it takes all the running you can do, to keep in the same place.) 소설 속 상황에 빗대어 진화의 원리를 설명하는 글이다. 마지막 문장 앞에 제시된 여우와 토끼의 예시에 따르면, 여우가 토끼를 더 많이 잡기 위해 달리기가 빨라지도록 진화하면, 그 여우보다도 빠른 토끼만이 살아남아 번식하게 되므로 토끼 또한 더 빨라지도록 진화하게 된다. 이것은 다시 여우의 달리기가 더 빨라지게 하는 원인으로 작용하므로, 결과적으로 두 종의 상황은 시간이 지나도 차이가 없다. 따라서 빈칸에 들어갈 말로 가장 적절한 것은 ① '제자리에 머무를 뿐이다'이다.

- discover ⓥ 발견하다
- evolutionary ⓐ 진화적인
- generation ⓝ 세대
- pass on 물려주다
- species ⓝ (생물) 종
- adapt to ~에 적응하다
- biologist ⓝ 생물학자
- principle ⓝ 원리
- thrive ⓥ 번성하다
- gene ⓝ 유전자
- run into ~을 우연히 만나다

구문 풀이

3행 They run and they run, but then Alice discovers that they're
접속사
still under the same tree that they started from.
선행사(the same + 명) → 목적격 관계대명사

★★ 문제 해결 꿀~팁 ★★

▶ 많이 틀린 이유는?
여우가 토끼를 더 많이 잡기 위해 더 빨리 뛰도록 진화해도, 토끼 또한 똑같이 진화하기 때문에 결국 둘 다 '제자리에 있는' 셈이라는 것이 글의 결론이다. ③은 두 동물이 '서로 절대 우연히 만나지 않는다'는 의미로, run이 있어 혼동될 수 있지만 의미상 연관이 없다.

▶ 문제 해결 방법은?
글에 인용구가 나오면 주제와 연관되는 경우가 많다. 여기서도 인용구 안의 to keep in the same place가 주제를 가리키는 핵심 표현이다.

★★★ 1등급 대비 고난도 3점 문제

11 지적 능력 발달에 있어 천성보다 중요한 양육 | 정답률 44% | 정답 ③

다음 빈칸에 들어갈 말로 가장 적절한 것을 고르시오. [3점]

① by themselves for survival – 생존을 위해 스스로
② free from social interaction – 사회적 상호작용 없이
✓ based on what is around you – 여러분 주변에 있는 것에 따라
④ depending on genetic superiority – 유전적 우월성에 따라
⑤ so as to keep ourselves entertained – 우리 자신을 계속 즐겁게 하기 위해

In a study at Princeton University in 1992, / research scientists looked at two different groups of mice.
1992년 프린스턴 대학의 한 연구에서, / 연구 과학자들은 두 개의 다른 쥐 집단을 관찰했다.

One group was made intellectually superior / by modifying the gene for the glutamate receptor.
한 집단은 지적으로 우월하게 만들어졌다. / 글루타민산염 수용체에 대한 유전자를 변형함으로써

Glutamate is a brain chemical / that is necessary in learning.
글루타민산염은 뇌 화학 물질이다. / 학습에 필수적인

The other group was genetically manipulated / to be intellectually inferior, / also done by modifying the gene for the glutamate receptor.
다른 집단도 유전적으로 조작되었다. / 지적으로 열등하도록 / 역시 글루타민산염 수용체에 대한 유전자를 변형함으로써 이루어진

The smart mice were then raised in standard cages, / while the inferior mice were raised in large cages / with toys and exercise wheels / and with lots of social interaction.
그 후 똑똑한 쥐들은 표준 우리에서 길러졌다. / 열등한 쥐들은 큰 우리에서 길러진 반면 / 장난감과 운동용 쳇바퀴가 있고 / 사회적 상호작용이 많은

At the end of the study, / although the intellectually inferior mice were genetically handicapped, / they were able to perform just as well / as their genetic superiors.
연구가 끝날 무렵, / 비록 지적 능력이 떨어지는 쥐들이 유전적으로 장애가 있었지만, / 그들은 딱 그만큼 잘 수행할 수 있었다. / 그들의 유전적인 우월군들만큼

This was a real triumph for nurture over nature.
이것은 천성에 대한 양육의 진정한 승리였다.
Genes are turned on or off / based on what is around you.
유전자는 작동하거나 멈춘다. / 여러분 주변에 있는 것에 따라

1992년 프린스턴 대학의 한 연구에서, 연구 과학자들은 두 개의 다른 쥐 집단을 관찰했다. 한 집단은 글루타민산염 수용체에 대한 유전자를 변형함으로써 지적으로 우월하게 만들어졌다. 글루타민산염은 학습에 필수적인 뇌 화학 물질이다. 다른 집단도 역시 글루타민산염 수용체에 대한 유전자를 변형함으로써, 지적으로 열등하도록 유전적으로 조작되었다. 그 후 똑똑한 쥐들은 표준 우리에서 길러진 반면에 열등한 쥐들은 장난감과 운동용 쳇바퀴가 있고 사회적 상호작용이 많은 큰 우리에서 길러졌다. 연구가 끝날 무렵, 비록 지적 능력이 떨어지는 쥐들이 유전적으로 장애가 있었지만, 그들은 딱 유전적인 우월군들만큼 잘 수행할 수 있었다. 이것은 천성(선천적 성질)에 대한 양육(후천적 환경)의 진정한 승리였다. 유전자는 여러분 주변에 있는 것에 따라 작동하거나 멈춘다.

Why? 왜 정답일까?

빈칸이 있는 문장 바로 앞에서 양육, 즉 후천적 환경이 타고난 천성을 이겼다(a real triumph for nurture over nature)는 말로 연구 결과를 정리하고 있다. 따라서 빈칸에 들어갈 말로 가장 적절한 것은 '환경, 양육'과 같은 의미의 ③ '여러분 주변에 있는 것에 따라'이다.

- intellectually ad 지적으로
- receptor n 수용체
- inferior a 열등한
- triumph n 승리
- free from ~ 없이, ~을 면하여
- modify v 수정하다, 바꾸다
- genetically ad 유전적으로
- handicapped a 장애가 있는
- nurture n 양육

구문 풀이

5행 The other group was genetically manipulated to be
　　　　　　　　　　　　　　　　　　　　선행사
intellectually inferior, (which was) also done by modifying the gene
　　　　　　　　　생략(계속적 용법)　　　과거분사
for the glutamate receptor.

★★ 문제 해결 꿀~팁 ★★

▶ 많이 틀린 이유는?
지적으로 우월하게(superior) 만들어진 쥐와 열등하게(inferior) 만들어진 쥐를 비교하는 실험 내용상 '유전적 우월함'을 언급하는 ④가 정답처럼 보인다. 하지만 실험의 결과를 보면, 결국 유전적으로 지능이 우월하게 만들어진 쥐와 열등하게 만들어진 쥐 사이에 차이가 없었다는 것이 핵심이다. 따라서 '유전적 우월함에 따라' 유전자가 작동하거나 작동하지 않을 수 있다는 의미를 완성하는 ④는 빈칸에 적절하지 않다.

▶ 문제 해결 방법은?
유전적으로 유도된 지능 차이보다도, 다른 어떤 요인이 쥐의 수행에 영향을 미칠 수 있었는지 살펴봐야 한다. 글 중반부를 보면, 열등한 쥐들이 자란 환경은 우월한 쥐들이 자란 환경에 비해 사회적 상호작용이 활발한 공간이었다고 한다. 나아가 빈칸 앞에서는 이 실험 결과가 유전보다도 양육, 즉 후천적 환경(nurture)의 중요성을 말해준다고 한다. 따라서 빈칸에도 '환경'과 관련된 내용이 들어가야 한다.

★★★ 1등급 대비 고난도 3점 문제

| 12 | 내륙 정착의 역사 | 정답률 32% | 정답 ⑤ |

다음 빈칸에 들어갈 말로 가장 적절한 것을 고르시오. [3점]

① ruining natural habitats – 자연 서식지를 파괴했다
② leveling the ground evenly – 땅을 고루 평평하게 했다
③ forming primitive superstitions – 원시적 미신을 형성했다
④ blaming their ancestors – 그들의 조상을 탓했다
✓ settling farther inland – 더 내륙 쪽으로 정착했다

The acceleration of human migration toward the shores / is a contemporary phenomenon, / but the knowledge and understanding of the potential risks / regarding coastal living / are not.
해안 쪽으로 사람들의 이동이 가속화된 것은 / 현대적인 현상이지만, / 잠재적 위험에 대한 지식과 이해는 / 해안 거주와 관련된 / 그렇지 않다.
Indeed, even at a time / when human-induced greenhouse-gas emissions / were not exponentially altering the climate, / warming the oceans, / and leading to rising seas, / our ancestors knew / how to better listen to and

---

respect / the many movements and warnings of the seas, / thus settling farther inland.
실제로, ~한 때조차도, / 인간이 유발한 온실 가스 배출이 / 기하급수적으로 기후를 변화시키지 않았고, / 바다를 온난화시키지 않았고, / 해수면 상승을 이끌지 않았을 (때조차도,) / 우리 조상들은 알고 있어서 / 어떻게 더 잘 듣고 존중할지를 / 바다의 많은 움직임과 경고를 / 더 내륙 쪽으로 정착했다.
For instance, along Japan's coast, / hundreds of so-called tsunami stones, / some more than six centuries old, / were put in place / to warn people not to build homes below a certain point.
예를 들어, 일본 해안가를 따라, / 수백 개의 이른바 쓰나미 스톤이, / 몇몇은 600년이 넘은 / 놓여졌다. / 특정 지점 아래로 집을 짓지 않을 것을 사람들에게 경고하기 위해
Over the world, / moon and tides, winds, rains and hurricanes / were naturally guiding humans' settlement choice.
전 세계에 걸쳐, / 달과 조석, 바람, 비와 허리케인은 / 자연스럽게 인간의 정착 선택을 안내했다.

해안 쪽으로 사람들의 이동이 가속화된 것은 현대적인 현상이지만, 해안 거주와 관련된 잠재적 위험에 대한 지식과 이해는 그렇지 않다. 실제로, 인간이 유발한 온실 가스 배출이 기하급수적으로 기후를 변화시키지 않았고, 바다를 온난화시키지 않았고, 해수면 상승을 이끌지 않았을 때조차도, 우리 조상들은 바다의 많은 움직임과 경고를 어떻게 더 잘 듣고 존중할지를 알고 있어서 더 내륙 쪽으로 정착했다. 예를 들어, 일본 해안가를 따라, 몇몇은 600년이 넘은 수백 개의 이른바 쓰나미 스톤이, 특정 지점 아래로 집을 짓지 않을 것을 사람들에게 경고하기 위해 놓여졌다. 전 세계에 걸쳐, 달과 조석, 바람, 비와 허리케인은 자연스럽게 인간의 정착 선택을 안내했다.

Why? 왜 정답일까?

첫 문장(~ but the knowledge and understanding of the potential risks regarding coastal living are not.)과 마지막 문장(Over the world, moon and tides, winds, rains and hurricanes were naturally guiding humans' settlement choice.)에서 사람들은 자연이 준 단서에 근거하여 해안 거주에 대한 위험을 인식하고 자연스럽게 내륙 쪽으로 더 자리를 잡게 되었다는 내용을 말하고 있으므로, 빈칸에 들어갈 말로 가장 적절한 것은 ⑤ '더 내륙 쪽으로 정착했다'이다.

- acceleration n 가속화
- contemporary a 현대적인, 동시대의
- regarding prep ~에 관하여
- human-induced 인간이 유발한
- alter v 바꾸다, 달라지게 하다
- migration n 이주, 이민
- phenomenon n 현상
- coastal a 해안(가)의
- exponentially ad 기하급수적으로
- in place 제자리에

구문 풀이

4행 Indeed, / even at a time [when human-induced greenhouse-
　　　　　　　　　　　　　　　　　　　　관계부사
gas emissions were not exponentially altering the climate, warming
　　　　　　　　　　　　　　　　　　과거진행1　　　　　　　과거진행2
the oceans, and leading to rising seas], / our ancestors knew
　　　과거진행3　　　　　　　　　　　　　주어　　　　동사
{how to better listen to and respect the many movements and
「how+to부정사(~하는 방법)」　　listen to와 respect의 공통 목적어
warnings of the seas}, thus settling farther inland.
　　　　　　　　　　　　분사구문

★★ 문제 해결 꿀~팁 ★★

▶ 많이 틀린 이유는?
소재가 낯설어 오답이 많이 나온 문제였다. ①은 서식지 파괴, ③은 미신을 언급하고 있는데 두 내용 모두 지문에서 언급된 바가 없다.

▶ 문제 해결 방법은?
글의 처음과 끝에 주목할 때, 달과 조석, 비, 바람, 허리케인 등 자연이 주는 힌트에 의해 인간은 해안 거주의 위험성을 오래전부터 이해해 왔고 이로 인해 '해안보다는 내륙 쪽으로 점점 이주해오게 되었다'는 내용이 주제임을 알 수 있다.

DAY 09 | 빈칸 추론 09

01 ②	02 ①	03 ③	04 ⑤	05 ②
06 ③	07 ③	08 ②	09 ①	10 ④
11 ①	12 ②			

---

01 야생 동물 피해 관리의 정의 정답률 56% | 정답 ②

다음 빈칸에 들어갈 말로 가장 적절한 것을 고르시오.

① cloning – 복제하지
✓ harming – 해를 끼치지
③ training – 훈련시키지
④ overfeeding – 먹이를 너무 많이 주지
⑤ domesticating – 길들이지

Some people have defined wildlife damage management / as the science and management of overabundant species, / but this definition is too narrow.
어떤 사람들은 야생 동물 피해 관리를 정의했지만, / 과잉 종들에 대한 과학과 관리로 / 이 정의는 너무 좁다.

All wildlife species act in ways / that harm human interests.
모든 야생 동물 종들은 방식으로 행동한다. / 인간의 이익에 해를 끼치는

Thus, all species cause wildlife damage, / not just overabundant ones.
따라서 모든 종이 야생 동물 피해를 야기한다. / 단지 과잉 종뿐만 아니라

One interesting example of this / involves endangered peregrine falcons in California, / which prey on another endangered species, / the California least tern.
이것의 흥미로운 한 사례는 / 캘리포니아의 멸종 위기에 처한 송골매인데, / 그것들은 또 다른 멸종 위기 종을 먹이로 한다. / 캘리포니아 작은 제비갈매기라는

Certainly, we would not consider peregrine falcons / as being overabundant, / but we wish that they would not feed on an endangered species.
분명히 우리는 송골매를 생각하지 않겠지만, / 과잉이라고 / 우리는 그것들이 멸종 위기에 처한 종들을 먹고 살지 않기를 바란다.

In this case, one of the negative values / associated with a peregrine falcon population / is that its predation reduces the population of another endangered species.
이런 경우에, 부정적인 가치들 중 하나는 / 송골매 개체 수와 관련된 / 그것의 포식이 또 다른 멸종 위기 종들의 개체 수를 감소시킨다는 것이다.

The goal of wildlife damage management in this case / would be to stop the falcons from eating the terns / without harming the falcons.
이런 경우에 야생 동물 피해 관리의 목표는 / 송골매가 작은 제비갈매기를 잡아먹지 못하게 하는 것일 것이다. / 송골매에 해를 끼치지 않으면서

어떤 사람들은 야생 동물 피해 관리를 과잉 종들에 대한 과학과 관리로 정의했지만, 이 정의는 너무 좁다. 모든 야생 동물 종들은 인간의 이익에 해를 끼치는 방식으로 행동한다. 따라서 단지 과잉 종뿐만 아니라 모든 종이 야생 동물 피해를 야기한다. 이것의 흥미로운 한 사례는 캘리포니아의 멸종 위기에 처한 송골매인데, 그것들은 캘리포니아 작은 제비갈매기라는 또 다른 멸종 위기 종을 먹이로 한다. 분명히 우리는 송골매를 과잉이라고 생각하지 않겠지만, 우리는 그것들이 멸종 위기에 처한 종들을 먹고 살지 않기를 바란다. 이런 경우에, 송골매 개체 수와 관련된 부정적인 가치들 중 하나는 그것의 포식이 또 다른 멸종 위기 종들의 개체 수를 감소시킨다는 것이다. 이런 경우에 야생 동물 피해 관리의 목표는 송골매에 해를 끼치지 않으면서 송골매가 작은 제비갈매기를 잡아먹지 못하게 하는 것일 것이다.

Why? 왜 정답일까?

빈칸 앞의 두 문장에서 송골매가 멸종 위기에 처한 작은 제비갈매기를 잡아먹고 살면 작은 제비갈매기 종의 개체 수가 감소하는 부정적 결과가 나타나기에 송골매가 과잉 개체는 아니지만 야생 동물 피해 관리의 대상이 될 수 있음을 설명하고 있다(Certainly, we would not consider peregrine falcons as being overabundant, but we wish that they would not feed on an endangered species.). 이를 근거로 볼 때, 야생 동물 피해 관리의 목표는 송골매와 작은 제비갈매기 모두가 적절한 개체 수를 유지하도록 관리하는 것이리라는 점을 유추할 수 있다. 따라서 빈칸에 들어갈 말로 가장 적절한 것은 ② '해를 끼치지'이다.

- **wildlife** ⓝ 야생 생물
- **definition** ⓝ 정의, 의미
- **involve** ⓥ 포함하다, 수반하다
- **prey on** ~을 먹이로 하다
- **predation** ⓝ 포식
- **train** ⓥ 교육시키다
- **domesticate** ⓥ 길들이다, 사육하다
- **overabundant** ⓐ 과잉의, 과도하게 풍부한
- **narrow** ⓥ 좁다
- **endangered** ⓐ 멸종 위기에 처한
- **feed on** ~을 먹고 살다
- **clone** ⓥ 복제하다
- **overfeed** ⓥ 너무 많이 먹이다[주다]

구문 풀이

11행 In this case, one of the negative values [associated with a peregrine falcon population] is {that its predation reduces the population of another endangered species}.
주어 / 과거분사(~와 연관된) / 동사 / { }: 주격 보어

---

02 광고 교환 정답률 58% | 정답 ①

다음 빈칸에 들어갈 말로 가장 적절한 것을 고르시오.

✓ trading space – 공간을 교환함
② getting funded – 자금을 지원받음
③ sharing reviews – 상품평을 공유함
④ renting factory facilities – 공장 시설을 빌림
⑤ increasing TV commercials – TV 광고를 늘림

Although many small businesses have excellent websites, / they typically can't afford aggressive online campaigns.
비록 많은 작은 사업체들이 훌륭한 웹 사이트를 가지고 있지만, / 보통 그들은 매우 적극적인 온라인 캠페인을 할 여유가 없다.

One way to get the word out / is through an advertising exchange, / in which advertisers place banners on each other's websites for free.
소문나게 하는 한 가지 방법은 / 광고 교환을 통해서이다. / 광고주들이 서로의 웹 사이트에 무료로 배너를 게시하는

For example, / a company selling beauty products / could place its banner on a site that sells women's shoes, / and in turn, / the shoe company could put a banner on the beauty product site.
예를 들어, / 미용 제품을 판매하는 회사는 / 여성 신발을 판매하는 사이트에 자신의 배너를 게시할 수 있고, / 그다음에는 / 그 신발 회사가 미용 제품 사이트에 배너를 게시할 수 있다.

Neither company charges the other; / they simply exchange ad space.
두 회사 모두 상대에게 비용을 청구하지 않는데, / 그들은 그저 광고 공간을 교환하는 것이다.

Advertising exchanges are gaining in popularity, / especially among marketers / who do not have much money / and who don't have a large sales team.
광고 교환은 인기를 얻고 있다. / 특히 마케팅 담당자들 사이에서 / 돈이 많지 않거나 / 대규모 영업팀이 없는

By trading space, / advertisers find new outlets / that reach their target audiences / that they would not otherwise be able to afford.
공간을 교환함으로써, / 광고주들은 새로운 (광고의) 출구를 찾는다. / 자신의 목표 고객과 접촉할 수 있는 / 그러지 않으면 그들이 접촉할 여유가 없는

비록 많은 작은 사업체들이 훌륭한 웹 사이트를 가지고 있지만, 그들은 보통 매우 적극적인 온라인 캠페인을 할 여유가 없다. 소문나게 하는 한 가지 방법은 광고주들이 서로의 웹 사이트에 무료로 배너를 게시하는 광고 교환을 통해서이다. 예를 들어, 미용 제품을 판매하는 회사는 여성 신발을 판매하는 사이트에 자신의 배너를 게시할 수 있고, 그다음에는 그 신발 회사가 미용 제품 사이트에 배너를 게시할 수 있다. 두 회사 모두 상대에게 비용을 청구하지 않는데, 그들은 그저 광고 공간을 교환하는 것이다. 광고 교환은 특히 돈이 많지 않거나 대규모 영업팀이 없는 마케팅 담당자들 사이에서 인기를 얻고 있다. 공간을 교환함으로써, 광고주들은 그러지 않으면 접촉할 여유가 없는 자신의 목표 고객과 접촉할 수 있는 새로운 (광고의) 출구를 찾는다.

Why? 왜 정답일까?

예시 앞의 주제문 'One way to get the word out is through an advertising exchange, in which advertisers place banners on each other's websites for free.'에서 작은 사업체들은 서로 웹 사이트에 무료로 배너를 게시하는 광고 교환을 통해 사업체를 홍보한다는 내용을 제시하므로, 빈칸에 들어갈 말로 가장 적절한 것은 ① '공간을 교환함'이다.

- **typically** ⓐⓓ 보통, 전형적으로
- **get the word out** ⓥ 말을 퍼뜨리다
- **for free** 공짜로, 무료로
- **charge** ⓥ (요금을) 청구하다, 부과하다
- **fund** ⓥ 기금을 지원하다 ⓝ 기금
- **commercial** ⓝ 광고 ⓐ 상업적인
- **afford** ⓥ ~할 여유가 있다
- **place** ⓥ (광고를) 게시하다[내다]
- **in turn** 차례로, 결국
- **gain in popularity** 인기를 얻다
- **facility** ⓝ 시설

구문 풀이

3행 One way to get the word out is through an advertising exchange, in which advertisers place banners on each other's websites for free.
주어 / 형용사적 용법 / 동사 / 보어(전명구) / 계속적 용법

DAY 09

03 유혹을 극복하는 방법 정답률 51% | 정답 ③

다음 빈칸에 들어갈 말로 가장 적절한 것을 고르시오.

① letting go of all-or-nothing mindset
양자택일의 사고방식을 버림
② finding reasons why you want to change
왜 변하고 싶은지 이유를 찾음
✓③ locking yourself out of your temptations
여러분 자신을 유혹으로부터 차단함
④ building a plan and tracking your progress
계획을 세워 진행 상황을 추적함
⑤ focusing on breaking one bad habit at a time
한 번에 하나의 나쁜 습관을 깨는 데 집중함

If you've ever made a poor choice, / you might be interested / in learning how to break that habit.
여러분이 한 번이라도 좋지 못한 선택을 한 적이 있다면, / 여러분은 관심이 있을지도 모른다. / 그런 습관을 깨는 방법을 배우는 데
One great way / to trick your brain into doing so / is to sign a "Ulysses Contract."
한 가지 좋은 방법은 / 여러분의 뇌를 속여 그렇게 하는 / 'Ulysses 계약'에 서명하는 것이다.
The name of this life tip / comes from the Greek myth about Ulysses, / a captain / whose ship sailed past the island of the Sirens, / a tribe of dangerous women / who lured victims to their death with their irresistible songs.
이 인생에 대한 조언의 이름은 / Ulysses에 관한 그리스 신화에서 유래되었는데, / 그는 선장이었다. / 그의 배가 사이렌의 섬을 지나던 / 위험한 여성 부족인 / 저항할 수 없는 노래를 통해 희생자들을 죽음으로 유혹한
Knowing that he would otherwise be unable to resist, / Ulysses instructed his crew / to stuff their ears with cotton / and tie him to the ship's mast / to prevent him from turning their ship towards the Sirens.
그렇게 하지 않으면 저항할 수 없다는 것을 알고, / Ulysses는 선원들에게 지시했다. / 귀를 솜으로 막고 / 자신을 배의 돛대에 묶으라고 / 그가 사이렌 쪽으로 배를 돌리지 못하게 막기 위해
It worked for him / and you can do the same thing / by locking yourself out of your temptations.
그것은 그에게 효과가 있었고, / 여러분은 똑같은 일을 할 수 있다. / 여러분 자신을 유혹으로부터 차단함으로써
For example, / if you want to stay off your cellphone / and concentrate on your work, / delete the apps that distract you / or ask a friend to change your password!
예를 들어, / 만약 여러분이 휴대폰을 멀리하고 / 일에 집중하고 싶다면, / 여러분의 주의를 산만하게 하는 앱들을 삭제하거나, / 친구에게 여러분의 비밀번호를 바꿔달라고 요청하라!

여러분이 한 번이라도 좋지 못한 선택을 한 적이 있다면, 그런 습관을 깨는 방법을 배우는 데 관심이 있을지도 모른다. 여러분의 뇌를 속여 그렇게 하는 한 가지 좋은 방법은 'Ulysses 계약'에 서명하는 것이다. 이 인생에 대한 조언의 이름은 Ulysses에 관한 그리스 신화에서 유래되었는데, 그는 저항할 수 없는 노래를 통해 희생자들을 죽음으로 유혹한 위험한 여성 부족인 사이렌의 섬을 지나던 배의 선장이었다. Ulysses는 그렇게 하지 않으면 저항할 수 없다는 것을 알고, 선원들에게 귀를 솜으로 막고 자신을 배의 돛대에 묶게 시켜 자신이 사이렌 쪽으로 배를 돌리지 못하게 했다. 그것은 그에게 효과가 있었고, 여러분은 여러분 자신을 유혹으로부터 차단함으로써 똑같은 일을 할 수 있다. 예를 들어, 만약 여러분이 휴대폰을 멀리하고 일에 집중하고 싶다면, 여러분의 주의를 산만하게 하는 앱들을 삭제하거나, 친구에게 여러분의 비밀번호를 바꿔달라고 요청하라!

Why? 왜 정답일까?

빈칸 앞에서 신화 속 인물 Ulysses는 선원들을 시켜 자기 몸을 돛대에 묶게 해서 사이렌의 노래에 유혹되려는 자기 자신을 막았다고 한다. 빈칸에는 이러한 Ulysses의 조치를 일반화할 수 있는 표현이 필요하므로, 답으로 가장 적절한 것은 ③ '여러분 자신을 유혹으로부터 차단함'이다. 일에 집중하기 위해 일에 도움이 안 되는 앱을 지우거나 친구를 통해 비밀번호를 바꾸게 하라는 내용 또한 '유혹에 넘어가지 않기'를 위한 예시에 해당한다.

- break a habit 습관을 깨다
- myth ⓝ 신화
- lure ⓥ 유혹하다
- instruct ⓥ 지시하다, 가르치다
- tie ⓥ 묶다
- distract ⓥ 산만하게 하다
- all-or-nothing ⓐ 양자택일의
- trick A into B A를 속여 B하게 하다
- sail ⓥ 항해하다
- irresistible ⓐ 저항할 수 없는
- stuff ⓥ (속을) 채우다, 막다
- mast ⓝ 돛대
- let go of ~을 놔주다, 내려놓다
- temptation ⓝ 유혹

구문 풀이

4행 The name of this life tip comes from the Greek myth about Ulysses, (a captain whose ship sailed past the island of the Sirens),
( ): Ulysses와 동격
{a tribe of dangerous women who lured victims to their death with their irresistible songs}. [ ]: the Sirens와 동격

04 자신의 발달 환경을 주도적으로 만드는 인간 정답률 53% | 정답 ⑤

다음 빈칸에 들어갈 말로 가장 적절한 것을 고르시오.

① mirrors of their generation – 자기 세대의 거울
② shields against social conflicts – 사회적 갈등을 막는 방패
③ explorers in their own career path – 자기 진로의 탐색가
④ followers of their childhood dreams – 어린 시절의 꿈을 좇는 사람
✓⑤ manufacturers of their own development – 자신의 발달을 생산하는 사람

The prevailing view among developmental scientists / is / that people are active contributors to their own development.
발달 과학자들 사이에서 지배적인 견해는 / ~이다. / 사람들이 자신의 발달에 능동적인 기여자라는 것이다.
People are influenced by the physical and social contexts / in which they live, / but they also play a role / in influencing their development / by interacting with, and changing, those contexts.
사람들은 물리적 및 사회적 환경의 영향을 받지만, / 자신이 사는 / 그들은 또한 역할을 한다. / 자신의 발달에 영향을 주는 데 있어 / 그 환경들과 상호 작용하고 그것을 변화시켜
Even infants influence the world around them / and construct their own development / through their interactions.
심지어 유아들도 자기 주변의 세상에 영향을 주고, / 자신의 발달을 구성한다. / 상호작용을 통해
Consider an infant / who smiles at each adult he sees; / he influences his world / because adults are likely to smile, / use "baby talk," / and play with him / in response.
유아를 생각해 보라. / 그가 바라보는 어른마다 미소 짓는 / 그는 자신의 세상에 영향을 준다. / 어른들은 미소 짓고, / '아기 말'을 사용하고, / 그와 함께 놀아줄 것이기 때문에 / 이에 반응하여
The infant brings adults into close contact, / making one-on-one interactions / and creating opportunities for learning.
그 유아는 어른들을 친밀한 연결로 끌어들여서, / 일대일 상호작용을 하고 / 학습의 기회를 만든다.
By engaging with the world around them, / thinking, / being curious, / and interacting with people, objects, and the world around them, / individuals of all ages / are manufacturers of their own development.
주변 세상의 관심을 끌고, / 생각하고, / 호기심을 가지고, / 주변 사람, 사물, 세상과 상호작용함으로써, / 모든 연령대의 개인들은 / '자신의 발달을 생산하는 사람'이다.

발달 과학자들 사이에서 지배적인 견해는 사람들이 자신의 발달에 능동적인 기여자라는 것이다. 사람들은 자신이 사는 물리적 및 사회적 환경의 영향을 받지만, 그들은 또한 그 환경들과 상호작용하고 그것을 변화시켜 자신의 발달에 영향을 주는 역할을 한다. 심지어 유아들도 자기 주변의 세상에 영향을 주고, 상호작용을 통해 자신의 발달을 구성한다. 그가 바라보는 어른마다 미소 짓는 유아를 생각해 보라. 어른들은 이에 반응하여 미소 짓고, '아기 말'을 사용하고, 그와 함께 놀아줄 것이기 때문에 그는 자신의 세상에 영향을 준다. 그 유아는 어른들을 친밀한 연결로 끌어들여서, 일대일 상호작용을 하고 학습의 기회를 만든다. 주변 세상의 관심을 끌고, 생각하고, 호기심을 가지고, 주변 사람, 사물, 세상과 상호작용함으로써, 모든 연령대의 개인들은 '자신의 발달을 생산하는 사람'이다.

Why? 왜 정답일까?

주제문인 첫 문장에서 인간은 자신의 발달에 능동적으로 기여하는 주체(~ people are active contributors to their own development.)라고 언급하므로, 빈칸에 들어갈 말로 가장 적절한 것은 ⑤ '자신의 발달을 생산하는 사람'이다.

- prevailing ⓐ 지배적인, 만연한
- baby talk 아기 말(말을 배우는 유아나 어린이에게 어른이 쓰는 말투)
- close ⓐ 친밀한
- generation ⓝ 세대
- conflict ⓝ 갈등
- manufacturer ⓝ 생산자
- developmental ⓐ 발달의
- one-on-one ⓐ 일대일의
- shield ⓝ 방패
- career path 진로

구문 풀이

8행 Consider an infant who smiles at each adult [he sees]; he
명령문(~하라) 목적어 주격 관계대명사
influences his world because adults are likely to smile, use "baby
~할 것이다 동사원형1 동사원형2
talk," and play with him in response. [ ]: 목적격 관계대명사절
동사원형3

05 수하물 찾는 시간에 관한 불평 해결 정답률 59% | 정답 ②

다음 빈칸에 들어갈 말로 가장 적절한 것을 고르시오. [3점]

① having them wait in line – 그들을 줄 서서 기다리게 한 것
✓② making them walk longer – 탑승객들을 더 오래 걷게 함
③ producing more advertisements – 더 많은 광고를 제작한 것

④ bothering them with complaints – 불평으로 그들을 성가시게 한 것
⑤ hiring more staff to handle bags – 수하물을 다루는 직원 수를 늘린 것

Houston Airport executives / faced plenty of complaints / regarding baggage claim time, / so they increased the number of baggage handlers.
Houston 공항의 임원은 / 많은 불평에 직면했고, / 수하물을 찾는 데 걸리는 시간에 관한 / 그래서 그들은 수하물 담당자들의 수를 늘렸다.

Although it reduced the average wait time to eight minutes, / complaints didn't stop.
이것이 기다리는 시간을 평균 8분으로 줄였음에도 불구하고 / 불평은 멈추지 않았다.

It took about a minute / to get from the arrival gate to baggage claim, / so the passengers spent seven more minutes / waiting for their bags.
약 1분의 시간이 걸려서 / 도착 게이트에서 수하물을 찾는 곳까지 도달하려면 / 탑승객들은 7분을 더 보냈다. / 자기 가방을 기다리며

The solution was / to move the arrival gates away from the baggage claim / so it took passengers about seven minutes / to walk there.
해결책은 / 도착 게이트를 수하물 찾는 곳으로부터 더 멀리 이동시키는 것이었고, / 그리하여 탑승객들에게 약 7분의 시간이 걸렸다. / 그곳까지 걸어가는 데

It resulted in complaints reducing to almost zero.
이는 불평이 거의 0으로 줄어드는 결과를 가져왔다.

Research shows / occupied time feels shorter than unoccupied time.
연구에서는 보여준다. / (어떤 행동으로) 소요한 시간이 빈 시간보다 더 짧게 느껴진다는 것을

People usually exaggerate / about the time they waited, / and what they find most bothersome / is time spent unoccupied.
사람들은 보통 과장하며, / 그들이 기다린 시간에 대해 / 그들이 가장 성가시다고 여기는 것은 / 비어있는 시간이다.

Thus, occupying the passengers' time / by making them walk longer / gave them the idea / they didn't have to wait as long.
따라서 시간을 소요시킨 것은 / 탑승객들을 더 오래 걷게 함으로써 / 그들에게 생각을 갖게 했다. / 그들이 그렇게 오래 기다릴 필요가 없다는

Houston 공항의 임원들은 수하물을 찾는 데 걸리는 시간에 관한 많은 불평에 직면하여, 수하물 담당자들의 수를 늘렸다. 이것이 기다리는 시간을 평균 8분으로 줄였음에도 불구하고 불평은 멈추지 않았다. 도착 게이트에서 수하물을 찾는 곳까지 도달하려면 약 1분의 시간이 걸려서 탑승객들은 자기 가방을 기다리며 7분을 더 보냈다. 해결책은 도착 게이트를 수하물 찾는 곳으로부터 더 멀리 이동시키는 것이었고, 그리하여 탑승객들이 수하물을 찾는 곳으로 걷는 데 약 7분의 시간이 걸렸다. 이는 불평이 거의 0으로 줄어드는 결과를 가져왔다. 연구에서는 (어떤 행동으로) 소요한 시간이 빈 시간보다 더 짧게 느껴진다는 것을 보여준다. 사람들은 보통 기다린 시간에 대해 과장하며, 그들이 가장 성가시다고 여기는 것은 (무언가 하지 않고) 비어있는 시간이다. 따라서 탑승객들을 더 오래 걷게 함으로써 시간을 소요시킨 것은 그들로 하여금 그렇게 오래 기다릴 필요가 없다는 생각을 갖게 했다.

Why? 왜 정답일까?

'The solution was to move the arrival gates away from the baggage claim so it took passengers about seven minutes to walk there.'에서 수하물을 기다리는 시간이 너무 길다는 불평에 대처하기 위한 해결책은 탑승객들이 걷는 시간을 1분에서 7분으로 늘리는 것이었다고 이야기하므로, 빈칸에 들어갈 말로 가장 적절한 것은 ② '탑승객들을 더 오래 걷게 함'이다.

- executive ⓝ 임원, 중역
- regarding prep ~에 관하여
- reduce ⓥ 줄이다, 감소시키다
- result in ~을 가져오다, ~을 초래하다
- exaggerate ⓥ 과장하다
- face ⓥ 직면하다, 맞서다
- baggage ⓝ 수하물, 짐
- solution ⓝ 해결책
- occupied ⓐ 차지된, 점거된
- bothersome ⓐ 성가신, 귀찮은

구문 풀이

5행 It took about a minute to get from the arrival gate to baggage
「take + 시간 + to부정사 : ~하는 데 …의 시간이 걸리다」
claim, / so the passengers spent seven more minutes waiting for their
「spend + 시간 + 동명사 : ~하는 데 …의 시간을 쓰다」
bags.

06 자전거 또는 오토바이를 탈 때 동승자의 역할   정답률 48% | 정답 ③

다음 빈칸에 들어갈 말로 가장 적절한 것을 고르시오. [3점]

① warn other people of danger – 다른 사람들에게 위험을 경고하도록
② stop the rider from speeding – 운전자가 과속하지 못하게 막도록
✓ mirror the rider's every move – 운전자의 모든 움직임을 따라하도록
④ relieve the rider's emotional anxiety – 운전자의 정서 불안을 완화해 주도록
⑤ monitor the road conditions carefully – 도로 상황을 면밀히 주시하도록

In Dutch bicycle culture, / it is common / to have a passenger on the backseat.
네덜란드의 자전거 문화에서, / 흔하다. / 뒷좌석에 동승자를 앉히는 것은

So as to follow the rider's movements, / the person on the backseat needs to hold on tightly.
자전거 운전자의 움직임을 따르기 위해서, / 뒷좌석에 앉은 사람은 꽉 잡을 필요가 있다.

Bicycles turn / not just by steering but also by leaning, / so the passenger needs to lean / the same way as the rider.
자전거는 방향을 바꾸는데 / 핸들을 조종하는 것만 아니라 몸을 기울임으로써 / 동승자는 몸을 기울일 필요가 있다. / 자전거 운전자와 같은 방향으로

A passenger who would keep sitting up straight / would literally be a pain in the behind.
뒷좌석에서 계속해서 똑바로 앉아 있는 동승자는 / 말 그대로 뒷좌석의 골칫거리가 될 것이다.

On motorcycles, / this is even more critical.
오토바이를 탈 때는, / 이것이 훨씬 더 중요하다.

Their higher speed requires more leaning on turns, / and lack of coordination can be disastrous.
오토바이의 더 높은 속도는 방향을 바꿀 때 몸을 더 많이 기울일 것을 요구하고, / 협응의 부족은 재앙이 될 수 있다.

The passenger is a true partner in the ride, / expected to mirror the rider's every move.
동승자는 주행 시 진정한 동반자이다. / 운전자의 모든 움직임을 따라하도록 기대되기 때문에

네덜란드의 자전거 문화에서, 뒷좌석에 동승자를 앉히는 것은 흔하다. 자전거 운전자의 움직임을 따르기 위해서, 뒷좌석에 앉은 사람은 꽉 잡을 필요가 있다. 자전거는 핸들을 조종하는 것뿐만 아니라 몸을 기울여서 방향을 바꾸기에 동승자는 자전거 운전자와 같은 방향으로 몸을 기울일 필요가 있다. 뒷좌석에서 계속해서 똑바로 앉아 있는 동승자는 말 그대로 뒷좌석의 골칫거리가 될 것이다. 오토바이를 탈 때는 이것이 훨씬 더 중요하다. 오토바이의 더 높은 속도는 방향을 바꿀 때 몸을 더 많이 기울일 것을 요구하고, 협응의 부족은 재앙이 될 수 있다. 동승자는 운전자의 모든 움직임을 따라하도록 기대되기 때문에 주행 시 진정한 동반자이다.

Why? 왜 정답일까?

자전거와 오토바이에서 동승자는 운전자의 움직임에 맞추어 같은 방향으로 몸을 기울이는 등 '협응'할 필요성이 있다는 내용의 글이다. 따라서 예시를 일반화하여 결론을 내리는 빈칸에 들어갈 말로 가장 적절한 것은 ③ '운전자의 모든 움직임을 따라하도록'이다.

- tightly ad 꽉, 단단히
- lean ⓥ (몸을) 기울이다
- critical ⓐ 중요한
- disastrous ⓐ 재앙의
- anxiety ⓝ 불안
- steer ⓥ (핸들을) 조종하다
- literally ad 말 그대로
- coordination ⓝ (신체의) 협응
- warn A of B ⓥ A에게 B를 경고하다

구문 풀이

2행 So as to follow the rider's movements, the person on the
~하기 위해서(= in order to ~)   주어
backseat needs to hold on tightly.
동사(~할 필요가 있다)

07 새로운 식민지의 이념적 기초가 된 Locke의 사상   정답률 41% | 정답 ③

다음 빈칸에 들어갈 말로 가장 적절한 것을 고르시오. [3점]

① foundations for reinforcing ties between European and colonial societies
유럽 사회와 식민 사회 간의 연결고리를 강조하는 기반
② new opportunities for European societies to value their tradition
유럽 사회가 그들의 전통을 중시할 새로운 기회
✓ an optimistic framework for those trying to form a different society
다른 사회를 형성하려는 사람들에게 낙관적인 틀
④ an example of the role that nature plays in building character
천성이 성격 형성에 행하는 역할의 예시
⑤ an access to expertise in the areas of philosophy and science
철학 및 과학 분야의 전문 지식에 대한 접근

The empiricist philosopher John Locke argued / that when the human being was first born, / the mind was simply a blank slate — a *tabula rasa* — / waiting to be written on by experience.
경험주의 철학자 John Locke는 주장했다. / 인간이 처음 태어났을 때, / 그 마음은 그저 빈 석판 — 백지 상태의 마음 — 이었다고 / 경험에 의해 기록되기를 기다리는

Locke believed / that our experience shapes / who we are and who we become — / and therefore he also believed / that, given different experiences, / human beings would have different characters.
Locke는 믿었고, / 우리의 경험이 형성한다 / 우리가 누구고 어떤 사람이 되어 갈지를 / 그래서 그는 또한 믿었다. / 다른 경험이 주어지면 / 인간은 다른 성격을 가지게 되리라고

The influence of these ideas was profound, / particularly for the new colonies in America, for example, / because these were conscious attempts / to make a new start and to form a new society.

DAY 09

이런 생각의 영향은 크게 나타났는데, / 가령 특히 미대륙의 새로운 식민지에서 / 왜냐하면 이들 식민지는 의식적인 시도였기 때문이었다. / 새로운 시작을 하고 새로운 사회를 형성하려는

The new society / was to operate on a different basis / from that of European culture, / which was based on the feudal system / in which people's place in society was almost entirely determined by birth, / and which therefore tended to emphasize innate characteristics.

새로운 사회는 / 기반에서 작동될 것이었는데, / 유럽 문화의 기반과는 다른 / 유럽 문화는 봉건 제도에 기반을 두었고, / 사람들의 사회적 지위가 거의 전적으로 출생에 의해 결정되는 / 따라서 그것은 선천적인 특성을 강조하는 경향이 있었다.

Locke's emphasis on the importance of experience / in forming the human being / provided an optimistic framework for those / trying to form a different society.

경험이 갖는 중요성에 대한 Locke의 강조는 / 인간의 형성에서의 / 사람들에게 낙관적인 틀을 제공했다. / 다른 사회를 형성하려는

경험주의 철학자 John Locke는 인간이 처음 태어났을 때, 그 마음은 경험에 의해 기록되기를 기다리는 그저 빈 석판 — 백지 상태의 마음 — 이었다고 주장했다. Locke는 우리의 경험이 우리가 누구이고 어떤 사람이 되어 갈지를 형성한다고 믿었고, 그래서 그는 또한 인간은 다른 경험이 주어지면 다른 성격을 가지게 되리라고 믿었다. 이런 생각의 영향은 가령 특히 미대륙의 새로운 식민지에서 크게 나타났는데, 왜냐하면 이들 식민지는 새로운 시작을 하고 새로운 사회를 형성하려는 의식적인 시도였기 때문이었다. 새로운 사회는 유럽 문화의 기반과는 다른 기반에서 작동될 것이었는데, 유럽 문화는 사람들의 사회적 지위가 거의 전적으로 출생에 의해 결정되는 봉건 제도에 기반을 두었고, 따라서 그것은 선천적인 특성을 강조하는 경향이 있었다. 인간의 형성에서 경험이 갖는 중요성에 대한 Locke의 강조는 <u>다른 사회를 형성하려는 사람들에게 낙관적인 틀을 제공했다.</u>

Why? 왜 정답일까?

John Locke의 백지 상태 가설이 초기 식민지의 이념적 배경으로 작용했다는 내용이다. 선도 악도 타고나지 않은 인간이 어떤 경험을 하는가에 따라 아예 다른 성격을 구축할 수 있다는 주장은 선천적 특성보다는 '후천적 경험'을 강조하는 것이었고, 이것은 출신 성분을 중시했던 유럽 봉건주의 사상과는 대척점에 있었기에 새로 태동하는 식민지 사회에 힘이 되었다(The influence of these ideas was profound ~ in America)는 것이다. 따라서 빈칸에 들어갈 말로 가장 적절한 것은 ③ '다른 사회를 형성하려는 사람들에게 낙관적인 틀(an optimistic framework for those trying to form a different society)'이다.

- **empiricist** ⓝ 경험주의자
- **tabula rasa** 백지 상태
- **colony** ⓝ 식민지
- **emphasize** ⓥ 강조하다
- **foundation** ⓝ 기반, 근본
- **slate** ⓝ 석판
- **profound** ⓐ 심오한, (영향이) 큰
- **feudal** ⓐ 봉건 제도의
- **innate** ⓐ 타고난, 선천적인
- **reinforce** ⓥ 강조하다, 강화하다, 증강하다

구문 풀이

11행 The new society was to operate on a different basis from
→지시대명사 = the basis)
that of European culture, which was based on the feudal system
　　　　　선행사　　　　　계속적 용법　　　　　선행사
[in which people's place in society was almost entirely determined by birth], and [which therefore tended to emphasize innate characteristics]. [ ] : the feudal system 수식

★★★ 1등급 대비 고난도 2점 문제

08 인간이 쉽게 과열되지 않는 이유 　　　정답률 44% | 정답 ②

다음 빈칸에 들어갈 말로 가장 적절한 것을 고르시오.

① hot weather – 더운 날씨
✔ a lack of fur – 털의 부족
③ muscle strength – 근력
④ excessive exercise – 과도한 운동
⑤ a diversity of species – 다양한 종들

Humans are champion long-distance runners.
인간들은 최고의 장거리 달리기 선수들이다.

As soon as a person and a chimp start running / they both get hot.
한 사람과 침팬지가 달리기를 시작하자마자 / 그들은 둘 다 더위를 느낀다.

Chimps quickly overheat; humans do not, / because they are much better at shedding body heat.
침팬지는 빠르게 체온이 오르지만, / 인간들은 그렇지 않은데, / 그들은 신체 열을 떨어뜨리는 것을 훨씬 잘하기 때문이다.

According to one leading theory, / ancestral humans lost their hair over successive generations / because less hair meant cooler, more effective long-distance running.

유력한 한 이론에 따르면, / 선조들은 잇따른 세대에 걸쳐서 털을 잃었다. / 적은 털이 더 시원하고 장거리 달리기에 더 효과적인 것을 의미하기 때문에

That ability let our ancestors outmaneuver and outrun prey.
그런 능력은 우리 조상들이 먹잇감을 이기고 앞질러서 달리게 했다.

Try wearing a couple of extra jackets / — or better yet, fur coats — / on a hot humid day / and run a mile.
여분의 재킷 두 개를 입는 것을 시도하고 / 혹은 더 좋게는, 털 코트를 / 덥고 습한 날에 / 1마일을 뛰어라.

Now, take those jackets off and try it again.
이제, 그 재킷을 벗고 다시 시도하라.

You'll see what a difference a lack of fur makes.
당신은 털의 부족이 만드는 차이점이 무엇인지 알 것이다.

인간들은 최고의 장거리 달리기 선수들이다. 한 사람과 침팬지가 달리기를 시작하자마자 그들은 둘 다 더위를 느낀다. 침팬지는 빠르게 체온이 오르지만, 인간들은 그렇지 않은데, 그들은 신체 열을 떨어뜨리는 것을 훨씬 잘하기 때문이다. 유력한 한 이론에 따르면, 털이 더 적으면 더 시원하고 장거리 달리기에 더 효과적인 것을 의미하기 때문에 선조들은 잇따른 세대에 걸쳐서 털을 잃었다. 그런 능력은 우리 조상들이 먹잇감을 이기고 앞질러서 달리게 했다. 덥고 습한 날에 여분의 재킷 두 개를 — 혹은 더 좋게는, 털 코트를 — 입는 것을 시도하고 1마일을 뛰어라. 이제, 그 재킷을 벗고 다시 시도하라. 당신은 <u>털의 부족</u>이 만드는 차이점이 무엇인지 알 것이다.

Why? 왜 정답일까?

'According to one leading theory, ancestral humans lost their hair over successive generations because less hair meant cooler, more effective long-distance running.'에서 털이 더 적으면 더 시원해지고 장거리 달리기를 더 잘하게 되므로 인간은 연이은 세대에 걸쳐 계속 털이 적어지게 되었다고 설명하고 있다. 따라서 빈칸에 들어갈 말로 가장 적절한 것은 ② '털의 부족'이다.

- **overheat** ⓥ 과열되다
- **ancestral** ⓐ 선조의, 조상의
- **generation** ⓝ 세대
- **outrun** ⓥ ~보다 빨리 달리다
- **lack** ⓝ 부족, 결여
- **leading** ⓐ 선도적인
- **successive** ⓐ 잇따른, 연속적인
- **effective** ⓐ 효과적인
- **humid** ⓐ 습한
- **excessive** ⓐ 과도한

구문 풀이

3행 Chimps quickly overheat; humans do not, because they
　　　　주어1　　　　동사1　　　　주어2　　　　　이유 접속사
　　　　　　　　　　　　　　　　　　　　→동사2(= do not overheat)
are much better at shedding body heat.
「be good at + 동명사 : ~을 잘하다」

★★ 문제 해결 꿀~팁 ★★

▶ **많이 틀린 이유는?**
인간이 침팬지와 다르게 장시간을 달려도 크게 과열되지 않는 근본적인 이유를 파악해야 한다. ①의 '더운 날씨'는 원인으로 지적되지 않았고, ④의 '과도한 운동' 또한 '장거리 달리기'를 비약시킨 표현에 불과하다.

▶ **문제 해결 방법은?**
글 중간에서 조상들이 '털을 잃어왔다'는 내용이 등장한 이유를 생각해 본다. 이는 인간이 다른 동물에 비해 '털이 적기 때문에' 체온 조절에 능하다는 내용을 보충하기 위한 것이다.

★★★ 1등급 대비 고난도 3점 문제

09 창의력의 위기 　　　정답률 31% | 정답 ①

다음 빈칸에 들어갈 말로 가장 적절한 것을 고르시오. [3점]

✔ unrivaled – 경쟁할 상대가 없지
② learned – 학습되지
③ universal – 보편적이지
④ ignored – 무시되지
⑤ challenged – 도전받지

Creativity is a skill / we usually consider uniquely human.
창의력은 능력이다. / 우리가 일반적으로 인간만이 고유하게 가지고 있다고 간주하는

For all of human history, / we have been the most creative beings on Earth.
인류 역사를 통틀어, / 우리는 지구상에서 가장 창의적인 존재였다.

Birds can make their nests, / ants can make their hills, / but no other species on Earth / comes close to the level of creativity / we humans display.
새는 둥지를 틀 수 있고, / 개미는 개미탑을 쌓을 수 있지만, / 지구상의 어떤 다른 종도 / 창의력 수준에 가까이 도달하지는 못한다. / 우리 인간이 보여주는

However, just in the last decade / we have acquired the ability / to do amazing things with computers, / like developing robots.

하지만, 불과 지난 10년 만에 / 우리는 능력을 습득하였다. / 컴퓨터로 놀라운 것을 할 수 있는 / 로봇 개발처럼

With the artificial intelligence boom of the 2010s, / computers can now recognize faces, / translate languages, / take calls for you, / write poems, / and beat players / at the world's most complicated board game, / to name a few things.
2010년대의 인공 지능의 급속한 발전으로 / 컴퓨터는, 이제 얼굴을 인식하고, / 언어를 번역하고, / 여러분을 대신해 전화를 받고, / 시를 쓸 수 있으며 / 선수들을 이길 수 있다. / 세계에서 가장 복잡한 보드게임에서 / 몇 가지를 언급하자면

All of a sudden, / we must face the possibility / that our ability to be creative is not unrivaled.
갑작스럽게, / 우리는 가능성에 직면해야 할 것이다. / 우리의 창의력이 경쟁할 상대가 없지 않게 되는

창의력은 우리가 일반적으로 인간만이 고유하게 가지고 있다고 간주하는 능력이다. 인류 역사를 통틀어, 우리는 지구상에서 가장 창의적인 존재였다. 새는 둥지를 틀 수 있고, 개미는 개미탑을 쌓을 수 있지만, 지구상의 어떤 다른 종도 우리 인간이 보여주는 창의력 수준에 가까이 도달하지는 못한다. 하지만, 불과 지난 10년 만에 우리는 로봇 개발처럼 컴퓨터로 놀라운 것을 할 수 있는 능력을 습득하였다. 2010년대의 인공 지능의 급속한 발전으로 컴퓨터는, 몇 가지를 언급하자면, 이제 얼굴을 인식하고, 언어를 번역하고, 여러분을 대신해 전화를 받고, 시를 쓸 수 있으며 세계에서 가장 복잡한 보드게임에서 선수들을 이길 수 있다. 갑작스럽게, 우리는 우리의 창의력이 __경쟁할 상대가 없지__ 않게 되는 가능성에 직면해야 할 것이다.

Why? 왜 정답일까?

빈칸 앞의 문장에서 컴퓨터는 얼굴 인식, 언어 번역, 전화 응대, 시 창작, 보드게임 경기 등 기존에 인간만의 영역으로 여겨졌던 다양한 활동을 할 수 있게 되었다고 언급하는 것으로 보아, 빈칸이 포함된 문장은 그간 인간만의 능력으로 간주되어 왔던 창의력도 컴퓨터의 능력에 포함될지도 모른다는 의미를 나타내야 한다. 따라서 빈칸에 들어갈 말로 가장 적절한 것은 ① '경쟁할 상대가 없지'이다.

- **creativity** ⑩ 창조성, 독창성
- **nest** ⑩ 둥지
- **display** ⓥ 드러내다, 내보이다
- **translate** ⓥ 번역하다
- **unrivaled** ⓐ 경쟁 상대가 없는
- **uniquely** 쪠 고유하게
- **come close to** ~에 근접하다
- **artificial intelligence** 인공 지능
- **complicated** ⓐ 복잡한
- **universal** ⓐ 일반적인, 보편적인

구문 풀이

3행 Birds can make their nests, ants can make their hills, but
no other species on Earth comes close to the level of creativity [(that)
　부정 주어　　　　　　　동사(단수)　　　　　생략(목적격 관계대명사)
we humans display].

★★ 문제 해결 꿀~팁 ★★

▶ 많이 틀린 이유는?
빈칸에 직접 대응시킬 주제문이 없고 추상적인 내용을 다루어 까다로운 지문이다. 최다 오답인 ④는 인공 지능의 발달로 인해 인간의 창의력이 '무시되지' 않을 가능성이 있다는 뜻인데, 이 글은 컴퓨터가 인간의 창의력을 따라잡을 수도 있다는 내용을 주로 다루고 있어 주제와 무관한 선택지이다. ⑤는 주제와 상충한다.

▶ 문제 해결 방법은?
글 중간에 역접의 연결어가 나오므로 전반부보다는 후반부에 무게를 실어 독해한다. 특히 빈칸이 마지막 문장에 있으므로 바로 앞의 예문을 읽고 이를 토대로 일반화된 결론을 추론해야 한다.

★★★ 1등급 대비 고난도 3점 문제

10 문제 해결에서 가정이 필요한 이유　　정답률 43% | 정답 ④

다음 빈칸에 들어갈 말로 가장 적절한 것을 고르시오. [3점]

① prevent violations of consumer rights
　소비자 권리 침해를 방지할
② understand the value of cultural diversity
　문화적 다양성의 가치를 이해할
③ guarantee the safety of experimenters in labs
　실험실에 있는 실험자의 안전을 보장할
✓ focus our thinking on the essence of the problem
　문제의 본질에 우리의 사고를 집중할
⑤ realize the differences between physics and economics
　물리학과 경제학의 차이를 깨달을

If you ask a physicist / how long it would take a marble to fall / from the top of a ten-story building, / he will likely answer the question / by assuming that the marble falls in a vacuum.

만약 당신이 물리학자에게 묻는다면, / 구슬이 떨어지는 데 시간이 얼마나 걸리는지 / 10층 건물 꼭대기에서 / 그는 그 질문에 답할 것 같다. / 진공상태에서 구슬이 떨어진다고 가정하고

In reality, the building is surrounded by air, / which applies friction to the falling marble / and slows it down.
실제로 건물은 공기로 둘러싸여 있는데, / 그것이 떨어지는 구슬에 마찰을 가하며 / 속도를 떨어뜨린다.

Yet the physicist will point out / that the friction on the marble is so small / that its effect is negligible.
그러나 그 물리학자는 지적할 것이다. / 구슬에 가해지는 마찰이 너무 작아서 / 그것의 영향은 무시할 수 있다는 점을

Assuming the marble falls in a vacuum / simplifies the problem / without substantially affecting the answer.
구슬이 진공상태에서 떨어진다고 가정하는 것은 / 그 문제를 단순화한다 / 그 답에 큰 영향을 주지 않고

Economists make assumptions for the same reason: / Assumptions can simplify the complex world / and make it easier to understand.
경제학자들도 같은 이유로 가정을 한다. / 가정은 복잡한 세상을 단순화하고 / 그것을 이해하는 것을 더 쉽게 만든다

To study the effects of international trade, for example, / we might assume / that the world consists of only two countries / and that each country produces only two goods.
예를 들어, 국제 무역의 효과를 연구하기 위해 / 우리는 가정할 수 있다. / 세상이 단 두 국가로만 구성되었고, / 각 국가가 두 가지 상품만을 생산한다고

By doing so, / we can focus our thinking on the essence of the problem.
그렇게 함으로써, / 우리는 문제의 본질에 우리의 사고를 집중할 수 있다.

Thus, we are in a better position / to understand international trade in the complex world.
따라서 우리는 더 나은 위치에 있게 된다. / 복잡한 세상에서 국제 무역을 이해하는

만약 당신이 10층 건물 꼭대기에서 구슬이 떨어지는 데 시간이 얼마나 걸리는지 물리학자에게 묻는다면, 그는 진공상태에서 구슬이 떨어진다고 가정하고 그 질문에 답할 것 같다. 실제로 건물은 공기로 둘러싸여 있는데, 그것이 떨어지는 구슬에 마찰을 가하며 속도를 떨어뜨린다. 그러나 그 물리학자는 구슬에 가해지는 마찰이 너무 작아서 그것의 영향은 무시할 수 있다는 점을 지적할 것이다. 구슬이 진공상태에서 떨어진다고 가정하는 것은 그 답에 큰 영향을 주지 않고 그 문제를 단순화한다. 경제학자들도 같은 이유로 가정을 한다. 가정은 복잡한 세상을 단순화하고 이해하는 것을 더 쉽게 만들 수 있다. 예를 들어, 국제 무역의 효과를 연구하기 위해 우리는 세상이 단 두 국가로만 구성되었고, 각 국가가 두 가지 상품만을 생산한다고 가정할 수 있다. 그렇게 함으로써, 우리는 문제의 본질에 우리의 사고를 집중할 수 있다. 따라서 우리는 복잡한 세상에서 국제 무역을 이해하는 더 나은 위치에 있게 된다.

Why? 왜 정답일까?

가정은 세상을 이해하기 쉽도록 더 단순하게 만들어주기 때문에(Assumptions can simplify the complex world and make it easier to understand.) 문제 해결에 도움이 된다는 내용을 다룬 글이므로, 빈칸에 들어갈 말로 가장 적절한 것은 ④ '문제의 본질에 우리의 사고를 집중할'이다.

- **physicist** ⑩ 물리학자
- **assume** ⓥ 가정하다, 추정하다
- **surround** ⓥ 둘러싸다
- **simplify** ⓥ 단순화하다
- **violation** ⑩ 침해, 위반, 위배
- **guarantee** ⓥ 보장하다
- **marble** ⑩ 구슬, 대리석
- **vacuum** ⑩ 진공, 공백
- **friction** ⑩ 마찰
- **substantially** 쪠 상당히, 많이
- **diversity** ⑩ 다양성

구문 풀이

12행 To study the effects of international trade, for example, / we
　　　~하기 위해
might assume {that the world consists of only two countries} and
　　　　　　　　~로 구성되다　　　{ } : might assume의 목적어
{that each country produces only two goods}.

★★ 문제 해결 꿀~팁 ★★

▶ 많이 틀린 이유는?
과학이나 경제학 등에서 문제를 해결하기 위해 특정한 상황을 '가정'하는 것이 왜 필요한지를 설명한 글이다. 오답 중 ②에는 '문화적 다양성'이라는 표현이 나오는데 이는 본문의 다른 부분에서 한 번도 쓰이지 않은 표현이다. ⑤의 경우에는, 본문에 언급된 '물리학', '경제학' 등의 단어를 포함하고 있지만, 본문의 내용은 두 학문 간 차이를 설명하는 것과는 관련이 없다.

▶ 문제 해결 방법은?
본문에서 '가정'의 기능을 설명한 표현은 'simplify', 'makes it easier to understand'이고, 이를 ④에서는 'focus ~ on the essence of the problem'이라는 말로 바꾸었다.

DAY 09

★★★ 1등급 대비 고난도 3점 문제

11　감정에 좌우되는 인간　정답률 25% | 정답 ①

다음 빈칸에 들어갈 말로 가장 적절한 것을 고르시오. [3점]

✓ cultivate both distance and a degree of detachment
거리감과 어느 정도의 분리감을 기르는

② find out some clues or hints to their occupation
그들의 직업에 대해 단서와 힌트를 찾아내는

③ learn to be more empathetic for them
그들에게 더 공감하는 법을 배우는

④ discover honesty in their character
그들의 성격에서 정직함을 발견하는

⑤ relieve their anxiety and worries
그들의 불안과 걱정을 완화시키는

We like to make a show / of how much our decisions are based / on rational considerations, / but the truth is / that we are largely governed by our emotions, / which continually influence our perceptions.
우리는 보여 주고 싶지만, / 우리의 결정이 얼마나 많이 근거하는지 / 이성적 고려에 / 진실은 / 우리가 감정에 주로 지배당하고 있고 / 이것은 계속적으로 우리의 인지에 영향을 준다는 것이다.

What this means is / that the people around you, / constantly under the pull of their emotions, / change their ideas by the day or by the hour, / depending on their mood.
이것이 의미하는 바는 / 여러분의 주변 사람들이 / 끊임없이 감정의 끌어당김 아래에 있는 / 날마다 혹은 시간마다 그들의 생각을 바꾼다는 것이다. / 그들의 기분에 따라서

You must never assume / that what people say or do in a particular moment / is a statement of their permanent desires.
여러분은 가정해서는 안 된다. / 사람들이 특정한 순간에 말하거나 행하는 것이 / 그들의 영구적인 바람에 대한 진술이라고

Yesterday they were in love with your idea; / today they seem cold.
어제 그들은 여러분의 아이디어를 좋아했지만, / 오늘은 냉담해 보인다.

This will confuse you / and if you are not careful, / you will waste valuable mental space / trying to figure out their real feelings, / their mood of the moment, / and their fleeting motivations.
이것이 여러분을 혼란스럽게 할 것이고, / 만약 여러분이 조심하지 않는다면, / 여러분은 소중한 정신적 공간을 허비할 것이다. / 그들의 실제 감정, / 그 순간 그들의 기분, / 그들의 빠르게 지나가는 열의를 알아내려고 노력하면서

It is best / to cultivate both distance and a degree of detachment / from their shifting emotions / so that you are not caught up in the process.
최선이다. / 거리감과 어느 정도의 분리감을 기르는 것이 / 그들의 변화하는 감정들로부터 / 여러분이 그 과정에 사로잡히지 않기 위해서는

우리는 우리의 결정이 얼마나 많이 이성적 고려에 근거하는지 보여 주고 싶지만, 진실은 우리가 감정에 주로 지배당하고 있고 이것은 계속적으로 우리의 인지에 영향을 준다는 것이다. 이것이 의미하는 바는 끊임없이 감정의 끌어당김 아래에 있는 여러분의 주변 사람들이 날마다 혹은 시간마다 그들의 기분에 따라서 그들의 생각을 바꾼다는 것이다. 여러분은 사람들이 특정한 순간에 말하거나 행하는 것이 그들의 영구적인 바람에 대한 진술이라고 가정해서는 안 된다. 어제 그들은 여러분의 아이디어를 좋아했지만, 오늘은 냉담해 보인다. 이것이 여러분을 혼란스럽게 할 것이고, 만약 여러분이 조심하지 않는다면, 여러분은 그들의 실제 감정, 그 순간 그들의 기분, 그들의 빠르게 지나가는 열의를 알아내려고 노력하면서 소중한 정신적 공간을 허비할 것이다. 여러분이 그 과정에 사로잡히지 않기 위해서는 그들의 변화하는 감정들로부터 거리감과 어느 정도의 분리감을 기르는 것이 최선이다.

Why? 왜 정답일까?

What this means 이하의 두 문장(~ people around you, ~, change ~, depending on their mood. You must never assume that what people say or do in a particular moment is a statement of their permanent desires.)에서 사람들은 감정의 영향을 쉽게 받기 때문에 상대방이 어떤 한 순간에 한 말과 행동을 가지고 그 사람의 영속적인 상태나 기분을 추측하려 해서는 안 된다고 이야기하므로, 빈칸에 들어갈 말로 가장 적절한 것은 ① '거리감과 어느 정도의 분리감을 기르는'이다.

- **rational** ⓐ 이성적인, 합리적인
- **continually** ⓐⓓ 계속적으로, 지속적으로
- **constantly** ⓐⓓ 끊임없이, 거듭
- **statement** ⓝ 진술
- **fleeting** ⓐ 순간적인, 빠르게 지나가는
- **consideration** ⓝ 고려, 고려 사항
- **perception** ⓝ 인지, 지각
- **depending on** ~에 따라, ~에 좌우되어
- **permanent** ⓐ 영속적인, 영구적인
- **caught up** ~에 사로잡힌

구문 풀이

1행 We like to make a show of {how much our decisions
~을 과시하다, 보여 주다　의문사(얼마나)
are based on rational considerations}, / but the truth is {that we are
~에 기반을 두다　　　　　　　　　　　병렬
largely governed by our emotions}, which continually influence our
{ }: 명사절　　선행사　계속적 용법
perceptions.

▶ **많이 틀린 이유는?**
인간은 순간적인 감정에 좌우되는 존재이므로 어떤 사람이 어떤 특정한 순간에 한 말로 인해 오래 고민할 필요가 없으며, 오히려 일정한 거리를 둘 필요가 있다는 내용을 다룬 글이다. 최다 오답은 ②인데 이는 빈칸 앞의 'trying to figure out their real feelings' 등에 한정된 주의를 기울였을 때 골랐을 법한 오답이다. 나아가 'occupation(직업)'이라는 소재 또한 지문에서 언급된 바가 없다.

▶ **문제 해결 방법은?**
'but the truth is ~', 'You must never assume ~' 등 주제문을 나타내는 단서가 있는 문장부터 읽어 내용의 논리적인 흐름을 잡도록 한다.

★★★ 1등급 대비 고난도 3점 문제

12　환금 작물 재배로 인한 아프리카의 물 부족 심화　정답률 43% | 정답 ②

다음 빈칸에 들어갈 말로 가장 적절한 것을 고르시오. [3점]

① lowering the prices of crops – 작물의 가격을 낮추고 있는

✓ making water shortages worse – 물 부족을 심화시키고 있는

③ making farmers' incomes lower – 농부의 수입을 낮추고 있는

④ producing goods with more profit – 더 많은 이윤과 함께 재화를 생산하고 있는

⑤ criticizing the unfair trade of water – 불공정한 물 거래를 비판하는

What do rural Africans think / as they pass fields of cash crops / such as sunflowers, roses, or coffee, / while walking five kilometers a day to collect water?
아프리카 농촌 사람들은 어떤 생각을 할까? / 그들이 환금 작물 밭을 지날 때 / 해바라기나 장미, 커피와 같은 / 물을 길러 하루에 5킬로미터씩 걸으며

Some African countries find it difficult / to feed their own people / or provide safe drinking water, / yet precious water is used / to produce export crops for European markets.
몇몇 아프리카 국가들은 어렵다는 것을 알게 되지만 / 자국민을 먹여 살리거나 / 그들에게 안전한 식수를 공급하는 것이 / 귀한 물은 사용된다. / 유럽 시장을 위한 수출용 작물을 기르는 데

But, African farmers cannot help but grow those crops / because they are one of only a few sources of income for them.
그러나, 아프리카 농부들은 그런 작물들을 기르지 않을 수 없는데 / 왜냐하면 그것이 몇 안 되는 수입원 중 하나이기 때문이다.

In a sense, / African countries are exporting their water / in the very crops they grow.
어떤 의미에서, / 아프리카 나라들은 물을 수출하고 있는 것이다. / 자기들이 기르는 작물의 형태로

They need water, / but they also need to export water / through the crops they produce.
그들은 물이 필요하지만, / 또한 그 물을 수출할 필요도 있다. / 그들이 길러내는 작물을 통해

Environmental pressure groups argue / that European customers / who buy African coffee or flowers / are making water shortages worse in Africa.
환경 (보호) 압력 단체들은 주장한다. / 유럽 고객들은 / 아프리카의 커피나 꽃을 사는 / 물 부족을 심화시키고 있는 것이라고

아프리카 농촌 사람들은 물을 길러 하루에 5킬로미터씩 걸으며, 해바라기나 장미, 커피와 같은 환금 작물 밭을 지날 때 어떤 생각을 할까? 몇몇 아프리카 국가들은 자국민을 먹여 살리거나 그들에게 안전한 식수를 공급하기 어려워하지만, 귀한 물은 유럽 시장을 위한 수출용 작물을 기르는 데 사용된다. 그러나, 아프리카 농부들은 그런 작물들을 기르지 않을 수 없는데 왜냐하면 그것이 몇 안 되는 수입원 중 하나이기 때문이다. 어떤 의미에서, 아프리카 나라들은 자기들이 기르는 작물의 형태로 물을 수출하고 있는 것이다. 그들은 물이 필요하지만, 또한 그들이 길러내는 작물을 통해 그 물을 수출할 필요도 있다. 환경 (보호) 압력 단체들은 아프리카의 커피나 꽃을 사는 유럽 고객들은 물 부족을 심화시키고 있는 것이라고 주장한다.

Why? 왜 정답일까?

아프리카의 몇몇 국가들에서 먹을 물을 활용하여 커피나 꽃 등 환금 작물을 재배함으로 인해 물 부족 현상이 심화되고 있음을 설명한 글이다. 'In a sense, African countries are exporting their water in the very crops they grow.'에서 환금 작물을 재배하는 아프리카 국가들은 결국 안 그래도 부족한 물을 수출하는 것이나 다름없다고 이야기했는데, 이를 통해 아프리카의 환금 작물을 사는 유럽 소비자들은 결국 자신들도 모르는 새에 아프리카의 물 부족 심화 현상을 부추기고 있는 것과 같다는 내용을 유추할 수 있다. 따라서 빈칸에 들어갈 말로 가장 적절한 것은 ② '물 부족을 심화시키고 있는'이다.

- rural ⓐ 농촌의, 시골의
- collect ⓥ 모으다
- precious ⓐ 귀중한, 귀한
- environmental ⓐ 환경의
- customer ⓝ 고객, 손님
- cash crop 환금 작물
- feed ⓥ 먹여 살리다, 먹이를 주다
- export ⓥ 수출하다
- pressure group 압력 단체

구문 풀이

3행 Some African countries find it difficult to feed their own
「find + 가목적어 + 목적격 보어 + 진목적어1 +
people or provide safe drinking water, / yet precious water is used
(to 생략) ─┘ 진목적어2   「be used to + 동사원형 : ~하기 위해 쓰다」
to produce export crops for European markets.

★★ 문제 해결 꿀~팁 ★★

▶ 많이 틀린 이유는?
본문에서 선택지를 그대로 대응시킬 말이 없고 한 번 더 생각해야 답을 고를 수 있기에 어려운 문제였다. 최다 오답인 ⑤는 주제와 반대되는 내용을 담고 있다.

▶ 문제 해결 방법은?
아프리카 사람들은 물이 부족하지만 돈을 벌기 위해 환금 작물을 재배할 수밖에 없는데, 유럽 사람들이 이를 자꾸 사면 결국에는 공급을 뒷받침하기 위해 재배가 이어지게 되고 식수 또한 자꾸 이 농사에 들어가게 된다. 이러한 연쇄 고리를 파악하면 '환금 작물 구매 → 물 부족 심화'라는 도식에 따라 답을 고를 수 있다.

---

01 ④	02 ④	03 ②	04 ②	05 ⑤
06 ③	07 ①	08 ①	09 ⑤	10 ③
11 ①	12 ④			

01   비슷한 사람들끼리 더 쉽게 시작되는 관계   정답률 56% | 정답 ④

다음 빈칸에 들어갈 말로 가장 적절한 것을 고르시오.

① information deficit – 정보 부족
② cultural adaptability – 문화적 적응력
③ meaning negotiation – 의미 협상
✔ behavioral coordination – 행동의 조화
⑤ unconditional acceptance – 무조건적 수용

Although a balance or harmony between partners / clearly develops over time in a relationship, / it is also a factor / in initial attraction and interest in a partner.
비록 파트너 사이의 균형이나 조화는 / 관계에서 시간이 지남에 따라 분명히 발전하지만 / 이것은 요인이기도 하다. / 파트너에 대한 초기 매력과 관심에 있어

That is, / to the extent / that two people share similar verbal and nonverbal habits in a first meeting, / they will be more comfortable with one another.
즉, / 정도만큼 / 두 사람이 첫 만남에서 비슷한 언어적 및 비언어적 습관을 공유하는 / 그들은 서로 더 편안할 것이다.

For example, / fast-paced individuals talk and move quickly / and are more expressive, / whereas slow-paced individuals have a different tempo / and are less expressive.
예를 들어, / 속도가 빠른 사람들은 빠르게 말을 하고 움직이며 / 더 표현하는 반면, / 속도가 느린 사람들은 속도가 다르며 / 덜 표현한다.

Initial interactions / between people at opposite ends of such a continuum / may be more difficult / than those between similar types.
초기 상호 작용은 / 이러한 연속체의 반대쪽 끝에 있는 사람들 간의 / 더 어려울 수 있다. / 유사한 유형들 간의 상호 작용보다

In the case of contrasting styles, / individuals may be less interested in pursuing a relationship / than if they were similar in interaction styles.
대비되는 유형인 경우 / 사람들은 관계 추구에 관심을 덜 보일 수 있다. / 그들이 상호 작용 유형 면에서 비슷한 경우보다

Individuals with similar styles, / however, / are more comfortable / and find that they just seem to "click" with one another.
비슷한 유형의 사람들은 / 그러나 / 더 편안하고, / 그야말로 서로 '즉시 마음이 통하는' 것 같다고 느낀다.

Thus, / behavioral coordination may provide a selection filter / for the initiation of a relationship.
따라서 / 행동의 조화는 선택 필터를 제공할 수 있다. / 관계의 시작을 위한

파트너 사이의 균형이나 조화는 관계에서 시간이 지남에 따라 분명히 발전하지만, 이것은 파트너에 대한 초기 매력과 관심의 요인이기도 하다. 즉, 두 사람은 첫 만남에서 비슷한 언어적 및 비언어적 습관을 공유하는 정도만큼 서로 더 편안할 것이다. 예를 들어, 속도가 빠른 사람들은 빠르게 말을 하고 움직이며 더 표현하는 반면, 속도가 느린 사람들은 속도가 다르며 덜 표현한다. 이러한 연속체의 반대쪽 끝에 있는 사람들 간의 초기 상호 작용은 유사한 유형보다 더 어려울 수 있다. 대비되는 유형인 경우 사람들은 상호 작용 유형이 비슷한 경우보다 관계 추구에 관심을 덜 보일 수 있다. 그러나 비슷한 유형의 사람들은 더 편안하고, 그야말로 서로 '즉시 마음이 통하는' 것 같다고 느낀다. 따라서 행동의 조화는 관계의 시작을 위한 선택 필터를 제공할 수 있다.

Why? 왜 정답일까?

첫 문장에서 사람들은 비슷하면 처음에 서로 매력을 느끼기 쉽다고 이야기한다(Although a balance or harmony between partners clearly develops over time in a relationship, it is also a factor in initial attraction and interest in a partner.). 따라서 빈칸에 들어갈 말로 가장 적절한 것은 a balance or harmony와 같은 의미인 ④ '행동의 조화(behavioral coordination)'이다.

- attraction ⓝ 끌림, 매력
- nonverbal ⓐ 비언어적인
- expressive ⓐ 표현적인, 잘 표현하는
- contrasting ⓐ 대비되는
- initiation ⓝ 시작
- adaptability ⓝ 적응력
- unconditional ⓐ 무조건적인
- verbal ⓐ 언어적인
- fast-paced ⓐ 속도가 빠른
- continuum ⓝ 연속체
- click ⓥ 잘 통하다, 맞다
- deficit ⓝ 부족, 적자
- coordination ⓝ 조화

구문 풀이

4행 That is, <u>to the extent that</u> two people share similar verbal
　　　　　　　~할 정도까지
and nonverbal habits in a first meeting, they will be more comfortable
with one another.

---

02 | 음식으로 아이를 달래는 것의 장단기적 영향 | 정답률 74% | 정답 ④

다음 빈칸에 들어갈 말로 가장 적절한 것을 고르시오.

① make friends – 친구를 사귀는
② learn etiquettes – 예절을 배우는
③ improve memory – 기억을 향상시키는
✔ manage emotions – 감정을 다스리는
⑤ celebrate achievements – 성취를 축하하는

When a child is upset, / the easiest and quickest way to calm them down / is to give them food.
아이가 화를 낼 때, / 아이를 진정시키는 가장 쉽고 가장 빠른 방법은 / 아이에게 음식을 주는 것이다.

This acts as a distraction / from the feelings they are having, / gives them something to do with their hands and mouth / and shifts their attention / from whatever was upsetting them.
이것은 주의를 돌리는 것으로 작용하고, / 아이가 가지고 있는 감정으로부터 / 손과 입으로 할 수 있는 무언가를 아이에게 제공하며, / 아이의 주의를 옮겨 가게 한다. / 화나게 하고 있는 것이 무엇이든 그것으로부터

If the food chosen is also seen as a treat / such as sweets or a biscuit, / then the child will feel 'treated' and happier.
또한 선택된 음식이 특별한 먹거리로 여겨지면, / 사탕이나 비스킷 같은 / 그 아이는 '특별한 대접을 받았다고' 느끼고 기분이 더 좋을 것이다.

In the shorter term / using food like this is effective.
단기적으로는 / 이처럼 음식을 이용하는 것은 효과적이다.

But in the longer term / it can be harmful / as we quickly learn / that food is a good way to manage emotions.
하지만 장기적으로는 / 그것은 해로울 수 있다. / 우리가 곧 알게 되기 때문에 / 음식이 감정을 다스리는 좋은 방법이라는 것을

Then as we go through life, / whenever we feel annoyed, anxious or even just bored, / <u>we turn to food to make ourselves feel better.</u>
그러면 우리가 삶을 살아가면서, / 짜증이 나거나, 불안하거나, 심지어 그저 지루함을 느낄 때마다, / 우리 자신의 기분을 더 좋게 만들기 위해 우리는 음식에 의존한다.

아이가 화를 낼 때, 아이를 진정시키는 가장 쉽고 가장 빠른 방법은 음식을 주는 것이다. 이것은 아이가 가지고 있는 감정으로부터 주의를 돌리는 것으로 작용하고, 손과 입으로 할 수 있는 무언가를 아이에게 제공하며, 화나게 하고 있는 것이 무엇이든 그것으로부터 아이의 주의를 옮겨 가게 한다. 또한 선택된 음식이 사탕이나 비스킷 같은 특별한 먹거리로 여겨지면, 그 아이는 '특별한 대접을 받았다고' 느끼고 기분이 더 좋을 것이다. 이처럼 음식을 이용하는 것은 단기적으로는 효과적이다. 하지만 음식이 감정을 다스리는 좋은 방법이라는 것을 우리가 곧 알게 되기 때문에 그것은 장기적으로는 해로울 수 있다. 그러면 우리가 삶을 살아가면서, 짜증이 나거나, 불안하거나, 심지어 그저 지루함을 느낄 때마다, 우리 자신의 기분을 더 좋게 만들기 위해 우리는 음식에 의존한다.

Why? 왜 정답일까?

화난 아이의 기분을 음식으로 달래주는 것이 단기적으로는 효과가 있지만 장기적으로는 아이가 기분이 좋지 않을 때 음식에 의존하게 하는 결과를 낳기 때문에 좋지 않을 수 있다는 내용을 다룬 글이다. 두 번째 문장과 세 번째 문장에서, 음식은 아이가 기분이 나쁠 때 주의를 돌려주는 효과가 있으며, 특히 그 음식이 특별한 먹거리로 여겨지는 경우 아이를 특히 더 기분 좋게 한다고 설명하고 있다. 또한 마지막 문장에서는 그리하여 우리가 장기적으로 '기분을 나아지게' 하고자 할 때 음식에 의존하는 결과가 나타날 수 있다고 한다. 따라서 빈칸에 들어갈 말로 가장 적절한 것은 ④ '감정을 다스리는'이다.

- distraction ⓝ 주의를 돌리는 것
- see A as B A를 B로 간주하다
- harmful ⓐ 해로운
- turn to ~에 의지하다
- achievement ⓝ 성취
- shift ⓥ 돌리다, 바꾸다
- treat ⓝ 간식 ⓥ 대접하다
- anxious ⓐ 불안한
- celebrate ⓥ 축하하다

구문 풀이

11행 Then as we go through life, whenever we feel annoyed,
　　　　　 접속사(~함에 따라)　　　　 복합관계부사(~할 때마다)　　2형식 동사 보어1
anxious or even just bored, we turn to food to make ourselves
　　보어2　　　　　　　보어3　주어 동사　 목적어 부사적 용법(목적) ⌐목적어
feel better.
원형부정사

---

03 | 정기적인 회의를 통한 창의력 향상 | 정답률 57% | 정답 ②

다음 빈칸에 들어갈 말로 가장 적절한 것을 고르시오. [3점]

① consumer complaints – 소비자 불만
✔ the regular meetings – 이 정기적인 회의들
③ traveling experiences – 여행 경험
④ flexible working hours – 유연한 근무 시간
⑤ the financial incentives – 재정적 인센티브

One CEO in one of Silicon Valley's most innovative companies / has what would seem like a boring, creativity-killing routine.
실리콘 밸리의 가장 혁신적인 회사들 중 한 회사의 최고 경영자는 / 지루하고 창의력을 해치는 듯 보이는 관례가 있다.

He holds a three-hour meeting / that starts at 9:00 A.M. one day a week.
그는 세 시간짜리 회의를 연다, / 일주일에 하루 오전 9시에 시작하는

It is never missed or rescheduled at a different time.
그 회의에 빠지거나 다른 시간으로 일정이 변경되는 일은 결코 없다.

It is mandatory — so much so / that even in this global firm / all the executives know never to schedule any travel / that will conflict with the meeting.
그것은 의무적인데 너무 그러하여 / 심지어 이 다국적 기업에서 / 모든 경영자들은 어떠한 이동 일정도 절대로 잡지 않아야 한다는 것을 알고 있다. / 그 회의 일정과 상충하는(그 회의와 시간이 겹치는)

At first glance / there is nothing particularly unique about this.
언뜻 보아, / 여기에 특별히 독특한 점은 없다.

But what *is* unique is the quality of ideas / that come out of <u>the regular meetings.</u>
그러나 *정말로* 독특한 것은 아이디어의 질이다. / 이 정기적인 회의들로부터 나오는

Because the CEO has eliminated the mental cost / involved in planning the meeting / or thinking about who will or won't be there, / people can focus on creative problem solving.
최고경영자는 정신적 비용을 없앴기 때문에, / 회의를 계획하거나 / 누가 회의에 참여하고 참여하지 않을지에 대해 생각하는 것과 관련된 / 사람들은 창의적인 문제 해결에 초점을 맞출 수 있다.

실리콘 밸리의 가장 혁신적인 회사들 중 한 회사의 최고 경영자는 지루하고 창의력을 해치는 듯 보이는 관례가 있다. 그는 일주일에 하루 오전 9시에 시작하는 세 시간짜리 회의를 연다. 그 회의에 빠지거나 다른 시간으로 일정이 변경되는 일은 결코 없다. 그것은 의무적인데 너무 그러하여 심지어 이 다국적 기업의 모든 경영자들은 그 회의와 시간이 겹치는 어떠한 이동 일정도 절대로 잡지 않아야 한다는 것을 알고 있다. 언뜻 보아, 여기에 특별히 독특한 점은 없다. 그러나 *정말로* 독특한 것은 이 정기적인 회의들로부터 나오는 아이디어의 질이다. 최고경영자는 회의를 계획하거나 누가 회의에 참여하고 참여하지 않을지에 대해 생각하는 것과 관련된 정신적 비용을 없앴기 때문에, 사람들은 창의적인 문제 해결에 초점을 맞출 수 있다.

Why? 왜 정답일까?

시간을 바꾸거나 불참할 수 없는 '정기적인' 회의(He holds a three-hour meeting that starts at 9:00 A.M. one day a week. It is never missed or rescheduled at a different time.)를 통해 불필요한 정신적 비용을 해소하고 (~ the CEO has eliminated the mental cost involved in planning the meeting ~) 창의력 증진에 시간을 투자하는 회사가 있음을 소개한 글이다. 따라서 빈칸에 들어갈 말로 가장 적절한 것은 ② '이 정기적인 회의들'이다.

- innovative ⓐ 혁신적인
- executive ⓝ 경영진, 중역
- eliminate ⓥ 없애다, 제거하다
- flexible ⓐ 유연한, 융통성 있는
- mandatory ⓐ 의무적인, 강제의
- at first glance 언뜻 보기에, 처음에는
- involved in ~와 관련된, ~에 연루된
- incentive ⓝ 인센티브, 상여금, 장려금

구문 풀이

5행 It is mandatory — so much so that even in this global firm all
　　　　　　　　　 매우 그러하므로 ~하다
the executives know never to schedule any travel [that will conflict with
　　　　　　　　　　　　　　　　　　　　　　주격 관계대명사　~와 상충되다
the meeting].

---

04 | 키워드 중심의 태그 시스템이 갖는 한계 | 정답률 47% | 정답 ②

다음 빈칸에 들어갈 말로 가장 적절한 것을 고르시오.

① a set of words that allow users to identify an individual object
　사용자가 각각의 사물을 식별할 수 있게 하는 일련의 단어
✔ a comprehensive description of what is happening in an image
　이미지에서 일어나고 있는 일에 대한 포괄적인 설명
③ a reliable resource for categorizing information by pictures
　사진으로 정보를 분류할 수 있는 믿을 만한 자원

④ a primary means of organizing a sequential order of words
단어의 순차적 순서를 구성하는 주요 수단
⑤ a useful filter for sorting similar but not identical images
유사하지만 똑같지는 않은 이미지를 분류하는 데 유용한 필터

Many people create and share pictures and videos on the Internet.
많은 사람이 사진과 영상을 만들어 인터넷에 공유한다.

The difficulty is finding what you want.
어려운 점은 여러분이 원하는 것을 찾는 것이다.

Typically, / people want to search using words / (rather than, say, example sketches).
일반적으로 / 사람들은 단어를 사용하여 검색하기를 원한다 / (예시 스케치 같은 것이 아니라)

Because most pictures don't come with words attached, / it is natural / to try and build tagging systems / that tag images with relevant words.
대부분의 사진에는 단어가 첨부되어 있지 않기 때문에, / 당연하다. / 태그 시스템을 써보고 만들어가는 것은 / 이미지에 관련 단어를 태그하는

The underlying machinery is straightforward / — we apply image classification and object detection methods / and tag the image with the output words.
기본적인 시스템은 간단하다 / 우리는 이미지 분류와 개체 감지 방법을 적용하고 / 출력된 단어로 이미지를 태그한다.

But tags aren't a comprehensive description / of what is happening in an image.
하지만 태그는 포괄적인 설명이 아니다. / 이미지에서 일어나고 있는 일에 대한

It matters who is doing what, / and tags don't capture this.
누가 무엇을 하고 있는지가 중요한데, / 태그는 이것을 포착하지 못한다.

For example, / tagging a picture of a cat in the street / with the object categories "cat", "street", "trash can" and "fish bones" / leaves out the information / that the cat is pulling the fish bones / out of an open trash can on the street.
예를 들어, / 거리에 있는 고양이의 사진을 태그하는 것은 / '고양이', '거리', '쓰레기통', '생선 뼈'라는 개체 범주로 / 정보를 빠뜨리게 된다. / 그 고양이가 생선 뼈를 빼내고 있다는 / 거리에 있는 열린 쓰레기통에서

많은 사람이 사진과 영상을 만들어 인터넷에 공유한다. 어려운 점은 여러분이 원하는 것을 찾는 것이다. 일반적으로 사람들은 (예시 스케치 같은 것이 아니라) 단어를 사용하여 검색하기를 원한다. 대부분의 사진에는 단어가 첨부되어 있지 않기 때문에, 이미지에 관련 단어를 태그하는 태그 시스템을 써보고 만들어가는 것은 당연하다. 기본적인 시스템은 간단한데, 이미지 분류와 개체 감지 방법을 적용하고 출력된 단어로 이미지를 태그한다. 하지만 태그는 이미지에서 일어나고 있는 일에 대한 포괄적인 설명이 아니다. 누가 무엇을 하고 있는지가 중요한데, 태그는 이것을 포착하지 못한다. 예를 들어, 거리에 있는 고양이의 사진을 '고양이', '거리', '쓰레기통', '생선 뼈'라는 개체 범주로 태그하는 것은 그 고양이가 거리에 있는 열린 쓰레기통에서 생선 뼈를 빼내고 있다는 정보를 빠뜨리게 된다.

Why? 왜 정답일까?

마지막 문장의 예시는 키워드 중심의 태그 시스템이 이미지 속의 상황을 묘사하지 못한다는 것을 보여준다. 즉 단어 중심으로 나열할 뿐, 어떤 행위가 일어나고 있는지 설명하지 못한다는(It matters who is doing what, and tags don't capture this.) 의미가 되도록 빈칸에 들어갈 말로 가장 적절한 것은 ② '이미지에서 일어나고 있는 일에 대한 포괄적인 설명'이다.

- attached ⓐ 부착된, 첨부된
- relevant ⓐ 관련 있는, 적절한
- classification ⓝ 분류
- leave out 빠뜨리다
- identify ⓥ 식별하다
- sequential ⓐ 순차적인
- tag ⓥ 태그를 달다, 꼬리표를 붙이다
- straightforward ⓐ 쉬운, 간단한
- detection ⓝ 감지
- pull out of ~에서 꺼내다
- comprehensive ⓐ 광범위한

구문 풀이

11행 For example, tagging a picture of a cat in the street with the
　　　　　　　　　　　　동명사구 주어
object categories "cat", "street", "trash can" and "fish bones"
leaves out the information {that the cat is pulling the fish bones out
동사(단수)　　　목적어　　　　　{ } : 동격(= the information)
of an open trash can on the street}.

05 식당 선택에 영향을 미치는 손님 수　　정답률 60% | 정답 ⑤

다음 빈칸에 들어갈 말로 가장 적절한 것을 고르시오.

① both restaurants are getting busier
두 식당 모두 더 붐비게 된다
② you and your friend start hesitating
당신과 친구는 망설이기 시작한다

③ your decision has no impact on others
당신의 결정은 다른 사람들의 결정에 영향이 없다
④ they reject what lots of other people do
그들은 많은 다른 사람들이 하는 일을 거부한다
✔ they decide to do the same as the other eight
그들도 다른 여덟 명과 같은 행동을 하기로 결정한다

We are more likely to eat in a restaurant / if we know that it is usually busy.
우리는 그 식당에서 식사할 가능성이 더 크다. / 우리가 어떤 식당이 대체로 붐빈다는 것을 알게 되면

Even when nobody tells us a restaurant is good, / our herd behavior determines our decision-making.
아무도 우리에게 어떤 식당이 좋다고 말하지 않을 때조차도, / 우리의 무리 행동은 우리의 의사를 결정한다.

Let's suppose / you walk toward two empty restaurants.
가정하자. / 당신이 두 개의 텅 빈 식당 쪽으로 걸어가고 있다고

You do not know which one to enter.
당신은 어느 곳에 들어가야 할지 모른다.

However, / you suddenly see / a group of six people enter one of them.
하지만, / 갑자기 당신은 보게 된다. / 여섯 명의 무리가 둘 중 하나의 식당으로 들어가는 것을

Which one are you more likely to enter, / the empty one or the other one?
당신은 어느 식당에 들어갈 가능성이 더 높겠는가? / 텅 빈 식당 혹은 나머지 식당 중

Most people would go into the restaurant / with people in it.
대부분의 사람들은 식당에 들어갈 것이다. / 사람들이 있는

Let's suppose / you and a friend go into that restaurant.
가정하자. / 당신과 친구가 그 식당에 들어간다고

Now, it has eight people in it.
이제, 그 식당 안에는 여덟 명이 있다.

Others see / that one restaurant is empty / and the other has eight people in it.
다른 사람들은 보게 된다. / 한 식당은 텅 비어 있고 / 다른 식당은 여덟 명이 있는 것을

So, they decide to do the same as the other eight.
그래서, 그들도 다른 여덟 명과 같은 행동을 하기로 결정한다.

어떤 식당이 대체로 붐빈다는 것을 알게 되면 우리가 그 식당에서 식사할 가능성이 더 크다. 아무도 우리에게 어떤 식당이 좋다고 말하지 않을 때조차도, 우리의 무리 행동은 우리의 의사를 결정한다. 당신이 두 개의 텅 빈 식당 쪽으로 걸어가고 있다고 가정하자. 당신은 어느 곳에 들어가야 할지 모른다. 하지만, 갑자기 당신은 여섯 명의 무리가 둘 중 하나의 식당으로 들어가는 것을 보게 된다. 당신은 텅 빈 식당 혹은 나머지 식당 중 어느 식당에 들어갈 가능성이 더 높겠는가? 대부분의 사람들은 사람들이 있는 식당에 들어갈 것이다. 당신과 친구가 그 식당에 들어간다고 가정하자. 이제, 그 식당 안에는 여덟 명이 있다. 다른 사람들은 한 식당은 텅 비어 있고 다른 식당은 여덟 명이 있는 것을 보게 된다. 그래서, 그들도 다른 여덟 명과 같은 행동을 하기로 결정한다.

Why? 왜 정답일까?

첫 문장인 'We are more likely to eat in a restaurant if we know that it is usually busy.'에서 우리는 붐비는 식당에서 식사할 가능성이 더 높다는 주제를 제시하고 이를 예를 들어 설명하는 글이다. 주제에 비추어볼 때, 빈칸 앞의 문장과 같이 텅 빈 식당과 여덟 명의 손님이 있는 식당을 각각 발견할 경우 사람들은 조금 더 붐비는 후자의 식당에서 식사를 하게 될 것임을 유추할 수 있다. 따라서 빈칸에 들어갈 말로 가장 적절한 것은 ⑤ '그들도 다른 여덟 명과 같은 행동을 하기로 결정한다'이다.

- decision-making 의사 결정
- suddenly ⓐ[ad] 갑자기
- impact ⓝ 영향, 충격
- suppose ⓥ 가정하다
- hesitate ⓥ 망설이다
- reject ⓥ 거부하다

구문 풀이

2행 Even when nobody tells us (that) a restaurant is good, /
　　　심지어 ~할 때에도　　　생략
our herd behavior determines our decision-making.
　　　주어　　　　　　　동사

06 공동체 의식을 증진하는 음악　　정답률 62% | 정답 ③

다음 빈칸에 들어갈 말로 가장 적절한 것을 고르시오. [3점]

① the foundation for social reform – 사회 개혁의 기초
② the feedback for pop culture – 대중문화에 대한 피드백
✔ the feeling of a community – 공동체라는 느낌
④ the access to traditional songs – 전통 노래에 대한 접근
⑤ the solution for copyright issues – 저작권 문제에 대한 해결책

Music connects people to one another / not only through a shared interest or hobby, / but also through emotional connections / to particular songs, communities, and artists.
음악은 사람들을 서로 연결시킨다. / 공통의 관심사나 취미를 통해서뿐만 아니라 / 감정적 연결을 통해서도 / 특정한 노래, 공동체, 그리고 예술가에 대한

DAY 10

The significance of others in the search for the self / is meaningful; / as Agger, a sociology professor, states, / "identities are largely social products, / formed in relation to others / and how we think they view us."

자신을 찾아가는 과정 속에서 다른 사람들의 중요성은 / 의미가 있다. / 사회학 교수인 Agger의 말처럼, / "정체성은 주로 사회적 산물이다. / 다른 사람들과의 관계로 형성되는 / 그리고 우리 생각에 그들이 우리를 어떻게 보느냐로

And Frith, a socio-musicologist, argues / that popular music has such connections.

그리고 사회음악학자인 Frith는 주장한다. / 대중음악이 그러한 연결을 가지고 있다고

For music fans, / the genres, artists, and songs / in which people find meaning, thus, / function as potential "places" / through which one's identity can be positioned / in relation to others; / they act as chains / that hold at least parts of one's identity in place.

그러므로 음악 팬들에게, / 장르, 예술가, 그리고 노래는 / 사람들이 의미를 찾는 / 잠재적인 '장소'로서 기능을 하는데, / 그 장소를 통해 자신의 정체성이 자리 잡을 수 있다. / 다른 사람들과 연관되어 / (말하자면) 그것은 사슬로서 역할을 한다. / 적어도 사람들의 정체성 일부를 제자리에 묶어두는

The connections / made through shared musical passions / provide a sense of safety and security / in the notion that there are groups of similar people / who can provide the feeling of a community.

연결은 / 공유된 음악적 열정을 통해 만들어진 / 안전과 안정감을 제공한다. / 비슷한 사람들의 집단이 있다는 점에서 / 공동체라는 느낌을 제공해 줄 수 있는

음악은 공통의 관심사나 취미를 통해서뿐만 아니라 특정한 노래, 공동체, 그리고 예술가에 대한 감정적 연결을 통해서도 사람들을 서로 연결시킨다. 자신을 찾아가는 과정 속에서 다른 사람들의 중요성은 의미가 있다. 사회학 교수인 Agger의 말처럼, "정체성은 주로 다른 사람들과의 관계와 우리 생각에 그들이 우리를 어떻게 보느냐로 형성되는 사회적 산물이다." 그리고 사회음악학자인 Frith는 대중음악이 그러한 연결을 가지고 있다고 주장한다. 그러므로 음악 팬들에게, 사람들이 의미를 찾는 장르, 예술가, 그리고 노래는 잠재적인 '장소'로서 기능을 하는데, 그 장소를 통해 자신의 정체성이 다른 사람들과 연관되어 자리 잡을 수 있다. 말하자면 그것은 적어도 사람들의 정체성 일부를 제자리에 묶어두는 사슬로서 역할을 한다. 공유된 음악적 열정을 통해 만들어진 연결은 공동체라는 느낌을 제공해 줄 수 있는 비슷한 사람들의 집단이 있다는 점에서 안전과 안정감을 제공한다.

Why? 왜 정답일까?

음악은 사람들이 정체성의 일부를 서로 공유하며 감정적인 유대감과 공동체 의식을 나눌 수 있는 장소와 같은 기능을 한다(~ function as potential "places" through which one's identity can be positioned in relation to others: ~)는 내용을 담은 글이다. 따라서 빈칸에 들어갈 말로 가장 적절한 것은 ③ '공동체라는 느낌'이다.

- significance ⓝ 중요성
- sociology ⓝ 사회학
- in relation to ~와 관련되어
- position ⓥ ~의 자리를 잡다
- notion ⓝ 개념, 관념, 생각
- meaningful ⓐ 의미 있는, 유의미한
- identity ⓝ 정체성
- function ⓥ 기능하다, 작용하다
- security ⓝ 안정, 안도감

구문 풀이

9행 For music fans, / the genres, artists, and songs [in which people find meaning], thus, function as potential "places" [through which one's identity can be positioned in relation to others]: / they act as chains [that hold at least parts of one's identity in place].

---

07 | 영화 속 외국어 대화에 자막이 없을 때의 효과 | 정답률 59% | 정답 ①

다음 빈칸에 들어갈 말로 가장 적절한 것을 고르시오. [3점]

✔ seeing the film from her viewpoint - 그녀의 시각에서 영화를 보고 있게
② impressed by her language skills - 그녀의 언어 능력에 감명받게
③ attracted to her beautiful voice - 그녀의 아름다운 목소리에 이끌리게
④ participating in a heated debate - 열띤 토론에 참여하게
⑤ learning the language used in the film - 영화에서 사용된 언어를 배우고 있게

Most times a foreign language is spoken in film, / subtitles are used / to translate the dialogue for the viewer.

영화에서 외국어가 사용되는 대부분의 경우 / 자막이 사용된다. / 관객을 위해 대화를 통역하려고

However, / there are occasions / when foreign dialogue is left unsubtitled / (and thus incomprehensible to most of the target audience).

하지만 / 경우가 있다. / 외국어 대화가 자막 없이 처리되는 / (그리하여 대부분의 주요 대상 관객이 이해하지 못하게)

This is often done / if the movie is seen / mainly from the viewpoint of a particular character / who does not speak the language.

흔히 이렇게 처리된다. / 영화가 보여지는 경우에 / 주로 특정한 등장인물의 관점에서 / 그 언어를 할 줄 모르는

Such absence of subtitles / allows the audience / to feel a similar sense of incomprehension and alienation / that the character feels.

그러한 자막의 부재는 / 관객이 ~하게 한다. / 비슷한 몰이해와 소외의 감정을 / 그 등장인물이 느끼는

An example of this / is seen in *Not Without My Daughter*.

이것의 한 예는 / *Not Without My Daughter*에서 볼 수 있다.

The Persian language dialogue / spoken by the Iranian characters / is not subtitled / because the main character Betty Mahmoody does not speak Persian / and the audience is seeing the film from her viewpoint.

페르시아어 대화는 / 이란인 등장인물들이 하는 / 자막 없이 처리되며 / 왜냐하면 주인공 Betty Mahmoody가 페르시아어를 하지 못하기 때문에 / 관객은 그녀의 시각에서 영화를 보고 있게 된다.

영화에서 외국어가 사용되는 대부분의 경우 관객을 위해 대화를 통역하려고 자막이 사용된다. 하지만 외국어 대화가 자막 없이 (그리하여 대부분의 주요 대상 관객이 이해하지 못하게) 처리되는 경우가 있다. 영화가 그 언어를 할 줄 모르는 특정한 등장인물의 관점에서 주로 보여지는 경우에 흔히 이렇게 처리된다. 그러한 자막의 부재는 관객이 그 등장인물이 느끼는 것과 비슷한 몰이해와 소외의 감정을 느끼게 한다. 이것의 한 예를 *Not Without My Daughter*에서 볼 수 있다. 주인공 Betty Mahmoody가 페르시아어를 하지 못하기 때문에 이란인 등장인물들이 하는 페르시아어 대화에는 자막이 없으며, 관객은 그녀의 시각에서 영화를 보고 있게 된다.

Why? 왜 정답일까?

외국어 대화가 자막 없이 사용되는 경우는 그 언어를 할 줄 모르는 특정 등장인물의 시점에서 사건을 보게 만든다(~ if the movie is seen mainly from the viewpoint of a particular character who does not speak the language.)는 설명으로 보아, 빈칸에 들어갈 말로 가장 적절한 것은 ① '그녀의 시각에서 영화를 보고 있게'이다.

- translate ⓥ 번역하다, 통역하다
- viewpoint ⓝ 관점, 시점
- occasion ⓝ 경우, 때
- absence ⓝ 부재

구문 풀이

3행 However, there are occasions [when foreign dialogue is left unsubtitled (and thus incomprehensible to most of the target audience)].

★★★ 1등급 대비 고난도 2점 문제

08 | 실수를 통한 이익 | 정답률 36% | 정답 ①

다음 빈칸에 들어갈 말로 가장 적절한 것을 고르시오.

✔ share the benefits - 이익들을 공유해서
② overlook the insights - 통찰력을 간과해서
③ develop creative skills - 창의력을 발달시켜서
④ exaggerate the achievements - 성취를 과장해서
⑤ underestimate the knowledge - 지식을 과소평가해서

One big difference between science and stage magic / is / that while magicians hide their mistakes from the audience, / in science / you make your mistakes in public.

과학과 무대 마술 사이의 한 가지 큰 차이점은 / ~이다. / 마술사들이 실수를 관중에게 숨기는 반면, / 과학에서는 / 공공연히 실수를 한다는 것

You show them off / so that everybody can learn from them.

당신은 실수를 드러내 보여준다. / 모두가 실수로부터 배울 수 있도록

This way, / you get the advantage of everybody else's experience, / and not just your own idiosyncratic path / through the space of mistakes.

이런 식으로, / 당신은 다른 모든 사람들의 경험이라는 이익을 얻는다. / 당신 자신만의 특유한 길뿐만 아니라, / 실수라는 영역을 거쳐 온

This, by the way, is another reason / why we humans are so much smarter / than every other species.

한편, 이는 또 다른 이유이다. / 왜 우리 인간이 훨씬 더 영리한지에 대한 / 다른 모든 종보다

It is not that our brains are bigger or more powerful, / or even that we have the ability / to reflect on our own past errors, / but that we share the benefits / that our individual brains have earned / from their individual histories of trial and error.

그것은 우리의 뇌가 더 크거나 더 강력해서, / 혹은 심지어 우리가 능력을 가져서가 아니라, / 우리 자신의 과거 실수들을 반추하는 / 우리가 이익들을 공유해서이다. / 우리 개개인들의 뇌가 얻어낸 / 각자 자신의 시행착오의 역사로부터

과학과 무대 마술 사이의 한 가지 큰 차이점은 마술사들이 실수를 관중에게 숨기는 반면, 과학에서는 공공연히 실수를 한다는 것이다. 당신은 모두가 실수로부터 배울 수 있도록 실수를 드러내 보여준다. 이런 식으로, 당신은 실수라는 영역을 거쳐 온 당신 자신만의 특유한 길(에서 얻은 이익)뿐만 아니라, 다른 모든 사람들의 경험이라는 이익을 얻는다. 한편, 이는 왜 우리 인간이 다른 모든 종보다 훨씬 더 영리한지에 대한 또 다른 이유이다. 그것은 우리의 뇌가 더 크거나 더 강력해서, 혹은 심지어 우리가 우리 자신의 과거 실수들을 반추하는 능력을 가져서가 아니라, 우리 개개인들의 뇌가 각자 자신의 시행착오의 역사로부터 얻어낸 <u>이익들을 공유해서</u>이다.

Why? 왜 정답일까?

'You show them off so that everybody can learn from them. This way, you get the advantage of everybody else's experience, ~'에서 서로 실수를 드러내 보여주면 실수를 통해 얻은 경험과 이익을 공유할 수 있다고 했다. 이를 근거로 볼 때, 인간이 똑똑한 이유를 설명하는 마지막 문장이 '실수로 인한 이익이 공유되기' 때문이라는 의미가 되어야 하므로, 빈칸에 들어갈 말로 가장 적절한 것은 ① '이익들을 공유해서'이다.

- advantage ⓝ 이점
- reflect on ~을 반추하다
- overlook ⓥ 간과하다, 못 보고 넘어가다
- underestimate ⓥ 과소평가하다
- species ⓝ (생물) 종
- trial and error 시행착오
- exaggerate ⓥ 과장하다

구문 풀이

9행 It is not {that our brains are bigger or more powerful}, or even
　　　　　 ⌐not＋A　　　　　　　　　　　　　　　　　 or A'＋
{that we have the ability to reflect on our own past errors}, but {that
　　　　　　　　　　　　　　　　　 but＋B : A나 A'가 아니라 B인 (A, A', B 자리에 모두 that절)
we share the benefits [that our individual brains have earned from
　　　　　　선행사　　　　　목적격 관·대
their individual histories of trial and error]}.

★★ 문제 해결 꿀~팁 ★★

▶ 많이 틀린 이유는?
첫 두 문장에서 모두가 배울 수 있도록 실수를 드러내 보이는 것을 글의 주된 소재로 언급하고 있다. 창의력 발달에 관해서는 언급되지 않으므로 ③은 답으로 적절하지 않다.
▶ 문제 해결 방법은?
'You show them[your mistakes] off so that everybody can learn from them. This way, you get the advantage of everybody else's experience, ~'에서 show off가 ①의 share로, advantage가 ①의 benefits로 재진술되었다.

★★★ 1등급 대비 고난도 3점 문제

09 쉽게 얻을 수 없는 것의 매력　　　　　 정답률 47% | 정답 ⑤

다음 빈칸에 들어갈 말로 가장 적절한 것을 고르시오. [3점]
① distrust - 불신
② difference - 차이
③ intelligence - 지능
④ irresponsibility - 무책임
✔ unavailability - 만날 수 없음

People are attracted to individuals and things / they cannot readily obtain.
사람들은 사람이나 사물에 이끌린다. / 그들이 쉽게 얻을 수 없는
In the case with things, / people are more attracted to a desired object / because it is out of their reach.
사물의 경우, / 사람들은 원하는 물건에 더 이끌린다. / 그것이 손에 닿지 않기 때문에
When the object of desire is finally gained, / the attraction for the object rapidly decreases.
마침내 원하는 물건을 얻게 되면, / 그 물건에 대한 매력은 빠르게 감소한다.
Christmas presents / provide a good example of this phenomenon.
크리스마스 선물이 / 이러한 현상의 적합한 예를 제공한다.
Toys children wanted all year long / are thrown away several days / after they are taken from gift boxes under the tree.
아이들이 일 년 내내 원했던 장난감은 / 며칠 뒤에 버려진다. / 그것이 트리 아래 선물 상자에서 꺼내진 후
The phenomenon also holds true for human interaction, / particularly in the early stages of a developing relationship.
그 현상은 사람들의 상호 작용에도 유효하다. / 특히 형성 중인 관계의 초기 단계에서
The common dating rule has scientific merit.
일반적인 데이트 규칙에는 과학적 가치가 있다.
An individual / should not always make himself or herself readily available / to the person / they are targeting for a longer-term relationship.
사람은 / 자기 자신을 항상 쉽게 만날 수 있는 상태로 만들어서는 안 된다. / 사람에게 / 장기적인 관계를 목표로 하고 있는

A certain level of <u>unavailability</u> / will make you more of a mystery and a challenge.
일정 정도의 만날 수 없음이 / 여러분을 더욱 신비롭고 도전적인 존재로 만들어 줄 것이다.

─────────────────────────

사람들은 쉽게 얻을 수 없는 사람이나 사물에 이끌린다. 사물의 경우, 사람들은 원하는 물건이 손에 닿지 않기 때문에 더 이끌린다. 마침내 원하는 물건을 얻게 되면, 그 물건에 대한 매력은 빠르게 감소한다. 크리스마스 선물이 이러한 현상의 적합한 예를 제공한다. 아이들이 일 년 내내 원했던 장난감은 트리 아래 선물 상자에서 꺼내진 후 며칠 뒤에 버려진다. 그 현상은 사람들의 상호 작용, 특히 관계가 형성되는 초기 단계에도 유효하다. 일반적인 데이트 규칙에는 과학적 가치가 있다. 사람은 장기적인 관계를 목표로 하고 있는 사람에게 자기 자신을 항상 쉽게 만나게 해서는 안 된다. 일정 정도의 만날 수 없음이 여러분을 더욱 신비롭고 도전적인 존재로 만들어 줄 것이다.

Why? 왜 정답일까?

사람들은 쉽게 얻을 수 없는 사람이나 사물에 이끌리고(People are attracted to individuals and things they cannot readily obtain.) 원하는 물건을 얻게 되면 그 물건에 대한 매력은 빠르게 감소한다고 한다. 이어서 빈칸 앞의 문장에서는 연인에게 '쉽게 얻기 어려운' 존재가 되어야 한다는 것을 말하고 있으므로, 빈칸에 들어갈 말로 가장 적절한 것은 ⑤ '만날 수 없음'이다.

- attract ⓥ (마음을) 끌다
- obtain ⓥ 얻다
- phenomenon ⓝ 현상
- target ⓥ 목표로 하다
- readily ⓐⓓ 쉽게, 손쉽게
- out of one's reach 손이 닿지 않는 곳에
- hold true (규칙·말 따위가) 유효하다

구문 풀이

7행 Toys [children wanted all year long] are thrown away several
　　　　　　 목적격 관계대명사 생략
days / after they are taken from gift boxes under the tree.
　　　 접속사

★★ 문제 해결 꿀~팁 ★★

▶ 많이 틀린 이유는?
첫 문장과 빈칸 바로 앞 문장에서 힌트를 찾을 수 있기에 쉬운 문제였지만, 정답 선택지의 어휘가 낯설었다면 어렵게 느껴졌을 문제이다. unavailability는 물건의 경우에는 '이용 불가능함', 사람의 경우에는 '만날 수 없음'을 뜻한다.
▶ 문제 해결 방법은?
단어 빈칸은 구 또는 절 빈칸과 달리 논리적 추론 능력에 더불어 어휘 실력까지 갖출 것을 요구하는 문항이다. 평소 필수 어휘집을 가까이 하여 단어 때문에 오답을 내는 경우가 없도록 대비한다.

★★★ 1등급 대비 고난도 3점 문제

10 생물의 진화 방향을 이끄는 실내 공간과 생활　　 정답률 46% | 정답 ③

다음 빈칸에 들어갈 말로 가장 적절한 것을 고르시오. [3점]
① produce chemicals to protect themselves
　스스로를 보호하고자 화학 물질을 만들어낼
② become extinct with the destroyed habitats
　파괴된 서식지와 함께 멸종할
✔ evolve the traits they need to thrive indoors
　실내에서 번성하기 위해 자신에게 필요한 특성들을 진화시킬
④ compete with outside organisms to find their prey
　먹잇감을 찾고자 야외 생물들과 경쟁할
⑤ break the boundaries between wildlife and humans
　야생 종과 인간 사이의 경계를 무너뜨릴

Our homes aren't just ecosystems, / they're unique ones, / hosting species / that are adapted to indoor environments / and pushing evolution in new directions.
우리의 집은 단순한 생태계가 아니라 / 그것은 독특한 곳이며, / 종들을 수용하고 / 실내 환경에 적응된 / 새로운 방향으로 진화를 밀어붙인다.
Indoor microbes, insects, and rats / have all evolved the ability / to survive our chemical attacks, / developing resistance to antibacterials, insecticides, and poisons.
실내 미생물, 곤충, 그리고 쥐들은 / 모두 능력을 진화시켰다. / 우리의 화학적 공격에서 살아남을 수 있는 / 항균제, 살충제, 독에 대한 내성을 키우면서
German cockroaches are known / to have developed a distaste for glucose, / which is commonly used as bait in roach traps.
독일 바퀴벌레는 알려져 있는데 / 포도당에 대한 혐오감을 발달시킨 것으로 / 이것은 바퀴벌레 덫에서 미끼로 흔히 사용된다.

Some indoor insects, / which have fewer opportunities to feed / than their outdoor counterparts, / seem to have developed the ability / to survive when food is limited.
일부 실내 곤충은 / 먹이를 잡아먹을 기회가 더 적은 / 야외에 있는 상대방에 비해 / 능력을 발달시킨 것으로 보인다. / 먹이가 제한적일 때 생존할 수 있는

Dunn and other ecologists have suggested / that as the planet becomes more developed and more urban, / more species will evolve the traits / they need to thrive indoors.
Dunn과 다른 생태학자들은 말했다. / 지구가 점점 더 발전되고 도시화되면서, / 더 많은 종들이 특성들을 진화시킬 것이라고 / 실내에서 번성하기 위해 자신에게 필요한

Over a long enough time period, / indoor living could drive our evolution, too.
충분히 긴 시간에 걸쳐, / 실내 생활은 또한 우리의 진화를 이끌 수 있었다.

Perhaps my indoorsy self represents the future of humanity.
아마도 실내 생활을 좋아하는 나의 모습은 인류의 미래를 대변할 것이다.

───────────────

우리의 집은 단순한 생태계가 아니라 독특한 곳이며, 실내 환경에 적응된 종들을 수용하고 새로운 방향으로 진화를 밀어붙인다. 실내 미생물, 곤충, 그리고 쥐들은 모두 항균제, 살충제, 독에 대한 내성을 키우면서 우리의 화학적 공격에서 살아남을 수 있는 능력을 진화시켰다. 독일 바퀴벌레는 바퀴벌레 덫에서 미끼로 흔히 사용되는 포도당에 대한 혐오감을 발달시킨 것으로 알려져 있다. 야외에 있는 상대방에 비해 먹이를 잡아먹을 기회가 더 적은 일부 실내 곤충은 먹이가 제한적일 때 생존할 수 있는 능력을 발달시킨 것으로 보인다. Dunn과 다른 생태학자들은 지구가 점점 더 발전되고 도시화되면서, 더 많은 종들이 실내에서 번성하기 위해 자신에게 필요한 특성들을 진화시킬 것이라고 말했다. 충분히 긴 시간에 걸쳐, 실내 생활은 또한 우리의 진화를 이끌 수 있었다. 아마도 실내 생활을 좋아하는 나의 모습은 인류의 미래를 대변할 것이다.

Why? 왜 정답일까?

첫 문장과 빈칸 뒤의 문장에서 집, 즉 실내 공간이 우리 진화를 이끌어 간다(indoor living could drive our evolution)는 주제를 반복하여 제시한다. 따라서 빈칸에 들어갈 말로 가장 적절한 것은 우리가 실내 생활에 필요한 방향으로 발전해 간다는 의미의 ③ '실내에서 번성하기 위해 자신에게 필요한 특성들을 진화시킬'이다.

- host ⓥ 접대하다, 주최하다
- resistance ⓝ 내성, 저항력
- insecticide ⓝ 살충제
- distaste ⓝ 혐오
- bait ⓝ 미끼
- ecologist ⓝ 생태학자
- extinct ⓐ 멸종한
- prey ⓝ 먹잇감
- microbe ⓝ 미생물
- antibacterial ⓐ 항균성의 ⓝ 항균제
- cockroach ⓝ 바퀴벌레
- glucose ⓝ 포도당
- counterpart ⓝ 상대방, 대응물
- represent ⓥ 표현하다, 나타내다
- habitat ⓝ 서식지

구문 풀이

6행 German cockroaches are known to have developed a
「be known + to have p.p. : ~했다고 알려지다(완료부정사)」
distaste for glucose, which is commonly used as bait in roach traps.
선행사   계속적 용법(보충 설명)

★★ 문제 해결 꿀~팁 ★★

▶ 많이 틀린 이유는?
chemical attacks 등 지엽적 소재만 보면 ①을 답으로 고르기 쉽다. 하지만 풀이의 핵심은 생태계의 생명체들이 '어떤 방향으로' 진화하도록 유도되어 왔는지를 파악하는 데 있다.

▶ 문제 해결 방법은?
빈칸 뒤를 보면 '실내 생활이 우리 진화를 이끌 수 있었다(indoor living could drive our evolution)'는 결론이 나온다. 이 결론과 동일한 말이 빈칸에도 들어갈 것이다.

★★★ 1등급 대비 고난도 3점 문제

| **11** | 홈 이점이 발휘되지 못하는 경우 | 정답률 19% | 정답 ① |

다음 빈칸에 들어갈 말로 가장 적절한 것을 고르시오. [3점]
✔ often welcome a road trip – 길을 떠나는 것을 흔히 반길
② avoid international matches – 국제적 경기를 피할
③ focus on increasing ticket sales – 티켓 매출을 높이는 데 집중할
④ want to have an eco-friendly stadium – 친환경적인 경기장을 갖기를 원할
⑤ try to advertise their upcoming games – 다가오는 경기를 광고하려 애쓸

───────────────

One dynamic that can change dramatically in sport / is the concept of the home-field advantage, / in which perceived demands and resources seem to play a role.
스포츠에서 극적으로 바뀔 수 있는 한 가지 역학은 / 홈 이점이라는 개념으로, / 여기에는 인식된 부담과 자원이 역할을 하는 것처럼 보인다.

Under normal circumstances, / the home ground would appear / to provide greater perceived resources / (fans, home field, and so on).
일반적인 상황에서, / 홈그라운드는 보일 것이다. / 인식된 자원을 더 많이 제공하는 것처럼 / (팬, 홈 경기장 등)

However, / researchers Roy Baumeister and Andrew Steinhilber / were among the first / to point out / that these competitive factors can change; / for example, / the success percentage for home teams / in the final games of a playoff or World Series / seems to drop.
하지만, / 연구원 Roy Baumeister와 Andrew Steinhilber는 / 최초의 사람들 중 하나였다. / 지적한 / 이러한 경쟁력이 있는 요소들이 바뀔 수도 있다고 / 예를 들어, / 홈 팀들의 성공률은 / 우승 결정전이나 미국 프로 야구 선수권의 마지막 경기에서 / 떨어지는 것처럼 보인다.

Fans can become part of the perceived demands / rather than resources / under those circumstances.
팬들은 인식된 부담의 일부가 될 수 있다. / 자원보다는 / 이러한 상황에서

This change in perception can also explain / why a team that's struggling at the start of the year / will often welcome a road trip / to reduce perceived demands and pressures.
이러한 인식의 변화는 또한 설명할 수 있다. / 왜 연초에 고전하는 팀이 / 길을 떠나는 것을 흔히 반길 것인지 / 인식된 부담과 압박을 줄이기 위해

───────────────

스포츠에서 극적으로 바뀔 수 있는 한 가지 역학은 홈 이점이라는 개념으로, 여기에는 인식되는 부담과 자원이 일조하는 것처럼 보인다. 일반적인 상황에서, 홈그라운드는 인식되는 자원(팬, 홈 경기장 등)을 더 많이 제공하는 것처럼 보일 것이다. 하지만, 연구원 Roy Baumeister와 Andrew Steinhilber는 이러한 경쟁력이 있는 요소들이 바뀔 수도 있다고 처음으로 지적한 사람 중 하나였다. 예를 들어, 우승 결정전이나 미국 프로 야구 선수권의 마지막 경기에서 홈 팀들의 성공률은 떨어지는 것처럼 보인다. 이러한 상황에서 팬들은 자원보다는 인식되는 부담의 일부가 될 수 있다. 이러한 인식의 변화는 왜 연초에 고전하는 팀이 인식되는 부담과 압박을 줄이기 위해 길을 떠나는 것(원정 경기를 가는 것)을 흔히 반길 것인지 또한 설명할 수 있다.

Why? 왜 정답일까?

홈그라운드의 이점은 부담에 대한 인식이나 자원에 의해 뒤집힐 수 있다(~ the concept of the home-field advantage, in which perceived demands and resources seem to play a role.)는 내용의 글이다. for example 뒤로 결승전 등 중요한 경기에서 팬들은 선수들에게 자원이 아닌 부담일 수 있기에 도리어 홈 팀의 성적이 부진해질 수 있다고 한다. 이를 근거로 볼 때, 마지막 문장은 부진하는 팀이 도리어 부담을 피하고자 '홈그라운드에서의 경기를 피한다'는 내용일 것이다. 따라서 빈칸에 들어갈 말로 가장 적절한 것은 ① '길을 떠나는 것을 흔히 반길'이다.

- play a role in ~에 역할을 하다, 일조하다
- perception ⓝ 인식
- competitive ⓐ 경쟁력 있는
- struggle ⓥ 고전하다, 분투하다

구문 풀이

1행 One dynamic [that can change dramatically in sport] is
주어(선행사)   주격 관계대명사   동사(단수)
the concept of the home-field advantage, in which perceived
보어(선행사)   「전치사+관계대명사」
demands and resources seem to play a role.

★★ 문제 해결 꿀~팁 ★★

▶ 많이 틀린 이유는?
home-field advantage만 보면 정답과 정반대되는 의미의 ②를 고르기 쉽다. 하지만 사실 이 글은 '홈 구장의 이점'을 긍정하는 글이 아니라 이 이점이 '없을 수도 있는' 경우에 대한 글이다.

▶ 문제 해결 방법은?
for example 뒤에서, 홈 팀의 결승전 승률이 '떨어지는' 것처럼 보인다는 예를 제시한다. 이 점이 어떤 결과를 불러올까 생각해보면, 연초에 고전 중인 팀은 오히려 '홈 팀에서 경기하기를 꺼릴' 수도 있다는 추론이 가능하다.

★★★ 1등급 대비 고난도 3점 문제

| **12** | 의뢰인의 속마음을 드러내준 의뢰인의 발 | 정답률 40% | 정답 ④ |

다음 빈칸에 들어갈 말로 가장 적절한 것을 고르시오. [3점]
① a signal of his politeness – 그의 공손함의 표시
② the subject of the conversation – 대화의 주제

③ expressing interest in my words – 내 말에 관심을 나타내고 있는
✔ the most honest communicators – 가장 정직한 의사 전달자
⑤ stepping excitedly onto the ground – 발을 경쾌하게 내딛고 있는

Recently I was with a client / who had spent almost five hours with me.
최근에 나는 고객과 함께 있었다. / 나와 거의 5시간을 보낸

As we were parting for the evening, / we reflected on what we had covered that day.
저녁을 위해 헤어지면서, / 우리는 그날 다룬 내용을 되새겼다.

Even though our conversation was very collegial, / I noticed / that my client was holding one leg at a right angle to his body, / seemingly wanting to take off on its own.
비록 우리의 대화가 매우 평등했음에도 불구하고, / 나는 알아챘는데, / 나의 고객이 한쪽 다리를 몸과 직각으로 두고 있다는 것을 / 외견상 (한쪽 다리가) 혼자서 떠나고 싶어 하는 것 같았다.

At that point I said, / "You really do have to leave now, don't you?"
그때 나는 말했다. / "지금 정말 가셔야 하죠, 그렇지 않나요?"라고

"Yes," he admitted.
"네."라고 그는 인정했다.

"I am so sorry. / I didn't want to be rude / but I have to call London and I only have five minutes!"
"정말 미안합니다. / 무례하게 굴고 싶지는 않았지만 / 전 런던에 전화해야 하는데 시간이 5분밖에 없어요!"

Here was a case / where my client's language and most of his body / revealed nothing but positive feelings.
이것은 상황이었다. / 내 의뢰인의 언어와 그의 몸의 대부분은 / 긍정적인 감정만을 드러냈던

His feet, however, were the most honest communicators, / and they clearly told me / that as much as he wanted to stay, duty was calling.
그러나 그의 발은 가장 정직한 의사 전달자였고 / 그것들은 내게 분명히 나타냈다. / 그가 남아있고 싶어 하지만 일이 그를 부르고 있다는 것을

최근에 나는 나와 거의 5시간을 보낸 고객과 함께 있었다. 저녁을 위해 헤어지면서, 우리는 그날 다룬 내용을 되새겼다. 비록 우리의 대화가 매우 평등했음에도 불구하고, 나는 나의 고객이 한쪽 다리를 몸과 직각으로 두고 있다는 것을 알아챘는데, 외견상 (한쪽 다리가) 혼자서 떠나고 싶어 하는 것 같았다. 그때 나는 "지금 정말 가셔야 하죠, 그렇지 않나요?"라고 말했다. "네."라고 그는 인정했다. "정말 미안합니다. 무례하게 굴고 싶지는 않았지만 런던에 전화해야 하는데 시간이 5분밖에 없어요!" 여기서 내 의뢰인의 언어와 그의 몸의 대부분은 긍정적인 감정만을 드러내고 있었다. 그러나 그의 발은 가장 정직한 의사 전달자였고 그것들은 그가 남아있고 싶어 하지만 해야 할 일이 있다는 것을 분명히 나타냈다.

Why? 왜 정답일까?

'~ I noticed that my client was holding one leg at a right angle to his body, seemingly wanting to take off on its own.'에서 필자는 의뢰인이 한쪽 발을 몸과 직각으로 위치하게 빼둔 것을 보고 의뢰인이 빨리 가야 한다고 생각하고 있음을 눈치챘다고 하므로, 빈칸에 들어갈 말로 가장 적절한 것은 발이 의뢰인의 속마음을 드러내 주었다는 의미를 나타내는 ④ '가장 정직한 의사 전달자'이다.

- reflect on ⓥ ~을 되새기다, 반추하다
- right angle ⓝ 직각
- rude ⓐ 무례한
- communicator ⓝ 의사 전달자
- cover ⓥ (기사 등에서) 다루다
- take off ⓥ 떠나다
- politeness ⓝ 공손함
- excitedly ⓐⓓ 신나게, 들떠서

구문 풀이

12행 His feet, however, were the most honest communicators,
주어1 / 동사1

and they clearly told me that as much as he wanted to stay, duty
주어2 / 동사2 / '(문두의) as + 원급 + as : ~하기는 하지만' / 주어
접속사(~것)

was calling.
동사

★★ 문제 해결 꿀~팁 ★★

▶ 많이 틀린 이유는?
일화가 나오면 부분적인 표현에 집중하기보다 이야기의 전체적인 흐름을 파악해야 한다. ①은 본문의 'I didn't want to be rude ~'만, ⑤는 '~ seemingly wanting to take off on its own.'만 보았을 때 각각 고르기 쉬운 오답이다.

▶ 문제 해결 방법은?
이 일화의 핵심은 필자의 고객이 말이나 몸 자체로 대체로 긍정적인 신호를 나타내고 있었음에도 불구하고 유일하게 '몸과 직각을 이루며 떠나고 싶어 하는 것처럼 보였던' 그의 발이 그의 진심을 대변해주고 있었다는 것이다. 이렇듯 이야기 흐름의 큰 줄기를 파악한 후 이를 토대로 추론할 수 있는 논리적인 결론을 선택지에서 찾도록 한다.

DAY 11 　글의 순서 01

01 ⑤	02 ②	03 ⑤	04 ③	05 ③
06 ④	07 ②	08 ②	09 ⑤	10 ③
11 ②	12 ④			

01　생산성과 노동 분업　정답률 68% | 정답 ⑤

주어진 글 다음에 이어질 글의 순서로 가장 적절한 것을 고르시오.

① (A) - (C) - (B)
② (B) - (A) - (C)
③ (B) - (C) - (A)
④ (C) - (A) - (B)
✔ (C) - (B) - (A)

Managers are always looking for ways / to increase productivity, / which is the ratio of costs to output in production.
관리자들은 항상 방법을 찾고 있는데, / 생산성을 높일 수 있는 / 이것은 생산에서 비용 대비 생산량의 비율이다.

Adam Smith, / writing when the manufacturing industry was new, / described a way / that production could be made more efficient, / known as the "division of labor."
Adam Smith는 / 제조 산업이 새로 등장했을 때 저술한 / 방식을 설명했다 / 생산이 더 효율적으로 될 수 있는 / 이것은 '노동 분업'으로 알려져 있다.

(C) Making most manufactured goods / involves several different processes / using different skills.
대부분의 공산품을 만드는 것은 / 여러 가지 다른 과정을 포함한다. / 다른 기술을 사용하는

Smith's example was the manufacture of pins: / the wire is straightened, / sharpened, / a head is put on, / and then it is polished.
Smith의 예는 핀의 제조였다. / 철사가 곧게 펴지고, / 뾰족해지고, / 머리가 끼워지고, / 그러고 나서 그것은 다듬어진다.

(B) One worker could do all these tasks, / and make 20 pins in a day.
한 명의 노동자가 이 모든 작업들을 할 수 있고, / 하루에 20개의 핀을 만들 수도 있다.

But this work can be divided into its separate processes, / with a number of workers each performing one task.
그러나 이 일은 별개의 과정으로 분리될 수 있다. / 많은 노동자가 각각 한 가지 작업을 수행하며

(A) Because each worker specializes in one job, / he or she can work much faster / without changing from one task to another.
각 노동자는 한 가지 작업을 전문으로 하기 때문에, / 이 사람은 훨씬 더 빠르게 일할 수 있다. / 한 작업에서 다른 작업으로 옮겨가지 않으면서

Now 10 workers can produce thousands of pins in a day / — a huge increase in productivity / from the 200 / they would have produced before.
이제 10명의 노동자가 하루에 수천 개의 핀을 생산할 수 있다. / 이는 큰 증가이다. / 이는 생산성의 큰 증가이다. / 200개로부터 / 이전에 그들이 생산했던

관리자들은 항상 생산성을 높일 수 있는 방법을 찾고 있는데, 생산성은 생산에서 비용 대비 생산량의 비율이다. 제조 산업이 새로 등장했을 때 저술한 Adam Smith는 생산이 더 효율적으로 될 수 있는 방식을 설명했고, 이것은 '노동 분업'으로 알려져 있다.

(C) 대부분의 공산품을 만드는 것은 다른 기술을 사용하는 여러 가지 다른 과정을 포함한다. Smith의 예는 핀의 제조였다. 철사를 곧게 펴고, 뾰족하게 만들고, 머리를 끼운 다음, 그것을 다듬는다.

(B) 한 명의 노동자가 이 모든 작업들을 할 수 있고, 하루에 20개의 핀을 만들 수도 있다. 그러나 이 일은 많은 노동자가 각각 한 가지 작업을 수행하며 별개의 과정으로 분리될 수 있다.

(A) 각 노동자는 한 가지 작업을 전문으로 하기 때문에, 이 사람은 한 작업에서 다른 작업으로 옮겨가지 않으면서 훨씬 더 빠르게 일할 수 있다. 이제 10명의 노동자가 하루에 수천 개의 핀을 생산할 수 있다. 이는 이전에 그들이 생산했던 200개로부터 생산성 측면에서 크게 증가한 것이다.

Why? 왜 정답일까?

'노동 분업'의 개념을 소개하는 주어진 글 뒤로, 핀 제조 과정을 예로 설명하는 (C), 이 제조 과정은 한 사람에 의해 수행될 수도 있지만, 분업으로 진행될 수도 있다고 설명하는 (B), 분업 상황의 장점을 소개하는 (A)가 차례로 이어져야 자연스럽다. 따라서 글의 순서로 가장 적절한 것은 ⑤ '(C) - (B) - (A)'이다.

- ratio ⓝ 비율
- manufacturing industry 제조업
- efficient ⓐ 효율적인
- output ⓝ 산출
- describe ⓥ 설명하다
- division of labor 분업

- specialize in ~에 특화되다
- involve ⓥ 포함하다, 수반하다
- sharpen ⓥ 뾰족하게 하다

- a number of 많은
- straighten ⓥ 곧게 펴다
- polish ⓥ 다듬다

구문 풀이

14행 But this work can be divided into its separate processes, with a number of workers each performing one task.
「with + 명사 + 분사 : ~이 …한 채로(부대상황 분사구문)」

---

02 식량 문제와 그 해결 정답률 64% | 정답 ②

주어진 글 다음에 이어질 글의 순서로 가장 적절한 것을 고르시오.

① (A) - (C) - (B) ✔(B) - (A) - (C)
③ (B) - (C) - (A) ④ (C) - (A) - (B)
⑤ (C) - (B) - (A)

With nearly a billion hungry people in the world, / there is obviously no single cause.
전 세계에 거의 10억 명의 굶주리는 사람들이 있는데, / 분명 원인이 단 하나만 있는 것은 아니다.
(B) However, / far and away the biggest cause is poverty.
그렇지만, / 가장 큰 원인은 단연 빈곤이다.
Seventy-nine percent of the world's hungry / live in nations / that are net exporters of food.
세계의 굶주리는 사람들의 79퍼센트가 / 나라에 살고 있다. / 식량 순 수출국인
How can this be?
어떻게 이럴 수가 있을까?
(A) The reason people are hungry in those countries / is / that the products produced there / can be sold on the world market for more / than the local citizens can afford to pay for them.
그러한 국가에서 사람들이 굶주리는 이유는 / ~이다. / 그곳에서 생산된 산물들이 / 세계 시장에서 더 비싸게 팔릴 수 있기 때문이다. / 현지 시민들이 그것들에 지불할 수 있는 것보다
In the modern age / you do not starve because you have no food, / you starve because you have no money.
현대에는 / 여러분이 식량이 없어서 굶주리는 것이 아니라, / 여러분은 돈이 없어서 굶주리는 것이다.
(C) So the problem really is / that food is, in the grand scheme of things, too expensive / and many people are too poor to buy it.
그래서 진짜 문제는 ~이다. / 식량이 거대한 체계로 볼 때 너무 비싸고 / 많은 사람들은 너무 가난하여 그것을 구매할 수 없다는 것
The answer will be / in continuing the trend of lowering the cost of food.
해답은 있을 것이다. / 식량의 가격을 낮추는 추세를 지속하는 데

전 세계에 거의 10억 명의 굶주리는 사람들이 있는데, 분명 원인이 단 하나만 있는 것은 아니다.
(B) 그렇지만, 가장 큰 원인은 단연 빈곤이다. 세계의 굶주리는 사람들의 79퍼센트가 식량 순 수출국에 살고 있다. 어떻게 이럴 수가 있을까?
(A) 그러한 국가에서 사람들이 굶주리는 이유는 그곳에서 생산된 산물들이 현지 시민들이 그것들에 지불할 수 있는 것보다 더 비싸게 세계 시장에서 팔릴 수 있기 때문이다. 현대에는 여러분이 식량이 없어서 굶주리는 것이 아니라, 돈이 없어서 굶주리는 것이다.
(C) 그래서 진짜 문제는 거대한 체계로 볼 때 식량이 너무 비싸고 많은 사람들은 너무 가난하여 그것을 구매할 수 없다는 것이다. 해답은 식량의 가격을 낮추는 추세를 지속하는 데 있을 것이다.

Why? 왜 정답일까?

식량 문제의 원인이 다양함을 언급하는 주어진 글 뒤로, 빈곤이 가장 큰 원인임을 제시하는 (B), 빈곤한 국가의 굶주리는 사람들은 말 그대로 돈이 없어서 굶주린다는 설명을 이어 가는 (A), 해결책을 언급하며 글을 맺는 (C)가 차례로 이어져야 한다. 따라서 글의 순서로 가장 적절한 것은 ② '(B) - (A) - (C)'이다.

- billion ⓝ 10억
- afford to ~할 여유가 되다
- poverty ⓝ 가난, 빈곤

- obviously ⓐⓓ 분명히
- starve ⓥ 굶주리다

구문 풀이

3행 The reason (that) people are hungry in those countries is
주어 / 생략 / 동사(단수)
that the products produced there can be sold on the world market
접속사(~것) / 조동사 수동태(조동사+be p.p.)
for more than the local citizens can afford to pay for them.

---

03 인간 창조에 관한 신화 정답률 60% | 정답 ⑤

주어진 글 다음에 이어질 글의 순서로 가장 적절한 것을 고르시오.

① (A) - (C) - (B) ② (B) - (A) - (C)
③ (B) - (C) - (A) ④ (C) - (A) - (B)
✔(C) - (B) - (A)

A god called Moinee was defeated / by a rival god called Dromerdeener / in a terrible battle up in the stars.
Moinee라는 신이 패배했다. / Dromerdeener이라는 이름의 라이벌 신에게 / 하늘 위 별에서 벌어진 끔찍한 전투에서
Moinee fell out of the stars down to Tasmania to die.
Moinee는 별에서 Tasmania로 떨어져 죽었다.
(C) Before he died, / he wanted to give a last blessing to his final resting place, / so he decided to create humans.
그가 죽기 전에 / 그는 최후의 안식처에 마지막 축복을 해주고 싶어서 / 인간을 창조하기로 결심했다.
But he was in such a hurry, / knowing he was dying, / that he forgot to give them knees; / and he absent-mindedly gave them big tails like kangaroos, / which meant they couldn't sit down.
그러나 그는 매우 서둘렀기에 / 자신이 죽어가고 있다는 것을 알고 / 그들에게 무릎을 만들어 주는 것을 잊었고, / 그는 아무 생각 없이 캥거루처럼 큰 꼬리를 만들어 주었는데, / 그것은 그들이 앉을 수 없다는 것을 의미했다.
(B) Then he died.
그리고 나서 그는 죽었다.
The people hated having kangaroo tails and no knees, / and they cried out to the heavens for help.
사람들은 캥거루 같은 꼬리가 있고 무릎이 없는 것을 싫어했고, / 그들은 도움을 얻고자 하늘에 외쳤다.
Dromerdeener heard their cry / and came down to Tasmania to see what the matter was.
Dromerdeener는 그들의 외침을 듣고 / 무엇이 문제인지 보려고 Tasmania로 내려왔다.
(A) He took pity on the people, / gave them bendable knees / and cut off their inconvenient kangaroo tails / so they could all sit down at last.
그는 사람들을 불쌍히 여겨서 / 그들에게 구부러지는 무릎을 만들어 주고, / 그들의 불편한 캥거루 꼬리를 잘라냈다. / 마침내 그들이 모두 앉을 수 있도록
Then they lived happily ever after.
그 후 사람들은 영원히 행복하게 살았다.

Moinee라는 신이 하늘 위 별에서 벌어진 끔찍한 전투에서 Dromerdeener이라는 이름의 라이벌 신에게 패배했다. Moinee는 별에서 Tasmania로 떨어져 죽었다.
(C) 죽기 전에 그는 최후의 안식처에 마지막 축복을 해주고 싶어서 인간을 창조하기로 결심했다. 그러나 그는 자신이 죽어가고 있다는 것을 알고 매우 서둘렀기에 그들에게 무릎을 만들어 주는 것을 잊고, 아무 생각 없이 캥거루처럼 큰 꼬리를 만들어 주었는데, 그것은 그들이 앉을 수 없다는 것을 의미했다.
(B) 그리고 나서 그는 죽었다. 사람들은 캥거루 같은 꼬리가 있고 무릎이 없는 것을 싫어했고, 도움을 얻고자 하늘에 외쳤다. Dromerdeener는 그들의 외침을 듣고 무엇이 문제인지 보려고 Tasmania로 내려왔다.
(A) 그는 사람들을 불쌍히 여겨서 그들에게 구부러지는 무릎을 만들어 주고, 마침내 그들이 모두 앉을 수 있도록 불편한 캥거루 꼬리를 잘라냈다. 그 후 사람들은 영원히 행복하게 살았다.

Why? 왜 정답일까?

Moinee라는 신이 Dromerdeener와의 싸움에서 패배해서 죽게 되었다는 내용의 주어진 글 뒤에는, Moinee가 죽기 전에 서둘러 인간을 만들었는데 무릎이 없고 대신에 꼬리가 달린 형태였다는 내용의 (C), 그의 사후 사람들이 불편함을 해결하고자 하늘에 도움을 요청했다는 내용의 (B), Dromerdeener가 이 외침을 듣고 내려와 꼬리를 없애고 무릎을 만들어 주었다는 내용의 (A)가 차례로 이어져야 한다. 따라서 글의 순서로 가장 적절한 것은 ⑤ '(C) - (B) - (A)'이다.

- defeat ⓥ 패배시키다
- take pity on ⓥ ~을 불쌍히 여기다
- inconvenient ⓐ 불편한
- resting place ⓝ 안식처

- fall out of ⓥ ~에서 떨어지다
- bendable ⓐ 구부릴 수 있는
- blessing ⓝ 축복
- absent-mindedly ⓐⓓ 아무 생각 없이

구문 풀이

14행 But he was in such a hurry, knowing he was dying, that he
「such ~ that … : 너무 ~해서 하다」
forgot to give them knees; and he absent-mindedly gave them big
~할 것을 잊다 / 선행사
tails like kangaroos, which meant they couldn't sit down.
계속적 용법

04 목표를 더 효율적으로 달성할 수 있는 방법 찾기 정답률 64% | 정답 ③

주어진 글 다음에 이어질 글의 순서로 가장 적절한 것을 고르시오.

① (A) – (C) – (B)
② (B) – (A) – (C)
✓③ (B) – (C) – (A)
④ (C) – (A) – (B)
⑤ (C) – (B) – (A)

When you look at a map, / you may conclude / — as commercial airline navigators once did — / that the best way to get from Amsterdam to Tokyo / is to head in an easterly direction / along what is known as the Mediterranean route.
여러분이 지도를 보면 / 여러분은 결론 내릴지도 모른다. / 민간 항공사 조종사들이 한때 그랬듯이 / 암스테르담에서 도쿄로 가는 가장 좋은 방법은 / 동쪽 방향으로 가는 것이라고 / 지중해 노선이라고 알려진 것을 따라서

(B) But look at a globe instead of a map, / and your perspective may change.
하지만 지도 대신 지구본을 보라. / 그러면 여러분의 관점이 바뀔지도 모른다.

Rather than heading east on the Mediterranean route, / commercial planes going from Amsterdam to Tokyo / now fly north!
지중해 노선상 동쪽으로 가기보다는 / 암스테르담에서 도쿄로 가는 민항기는 / 이제 북쪽으로 비행한다!

That's right.
그것이 맞다.

(C) They take what is known as the 'polar route,' / flying over the North Pole to Alaska, and then west to Tokyo — / for a savings of roughly 1,500 miles!
그들은 '북극 노선'이라고 알려진 것을 택해, / 북극을 넘어 알래스카로 비행하고 그러고 나서 도쿄를 향해 서쪽으로 비행한다! / 대략 1,500마일을 절약하기 위해

What is the lesson here?
여기에서 교훈이 무엇인가?

(A) After you've decided on a goal, / work hard to accomplish it, / but keep looking for ways / of achieving the goal more efficiently, / perhaps from a different angle.
여러분이 목표를 정한 뒤 / 그것을 달성하기 위해 열심히 노력하되, / 방법을 계속 찾아라. / 그 목표를 더 효율적으로 달성하기 위한 / 아마도 다른 관점에서

This approach is sometimes known as *reframing*.
때때로 이 접근 방식은 *재구성*이라고 알려져 있다.

민간 항공사 조종사들이 한때 그랬듯이 지도를 보면 여러분은 암스테르담에서 도쿄로 가는 가장 좋은 방법은 지중해 노선이라고 알려진 것을 따라서 동쪽 방향으로 가는 것이라고 결론 내릴지도 모른다.

(B) 하지만 지도 대신 지구본을 보면, 관점이 바뀔지도 모른다. 지중해 노선상 동쪽으로 가기보다는 암스테르담에서 도쿄로 가는 민항기는 이제 북쪽으로 비행한다! 그것이 맞다.

(C) 대략 1,500마일을 절약하기 위해, 그들은 '북극 노선'이라고 알려진 것을 택해, 북극을 넘어 알래스카로 비행하고 그러고 나서 도쿄를 향해 서쪽으로 비행한다! 여기에서 교훈이 무엇인가?

(A) 목표를 정한 뒤 그것을 달성하기 위해 열심히 노력하되, 아마도 다른 관점에서 그 목표를 더 효율적으로 달성하기 위한 방법을 계속 찾아라. 때때로 이 접근 방식은 *재구성*이라고 알려져 있다.

Why? 왜 정답일까?

암스테르담에서 도쿄로 가는 가장 좋은 방법은 지중해 노선이라고 알려진 것을 따라서 동쪽 방향으로 가는 것이라는 주어진 글 다음에 지도 대신 지구본을 보면 우리의 관점이 바뀔지도 모른다면서 동쪽으로 가기보다는 북쪽으로 비행하는 것이 맞다고 하는 **(B)**, 다음에 약 **1500**마일을 절약하기 위해 북극을 넘어 알래스카로 비행하고 서쪽을 향해 도쿄로 비행한다는 **(C)**가 이어진 후 다른 관점에서 목표를 더 효율적으로 달성하기 위한 방법을 계속 찾으라고 하며 이 접근 방식을 재구성이라고 말하는 **(A)**가 오는 것이 자연스럽다. 따라서 주어진 글 다음에 이어질 글의 순서로 가장 적절한 것은 ③ '**(B)** – **(C)** – **(A)**'이다.

● **conclude** ⓥ 결론을 내리다
● **navigator** ⓝ 조종사, 항해사
● **accomplish** ⓥ 달성하다, 이룩하다
● **efficiently** [ad] 효율적으로, 능률적으로
● **perspective** ⓝ 관점
● **commercial** ⓐ 민영의, 상업의
● **Mediterranean** ⓐ 지중해의
● **achieve** ⓥ 달성하다, 성취하다
● **reframe** ⓥ 재구성하다
● **roughly** [ad] 대략

구문 풀이

1행 When you look at a map, / you may conclude — as commercial
접속사(~할 때)
airline navigators once did — [that the best way {to get from Amsterdam
접속사   형용사적 용법
to Tokyo}] is to head in an easterly direction along [what is known
is의 보어   관계대명사(~것)
as the Mediterranean route].

---

05 색의 물리적 특성에 대한 연구 정답률 56% | 정답 ③

주어진 글 다음에 이어질 글의 순서로 가장 적절한 것을 고르시오.

① (A) – (C) – (B)
② (B) – (A) – (C)
✓③ (B) – (C) – (A)
④ (C) – (A) – (B)
⑤ (C) – (B) – (A)

The scientific study / of the physical characteristics of colors / can be traced back to Isaac Newton.
과학적 연구는 / 색의 물리적 특성에 관한 / Isaac Newton으로 거슬러 갈 수 있다.

(B) One day, he spotted a set of prisms / at a big county fair.
어느 날, 그는 프리즘 한 세트를 발견했다. / 큰 장터에서

He took them home / and began to experiment with them.
그는 그것들을 집으로 가져와서 / 실험하기 시작했다.

In a darkened room / he allowed a thin ray of sunlight / to fall on a triangular glass prism.
암실에서 / 그는 가느다란 태양광 한 줄기가 ~하게 했다. / 삼각 유리 프리즘 위에 떨어지게

(C) As soon as the white ray hit the prism, / it separated into the familiar colors of the rainbow.
그 백색광이 프리즘에 부딪치자마자 / 그것은 친숙한 무지개 색으로 분리되었다.

This finding was not new, / as humans had observed the rainbow / since the beginning of time.
이 발견은 새로운 것이 아니었다. / 사람들은 무지개를 관찰해 왔기 때문에, / 태초 이래로

(A) It was only when Newton placed a second prism / in the path of the spectrum / that he found something new.
Newton이 두 번째 프리즘을 놓았을 때가, / 스펙트럼의 경로에 / 그가 새로운 점을 발견한 것은

The composite colors produced a white beam.
합성된 색은 흰 빛줄기를 만들어냈다.

Thus he concluded / that white light can be produced / by combining the spectral colors.
그래서 그는 결론 내렸다. / 백색광이 만들어질 수 있다고 / 스펙트럼 색을 혼합하여

색의 물리적 특성에 관한 과학적 연구는 Isaac Newton으로 거슬러 갈 수 있다.

(B) 어느 날, 그는 큰 장터에서 프리즘 한 세트를 발견했다. 그는 그것들을 집으로 가져와서 실험하기 시작했다. 그는 암실에서 가느다란 태양광 한 줄기가 삼각 유리 프리즘 위에 떨어지게 하였다.

(C) 그 백색광은 프리즘에 부딪치자마자 친숙한 무지개 색으로 분리되었다. 사람들은 태초 이래로 무지개를 관찰해 왔기 때문에, 이 발견은 새로운 것이 아니었다.

(A) Newton이 새로운 점을 발견한 것은 스펙트럼의 경로에 두 번째 프리즘을 놓았을 때였다. 합성된 색은 흰 빛줄기를 만들어냈다. 그래서 그는 스펙트럼 색을 혼합하여 백색광이 만들어질 수 있다고 결론 내렸다.

Why? 왜 정답일까?

색의 물리적 특성에 관한 연구를 화제로 꺼내는 주어진 글 뒤에는, **Newton**이 프리즘을 가지고 빛의 색깔에 대해서 실험하기 시작했다는 내용의 **(B)**, 실험의 구체적인 내용을 다루는 **(C)**, 실험에서 발견된 새로운 결론을 소개하는 **(A)**가 차례로 이어지는 것이 적절하다. 따라서 글의 순서로 가장 적절한 것은 ③ '**(B)** – **(C)** – **(A)**'이다.

● **characteristic** ⓝ 특성, 특징
● **path** ⓝ 경로, 길
● **combine** ⓥ 합치다, 결합하다
● **spot** ⓥ 발견하다, 찾다, 알아채다
● **familiar** ⓐ 익숙한
● **be traced back to** ~로 거슬러 올라가다
● **conclude** ⓥ 결론을 내리다, 완결 짓다
● **spectral** ⓐ 스펙트럼의
● **separate into** ~로 분리되다, 분리하다
● **observe** ⓥ 관찰하다, 보다

구문 풀이

3행 It was {only when Newton placed a second prism in the path
「it is + 〔강조어구〕+
of the spectrum} that {he found something new}.
that + 〔나머지 문장〕: 강조구문

---

06 두 변인 사이의 인과관계를 연구할 때 주의할 점 정답률 56% | 정답 ④

주어진 글 다음에 이어질 글의 순서로 가장 적절한 것을 고르시오.

① (A) – (C) – (B)
② (B) – (A) – (C)
③ (B) – (C) – (A)
✓④ (C) – (A) – (B)
⑤ (C) – (B) – (A)

Even though two variables seem to be related, / there may not be a causal relationship.

비록 두 변인이 관련된 것처럼 보일지라도 / 인과 관계가 없을 수도 있다.

(C) In fact, / the two variables may merely seem to be associated with each other / due to the effect of some third variable.
사실, / 그 두 변인은 단지 서로 관련된 것처럼 보일지도 모른다. / 어떤 제3 변인의 영향으로

Sociologists call such misleading relationships spurious.
사회학자들은 이러한 오해의 소지가 있는 관계를 허위라고 부른다.

A classic example is the apparent association / between children's shoe size and reading ability.
전형적인 예는 명백한 연관성이다. / 아이들의 신발 크기와 읽기 능력 사이의

It seems / that as shoe size increases, / reading ability improves.
~한 것처럼 보인다. / 신발 크기가 커질수록, / 읽기 능력이 향상되는

(A) Does this mean / that the size of one's feet (independent variable) / causes an improvement in reading skills (dependent variable)?
이것이 의미하는가? / 사람의 발 크기(독립 변인)가 / 읽기 능력(종속 변인)의 향상을 유발한다는 것을

Certainly not.
물론 아니다.

This false relationship is caused by a third factor, age, / that is related to shoe size as well as reading ability.
이러한 허위 관계는 제3 변인인 연령에 의해 발생한다. / 읽기 능력은 물론 신발 크기와도 관련이 있는

(B) Hence, / when researchers attempt to make causal claims / about the relationship between an independent and a dependent variable, / they must control for — or rule out — other variables / that may be creating a spurious relationship.
따라서, / 연구자들이 인과 관계를 주장하려고 할 때 / 독립 변인과 종속 변인 사이의 관계에 대한 / 그들은 다른 변인들을 통제하거나 배제해야만 한다. / 허위 관계를 만들어 낼 수도 있는

비록 두 변인이 관련된 것처럼 보일지라도 인과 관계가 없을 수도 있다.

(C) 사실, 그 두 변인은 어떤 제3 변인의 영향으로 단지 서로 관련된 것처럼 보일지도 모른다. 사회학자들은 이러한 오해의 소지가 있는 관계를 허위라고 부른다. 전형적인 예는 아이들의 신발 크기와 읽기 능력 사이의 명백한 연관성이다. 신발 크기가 커질수록, 읽기 능력이 향상되는 것처럼 보인다.

(A) 이것이 사람의 발 크기(독립 변인)가 읽기 능력(종속 변인)의 향상을 유발한다는 것을 의미하는가? 물론 아니다. 이러한 허위 관계는 읽기 능력은 물론 신발 크기와도 관련이 있는 제3 변인인 연령에 의해 발생한다.

(B) 따라서, 연구자들이 독립 변인과 종속 변인 사이의 관계에 대한 인과 관계를 주장하려고 할 때 그들은 허위 관계를 만들어 낼 수도 있는 다른 변인들을 통제하거나 배제해야만 한다.

Why? 왜 정답일까?

어떤 두 변인의 인과 관계를 연구할 때 주의할 점에 관해 설명한 글이다. 주어진 글에서 언뜻 관련되어 보이는 두 요인 간에도 인과 관계가 없을 수 있다는 점을 언급한 뒤, (C)는 두 변인 사이에 제3의 변인이 관여되어서 두 변인이 표면적으로 관련되어 보일 수 있기 때문임을 설명한다. 이어서 (C)의 후반부에는 신발 크기와 읽기 능력이라는 두 가지 변인 사이 관계가 예로 제시되는데, (A)는 이 두 변인 사이에 연령이라는 제3의 변인이 영향을 미치고 있음을 지적한다. (B)는 (C)와 (A)의 내용을 토대로 두 변인 사이의 인과 관계를 연구할 때에는 영향을 미칠 수 있는 다른 변인들에 대한 통제가 필수적이라는 결론 (Hence)을 이끌어 낸다. 따라서 글의 순서로 가장 적절한 것은 ④ '(C) – (A) – (B)'이다.

- **causal relationship** 인과 관계
- **factor** ⓝ 요인
- **associated with** ~와 연관된
- **apparent** ⓐ 명백한
- **improvement** ⓝ 향상, 개선
- **rule out** 배제하다
- **misleading** ⓐ 잘못된, 오도하는

구문 풀이

8행 Hence, when researchers attempt to make causal claims
         접속사(~할 때)   ~하려고 시도하다
about the relationship between an independent and a dependent
                                                                        주격 관계대명사
variable, they must control for — or rule out — other variables [that
              주어   동사   삽입구(동사2)   목적어(선행사)
may be creating a spurious relationship].

---

07 패턴을 찾는 인간의 특성 정답률 50% | 정답 ②

주어진 글 다음에 이어질 글의 순서로 가장 적절한 것을 고르시오. [3점]

① (A) – (C) – (B)   ✔ (B) – (A) – (C)
③ (B) – (C) – (A)   ④ (C) – (A) – (B)
⑤ (C) – (B) – (A)

The next time you're out under a clear, dark sky, / look up.
다음에 여러분이 맑고 어두운 하늘 아래에 있을 때 / 위를 올려다보아라.

If you've picked a good spot for stargazing, / you'll see a sky full of stars, / shining and twinkling / like thousands of brilliant jewels.
만약 여러분이 별을 보기에 좋은 장소를 골랐다면, / 여러분은 별로 가득한 하늘을 보게 될 것이다. / 빛나고 반짝거리는 / 수천 개의 광채가 나는 보석처럼

(B) But this amazing sight of stars / can also be confusing.
하지만 이 놀라운 별들의 광경은 / 또한 혼란스러울 수도 있다.

Try and point out a single star to someone.
어떤 사람에게 별 하나를 가리켜 보라.

Chances are, that person will have a hard time / knowing exactly which star you're looking at.
아마 그 사람은 어려울 것이다. / 여러분이 어떤 별을 보고 있는지를 정확하게 알기

(A) It might be easier / if you describe patterns of stars.
그것은 더 쉬워질 수도 있다. / 만약 여러분이 별의 패턴을 묘사한다면

You could say something like, / "See that big triangle of bright stars there?"
여러분은 말을 할 수 있을 것이다. / "저기 큰 삼각형을 이루는 밝은 별들이 보이세요?"와 같은

Or, "Do you see those five stars / that look like a big letter W?"
혹은, "저 다섯 개의 별이 보이세요? / 대문자 W처럼 보이는"

(C) When you do that, / you're doing exactly what we all do / when we look at the stars.
여러분이 그렇게 하면, / 여러분은 우리 모두가 하는 것을 정확하게 하고 있는 것이다. / 우리가 별을 바라볼 때

We look for patterns, / not just so that we can point something out to someone else, / but also because that's what we humans have always done.
우리는 패턴을 찾는다. / 다른 사람에게 어떤 것을 가리켜 보여주기 위해서뿐만 아니라, / 그렇게 하는 것이 우리 인간이 항상 해왔던 것이기도 하기 때문에

다음에 여러분이 맑고 어두운 하늘 아래에 있을 때 위를 올려다보아라. 만약 여러분이 별을 보기에 좋은 장소를 골랐다면, 수천 개의 광채가 나는 보석처럼 빛나고 반짝거리는 별로 가득한 하늘을 보게 될 것이다.

(B) 하지만 이 놀라운 별들의 광경은 또한 혼란스러울 수도 있다. 어떤 사람에게 별 하나를 가리켜 보라. 아마 그 사람은 여러분이 어떤 별을 보고 있는지를 정확하게 알기 어려울 것이다.

(A) 만약 여러분이 별의 패턴을 묘사한다면 그것은 더 쉬워질 수도 있다. "저기 큰 삼각형을 이루는 밝은 별들이 보이세요?"와 같은 말을 할 수 있을 것이다. 혹은, "대문자 W처럼 보이는 저 다섯 개의 별이 보이세요?"라고 말할 수도 있을 것이다.

(C) 여러분이 그렇게 하면, 여러분은 우리가 별을 바라볼 때 우리 모두가 하는 것을 정확하게 하고 있는 것이다. 우리는 다른 사람에게 어떤 것을 가리켜 보여주기 위해서뿐만 아니라, 그렇게 하는 것이 우리 인간이 항상 해왔던 것이기도 하기 때문에 패턴을 찾는다.

Why? 왜 정답일까?

밤하늘 가득한 별을 바라보는 내용으로 시작하는 주어진 글 뒤에는, 어떤 사람에게 별 하나를 가리킨다면 정확히 어떤 별인지 파악하기 어려워할 것이라는 내용의 (B), 이때 별의 일정한 패턴을 묘사해주면 이해를 도울 수 있다는 내용의 (A), 이렇듯 패턴을 찾는 것이 인간 행동의 특징이라는 결론을 내리는 (C)가 차례로 이어지는 것이 자연스럽다. 따라서 글의 순서로 가장 적절한 것은 ② '(B) – (A) – (C)'이다.

- **spot** ⓝ 특정한 곳
- **twinkle** ⓥ 반짝거리다
- **describe** ⓥ 묘사하다
- **sight** ⓝ 보기, 봄
- **point out** 가리키다
- **exactly** ⓐⓓ 정확히
- **stargazing** ⓝ 별 보기
- **brilliant** ⓐ 눈부신, 훌륭한
- **amazing** ⓐ 놀라운
- **confuse** ⓥ 혼란시키다, 혼란스럽게 만들다
- **chances are that** ~할 가능성이 있다

구문 풀이

10행 Chances are, that person will have a hard time knowing
        ~할 가능성이 있다   「have a hard time + 동명사 : ~하는 데 어려움이 있다」
exactly which star you're looking at.
        의문형용사(어떤)

---

08 결정의 형성 정답률 72% | 정답 ②

주어진 글 다음에 이어질 글의 순서로 가장 적절한 것을 고르시오. [3점]

① (A) – (C) – (B)   ✔ (B) – (A) – (C)
③ (B) – (C) – (A)   ④ (C) – (A) – (B)
⑤ (C) – (B) – (A)

Maybe you've heard this joke: / "How do you eat an elephant?"
아마 여러분은 이 농담을 들어본 적이 있을 것이다. / "코끼리를 어떻게 먹지?"

The answer is "one bite at a time."

(B) So, how do you "build" the Earth?
그렇다면, 여러분은 어떻게 지구를 '건설'하는가?

That's simple, too: / one atom at a time.
이것도 간단하다. / 한 번에 하나의 원자이다.

Atoms are the basic building blocks of crystals, / and since all rocks are made up of crystals, / the more you know about atoms, / the better.
원자는 결정의 기본 구성 요소이고, / 모든 암석은 결정으로 이루어져 있기 때문에, / 여러분이 원자에 대해 더 많이 알수록 / 더 좋다.

Crystals come in a variety of shapes / that scientists call *habits*.
결정은 다양한 모양으로 나온다. / 과학자들이 습성이라고 부르는

(A) Common crystal habits / include squares, triangles, and six-sided hexagons.
일반적인 결정 습성은 / 사각형, 삼각형, 육면의 육각형을 포함한다.

Usually crystals form / when liquids cool, / such as when you create ice cubes.
보통 결정이 형성된다. / 액체가 차가워질 때 / 여러분이 얼음을 만들 때와 같이

Many times, / crystals form in ways / that do not allow for perfect shapes.
많은 경우, / 결정은 방식으로 형성된다. / 완벽한 모양을 허용하지 않는

If conditions are too cold, too hot, / or there isn't enough source material, / they can form strange, twisted shapes.
조건이 너무 차갑거나, 너무 뜨겁거나, / 혹은 원천 물질이 충분하지 않으면 / 그것들은 이상하고 뒤틀린 모양을 형성할 수 있다.

(C) But when conditions are right, / we see beautiful displays.
하지만 조건이 맞을 때, / 우리는 아름다운 배열을 본다.

Usually, / this involves a slow, steady environment / where the individual atoms have plenty of time to join / and fit perfectly into what's known as the *crystal lattice*.
보통, / 이것은 느리고 안정적인 환경을 수반한다. / 개별적인 원자들이 충분한 시간을 들여 결합해서 / *결정격자*라고 알려진 것에 완벽하게 들어맞게 되는

This is the basic structure of atoms / that is seen time after time.
이것은 원자의 기본적인 구조이다. / 반복하여 보이는

아마 여러분은 이 농담을 들어본 적이 있을 것이다. "코끼리를 어떻게 먹지?" 정답은 '한 번에 한 입'이다.

(B) 그렇다면, 여러분은 어떻게 지구를 '건설'하는가? 이것도 간단하다. 한 번에 하나의 원자이다. 원자는 결정의 기본 구성 요소이고, 모든 암석은 결정으로 이루어져 있기 때문에, 여러분은 원자에 대해 더 많이 알수록 더 좋다. 결정은 과학자들이 습성이라고 부르는 다양한 모양으로 나온다.

(A) 일반적인 결정 습성은 사각형, 삼각형, 육면의 육각형을 포함한다. 보통 여러분이 얼음을 만들 때와 같이 액체가 차가워질 때 결정이 형성된다. 많은 경우, 결정은 완벽한 모양을 허용하지 않는 방식으로 형성된다. 조건이 너무 차갑거나, 너무 뜨겁거나, 혹은 원천 물질이 충분하지 않으면 이상하고 뒤틀린 모양을 형성할 수 있다.

(C) 하지만 조건이 맞을 때, 우리는 아름다운 배열을 본다. 보통, 이것은 개별적인 원자들이 충분한 시간을 들여 결합해서 *결정격자*라고 알려진 것에 완벽하게 들어맞게 되는 느리고 안정적인 환경을 수반한다. 이것은 반복하여 보이는 원자의 기본적인 구조이다.

Why? 왜 정답일까?

주어진 글에 '코끼리를 어떻게 먹나'라는 물음에 '한 번에 한 입씩' 먹으면 된다는 농담이 있다고 하는데, (B)는 이것이 지구가 만들어진 과정에도 적용될 수 있다면서 결정의 습성을 언급한다. (A)는 이 결정의 습성을 설명하면서, 많은 경우 결정이 뒤틀린 모양으로 형성된다고 언급하는데, (C)는 But으로 흐름을 반전시키며 아름다운 배열을 지닌 결정도 만들어진다고 설명한다. 따라서 글의 순서로 가장 적절한 것은 ② 'B) – (A) – (C)'이다.

- **bite** ⓝ 한 입 (베어문 조각) ⓥ 베어 물다
- **hexagon** ⓝ 육각형
- **ice cube** 얼음 조각
- **twisted** ⓐ 뒤틀린
- **be made up of** ~로 구성되다
- **plenty of** 많은
- **lattice** ⓝ 격자 (모양)
- **crystal** ⓝ 결정
- **liquid** ⓝ 액체
- **allow for** ~을 허용하다
- **atom** ⓝ 원자
- **steady** ⓐ 안정된, 꾸준한
- **fit into** ~에 들어 맞다
- **time after time** 자주, 매번, 되풀이해서

구문 풀이

17행 Usually, this involves a slow, steady environment [where the
　　　　　　　　　　　　　　　　　　　　　선행사(상황)　　　　　관계부사
individual atoms have plenty of time to join and fit perfectly into
　　　　　　　　　　　　　　　　　　　　　형용사적 용법　　　　　전치사
{what's known as the *crystal lattice*}].
　　　　　명사절

주어진 글 다음에 이어질 글의 순서로 가장 적절한 것을 고르시오. [3점]

① (A) – (C) – (B)　　　　　② (B) – (A) – (C)
③ (B) – (C) – (A)　　　　　④ (C) – (A) – (B)
✔(C) – (B) – (A)

Each beech tree grows in a particular location / and soil conditions can vary greatly / in just a few yards.
각각의 너도밤나무는 고유한 장소에서 자라고 / 토양의 조건들은 크게 달라질 수 있다. / 단 몇 야드 안에서도

The soil can have a great deal of water / or almost no water.
토양은 물이 많거나 / 거의 없을 수도 있다.

It can be full of nutrients or not.
그것은 영양분이 가득할 수도 있고 아닐 수도 있다.

(C) Accordingly, / each tree grows more quickly or more slowly / and produces more or less sugar, / and thus you would expect every tree / to be photosynthesizing at a different rate.
이에 따라, / 각 나무는 더 빨리 혹은 더 느리게 자라고 / 더 많거나 더 적은 당분을 생산하는데, / 그래서 여러분은 모든 나무가 ~할 거라고 기대할 것이다. / 다른 정도로 광합성을 할 거라고

(B) However, the rate is the same.
그러나 그 정도는 동일하다.

Whether they are thick or thin, / all the trees of the same species / are using light / to produce the same amount of sugar per leaf.
그것들이 굵든 가늘든 간에, / 같은 종의 모든 나무들은 / 빛을 사용하고 있다. / 이파리당 같은 양의 당을 생산하기 위해

Some trees have plenty of sugar / and some have less, / but the trees equalize this difference between them / by transferring sugar.
어떤 나무들은 충분한 당을 지니고 / 어떤 것들은 더 적게 지니지만, / 나무들은 그들 사이의 이 차이를 균등하게 한다. / 당을 전달하여

(A) This is taking place underground through the roots.
이것은 뿌리들을 통해 지하에서 일어나고 있다.

Whoever has an abundance of sugar / hands some over; / whoever is running short / gets help.
풍부한 당을 가진 나무가 누구든 간에 / 일부를 건네주고, / 부족해지는 나무는 누구든 간에 / 도움을 받는다.

Their network acts as a system / to make sure that no trees fall too far behind.
그들의 연결망은 시스템 역할을 한다. / 그 어떤 나무도 너무 뒤처지지 않는 것을 확실히 하기 위한

각각의 너도밤나무는 고유한 장소에서 자라고 토양의 조건들은 단 몇 야드 안에서도 크게 달라질 수 있다. 토양은 물이 많거나 거의 없을 수도 있다. 영양분이 가득할 수도 있고 아닐 수도 있다.

(C) 이에 따라, 각 나무는 더 빨리 혹은 더 느리게 자라고 더 많거나 더 적은 당분을 생산하는데, 그래서 여러분은 모든 나무가 다른 정도로 광합성을 할 거라고 기대할 것이다.

(B) 그러나 그 정도는 동일하다. 굵든 가늘든 간에, 같은 종의 모든 나무들은 빛을 사용하여 이파리당 같은 양의 당을 생산하고 있다. 어떤 나무들은 충분한 당을 지니고 어떤 것들은 더 적게 지니지만, 나무들은 당을 전달하여 그들 사이의 이 차이를 균등하게 한다.

(A) 이것은 뿌리들을 통해 지하에서 일어나고 있다. 풍부한 당을 가진 나무가 누구든 간에 일부를 건네주고, 부족해지는 나무는 누구든 간에 도움을 받는다. 그들의 연결망은 그 어떤 나무도 너무 뒤처지지 않는 것을 확실히 하기 위한 시스템 역할을 한다.

Why? 왜 정답일까?

너도밤나무가 자라는 토양 조건이 상이할 수 있다는 내용의 주어진 글 뒤로, (C)는 그래서(Accordingly) 광합성 정도가 나무마다 다를 것이라는 추측이 나올 수 있다고 한다. However로 시작하는 (B)는 사실은 그렇지 않다고 하며, 나무들끼리 서로 당을 주고받기 때문에 차이가 조절된다는 설명을 이어 간다. (A)는 이러한 '주고받음'이 뿌리를 통해 이뤄진다는 보충 설명과 함께, 나무끼리의 연결망이 각 나무에게 도움이 된다는 결론을 제시한다. 따라서 글의 순서로 가장 적절한 것은 ⑤ 'C) – (B) – (A)'이다.

- **beech tree** 너도밤나무
- **abundance** ⓝ 풍부함
- **run short** 부족해지다
- **equalize** ⓥ 동등하게 하다
- **photosynthesize** ⓥ 광합성하다
- **a great deal of** 많은
- **hand over** 건네주다
- **fall behind** 뒤처지다
- **transfer** ⓥ 전달하다

구문 풀이

6행 [Whoever has an abundance of sugar] hands some over;
　　　　　주어1　　　　　　　　　　　　　　　동사1(단수)
[whoever is running short] gets help. [ ]: 복합관계대명사절(~하는 누구든지)
　　주어2　　　　　　　　　동사2(단수)

★★★ 1등급 대비 고난도 2점 문제

10 현실적인 낙관론자와 비현실적인 낙관론자   정답률 35% | 정답 ③

주어진 글 다음에 이어질 글의 순서로 가장 적절한 것을 고르시오.

① (A) − (C) − (B)   ② (B) − (A) − (C)
✔③ (B) − (C) − (A)   ④ (C) − (A) − (B)
⑤ (C) − (B) − (A)

To be successful, / you need to understand the vital difference / between believing you will succeed, / and believing you will succeed easily.
성공하려면 / 당신은 중요한 차이를 이해할 필요가 있다. / 당신이 성공할 것이라고 믿는 것과 / 당신이 쉽게 성공할 것이라고 믿는 것 사이의

(B) Put another way, it's the difference / between being a realistic optimist, / and an unrealistic optimist.
다시 말해서, 그것은 차이이다. / 현실적인 낙관주의자가 되는 것과 / 비현실적인 낙관주의자가 되는 것 사이의

Realistic optimists believe they will succeed, / but also believe they have to make success happen / — through things like careful planning / and choosing the right strategies.
현실적인 낙관주의자들은 그들이 성공할 것이라고 믿을 뿐만 아니라, / 그들이 성공이 일어나도록 만들어야 한다고 믿는다. / 신중한 계획 같은 일을 통해 / 그리고 적절한 전략을 선택하는 일 등

(C) They recognize the need / for giving serious thought / to how they will deal with obstacles.
그들은 필요가 있다는 것을 인식한다. / 심각하게 고려할 / 그들이 장애물을 다룰 방법에 대해

This preparation only increases their confidence / in their own ability to get things done.
이런 준비만이 자신감을 높여 준다. / 일을 수행하는 그들 자신의 능력에 대한

(A) Unrealistic optimists, on the other hand, / believe that success will happen to them / — that the universe will reward them / for all their positive thinking, / or that somehow they will be transformed overnight / into the kind of person / for whom obstacles don't exist anymore.
반면에, 비현실적인 낙관주의자들은 / 성공이 그들에게 일어날 것이라고, / 즉 우주가 그들에게 보상할 것이라고 믿거나, / 자신의 모든 긍정적인 사고에 대해 / 혹은 어떤 식으로든 그들이 하룻밤 사이에 변모할 것이라고 믿는다. / 그런 종류의 사람으로 / 장애물이 더 이상 없는

성공하려면 당신은 당신이 성공할 것이라고 믿는 것과 당신이 쉽게 성공할 것이라고 믿는 것 사이의 중요한 차이를 이해할 필요가 있다.

(B) 다시 말해서, 그것은 현실적인 낙관주의자가 되는 것과 비현실적인 낙관주의자가 되는 것 사이의 차이이다. 현실적인 낙관주의자들은 그들이 성공할 것이라고 믿을 뿐만 아니라, 그들이 신중한 계획과 적절한 전략을 선택하는 일 등을 통해 성공이 일어나도록 만들어야 한다고 믿는다.

(C) 그들은 그들이 장애물을 다룰 방법에 대해 심각하게 고려할 필요가 있다는 것을 인식한다. 이런 준비만이 일을 수행하는 그들 자신의 능력에 대한 자신감을 높여 준다.

(A) 반면에, 비현실적인 낙관론자들은 성공이 그들에게 일어날 것이라고, 즉 우주가 그들에게 자신의 모든 긍정적인 사고에 대해 보상할 것이라고 믿거나, 혹은 어떤 식으로든 그들이 하룻밤 사이에 장애물이 더 이상 없는 그런 종류의 사람으로 변모할 것이라고 믿는다.

Why? 왜 정답일까?

스스로 성공하리라 믿는 것과 쉽게 성공하리라고 믿는 것 사이의 차이를 구별할 필요가 있다고 언급한 주어진 글 뒤에는, 이를 현실적인 낙관론과 비현실적인 낙관론의 차이로 다시 언급하며 현실적인 낙관론자들에 관해 구체적으로 설명하기 시작하는 (B), 설명을 이어가는 (C), on the other hand로 흐름을 반전시키며 비현실적인 낙관론자에 관해 언급하는 (A)가 차례로 이어져야 자연스럽다. 따라서 글의 순서로 가장 적절한 것은 ③ '(B) − (C) − (A)'이다.

- vital ⓐ 중요한
- optimist ⓝ 낙관론자
- transform ⓥ 변모하다
- obstacle ⓝ 장애물
- strategy ⓝ 전략
- unrealistic ⓐ 비현실적인
- somehow 〔ad〕 어떤 식으로든
- overnight 〔ad〕 하룻밤 사이에
- put another way 다시 말해서
- preparation ⓝ 준비

구문 풀이

4행   Unrealistic optimists, on the other hand, believe that success
         주어   동사   접속사1
will happen to them — that the universe will reward them for all their
                   접속사2
positive thinking, or that somehow they will be transformed overnight
               접속사3   조동사 수동태
into the kind of person [for whom obstacles don't exist anymore].
      선행사   「전치사+목적격 관계대명사」   자동사

★★★ 문제 해결 꿀~팁 ★★

▶ 많이 틀린 이유는?
(B) 이후 단락의 순서를 정확하게 잡는 것이 풀이의 관건이다. (C)의 They 뒤에서 'giving serious thought to how they will deal with obstacles'는 (B)의 'they have to make success happen'에 이어진다. 즉 현실적 낙관주의자는 성공하기 위해서 자신이 장애물을 처리해야 함을 이해하고 있으며, 구체적인 처리 방법을 고민하는 사람들이라는 설명이 (B) − (C)에 연달아 제시된다.

▶ 문제 해결 방법은?
순서 문제에서 대명사와 연결어는 중요한 단서이다. (A)의 on the other hand를 통해 이 글이 크게 보아 '현실적 낙관주의자 vs. 비현실적 낙관주의자'를 대조하는 글임을 파악한 뒤, (C)의 They가 둘 중 어느 대상을 가리키는지를 파악하는 데 주력하면 쉽게 답을 고를 수 있다.

★★★ 1등급 대비 고난도 3점 문제

11 광물의 형성   정답률 42% | 정답 ②

주어진 글 다음에 이어질 글의 순서로 가장 적절한 것을 고르시오. [3점]

① (A) − (C) − (B)   ✔② (B) − (A) − (C)
③ (B) − (C) − (A)   ④ (C) − (A) − (B)
⑤ (C) − (B) − (A)

Natural processes form minerals in many ways.
자연 과정은 많은 방법으로 광물을 형성한다.

For example, / hot melted rock material, / called magma, / cools / when it reaches the Earth's surface, / or even if it's trapped below the surface.
예를 들어, / 뜨거운 용암 물질은 / 마그마라고 불리는 / 식는다. / 그것이 지구의 표면에 도달할 때, / 또는 그것이 심지어 표면 아래에 갇혔을 때도

As magma cools, / its atoms lose heat energy, / move closer together, / and begin to combine into compounds.
마그마가 식으면서 / 마그마의 원자는 열에너지를 잃고, / 서로 더 가까이 이동해 / 화합물로 결합하기 시작한다.

(B) During this process, / atoms of the different compounds / arrange themselves into orderly, repeating patterns.
이 과정 동안, / 서로 다른 화합물의 원자가 / 질서 있고 반복적인 패턴으로 배열된다.

The type and amount of elements / present in a magma / partly determine / which minerals will form.
원소의 종류와 양이 / 마그마에 존재하는 / 부분적으로 결정한다. / 어떤 광물이 형성될지를

(A) Also, / the size of the crystals that form / depends partly / on how rapidly the magma cools.
또한, / 형성되는 결정의 크기는 / 부분적으로는 달려 있다. / 마그마가 얼마나 빨리 식나에

When magma cools slowly, / the crystals that form / are generally large enough / to see with the unaided eye.
마그마가 천천히 식으면, / 형성되는 결정은 / 대개 충분히 크다. / 육안으로 볼 수 있을 만큼

(C) This is because the atoms have enough time / to move together and form into larger crystals.
이것은 원자가 충분한 시간을 가지기 때문이다. / 함께 이동해 더 큰 결정을 형성할

When magma cools rapidly, / the crystals that form / will be small.
마그마가 빠르게 식으면, / 형성되는 결정은 / 작을 것이다.

In such cases, / you can't easily see individual mineral crystals.
이런 경우에는 / 여러분은 개별 광물 결정을 쉽게 볼 수 없다.

자연 과정은 많은 방법으로 광물을 형성한다. 예를 들어, 마그마라고 불리는 뜨거운 용암 물질은 지구의 표면에 도달할 때, 또는 심지어 표면 아래에 갇혔을 때도 식는다. 마그마가 식으면서 마그마의 원자는 열에너지를 잃고, 서로 더 가까이 이동해 화합물로 결합하기 시작한다.

(B) 이 과정 동안, 서로 다른 화합물의 원자가 질서 있고 반복적인 패턴으로 배열된다. 마그마에 존재하는 원소의 종류와 양이 어떤 광물이 형성될지를 부분적으로 결정한다.

(A) 또한, 형성되는 결정의 크기는 부분적으로는 마그마가 얼마나 빨리 식나에 달려 있다. 마그마가 천천히 식으면, 형성되는 결정은 대개 육안으로 볼 수 있을 만큼 충분히 크다.

(C) 이것은 원자가 함께 이동해 더 큰 결정을 형성할 충분한 시간을 가지기 때문이다. 마그마가 빠르게 식으면, 형성되는 결정은 작을 것이다. 이런 경우에는 개별 광물 결정을 쉽게 볼 수 없다.

Why? 왜 정답일까?

마그마가 식을 때 광물이 형성될 수 있다는 내용의 주어진 글 뒤로, '이 식어가는 과정' 동안 마그마 속 원소의 종류나 양에 따라 어떤 종류의 광물이 형성될지 결정된다고 설명하

는 (B)가 먼저 연결된다. 이어서 Also로 시작하는 (A)는 추가로 마그마가 식는 속도에 따라 광물의 크기가 결정된다고 언급한다. 마지막으로 (C)는 (A) 후반부에서 언급되었듯이 마그마가 천천히 식을 때 광물의 크기가 커지는 이유에 관해 보충 설명한다. 따라서 글의 순서로 가장 적절한 것은 ② '(B) – (A) – (C)'이다.

- form ⓥ 형성하다
- melt ⓥ 녹이다, 녹다
- trap ⓥ 가두다
- combine into ~로 결합되다
- partly [ad] 부분적으로
- with the unaided eye 육안으로
- orderly ⓐ 질서 있는
- in such cases 이런 경우에
- mineral ⓝ 광물
- surface ⓝ 표면
- atom ⓝ 원자
- compound ⓝ 화합물
- rapidly [ad] 빠르게
- arrange ⓥ 배열하다
- element ⓝ 원소, 구성요소

구문 풀이

7행 Also, the size of the crystals that form depends partly on how rapidly the magma cools.
「how + 형/부 + 주어 + 동사 : 얼마나 ~한지」

★★ 문제 해결 꿀~팁 ★★

▶ 많이 틀린 이유는?
(B)는 마그마가 식는 속도에 따라 그로 인해 만들어지는 결정의 종류가 달라질 수 있다는 내용으로 끝나는데, (C)를 보면 갑자기 결정의 '크기'가 커지는 이유를 언급한다. (C)에 앞서 '크기'를 처음 언급하는 단락은 Also로 시작하는 (A)이다. (A)에서 먼저 size를 언급해줘야 크기가 커지는 '이유'를 설명하는 (C)가 자연스럽게 연결된다.

▶ 문제 해결 방법은?
(A)와 (C)가 둘 다 '크기'를 언급하고 있지만, (B)에는 '크기'에 관한 언급이 없다. 따라서 Also가 있는 (A)를 먼저 연결해 '크기'에 관한 내용을 추가한다는 뜻을 밝히고, 뒤이어 (C)를 연결해야 논리적 흐름이 자연스러워진다.

★★★ 1등급 대비 고난도 3점 문제

12 큰 요청을 하기 앞서 작은 요청을 하는 것의 효과 | 정답률 37% | 정답 ④

주어진 글 다음에 이어질 글의 순서로 가장 적절한 것을 고르시오. [3점]

① (A) – (C) – (B)
② (B) – (A) – (C)
③ (B) – (C) – (A)
✔ ④ (C) – (A) – (B)
⑤ (C) – (B) – (A)

In a study, / a researcher pretending to be a volunteer / surveyed a California neighborhood, / asking residents / if they would allow a large sign / reading "Drive Carefully" / to be displayed on their front lawns.
한 연구에서, / 자원봉사자로 가장한 연구자가 / 한 캘리포니아 동네에서 설문조사했다. / 주민들에게 물으면서 / 그들이 큰 표지판을 허락할지를 / '운전 조심'이라고 쓰인 / 그들의 앞마당에 세워 두는 것을

(C) To help them understand what it would look like, / the volunteer showed his participants / a picture of the large sign / blocking the view of a beautiful house.
그것이 어떻게 보일지에 대한 이해를 돕기 위해, / 그 자원봉사자는 참여자들에게 보여주었다. / 큰 표지판 사진을 / 아름다운 집의 전망을 막는

Naturally, most people refused, / but in one particular group, / an incredible 76 percent actually approved.
당연하게도 대부분의 사람들은 거절했지만, / 어떤 특정 그룹에서 / 놀랍게도 76퍼센트가 실제로 승낙했다.

(A) The reason that they agreed was this: / two weeks earlier, / these residents had been asked by another volunteer / to make a small commitment / to display a tiny sign / that read "Be a Safe Driver" / in their windows.
그들이 동의한 이유는 이것이다. / 2주 전에, / 이 주민들은 다른 자원봉사자로부터 요청받은 적이 있었다. / 작은 약속을 하도록 / 아주 작은 표지판을 붙인다는 / '안전운전자가 되세요'라고 쓰인 / 그들의 창문에

(B) Since it was such a small and simple request, / nearly all of them agreed.
그것이 아주 작고 간단한 요청이었기 때문에, / 그들 거의 모두가 동의했다.

The astonishing result was / that the initial small commitment / deeply influenced their willingness / to accept the much larger request two weeks later.
놀라운 결과는 / 처음의 작은 약속이 / 그들의 의향에 깊은 영향을 끼쳤다는 것이다. / 2주 후의 훨씬 더 큰 요청을 받아들이려는

한 연구에서, 자원봉사자로 가장한 연구자가 한 캘리포니아 동네에서 주민들에게 그들의 앞마당에 '운전 조심'이라고 쓰인 큰 표지판을 세워 두는 것을 허락할지를 설문조사했다.

(C) 그것이 어떻게 보일지에 대한 이해를 돕기 위해, 그 자원봉사자는 참여자들에게 아름다운 집의 전망을 막는 큰 표지판 사진을 보여주었다. 당연하

게도 대부분의 사람들은 거절했지만, 어떤 특정 그룹에서 놀랍게도 76퍼센트가 실제로 승낙했다.

(A) 그들이 동의한 이유는 이것이다. 2주 전에, 이 주민들은 다른 자원봉사자로부터 '안전운전자가 되세요'라고 쓰인 아주 작은 표지판을 창문에 붙인다는 작은 약속을 하도록 요청받은 적이 있었다.

(B) 그것이 아주 작고 간단한 요청이었기 때문에, 그들 거의 모두가 동의했다. 놀라운 결과는, 처음의 작은 약속이 그들이 2주 후의 훨씬 더 큰 요청을 기꺼이 받아들이는 데 깊은 영향을 끼쳤다는 것이다.

Why? 왜 정답일까?

주어진 글에서 자원봉사자로 가장한 연구자가 동네 주민들에게 '운전 조심'이라고 쓰인 큰 표지판을 세우는 것에 동의해줄지를 물어보았다고 언급한 데 이어, (C)는 이 연구자(the volunteer)가 대체로 거절의 답변을 얻은 가운데 한 집단에서 다수의 승낙을 받아냈다는 결과를 소개한다. (A)는 (C)에서 언급된 '동의해준 사람들'을 they로 지칭하며, 이들은 실험 2주 전 아주 작은 표지판을 창문에 붙여달라는 요청을 받은 적이 있었다고 설명한다. (B)은 '작은 표지판을 창문에 붙이는 것'을 it으로 가리키며, 이렇듯 작은 요청을 먼저 받은 후 큰 요청을 받았기에 주민들의 선택이 다른 집단과 달라졌다는 최종적 해석을 제시한다. 따라서 글의 순서로 가장 적절한 것은 ④ '(C) – (A) – (B)'이다.

- pretend ⓥ ~인 체하다
- make a commitment 약속하다
- astonishing ⓐ 놀라운
- willingness ⓝ 의향, ~하려는 마음
- block ⓥ 막다, 차단하다
- display ⓥ 전시하다
- tiny ⓐ 아주 작은
- initial ⓐ 처음의, 초기의
- incredible ⓐ 믿을 수 없는, 놀라운
- approve ⓥ 승인하다

구문 풀이

1행 In a study, a researcher (pretending to be a volunteer) surveyed
주어 ⌣ 동사
a California neighborhood, asking residents {if they would allow
분사구문 간접목적어 5형식 동사
a large sign (reading "Drive Carefully") to be displayed on their front
목적어 ⌣ 목적격 보어
lawns}. 〔 〕: 직접목적어

★★ 문제 해결 꿀~팁 ★★

▶ 많이 틀린 이유는?
(B)와 (C)의 첫 문장에 모두 it이 나오므로 it이 가리키는 바를 잘 찾아야 한다.
(B)의 it은 '작고 간단한 요청'이고, (C)의 it은 '아름다운 집 정경을 모두 가릴 만큼 큰 표지판'이다. 주어진 글에 등장하는 a large sign은 둘 중 (C)의 it과 연결되므로, 선택지 중 (B)로 시작하는 ②와 ③은 답에서 제외된다.

▶ 문제 해결 방법은?
대명사 힌트에 주목하면 답을 쉽게 고를 수 있다.
주어진 글의 a large sign이 (C)의 it, (C)의 an incredible 76 percent가 (A)의 they, (A)의 'to display a tiny sign ~'이 (B)의 it으로 연결되고 있다.

DAY 12 　　글의 순서 02

01 ③	02 ②	03 ⑤	04 ⑤	05 ⑤
06 ②	07 ⑤	08 ②	09 ②	10 ④
11 ②	12 ④			

01　기타가 소리를 내는 과정　정답률 63% | 정답 ③

주어진 글 다음에 이어질 글의 순서로 가장 적절한 것을 고르시오.

① (A) – (C) – (B)　　　② (B) – (A) – (C)
✔(B) – (C) – (A)　　　④ (C) – (A) – (B)
⑤ (C) – (B) – (A)

When you pluck a guitar string / it moves back and forth hundreds of times every second.
여러분이 기타 줄을 뜯을 때 / 그것은 매초 수백 번 이리저리 움직인다.
(B) Naturally, / this movement is so fast / that you cannot see it / — you just see the blurred outline of the moving string.
당연히, / 이 움직임은 너무 빨라서 / 여러분이 볼 수 없다. / 여러분은 그저 움직이는 줄의 흐릿한 윤곽만 본다.
Strings vibrating in this way on their own / make hardly any noise / because strings are very thin / and don't push much air about.
이렇게 스스로 진동하는 줄들은 / 거의 소리가 나지 않는데, / 이는 줄이 매우 가늘고 / 많은 공기를 밀어내지 못하기 때문이다.
(C) But if you attach a string to a big hollow box / (like a guitar body), / then the vibration is amplified / and the note is heard loud and clear.
하지만 여러분이 속이 빈 커다란 상자에 줄을 달면, / (기타 몸통 같이) / 그 진동은 증폭되어 / 그 음이 크고 선명하게 들린다.
The vibration of the string is passed on / to the wooden panels of the guitar body, / which vibrate back and forth / at the same rate as the string.
그 줄의 진동은 전달된다 / 기타 몸통의 나무판으로 / 그리고 그것은 이리저리 떨린다. / 결과 같은 정도로
(A) The vibration of the wood / creates more powerful waves in the air pressure, / which travel away from the guitar.
그 나무의 진동은 / 공기의 압력에 더 강력한 파동을 만들어 내고 / 그것은 기타로부터 멀리 퍼진다.
When the waves reach your eardrums / they flex in and out / the same number of times a second / as the original string.
그 파동이 여러분의 고막에 도달할 때 / 그것은 굽이쳐 들어가고 나온다. / 초당 동일한 횟수로 / 원래의 줄과

여러분이 기타 줄을 뜯을 때 그것은 매초 수백 번 이리저리 움직인다.

(B) 당연히, 이 움직임은 너무 빨라서 여러분이 볼 수 없다. 여러분은 그저 움직이는 줄의 흐릿한 윤곽만 본다. 이렇게 스스로 진동하는 줄들은 거의 소리가 나지 않는데, 이는 줄이 매우 가늘어 많은 공기를 밀어내지 못하기 때문이다.

(C) 하지만 여러분이 (기타 몸통 같이) 속이 빈 커다란 상자에 줄을 달면, 그 진동은 증폭되어 그 음이 크고 선명하게 들린다. 그 줄의 진동은 기타 몸통의 나무판으로 전달되어 줄과 같은 정도로 이리저리 떨린다.

(A) 그 나무의 진동은 공기의 압력에 더 강력한 파동을 만들어 내어 기타로부터 멀리 퍼진다. 그 파동이 여러분의 고막에 도달할 때 원래의 줄과 초당 동일한 횟수로 굽이쳐 들어가고 나온다.

Why? 왜 정답일까?

기타 줄을 뜯으면 줄이 떨린다는 주어진 글에 이어, (B)는 우리가 이 움직임을 평소에는 볼 수 없으며, 혼자서 진동하는 줄은 공기를 충분히 밀어내지 못해 소리도 내지 못한다고 언급한다. (C)는 But으로 흐름을 반전시키며, 줄을 기타 몸통 같은 상자에 달아서 진동을 증폭시키는 상황을 제시하고, (A)는 이 진동이 소리로 나오게 된다는 내용으로 글을 맺는다. 따라서 글의 순서로 가장 적절한 것은 ③ '(B) – (C) – (A)'이다.

- pluck ⓥ (현악기를) 뜯다
- vibration ⓝ 진동
- flex ⓥ (관절을) 구부리다
- attach A to B A를 B에 부착하다
- amplify ⓥ 증폭시키다
- string ⓝ 줄, 현악기
- eardrum ⓝ 고막
- thin ⓐ 얇은
- hollow ⓐ (속이) 빈
- rate ⓝ 속도, 비율

구문 풀이

10행　Strings (vibrating in this way on their own) make hardly any
　　　　주어　　현재분사　　　　　　　　　　　동사(복수)　거의 전혀 ~않다
noise because strings are very thin and don't push much air about.

02　스포츠에 활용되는 공의 특징　정답률 56% | 정답 ②

주어진 글 다음에 이어질 글의 순서로 가장 적절한 것을 고르시오.

① (A) – (C) – (B)　　　✔(B) – (A) – (C)
③ (B) – (C) – (A)　　　④ (C) – (A) – (B)
⑤ (C) – (B) – (A)

Almost all major sporting activities / are played with a ball.
거의 모든 주요 스포츠 활동은 / 공을 갖고 행해진다.
(B) The rules of the game / always include rules / about the type of ball that is allowed, / starting with the size and weight of the ball.
경기의 규칙들은 / 규칙들을 늘 포함하고 있다. / 허용되는 공의 유형에 관한 / 공의 크기와 무게부터 시작해서
The ball must also have a certain stiffness.
공은 또한 특정 정도의 단단함을 갖추어야 한다.
(A) A ball might have the correct size and weight / but if it is made as a hollow ball of steel / it will be too stiff / and if it is made from light foam rubber with a heavy center / it will be too soft.
공이 적절한 크기와 무게를 갖출 수 있으나 / 그것이 속이 빈 강철 공으로 만들어지면 / 그것은 너무 단단할 것이고, / 그것이 무거운 중심부를 가진 가벼운 발포 고무로 만들어지면 / 그 공은 너무 물렁할 것이다.
(C) Similarly, along with stiffness, / a ball needs to bounce properly.
마찬가지로, 단단함과 더불어 / 공은 적절히 튈 필요가 있다.
A solid rubber ball / would be too bouncy for most sports, / and a solid ball made of clay / would not bounce at all.
순전히 고무로만 된 공은 / 대부분의 스포츠에 지나치게 잘 튈 것이고, / 순전히 점토로만 만든 공은 / 전혀 튀지 않을 것이다.

거의 모든 주요 스포츠 활동은 공을 갖고 행해진다.

(B) 경기의 규칙들은 공의 크기와 무게부터 시작해서 허용되는 공의 유형에 관한 규칙들을 늘 포함하고 있다. 공은 또한 특정 정도의 단단함을 갖추어야 한다.

(A) 공이 적절한 크기와 무게를 갖출 수 있으나 속이 빈 강철 공으로 만들어지면 그것은 너무 단단할 것이고, 무거운 중심부를 가진 가벼운 발포 고무로 만들어지면 그 공은 너무 물렁할 것이다.

(C) 마찬가지로, 공은 단단함과 더불어 적절히 튈 필요가 있다. 순전히 고무로만 된 공은 대부분의 스포츠에 지나치게 잘 튈 것이고, 순전히 점토로만 만든 공은 전혀 튀지 않을 것이다.

Why? 왜 정답일까?

스포츠에 활용되는 공이 갖추어야 할 특징에 관해 설명한 글이다. 먼저 주어진 글에서 공이 스포츠에서 널리 쓰인다는 내용을 제시한 데 이어, (B)에서는 경기 규칙을 보면 어떤 공이 사용되어야 하는지를 명시하고 있다는 내용과 함께 공이 단단함을 갖추어야 한다는 점을 언급한다. 이어서 (A)는 공이 적절한 크기나 무게를 갖추더라도 강철로 되어 있다면 지나치게 단단할 것이고, 역으로 (매트리스에 주로 활용되는) 발포 고무로 만들어진다면 너무 물렁할 것이라는 보충 설명을 제시한다. 이러한 (A)의 내용에 Similarly로 연결되는 (C)는 단단함과 더불어 필요한 특징으로서 잘 튀어오르는 속성을 언급하고 있다. 따라서 글의 순서로 가장 적절한 것은 ② '(B) – (A) – (C)'이다.

- major ⓐ 주요한
- steel ⓝ 강철
- rubber ⓝ 고무
- bounce ⓥ 튀어오르다
- solid ⓐ 순수한(다른 물질이 섞이지 않은)
- hollow ⓐ (속이) 빈
- stiff ⓐ 단단한
- certain ⓐ 확실한, 틀림없는
- properly 〔ad〕 적절히
- clay ⓝ 점토

구문 풀이

3행　A ball might have the correct size and weight but if it is made
　　　주어　　동사　　　　　　　　　　　　　조건 접속사1↵　현재시제1
as a hollow ball of steel it will be too stiff and if it is made from light
전치사(~로서)　　　　　　미래시제1　조건 접속사2↵　현재시제2(~으로 만들어지다)
foam rubber with a heavy center it will be too soft.
　　　　　　　　　　　　　　　　　미래시제2

03　인간이 배가 불러도 음식을 계속 먹는 이유　정답률 50% | 정답 ⑤

주어진 글 다음에 이어질 글의 순서로 가장 적절한 것을 고르시오.

① (A) – (C) – (B)　　　② (B) – (A) – (C)
③ (B) – (C) – (A)　　　④ (C) – (A) – (B)
✔(C) – (B) – (A)

When we compare human and animal desire / we find many extraordinary differences.

우리가 인간과 동물의 욕망을 비교할 때 / 우리는 많은 특별한 차이점을 발견한다.
Animals tend to eat with their stomachs, / and humans with their brains.
동물은 위장으로 먹는 경향이 있고, / 인간은 뇌로 먹는 경향이 있다.
(C) When animals' stomachs are full, they stop eating, / but humans are never sure when to stop.
동물은 배가 부르면 먹는 것을 멈추지만, / 인간은 언제 멈춰야 할지 결코 확신하지 못한다.
When they have eaten as much as their bellies can take, / they still feel empty, / they still feel an urge for further gratification.
인간은 배에 담을 수 있는 만큼 먹었을 때, / 그들은 여전히 허전함을 느끼고 / 여전히 추가적인 만족감에 대한 충동을 느낀다.
(B) This is largely due to anxiety, / to the knowledge that a constant supply of food is uncertain.
이것은 주로 불안감 때문이다. / 지속적인 식량 공급이 불확실하다는 인식에 따른
Therefore, they eat as much as possible / while they can.
그러므로 그들은 가능한 한 많이 먹는다. / 그들이 먹을 수 있을 때
(A) It is due, also, to the knowledge / that, in an insecure world, pleasure is uncertain.
또한, 그것은 인식 때문이다. / 불안정한 세상에서 즐거움이 불확실하다는
Therefore, the immediate pleasure of eating / must be exploited to the full, / even though it does violence to the digestion.
따라서 즉각적인 먹는 즐거움은 / 충분히 이용되어야 한다. / 그것이 소화에 무리가 되더라도

인간과 동물의 욕망을 비교할 때 우리는 많은 특별한 차이점을 발견한다. 동물은 위장으로, 인간은 뇌로 먹는 경향이 있다.
(C) 동물은 배가 부르면 먹는 것을 멈추지만, 인간은 언제 멈춰야 할지 결코 확신하지 못한다. 인간은 배에 담을 수 있는 만큼 먹었을 때, 그들은 여전히 허전함을 느끼고 여전히 추가적인 만족감에 대한 충동을 느낀다.
(B) 이것은 주로 지속적인 식량 공급이 불확실하다는 인식에 따른 불안감 때문이다. 그러므로 그들은 먹을 수 있을 때 가능한 한 많이 먹는다.
(A) 또한, 그것은 불안정한 세상에서 즐거움이 불확실하다는 인식 때문이다. 따라서 즉각적인 먹는 즐거움을 소화에 무리가 되더라도 충분히 이용하여야 한다.

Why? 왜 정답일까?

동물과 인간의 욕망에는 차이가 있음을 언급하며 식욕의 예를 들기 시작하는 주어진 글 뒤에는, 동물의 경우 배가 부르면 먹는 것을 멈추지만 인간은 그렇지 않다고 설명하는 (C), 인간이 배가 불러도 계속 먹는 이유를 설명하는 (B), 이유를 추가하는 (A)가 차례로 이어져야 한다. 따라서 글의 순서로 가장 적절한 것은 ⑤ '(C) – (B) – (A)'이다.

● extraordinary ⓐ 특별한
● uncertain ⓐ 불확실한
● exploit ⓥ 이용하다
● digestion ⓝ 소화
● constant ⓐ 지속적인
● insecure ⓐ 불안정한
● immediate ⓐ 즉각적인
● do violence ⓥ ~을 해치다
● anxiety ⓝ 불안
● urge ⓝ 충동

구문 풀이

5행 It is due, also, to the knowledge that, in an insecure world,
　　　　　　　「due to + 명사 : ~ 때문에」　　　동격 접속사
pleasure is uncertain.
주어　　동사　　보어

---

04 정전기의 예시와 원리　　　정답률 73% | 정답 ⑤

주어진 글 다음에 이어질 글의 순서로 가장 적절한 것을 고르시오.

① (A) – (C) – (B)
② (B) – (A) – (C)
③ (B) – (C) – (A)
④ (C) – (A) – (B)
✔ (C) – (B) – (A)

Use a plastic pen / and rub it on your hair about ten times / and then hold the pen / close to small pieces of tissue paper or chalk dust.
플라스틱 펜을 이용하여 / 약 열 번을 머리카락에 문지른 뒤 / 그 펜을 가져가라. / 작은 휴지 조각이나 분필 가루 근처로
(C) You will find / that the bits of paper or chalk dust / cling to the pen.
여러분은 발견하게 될 것이다. / 휴지 조각이나 분필 가루가 / 펜에 달라붙는 것을
What you have done there is / to create a form of electricity / called static electricity.
여러분이 한 일은 / 전기의 한 형태를 만든 것이다. / 정전기라고 불리는
(B) This kind of electricity / is produced by friction, / and the pen becomes electrically charged.
이 유형의 전기는 / 마찰에 의해 만들어지고, / 그 펜은 전기를 띠게 된다.
Static electricity is also found in the atmosphere.

정전기는 대기에서도 발견된다.
(A) During a thunderstorm, / clouds may become charged / as they rub against each other.
뇌우가 몰아치는 동안, / 구름은 전기를 띠게 될 수 있다. / 그것들이 서로 마찰되면서
The lightning that we often see during a storm / is caused by a large flow of electrical charges / between charged clouds and the earth.
폭풍이 몰아치는 동안 우리가 종종 보는 번개는 / 커다란 전하의 흐름으로 야기된다. / 전기를 띤 구름과 지면 사이의

플라스틱 펜을 이용하여 약 열 번을 머리카락에 문지른 뒤 그 펜을 작은 휴지 조각이나 분필 가루에 가까이 가져가라.
(C) 여러분은 휴지 조각이나 분필 가루가 펜에 달라붙는 것을 발견하게 될 것이다. 여러분이 한 일은 정전기라고 불리는 전기의 한 형태를 만든 것이다.
(B) 이 유형의 전기는 마찰에 의해 만들어지고, 그 펜은 전기를 띠게 된다. 정전기는 대기에서도 발견된다.
(A) 뇌우가 몰아치는 동안, 구름은 서로 마찰되면서 전기를 띠게 될 수 있다. 폭풍이 몰아치는 동안 우리가 종종 보는 번개는 전기를 띤 구름과 지면 사이 커다란 전하의 흐름으로 야기된다.

Why? 왜 정답일까?

정전기를 간단히 만들어볼 수 있는 단계를 소개하는 주어진 글 뒤에는, 그 결과 생긴 것이 정전기임을 짚어주는 (C), 정전기가 왜 생기는지 설명하며 이것이 대기에서도 발견된다고 이야기한 (B), 대기에서의 예를 상술하는 (A)가 차례로 이어지는 것이 자연스럽다. 따라서 주어진 글 다음에 이어질 글의 순서로 가장 적절한 것은 ⑤ '(C) – (B) – (A)'이다.

● rub ⓥ 문지르다
● thunderstorm ⓝ 뇌우
● lightning ⓝ 번개
● static electricity 정전기
● cling to ~에 달라붙다, ~에 매달리다
● dust ⓝ (미세한) 가루, 먼지
● charged ⓐ 전기를 띤
● friction ⓝ 마찰
● atmosphere ⓝ 대기
● create ⓥ 만들다, 창조하다

구문 풀이

5행 The lightning [that we often see during a storm] is caused
　　　 주어　　　 목적격 관계대명사　　　　　　　　동사(단수)
by a large flow of electrical charges between charged clouds and
　　　　　　　　　　　　　　　　　　　「between A and B : A와 B 사이」
the earth.

---

05 대인 관계의 메시지　　　정답률 37% | 정답 ⑤

주어진 글 다음에 이어질 글의 순서로 가장 적절한 것을 고르시오.

① (A) – (C) – (B)
② (B) – (A) – (C)
③ (B) – (C) – (A)
④ (C) – (A) – (B)
✔ (C) – (B) – (A)

Interpersonal messages / combine content and relationship dimensions.
대인 관계에서의 메시지는 / 내용 차원과 관계 차원을 결합시킨다.
That is, they refer to the real world, / to something external to both speaker and listener; / at the same time / they also refer to the relationship between parties.
즉, 그것들은 실제 세계를 지칭하며, / 화자와 청자 모두에게 외부적인 대상인 / 동시에 / 당사자들 사이의 관계를 지칭하기도 한다.
(C) For example, a supervisor may say to a trainee, / "See me after the meeting."
예를 들어, 한 관리자가 한 수습 직원에게 말할 수 있다. / "회의 끝나고 저 좀 봅시다."라고
This simple message has a content message / that tells the trainee / to see the supervisor after the meeting.
이 간단한 메시지는 내용 메시지를 담고 있다. / 수습 직원에게 전달하는 / 회의 후에 관리자를 만나야 한다는 것을
(B) It also contains a relationship message / that says something about the connection / between the supervisor and the trainee.
그것은 또한 관계 메시지를 포함하고 있다. / 관계에 대해 무언가를 말해 주는 / 관리자와 수습 직원 사이의
Even the use of the simple command / shows there is a status difference / that allows the supervisor to command the trainee.
이 간단한 명령의 사용도 / 지위의 차이가 존재한다는 것을 보여 준다. / 관리자가 그 수습 직원에게 명령할 수 있게 하는
(A) You can appreciate this most clearly / if you visualize the same command / being made by the trainee to the supervisor.
당신은 이것을 아주 명확하게 이해할 수 있을 것이다. / 만약 같은 명령을 상상해 본다면 / 수습 직원이 관리자에게 내리고 있는
It appears awkward and out of place, / because it violates the normal relationship / between supervisor and trainee.
그것은 어색하고 상황에 맞지 않아 보인다. / 그것이 일반적인 관계를 위반하기 때문에 / 관리자와 수습 직원 사이의

대인 관계에서의 메시지에는 내용 차원과 관계 차원이 결합되어 있다. 즉, 그것들은 화자와 청자 모두에게 외부적인 대상인 실제 세계를 지칭하며, 동시에 당사자들 사이의 관계를 지칭하기도 한다.

(C) 예를 들어, 한 관리자가 한 수습 직원에게 "회의 끝나고 저 좀 봅시다."라고 말할 수 있다. 이 간단한 메시지는 수습 직원이 회의 후에 관리자를 만나야 한다는 것을 전달하는 내용 메시지를 담고 있다.

(B) 그것은 또한 관리자와 수습 직원 사이의 관계에 대해 무언가를 말해 주는 관계 메시지를 포함하고 있다. 이 간단한 명령의 사용도 관리자가 그 수습 직원에게 명령할 수 있게 하는 지위의 차이가 존재한다는 것을 보여 준다.

(A) 만약 수습 직원이 관리자에게 같은 명령을 내린다고 상상해 본다면 당신은 이것을 아주 명확하게 이해할 수 있을 것이다. 그것은 관리자와 수습 직원 사이의 일반적인 관계를 위반하기 때문에 어색하고 상황에 맞지 않아 보인다.

Why? 왜 정답일까?

대인 관계에서의 메시지에 내용 차원과 관계 차원이 존재한다는 내용의 주어진 글 뒤에는, 관리자가 수습 직원을 부르는 예로 내용 메시지를 먼저 언급하는 (C), 관계 메시지를 이어서 언급하는 (B), 반대의 상황을 가정하며 예시에 대한 설명을 확장하는 (A)가 차례로 이어져야 한다. 따라서 글의 순서로 가장 적절한 것은 ⑤ '(C) − (B) − (A)'이다.

- **interpersonal** ⓐ 대인 관계와 관련된
- **dimension** ⓝ 차원
- **external** ⓐ 외부의, 외부적인
- **visualize** ⓥ 상상하다, 마음속에 그리다
- **out of place** (상황 등에) 어울리지 않는
- **normal** ⓐ 보통의
- **command** ⓝ 명령 ⓥ 명령하다
- **content** ⓝ 내용물
- **refer to** ~을 지칭하다, 가리키다, 언급하다
- **appreciate** ⓥ 이해하다
- **awkward** ⓐ 어색한, 불편한, 곤란한
- **violate** ⓥ 위반하다, 어기다
- **trainee** ⓝ 교육을 받는 사람
- **status** ⓝ 지위, 상태

구문 풀이

13행 Even the use of the simple command shows {(that) there is
주어 〔동사〕 생략(접속사)
a status difference [that allows the supervisor to command the
주격 관계대명사 allows의 목적격 보어
trainee]}. 〔 〕: 목적어

---

06 작가가 되고 싶었던 Charles Dickens   정답률 65% | 정답 ②

주어진 글 다음에 이어질 글의 순서로 가장 적절한 것을 고르시오.

① (A) − (C) − (B)   ✔ (B) − (A) − (C)
③ (B) − (C) − (A)   ④ (C) − (A) − (B)
⑤ (C) − (B) − (A)

In early 19th century London, / a young man named Charles Dickens / had a strong desire to be a writer.
19세기 초반 런던, / Charles Dickens라는 이름의 젊은이는 / 작가가 되려는 강한 열망을 갖고 있었다.

But everything seemed to be against him.
하지만 모든 것이 그에게 불리한 것 같았다.

(B) He had never been able to attend school / for more than four years.
그는 학교에 다닌 적이 없었다. / 4년 이상

His father had been in jail / because he couldn't pay his debts, / and this young man often knew the pain of hunger.
그의 아버지는 감옥에 있었고, / 그가 자기 빚을 갚지 못했기에 / 이 젊은이는 자주 배고픔의 고통을 알았다.

(A) Moreover, / he had so little confidence / in his ability to write / that he mailed his writings secretly at night to editors / so that nobody would laugh at him.
더구나, / 그는 자신감이 너무 없어서 / 자신의 글재주에 / 그는 밤에 몰래 편집자들에게 자신의 글을 우편으로 보냈다. / 그 누구도 자신을 비웃지 못하도록

Story after story was refused.
작품들마다 거절을 당했다.

(C) But one day, / one editor recognized and praised him.
하지만 어느 날, / 한 편집장이 그를 알아보고 칭찬해 주었다.

The praise / that he received from getting one story in print / changed his whole life.
칭찬은 / 하나의 이야기를 출판하여 그가 얻은 / 그의 일생을 바꾸어 놓았다.

His works have been widely read / and still enjoy great popularity.
그의 작품들은 널리 읽히게 되었고 / 여전히 엄청난 인기를 누린다.

19세기 초반 런던, Charles Dickens라는 이름의 젊은이는 작가가 되려는 강한 열망을 갖고 있었다. 하지만 모든 것이 그에게 불리한 것 같았다.

(B) 그는 4년 이상 학교에 다닌 적이 없었다. 그의 아버지는 빚을 갚지 못해 감

옥에 있었고, 이 젊은이는 자주 배고픔의 고통을 알았다.

(A) 더구나, 그는 자신의 글재주에 자신감이 너무 없어서 그 누구도 자신을 비웃지 못하도록 밤에 몰래 편집자들에게 자신의 글을 우편으로 보냈다. 작품들마다 거절을 당했다.

(C) 하지만 어느 날, 한 편집장이 그를 알아보고 칭찬해 주었다. 하나의 이야기를 출판하여 그가 얻은 칭찬은 그의 일생을 바꾸어 놓았다. 그의 작품들은 널리 읽히게 되었고 여전히 엄청난 인기를 누린다.

Why? 왜 정답일까?

Charles Dickens는 작가가 되고자 했지만 상황이 그에게 불리했다는 내용의 주어진 글 뒤에는 구체적으로 그의 불리한 조건을 묘사한, 즉 그의 교육 및 가정이 모두 불우했음을 이야기한 (B), 이어서 그가 스스로의 글재주에도 자신 없어 했다는 내용의 (A)가 차례로 나오는 것이 적절하다. '하지만' 결국 그가 작가로서 성공을 거두게 되었다는 내용의 (C)는 마지막에 나오는 것이 자연스럽다. 따라서 주어진 글 다음에 이어질 글의 순서로 가장 적절한 것은 ② '(B) − (A) − (C)'이다.

- **desire** ⓝ 열망, 갈망
- **secretly** ⓐ𝒹 몰래
- **jail** ⓝ 교도소
- **recognize** ⓥ 알아보다, 인정하다
- **whole** ⓐ 전체의
- **confidence** ⓝ 자신감, 믿음
- **refuse** ⓥ 거절하다
- **debt** ⓝ 빚, 부채
- **praise** ⓥ 칭찬하다
- **widely** ⓐ𝒹 널리

구문 풀이

4행 Moreover, / he had so little confidence in his ability to write
접속부사(첨가) 「so + 형용사」
that he mailed his writings secretly at night to editors / so that nobody
「that + 주어 + 동사 : 너무 ~해서 …하다」 ~하도록
would laugh at him.
~을 비웃다

---

07 색상이 무게에 대한 인식에 미치는 영향   정답률 42% | 정답 ⑤

주어진 글 다음에 이어질 글의 순서로 가장 적절한 것을 고르시오.

① (A) − (C) − (B)   ② (B) − (A) − (C)
③ (B) − (C) − (A)   ④ (C) − (A) − (B)
✔ (C) − (B) − (A)

Color can impact / how you perceive weight.
색상은 영향을 줄 수 있다. / 여러분이 무게를 인식하는 방식에

Dark colors look heavy, / and bright colors look less so.
어두운 색은 무거워 보이고, / 밝은 색은 덜 그렇게 보인다.

Interior designers often paint darker colors / below brighter colors / to put the viewer at ease.
실내 디자이너들은 종종 더 어두운 색을 칠한다. / 더 밝은 색 아래에 / 보는 사람을 편안하게 해 주기 위해

(C) Product displays work the same way.
상품 전시도 같은 방식으로 작동한다.

Place bright-colored products higher / and dark-colored products lower, / given that they are of similar size.
밝은 색의 상품을 더 높이 배치하라. / 어두운 색의 상품을 더 낮게 / 상품들이 비슷한 크기라면

This will look more stable / and allow customers to comfortably browse the products / from top to bottom.
이것은 더 안정적으로 보이고 / 고객이 편안하게 상품들을 훑어볼 수 있도록 해 준다. / 위에서 아래로

(B) In contrast, / shelving dark-colored products on top / can create the illusion / that they might fall over, / which can be a source of anxiety for some shoppers.
반대로 / 어두운 색의 상품을 선반 맨 위에 두는 것은 / 착각을 불러일으킬 수 있으며, / 상품들이 떨어질 수 있다는 / 이것은 일부 구매자들에게 불안감의 원인이 될 수 있다.

Black and white, / which have a brightness of 0% and 100%, respectively, / show the most dramatic difference / in perceived weight.
검은색과 흰색은 / 명도가 각각 0%와 100%인 / 가장 극적인 차이를 보여준다. / 인식된 무게의

(A) In fact, / black is perceived / to be twice as heavy as white.
사실, / 검은색은 인식된다. / 흰색보다 두 배 무겁게

Carrying the same product in a black shopping bag, / versus a white one, / feels heavier.
같은 상품을 검은색 쇼핑백에 담아 드는 것이 / 흰색 쇼핑백보다 / 더 무겁게 느껴진다.

So, / small but expensive products / like neckties and accessories / are often sold / in dark-colored shopping bags or cases.
따라서 / 작지만 값비싼 상품들은 / 넥타이와 액세서리와 같이 / 대체로 판매된다. / 어두운 색의 쇼핑백 또는 케이스에 담겨

색상은 여러분이 무게를 인식하는 방식에 영향을 줄 수 있다. 어두운 색은 무거

위 보이고, 밝은 색은 덜 그렇게 보인다. 실내 디자이너들은 보는 사람을 편안하게 해 주기 위해 종종 더 밝은 색 아래에 더 어두운 색을 칠한다.

(C) 상품 전시도 같은 방식으로 작용한다. 상품들이 비슷한 크기라면, 밝은 색의 상품을 더 높이, 어두운 색의 상품을 더 낮게 배치하라. 이것은 더 안정적으로 보이고 고객이 편안하게 상품들을 위에서 아래로 훑어볼 수 있도록 해 준다.

(B) 반대로 어두운 색의 상품을 선반 맨 위에 두는 것은 상품들이 떨어질 수 있다는 착각을 불러일으킬 수 있으며, 이것은 일부 구매자들에게 불안감의 원인이 될 수 있다. 명도가 각각 0%와 100%인 검은색과 흰색은 인식된 무게의 가장 극적인 차이를 보여준다.

(A) 사실, 검은색은 흰색보다 두 배 무겁게 인식된다. 같은 상품을 흰색 쇼핑백보다 검은색 쇼핑백에 담아 드는 것이 더 무겁게 느껴진다. 따라서 넥타이와 액세서리와 같이 작지만 값비싼 상품들은 대체로 어두운 색의 쇼핑백 또는 케이스에 담겨 판매된다.

Why? 왜 정답일까?

색상이 무게를 인식하는 데 영향을 미칠 수 있다고 말하며 실내 디자이너들이 이러한 사실을 활용하고 있다는 내용의 주어진 글 뒤에는, 상품 전시에서도 같은 사실을 활용하여 어두운 색의 상품을 더 낮게 배치하는 예를 언급하는 (C), 어두운 상품을 위에 두는 경우를 대조하며 선명한 검은색과 흰색이 가장 극적인 차이를 보일 수 있다는 내용을 이어서 언급하는 (B), 흑백의 무게감 대비와 관련된 사례를 드는 (A)가 차례로 연결되어야 자연스럽다. 따라서 글의 순서로 가장 적절한 것은 ⑤ '(C) − (B) − (A)'이다.

- **impact** ⓥ 영향을 주다 ⓝ 영향
- **at ease** 편안한, 걱정 없는
- **illusion** ⓝ 착각, 환상
- **brightness** ⓝ 명도, 밝음
- **dramatic** ⓐ 극적인
- **browse** ⓥ 훑어보다, 둘러보다
- **perceive** ⓥ 인식하다, 인지하다
- **shelve** ⓥ 선반에 얹다
- **anxiety** ⓝ 불안, 염려, 걱정거리
- **respectively** ⓐⓓ 각각
- **stable** ⓐ 안정적인

구문 풀이

11행 In contrast, / shelving dark-colored products on top can create
　　　　　　　동명사구 주어　　　　　　　　　　　　동사
the illusion {that they might fall over}, which can be a source of anxiety
　　　{ } : the illusion과 동격　　계속적 용법(= the illusion)
for some shoppers.

08　시계의 발명　　　정답률 78% | 정답 ②

주어진 글 다음에 이어질 글의 순서로 가장 적절한 것을 고르시오. [3점]
① (A) − (C) − (B)　　✔ (B) − (A) − (C)
③ (B) − (C) − (A)　　④ (C) − (A) − (B)
⑤ (C) − (B) − (A)

Up until about 6,000 years ago, / most people were farmers.
약 6,000년 전까지 / 대부분의 사람들은 농부였다.

Many lived in different places throughout the year, / hunting for food / or moving their livestock to areas with enough food.
많은 사람들은 일 년 내내 여러 장소에서 살았고, / 식량을 찾아다니거나 / 가축을 충분한 먹이가 있는 지역으로 옮겼다.

(B) There was no need to tell the time / because life depended on natural cycles, / such as the changing seasons or sunrise and sunset.
시간을 알 필요가 없었다. / 삶이 자연적인 주기에 달려 있기 때문에 / 변화하는 계절이나 일출과 일몰 같은

Gradually more people started to live in larger settlements, / and some needed to tell the time.
점점 더 많은 사람들이 더 큰 정착지에서 살기 시작했고, / 어떤 사람들은 시간을 알 필요가 있었다.

(A) For example, / priests wanted to know / when to carry out religious ceremonies.
예를 들어, / 성직자들은 알고 싶었다. / 언제 종교적인 의식을 수행해야 하는지

This was when people first invented clocks / — devices that show, measure, and keep track of passing time.
이때 사람들이 처음으로 발명했다. / 시간을 보여주고, 측정하고, 흐르는 시간을 추적하는 장치인 시계를

(C) Clocks have been important ever since.
시계는 그 이후로도 중요했다.

Today, / clocks are used for important things / such as setting busy airport timetables / — if the time is incorrect, / aeroplanes might crash into each other / when taking off or landing!
오늘날, / 시계는 중요한 일에 사용된다. / 바쁜 공항 시간표를 설정하는 것과 같은 / 만약 시간이 부정확하다면, / 비행기는 서로 충돌할지도 모른다! / 이륙하거나 착륙할 때

약 6,000년 전까지 대부분의 사람들은 농부였다. 많은 사람들은 일 년 내내 여러 장소에서 살았고, 식량을 찾아다니거나 가축을 충분한 먹이가 있는 지역으로 옮겼다.

(B) 변화하는 계절이나 일출과 일몰 같은 자연적인 주기에 삶이 달려 있었기 때문에 시간을 알 필요가 없었다. 점점 더 많은 사람들이 더 큰 정착지에서 살기 시작했고, 어떤 사람들은 시간을 알 필요가 있었다.

(A) 예를 들어, 성직자들은 언제 종교적인 의식을 수행해야 하는지 알고 싶었다. 이때 사람들이 시간을 보여주고, 측정하고, 흐르는 시간을 추적하는 장치인 시계를 처음으로 발명했다.

(C) 시계는 그 이후로도 중요했다. 오늘날, 시계는 바쁜 공항 시간표를 설정하는 것과 같은 중요한 일에 사용된다. 만약 시간이 부정확하다면, 비행기는 이륙하거나 착륙할 때 서로 충돌할지도 모른다!

Why? 왜 정답일까?

사람들이 대부분 농부였던 시절을 언급하는 주어진 글 뒤로, 이때는 시계가 필요 없었다는 내용으로 시작하는 (B)가 연결된다. 한편, (B)의 후반부는 그러다 일부 사람들이 시계를 필요로 하기 시작했다는 내용이고, (A)는 그런 사람들의 예로 성직자를 언급한다. (C)는 시계가 처음 발명된 이후로 시계의 중요성이 높아졌고, 오늘날에도 시계가 중요한 역할을 담당하고 있음을 설명한다. 따라서 글의 순서로 가장 적절한 것은 ② '(B) − (A) − (C)'이다.

- **hunt for** ~을 사냥하다
- **carry out** 수행하다
- **device** ⓝ 장치
- **keep track of** ~을 추적하다, 기록하다
- **gradually** ⓐⓓ 점차
- **tell the time** 시간을 알다
- **take off** 이륙하다
- **livestock** ⓝ 가축
- **religious** ⓐ 종교적인
- **measure** ⓥ 측정하다
- **natural cycle** 자연적 주기
- **settlement** ⓝ 정착(지)
- **crash into** ~에 충돌하다
- **land** ⓥ 착륙하다

구문 풀이

14행 Today, clocks are used for important things such as setting busy airport timetables — if the time is incorrect, aeroplanes might crash into each other when taking off or landing!
접속사를 포함한 분사구문(= when they take off or land)

09　좋은 음악과 나쁜 음악　　　정답률 61% | 정답 ②

주어진 글 다음에 이어질 글의 순서로 가장 적절한 것을 고르시오. [3점]
① (A) − (C) − (B)　　✔ (B) − (A) − (C)
③ (B) − (C) − (A)　　④ (C) − (A) − (B)
⑤ (C) − (B) − (A)

Robert Schumann once said, / "The laws of morals are those of art."
Robert Schumann은 언젠가 말했다. / "도덕의 법칙은 예술의 법칙이다."라고

What the great man is saying here / is that there is good music and bad music.
여기서 이 위인이 말하고 있는 것은 / 좋은 음악과 나쁜 음악이 있다는 것이다.

(B) The greatest music, / even if it's tragic in nature, / takes us to a world higher than ours; / somehow the beauty uplifts us.
가장 위대한 음악은, / 심지어 그것이 사실상 비극적일지라도, / 우리의 세상보다 더 높은 세상으로 우리를 데려간다. / 어떻게든지 아름다움은 우리를 고양시킨다.

Bad music, on the other hand, degrades us.
반면에 나쁜 음악은 우리를 격하시킨다.

(A) It's the same with performances: / a bad performance isn't necessarily the result of incompetence.
연주도 마찬가지다. / 나쁜 연주가 반드시 무능의 결과는 아니다.

Some of the worst performances occur / when the performers, / no matter how accomplished, / are thinking more of themselves / than of the music they're playing.
최악의 연주 중 일부는 발생한다. / 연주자들이 ~할 때 / 아무리 숙달되었더라도 / 자기 자신을 더 생각하고 있을 / 연주하고 있는 곡보다

(C) These doubtful characters aren't really listening / to what the composer is saying / — they're just showing off, / hoping that they'll have a great 'success' with the public.
이 미덥지 못한 사람들은 정말로 듣고 있는 것이 아니다. / 작곡가가 말하는 것을 / 그들은 그저 뽐내고 있을 뿐이다. / 그들이 대중적으로 큰 '성공'을 거두기를 바라며

The performer's basic task / is to try to understand the meaning of the music, / and then to communicate it honestly to others.
연주자의 기본 임무는 / 음악의 의미를 이해하려고 노력하고서, / 그것을 다른 사람들에게 정직하게 전달하는 것이다.

Robert Schumann은 "도덕의 법칙은 예술의 법칙이다."라고 말한 적이 있다. 여기서 이 위인이 말하고 있는 것은 좋은 음악과 나쁜 음악이 있다는 것이다.

(B) 가장 위대한 음악은, 심지어 그것이 사실상 비극적일지라도, 우리의 세상보다 더 높은 세상으로 우리를 데려가며, 아름다움은 어떻게든지 우리를 고양시킨다. 반면에 나쁜 음악은 우리를 격하시킨다.

(A) 연주도 마찬가지다. 나쁜 연주가 반드시 무능의 결과는 아니다. 최악의 연주 중 일부는 연주자들이 아무리 숙달되었더라도 연주하고 있는 곡보다 자기 자신을 더 생각하고 있을 때 발생한다.

(C) 이 미덥지 못한 사람들은 작곡가가 말하는 것을 정말로 듣고 있는 것이 아니다. 그들은 대중적으로 큰 '성공'을 거두기를 바라며 그저 뽐내고 있을 뿐이다. 연주자의 기본 임무는 음악의 의미를 이해하려고 노력하고서, 그것을 다른 사람들에게 정직하게 전달하는 것이다.

Why? 왜 정답일까?

음악에 좋은 음악과 나쁜 음악이 있음을 언급하는 주어진 글 뒤로, 두 음악의 특징을 풀어 설명하는 (B), 연주에도 나쁜 연주와 좋은 연주가 있음을 덧붙이는 (A), (A)에서 언급된 최악의 연주자를 These doubtful characters로 가리키는 (C)가 차례로 연결된다. 따라서 글의 순서로 가장 적절한 것은 ② '(B) – (A) – (C)'이다.

- accomplished ⓐ 숙달된, 기량이 뛰어난
- doubtful ⓐ 미심쩍은
- show off 과시하다, 뽐내다
- uplift ⓥ 고양시키다, 들어올리다
- composer ⓝ 작곡가

구문 풀이

5행 Some of the worst performances occur when the performers, no matter how accomplished (they are), are thinking more of themselves than of the music they're playing.
「no matter how + 형/부 + 주어 + 동사 : 아무리 ~할지라도」

★★★ **1등급 대비 고난도 2점 문제**

| 10 | 농경 생활로 인한 인간 사회의 변화 | 정답률 36% | 정답 ④ |

주어진 글 다음에 이어질 글의 순서로 가장 적절한 것을 고르시오.

① (A) – (C) – (B) ② (B) – (A) – (C)
③ (B) – (C) – (A) ✔ (C) – (A) – (B)
⑤ (C) – (B) – (A)

In the Old Stone Age, / small bands of 20 to 60 people / wandered from place to place / in search of food.
구석기 시대에는 / 20 ~ 60명의 작은 무리가 / 여기저기 돌아다녔다. / 먹을 것을 찾아

Once people began farming, / they could settle down near their farms.
일단 사람들이 농사를 짓기 시작하면서, / 그들은 자신의 농경지 근처에 정착할 수 있었다.

(C) As a result, / towns and villages grew larger.
그 결과, / 도시와 마을이 더 커졌다.

Living in communities / allowed people / to organize themselves more efficiently.
공동체 생활은 / 사람들이 ~하게 했다. / 더 효율적으로 조직되게

They could divide up the work / of producing food and other things they needed.
그들은 일을 나눌 수 있었다. / 식량과 자신들에게 필요한 다른 것들을 생산하는

(A) While some workers grew crops, / others built new houses and made tools.
어떤 노동자들은 농작물을 재배하는 한편, / 다른 노동자들은 새로운 집을 짓고 도구를 만들었다.

Village dwellers also learned to work together / to do a task faster.
마을 거주자들은 또한 함께 일하는 법도 익혔다. / 일을 더 빨리 하려고

(B) For example, / toolmakers could share the work / of making stone axes and knives.
예를 들어, / 도구 제작자들은 작업을 함께 할 수 있었다. / 돌도끼와 돌칼을 만드는

By working together, / they could make more tools / in the same amount of time.
함께 일하여 / 그들은 더 많은 도구를 만들 수 있었다. / 같은 시간 안에

구석기 시대에는 20 ~ 60명의 작은 무리가 먹을 것을 찾아 여기저기 돌아다녔다. 일단 농사를 짓기 시작하면서, 사람들은 자신의 농경지 근처에 정착할 수 있었다.

(C) 그 결과, 도시와 마을이 더 커졌다. 공동체 생활을 통해 사람들은 더 효율적으로 조직될 수 있었다. 그들은 식량과 자신들에게 필요한 다른 것들을 생산하는 일을 나눌 수 있었다.

(A) 어떤 노동자들은 농작물을 재배하는 한편, 다른 노동자들은 새로운 집을 짓고 도구를 만들었다. 마을 거주자들은 또한 일을 더 빨리 하려고 함께 일하는 법도 익혔다.

(B) 예를 들어, 도구 제작자들은 돌도끼와 돌칼을 만드는 작업을 함께 할 수 있었다. 그들은 함께 일하여 같은 시간 안에 더 많은 도구를 만들 수 있었다.

Why? 왜 정답일까?

농경이 시작되면서 사람들이 정착할 수 있었다는 내용의 주어진 글 뒤로, '그 결과' 도시와 마을이 생기고 사람들이 일을 분배할 수 있게 되었다고 설명하는 (C)가 먼저 연결된다. 이어서 (A)는 (C)에서 언급된 '분업'이 어떻게 이루어졌는지 언급하며, 사람들이 함께 일하는 법 또한 배우게 되었다고 이야기한다. (B)에서는 '함께 작업'하는 상황의 예를 제시하며 (A)를 보충 설명한다. 따라서 글의 순서로 가장 적절한 것은 ④ '(C) – (A) – (B)'이다.

- Old Stone Age 구석기 시대
- wander ⓥ 돌아다니다, 배회하다
- settle down 정착하다
- dweller ⓝ 거주자
- community ⓝ 공동체, 지역사회
- efficiently ⓐⓓ 효율적으로
- band ⓝ (소규모) 무리
- in search of ~을 찾아서
- crop ⓝ 작물
- axe ⓝ 도끼
- organize ⓥ 조직하다, 정리하다
- divide up ~을 나누다

구문 풀이

3행 Once people began farming, they could settle down near their farms.
접속사(일단 ~한다면)

★★ **문제 해결 꿀~팁** ★★

▶ 많이 틀린 이유는?

글을 자세히 읽지 않고 연결어 중심으로만 보면, (B)가 주어진 글의 예시(For example)이고 (C)가 전체 글의 결론(As a result)일 것이라고 잘못 추론할 수 있다. 하지만, 내용적 단서가 중요하다. 주어진 글은 사람들이 농경을 시작하며 정착했다는 내용인데, (B)는 갑자기 '도구 제작자'를 언급하며, 이들이 업무를 분업해 담당했다는 설명을 제시하고 있다. 서로 전혀 다른 키워드로 보아 (B)가 주어진 글에 대한 예시라고 보기 어렵기 때문에 ②를 답으로 고르는 것은 적절하지 않다.

▶ 문제 해결 방법은?

사람들이 농경지 근처에 정착하여 살게 되면서, 마을이 성장하고 분업화가 일어나(C), 누구는 농사를 짓고 누구는 도구를 만드는 한편 공동 작업도 활성화되었으며(A), 공동 작업으로 더 쉽고 빠른 작업이 가능해졌다(B)는 흐름이다.

★★★ **1등급 대비 고난도 3점 문제**

| 11 | 소수 집단과 다수 집단의 건강 지표 차이 | 정답률 38% | 정답 ② |

주어진 글 다음에 이어질 글의 순서로 가장 적절한 것을 고르시오. [3점]

① (A) – (C) – (B) ✔ (B) – (A) – (C)
③ (B) – (C) – (A) ④ (C) – (A) – (B)
⑤ (C) – (B) – (A)

Many studies have shown / that people's health and subjective well-being / are affected by ethnic relations.
많은 연구들이 보여주었다. / 사람들의 건강과 주관적 웰빙이 / 민족 관계에 의해 영향을 받는다는 것을

Members of minority groups in general / have poorer health outcomes / than the majority group.
소수 집단의 구성원이 일반적으로 / 더 좋지 않은 건강 결과를 보인다. / 다수 집단보다

(B) But that difference remains / even when obvious factors, / such as social class and access to medical services / are controlled for.
그러나 그러한 차이가 남아 있다 / 명백한 요소들이 / 사회 계층과 의료 서비스에 대한 접근성 같은 / 통제될 때조차도

This suggests / that dominance relations have their own effect / on people's health.
이것은 보여 준다. / 우세 관계가 그 자체의 영향을 미친다는 것을 / 사람들의 건강에

How could that be the case?
어떻게 그럴 수 있을까?

(A) One possible answer is stress.
한 가지 가능한 답은 스트레스이다.

From multiple physiological studies, / we know / that encounters with members of other ethnic-racial categories, / even in the relatively safe environment of laboratories, / trigger stress responses.
다수의 생리학적 연구를 통해 / 우리는 안다. / 다른 민족적-인종적 범주의 구성원들과 마주치는 것이 / 비교적 안전한 실험실 환경에서조차도 / 스트레스 반응을 유발한다는 것을

(C) Minority individuals / have many encounters with majority individuals, / each of which may trigger such responses.
소수 집단의 개인들은 / 다수 집단의 개인들과 많은 마주침을 가지며, / 각각의 마주침은 이러한 반응을 유발할 지도 모른다.

However minimal these effects may be, / their frequency may increase total stress, / which would account for / part of the health disadvantage of minority individuals.
이러한 영향이 아무리 작을지라도 / 그것의 빈번한 발생이 총체적 스트레스를 증가시킬지도 모르며 / 이는 설명할 것이다. / 소수 집단 개인들의 건강상 불이익의 일부를

많은 연구들이 사람들의 건강과 주관적 웰빙이 민족 관계에 의해 영향을 받는다는 것을 보여주었다. 소수 집단의 구성원들이 일반적으로 다수 집단보다 더 좋지 않은 건강 결과를 보인다.

(B) 그러나 사회 계층과 의료 서비스에 대한 접근성 같은 명백한 요소들이 통제될 때조차도 그러한 차이가 남아 있다. 이것은 우세 관계가 사람들의 건강에 자체적인 영향을 미친다는 것을 보여 준다. 어떻게 그럴 수 있을까?

(A) 한 가지 가능한 답은 스트레스이다. 다수의 생리학적 연구를 통해 우리는 비교적 안전한 실험실 환경에서조차도 다른 민족적-인종적 범주의 구성원들과 마주치는 것이 스트레스 반응을 유발한다는 것을 안다.

(C) 소수 집단의 개인들은 다수 집단의 개인들과 많이 마주치며, 각각의 마주침은 이러한 반응을 유발할지도 모른다. 이러한 영향이 아무리 작을지라도 그것의 빈번한 발생이 총체적 스트레스를 증가시킬지도 모르며 이는 소수 집단 개인들의 건강상 불이익의 일부를 설명할 것이다.

Why? 왜 정답일까?

소수 집단의 구성원들이 대체로 다수 집단의 구성원보다 건강이 더 좋지 않다는 일반적인 내용을 제시하는 주어진 글 뒤에는, 심지어 사회 계층이나 의료 서비스에 대한 접근성 등 다른 요소들이 통제되었을 때조차 왜 이러한 결과가 나타나는지 자문하는 (B), 그 답이 스트레스에 있음을 제시하는 (A), 답을 보충 설명하는 (C)가 차례로 이어지는 것이 자연스럽다. 따라서 글의 순서로 가장 적절한 것은 ② '(B) – (A) – (C)'이다.

- subjective ⓐ 주관적인
- physiological ⓐ 생리학적인
- trigger ⓥ 유발하다
- have an effect on ⓥ ~에 영향을 미치다
- account for ⓥ ~을 설명하다
- ethnic ⓐ 민족적인
- encounter ⓝ 마주침 ⓥ 마주치다
- dominance ⓝ 우세
- frequency ⓝ 빈도
- disadvantage ⓝ 불이익

구문 풀이

17행 However minimal these effects may be, / their frequency may
「however + 형용사/부사 + 주어 + 동사 : 아무리 ~하더라도」
increase total stress, which would account for part of the health
계속적 용법(주절 부연)
disadvantage of minority individuals.

★★ 문제 해결 꿀~팁 ★★

▶ 많이 틀린 이유는?
주어진 글의 Members of minority groups만 보고 바로 (C)를 연결시켜서는 안 된다. 주어진 글의 마지막 문장은 전체적으로 볼 때 소수 집단 사람들과 다수 집단 사람들의 건강 지표상 차이를 언급하는 내용이어서, 이를 (B)에서 that difference 로 요약하는 것이다.

▶ 문제 해결 방법은?
주어진 글이 마지막 문장이 (B)의 that difference로, (B)의 'How could that be the case?'라는 질문이 (A)의 One possible answer라는 답으로 연결된다는 것을 파악하면 쉽게 정답을 찾을 수 있다.

★★★ 1등급 대비 고난도 3점 문제

12 AI 로봇과 일반 로봇의 차이   정답률 40% | 정답 ④

주어진 글 다음에 이어질 글의 순서로 가장 적절한 것을 고르시오. [3점]

① (A) – (C) – (B)
② (B) – (A) – (C)
③ (B) – (C) – (A)
✔ (C) – (A) – (B)
⑤ (C) – (B) – (A)

The basic difference / between an AI robot and a normal robot / is the ability of the robot and its software / to make decisions, / and learn and adapt to its environment / based on data from its sensors.
기본적 차이는 / AI 로봇과 보통 로봇의 / 로봇과 그것의 소프트웨어의 능력이다. / 결정을 내리고, / 학습하여 환경에 적응하는 / 센서로부터 얻는 데이터에 기반하여

(C) To be a bit more specific, / the normal robot shows deterministic behaviors.
좀 더 구체적으로 말해서 / 보통 로봇은 결정론적인(이미 정해진) 행동을 보인다.

That is, / for a set of inputs, / the robot will always produce the same output.
다시 말해, / 일련의 입력에 대해 / 그 로봇은 항상 똑같은 결과를 만들 것이다.

(A) For instance, / if faced with the same situation, / such as running into an obstacle, / then the robot will always do the same thing, / such as go around the obstacle to the left.
예를 들어, / 동일한 상황에 직면한다면 / 장애물을 우연히 마주치는 것과 같이 / 그 로봇은 항상 똑같은 행동을 할 것이다. / 그 장애물을 왼쪽으로 돌아서 가는 것과 같이

An AI robot, / however, / can do two things the normal robot cannot: / make decisions and learn from experience.
AI 로봇은 / 하지만 / 보통 로봇이 할 수 없는 두 가지, / 즉, 결정을 내리고 경험으로부터 학습하는 것을 할 수 있다.

(B) It will adapt to circumstances, / and may do something different / each time a situation is faced.
그것은 환경에 적응할 것이고, / 다른 행동을 할 수 있다. / 어떤 상황에 직면할 때마다

The AI robot may try to push the obstacle out of the way, / or make up a new route, / or change goals.
AI 로봇은 경로에서 장애물을 밀어내거나 / 새로운 경로를 만들거나 / 목표를 바꾸려 할 수도 있다.

AI 로봇과 일반 로봇의 근본적 차이는 센서로부터 얻는 데이터에 기반하여 결정을 내리고 학습하여 환경에 적응하는 로봇과 그것의 소프트웨어의 능력이다.

(C) 좀 더 구체적으로 말해서 일반 로봇은 결정론적인 행동을 보인다. 즉, 일련의 입력에 대해 그 로봇은 항상 똑같은 결과를 만들 것이다.

(A) 예를 들어, 장애물을 우연히 마주치는 것과 같이 동일한 상황에 직면한다면 그 로봇은 그 장애물을 왼쪽으로 돌아서 가는 것과 같이 항상 똑같은 행동을 할 것이다. 하지만 AI 로봇은 일반 로봇이 할 수 없는 두 가지, 즉, 결정을 내리는 것과 경험으로부터 학습하는 것을 할 수 있다.

(B) 그것은 환경에 적응할 것이고, 어떤 상황에 직면할 때마다 다른 행동을 할 수 있다. AI 로봇은 경로에서 장애물을 밀어내거나 새로운 경로를 만들거나 아니면 목표를 바꾸려 할 수 있다.

Why? 왜 정답일까?

AI 로봇과 일반 로봇의 차이를 화두로 제시하는 주어진 글 다음에는, 차이를 구체적으로 언급하겠다고 말하며 먼저 일반 로봇의 특징을 설명하는 (C), 일반 로봇의 활동에 대한 예를 제시한 뒤 however를 통해 AI 로봇으로 화제를 전환하는 (A), 문단 첫 머리의 It으로 AI 로봇을 받아 그 특징을 설명하는 (B)가 차례로 이어지는 것이 자연스럽다. 따라서 글의 순서로 가장 적절한 것은 ④ '(C) – (A) – (B)'이다.

- difference ⓝ 차이점
- adapt to ~에 적응하다
- run into ~을 우연히 마주치다
- circumstances ⓝ 사정, 상황
- specific ⓐ 구체적인
- produce ⓥ 생산하다
- decision ⓝ 결정, 판단
- faced with ~에 직면한
- obstacle ⓝ 장애물, 방해물
- push ~ out of the way ~을 밀어내다
- input ⓝ 입력, 투입
- output ⓝ 산출, 결과

구문 풀이

1행 The basic difference between an AI robot and a normal robot
주어
is the ability of the robot and its software to make decisions, and
동사 주격 보어 형용사적 용법1
(to) learn and (to) adapt to its environment based on data from its sensors.
형용사적 용법2 형용사적 용법3 ~에 기반하여

★★ 문제 해결 꿀~팁 ★★

▶ 많이 틀린 이유는?
주어진 글 뒤에 가장 먼저 이어지는 단락을 찾는 것이 풀이의 관건이다. 주어진 글에서 AI 로봇과 일반 로봇이라는 두 가지 소재를 모두 제시하므로, (B)와 같이 단수대명사 It이 뒤에 이어질 경우 이 It이 무엇을 가리키는지가 불분명해진다.

▶ 문제 해결 방법은?
'To be a bit more specific'은 주어진 글에서 언급된 AI 로봇과 일반 로봇 중 어느 한 대상을 특정하여 언급할 것임을 알리는 신호어이다. 신호어의 기능을 잘 파악하면 순서 문제 풀이 시간을 단축하는 데 도움이 된다.

DAY 13 글의 순서 03

01 ③	02 ⑤	03 ⑤	04 ②	05 ⑤
06 ①	07 ②	08 ②	09 ⑤	10 ④
11 ⑤	12 ⑤			

---

01 노동의 자동화로 인한 일자리 위기   정답률 58% | 정답 ③

주어진 글 다음에 이어질 글의 순서로 가장 적절한 것을 고르시오.

① (A) – (C) – (B) ② (B) – (A) – (C)
✓③ (B) – (C) – (A) ④ (C) – (A) – (B)
⑤ (C) – (B) – (A)

Things are changing.
상황이 변하고 있다.
It has been reported / that 42 percent of jobs in Canada / are at risk, / and 62 percent of jobs in America / will be in danger / due to advances in automation.
보도되었다. / 캐나다의 일자리 중 42퍼센트가 / 위기에 처했으며, / 미국의 일자리 중 62퍼센트가 / 위기에 처할 것이라고 / 자동화의 발전으로 인해
(B) You might say / that the numbers seem a bit unrealistic, / but the threat is real.
여러분은 말할지 모른다 / 그 숫자들이 약간 비현실적으로 보인다고 / 하지만 그 위험은 현실이다.
One fast food franchise has a robot / that can flip a burger in ten seconds.
한 패스트푸드 체인점은 로봇을 가지고 있다. / 10초 안에 버거 하나를 뒤집을 수 있는
It is just a simple task / but the robot could replace an entire crew.
그것은 단지 단순한 일일 뿐이지만, / 그 로봇은 전체 직원을 대체할 수도 있다.
(C) Highly skilled jobs are also at risk.
고도로 숙련된 직업들 또한 위기에 처해 있다.
A supercomputer, / for instance, / can suggest available treatments / for specific illnesses / in an automated way, / drawing on the body of medical research and data on diseases.
슈퍼컴퓨터는 / 예를 들면, / 이용 가능한 치료법을 제안할 수 있다. / 특정한 질병들에 대해 / 자동화된 방식으로 / 질병에 대한 방대한 양의 의학 연구와 데이터를 이용하여
(A) However, / what's difficult to automate / is the ability / to creatively solve problems.
하지만, / 자동화하기 어려운 것은 / 능력이다. / 문제를 창의적으로 해결하는
Whereas workers in "doing" roles / can be replaced by robots, / the role of creatively solving problems / is more dependent on an irreplaceable individual.
'하는' 역할의 노동자들은 / 로봇들에 의해 대체될 수 있는 반면에, / 창의적으로 문제를 해결하는 역할은 / 대체 불가능한 개인에 더 의존한다.

상황이 변하고 있다. 캐나다의 일자리 중 42퍼센트가 위기에 처했으며, 미국의 일자리 중 62퍼센트가 자동화의 발전으로 인해 위기에 처할 것이라고 보도되었다.

(B) 여러분은 그 숫자들이 약간 비현실적으로 보인다고 말할지 모르지만, 그 위험은 현실이다. 한 패스트푸드 체인점은 10초 안에 버거 하나를 뒤집을 수 있다. 그것은 단지 단순한 일일 뿐이지만, 로봇은 전체 직원을 대체할 수도 있다.

(C) 고도로 숙련된 직업들 또한 위기에 처해 있다. 예를 들면, 슈퍼컴퓨터는 질병에 대한 방대한 양의 의학 연구와 데이터를 이용하여 특정한 질병들에 대해 이용 가능한 치료법을 자동화된 방식으로 제안할 수 있다.

(A) 하지만, 자동화하기 어려운 것은 문제를 창의적으로 해결하는 능력이다. '(기계적인 일을) 하는' 역할의 노동자들은 로봇들에 의해 대체될 수 있는 반면에, 창의적으로 문제를 해결하는 역할은 대체 불가능한 개인에 더 의존한다.

Why? 왜 정답일까?

노동 시장의 상황이 변하고 있다며 경각심을 일깨우는 주어진 글 뒤로, 주어진 글에 언급된 수치들을 the numbers로 지칭하는 (B)가 연결된다. (B)에서는 '이 수치들'이 비현실적인 것 같아도 사실적임을 보충 설명하는데, (C)는 여기에 이어 고도로 숙련된 직군 또한(also) 위기에 처해 있다고 설명한다. 마지막으로 상황을 반전시키는(However) (A)는 자동화하기 어려운 대상으로 인간의 창의적 문제 해결 능력을 언급한다. 따라서 글의 순서로 가장 적절한 것은 ③ '(B) – (C) – (A)'이다.

- at risk 위험에 처한
- replace ⓥ 대체하다
- unrealistic ⓐ 비현실적인
- crew ⓝ (전체) 직원, 승무원
- automation ⓝ 자동화
- irreplaceable ⓐ 대체할 수 없는
- flip ⓥ 뒤집다
- draw on ～을 이용하다

구문 풀이

1행 It has been reported [that 42 percent of jobs in Canada are
가주어
at risk, and 62 percent of jobs in America will be in danger due to advances in automation]. [ ] : 진주어

---

02 아기가 사람 얼굴을 선호하는 이유   정답률 69% | 정답 ⑤

주어진 글 다음에 이어질 글의 순서로 가장 적절한 것을 고르시오.

① (A) – (C) – (B) ② (B) – (A) – (C)
③ (B) – (C) – (A) ④ (C) – (A) – (B)
✓⑤ (C) – (B) – (A)

Starting from birth, / babies are immediately attracted to faces.
태어나면서부터, / 아기는 즉각적으로 사람 얼굴에 끌린다.
Scientists were able to show this / by having babies look at two simple images, / one that looks more like a face than the other.
과학자들은 이것을 보여줄 수 있었다. / 아기에게 간단한 두 개의 이미지를 보여줌으로써 / 하나가 다른 것에 비해 더 사람 얼굴처럼 보이는 이미지
(C) By measuring where the babies looked, / scientists found / that the babies looked at the face-like image more / than they looked at the non-face image.
아기가 바라보는 곳을 유심히 살펴보면서, / 과학자들은 발견하게 되었다. / 아기가 얼굴처럼 보이는 이미지를 더 바라본다는 것을 / 그들이 얼굴처럼 보이지 않는 이미지를 보는 것보다
Even though babies have poor eyesight, / they prefer to look at faces.
아기는 시력이 좋지 않음에도 불구하고 / 그들은 얼굴을 보는 것을 더 좋아한다.
But why?
그런데 왜 그럴까?
(B) One reason babies might like faces / is because of something called evolution.
아기가 얼굴을 좋아하는 것 같은 하나의 이유는 / 진화라고 불리는 것 때문이다.
Evolution involves changes / to the structures of an organism(such as the brain) / that occur over many generations.
진화는 변화를 수반한다. / 유기체 구조(뇌와 같은 것)에 있어서의 / 여러 세대를 거쳐 발생하는
(A) These changes help the organisms to survive, / making them alert to enemies.
이런 변화들은 유기체가 생존하도록 도와준다. / 적들을 경계하게 해서
By being able to recognize faces / from afar or in the dark, / humans were able to know / someone was coming / and protect themselves from possible danger.
얼굴을 알아볼 수 있음으로써, / 멀리서 또는 어둠 속에서 / 인간은 알 수 있었고 / 누군가 다가오는지 / 있을 법한 위험으로부터 자신을 보호할 수 있었다.

태어나면서부터, 아기는 즉각적으로 사람 얼굴에 끌린다. 과학자들은 아기에게 간단한 두 개의 이미지, 하나가 다른 것에 비해 더 사람 얼굴처럼 보이는 이미지를 보여줌으로써 이것을 보여줄 수 있었다.

(C) 과학자들은 아기가 바라보는 곳을 유심히 살펴보면서, 아기가 얼굴처럼 보이지 않는 이미지보다는 얼굴처럼 보이는 이미지를 더 바라본다는 것을 발견하게 되었다. 아기는 시력이 좋지 않음에도 불구하고 얼굴을 보는 것을 더 좋아한다. 그런데 왜 그럴까?

(B) 아기가 얼굴을 좋아하는 것 같은 하나의 이유는 진화라고 불리는 것 때문이다. 진화는 여러 세대를 거쳐 발생하는 유기체 구조(뇌와 같은 것)의 변화를 수반한다.

(A) 이런 변화들은 적들을 경계하게 해서 유기체가 생존하도록 도와준다. 멀리서 또는 어둠 속에서 얼굴을 알아볼 수 있음으로써, 인간은 누군가가 다가오는지 알 수 있었고 있을 법한 위험으로부터 자신을 보호할 수 있었다.

Why? 왜 정답일까?

주어진 글에서 아기들은 태어나면서부터 사람 얼굴에 끌리고, 이를 뒷받침하는 실험이 있다고 언급한다. (C)는 주어진 글의 실험에 따르면 아기들이 시력이 좋지 않은데도 불구하고 얼굴 이미지를 선호하는데 '왜 그런 것인지' 의문을 던진다. (B)는 (C)에서 제시된 질문에 '진화' 때문이라는 답을 제시한다. (A)는 (B)에서 언급된 '진화'를 보충 설명하는 내용이다. 따라서 글의 순서로 가장 적절한 것은 ⑤ '(C) – (B) – (A)'이다.

- alert ⓐ 경계하는
- structure ⓝ 구조
- evolution ⓝ 진화
- eyesight ⓝ 시력

구문 풀이

10행 One reason [babies might like faces] is because of something
주어 / 동사(단수) / 전치사 / 명사
called evolution.
과거분사

---

03 페루의 독립과 노예 해방 정답률 56% | 정답 ⑤

주어진 글 다음에 이어질 글의 순서로 가장 적절한 것을 고르시오.

① (A) – (C) – (B)
② (B) – (A) – (C)
③ (B) – (C) – (A)
④ (C) – (A) – (B)
✓ (C) – (B) – (A)

In 1824, Peru won its freedom from Spain.
1824년, 페루는 스페인으로부터 독립했다.

Soon after, / Simón Bolívar, / the general who had led the liberating forces, / called a meeting / to write the first version of the constitution / for the new country.
독립 직후, / Simón Bolívar는 / 해방군을 이끌었던 장군인 / 회의를 소집하였다. / 헌법의 초안을 작성하기 위해 / 새 나라를 위한

(C) After the meeting, / the people wanted to do something special for Bolívar / to show their appreciation / for all he had done for them, / so they offered him / a gift of one million pesos, / a very large amount of money in those days.
회의가 끝난 후, / 사람들은 그에게 특별한 것을 해 주고 싶어 했다. / 감사의 표시로 / 그가 그들을 위해 해 준 모든 것에 대한 / 그래서 그들은 그에게 주었다. / 1백만 페소를 선물로 / 그 당시 매우 많은 돈인

(B) Bolívar accepted the gift and then asked, / "How many slaves are there in Peru?"
Bolívar는 선물을 받고 나서 물었다. / "페루에 노예가 몇 명입니까?"

He was told / there were about three thousand.
그는 들었다. / 대략 3천 명이 있다는 답을

"And how much does a slave sell for?" / he wanted to know.
"그리고 노예 한 명은 얼마에 팔립니까?" / 그는 알고 싶어 했다.

"About 350 pesos for a man," / was the answer.
"한 사람당 약 350페소입니다."라는 / 대답이 있었다.

(A) "Then," said Bolívar, / "I'll add whatever is necessary to this million pesos / you have given me / and I will buy all the slaves in Peru / and set them free.
"그렇다면,"이라고 Bolívar가 말했다. / "나는 이 1백만 페소에 필요한 것은 무엇이든 다 더할 것입니다 / 당신들이 나에게 준 / 그리고 나는 페루에 있는 모든 노예를 사서 / 그들을 해방시켜 주겠습니다.

It makes no sense to free a nation, / unless all its citizens enjoy freedom as well."
한 국가를 해방시킨다는 것은 의미가 없습니다. / 모든 시민 또한 자유를 누리지 못한다면"

1824년, 페루는 스페인으로부터 독립했다. 독립 직후, 해방군을 이끌었던 장군인 Simón Bolívar는 새 나라를 위한 헌법의 초안을 작성하기 위해 회의를 소집하였다.

(C) 회의가 끝난 후, 사람들은 Bolívar가 그들을 위해 해 준 모든 것에 대한 감사의 표시로 그에게 특별한 것을 해 주고 싶어 했다. 그래서 그들은 그 당시 매우 많은 돈인 1백만 페소를 그에게 선물로 주었다.

(B) Bolívar는 선물을 받고 나서 물었다. "페루에 노예가 몇 명입니까?" 그는 대략 3천 명이 있다는 답을 들었다. "그리고 노예 한 명은 얼마에 팔립니까?" 그는 알고 싶어 했다. "한 사람당 약 350페소입니다."라는 대답이 있었다.

(A) Bolívar가 말했다. "그렇다면, 나는 당신들이 나에게 준 이 1백만 페소에 필요한 것은 무엇이든 다 더해 페루에 있는 모든 노예를 사서 그들을 해방시켜 주겠습니다. 모든 시민 또한 자유를 누리지 못한다면, 한 국가를 해방시킨다는 것은 의미가 없습니다."

Why? 왜 정답일까?

페루가 스페인으로부터 독립한 이후로 해방군의 장군인 **Bolívar**가 회의를 소집했다는 내용의 주어진 글 뒤에는, 회의 이후 사람들이 그의 공을 치하하여 돈 1백만 페소를 주었다는 내용의 **(C)**, 이를 받은 장군이 전국에 노예가 얼마나 있으며 한 명당 얼마에 팔리는지를 물었다는 내용의 **(B)**, 그가 자신이 받은 돈에 필요한 추가 금액을 보태 모든 노예를 사서 해방시켜주기를 원했다는 내용의 **(A)**가 차례로 이어지는 것이 자연스럽다. 따라서 글의 순서로 가장 적절한 것은 ⑤ '**(C) – (B) – (A)**'이다.

- **win freedom** 독립하다, 자유를 얻다
- **liberate** ⓥ 해방시키다, 자유롭게 하다
- **general** ⓝ 장군
- **call a meeting** 회의를 소집하다

- **version** ⓝ 판, 형태
- **slave** ⓝ 노예
- **nation** ⓝ 국가
- **citizen** ⓝ 시민
- **freedom** ⓝ 자유
- **meeting** ⓝ 회의
- **amount** ⓝ 액수, 금액
- **peso** ⓝ 페소(화폐 단위)
- **set free** 해방시키다
- **unless** conj ⋯하지 않는다면
- **enjoy** ⓥ 누리다
- **sell for** (얼마에) 팔리다[팔다]
- **appreciation** ⓝ 감사, 이해

구문 풀이

7행 It makes no sense to free a nation, / unless all its citizens
가주어 / 진주어 / 조건 접속사(= if ~ not)
enjoy freedom as well."
~도, 또한

---

04 과학과 예술의 근간인 협업 정답률 58% | 정답 ②

주어진 글 다음에 이어질 글의 순서로 가장 적절한 것을 고르시오.

① (A) – (C) – (B)
✓ (B) – (A) – (C)
③ (B) – (C) – (A)
④ (C) – (A) – (B)
⑤ (C) – (B) – (A)

Collaboration is the basis / for most of the foundational arts and sciences.
협업은 기반이다. / 대부분의 기초 예술과 과학의

(B) It is often believed / that Shakespeare, like most playwrights of his period, / did not always write alone, / and many of his plays are considered collaborative / or were rewritten after their original composition.
흔히 믿어지고, / 셰익스피어는, 당대 대부분의 극작가처럼, / 늘 혼자 작품을 썼던 것은 아니라고 / 그의 희곡 중 다수가 협업을 한 것으로 여겨지거나 / 최초의 창작 후에 개작되었다.

Leonardo Da Vinci made his sketches individually, / but he collaborated with other people / to add the finer details.
레오나르도 다빈치는 혼자서 스케치를 그렸지만, / 다른 사람들과 협업했다. / 더 세밀한 세부 묘사를 더 하기 위해

(A) For example, / his sketches of human anatomy / were a collaboration with Marcantonio della Torre, / an anatomist from the University of Pavia.
예를 들어, / 인체의 해부학적 구조를 그린 그의 스케치는 / Marcantonio della Torre와 협업한 것이었다. / Pavia 대학의 해부학자인

Their collaboration is important / because it marries the artist with the scientist.
그들의 협업은 중요하다. / 예술가와 과학자가 결합한 것이어서

(C) Similarly, / Marie Curie's husband stopped his original research / and joined Marie in hers.
마찬가지로, / Marie Curie의 남편은 원래 자신이 하던 연구를 중단하고 / Marie의 연구를 함께 했다.

They went on to collaboratively discover radium, / which overturned old ideas / in physics and chemistry.
그들은 더 나아가 협업으로 라듐을 발견했고, / 그것은 기존 개념들을 뒤집었다. / 물리학과 화학에서의

협업은 대부분의 기초 예술과 과학의 기반이다.

(B) 셰익스피어는, 당대 대부분의 극작가처럼, 늘 혼자 작품을 썼던 것은 아니라고 흔히 믿어지고, 그의 희곡 중 다수가 협업을 한 것으로 여겨지거나 최초의 창작 후에 개작되었다. 레오나르도 다빈치는 혼자서 스케치를 했지만, 더 세밀한 세부 묘사를 더하기 위해 다른 사람들과 협업했다.

(A) 예를 들어, 그의 인체 해부 구조 스케치는 Pavia 대학의 해부학자인 Marcantonio della Torre와 협업한 것이었다. 그들의 협업은 예술가와 과학자가 결합한 것이어서 중요하다.

(C) 마찬가지로, Marie Curie의 남편은 원래 자신이 하던 연구를 중단하고 Marie의 연구를 함께 했다. 그들은 더 나아가 협업으로 라듐을 발견했고, 그것은 물리학과 화학의 오래된 개념들을 뒤집었다.

Why? 왜 정답일까?

협업이 기초 예술과 과학의 기반임을 언급한 주어진 글 뒤에는, 셰익스피어와 레오나르도 다빈치의 예를 제시하는 **(B)**, 다빈치를 단락 초반에서 **his**로 받아 그의 스케치 중 협동 작업의 사례를 언급하는 **(A)**, 이어서 추가 사례를 제시하는 **Similarly** 뒤로 과학에서의 예로서 퀴리 부부를 언급하는 **(C)**가 차례로 연결되는 것이 자연스럽다. 따라서 글의 순서로 가장 적절한 것은 ② '**(B) – (A) – (C)**'이다.

- **collaboration** ⓝ 협업, 협동, 공동 작업
- **foundational** ⓐ 기초적인, 기본의
- **anatomist** ⓝ 해부학자
- **playwright** ⓝ 극작가
- **rewrite** ⓥ 개작하다, 다시 쓰다
- **basis** ⓝ 근거, 이유
- **sketch** ⓝ 개요
- **marry** ⓥ 결합시키다
- **period** ⓝ 기간, 시기
- **composition** ⓝ 작성, 작곡, 작품

- **individually** [ad] 개인적으로, 따로
- **join** [v] 합류하다
- **fine** [a] 세밀한, 섬세한, 촘촘한
- **overturn** [v] 뒤엎다, 전복시키다

구문 풀이

8행 주어1(가주어)
It is often believed {that Shakespeare, like most playwrights
　　　　동사1　　　　　　주어
of his period, did not always write alone}, and many of his plays
　　　　　　　　동사　　　　　　{　}: 진주어　　　주어2
are considered collaborative or were rewritten after their original
동사2　　　　　보어(형용사)　　　　동사3
composition.

---

05 자기 통제에 대한 과신과 습관 고치기　정답률 56% | 정답 ⑤

주어진 글 다음에 이어질 글의 순서로 가장 적절한 것을 고르시오.
① (A) - (C) - (B)　② (B) - (A) - (C)
③ (B) - (C) - (A)　④ (C) - (A) - (B)
✔ (C) - (B) - (A)

No one likes to think they're average, / least of all below average.
누구도 자신이 평균이라고 생각하기를 좋아하지 않으며, / 자신을 평균 이하라고 생각하는 사람은 극히 드물다.

(C) When asked by psychologists, / most people rate themselves above average / on all manner of measures / including intelligence, looks, health, and so on.
심리학자들에게 질문을 받았을 때, / 대부분의 사람들은 자신들이 평균 이상이라고 평가한다. / 모든 척도들에서 / 지능, 외모, 건강 등을 포함한

Self-control is no different: / people consistently overestimate their ability to control themselves.
자기 통제 또한 다르지 않아서, / 사람들은 자기 자신을 통제할 수 있는 능력을 지속적으로 과대평가한다.

(B) This over-confidence in self-control / can lead people to assume / they'll be able to control themselves in situations / in which, it turns out, they can't.
자기 통제에 대한 이러한 과신은 / 그들이 가정하도록 이끈다. / 상황에서 스스로를 통제할 수 있다고 / (그들이 자신을) 통제할 수 없다고 밝혀지는

This is why / trying to stop an unwanted habit / can be an extremely frustrating task.
이러한 이유로 / 원하지 않는 습관을 멈추려 노력하는 것은 / 매우 좌절감을 주는 일이 될 수 있다.

(A) Over the days and weeks / from our resolution to change, / we start to notice it popping up again and again.
며칠과 몇 주에 걸쳐, / 변화하고자 결심한 순간부터 / 우리는 그것이 반복적으로 불쑥 나타나는 것을 알아채기 시작한다.

The old habit's well-practiced performance / is beating our conscious desire for change into submission.
그 오래된 습관의 길들여진 행동은 / 변화를 향한 우리의 의식적인 욕구를 굴복시킨다.

누구도 자신이 평균이라고 생각하기를 좋아하지 않으며, 자신을 평균 이하라고 생각하는 사람은 극히 드물다.

(C) 심리학자들에게 질문을 받았을 때, 대부분의 사람들은 지능, 외모, 건강 등을 포함한 모든 척도들에서 자신들이 평균 이상이라고 평가한다. 자기 통제 또한 다르지 않아서, 사람들은 자기 자신을 통제할 수 있는 능력을 지속적으로 과대평가한다.

(B) 자기 통제에 대한 이러한 과신은 그들이 통제할 수 없다고 밝혀지는 상황에서 스스로를 통제할 수 있다고 가정하도록 이끈다. 이러한 이유로 원하지 않는 습관을 멈추려 노력하는 것은 매우 좌절감을 주는 일이 될 수 있다.

(A) 변화하고자 결심한 순간부터 며칠과 몇 주에 걸쳐, 우리는 그것(원하지 않는 습관)이 반복적으로 불쑥 나타나는 것을 알아채기 시작한다. 그 오래된 습관의 길들여진 행동은 변화를 향한 우리의 의식적인 욕구를 굴복시킨다.

Why? 왜 정답일까?

사람들은 스스로를 평균 혹은 그 이하라고 생각하지 않는다는 내용의 주어진 글 뒤에는, 사람들이 자기 통제 능력 또한 과대평가하는 경향을 보인다는 내용의 **(C)**, 그리하여 변하지 않는 습관을 고치려 할 때 사람들이 좌절감을 경험할 수 있다는 내용의 **(B)**, 습관 고치기의 어려움을 설명한 **(A)**가 차례로 이어지는 것이 적절하다. 따라서 글의 순서로 가장 적절한 것은 ⑤ '(C) - (B) - (A)'이다.

- **average** [n] 평균
- **pop up** 불쑥 나타나다, 튀어나오다
- **conscious** [a] 의식적인
- **over-confidence** 과신
- **extremely** [ad] 매우, 극도로
- **rate** [v] 평가하다, 등급을 매기다
- **resolution** [n] 결심, 다짐
- **well-practiced** 잘 길들여진
- **submission** [n] 굴복, 항복
- **turn out** ~라고 밝혀지다, 판명되다
- **frustrating** [a] 좌절감을 주는
- **consistently** [ad] 지속적으로, 일관되게

구문 풀이

8행 This over-confidence in self-control can lead people
to assume {they'll be able to control themselves in situations
to부정사: ~이 …하도록 이끌다　{　}: 명사절　선행사
[in which, (it turns out), they can't]}.
( ): 삽입절　= can't control themselves

---

06 더 나은 것을 위한 지속된 추구　정답률 50% | 정답 ①

주어진 글 다음에 이어질 글의 순서로 가장 적절한 것을 고르시오.
✔ (A) - (C) - (B)　② (B) - (A) - (C)
③ (B) - (C) - (A)　④ (C) - (A) - (B)
⑤ (C) - (B) - (A)

Students work to get good grades / even when they have no interest in their studies.
학생들은 좋은 성적을 얻기 위해 공부한다. / 그들이 공부에 관심이 없을 때에도

People seek job advancement / even when they are happy with the jobs / they already have.
사람들은 승진을 추구한다. / 심지어 그들이 직업에 만족할 때에도 / 그들이 이미 가지고 있는

(A) It's like being in a crowded football stadium, / watching the crucial play.
그것은 마치 사람들로 붐비는 축구 경기장에 있는 것과 같다. / 중요한 경기를 관람하면서

A spectator several rows in front / stands up to get a better view, / and a chain reaction follows.
몇 줄 앞에 있는 한 관중이 / 더 잘 보기 위해 일어서고, / 뒤이어 연쇄 반응이 일어난다.

(C) Soon everyone is standing, / just to be able to see as well as before.
곧 모든 사람들이 일어서게 된다. / 단지 이전처럼 잘 보기 위해

Everyone is on their feet rather than sitting, / but no one's position has improved.
모두가 앉기보다는 일어서지만, / 그 누구의 위치도 나아지지 않았다.

(B) And if someone refuses to stand, / he might just as well not be at the game at all.
그리고 만약 누군가가 일어서기를 거부한다면, / 그는 경기에 있지 않는 편이 나을 것이다.

When people pursue goods that are positional, / they can't help being in the rat race.
사람들이 위치상의 이익을 추구할 때, / 그들은 치열하고 무의미한 경쟁을 하지 않을 수 없다.

To choose not to run is to lose.
뛰지 않기로 선택하는 것은 지는 것이다.

학생들은 심지어 공부에 관심이 없을 때에도 좋은 성적을 얻기 위해 공부한다. 사람들은 심지어 이미 가지고 있는 직업에 만족할 때에도 승진을 추구한다.

(A) 그것은 마치 사람들로 붐비는 축구 경기장에서 중요한 경기를 관람하는 것과 같다. 몇 줄 앞에 있는 한 관중이 더 잘 보기 위해 일어서고, 뒤이어 연쇄 반응이 일어난다.

(C) 단지 이전처럼 잘 보기 위해 곧 모든 사람들이 일어서게 된다. 모두가 앉기보다는 일어서지만, 그 누구의 위치도 나아지지 않았다.

(B) 그리고 만약 누군가가 일어서기를 거부한다면, 그는 경기에 있지 않는 편이 나을 것이다. 사람들이 위치상의 이익를 추구할 때, 그들은 치열하고 무의미한 경쟁을 하지 않을 수 없다. 뛰지 않기로 선택하는 것은 지는 것이다.

Why? 왜 정답일까?

주어진 글에서 학생들과 직장인들의 예를 들어 사람들은 계속 더 나은 것을 추구한다는 점을 언급한 데 이어, **(A)**는 축구 경기장의 비유를 소개하고 있다. **(A)**의 마지막 부분은 한 사람이 더 잘 보려고 일어서면 연쇄 반응이 일어난다는 내용으로 끝나고, **(C)**는 결국 모든 사람이 일어나게 된다고 설명한다. **(B)**는 일어서기를 거부하는 누군가가 있다면 그 사람은 경기장에 없는 편이 나을 것임을 언급하며 비유를 마무리한다. 따라서 글의 순서로 가장 적절한 것은 ① '(A) - (C) - (B)'이다.

- **job advancement** [n] 승진
- **crucial** [a] 중요한
- **improve** [v] 나아지다, 개선되다
- **crowded** [a] 붐비는
- **positional** [a] 위치상의

구문 풀이

9행 And if someone refuses to stand, he might just as well not be
조건 접속사　「refuse+to부정사: ~하기를 거부하다」「might as well not+동사원형:
at the game at all.　~하지 않는 것이 낫다」

---

07 설득의 기술
정답률 64% | 정답 ②

주어진 글 다음에 이어질 글의 순서로 가장 적절한 것을 고르시오.

① (A) – (C) – (B) ✔ ② (B) – (A) – (C)
③ (B) – (C) – (A) ④ (C) – (A) – (B)
⑤ (C) – (B) – (A)

Making a small request / that people will accept / will naturally increase the chances / of their accepting a bigger request afterwards.
작은 요구를 하는 것은 / 사람들이 수락할 / 가능성을 자연스럽게 증가시킬 것이다. / 나중에 그들이 더 큰 요구를 수락할

(B) For instance, / a salesperson might request you to sign a petition / to prevent cruelty against animals.
예를 들어, / 한 판매원이 여러분에게 청원서에 서명하도록 요구할지도 모른다. / 동물들에 대한 잔인함을 막기 위한

This is a very small request, / and most people will do what the salesperson asks.
이것은 아주 작은 요구이고 / 대부분의 사람들은 판매원이 요구하는 바를 할 것이다.

(A) After this, the salesperson asks you / if you are interested / in buying any cruelty-free cosmetics from their store.
그 이후에 판매원은 여러분에게 물어본다. / 여러분이 관심이 있는지를 / 잔인함을 가하지 않은 어떤 화장품을 자신의 매장에서 사는 것에

Given the fact / that most people agree to the prior request / to sign the petition, / they will be more likely to purchase the cosmetics.
사실을 고려하면 / 이전 요구에 사람들이 동의한다는 / 청원서에 서명해 달라는 / 그들이 화장품을 구매할 가능성이 더 높을 것이다.

(C) They make such purchases / because the salesperson takes advantage of a human tendency / to be consistent in their words and actions.
그들은 그러한 구매를 한다. / 그 판매원이 인간의 경향을 이용하기 때문에 / 자기 말과 행동에 있어 일관되고자 하는

People want to be consistent / and will keep saying yes / if they have already said it once.
사람들은 일관되기를 원하며 / 계속 예라고 말할 것이다. / 만약 자신이 이미 한번 그렇게 말했다면

사람들이 수락할 작은 요구를 하는 것은 나중에 그들이 더 큰 요구를 수락할 가능성을 자연스럽게 증가시킬 것이다.

(B) 예를 들어 한 판매원이 여러분에게 동물들에 대한 잔인함을 막기 위한 청원서에 서명하도록 요구할지도 모른다. 이것은 아주 작은 요구이고 대부분의 사람들은 판매원이 요구하는 바를 할 것이다.

(A) 그 이후에 판매원은 여러분에게 (동물들에게) 잔인함을 가하지 않은 어떤 화장품을 자신의 매장에서 사는 것에 관심이 있는지를 물어본다. 청원서에 서명해 달라는 이전 요구에 사람들이 동의한다는 사실을 고려하면 그들이 화장품을 구매할 가능성이 더 높을 것이다.

(C) 그 판매원이 자기 말과 행동에 있어 일관되고자 하는 인간의 경향을 이용하기 때문에 그들은 그러한 구매를 한다. 사람들은 일관되기를 원하며 만약 자신이 이미 한번 그렇게 말했다면 계속 예라고 말할 것이다.

Why? 왜 정답일까?

작은 요구를 먼저 한 후 큰 요구를 제시하면 사람들이 큰 요구를 수용할 가능성이 높아질 수 있다고 언급한 주어진 글 뒤에는, 판매원이 먼저 동물 학대에 반대하는 청원서를 작성해달라고 부탁하는 예를 제시하는 (B), 이후에 판매원이 동물에게 해를 가하지 않은 화장품 구매를 권유한다는 내용의 (A), 이 경우 사람들이 화장품 구매까지 하게 될 가능성이 높아지는 이유를 설명하는 (C)가 차례로 이어지는 것이 자연스럽다. 따라서 글의 순서로 가장 적절한 것은 ② '(B) – (A) – (C)'이다.

- cruelty ⓝ 잔인함
- take advantage of ⓥ ~을 이용하다
- consistent ⓐ 일관적인

구문 풀이

1행 Making a small request [that people will accept] will naturally
동명사구 주어 / 선행사 / 동사구
increase the chances of their accepting a bigger request afterwards.
의미상 주어 동명사(of의 목적어)

Ethical and moral systems / are different for every culture.
윤리적 그리고 도덕적 체계는 / 모든 문화마다 다르다.

According to cultural relativism, / all of these systems are equally valid, / and no system is better than another.
문화 상대주의에 따르면, / 이 모든 체계는 똑같이 타당하며 / 어떠한 체계도 다른 체계보다 우수하지 않다.

(B) The basis of cultural relativism / is the notion / that no true standards of good and evil actually exist.
문화 상대주의의 기본은 / 개념이다. / 선과 악의 진정한 기준이 실제로 존재하지 않는다는

Therefore, / judging whether something is right or wrong / is based on individual societies' beliefs, / and any moral or ethical opinions are affected / by an individual's cultural perspective.
그러므로 / 무언가가 옳은지 또는 그른지를 판단하는 것은 / 개별 사회의 신념에 근거하며, / 도덕적 또는 윤리적 견해는 영향을 받는다. / 개인의 문화적 관점에 의해

(A) There exists an inherent logical inconsistency / in cultural relativism, / however.
내재적인 논리적 모순이 존재한다. / 문화 상대주의에는 / 그러나

If one accepts the idea / that there is no right or wrong, / then there exists no way / to make judgments in the first place.
만일 생각을 받아들이면, / 옳고 그름이 없다는 / 방법이 존재하지 않는다. / 애초에 판단할

To deal with this inconsistency, / cultural relativism creates "tolerance."
이 모순을 해결하기 위해 / 문화 상대주의는 '관용'을 만들어 낸다.

(C) However, / with tolerance comes intolerance, / which means / that tolerance must imply some sort of ultimate good.
그러나 / 관용에는 불관용이 따르며, / 이것은 의미한다. / 관용이 일종의 궁극적인 선을 내포하고 있음에 틀림없다는 것을

Thus, / tolerance also goes against / the very notion of cultural relativism, / and the boundaries of logic / make cultural relativism impossible.
따라서 / 관용 또한 반하는 것이며, / 문화 상대주의의 바로 그 개념에 / 논리의 영역이 / 문화 상대주의를 불가능하게 만든다.

윤리적 그리고 도덕적 체계는 모든 문화마다 다르다. 문화 상대주의에 따르면, 이 모든 체계는 똑같이 타당하며 어떠한 체계도 다른 체계보다 우수하지 않다.

(B) 문화 상대주의의 기본은 선과 악의 진정한 기준이 실제로 존재하지 않는다는 개념이다. 그러므로 무언가가 옳은지 또는 그른지를 판단하는 것은 개별 사회의 신념에 근거하며, 어떤 도덕적 또는 윤리적 견해는 개인의 문화적 관점에 의해 영향을 받는다.

(A) 그러나 문화 상대주의에는 내재적인 논리적 모순이 존재한다. 만일 옳고 그름이 없다는 생각을 받아들이면, 애초에 판단할 방법이 존재하지 않는다. 이 모순을 해결하기 위해 문화 상대주의는 '관용'을 만들어 낸다.

(C) 그러나 관용에는 불관용이 따르며, 이것은 관용이 일종의 궁극적인 선을 내포하고 있음에 틀림없다는 것을 의미한다. 따라서 관용 또한 문화 상대주의의 바로 그 개념에 반하는 것이며, 논리의 영역이 문화 상대주의를 불가능하게 만든다.

Why? 왜 정답일까?

문화 상대주의에 따르면 서로 다른 체계 간에 우열이 존재하지 않는다는 내용의 주어진 글 뒤에는, 그렇기에 선악의 진정한 기준이 없으며 어떤 행위의 옳고 그름을 판단하는 것은 개별 사회의 몫이라는 내용의 (B)가 먼저 연결된다. 이어서 (A)는 however로 흐름을 반전시키며 문화 상대주의의 모순을 지적하고, 이 모순을 해결하기 위해 관용이 등장한다는 점을 언급한다. 마지막으로 (C)는 다시금 However로 흐름을 뒤집으며 관용 또한 한계를 지닌 개념임을 설명한다. 따라서 글의 순서로 가장 적절한 것은 ② '(B) – (A) – (C)'이다.

- relativism ⓝ 상대주의
- equally ⓐ 똑같이, 동등하게
- valid ⓐ 타당한, 유효한, 정당한
- inherent ⓐ 내재하는, 본질적인
- inconsistency ⓝ 모순, 불일치
- perspective ⓝ 관점, 견해
- go against ~에 반대하다, 저항하다
- boundary ⓝ 경계, 한계

구문 풀이

17행 However, with tolerance comes intolerance, which means
「부사구+동사+주어 : 도치 구문」 / 계속적 용법
{that tolerance must imply some sort of ultimate good}.
{ } : 명사절

---

08 문화 상대주의의 내재적 모순
정답률 58% | 정답 ②

주어진 글 다음에 이어질 글의 순서로 가장 적절한 것을 고르시오. [3점]

① (A) – (C) – (B) ✔ ② (B) – (A) – (C)
③ (B) – (C) – (A) ④ (C) – (A) – (B)
⑤ (C) – (B) – (A)

---

09 흡혈귀가 존재했을 수 없는 이유
정답률 62% | 정답 ⑤

주어진 글 다음에 이어질 글의 순서로 가장 적절한 것을 고르시오. [3점]

① (A) – (C) – (B) ② (B) – (A) – (C)
③ (B) – (C) – (A) ④ (C) – (A) – (B)
✔ ⑤ (C) – (B) – (A)

According to legend, / once a vampire bites a person, / that person turns into a vampire / who seeks the blood of others.
전설에 따르면, / 흡혈귀가 사람을 물면 / 그 사람은 흡혈귀로 변한다. / 다른 사람의 피를 갈구하는

A researcher came up with some simple math, / which proves that these highly popular creatures can't exist.
한 연구자는 간단한 계산법을 생각해냈다. / 이 잘 알려진 존재가 실존할 수 없다는 것을 증명하는

(C) University of Central Florida physics professor / Costas Efthimiou's work breaks down the myth.
University of Central Florida의 물리학과 교수인 / Costas Efthimiou의 연구가 그 미신을 무너뜨렸다.

Suppose / that on January 1st, 1600, / the human population was just over five hundred million.
가정해 보자. / 1600년 1월 1일에 / 인구가 5억 명이 넘는다고

(B) If the first vampire came into existence / that day and bit one person a month, / there would have been two vampires by February 1st, 1600.
그날 최초의 흡혈귀가 생겨나서 / 한 달에 한 명을 물었다면, / 1600년 2월 1일까지 흡혈귀가 둘 있었을 것이다.

A month later there would have been four, / the next month eight, / then sixteen, / and so on.
한 달 뒤면 넷이 되었을 것이고 / 그다음 달은 여덟, / 그리고 열여섯 / 등등이 되었을 것이다.

(A) In just two-and-a-half years, / the original human population / would all have become vampires / with no humans left.
불과 2년 반 만에, / 원래의 인류는 / 모두 흡혈귀가 되었을 것이다. / 인간이 하나도 남지 않은 채로

But look around you.
하지만 주위를 둘러보라.

Have vampires taken over the world?
흡혈귀가 세상을 정복하였는가?

No, because there's no such thing.
아니다. 왜냐하면 흡혈귀는 존재하지 않으니까.

전설에 따르면, 흡혈귀가 사람을 물면 그 사람은 다른 사람의 피를 갈구하는 흡혈귀로 변한다. 한 연구자는 이 대단히 잘 알려진 존재가 실존할 수 없다는 것을 증명하는 간단한 계산법을 생각해냈다.

(C) University of Central Florida의 물리학과 교수 Costas Efthimiou의 연구가 그 미신을 무너뜨렸다. 1600년 1월 1일에 인구가 막 5억 명을 넘겼다고 가정해 보자.

(B) 그날 최초의 흡혈귀가 생겨나서 한 달에 한 명을 물었다면, 1600년 2월 1일까지 흡혈귀가 둘 있었을 것이다. 한 달 뒤면 넷, 그다음 달은 여덟, 그리고 열여섯 등등으로 계속 늘어났을 것이다.

(A) 불과 2년 반 만에, 원래의 인류는 모두 흡혈귀가 되어 더 이상 남아 있지 않았을 것이다. 하지만 주위를 둘러보라. 흡혈귀가 세상을 정복하였는가? 아니다. 왜냐하면 흡혈귀는 존재하지 않으니까.

Why? 왜 정답일까?

흡혈귀가 존재했음을 부정하는 계산식을 생각해낸 사람이 있다는 내용의 주어진 글 뒤에는, 먼저 1600년 1월 1일에 인구가 5억 명이 넘었다고 가정해 보자며 계산식에 관해 설명하기 시작하는 (C)가 연결된다. 이어서 (B)는 (C)에서 언급한 날짜를 that day로 가리키며, 흡혈귀가 달마다 두 배씩 늘어가는 상황을 가정해 보자고 설명한다. 마지막으로 (A)는 (C)-(B)의 상황이 성립한다면 5억 명의 사람들이 불과 2년 반 만에 모두 흡혈귀로 변했을 것인데, 인류는 현재까지 지속되고 있으므로 흡혈귀가 존재했을 수 없다는 결론을 제시하고 있다. 따라서 글의 순서로 가장 적절한 것은 ⑤ '(C) - (B) - (A)'이다.

- **legend** ⓝ 전설
- **come into existence** 생기다, 나타나다
- **myth** ⓝ 미신, (잘못된) 통념
- **take over** ~을 지배하다, 장악하다
- **break down** 무너뜨리다

구문 풀이

[6행] In just two-and-a-half years, the original human population would all have become vampires with no humans left.
「would have + 과거분사 : ~했을 것이다 (가정법 과거완료 주절)」 「with + 명사 + 과거분사 : ~이 …된 채로」

---

10 고도로 복잡해진 소프트웨어와 그에 따른 부작용 | 정답률 51% | 정답 ④

주어진 글 다음에 이어질 글의 순서로 가장 적절한 것을 고르시오.

① (A) - (C) - (B)
② (B) - (A) - (C)
③ (B) - (C) - (A)
④ ✔ (C) - (A) - (B)
⑤ (C) - (B) - (A)

The growing complexity of computer software / has direct implications for our global safety and security, / particularly as the physical objects upon

---

which we depend / — things like cars, airplanes, bridges, tunnels, and implantable medical devices — / transform themselves into computer code.
컴퓨터 소프트웨어 복잡성의 증가는 / 전 세계의 안전과 보안에 직접적인 영향을 주는데, / 특히 우리가 의존하는 물리적 대상이 / 즉 자동차, 비행기, 교량, 터널, 이식형 의료 기기와 같은 것들 / 컴퓨터 코드로 변해감에 따라 그렇다.

(C) Physical things are increasingly becoming information technologies.
물리적 사물은 점점 더 정보 기술이 되어가고 있다.

Cars are "computers we ride in," / and airplanes are nothing more than "flying Solaris boxes / attached to bucketfuls of industrial control systems."
자동차는 '우리가 타는 컴퓨터'이고, / 비행기는 '비행 솔라리스 박스'에 불과하다. / '수많은 산업 제어 시스템에 부착된'

(A) As all this code grows in size and complexity, / so too do the number of errors and software bugs.
이 모든 코드가 크기와 복잡성이 증가함에 따라, / 오류와 소프트웨어 버그 수 또한 증가한다.

According to a study by Carnegie Mellon University, / commercial software typically has twenty to thirty bugs / for every thousand lines of code / — 50 million lines of code means / 1 million to 1.5 million potential errors / to be exploited.
Carnegie Mellon 대학교의 연구에 따르면, / 상용 소프트웨어에는 보통 20〜30개의 버그가 있어서, / 코드 1,000줄당 / 5천만 줄의 코드는 의미한다. / 1백만〜150만 개의 잠재적 오류가 / 악의적으로 이용될 수 있다는 것을

(B) This is the basis for all malware attacks / that take advantage of these computer bugs / to get the code to do something / it was not originally intended to do.
이것이 바로 모든 악성 소프트웨어 공격의 근간이다. / 이 컴퓨터 버그를 이용하는 / 코드가 뭔가를 하게 하려고 / 그것이 원래 하도록 의도되지 않은

As computer code grows more elaborate, / software bugs flourish and security suffers, / with increasing consequences for society at large.
컴퓨터 코드가 더 정교해짐에 따라, / 소프트웨어 버그는 창궐하고 보안은 악화되어, / 사회 전반에 미치는 영향이 커진다.

컴퓨터 소프트웨어 복잡성의 증가는 전 세계의 안전과 보안에 직접적인 영향을 주는데, 우리가 의존하는 물리적 대상, 즉 자동차, 비행기, 교량, 터널, 이식형 의료 기기와 같은 것들이 컴퓨터 코드로 변해감에 따라 특히 그렇다.

(C) 물리적 사물은 점점 더 정보 기술이 되어가고 있다. 자동차는 '우리가 타는 컴퓨터'이고, 비행기는 '수많은 산업 제어 시스템에 부착된 비행 솔라리스 박스'에 불과하다.

(A) 이 모든 코드가 크기와 복잡성이 증가함에 따라, 오류와 소프트웨어 버그 수 또한 증가한다. Carnegie Mellon 대학교의 연구에 따르면, 상용 소프트웨어에는 보통 코드 1,000줄당 20~30개의 버그가 있어서, 5천만 줄의 코드는 1백만~150만 개의 잠재적 오류가 악의적으로 이용될 수 있다는 것을 의미한다.

(B) 이것이 바로 컴퓨터 버그를 이용해 코드가 원래 의도되지 않은 작업을 하게 하는 모든 악성 소프트웨어 공격의 근간이다. 컴퓨터 코드가 더 정교해짐에 따라, 소프트웨어 버그는 창궐하고 보안은 악화되어, 사회 전반에 미치는 영향이 커진다.

Why? 왜 정답일까?

주어진 글은 컴퓨터 소프트웨어의 복잡성에 관해 언급하며 물리적 대상이 컴퓨터 코드로 변해가고 있다고 이야기한다. (C)는 이 컴퓨터 코드를 '정보 기술'로 일반화하며, 자동차와 비행기의 변모를 예로 든다. 이어서 (A)는 코드의 복잡성 증가에 따라 오류의 수 또한 증가한다고 설명하고, (C)는 이런 점이 바로 악성 소프트웨어 공격으로 이어질 여지가 있다고 언급한다. 따라서 글의 순서로 가장 적절한 것은 ④ '(C) - (A) - (B)'이다.

- **complexity** ⓝ 복잡성
- **physical** ⓐ 물리적인
- **medical device** 의료 기기
- **commercial** ⓐ 상용의, 상업적인
- **exploit** ⓥ 악용하다, 착취하다
- **originally** [ad] 원래
- **at large** 전체적인, 대체적인
- **attached to** ~에 부착된
- **implication** ⓝ 영향
- **implantable** ⓐ (체내에) 심을 수 있는
- **software bug** 소프트웨어 버그
- **typically** [ad] 보통
- **take advantage of** ~을 이용하다
- **flourish** ⓥ 번성하다
- **nothing more than** ~에 불과한
- **bucketfuls of** 수많은

구문 풀이

[1행] The growing complexity of computer software has direct implications for our global safety and security, particularly as
접속사
the physical objects [upon which we depend] — (things like cars,
주어   ( ): 삽입구
airplanes, bridges, tunnels, and implantable medical devices) —
transform themselves into computer code.
동사(복수)

★★★ 1등급 대비 고난도 2점 문제

11 반사면을 활용하여 암호 메시지 작성하기   정답률 40% | 정답 ⑤

주어진 글 다음에 이어질 글의 순서로 가장 적절한 것을 고르시오.

① (A) − (C) − (B)   ② (B) − (A) − (C)
③ (B) − (C) − (A)   ④ (C) − (A) − (B)
✓(C) − (B) − (A)

Mirrors and other smooth, shiny surfaces / reflect light.
거울과 부드럽고, 광택이 나는 다른 표면들은 / 빛을 반사한다.

We see reflections from such surfaces / because the rays of light form an image on the retina of our eyes.
우리는 그런 표면들로부터 반사된 것을 본다. / 광선이 우리 눈의 망막에 이미지를 형성하기 때문에

(C) Such images are always reversed.
그런 이미지들은 항상 거꾸로 되어 있다.

Look at yourself in a mirror, / wink your right eye / and your left eye seems to wink back at you.
거울에 비친 여러분의 모습을 보며 / 오른쪽 눈을 깜박여 보아라, / 그러면 왼쪽 눈이 여러분에게 눈을 깜박이는 것처럼 보일 것이다.

You can use a mirror / to send a coded message to a friend.
여러분은 거울을 사용하여 / 친구에게 암호로 된 메시지를 보낼 수 있다.

(B) Stand a mirror upright on the table, / so that a piece of paper on the table can be clearly seen in the mirror.
거울을 탁자 위에 수직으로 세워라, / 탁자 위에 놓인 한 장의 종이가 거울 속에 명확하게 보일 수 있도록

Now write a message that looks right / when you look in the mirror.
이제 정상적으로 보이는 메시지를 적어라. / 거울을 볼 때

(A) Keep your eyes on the reflected image / while you are writing / and not on your paper.
반사되는 이미지를 계속 보아라, / 여러분이 쓰는 동안 / 종이가 아니라

After a little practice, / it will be easier to write "backwards."
조금 연습을 하고 나면, / '거꾸로' 쓰는 것이 더 쉬울 것이다.

When your friend receives such a message / he will be able to read it / by holding the paper up to a mirror.
여러분의 친구가 그런 메시지를 받으면, / 그는 그것을 읽을 수 있을 것이다. / 그 종이를 거울에 비춰 봄으로써

거울과 부드럽고 광택이 나는 다른 표면들은 빛을 반사한다. 광선이 우리 눈의 망막에 이미지를 형성하기 때문에 우리는 그런 표면들로부터 반사된 것을 본다.

(C) 그런 이미지들은 항상 거꾸로 되어 있다. 거울에 비친 여러분의 모습을 보며 오른쪽 눈을 깜박여 보아라. 그러면 왼쪽 눈이 여러분에게 눈을 깜박이는 것처럼 보일 것이다. 여러분은 거울을 사용하여 친구에게 암호로 된 메시지를 보낼 수 있다.

(B) 탁자 위에 놓인 한 장의 종이가 거울 속에 명확하게 보일 수 있도록 거울을 탁자 위에 수직으로 세워라. 이제 거울을 볼 때 정상적으로 보이는 메시지를 적어라.

(A) 쓰는 동안 종이가 아니라 반사되는 이미지를 계속 보아라. 조금 연습을 하고 나면, '거꾸로' 쓰는 것이 더 쉬울 것이다. 여러분의 친구가 그런 메시지를 받으면, 그는 그 종이를 거울에 비춰 봄으로써 그것을 읽을 수 있을 것이다.

Why? 왜 정답일까?

거울 등 반짝이는 표면은 빛을 반사한다는 것을 언급하는 주어진 글 뒤에는, 반사된 이미지는 늘 거꾸로 되어 있기에 이를 활용하면 친구에게 암호 메시지를 보낼 수 있다는 내용의 (C), 거울을 이용하여 암호 메시지를 쓰는 방법을 설명하는 내용의 (B), 쓰는 동안 주의할 점을 언급한 후 몇 번의 연습을 거치면 친구에게 메시지를 잘 전달할 수 있다는 결론으로 이어지는 (A)가 차례로 이어져야 한다. 따라서 글의 순서로 가장 적절한 것은 ⑤ '(C) − (B) − (A)'이다.

- **reflection** ⑪ (거울 등에) 반사된 것
- **reverse** ⓥ 뒤집다
- **upright** ⑩ 똑바로
- **coded** ⑧ 암호화된, 부호화된

구문 풀이

7행 When your friend receives such a message he will be able
  접속사(~할 때)   「such a+(형)+명 : 그러한 (~한) …」
to read it by holding the paper up to a mirror.
  ~함으로써

★★ 문제 해결 꿀~팁 ★★

▶ 많이 틀린 이유는?
주어진 글의 Mirrors만 보고 기계적으로 (B)를 연결해서는 안 된다. 주어진 글에 '메시지'에 관한 언급이 없는데 (B)에서는 갑자기 거울을 세워놓고 종이를 꺼내 '메시지'

를 써 볼 것을 지시하고 있다. 더구나 주어진 글의 특정 표현이나 어구가 (B)에서 재진술되거나 반복되지 않는 것으로 보아, 주어진 글 뒤에 (B)가 나올 수 없다.

▶ 문제 해결 방법은?
주어진 글 후반부의 an image를 (C)의 Such images와 대응시킨 후, 나머지 두 단락은 전체적으로 가볍게 훑으며 논리적인 흐름에 맞게 순서를 연결시키도록 한다.

★★★ 1등급 대비 고난도 3점 문제

12 생산성이 최악일 때 오히려 더 발휘되는 창의성   정답률 44% | 정답 ⑤

주어진 글 다음에 이어질 글의 순서로 가장 적절한 것을 고르시오. [3점]

① (A) − (C) − (B)   ② (B) − (A) − (C)
③ (B) − (C) − (A)   ④ (C) − (A) − (B)
✓(C) − (B) − (A)

Most people have a perfect time of day / when they feel they are at their best, / whether in the morning, evening, or afternoon.
대부분의 사람들은 완벽한 시간을 갖는다. / 하루 중 그들이 최고의 상태에 있다고 느끼는 / 아침이든 저녁이든 혹은 오후든

(C) Some of us are night owls, / some early birds, / and others in between / may feel most active during the afternoon hours.
우리 중 몇몇은 저녁형 인간이고, / 몇몇은 아침형 인간이며, / 그 사이에 있는 누군가는 / 오후의 시간 동안 가장 활력을 느낄지도 모른다.

If you are able to organize your day / and divide your work, / make it a point / to deal with tasks that demand attention / at your best time of the day.
여러분이 하루를 계획할 수 있다면 / 그리고 업무를 분배할 / ~하기로 정하라. / 집중을 요구하는 과업을 처리하기로 / 하루 중 최적의 시간에

(B) However, / if the task you face demands creativity and novel ideas, / it's best to tackle it / at your "worst" time of day!
그러나, / 만약 여러분이 직면한 과업이 창의성과 새로운 아이디어를 요구한다면, / 처리하는 것이 최선이다! / 하루 중 '최악의' 시간에

So if you are an early bird, / make sure to attack your creative task in the evening, / and vice versa for night owls.
그래서 만약 여러분이 아침형 인간이라면 / 반드시 저녁에 창의적인 작업에 착수하고, / 저녁형 인간이라면 반대로 하라.

(A) When your mind and body / are less alert than at your "peak" hours, / the muse of creativity awakens / and is allowed to roam more freely.
여러분의 정신과 신체가 / '정점' 시간보다 주의력이 덜할 때, / 창의성의 영감이 깨어나 / 더 자유롭게 거니는 것이 허용된다.

In other words, / when your mental machinery is loose / rather than standing at attention, / the creativity flows.
다시 말해서, / 여러분의 정신 기제가 느슨하게 풀려있을 때 / 차렷 자세로 있을 때보다 / 창의성이 샘솟는다.

대부분의 사람들은 아침이든 저녁이든 혹은 오후든, 하루 중 그들이 최고의 상태에 있다고 느끼는 완벽한 시간을 갖는다.

(C) 우리 중 몇몇은 저녁형 인간이고, 몇몇은 아침형 인간이며, 그 사이에 있는 누군가는 오후의 시간 동안 가장 활력을 느낄지도 모른다. 여러분이 하루를 계획하고 업무를 분배할 수 있다면, 집중을 요구하는 과업을 하루 중 최적의 시간에 처리하기로 정하라.

(B) 그러나, 만약 여러분이 직면한 과업이 창의성과 새로운 아이디어를 요구한다면, 하루 중 '최악의' 시간에 처리하는 것이 최선이다! 그래서 만약 여러분이 아침형 인간이라면 반드시 저녁에 창의적인 작업에 착수하고, 저녁형 인간이라면 반대로 하라.

(A) 여러분의 정신과 신체가 '정점' 시간보다 주의력이 덜할 때, 창의성의 영감이 깨어나 더 자유롭게 거니는 것이 허용된다. 다시 말해서, 여러분의 정신 기제가 차렷 자세로 있을 때보다(힘과 긴장이 바짝 들어가 있을 때보다) 느슨하게 풀려있을 때 창의성이 샘솟는다.

Why? 왜 정답일까?

사람들에게는 자기 신체와 잘 맞는 시간이 있다고 언급하는 주어진 글 뒤로, 집중력이 필요한 과업은 최적의 시간대에 처리해야 한다는 (C), '반면에' 창의성이 필요한 과업은 최악의 시간대에 처리하는 것이 좋다는 (B), 그 이유를 보충 설명하는 (A)가 연결되어야 자연스럽다. 따라서 글의 순서로 가장 적절한 것은 ⑤ '(C) − (B) − (A)'이다.

- **whether A or B** A이든 B이든
- **stand at attention** 차렷 자세를 취하다
- **tackle** ⓥ 해결하다, 처리하다, 다루다
- **loose** ⑧ 느슨한
- **novel** ⑧ 새로운, 신기한
- **early bird** 아침형 인간

DAY 13

- vice versa 그 반대도 같다
- make it a point to ~하기로 정하다, 으레 ~하다
- night owl 저녁형 인간

구문 풀이

14행 Some of us are night owls, some (are) early birds, and others
주어1　　　　　　　　주어2(여럿 중 일부)↵ 생략(중복)　　　　　　주어3(또 다른 일부)
in between may feel most active during the afternoon hours.

★★ 문제 해결 꿀~팁 ★★

▶ 많이 틀린 이유는?

(C) – (A)를 잘못 연결하기 쉽지만, (C)는 '정점' 시간에 수행할 과업(= 집중력이 필요한 일)을 언급하는 반면 (A)는 정점 시간이 '아닐' 때 수행할 과업(= 창의력이 필요한 일)을 언급한다. 즉 두 단락은 다루는 소재가 다르므로 적절한 흐름 전환의 연결어가 없으면 연결될 수 없다.

▶ 문제 해결 방법은?

하루 중 최적의 시간대가 개인마다 다르다는 주어진 글 뒤로, 누구는 아침이 좋고, 또 누구는 밤이 좋으니 각자 정점의 시간마다 집중력이 필요한 일을 처리하는 것이 좋다는 (C)가 먼저 연결된다. 즉 주어진 글과 (C)는 '일반적 내용 – 구체적 사례'의 흐름으로 자연스럽게 연결된다. 이어서 (A), (B)는 모두 (C)와는 달리 '창의력 과업을 수행하기 좋은 시간대'에 관한 내용인데, 이렇듯 흐름이나 소재가 달라질 때는 역접어가 있는 단락을 먼저 연결해야 한다. 따라서 (B) – (A)의 순서가 적합하다.

DAY 14　글의 순서 04

01 ③	02 ②	03 ③	04 ②	05 ②
06 ②	07 ④	08 ③	09 ②	10 ⑤
11 ③	12 ④			

01　과거 시골 건축업자들의 건축 양식　　정답률 58% | 정답 ③

주어진 글 다음에 이어질 글의 순서로 가장 적절한 것을 고르시오.

① (A) – (C) – (B)　　　② (B) – (A) – (C)
✔ (B) – (C) – (A)　　　④ (C) – (A) – (B)
⑤ (C) – (B) – (A)

Toward the end of the 19th century, / a new architectural attitude emerged.
19세기 말이 되면서, / 새로운 건축학적 사고방식이 나타났다.
Industrial architecture, / the argument went, / was ugly and inhuman; / past styles had more to do with pretension / than what people needed in their homes.
산업 건축은 / 그 주장에 따르면, / 추하고 비인간적이었다. / 과거의 스타일은 허세와 더욱 관련이 있었다. / 사람들이 자기 집에서 필요로 했던 것보다는
(B) Instead of these approaches, / why not look at the way / ordinary country builders worked in the past?
이러한 접근 대신에, / 방식을 살펴보는 것은 어떠한가? / 평범한 시골 건축업자들이 과거에 일했던
They developed their craft skills over generations, / demonstrating mastery of both tools and materials.
그들은 세대를 거쳐 공예 기술을 발전시켰다. / 도구와 재료 둘 다에 숙달한 기술을 보이며
(C) Those materials were local, / and used with simplicity — / houses built this way / had plain wooden floors and whitewashed walls inside.
그 재료는 지역적이고, / 단순하게 사용되었는데, / 이러한 방식으로 건축된 집들은 / 실내가 평범한 나무 바닥과 회반죽을 칠한 벽으로 되어 있었다.
(A) But they supplied people's needs perfectly / and, at their best, had a beauty / that came from the craftsman's skill / and the rootedness of the house in its locality.
그러나 그것들은 사람들의 필요를 완벽하게 충족시켰고, / 가장 좋은 경우 아름다움을 갖추고 있었다. / 장인의 솜씨에서 비롯된 / 그리고 그 집이 그 지역에 뿌리내림으로써 비롯된

19세기 말이 되면서, 새로운 건축학적 사고방식이 나타났다. 그 주장에 따르면, 산업 건축은 추하고 비인간적이었다. 과거의 스타일은 사람들이 자기 집에서 필요로 했던 것보다는 허세와 더욱 관련이 있었다.

(B) 이러한 접근 대신에, 평범한 시골 건축업자들이 과거에 일했던 방식을 살펴보는 것은 어떠한가? 그들은 도구와 재료 둘 다에 숙달한 기술을 보이며, 세대를 거쳐 공예 기술을 발전시켰다.

(C) 그 재료는 지역적이었고, 단순하게 사용되었는데, 이러한 방식으로 건축된 집들은 실내가 평범한 나무 바닥과 회반죽을 칠한 벽으로 되어 있었다.

(A) 그러나 그것들은 사람들의 필요를 완벽하게 충족시켰고, 가장 좋은 경우 장인의 솜씨와 집이 그 지역에 뿌리내리며 비롯된 아름다움을 갖추고 있었다.

Why? 왜 정답일까?

산업 건축 양식을 언급하는 주어진 글 뒤로, '이 접근법' 대신 평범한 시골 건축업자들의 작업 방식을 살펴보겠다고 언급하는 (B), (B)에서 언급된 재료를 Those materials로 받으며 이것들이 단순하게 사용되었다고 설명하는 (C), '그래도' 이렇게 건축된 집들은 사람들의 필요만큼은 완벽하게 충족시켰다는 내용의 (A)가 차례로 연결된다. 따라서 글의 순서로 가장 적절한 것은 ③ '(B) – (C) – (A)'이다.

- architectural ⓐ 건축의
- inhuman ⓐ 비인간적인
- rootedness ⓝ 뿌리내림, 고착, 정착
- demonstrate ⓥ 입증하다
- plain ⓐ 평범한, 단순한
- emerge ⓥ 나타나다, 출현하다
- craftsman ⓝ 장인
- locality ⓝ (~이 존재하는) 지역, 곳
- mastery ⓝ 숙달한 기술

구문 풀이

2행 Industrial architecture, (the argument went), was ugly and
　　　　　　주어1　　　　　( ): 삽입절　　　동사1
inhuman; past styles had more to do with pretension than {what
　　　　　　주어2　　동사2(~와 더 관련이 있었다)　　　　관계대명사(~것)
people needed in their homes}.

02 미디어상의 잘못된 정보 공유 문제 　정답률 65% | 정답 ②

주어진 글 다음에 이어질 글의 순서로 가장 적절한 것을 고르시오.

① (A) − (C) − (B)　　　✔(B) − (A) − (C)
③ (B) − (C) − (A)　　　④ (C) − (A) − (B)
⑤ (C) − (B) − (A)

People spend much of their time / interacting with media, / but that does not mean / that people have the critical skills / to analyze and understand it.
사람들은 많은 시간을 소비하지만, / 미디어를 이용해 상호작용하는 데 / 그렇다고 해서 뜻하지는 않는다. / 사람들이 중요한 기술을 가지고 있다는 것을 / 미디어를 분석하고 이해하는 데

(B) One well-known study from Stanford University in 2016 / demonstrated / that youth are easily fooled by misinformation, / especially when it comes through social media channels.
2016년 Stanford 대학의 잘 알려진 한 연구는 / 보여주었다. / 젊은이들이 잘못된 정보에 쉽게 속는다는 것을 / 특히 그것이 소셜 미디어 채널을 통해 올 때

This weakness is not found only in youth, however.
그러나 이러한 약점은 젊은이에게서만 발견되는 것은 아니다.

(A) Research from New York University found / that people over 65 / shared seven times as much misinformation / as their younger counterparts.
New York 대학의 조사에서 밝혔다. / 65세 이상의 사람들이 / 7배나 더 많은 잘못된 정보를 공유한다고 / 젊은이들보다

All of this raises a question:
이 모든 것이 의문을 제기한다.

What's the solution to the misinformation problem?
잘못된 정보 문제에 대한 해결책은 무엇인가?

(C) Governments and tech platforms / certainly have a role / to play in blocking misinformation.
정부와 기술 플랫폼은 / 분명 해야 할 역할을 가지고 있다. / 잘못된 정보를 막아내는 데 있어

However, / every individual needs to take responsibility / for combating this threat / by becoming more information literate.
그러나 / 모든 개인은 책임을 지닐 필요가 있다. / 이러한 위협에 맞서 싸울 / 정보를 더 잘 분별함으로써

사람들은 미디어를 이용해 상호작용하는 데 많은 시간을 소비하지만, 그렇다고 해서 사람들이 미디어를 분석하고 이해하는 데 중요한 기술을 가지고 있는 것은 아니다.

(B) 2016년 Stanford 대학의 잘 알려진 한 연구는 특히 정보가 소셜 미디어 채널을 통해 올 때 젊은이들이 잘못된 정보에 쉽게 속는다는 것을 보여주었다. 그러나 이러한 약점은 젊은이에게서만 발견되는 것은 아니다.

(A) New York 대학의 조사에서 65세 이상의 사람들이 젊은이들보다 7배나 더 많은 잘못된 정보를 공유한다고 밝혔다. 이 모든 것이 (다음의) 의문을 제기한다. 잘못된 정보 문제에 대한 해결책은 무엇인가?

(C) 정부와 기술 플랫폼은 분명 잘못된 정보를 막아내는 데 있어 해야 할 역할을 가지고 있다. 그러나 모든 개인은 정보를 더 잘 분별함으로써 이러한 위협에 맞서 싸울 책임을 지닐 필요가 있다.

Why? 왜 정답일까?

주어진 글에서 오늘날 사람들은 미디어를 많이 쓰고 있음에도 미디어를 분석하고 이해하는 데 필요한 능력을 갖추고 있지는 못하다고 지적한다. 이어서 (B)는 한 연구를 사례로 들며, 특히 젊은이들이 잘못된 정보에 쉽게 속는다는 점을 언급한다. (A)에서는 (B)의 말미에서 언급된 대로 '젊은 사람들뿐 아니라' 65세 이상의 연령대에서도 잘못된 정보 공유 문제가 발생한다고 언급한다. 이어서 (C)는 (A)의 마지막에 제시된, 정보 공유 문제에 대한 해결책을 묻는 질문에 대해 정부와 개인의 역할을 나누어 답하고 있다. 따라서 글의 순서로 가장 적절한 것은 ② '(B) − (A) − (C)'이다.

- interact with ~와 상호 작용하다
- misinformation ⓝ 오보, 잘못된 정보
- well-known ⓐ 잘 알려진
- fool ⓥ 속이다
- weakness ⓝ 약점
- government ⓝ 정부
- take responsibility for ~을 책임지다
- literate ⓐ ~을 다룰 줄 아는
- analyze ⓥ 분석하다
- raise a question 의문을 제기하다
- demonstrate ⓥ 입증하다
- especially ⓐⓓ 특히
- youth ⓝ 젊은이
- block ⓥ 막다, 차단하다
- combat ⓥ 싸우다

구문 풀이

1행 People spend much of their time interacting with media, but
　　　　　　　　　　「spend+시간+동명사 : ~하는 데 …을 소비하다」
that does not mean that people have the critical skills to analyze and
지시대명사(but 앞 문장)　접속사(~것)　　　　　　　　형용사적 용법1
understand it.
형용사적 용법2

---

03 신뢰 수준의 차이 　정답률 65% | 정답 ③

주어진 글 다음에 이어질 글의 순서로 가장 적절한 것을 고르시오.

① (A) − (C) − (B)　　　② (B) − (A) − (C)
✔(B) − (C) − (A)　　　④ (C) − (A) − (B)
⑤ (C) − (B) − (A)

Suppose / that you are busy working on a project one day / and you have no time to buy lunch.
가정해 보자, / 여러분이 어느 날 프로젝트를 하느라 바빠서 / 점심 식사를 살 시간이 없다고

All of a sudden your best friend shows up / with your favorite sandwich.
갑자기 가장 친한 친구가 나타난다. / 여러분이 가장 좋아하는 샌드위치를 들고

(B) He tells you that he knows you are busy / and he wants to help you out / by buying you the sandwich.
그는 여러분이 바쁘다는 것을 알고 있으며, / 돕고 싶다고 말한다. / 여러분에게 샌드위치를 사 주어

In this case, / you are very likely to appreciate your friend's help.
이런 경우에, / 여러분은 친구의 도움에 고마워할 가능성이 높다.

(C) However, / if a stranger shows up with the same sandwich / and offers it to you, / you won't appreciate it.
그러나 / 만약 낯선 사람이 같은 샌드위치를 들고 나타나 / 그것을 여러분에게 준다면, / 여러분은 그것을 고마워하지 않을 것이다.

Instead, you would be confused.
대신에, 여러분은 혼란스러울 것이다.

You would likely think / "Who are you, / and how do you know what kind of sandwich I like to eat?"
여러분은 생각하기가 쉽다. / "당신은 누군데, / 제가 어떤 종류의 샌드위치를 먹고 싶은지 어떻게 아세요?"라고

(A) The key difference between these two cases / is the level of trust.
이 두 경우의 주요한 차이점은 / 신뢰 수준이다.

You trust your best friend so much / that you won't worry about him knowing you too well, / but you certainly would not give the same level of trust / to a stranger.
여러분은 가장 친한 친구를 아주 많이 믿어서 / 그 친구가 여러분을 너무 잘 알고 있다는 것에 대해 걱정하지 않겠지만, / 여러분은 분명히 같은 수준의 신뢰를 주지 않을 것이다. / 낯선 사람에게는

여러분이 어느 날 프로젝트를 하느라 바빠서 점심 식사를 살 시간이 없다고 가정해 보자. 갑자기 가장 친한 친구가 여러분이 가장 좋아하는 샌드위치를 들고 나타난다.

(B) 그는 여러분이 바쁘다는 것을 알고 있으며, 샌드위치를 사 주어 돕고 싶다고 말한다. 이런 경우에, 여러분은 친구의 도움에 고마워할 가능성이 높다.

(C) 그러나 만약 낯선 사람이 같은 샌드위치를 들고 나타나 그것을 여러분에게 준다면, 여러분은 그것을 고마워하지 않을 것이다. 대신에, 혼란스러울 것이다. 여러분은 "당신은 누군데, 제가 어떤 종류의 샌드위치를 먹고 싶은지 어떻게 아세요?"라고 생각하기가 쉽다.

(A) 이 두 경우의 주요한 차이점은 신뢰 수준이다. 여러분은 가장 친한 친구를 아주 많이 믿어서 그 친구가 여러분을 너무 잘 알고 있다는 것에 대해 걱정하지 않겠지만, 낯선 사람에게는 분명히 같은 수준의 신뢰를 주지 않을 것이다.

Why? 왜 정답일까?

바쁘게 일하고 있는 도중 가장 친한 친구가 샌드위치를 들고 나타나는 경우를 언급한 주어진 글에 이어, (B)에서는 그 친구(He)가 베푼 친절에 고마운 감정을 느낄 가능성이 크다는 점을 이야기한다. (C)에서는 However로 흐름을 반전하며 낯선 사람이 샌드위치를 갖다 주는 경우를 언급하는데, (A)는 두 경우의 차이점(The key difference between these two cases)으로서 샌드위치에 대한 신뢰 수준을 언급한다. 따라서 글의 순서로 가장 적절한 것은 ③ '(B) − (C) − (A)'이다.

- all of a sudden 갑자기
- certainly ⓐⓓ 틀림없이
- confused ⓐ 혼란스러운
- show up 나타나다
- appreciate ⓥ 고마워하다

구문 풀이

6행 You trust your best friend so much that you won't worry
　　전치사　　　　　　　　「so+형/부+that : 너무 ~해서 …하다」
about him knowing you too well, / but you certainly would not give
　　의미상 주어 →동명사(about의 목적어)
the same level of trust to a stranger.

---

04 행동의 변화를 이끌어내는 것 　정답률 57% | 정답 ②

주어진 글 다음에 이어질 글의 순서로 가장 적절한 것을 고르시오.

① (A) − (C) − (B)　　　✔(B) − (A) − (C)

③ (B) − (C) − (A)   ④ (C) − (A) − (B)
⑤ (C) − (B) − (A)

We make decisions / based on what we *think* we know.
우리는 결정을 한다. / 우리가 안다고 *생각하는* 것을 기반으로
It wasn't too long ago / that the majority of people believed / the world was flat.
그다지 오래되지 않았다. / 대다수의 사람들이 믿었던 것은 / 세상이 편평하다고
(B) This perceived truth impacted behavior.
이렇게 인지된 사실은 행동에 영향을 미쳤다.
During this period, / there was very little exploration.
이 기간에는 / 탐험이 거의 없었다.
People feared / that if they traveled too far / they might fall off the edge of the earth.
사람들은 두려워했다. / 만약 그들이 너무 멀리 가면 / 그들이 지구의 가장자리에서 떨어질까 봐
So for the most part / they didn't dare to travel.
그래서 대체로 / 그들은 감히 이동하지 않았다.
(A) It wasn't until that minor detail was revealed / — the world is round — / that behaviors changed on a massive scale.
그런 사소한 사항이 드러나고 나서였다. / 세상은 둥글다 / 비로소 대대적으로 행동이 변화한 것은
Upon this discovery, / societies began to travel across the planet.
이것이 발견된 후 곧, / 사람들은 세상을 돌아다니기 시작했다.
Trade routes were established; / spices were traded.
무역 경로가 만들어졌으며, / 향신료가 거래되었다.
(C) New ideas, like mathematics, / were shared / between societies / which allowed for all kinds of innovations and advancements.
수학 같은 새로운 개념이 / 공유되었다. / 사회들 사이에 / 모든 종류의 혁신과 진보를 고려했던
The correction of a simple false assumption / moved the human race forward.
단순한 잘못된 가정의 수정이 / 인류를 앞으로 나아가게 했다.

우리는 우리가 안다고 *생각하는* 것을 기반으로 결정을 한다. 대다수의 사람들이 세상이 편평하다고 믿었던 것은 그다지 오래되지 않았다.

(B) 이렇게 인지된 사실은 행동에 영향을 미쳤다. 이 기간에는 탐험이 거의 없었다. 사람들은 만약 너무 멀리 가면 지구의 가장자리에서 떨어질까 봐 두려워했다. 그래서 대체로 그들은 감히 이동하지 않았다.

(A) 대대적으로 행동이 변화한 것은 비로소 그런 사소한 사항 — 세상은 둥글다 — 이 드러나고 나서였다. 이것이 발견된 후 곧, 사람들은 세상을 돌아다니기 시작했다. 무역 경로가 만들어졌으며, 향신료가 거래되었다.

(C) 모든 종류의 혁신과 진보를 고려했던 사회들 사이에 수학 같은 새로운 개념이 공유되었다. 단순한 잘못된 가정의 수정이 인류를 앞으로 나아가게 했다.

Why? 왜 정답일까?

인간은 본래 세상이 편평하다고 믿었음을 언급하는 주어진 글 뒤에는, 사람들의 이러한 믿음이 행동에도 영향을 미쳤기에 옛날에는 탐험이 잘 이루어지지 않았다고 설명하는 (B), 지구는 둥글다는 믿음이 퍼지면서 인간은 탐험과 무역을 시작했다고 언급하는 (A), 앞의 내용을 토대로 잘못된 가정의 수정이 인류를 진보시켰다는 결론을 내리는 (C)가 차례로 이어져야 한다. 따라서 글의 순서로 가장 적절한 것은 ② '(B) − (A) − (C)'이다.

- **majority** ⓝ 다수, 가장 많은 수
- **massive** ⓐ 대대적인, 거대한
- **impact** ⓥ 영향을 미치다 ⓝ 영향
- **for the most part** 대체로
- **innovation** ⓝ 혁신
- **assumption** ⓝ 가정
- **flat** ⓐ 편평한
- **establish** ⓥ 만들다, 설립하다
- **exploration** ⓝ 탐험
- **dare** ⓥ 감히 ~하다
- **correction** ⓝ 수정, 교정

구문 풀이

4행 It wasn't until that minor detail was revealed — (the world is
「it is[was] not until+   A+
round) — that behaviors changed on a massive scale.
( ): 동격   that+B : A하고 나서야 B하다[했다]」
(= that minor detail)

---

05 거래의 발생 과정   정답률 56% | 정답 ②

주어진 글 다음에 이어질 글의 순서로 가장 적절한 것을 고르시오.
① (A) − (C) − (B)   ✔(B) − (A) − (C)
③ (B) − (C) − (A)   ④ (C) − (A) − (B)
⑤ (C) − (B) − (A)

Trade will not occur / unless both parties want what the other party has to offer.
거래는 발생하지 않는다. / 양쪽 모두가 상대방이 제공해야 하는 것을 원하지 않으면
(B) This is referred to as the double coincidence of wants.
이것은 필요의 이중적 일치라고 불린다.
Suppose a farmer wants to trade eggs with a baker / for a loaf of bread.
농부가 제빵사와 계란을 거래하기를 원한다고 가정하자. / 빵 한 덩이를 얻기 위해
If the baker has no need or desire for eggs, / then the farmer is out of luck / and does not get any bread.
만약 제빵사가 계란에 대한 필요나 욕구가 없다면, / 농부는 운이 없으며 / 아무 빵도 얻지 못한다.
(A) However, if the farmer is enterprising / and utilizes his network of village friends, / he might discover / that the baker is in need of some new cast-iron trivets / for cooling his bread, / and it just so happens / that the blacksmith needs a new lamb's wool sweater.
그러나 만약에 농부가 사업성이 좋고 마을 친구들의 네트워크를 활용한다면, / 그는 발견할지도 모르며, / 제빵사가 새 무쇠 주철 삼각 거치대를 필요로 한다는 것을 / 그의 빵을 식힐 / 때마침 / 대장장이는 새로운 양털 스웨터를 필요로 한다.
(C) Upon further investigation, / the farmer discovers / that the weaver has been wanting an omelet for the past week.
더 자세한 조사로, / 그 농부는 알게 된다. / 직조공이 지난주 내내 오믈렛을 원하고 있었다는 것을
The farmer will then trade the eggs for the sweater, / the sweater for the trivets, / and the trivets for his fresh-baked loaf of bread.
그러면 그 농부는 계란을 스웨터와 거래할 것이다. / 스웨터를 삼각 거치대와, / 그리고 삼각 거치대를 제빵사가 갓 구운 빵 한 덩이와

양쪽 모두가 상대방이 제공해야 하는 것을 원하지 않으면 거래는 발생하지 않는다.

(B) 이것은 필요의 이중적 일치라고 불린다. 농부가 빵 한 덩이를 얻기 위해 제빵사와 계란을 거래하기를 원한다고 가정해보자. 만약 제빵사가 계란에 대한 필요나 욕구가 없다면, 농부는 운이 없으며 아무 빵도 얻지 못한다.

(A) 그러나 만약에 농부가 사업성이 좋고 마을 친구들의 네트워크를 활용한다면, 그는 제빵사가 그의 빵을 식힐 새 무쇠 주철 삼각 거치대를 필요로 한다는 것을 발견할지도 모르며, 때마침 대장장이는 새로운 양털 스웨터를 필요로 한다.

(C) 더 자세한 조사로, 그 농부는 직조공이 지난주 내내 오믈렛을 원하고 있었다는 것을 알게 된다. 그러면 그 농부는 계란을 스웨터와, 스웨터를 삼각 거치대와, 삼각 거치대를 제빵사가 갓 구운 빵 한 덩이와 거래할 것이다.

Why? 왜 정답일까?

필요의 이중적 일치로 인해 거래가 생겨나는 과정을 설명한 글이다. 거래의 양쪽 상대방이 서로에게 원하는 것을 제공할 수 없다면 거래가 생겨나지 않는다는 내용의 주어진 글 뒤에는, 거래가 발생하지 않는 상황의 예를 드는 (B), (B)의 흐름을 반전하며 다양한 필요가 있는 상황을 언급하는 (A), 그 필요를 서로 맞추면 거래가 발생한다는 내용을 제시하는 (C)가 차례로 이어지는 것이 자연스럽다. 따라서 글의 순서로 가장 적절한 것은 ② '(B) − (A) − (C)'이다.

- **trade** ⓝ 거래, 무역
- **enterprising** ⓐ 사업성이 좋은, 진취적인
- **in need of** ~을 필요로 하는
- **coincidence** ⓝ 우연의 일치
- **weaver** ⓝ 직조공, 방직공, 베 짜는 사람
- **unless** conj ~하지 않다면
- **utilize** ⓥ 활용하다, 이용하다
- **blacksmith** ⓝ 대장장이
- **investigation** ⓝ 조사, 수사, 연구

구문 풀이

3행 However, if the farmer is enterprising and utilizes his network
만약 ~라면   동사1   동사2
of village friends, / he might discover that the baker is in need of
명사절 접속사   ~을 필요로 하는
some new cast-iron trivets for cooling his bread, and it just so happens
때마침 우연히 ~하다
that the blacksmith needs a new lamb's wool sweater.

---

06 정보 공개에 관한 문화별 견해 차이   정답률 65% | 정답 ②

주어진 글 다음에 이어질 글의 순서로 가장 적절한 것을 고르시오. [3점]
① (A) − (C) − (B)   ✔(B) − (A) − (C)
③ (B) − (C) − (A)   ④ (C) − (A) − (B)
⑤ (C) − (B) − (A)

Ideas about how much disclosure is appropriate / vary among cultures.
얼마나 많은 정보를 공개하는 것이 적절한지에 관한 생각은 / 문화마다 다르다.

(B) Those born in the United States / tend to be high disclosers, / even showing a willingness / to disclose information about themselves to strangers.
미국에서 태어난 사람들은 / 정보를 많이 공개하려는 경향이 있고, / 기꺼이 의향을 보이기까지 한다. / 자기 자신에 관한 정보를 낯선 이에게 공개하려는

This may explain / why Americans seem particularly easy to meet / and are good at cocktail-party conversation.
이것은 설명할 수 있다. / 왜 미국인들이 특히 만나기 편해 보이고 / 칵테일 파티에서 대화하는 것에 능한지를

(A) On the other hand, / Japanese tend to do little disclosing about themselves to others / except to the few people with whom they are very close.
반면에, / 일본인들은 타인에게 자신에 관한 정보를 거의 공개하지 않는 경향이 있다. / 자신과 매우 친한 소수의 사람들을 제외하고는

In general, Asians do not reach out to strangers.
일반적으로 아시아인들은 낯선 이에게 관심을 내보이지 않는다.

(C) They do, however, show great care for each other, / since they view harmony as essential to relationship improvement.
그러나 그들은 서로를 매우 배려하는 모습을 보인다. / 그들이 조화를 관계 발전에 필수적이라고 간주하기 때문에

They work hard / to prevent those they view as outsiders / from getting information they believe to be unfavorable.
그들은 열심히 노력한다. / 그들이 외부인이라고 간주하는 사람들이 (~하지) 못하게 하려고 / 자신이 불리하다고 생각하는 정보를 얻는 것을

얼마나 많은 정보를 공개하는 것이 적절한지에 관한 생각은 문화마다 다르다.

(B) 미국에서 태어난 사람들은 정보를 많이 공개하려는 경향이 있고, 자기 자신에 관한 정보를 낯선 이에게 기꺼이 공개하려는 의향을 보이기까지 한다. 이것은 왜 미국인들이 특히 만나기 편해 보이고 칵테일 파티에서 대화하는 것에 능한지를 설명할 수 있다.

(A) 반면에, 일본인들은 자신과 매우 친한 소수의 사람들을 제외하고는 타인에게 자신에 관한 정보를 거의 공개하지 않는 경향이 있다. 일반적으로 아시아인들은 낯선 이에게 관심을 내보이지 않는다.

(C) 그러나 그들은 조화를 관계 발전에 필수적이라고 간주하기 때문에 서로를 매우 배려하는 모습을 보인다. 그들은 자신이 불리하다고 생각하는 정보를 외부인이라고 간주되는 사람들이 얻지 못하게 하려고 열심히 노력한다.

Why? 왜 정답일까?

정보 공개에 대한 생각이 문화마다 다르다고 언급한 주어진 글 뒤에는, 미국인들의 예를 들기 시작하는 (B), 일본인의 예를 대조하는 (A), 일본인들이 자신에 대한 정보를 공개하려 하지는 않지만 조화를 중시하기 때문에 서로 배려를 하기 위해 애쓴다는 내용을 덧붙이는 (C)가 차례로 이어져야 한다. 따라서 글의 순서로 가장 적절한 것은 ② '(B) – (A) – (C)'이다.

- appropriate ⓐ 적절한
- close ⓐ 친한, 가까운
- willingness ⓝ 기꺼이 ~하려는 마음
- unfavorable ⓐ 불리한, 호의적이 아닌
- vary ⓥ 다르다
- reach out to ⓥ ~에게 관심을 보이다
- essential ⓐ 필수적인, 본질적인

구문 풀이

14행 They work hard to prevent those [they view as outsiders] from
「prevent + A + from + 동명사 : A가 ~하지 못하게 하다」
getting information [they believe to be unfavorable].
선행사

---

07 고대 그리스 문명과 신화 　　　정답률 67% | 정답 ④

주어진 글 다음에 이어질 글의 순서로 가장 적절한 것을 고르시오.

① (A) – (C) – (B)
② (B) – (A) – (C)
③ (B) – (C) – (A)
✔ (C) – (A) – (B)
⑤ (C) – (B) – (A)

For its time, / ancient Greek civilization was remarkably advanced.
그 당시, / 고대 그리스 문명은 놀라울 정도로 진보했었다.

The Greeks figured out mathematics, geometry, and calculus / long before calculators were available.
그리스인들은 수학, 기하학, 미적분학을 이해했다. / 계산기를 이용할 수 있기 훨씬 전에

Centuries before telescopes were invented, / they proposed / that the earth might rotate on an axis / or revolve around the sun.
망원경이 발명되기 수세기 전, / 그들은 제안했다. / 지구가 축을 중심으로 회전하거나, / 혹은 태양 주변을 돌지도 모른다고

(C) Along with these mathematical, scientific advances, / the Greeks produced some of the early dramatic plays and poetry.
이러한 수학적, 과학적 진보와 함께, / 그리스인들은 몇몇 초기 연극과 시를 만들었다.

In a world / ruled by powerful kings and bloodthirsty warriors, / the Greeks even developed the idea of democracy.
세상에서 / 강력한 왕이나 피에 굶주린 전사에 의해 지배되는 / 그리스인들은 심지어 민주주의에 대한 생각도 발전시켰다.

(A) But they were still a primitive people.
하지만 그들은 여전히 원시적인 사람들이었다.

There were many aspects of the world around them / that they didn't understand very well.
주변 세상의 많은 측면들이 있었다. / 그들이 잘 이해하지 못했던

They had big questions, / like *Why are we here?* / and *Why is smoke coming out of that nearby volcano?*
그들은 커다란 의문점을 가졌다. / '왜 우리가 여기에 존재하는가?' 그리고 '왜 저 근처의 화산에서 연기가 나오고 있는가?'와 같은

(B) Myths provided answers to those questions.
신화는 그러한 질문에 답을 제공했다.

They were educational tools, / passing knowledge from one generation to the next.
그것은 교육적 도구였다. / 한 세대에서 다음 세대로 지식을 전달하는

They also taught morality / and conveyed truth about the complexity of life.
그것은 또한 도덕성을 가르쳤고 / 삶의 복잡성에 관한 진실을 전달했다.

In this way, / the Greeks were able to understand right and wrong in their lives.
이런 방식으로, / 그리스인들은 그들의 삶에서 옳고 그름을 이해할 수 있었다.

그 당시, 고대 그리스 문명은 놀라울 정도로 진보했었다. 그리스인들은 계산기를 이용할 수 있기 훨씬 전에 수학, 기하학, 미적분학을 이해했다. 망원경이 발명되기 수세기 전, 그들은 지구가 축을 중심으로 회전하거나, 혹은 태양 주변을 돌지도 모른다고 제안했다.

(C) 이러한 수학적, 과학적 진보와 함께, 그리스인들은 몇몇 초기 연극과 시를 만들었다. 강력한 왕이나 피에 굶주린 전사에 의해 지배되는 세상에서 그리스인들은 심지어 민주주의에 대한 생각도 발전시켰다.

(A) 하지만 그들은 여전히 원시적인 사람들이었다. 그들이 잘 이해하지 못했던 주변 세상의 많은 측면들이 있었다. 그들은 '왜 우리가 여기에 존재하는가?' 그리고 '왜 저 근처의 화산에서 연기가 나오고 있는가?'와 같은 커다란 의문점을 가졌다.

(B) 신화는 그러한 질문에 답을 제공했다. 그것은 한 세대에서 다음 세대로 지식을 전달하는 교육적 도구였다. 그것은 또한 도덕성을 가르쳤고 삶의 복잡성에 관한 진실을 전달했다. 이런 방식으로, 그리스인들은 그들의 삶에서 옳고 그름을 이해할 수 있었다.

Why? 왜 정답일까?

주어진 글에서 그리스 문명의 수학·과학적 진보를 언급한 데 이어, (C)에서는 그리스 문명의 예술적·정치적 측면의 진보를 이야기한다. (A)에서는 But으로 흐름을 반전시키며 이들이 여전히 몇 가지 커다란 의문점을 해결하지 못한 채 원시적인 면모를 지니고 있었음을 지적하는데, (B)에서는 그 의문에 대한 답을 신화가 제시해주었다는 내용을 제시한다. 따라서 글의 순서로 가장 적절한 것은 ④ '(C) – (A) – (B)'이다.

- civilization ⓝ 문명
- geometry ⓝ 기하학
- axis ⓝ 축, 축선, 중심
- revolve around ~의 주위를 돌다
- generation ⓝ 세대
- convey ⓥ 전달하다, 전하다
- democracy ⓝ 민주주의
- remarkably ⓐ 놀라울 정도로, 두드러지게
- calculus ⓝ 미적분학
- rotate ⓥ 회전하다, 회전시키다
- primitive ⓐ 원시의, 원시적인
- morality ⓝ 도덕, 도덕성, 도덕률
- complexity ⓝ 복잡성

구문 풀이

4행 Centuries before telescopes were invented, / they proposed
~하기 수 세기 전에
{that the earth might rotate on an axis or revolve around the sun}.
접속사　　　　　　동사1　　　　　　　　동사2　　　[ ] : proposed의 목적어

---

08 시간 투자에 대한 결정 　　　정답률 49% | 정답 ③

주어진 글 다음에 이어질 글의 순서로 가장 적절한 것을 고르시오. [3점]

① (A) – (C) – (B)
② (B) – (A) – (C)
✔ (B) – (C) – (A)
④ (C) – (A) – (B)
⑤ (C) – (B) – (A)

One of the most essential decisions / any of us can make / is how we invest our time.
가장 필수적인 결정 가운데 하나는 / 우리 중 누구라도 할 수 있는 / 우리가 시간을 어떻게 투자하는가이다.
(B) Of course, / how we invest time / is not our decision alone to make.
물론, / 시간을 어떻게 투자하는가는 / 우리가 혼자 하는 결정은 아니다.
Many factors determine / what we should do / either because we are members of the human race, / or because we belong to a certain culture and society.
많은 요인이 결정 내린다. / 우리가 무엇을 해야 하는지를 / 우리가 인류의 일원이라는 이유로, / 혹은 우리가 특정한 문화와 사회에 속한다는 이유로,
(C) Nevertheless, / there is room for personal choice, / and control over time / is to a certain extent in our hands.
그럼에도 불구하고, / 개인적인 선택을 위한 여지는 있고, / 시간에 대한 통제는 / 어느 정도 우리의 손 안에 있다.
Even in the most oppressive decades of the Industrial Revolution, / people didn't give up their free will / when it came to time.
심지어 가장 억압적이었던 산업 혁명 기간의 수십 년 동안에도, / 사람들은 자신의 자유 의지를 포기하지 않았다. / 시간에 있어
(A) During this period, / people worked for more than eighty hours a week in factories.
이 시기 동안, / 사람들은 공장에서 80시간 이상을 일했다.
But there were some / who spent their few precious free hours / reading books or getting involved in politics / instead of following the majority into the pubs.
하지만 일부 사람들이 있었다. / 얼마 안 되는 귀중한 자유 시간을 보내는 / 책을 읽거나 정치에 참여하면서 / 그저 다수를 좇아 술집에 가는 대신

우리 중 누구라도 할 수 있는 가장 필수적인 결정 가운데 하나는 우리가 시간을 어떻게 투자하는가이다.

(B) 물론, 시간을 어떻게 투자하는가는 우리가 혼자 하는 결정은 아니다. 우리가 인류의 일원이라는 이유로, 혹은 우리가 특정한 문화와 사회에 속한다는 이유로, 많은 요인이 우리가 무엇을 해야 하는지를 결정 내린다.

(C) 그럼에도 불구하고, 개인적인 선택을 위한 여지는 있고, 시간에 대한 통제는 어느 정도 우리의 손 안에 있다. 심지어 가장 억압적이었던 산업 혁명 기간의 수십 년 동안에도, 사람들은 시간에 있어 자신의 자유 의지를 포기하지 않았다.

(A) 이 시기 동안, 사람들은 공장에서 80시간 이상을 일했다. 하지만 얼마 안 되는 자유 시간 동안 그저 다수를 좇아 술집에 가는 대신 책을 읽거나 정치에 참여하는 일부 사람들이 있었다.

Why? 왜 정답일까?

'how we invest time'이라는 표현을 통해 '어떻게 시간을 투자하는가'에 관한 결정은 가장 필수적인 결정 중 하나임을 이야기한 주어진 글 뒤에는, 같은 표현을 반복하며 이 결정에는 여러 요인이 개입된다고 설명한 (B), 그럼에도 불구하고 어느 정도는 개인적인 선택의 여지와 통제력이 있다는 내용의 (C), 산업 혁명 시기의 예를 (C)에 이어 설명하는 (A)가 차례로 이어져야 자연스럽다. 따라서 주어진 글 다음에 이어질 글의 순서로 가장 적절한 것은 ③ '(B) – (C) – (A)'이다.

- **essential** ⓐ 필수적인, 본질적인
- **politics** ⓝ 정치
- **pub** ⓝ 주점
- **certain** ⓐ 특정한
- **room** ⓝ 여지
- **oppressive** ⓐ 억압적인, 억압하는
- **when it comes to** ~에 있어
- **invest** ⓥ 투자하다
- **majority** ⓝ 다수
- **belong to** ~에 속하다
- **nevertheless** ⓐⓓ 그럼에도 불구하고
- **extent** ⓝ 정도
- **Industrial Revolution** 산업 혁명

구문 풀이

4행 But / there were some [who spent their few precious free
주격 관계대명사   「spend + 시간 +
hours reading books or getting involved in politics instead of following
동명사1 + 동명사2 : ~하는 데 시간을 쓰다」   ~ 대신에   동명사
the majority into the pubs].

---

09 적응적 가소성   정답률 57% | 정답 ②

주어진 글 다음에 이어질 글의 순서로 가장 적절한 것을 고르시오.

① (A) – (C) – (B)   ✔ (B) – (A) – (C)
③ (B) – (C) – (A)   ④ (C) – (A) – (B)
⑤ (C) – (B) – (A)

A fascinating species of water flea / exhibits a kind of flexibility / that evolutionary biologists call *adaptive plasticity*.
물벼룩이라는 매혹적인 종은 / 일종의 유연성을 보여 준다. / 진화생물학자들이 적응적 가소성이라고 부르는
(B) If the baby water flea is developing into an adult in water / that includes the chemical signatures of creatures / that prey on water fleas, / it develops a helmet and spines / to defend itself against predators.
만일 새끼 물벼룩이 물에서 성체로 발달하고 있으면, / 생물의 화학적인 특징을 포함하는 / 물벼룩을 잡아먹고 사는 / 그것은 머리 투구와 가시 돌기를 발달시킨다. / 자신을 포식자로부터 지키기 위해
If the water around it / doesn't include the chemical signatures of predators, / the water flea doesn't develop these protective devices.
만일 주변의 물이 / 포식자의 화학적인 특징을 포함하지 않으면, / 그 물벼룩은 이러한 보호 장치를 발달시키지 않는다.
(A) That's a clever trick, / because producing spines and a helmet is costly, / in terms of energy, / and conserving energy is essential / for an organism's ability to survive and reproduce.
이것은 영리한 묘책인데, / 가시 돌기와 머리 투구를 만드는 것은 비용이 많이 들고, / 에너지 면에서 / 에너지를 보존하는 것은 핵심적이기 때문이다. / 살아남고 생식하는 유기체의 능력을 위해
The water flea only expends the energy / needed to produce spines and a helmet / when it needs to.
물벼룩은 오직 에너지를 소모한다. / 가시 돌기와 머리 투구를 만드는 데 필요한 / 그것이 필요할 때만
(C) So it may well be / that this plasticity is an adaptation: / a trait that came to exist in a species / because it contributed to reproductive fitness.
그러므로 아마 ~일 것이다. / 이러한 가소성은 적응일 / 즉 생물 종에 존재하게 된 특징 / 그것이 생식의 적합성에 이바지하기 때문에
There are many cases, / across many species, / of adaptive plasticity.
많은 사례가 있다. / 많은 종에 걸쳐 / 적응적 가소성의
Plasticity is conducive to fitness / if there is sufficient variation in the environment.
가소성은 적합성에 도움이 된다. / 환경에 충분한 차이가 있을 때

물벼룩이라는 매혹적인 종은 진화생물학자들이 적응적 가소성이라고 부르는 일종의 유연성을 보여 준다.

(B) 만일 새끼 물벼룩이 물벼룩을 잡아먹고 사는 생물의 화학적인 (고유한) 특징을 포함하는 물에서 성체로 발달하고 있으면, 그것은 자신을 포식자로부터 지키기 위해 머리 투구와 가시 돌기를 발달시킨다. 만일 주변의 물이 포식자의 화학적인 특징을 포함하지 않으면, 그 물벼룩은 이러한 보호 장치를 발달시키지 않는다.

(A) 이것은 영리한 묘책인데, 에너지 면에서 가시 돌기와 머리 투구를 만드는 것은 비용이 많이 들고, 에너지를 보존하는 것은 살아남고 생식하는 유기체의 능력을 위해 핵심적이기 때문이다. 물벼룩은 오직 필요할 때만 가시 돌기와 머리 투구를 만드는 데 필요한 에너지를 소모한다.

(C) 그러므로 이러한 가소성은 아마 적응일 텐데, 즉 그것은 생식의 적합성에 이바지하기 때문에 생물 종에 존재하게 된 특징이다. 많은 종에 걸쳐 적응적 가소성의 많은 사례가 있다. 가소성은 환경에 충분한 차이가 있을 때 적합성에 도움이 된다.

Why? 왜 정답일까?

물벼룩이 적응적 가소성을 보여주는 예시라고 언급하는 주어진 글 뒤로, 물벼룩이 환경에 따라 가시 돌기와 머리 투구를 발달시킬지 결정한다고 설명하는 (B), '이것'이 영리한 묘책인 이유를 설명하는 (A), So로 시작하며 결론을 내리는 (C)가 차례로 연결되어야 한다. 따라서 글의 순서로 가장 적절한 것은 ② '(B) – (A) – (C)'이다.

- **fascinating** ⓐ 매력적인
- **evolutionary** ⓐ 진화의
- **adaptive** ⓐ 적응의, 적응할 수 있는
- **clever** ⓐ 영리한
- **costly** ⓐ 비용이 많이 드는
- **conserve** ⓥ 보존하다
- **reproduce** ⓥ 번식하다, 재생하다
- **expend** ⓥ 쓰다, 들이다
- **signature** ⓝ 특징
- **defend against** ~로부터 보호하다
- **may well** 아마 ~일 것이다
- **fitness** ⓝ 적합성
- **variation** ⓝ 차이, 변주
- **species** ⓝ (생물) 종
- **biologist** ⓝ 생물학자
- **plasticity** ⓝ 가소성
- **spine** ⓝ 가시 돌기
- **in terms of** ~의 면에서
- **essential** ⓐ 필수적인
- **flea** ⓝ 벼룩
- **chemical** ⓐ 화학적인
- **prey on** ~을 먹고 살다
- **protective** ⓐ 보호하는
- **adaptation** ⓝ 적응
- **conducive** ⓐ 도움이 되는

구문 풀이

7행 The water flea only expends the energy needed to produce spines and a helmet when it needs to.
대부정사(= to produce spines and a helmet)

---

10 수위 차이가 있는 두 수역 간에 운하 건설하기   정답률 60% | 정답 ⑤

주어진 글 다음에 이어질 글의 순서로 가장 적절한 것을 고르시오.
① (A) − (C) − (B)
② (B) − (A) − (C)
③ (B) − (C) − (A)
④ (C) − (A) − (B)
✔ (C) − (B) − (A)

When two natural bodies of water stand at different levels, / building a canal between them / presents a complicated engineering problem.
두 곳의 자연 수역이 서로 수위가 다를 때, / 둘 사이에 운하를 건설하는 것은 / 복잡한 공학적 문제를 만들어 낸다.
(C) To make up for the difference in level, / engineers build one or more water "steps," / called locks, / that carry ships or boats up or down / between the two levels.
수위의 차이를 보전하기 위해 / 공학자들은 하나 이상의 물 '계단'을 만든다. / 로크라고 부르는, / 배나 보트를 위아래로 운반하는, / 두 수위 사이에서
A lock is an artificial water basin.
로크는 인공적인 물웅덩이이다.
It has a long rectangular shape / with concrete walls and a pair of gates at each end.
그것은 긴 직사각형 모양을 하고 있다. / 콘크리트 벽과 양 끝에 한 쌍의 문이 있는
(B) When a vessel is going upstream, / the upper gates stay closed / as the ship enters the lock at the lower water level.
선박이 상류로 올라가고 있을 때는, / 위쪽 문은 닫혀 있다. / 배가 더 낮은 수위에 있는 잠금장치에 들어서는 동안
The downstream gates are then closed / and more water is pumped into the basin.
그러고 나서 하류의 문이 닫히고 / 더 많은 물이 웅덩이 안으로 양수된다.
The rising water lifts the vessel / to the level of the upper body of water.
상승하는 물이 선박을 끌어올린다. / 위쪽의 물 높이 수준까지
(A) Then the upper gates open / and the ship passes through.
그러고 나면 위쪽 문이 열리고 / 배가 통과한다.
For downstream passage, / the process works the opposite way.
하류 통행의 경우, / 그 과정은 정반대로 작동한다.
The ship enters the lock from the upper level, / and water is pumped from the lock / until the ship is in line with the lower level.
배가 위쪽 수위의 로크로 들어오고, / 물이 로크로부터 양수된다. / 배가 더 낮은 수위와 일치할 때까지

───────────────

두 곳의 자연 수역이 서로 수위가 다를 때, 둘 사이에 운하를 건설하는 것은 복잡한 공학적 문제를 만들어 낸다.
(C) 수위의 차이를 보전하기 위해 공학자들은 두 수위 사이에서 배나 보트를 위아래로 운반하는, 로크라고 부르는 하나 이상의 물 '계단'을 만든다. 로크는 인공적인 물웅덩이이다. 그것은 콘크리트 벽과 양 끝에 한 쌍의 문이 있는 긴 직사각형 모양을 하고 있다.
(B) 선박이 상류로 올라가고 있을 때는, 배가 더 낮은 수위에 있는 잠금장치에 들어서는 동안 위쪽 문은 닫혀 있다. 그러고 나서 하류의 문이 닫히고 더 많은 물이 웅덩이 안으로 양수된다. 상승하는 물이 선박을 위쪽의 물 높이 수준까지 끌어올린다.
(A) 그러고 나면 위쪽 문이 열리고 배가 통과한다. 하류 통행의 경우, 그 과정은 정반대로 작동한다. 배가 위쪽 수위의 로크로 들어오고, 배가 더 낮은 수위와 일치할 때까지 물이 로크로부터 양수된다.

Why? 왜 정답일까?

주어진 글은 수위가 다른 두 자연 수역 사이에 운하를 건설하는 것을 화제로 제시한다. 먼저 (C)는 '두 수역의 수위 차이'를 보전하기 위해 하나 이상의 물 계단인 '로크'가 만들어진다고 설명한다. 이어서 (B)는 선박이 상류로 올라갈 때를 예로 들어, 로크의 두 문이 어떻게 작용하는지 설명하기 시작한다. Then으로 시작하는 (A)는 (B)의 과정을 뒤이어 설명한다. 따라서 글의 순서로 가장 적절한 것은 ⑤ '(C) − (B) − (A)'이다.

- **body of water** 수역, 물줄기
- **complicated** ⓐ 복잡한
- **downstream** ⓝ 하류의 ad 하류로
- **vessel** ⓝ 선박
- **basin** ⓝ 물웅덩이, 괸 물, (하천) 유역
- **make up for** ~을 보전하다, 보상하다
- **rectangular** ⓐ 직사각형의
- **canal** ⓝ 운하
- **engineering** ⓝ 공학
- **in line with** ~에 맞춰서, ~와 함께
- **upstream** ad 상류로 ⓐ 상류의
- **lift** ⓥ 들어올리다
- **artificial** ⓐ 인공적인

구문 풀이

15행 To make up for the difference in level, engineers build one
       목적(~하기 위해)
or more water "steps," (called locks), that carry ships or boats up or
        선행사   ( ): 과거분사구   주격 관계대명사
down between the two levels.

---

11 전자 상거래의 성장   정답률 42% | 정답 ③

주어진 글 다음에 이어질 글의 순서로 가장 적절한 것을 고르시오.
① (A) − (C) − (B)
② (B) − (A) − (C)
✔ (B) − (C) − (A)
④ (C) − (A) − (B)
⑤ (C) − (B) − (A)

Roughly twenty years ago, / brick-and-mortar stores began to give way to electronic commerce.
대략 20년 전, / 오프라인 거래 상점이 전자 상거래(온라인)로 바뀌기 시작했다.
For good or bad, / the shift fundamentally changed consumers' perception of the shopping experience.
좋든 나쁘든 간에, / 그 변화는 쇼핑 경험에 대한 소비자의 인식을 근본적으로 바꾸었다.
(B) Nowhere was the shift more obvious / than with book sales, / which is how online bookstores got their start.
그 변화가 더 분명한 곳은 없었는데 / 책 판매보다 / 그렇게 해서 온라인 서점이 시작되었다.
Physical bookstores simply could not stock / as many titles as a virtual bookstore could.
물리적인 서점은 그야말로 구비할 수 없었다. / 가상 서점이 할 수 있는 만큼 많은 서적을
There is only so much space available on a shelf.
딱 책꽂이 위의 공간만큼만 이용 가능했다.
(C) In addition to greater variety, / online bookstores were also able to offer aggressive discounts / thanks to their lower operating costs.
더 많은 다양성뿐만 아니라 / 온라인 서점은 또한 대단히 적극적으로 할인을 제공할 수 있었다. / 그들의 더 낮은 운영비 덕분에
The combination of lower prices and greater selection / led to the slow, steady rise of online bookstores.
더 낮은 가격과 더 많은 선택의 결합은 / 온라인 서점의 느리지만 꾸준한 상승으로 이어졌다.
(A) Before long, / the e-commerce book market / naturally expanded to include additional categories, / like CDs and DVDs.
머지않아 / 전자 상거래 책 시장은 / 추가적인 항목을 포함하도록 자연스럽게 확장되었다. / CD와 DVD 같은
E-commerce soon snowballed / into the enormous industry it is today, / where you can buy everything / from toilet paper to cars online.
전자 상거래는 곧 눈덩이처럼 불어났고, / 오늘날의 거대 산업으로 / 여기서 여러분은 모든 것을 온라인으로 살 수 있다. / 화장실 휴지에서 자동차까지

───────────────

대략 20년 전 오프라인 거래 상점이 전자 상거래(온라인)로 바뀌기 시작했다. 좋든 나쁘든 간에 그 변화는 쇼핑 경험에 대한 소비자의 인식을 근본적으로 바꾸었다.
(B) 그 변화가 책 판매보다 더 분명한 곳은 없었는데, 그렇게 해서 온라인 서점이 시작되었다. 물리적인 서점은 가상 서점이 할 수 있는 만큼 많은 서적을 그야말로 구비할 수 없었다. 딱 책꽂이 위의 공간만큼만 이용 가능했다.
(C) 더 많은 다양성뿐만 아니라 온라인 서점은 또한 더 낮은 운영비 덕분에 대단히 적극적으로 할인을 제공할 수 있었다. 더 싼 가격과 더 많은 선택의 결합은 온라인 서점의 느리지만 꾸준한 상승으로 이어졌다.
(A) 머지않아 전자 상거래 책 시장은 CD와 DVD 같은 추가적인 항목을 포함하도록 자연스럽게 확장되었다. 전자 상거래는 곧 오늘날의 거대 산업으로 눈덩이처럼 불어났고, 여기서 여러분은 화장실 휴지에서 자동차까지 모든 것을 온라인으로 살 수 있다.

Why? 왜 정답일까?

주어진 글은 약 20년 전 전자 상거래가 시작되어 쇼핑에 대한 인식을 변화시켰다는 일반적인 내용을 제시한다. 이어서 (B)는 특히 온라인 서점의 사례를 언급하며, 물리적 서점에 비해 온라인 서점이 공간적 이점을 지녔다고 설명한다. (C)는 온라인 서점이 또한 가격 우위를 지녔음을 언급하고, (A)는 온라인 서점 분야가 CD, DVD 등으로 확장되었음을 설명한다. 따라서 글의 순서로 가장 적절한 것은 ③ '(B) − (C) − (A)'이다.

- **roughly** ad 약, 대략
- **shift** ⓥ 바꾸다
- **electronic commerce** 전자 상거래
- **experience** ⓝ 경험
- **e-commerce** ⓝ 전자 상거래
- **expand** ⓥ 확장되다
- **snowball** ⓥ 눈덩이처럼 커지다
- **toilet paper** (화장실용) 화장지
- **title** ⓝ 서적, 출판물
- **offer** ⓥ 제공하다
- **operating cost** 운영비
- **steady** ⓐ 꾸준한
- **brick-and-mortar** ⓐ 오프라인 거래의
- **give way to** ~로 바뀌다
- **perception** ⓝ 인식
- **before long** 머지않아, 오래지 않아
- **naturally** ad 자연스럽게
- **additional** ⓐ 추가의
- **enormous** ⓐ 거대한
- **obvious** ⓐ 분명한
- **shelf** ⓝ 책꽂이
- **aggressive** ⓐ 공격적인, 적극적인
- **combination** ⓝ 결합

10행 Nowhere was the shift more obvious than with book sales,
「장소 부사구+동사+주어 : 도치 구문」
which is how online bookstores got their start.
계속적 용법(선행사 : 앞 문장)

★★ 문제 해결 꿀~팁 ★★

▶ 많이 틀린 이유는?
(B) 이후 (A)와 (C)의 순서를 잘 잡는 것이 관건이다. (B)에서 온라인 서점이 오프라인 서점보다 책을 다양하게 구비했다는 장점을 소개한 후, (A)는 온라인 서점 시장이 다른 부문으로 확장되었다는 내용을, (C)는 온라인 서점의 추가적 장점을 언급한다. 흐름상 (C)에서 온라인 서점의 장점에 관한 설명을 마무리하고, (A)에서 이 장점을 바탕으로 다른 상품 분야로의 확장이 가능했다는 결론을 내리는 것이 자연스럽다. 따라서 ② '(B) – (A) – (C)'는 답으로 부적절하다.

▶ 문제 해결 방법은?
(B)의 as many titles as a virtual bookstore가 (C)의 greater variety로 연결된다. 이어서 (C)의 결론인 the slow, steady rise of online bookstores가 (A)의 the e-commerce book market naturally expanded to include additional categories로 연결되며, 온라인 서점 사업이 책을 넘어 CD, DVD 등 다양한 부문으로 확장되었다는 최종적 결론에 이르고 있다.

★★★ 1등급 대비 고난도 3점 문제

| 12 | 협상에서 고려할 문제 | 정답률 43% | 정답 ④ |

주어진 글 다음에 이어질 글의 순서로 가장 적절한 것을 고르시오. [3점]
① (A) – (C) – (B)　　　　② (B) – (A) – (C)
③ (B) – (C) – (A)　　　✔(C) – (A) – (B)
⑤ (C) – (B) – (A)

In negotiation, / there often will be issues / that you do not care about /
— but that the other side cares about very much!
협상에서 / 문제가 종종 있을 것이다! / 당신은 신경 쓰지 않지만 / 상대방은 굉장히 많이 신경 쓰는
It is important to identify these issues.
이런 문제들을 확인하는 것이 중요하다.
(C) For example, / you may not care / about whether you start your new job in June or July.
예를 들어, / 당신은 신경쓰지 않는다. / 당신이 새 직업을 6월에 시작하든 7월에 시작하든
But if your potential boss strongly prefers / that you start as soon as possible, / that's a valuable piece of information.
하지만 당신의 상사가 될 사람은 강력히 선호한다면, / 여러분이 가능한 한 빨리 일을 시작하는 것을 / 이는 귀한 정보가 된다.
(A) Now you are in a position / to give her something / that she values (at no cost to you) / and get something of value in return.
이제 당신은 위치에 있다. / 무언가를 상대방에게 주고, / (당신에게는 부담이 없지만) 상대방이 중요시하는 / 보답으로 가치 있는 것을 받을
For example, / you might start a month earlier / and receive a larger bonus for doing so.
예를 들어, / 당신은 한 달 먼저 일을 시작하고 / 그렇게 함으로써 더 큰 보너스를 받을 수도 있다.
(B) Similarly, when purchasing my home, / I discovered / that the seller was very interested / in closing the deal as soon as possible.
마찬가지로, 내가 집을 살 때, / 나는 알아냈다. / 판매자가 큰 관심이 있음을 / 가급적 빨리 거래를 마무리짓는 데
So I agreed to close one month earlier than originally offered, / and the seller agreed to a lower price.
그래서 나는 원래 제시된 것보다 한 달 먼저 거래를 매듭짓기로 했고, / 판매자는 더 낮은 가격에 동의해 주었다.

협상에서 당신은 신경 쓰지 않지만 상대방은 굉장히 많이 신경 쓰는 문제가 종종 있을 것이다! 이런 문제들을 확인하는 것이 중요하다.

(C) 예를 들어, 당신은 새 직업을 6월에 시작하든 7월에 시작하든 신경쓰지 않는다. 하지만 당신의 상사가 될 사람은 여러분이 가능한 한 빨리 일을 시작하는 것을 강력히 선호한다면, 이는 귀한 정보가 된다.

(A) 이제 당신은 (당신에게는 부담이 없지만) 상대방이 중요시하는 무언가를 상대방에게 주고, 보답으로 가치 있는 것을 받을 위치에 있다. 예를 들어, 당신은 한 달 먼저 일을 시작하고 그렇게 함으로써 더 큰 보너스를 받을 수도 있다.

(B) 마찬가지로, 내가 집을 살 때, 나는 판매자가 가급적 빨리 거래를 마무리 짓는 데 큰 관심이 있음을 알아냈다. 그래서 나는 원래 제시된 것보다 한 달 먼저 거래를 매듭짓기로 했고, 판매자는 더 낮은 가격에 동의해 주었다.

주어진 글은 협상에서 한 당사자는 그다지 신경 쓰지 않지만 다른 당사자는 굉장히 신경 쓰는 문제가 있을 수 있고 이를 잘 파악하는 것이 중요하다는 내용을 말하는데 For example로 시작하는 (C)에서는 근무 시점에 대해 협상의 두 당사자가 생각의 차이를 갖고 있는 경우를 예로 든다. 이어서 (A)에서는 빠른 근무를 원하는 상사의 생각을 잘 파악하면 사원은 그 생각을 접수하는 대신 다른 보상을 받게 될 수도 있음을 덧붙여 이야기한다. Similarly로 시작하는 (B)에서는 (A)에서 마무리된 예시에 이어 다른 예시를 언급하는데, 필자 자신이 집을 살 때 판매자가 중요시하는 문제를 헤아려 자신에게도 이득이 되는 성공적인 거래를 제안할 수 있었다는 내용을 제시한다. 따라서 주어진 글 다음에 이어질 글의 순서로 가장 적절한 것은 ④ '(C) – (A) – (B)'이다.

- negotiation ⓝ 협상
- value ⓝ 가치
- in return 보답으로, 답례로
- similarly ⓐⓓ 비슷하게
- close a deal 거래를 매듭짓다
- agree to ~에 동의하다
- identify ⓥ 확인하다
- at no cost to ~에게 부담이 없는
- receive ⓥ 받다
- purchase ⓥ 사다, 구매하다
- originally ⓐⓓ 원래
- potential ⓐ 가능성이 있는, 잠재적인

1행 In negotiation, there often will be issues [that you do not care about]
목적격 관계대명사1
— but [that the other side cares about very much!]
목적격 관계대명사2

★★ 문제 해결 꿀~팁 ★★

▶ 많이 틀린 이유는?
'Similarly(마찬가지로)'는 앞에서 한 가지 예가 나오고 뒤에서 다른 예가 이어질 때 나오는 연결어다. 이 문제는 (C)와 (A)에 각각 예시가 나오므로 어느 단락 뒤에 (B)가 이어질지를 파악해야 한다는 점에서 어려운 문제였다.

▶ 문제 해결 방법은?
⑤와 같이 (C) 뒤에 (B)가 이어진다면 (A)는 '상사와의 협상' 내용이 아니라 '집을 사는' 예시에 관해 부연했을 것이다.
(C) – (A)의 소재가 같으므로 일단 잇고 (A) 마지막에 새로 소개되는 예시와 (B)의 예가 '마찬가지로'로 연결된다는 점에 유의한다.

글 뒤에는, Douglas가 그린 것이 손이었다는 내용의 (B), 아이들이 누구의 손인지 맞춰 보려 했다는 내용의 (C), 나중에 Douglas가 그것이 선생님의 손임을 말했다는 내용의 (A)가 차례로 이어져야 자연스럽다. 따라서 글의 순서로 가장 적절한 것은 ③ '(B) – (C) – (A)'이다.

- **turkey** ⓝ 칠면조
- **immediately** [ad] 즉시
- **raise** ⓥ 기르다, 키우다
- **responsive** ⓐ 관심을 보이는
- **attract one's interest** ~의 관심을 끌다

구문 풀이

1행 Mrs. Klein told her first graders to draw a picture of something to be thankful for.
동사 · 목적어 · 목적격 보어 · 대명사(-thing) · 형용사적 용법

DAY 15 — 글의 순서 05

01 ③	02 ②	03 ③	04 ②	05 ②
06 ⑤	07 ②	08 ②	09 ③	10 ②
11 ⑤	12 ②			

---

01 선생님에게 그림으로 감사를 표현한 Douglas · 정답률 79% | 성답 ③

주어진 글 다음에 이어질 글의 순서로 가장 적절한 것을 고르시오.

① (A) – (C) – (B)
② (B) – (A) – (C)
✓③ (B) – (C) – (A)
④ (C) – (A) – (B)
⑤ (C) – (B) – (A)

Mrs. Klein told her first graders / to draw a picture of something to be thankful for.
Klein 선생님은 1학년 학생들에게 말했다. / 감사히 여기는 것을 그려보라고

She thought / that most of the class would draw turkeys or Thanksgiving tables.
그녀는 생각했다. / 반 아이들 대부분이 칠면조나 추수감사절 식탁을 그릴 것으로

But Douglas drew something different.
하지만 Douglas는 색다른 것을 그렸다.

(B) Douglas was a boy / who usually spent time alone and stayed around her / while his classmates went outside together during break time.
Douglas는 소년이었다. / 보통 혼자 시간을 보내고 그녀 주변에 머무르는 / 그의 반 친구들이 쉬는 시간에 함께 밖으로 나가 있는 동안

What the boy drew was a hand.
그 소년이 그린 것은 손이었다.

But whose hand?
그런데 누구의 손일까?

His image immediately attracted the other students' interest.
그의 그림은 즉시 다른 학생들의 관심을 끌었다.

(C) So, / everyone rushed to talk / about whose hand it was.
그래서, / 모두가 앞다투어 말하려 했다. / 그것이 누구의 손인지에 관해

"It must be the hand of God / that brings us food," / said one student.
"그것은 신의 손이 틀림없어. / 우리에게 음식을 가져다주는" / 한 학생이 말했다.

"A farmer's," / said a second student, / "because they raise the turkeys."
"농부의 손이야," / 두 번째 학생이 말했다. / "왜냐하면 그들은 칠면조를 기르거든."이라고

"It looks more like a police officer's," / added another, / "they protect us."
"경찰관의 손과 더 비슷해 보여," / 또 다른 학생이 덧붙였다. / "그들은 우리를 보호해 줘."라고

(A) The class was so responsive / that Mrs. Klein had almost forgotten about Douglas.
반 아이들이 몹시 호응해서 / Klein 선생님은 Douglas에 대해 하마터면 잊어버릴 뻔했다.

After she had the others at work on another project, / she asked Douglas whose hand it was.
그녀가 나머지 아이들에게 다른 과제를 하도록 지도한 후, / 그녀는 Douglas에게 그 손이 누구 손인지 물었다.

He answered softly, / "It's yours. Thank you, Mrs. Klein."
그는 조용히 대답했다. / "선생님 손이에요. 고마워요, Klein 선생님."이라고

Klein 선생님은 1학년 학생들에게 감사히 여기는 것을 그려보라고 말했다. 그녀는 반 아이들 대부분이 칠면조나 추수감사절 식탁을 그릴 것으로 생각했다. 하지만 Douglas는 색다른 것을 그렸다.

(B) Douglas는 그의 반 친구들이 쉬는 시간에 함께 밖으로 나가 있는 동안, 보통 혼자 시간을 보내고 그녀 주변에 머무르는 소년이었다. 그 소년이 그린 것은 손이었다. 그런데 누구의 손일까? 그의 그림은 즉시 다른 학생들의 관심을 끌었다.

(C) 그래서, 모두들 그것이 누구의 손인지에 관해 앞다투어 말하려 했다. "그것은 우리에게 음식을 가져다주는 신의 손이 틀림없어."라고 한 학생이 말했다. "농부의 손이야, 왜냐하면 그들은 칠면조를 기르거든."이라고 두 번째 학생이 말했다. "경찰관의 손과 더 비슷해 보여, 그들은 우리를 보호해 줘."라고 또 다른 학생이 덧붙였다.

(A) 반 아이들의 호응에 Klein 선생님은 Douglas에 대해 하마터면 잊어버릴 뻔했다. 그녀는 나머지 아이들에게 다른 과제를 하도록 지도한 후, Douglas에게 그 손이 누구 손인지 물었다. "선생님 손이에요. 고마워요, Klein 선생님."이라고 그는 조용히 대답했다.

Why? 왜 정답일까?

고마운 것을 그려보는 시간에 Douglas가 무언가 색다른 것을 그렸다는 내용의 주어진

---

02 적목 현상이 일어나는 이유 · 정답률 81% | 정답 ②

주어진 글 다음에 이어질 글의 순서로 가장 적절한 것을 고르시오.

① (A) – (C) – (B)
✓② (B) – (A) – (C)
③ (B) – (C) – (A)
④ (C) – (A) – (B)
⑤ (C) – (B) – (A)

Imagine yourself at a party.
파티에 있는 자신을 상상해 보라.

It is dark / and a group of friends ask you to take a picture of them.
어두운데 / 친구들이 사진을 찍어 달라고 요청한다.

You grab your camera, point, and shoot your friends.
당신은 카메라를 잡고 친구들을 향해 사진을 찍는다.

(B) The camera automatically turns on the flash / as there is not enough light available / to produce a correct exposure.
카메라는 자동으로 플래시를 켠다. / 사용할 수 있는 빛이 충분하지 않기 때문에 / 정확한 노출을 만들어 내기 위해

The result is / half of your friends appear in the picture / with two bright red circles / instead of their eyes.
그 결과 / 친구 중 절반은 사진에 나온다. / 두 개의 밝은 빨간색 원과 함께 / 그들의 눈 대신

(A) This is a common problem / called the *red-eye effect*.
이것은 흔한 문제이다. / *적목(赤目)* 현상이라고 불리는

It is caused / because the light from the flash / penetrates the eyes through the pupils, / and then gets reflected to the camera / from the back of the eyes / where a large amount of blood is present.
그것은 발생한다. / 플래시에서 나오는 빛 때문에 / 동공을 통해 눈을 통과한 뒤, / 카메라로 반사되는 / 눈 뒤쪽으로부터 / 다량의 피가 있는

(C) This blood is the reason / why the eyes look red in the photograph.
이 피가 이유이다. / 사진에서 눈이 빨갛게 보이는

This effect is more noticeable / when there is not much light in the environment.
이 현상은 더욱 두드러진다. / 주위에 빛이 많지 않을 때

This is because pupils dilate when it is dark, / allowing more light to get inside the eye / and producing a larger red-eye effect.
이는 어두울 때 동공이 팽창하기 때문이다. / 더 많은 빛이 눈 안쪽으로 들어오게 하면서 / 더 큰 적목 현상을 일으키면서

파티에 있는 자신을 상상해 보라. 어두운데 친구들이 사진을 찍어 달라고 요청한다. 카메라를 잡고 친구들을 향해 사진을 찍는다.

(B) 정확한 노출을 만들어 내기 위해 사용할 수 있는 빛이 충분하지 않기 때문에 카메라는 자동으로 플래시를 켠다. 그 결과 친구 중 절반은 눈 대신 두 개의 밝은 빨간색 원과 함께 사진에 나온다.

(A) 이것은 *적목(赤目)* 현상이라고 불리는 흔한 문제이다. 그것은 플래시에서 나오는 빛이 동공을 통해 눈을 통과한 뒤, 다량의 피가 있는 눈 뒤쪽으로부터 카메라로 반사되기 때문에 발생한다.

(C) 이 피 때문에 사진에서 눈이 빨갛게 보인다. 이 현상은 주위에 빛이 많지 않을 때 더욱 두드러진다. 이는 어두울 때 동공이 팽창하여, 더 많은 빛이 눈 안쪽으로 들어오게 하면서 더 큰 적목 현상을 일으키기 때문이다.

Why? 왜 정답일까?

적목 현상이 일어나는 이유를 설명한 글이다. 주어진 글에서 어두운 파티장에서 친구들의 사진을 찍어줄 때를 생각해 보라고 언급한 후, (B)는 이 경우 빛이 충분하지 않아 자동으로 카메라 플래시가 터지고, 이후 사진을 보면 눈 대신 붉은 원이 보이게 된다는 설명을 제시한다. (A)는 (B)에 소개된 현상을 This로 받으며 이를 '적목 현상'이라는 용어로 정리한다. 한편 (A)의 후반부에서는 카메라 플래시에서 나온 빛이 눈을 통과한 후 피가 몰려 있는 눈 뒤쪽으로부터 다시 반사되기 때문에 적목 현상이 일어난다고 설명하는

데, (C)는 바로 이 피(This blood) 때문에 사진에서 눈이 붉게 나오는 것이라고 언급한다. 따라서 글의 순서로 가장 적절한 것은 ② '(B) – (A) – (C)'이다.

- **grab** ⓥ 붙잡다
- **present** ⓐ 존재하는
- **exposure** ⓝ 노출
- **reflect** ⓥ 반사하다
- **automatically** ⓐ 자동으로
- **noticeable** ⓐ 두드러지는

구문 풀이

4행 It is caused because the light from the flash penetrates the
접속사(~ 때문에)　주어　　　　　동사1
eyes through the pupils, and then gets reflected to the camera from
동사2(수동태)
the back of the eyes [where a large amount of blood is present].
장소 선행사　　　관계부사

---

03 조카에게 빠른 답장을 받은 Carnegie　　정답률 54% | 정답 ③

주어진 글 다음에 이어질 글의 순서로 가장 적절한 것을 고르시오.
① (A) – (C) – (B)
② (B) – (A) – (C)
✔(B) – (C) – (A)
④ (C) – (A) – (B)
⑤ (C) – (B) – (A)

Andrew Carnegie, the great early-twentieth-century businessman, / once heard his sister complain about her two sons.
20세기 초반의 위대한 사업가 Andrew Carnegie는 / 언젠가 누이가 자기 두 아들에 대해 불평하는 것을 들었다.

(B) They were away at college / and rarely responded to her letters.
그들은 멀리서 대학을 다니면서 / 어머니의 편지에 좀처럼 답장을 하지 않고 있었다.

Carnegie told her / that if he wrote them / he would get an immediate response.
Carnegie는 그녀에게 이야기했다. / 자신이 그들에게 편지를 쓰면 / 자신은 즉각적인 답장을 받을 것이라고

(C) He sent off two warm letters to the boys, / and told them / that he was happy / to send each of them a check for a hundred dollars / (a large sum in those days).
그는 다정한 편지 두 통을 조카들에게 보냈고, / 이야기했다. / 그가 기쁘다는 것을 / 그들 각자에게 100달러짜리 수표를 보내게 되어 / (당시 큰 액수였던)

Then he mailed the letters, / but didn't enclose the checks.
그런 다음 그는 편지를 부쳤지만, / 수표를 동봉하지는 않았다.

(A) Within days / he received warm grateful letters from both boys, / who noted at the letters' end / that he had unfortunately forgotten to include the check.
며칠 안에 / 그는 두 조카에게서 다정한 감사 편지를 받았는데, / 그들은 편지 말미에 언급했다. / 삼촌이 안타깝게도 수표를 함께 보내는 것을 잊었음을

If the check had been enclosed, / would they have responded so quickly?
만일 수표가 동봉되었더라면, / 그들이 그토록 빨리 답장을 보냈을까?

20세기 초반의 위대한 사업가 Andrew Carnegie는 언젠가 누이가 자기 두 아들에 대해 불평하는 것을 들었다.

(B) 그들은 멀리서 대학을 다니면서 어머니의 편지에 좀처럼 답장을 하지 않고 있었다. Carnegie는 자신이 그들에게 편지를 쓰면 자신은 즉각적인 답장을 받을 것이라고 이야기했다.

(C) 그는 다정한 편지 두 통을 조카들에게 보냈고, 그들 각자에게 (당시 큰 액수였던) 100달러짜리 수표를 보내게 되어 기쁘다는 것을 이야기했다. 그런 다음 그는 편지를 부쳤지만, 수표를 동봉하지는 않았다.

(A) 며칠 안에 그는 두 조카에게서 다정한 감사 편지를 받았는데, 그들은 편지 말미에 삼촌이 안타깝게도 수표를 함께 보내는 것을 잊었음을 언급했다. 만일 수표가 동봉되었더라면, 그들이 그토록 빨리 답장을 보냈을까?

Why? 왜 정답일까?

주어진 글에서는 Carnegie가 누이가 두 아들에 대해 불평하는 것을 들었다는 이야기가 나오는데 (B)에서는 이 '두 아들'을 They로 부르며 이들이 어머니의 편지에 좀처럼 답을 하지 않았다는 이야기를 이어간다. 한편 (B)의 마지막 부분에는 Carnegie가 자신이 편지를 쓴다면 바로 답을 받을 수 있다고 말했다는 내용이 나오는데 (C)에서는 Carnegie가 조카들에게 '수표를 보내게 되어 기쁘다'라고 편지를 쓰면서 수표는 보내지 않았다는 내용을 이어서 제시한다. 마지막으로 (A)에서는 Carnegie가 며칠만에 조카들로부터 답장을 받았고 이는 수표를 동봉한다고 말했으면서 실제로 동봉되지는 않았기 때문이었다는 내용을 말한다. 따라서 주어진 글 다음에 이어질 글의 순서로 가장 적절한 것은 ③ '(B) – (C) – (A)'이다.

- **businessman** ⓝ 사업가
- **complain** ⓥ 불평하다

- **grateful** ⓐ 감사해하는, 고마워하는
- **unfortunately** ⓐ 안타깝게도, 불행히도
- **rarely** ⓐ 좀처럼 ~하지 않는
- **send off** 보내다, 발송하다
- **note** ⓥ 언급하다, 말하다
- **check** ⓝ 수표
- **immediate** ⓐ 즉각적인, 즉시의
- **mail** ⓥ (우편물을) 부치다, 보내다

구문 풀이

4행 Within days / he received warm grateful letters from both boys,
→ 관계대명사(계속적 용법)
who noted (at the letters' end) that he had unfortunately forgotten to
동사　　　　　　　접속사　　　「forget to + 동사원형 :
include the check.　　　　　　　　　　　　　　(미래에) ~하는 것을 잊다」

---

04 박테리아의 이로운 점과 해로운 점　　정답률 77% | 정답 ②

주어진 글 다음에 이어질 글의 순서로 가장 적절한 것을 고르시오.
① (A) – (C) – (B)
✔(B) – (A) – (C)
③ (B) – (C) – (A)
④ (C) – (A) – (B)
⑤ (C) – (B) – (A)

We always have a lot of bacteria around us, / as they live almost everywhere / — in air, soil, in different parts of our bodies, / and even in some of the foods we eat.
우리 주변에는 항상 많은 박테리아가 있는데, / 왜냐하면 그것은 거의 모든 곳에 살고 있기 때문이다. / 즉 공기, 토양, 우리 몸의 다양한 부분들, / 그리고 심지어 우리가 먹는 몇몇 음식 속에도

But do not worry!
하지만 걱정하지 마라!

(B) Most bacteria are good for us.
대부분의 박테리아는 우리에게 유익하다.

Some live in our digestive systems / and help us digest our food, / and some live in the environment / and produce oxygen / so that we can breathe and live on Earth.
어떤 것은 우리의 소화 기관에 살면서 / 우리가 음식을 소화시키는 것을 도와주고, / 어떤 것은 주변에 살면서 / 산소를 만들어낸다. / 우리가 지구에서 숨 쉬고 살 수 있도록

(A) But unfortunately, / a few of these wonderful creatures / can sometimes make us sick.
하지만 불행하게도, / 몇몇 이런 훌륭한 생명체들이 / 때로는 우리를 병들게 할 수 있다.

This is when we need to see a doctor, / who may prescribe medicines to control the infection.
이때가 우리가 의사에게 진찰을 받아야 할 때인데 / 의사는 감염을 통제할 수 있도록 약을 처방해 줄 수 있다.

(C) But what exactly are these medicines / and how do they fight with bacteria?
그런데 이런 약은 정확히 무엇이고 / 어떻게 박테리아와 싸울까?

These medicines are called "antibiotics," / which means "against the life of bacteria."
이런 약은 '항생제'라고 불리는데, / '박테리아의 생명에 대항하는 것'을 의미한다.

Antibiotics either kill bacteria / or stop them from growing.
항생제는 박테리아를 죽이거나 / 또는 그것이 증식하는 것을 막는다.

우리 주변에는 항상 많은 박테리아가 있는데, 왜냐하면 그것은 거의 모든 곳, 즉 공기, 토양, 우리 몸의 다양한 부분들, 그리고 심지어 우리가 먹는 몇몇 음식 속에도 살고 있기 때문이다. 하지만 걱정하지 마라!

(B) 대부분의 박테리아는 우리에게 유익하다. 어떤 것은 우리의 소화 기관에 살면서 우리가 음식을 소화시키는 것을 도와주고, 어떤 것은 주변에 살면서 우리가 지구에서 숨 쉬고 살 수 있도록 산소를 만들어낸다.

(A) 하지만 불행하게도, 몇몇 이런 훌륭한 생명체들이 때로는 우리를 병들게 할 수 있다. 이때가 우리가 의사에게 진찰을 받아야 할 때인데 의사는 감염을 통제할 수 있도록 약을 처방해 줄 수 있다.

(C) 그런데 이런 약은 정확히 무엇이고 어떻게 박테리아와 싸울까? 이런 약은 '항생제'라고 불리는데, '박테리아의 생명에 대항하는 것'을 의미한다. 항생제는 박테리아를 죽이거나 또는 그것이 증식하는 것을 막는다.

Why? 왜 정답일까?

박테리아는 도처에 있지만 걱정할 필요는 없다는 내용의 주어진 글 뒤에는, 박테리아가 대체로 유익하다고 설명하는 (B), 하지만 불행히도 일부는 우리에게 해를 끼치기도 한다는 내용의 (A), 박테리아 감염이 있을 때 항생제가 이용된다는 내용의 (C)가 차례로 이어지는 것이 자연스럽다. 따라서 글의 순서로 가장 적절한 것은 ② '(B) – (A) – (C)'이다.

- **bacteria** ⓝ 세균, 박테리아
- **unfortunately** ⓐ 불행하게도
- **prescribe** ⓥ 처방하다
- **soil** ⓝ 토양
- **creature** ⓝ 창조물, 생물
- **medicine** ⓝ 의학, 약, 약물

- infection ⓝ 감염
- digest ⓥ 소화하다
- oxygen ⓝ 산소
- against prep ~에 맞서, 반대하여
- digestive system 소화기관
- produce ⓥ 생산하다
- antibiotic ⓝ 항생제

- implicit ⓐ 내재적인, 암묵적인
- specific ⓐ 특정한, 구체적인
- imprint ⓥ 각인시키다, 새기다
- explicit ⓐ 외재적인, 외현적인, 명확한
- consciously ⓐⓓ 의식적으로
- autonomic ⓐ 자동화의, 자율적인

구문 풀이

1행 We always have a lot of bacteria around us, as they live almost
이유 접속사
everywhere — in air, soil, in different parts of our bodies, and even
전명구1 　　　　전명구2
in some of the foods [we eat].
전명구3

구문 풀이

11행 Implicit memories are imprinted in the brain's autonomic
~에 각인되다
portion; that is why (even after years of not riding a bike) you still
그것이 ~한 이유이다　　( ) : 시간 부사구　　　　　주어
know how to ride.
동사 ~하는 방법

---

05 내재적 기억과 외재적 기억　정답률 65% | 정답 ②

주어진 글 다음에 이어질 글의 순서로 가장 적절한 것을 고르시오.

① (A) – (C) – (B)　　✔ (B) – (A) – (C)
③ (B) – (C) – (A)　　④ (C) – (A) – (B)
⑤ (C) – (B) – (A)

06 대접받고 싶은 대로 상대를 대접한다는 규칙의 맹점　정답률 58% | 정답 ⑤

주어진 글 다음에 이어질 글의 순서로 가장 적절한 것을 고르시오. [3점]

① (A) – (C) – (B)　　② (B) – (A) – (C)
③ (B) – (C) – (A)　　④ (C) – (A) – (B)
✔ (C) – (B) – (A)

Memory has two types / — implicit and explicit memory.
기억은 두 가지 종류가 있는데, / 내재적 기억과 외재적 기억이다.

When you learn things / without really thinking about it, / it's implicit memory or body memory.
여러분이 무언가를 배울 때, / 그것에 대해서 진정으로 생각하지 않고서 / 그것은 내재적 기억 혹은 신체 기억이다.

Knowing how to breathe when you were born / is an implicit memory.
태어났을 때 호흡하는 법을 아는 것은 / 내재적 기억이다.

(B) No one taught this to you.
아무도 여러분에게 이것을 가르쳐 주지 않았다.

Some of the things / you've learned since childhood / also become implicit memories.
~한 것 중 일부는 / 어릴 적부터 여러분이 배운 (것 중) / 또한 내재적 기억들이 된다.

Implicit memories are imprinted / in the brain's autonomic portion; / that is why even after years of not riding a bike / you still know how to ride.
내재적 기억들은 각인되는데, / 뇌의 자동화 부분에 / 이 때문에 여러분은 자전거를 수년 동안 타지 않고서도 / 여전히 자전거 타는 법을 알고 있다.

(A) Explicit memories, on the other hand, / are the memories or the specific things / that you consciously try to recall.
반면에 외재적 기억들은 / 기억들 혹은 특정한 것들이다. / 여러분이 의식적으로 기억하려고 노력하는

You use explicit memory every day on a conscious level.
여러분은 매일 의식적 차원에서 외재적 기억을 사용한다.

(C) Trying to find the keys, / trying to remember when an event is supposed to take place, / where it's going to be held, / and with whom you are going.
열쇠를 찾기 위해 노력하는 것, / 행사가 언제 개최되는지 기억하려고 노력하는 것. / 어디서 그것이 개최되는지, / 그리고 누구와 함께 그 행사에 가야 하는지

Explicit memories are the tasks / you have written down on your calendar or planner.
외재적 기억들은 과업들이다. / 여러분이 여러분의 달력이나 일정표에 적어왔던

기억은 두 가지 종류가 있는데, 내재적 기억과 외재적 기억이다. 여러분이 무언가에 대해서 진정으로 생각하지 않고서 그것을 배울 때, 그것은 내재적 기억 혹은 신체 기억이다. 태어났을 때 호흡하는 법을 아는 것은 내재적 기억이다.

(B) 아무도 여러분에게 이것을 가르쳐 주지 않았다. 또한 어릴 적부터 여러분이 배운 것 중 일부는 내재적 기억들이 된다. 내재적 기억들은 뇌의 자동화 부분에 각인되는데, 이 때문에 여러분은 사선거를 수년 동안 나시 않고서도 여전히 자전거 타는 법을 알고 있다.

(A) 반면에 외재적 기억들은 여러분이 의식적으로 기억하려고 노력하는 기억들 혹은 특정한 것들이다. 여러분은 매일 의식적 차원에서 외재적 기억을 사용한다.

(C) 열쇠를 찾기 위해 노력하는 것, 행사가 언제 개최되는지, 어디서 그것이 개최되는지, 그리고 누구와 함께 그 행사에 가야 하는지 기억하려고 노력하는 것. 외재적 기억들은 여러분이 여러분의 달력이나 일정표에 적어왔던 과업들이다.

Why? 왜 정답일까?

주어진 글에서 기억에는 내재적 기억과 외재적 기억이 있음을 말한 뒤 숨 쉬는 행위의 예를 들어 내재적 기억에 관한 이야기를 시작하는데, (B)에서는 이것이 아무에게도 배우지 않은 기억임을 설명한다. (A)에서는 화제를 전환하여(~ on the other hand, ~) 외재적 기억에 관해 말하고, (C)에서는 외재적 기억의 예를 든다. 따라서 글의 순서로 가장 적절한 것은 ② '(B) – (A) – (C)'이다.

Understanding how to develop / respect for and a knowledge of other cultures / begins with reexamining the golden rule: / "I treat others / in the way I want to be treated."
발달시키는 방법을 이해하는 것은 / 다른 문화에 대한 존중과 지식을 / 다음의 황금률을 재점검해보는 일에서 시작된다. / "나는 상대를 대접한다. / 내가 대접받고 싶은 대로"

(C) This rule makes sense on some level; / if we treat others as well as we want to be treated, / we will be treated well in return.
이 법칙은 어느 수준에서는 일리가 있다. / 만약 우리가 다른 사람들을 우리가 대접받고 싶은 만큼 대접한다면 / 우리는 보답으로 잘 대접받게 될 것이다.

This rule works well in a monocultural setting, / where everyone is working within the same cultural framework.
이 법칙은 단일 문화 환경에서는 잘 통한다. / 모든 사람이 같은 문화적 틀 안에서 일하는

(B) In a multicultural setting, however, / where words, gestures, beliefs, and views / may have different meanings, / this rule has an unintended result; / it can send a message / that my culture is better than yours.
그러나 다문화 환경에서는 / 단어, 제스처, 신념과 관점이 / 다른 의미를 지닐지도 모르는 / 이 법칙이 의도치 않은 결과를 낳는다. / 그것은 메시지를 줄 수 있다. / 나의 문화가 상대의 것보다 낫다는

(A) It can also create a frustrating situation / where we believe we are doing what is right, / but what we are doing is not being interpreted / in the way in which it was meant.
그것은 또한 답답한 상황을 낳을 수도 있다. / 우리가 자신이 하는 것이 옳다고 믿지만, / 그러나 우리가 하는 일이 해석되지 않는 / 그것이 의도된 방식으로

This miscommunication can lead to problems.
이러한 의사소통 오류는 문제를 야기할 수 있다.

다른 문화에 대한 존중과 지식을 발달시키는 방법을 이해하는 것은 다음의 황금률을 재점검해보는 일에서 시작된다. "나는 상대를 내가 대접받고 싶은 대로 대접한다."

(C) 이 법칙은 어느 수준에서는 일리가 있다. 만약 다른 사람들을 우리가 대접받고 싶은 만큼 대접한다면 우리는 보답으로 잘 대접받게 될 것이다. 이 법칙은 모든 사람이 같은 문화적 틀 안에서 일하는 단일 문화 환경에서는 잘 통한다.

(B) 그러나 단어, 제스처, 신념과 관점이 다른 의미를 지닐지도 모르는 다문화 환경에서는 이 법칙이 의도치 않은 결과를 낳는다. 그것은 나의 문화가 상대의 것보다 낫다는 메시지를 줄 수 있다.

(A) 그것은 또한 우리가 하는 것이 옳다고 믿지만, 그것이 의도된 방식으로 해석되지 않는 답답한 상황을 낳을 수도 있다. 이러한 의사소통 오류는 문제를 야기할 수 있다.

Why? 왜 정답일까?

자신이 대접받기를 원하는 대로 상대를 대접한다는 황금률을 다시 살펴봐야 한다는 주어진 글 뒤로, 이 법칙(This rule)이 단일 문화 환경에서는 잘 통한다는 내용의 (C), 하지만(however) 다문화 환경에서는 잘 안 통할 수 있다는 내용의 (B), 안 통할 때 생기는 문제에 관해 부연하는 (A)가 차례로 이어져야 자연스럽다. 따라서 글의 순서로 가장 적절한 것은 ⑤ '(C) – (B) – (A)'이다.

- reexamine ⓥ 재점검하다
- frustrating ⓐ 답답한, 좌절스러운
- miscommunication ⓝ 의사소통 오류
- unintended ⓐ 의도되지 않은
- in return 보답으로, 반응으로
- golden rule 황금률
- interpret ⓥ 해석하다, 이해하다
- multicultural ⓐ 다문화의
- make sense 일리가 있다, 의미가 통하다
- monocultural ⓐ 단일 문화의

구문 풀이

5행 It can also create a frustrating situation [where we believe
(that) we are doing what is right, but what we are doing is not being
interpreted in the way [in which it was meant]].

구문 풀이

3행 The output of the microbes — rich humus and soil — is in turn
the very material [from which a new oak tree may grow].
전치사 + 관계대명사 = where(관계부사)

---

07 자연의 순환 과정   정답률 69% | 정답 ②

주어진 글 다음에 이어질 글의 순서로 가장 적절한 것을 고르시오. [3점]

① (A) - (C) - (B)   ✔ (B) - (A) - (C)
③ (B) - (C) - (A)   ④ (C) - (A) - (B)
⑤ (C) - (B) - (A)

Why does garbage exist in the human system / but not more broadly in nature?
왜 쓰레기가 인간 체계에는 존재하지만 / 자연에는 더 널리 존재하지 않는가?

(B) Nature is a beautiful harmony of systems / whereby every system's output / is a useful input for other systems.
자연은 체계의 아름다운 조화이다. / 모든 체계의 산출물이 / 다른 체계에 유용한 투입물이 되는

An acorn that falls from a tree / is an important input / for a squirrel that eats it.
나무에서 떨어지는 도토리는 / 중요한 투입물이다. / 이를 먹는 다람쥐에게

The by-product of that delicious meal / — the squirrel's poop — / is an important input / for the microbes that consume it.
그 맛있는 식사의 부산물인 / 다람쥐 배설물은 / 중요한 투입물이다. / 이를 섭취하는 미생물에게

(A) The output of the microbes / — rich humus and soil — / is in turn the very material / from which a new oak tree may grow.
미생물의 산출물인 / 비옥한 부엽토와 토양은 / 결국 바로 그 물질이다. / 그것에서 새로운 떡갈나무가 자랄 수 있는

Even the carbon dioxide / that the squirrel breathes out / is what that tree may breathe in.
심지어 이산화탄소는 / 다람쥐가 내쉬는 / 그 나무가 들이쉴 수도 있는 것이다.

(C) This cycle is the fundamental reason / why life has thrived on our planet for millions of years.
이러한 순환은 근본적인 이유이다. / 생명이 수백만 년 동안 우리 지구에서 번창해 왔던

It's like the Ouroboros / — the ancient symbol / depicting a snake or dragon / eating its own tail; / in a way, / nature truly is a constant cycle of consuming itself.
이는 Ouroboros와 같다. / 고대 상징물인 / 뱀 또는 용을 그린 / 자신의 꼬리를 먹는 / 어떤 면에서 / 자연은 진정 그것 자신을 소비하는 끊임없는 순환이다.

왜 쓰레기가 인간 체계에는 존재하지만 자연에는 더 널리 존재하지 않는가?

(B) 자연은 모든 체계의 산출물이 다른 체계에 유용한 투입물이 되는 체계의 아름다운 조화이다. 나무에서 떨어지는 도토리는 이를 먹는 다람쥐에게 중요한 투입물이다. 그 맛있는 식사의 부산물인 다람쥐 배설물은 이를 섭취하는 미생물에게 중요한 투입물이다.

(A) 미생물의 산출물인 비옥한 부엽토와 토양은 결국 그것에서 새로운 떡갈나무가 자랄 수 있는 바로 그 물질이다. 심지어 다람쥐가 내쉬는 이산화탄소는 그 나무가 들이쉴 수도 있는 것이다.

(C) 이러한 순환은 생명이 수백만 년 동안 우리 지구에서 번창해 왔던 근본적인 이유이다. 이는 자신의 꼬리를 먹는 뱀 또는 용을 그린 고대 상징물인 Ouroboros와 같다. 어떤 면에서 자연은 진정 그것 자신을 소비하는 끊임없는 순환이다.

Why? 왜 정답일까?

자연에는 왜 쓰레기가 존재하지 않는지 묻는 주어진 글 다음에 자연은 모든 체계의 산출물이 다른 체계에 유용한 투입물이 되는 아름다운 조화라고 하며 다람쥐를 예로 드는 **(B)** 가 오고, 미생물의 산출물인 부엽토와 토양, 그리고 다람쥐가 내쉬는 이산화탄소에 관해서 얘기하는 **(A)**가 이어진 후 이런 순환에 대해서 설명하는 **(C)**가 연결되는 것이 자연스럽다. 따라서 주어진 글 다음에 이어질 글의 순서로 가장 적절한 것은 ② '**(B) - (A) - (C)**'이다.

- **exist** ⓥ 존재하다, 현존하다
- **in turn** 결국
- **whereby** [ad] 그래서, 그것에 의하여
- **by-product** 부산물
- **consume** ⓥ 소비하다, 먹다
- **thrive** ⓥ 번창하다
- **constant** ⓐ 끊임없는, 계속되는
- **humus** ⓝ 부엽토
- **oak tree** 떡갈나무
- **acorn** ⓝ 도토리
- **poop** ⓝ 배설물
- **fundamental** ⓐ 근본적인
- **depict** ⓥ 그리다, 묘사하다

---

08 문제 해결을 위한 설계 계획의 중요성   정답률 49% | 정답 ②

주어진 글 다음에 이어질 글의 순서로 가장 적절한 것을 고르시오. [3점]

① (A) - (C) - (B)   ✔ (B) - (A) - (C)
③ (B) - (C) - (A)   ④ (C) - (A) - (B)
⑤ (C) - (B) - (A)

If you start collecting and analyzing data / without first clarifying the question / you are trying to answer, / you're probably doing yourself more harm than good.
만약 여러분이 데이터를 수집하고 분석하기 시작한다면, / 질문을 먼저 분명히 하지 않은 채 / 여러분이 답하고자 하는 / 아마도 자신에게 득보다 실이 많은 일을 하고 있는 것이다.

(B) You'll end up drowning in a flood of information / and realize only later / that most of that research was a waste of time.
여러분은 결국 정보의 홍수에 빠지게 될 것이고, / 나중에야 비로소 깨닫게 될 것이다. / 그 조사의 대부분이 시간 낭비였다는 것을

To avoid this problem, / you should develop a problem-solving design plan / before you start collecting information.
이러한 문제를 피하기 위해서, / 여러분은 문제 해결 설계 계획을 세워야 한다. / 정보를 수집하기 전에

(A) In the design plan, / you clarify the issues you are trying to solve, / state your hypotheses, / and list what is required to prove those hypotheses.
그 설계 계획에서, / 여러분은 여러분이 해결하려는 문제를 분명히 하고, / 여러분의 가설을 진술하고, / 그 가설들을 증명하는 데 필요한 것을 열거한다.

Developing this plan / before you start researching / will greatly increase your problem-solving productivity.
이러한 계획을 세우는 것이 / 조사를 시작하기 전에 / 여러분의 문제 해결의 생산성을 크게 증가시킬 것이다.

(C) In addition, putting your plan down on paper / will not only clarify your thoughts.
게다가, 여러분의 계획을 종이에 적는 것은 / 여러분의 생각을 분명하게 해 주는 것만은 아니다.

If you're working in a group, / this plan will also help your team focus on what to do / and provide the starting point for your group brainstorming.
만약 여러분이 그룹으로 일하는 경우, / 이 계획은 또한 여러분의 팀이 해야 할 일에 집중하도록 도와주고, / 그룹의 브레인스토밍을 위한 시작점을 제공할 것이다.

만약 여러분이 답하고자 하는 질문을 먼저 분명히 하지 않은 채 데이터를 수집하고 분석하기 시작한다면, 아마도 자신에게 득보다 실이 많은 일을 하고 있는 것이다.

(B) 여러분은 결국 정보의 홍수에 빠지게 될 것이고, 나중에야 비로소 그 조사의 대부분이 시간 낭비였다는 것을 깨닫게 될 것이다. 이러한 문제를 피하기 위해서, 여러분은 정보를 수집하기 전에 문제 해결 설계 계획을 세워야 한다.

(A) 그 설계 계획에서, 여러분은 해결하려는 문제를 분명히 하고, 여러분의 가설을 진술하고, 그 가설들을 증명하는 데 필요한 것을 열거한다. 조사를 시작하기 전에 이러한 계획을 세우는 것이 여러분의 문제 해결의 생산성을 크게 증가시킬 것이다.

(C) 게다가, 여러분의 계획을 종이에 적는 것은 여러분의 생각을 분명하게 해 주는 것만은 아니다. 만약 여러분이 그룹으로 일하는 경우, 이 계획은 또한 여러분의 팀이 해야 할 일에 집중하도록 도와주고, 그룹의 브레인스토밍을 위한 시작점을 제공할 것이다.

Why? 왜 정답일까?

주어진 글에서 해결하려는 문제를 사전에 명확히 하지 않은 채 일에 뛰어들면 득보다 실이 많아질 수 있다고 말한 데 이어, **(B)**에서는 구체적으로 어떤 '실'이 생기는지 예를 들고 있다. 한편 **(B)**의 마지막 부분에서 '계획을 세워야 한다'는 내용이 언급되고, **(A)**에서는 이 계획(In the design plan)에 어떤 내용이 포함되어야 하는지 설명한다. **(C)**에서는 계획의 장점이 추가로 언급되고 있다. 따라서 글의 순서로 가장 적절한 것은 ② '**(B) - (A) - (C)**'이다.

- **analyze** ⓥ 분석하다
- **do more harm than good** 득(得)보다 실(失)이 많다
- **state** ⓥ 진술하다, 쓰다
- **productivity** ⓝ 생산성
- **flood** ⓝ 홍수
- **clarify** ⓥ 분명하게 하다
- **develop** ⓥ 개발하다
- **drown** ⓥ (물에) 빠지다
- **put ~ down** ~을 적다

4행 In the design plan, you clarify the issues [you are trying to
동사1
solve], state your hypotheses, and list {what is required to prove
동사2   동사3   ~하기 위해 필요하다
those hypotheses}.
{ }: 목적어

---

09 수학과 화학에서의 기호 사용   정답률 61% | 정답 ③

주어진 글 다음에 이어질 글의 순서로 가장 적절한 것을 고르시오. [3점]

① (A) – (C) – (B)　　　② (B) – (A) – (C)
✔(B) – (C) – (A)　　　④ (C) – (A) – (B)
⑤ (C) – (B) – (A)

If you had to write a math equation, / you probably wouldn't write, /
"Twenty-eight plus fourteen equals forty-two."
만일 여러분이 수학 등식을 써야 한다면, / 여러분은 아마 쓰지 않을 것이다. / '스물여덟 더하기 열넷은 마흔둘과
같다.'라고

It would take too long to write / and it would be hard to read quickly.
그것은 쓰는 데 너무 오래 걸리고 / 빨리 읽기가 어려울 것이다.

(B) You would write, "28 + 14 = 42."
여러분은 '28 + 14 = 42'라고 쓸 것이다.

Chemistry is the same way.
화학도 마찬가지이다.

Chemists have to write chemical equations all the time, / and it would take
too long to write and read / if they had to spell everything out.
화학자들은 항상 화학 방정식을 써야 하고, / 쓰고 읽는 데 너무 오래 걸릴 것이다. / 만약 그들이 모든 것을 상세
히 다 써야 한다면

(C) So chemists use symbols, / just like we do in math.
그래서 화학자들은 기호를 사용한다. / 우리가 수학에 하는 것처럼

A chemical formula lists all the elements / that form each molecule / and
uses a small number / to the bottom right of an element's symbol / to stand
for the number of atoms of that element.
화학식은 모든 원소를 나열하고 / 각 분자를 구성하는 / 작은 숫자를 사용한다. / 원소 기호의 오른쪽 아래에 /
그 원소의 원자 수를 나타내기 위해

(A) For example, / the chemical formula for water is H_2O.
예를 들어, / 물의 화학식은 H_2O이다.

That tells us / that a water molecule is made up / of two hydrogen ("H" and
"2") atoms / and one oxygen ("O") atom.
그것은 우리에게 말해 준다. / 하나의 물 분자는 이루어져 있다는 것을 / 두 개의 수소 원자('H'와 '2')와 / 하나의
산소 원자('O')로

만일 여러분이 수학 등식을 써야 한다면, 여러분은 아마 '스물여덟 더하기 열
넷은 마흔둘과 같다.'라고 쓰지 않을 것이다. 그것은 쓰는 데 너무 오래 걸리고
빨리 읽기가 어려울 것이다.

(B) 여러분은 '28 + 14 = 42'라고 쓸 것이다. 화학도 마찬가지이다. 화학자들은
항상 화학 방정식을 써야 하고, 만약 그들이 모든 것을 상세히 다 써야 한
다면 쓰고 읽는 데 너무 오래 걸릴 것이다.

(C) 그래서 화학자들은 우리가 수학에서 하는 것처럼 기호를 사용한다. 화학식
은 각 분자를 구성하는 모든 원소를 나열하고 그 원소의 원자 수를 나타내
기 위해 원소 기호의 오른쪽 아래에 작은 숫자를 사용한다.

(A) 예를 들어, 물의 화학식은 H_2O이다. 그것은 우리에게 하나의 물 분자는 두
개의 수소 원자('H'와 '2')와 하나의 산소 원자('O')로 이루어져 있다는 것을
말해 준다.

Why? 왜 정답일까?

주어진 글에서 우리가 수학 등식을 쓸 때 말로 풀어쓰지 않을 것이라 언급한 데 이어, **(B)**
에서는 우리가 '28 + 14 = 42'와 같이 '기호'를 사용할 것이라고 설명한다. 이어서 **(C)**는
(B)의 후반부에 이어 화학에서도 기호 사용이 필요하다고 언급하며, 특히 화학식의 경우
원소 기호 아래 작은 숫자를 사용하여 원자 수를 나타낸다는 내용을 덧붙인다. **For
example**로 시작하는 **(A)**는 **(C)**에서 언급한 아래 첨자 사용을 보여줄 수 있는 예로
H_2O를 제시한다. 따라서 글의 순서로 가장 적절한 것은 ③ '(B) – (C) – (A)'이다.

- **equation** ⑪ 방정식, 등식
- **be made up of** ~으로 구성되다
- **atom** ⑪ 원자
- **chemist** ⑪ 화학자
- **list** ⓥ 나열하다, 열거하다
- **bottom** ⑪ 아래
- **equal** ⓥ 같다
- **hydrogen** ⑪ 수소
- **chemistry** ⑪ 화학
- **spell out** 상세히 말하다
- **element** ⑪ 원소, 요소
- **stand for** ~을 나타내다[대표하다]

1행 If you had to write a math equation, you probably wouldn't
「if + 주어 + 과거 동사 ~, 주어 + 조동사 과거형 + 동사원형 : 가정법 과거(현재 사실의 반대 가정)」
write, "Twenty-eight plus fourteen equals forty-two."

---

10 인간을 만물의 척도로 보는 가정의 맹점   정답률 50% | 정답 ②

주어진 글 다음에 이어질 글의 순서로 가장 적절한 것을 고르시오.

① (A) – (C) – (B)　　　✔(B) – (A) – (C)
③ (B) – (C) – (A)　　　④ (C) – (A) – (B)
⑤ (C) – (B) – (A)

In the fifth century *B.C.E.*, / the Greek philosopher Protagoras pronounced, /
"Man is the measure of all things."
기원전 5세기에, / 그리스의 철학자 Protagoras는 선언했다. / "인간이 만물의 척도이다."라고

In other words, / we feel entitled to ask the world, / "What good are you?"
다시 말해서, / 우리는 세상을 향해 물어볼 자격이 있다고 느낀다. / "당신은 무슨 쓸모가 있는가?"라고

(B) We assume / that we are the world's standard, / that all things should be
compared to us.
우리는 추정한다. / 우리가 세상의 기준이라고 / 즉, 모든 것이 우리와 비교되어야 한다고

Such an assumption makes us overlook a lot.
그런 추정은 우리로 하여금 많은 것을 간과하게 한다.

(A) Abilities said to "make us human" / — empathy, communication, grief,
toolmaking, and so on — / all exist to varying degrees / among other minds /
sharing the world with us.
'우리를 인간답게 만들어 준다고' 일컬어지는 능력들, / 즉 공감, 의사소통, 슬픔, 도구 만들기 등은 / 다양한 정도
로 다 존재한다. / 지력을 지닌 다른 존재들 사이에서도 / 우리와 세상을 공유하는

Animals with backbones (fishes, amphibians, reptiles, birds, and mammals)
all / share the same basic skeleton, organs, nervous systems, hormones, and
behaviors.
척추동물(어류, 양서류, 파충류, 조류, 포유류)은 모두 / 동일한 기본 골격, 장기, 신경계, 호르몬, 행동을 공유
한다.

(C) Just as / different models of automobiles each / have an engine, drive
train, four wheels, doors, and seats, / we differ / mainly in terms of our
outside contours and a few internal tweaks.
~과 마찬가지로 / 다양한 자동차의 모델들이 각각 / 엔진, 동력 전달 체계, 네 바퀴, 문, 좌석을 가지고 있는 것 /
우리는 다르다. / 주로 우리의 외부 윤곽과 몇 가지 내부적인 조정 면에서

But like naive car buyers, / most people see only animals' varied exteriors.
하지만 순진한 자동차 구매자들처럼, / 대부분의 사람들은 오직 동물들의 다양한 겉모습만을 본다.

기원전 5세기에, 그리스의 철학자 Protagoras는 "인간이 만물의 척도이다."라고
선언했다. 다시 말해서, 우리는 세상을 향해 "당신은 무슨 쓸모가 있는가?"라고
물어볼 자격이 있다고 느낀다.

(B) 우리는 우리가 세상의 기준이라고, 즉 모든 것이 우리와 비교되어야 한다
고 추정한다. 그런 추정은 우리로 하여금 많은 것을 간과하게 한다.

(A) '우리를 인간답게 만들어 준다고' 일컬어지는 능력들, 즉 공감, 의사소통,
슬픔, 도구 만들기 등은 모두 우리와 세상을 공유하는, 지력을 지닌 다른
존재들 사이에서도 다양한 정도로 다 존재한다. 척추동물(어류, 양서류,
파충류, 조류, 포유류)은 모두 동일한 기본 골격, 장기, 신경계, 호르몬,
행동을 공유한다.

(C) 다양한 자동차의 모델들이 각각 엔진, 동력 전달 체계, 네 바퀴, 문, 좌석을
가지고 있는 것과 마찬가지로, 우리는 주로 우리의 외부 윤곽과 몇 가지
내부적인 조정 면에서 다르다. 하지만 순진한 자동차 구매자들처럼, 대부
분의 사람들은 오직 동물들의 다양한 겉모습만을 본다.

Why? 왜 정답일까?

'인간은 만물의 척도'라는 가정을 제시하는 주어진 글 뒤에는, 이것이 곧 인간이 스스로를
만물에 대한 비교 기준으로 여기고 있음을 의미한다고 설명하는 **(B)**, 이러한 인간 중심적
가정의 맹점을 지적하는 **(A)**, 다른 동물들에 대한 우리의 태도를 자동차 구매자에 빗대어
지적하는 **(C)**가 차례로 연결되어야 한다. 따라서 글의 순서로 가장 적절한 것은 ② '(B)
– (A) – (C)'이다.

- **philosopher** ⑪ 철학자
- **entitled** ⓐ 자격이 있는
- **grief** ⑪ 슬픔
- **reptile** ⑪ 파충류
- **overlook** ⓥ 간과하다, 무시하다
- **exterior** ⑪ 겉모습, 외부 ⓐ 외부의
- **pronounce** ⓥ 선언하다
- **empathy** ⑪ 공감, 감정 이입
- **amphibian** ⑪ 양서류
- **assumption** ⑪ 가정
- **naive** ⓐ 순진한, 세상을 잘 모르는

DAY 15

구문 풀이

12행 We assume that we are the world's standard, that all things
접속사1　　　　　　　接속사2(앞의 that절 동격)↵
should be compared to us.
조동사 수동태

- literary ⓐ 문학의
- boldly ⓐ 뚜렷하게, 대담하게
- analytical ⓐ 분석적인
- generalization ⓝ 일반화
- nature ⓝ 본질, 본성
- implication ⓝ 함축, 암시
- interpret ⓥ 해석하다

구문 풀이

4행 What a text implies is often of great interest to us.
주어(명사절)　　　동사(단수)　보어(= greatly interesting)

★★★ 1등급 대비 고난도 3점 문제

11 문학 텍스트의 이해　　　　　정답률 43% | 정답 ⑤

주어진 글 다음에 이어질 글의 순서로 가장 적절한 것을 고르시오. [3점]

① (A) – (C) – (B)　　　　② (B) – (A) – (C)
③ (B) – (C) – (A)　　　　④ (C) – (A) – (B)
✔(C) – (B) – (A)

Literary works, / by their nature, / suggest rather than explain; / they imply rather than state their claims boldly and directly.
문학 작품들은 / 그 본질상 / 설명하기보다는 암시하는데, / 그들은 그들의 주장을 뚜렷하고 직접적으로 진술하기보다는 함축한다.

(C) This broad generalization, / however, / does not mean / that works of literature do not include direct statements.
이 넓은 일반화는 / 그러나 / 뜻하지 않는다. / 문학 작품들이 직접적인 진술을 포함하지 않는다는 것을

Depending on when they were written and by whom, / literary works may contain large amounts of direct telling / and lesser amounts of suggestion and implication.
그들이 언제 그리고 누구에 의해 쓰였는지에 따라 / 문학 작품들은 많은 양의 직접적 말하기를 포함할 수도 있다. / 그리고 더 적은 양의 암시와 함축을

(B) But whatever the proportion of a work's showing to telling, / there is always something for readers to interpret.
하지만 작품에서 말하기 대 보여 주기의 비율이 어떻든 간에 / 독자가 해석해야 하는 무언가가 항상 존재한다.

Thus we ask the question / "What does the text suggest?" / as a way to approach literary interpretation, / as a way to begin thinking about a text's implications.
그러므로 우리는 질문을 한다. / "그 텍스트가 무엇을 암시하는가?"라는 / 문학적 해석에 접근하는 방법이자 / 텍스트의 함축에 대해 생각하기 시작하는 방법으로

(A) What a text implies / is often of great interest to us.
텍스트가 무엇을 함축하는지는 / 종종 우리에게 매우 흥미롭다.

And / our work of figuring out a text's implications / tests our analytical powers.
그리고 / 텍스트의 함축을 알아내는 우리의 작업은 / 우리의 분석적 능력을 시험한다.

In considering what a text suggests, / we gain practice in making sense of texts.
텍스트가 무엇을 암시하는지를 고려하는 과정에서 / 우리는 텍스트를 이해하는 기량을 얻게 된다.

문학 작품들은 그 본질상 설명하기보다는 암시하는데, 그들은 주장을 뚜렷하게 직접적으로 진술하기보다는 함축한다.

(C) 그러나 이 넓은 일반화는 문학 작품들이 직접적인 진술을 포함하지 않는다는 뜻은 아니다. 그들이 언제 누구에 의해 쓰였는지에 따라, 문학 작품들은 많은 양의 직접적 말하기와 더 적은 양의 암시와 함축을 포함할 수도 있다.

(B) 하지만 작품에서 말하기 대 보여 주기의 비율이 어떻든 간에 독자가 해석해야 하는 무언가가 항상 존재한다. 그러므로 우리는 문학적 해석에 접근하는 방법이자 텍스트의 함축에 대해 생각하기 시작하는 방법으로 "그 텍스트가 무엇을 암시하는가?"라는 질문을 한다.

(A) 텍스트가 무엇을 함축하는지는 종종 우리에게 매우 흥미롭다. 그리고 텍스트의 함축을 알아내는 작업은 우리의 분석적 능력을 시험한다. 텍스트가 무엇을 암시하는지를 고려하는 과정에서 우리는 텍스트를 이해하는 기량을 얻게 된다.

Why? 왜 정답일까?

주어진 글은 문학 작품의 특징으로 함축적 진술을 언급한다. 이어서 (C)는 however로 주의를 환기하며 문학 작품 안에 직접적 진술이 전혀 없지는 않다는 점을 상기시킨다. 한편 But으로 시작하는 (B)는 직접적 진술과 함축적 진술의 비율이 어떻든 간에 문학 텍스트에는 항상 독자가 해석해야 하는 부분이 있으며, 이 때문에 우리가 '그 텍스트가 무엇을 암시하는지' 자문하게 된다고 언급한다. (A)는 (B)의 "What does the text suggest?"를 What a text implies로 바꾸어 표현하며, 텍스트가 함축하는 바를 알아내는 과정에서 우리가 텍스트를 이해하는 능력을 기르게 된다고 설명한다. 따라서 글의 순서로 가장 적절한 것은 ⑤ '(C) – (B) – (A)'이다.

★★ 문제 해결 꿀~팁 ★★

▶ 많이 틀린 이유는?
(B)와 (C)의 순서를 잘 파악하는 것이 관건이다. 얼핏 보면 주어진 글의 imply rather than state가 (B)의 showing과 telling으로 바로 연결되는 것 같지만, (B)의 핵심은 '독자의 해석과 이해'에 관한 것이다. 이에 반해 (C)는 주어진 글과 마찬가지로 문학적인 글의 말하기 방식에 관해서 다루고 있으므로, 화제의 흐름상 (C)가 먼저 나온 뒤 (B)로 전환되는 것이 자연스럽다.

▶ 문제 해결 방법은?
주어진 글의 'Literary works ~ imply rather than state their claims boldly and directly.'가 (C)의 This broad generalization으로 이어지고, (C)의 literary works may contain large amounts of direct telling and lesser amounts of suggestion and implication이 (B)의 the proportion of a work's showing to telling으로 연결된다. 즉 (C)까지 문학 작품 속의 말하기와 보여주기(의 비중)에 관해 설명한 뒤, (B)에서 '그 비중에 상관없이' 독자가 해석할 부분이 있다는 내용으로 넘어가는 흐름임을 파악하도록 한다.

★★★ 1등급 대비 고난도 3점 문제

12 상관관계와 인과관계의 별개성　　　정답률 46% | 정답 ②

주어진 글 다음에 이어질 글의 순서로 가장 적절한 것을 고르시오. [3점]

① (A) – (C) – (B)　　　　✔(B) – (A) – (C)
③ (B) – (C) – (A)　　　　④ (C) – (A) – (B)
⑤ (C) – (B) – (A)

From a correlational observation, / we conclude / that one variable is related to a second variable.
상관관계의 관찰로부터 / 우리는 결론을 내린다. / 하나의 변인이 제2의 변인과 연관되어 있다고

But neither behavior / could be directly causing the other / even though there is a relationship.
그러나 둘 중 어느 행동도 / 다른 행동을 직접적으로 초래하지 않을 수 있다. / 관련성이 있다 하더라도

(B) The following example will illustrate / why it is difficult to make causal statements / on the basis of correlational observation.
다음 예는 보여줄 것이다. / 인과관계의 진술을 하는 것이 왜 어려운지를 / 상관관계의 관찰에 기초하여

The researchers at the U.S. Army / conducted a study of motorcycle accidents, / attempting to correlate the number of accidents with other variables / such as socioeconomic level and age.
미 육군 연구원들은 / 오토바이 사고에 관한 연구를 수행했다. / 사고의 수를 다른 변인과 연관시키려는 시도를 하여 / 사회 경제적 수준 및 나이와 같은

(A) They found / the best predictor / to be the number of tattoos / the rider had.
그들은 발견했다. / 최상의 예측 변인이 / 문신의 수라는 것을 / 오토바이를 타는 사람이 지닌

It would be a ridiculous error / to conclude / that tattoos cause motorcycle accidents / or that motorcycle accidents cause tattoos.
우스꽝스러운 오류가 될 것이다. / 결론 내리는 것은 / 문신이 오토바이 사고를 초래한다거나 / 오토바이 사고가 문신을 초래한다고

(C) Obviously, a third variable is related to both / — perhaps preference for risk.
명백히, 제3의 변인이 둘 다와 관련이 있는데, / 아마 위험에 대한 선호일 것이다.

A person who is willing to take risks / likes to be tattooed / and also takes more chances on a motorcycle.
위험을 기꺼이 감수하려는 사람은 / 문신 새기는 것을 좋아할 것이며 / 오토바이도 탈 가능성이 더 높다.

상관관계의 관찰로부터 우리는 하나의 변인이 제2의 변인과 연관되어 있다고 결론을 내린다. 그러나 관련성이 있다 하더라도 둘 중 어느 행동도 다른 행동을 직접적으로 초래하지 않을 수 있다.

(B) 다음 예는 상관관계의 관찰에 기초하여 인과관계의 진술을 하는 것이 왜 어려운지를 보여줄 것이다. 미 육군 연구원들은 사고의 수를 사회 경제적 수준 및 나이와 같은 다른 변인과 연관시키려는 시도를 하여 오토바이 사고에 관한 연구를 수행했다.

(A) 그들은 최상의 예측 변인이 오토바이를 타는 사람이 지닌 문신의 수라는 것을 발견했다. 문신이 오토바이 사고를 초래한다거나 오토바이 사고가 문신을 초래한다고 결론 내리는 것은 우스꽝스러운 오류가 될 것이다.

(C) 명백히, 제3의 변인이 둘 다와 관련이 있는데, 아마 위험에 대한 선호도일 것이다. 위험을 기꺼이 감수하려는 사람은 문신 새기는 것을 좋아할 것이며 오토바이도 탈 가능성이 더 높다.

Why? 왜 정답일까?

상관관계의 관찰에서 바로 인과관계를 추론하기는 어렵다는 내용의 주어진 글 뒤에는, 오토바이 사고 수의 예를 언급하기 시작한 **(B)**, 연구 결과 문신 수와 사고의 수가 서로 상관관계가 있다는 점이 드러났지만 이 두 변인을 인과관계로 엮으면 우스꽝스러울 것이라는 내용의 **(A)**, 오히려 제3의 변인이 어느 정도 관련되어 있을 것이라는 추가적인 해석을 제시하는 **(C)**가 차례로 이어지는 것이 자연스럽다. 따라서 주어진 글 다음에 이어질 글의 순서로 가장 적절한 것은 ② '**(B) – (A) – (C)**'이다.

- **correlational** ⓐ 상관관계의
- **variable** ⓝ (실험에서) 변인, 변수
- **ridiculous** ⓐ 우스꽝스러운
- **causal** ⓐ 인과관계의, 인과의
- **attempt** ⓥ 시도하다
- **socioeconomic** ⓐ 사회 경제적인
- **be willing to** 기꺼이 ~하다
- **conclude** ⓥ 결론 짓다
- **directly** ⓐⓓ 직접적으로
- **illustrate** ⓥ 보여주다, 예증하다
- **conduct** ⓥ (수행)하다
- **correlate** ⓥ 연관시키다
- **obviously** ⓐⓓ 명백히, 분명히

구문 풀이

6행 It would be a ridiculous error to conclude [that tattoos cause
(가주어) (진주어) (접속사(~것))
motorcycle accidents] or [that motorcycle accidents cause tattoos].
(접속사(~것))

★★ 문제 해결 꿀~팁 ★★

▶ 많이 틀린 이유는?
상관관계와 인과관계의 개념을 구별하는 까다로운 내용의 지문으로, 내용을 속속들이 파악하기보다 단서 중심으로 답을 찾는 데 주력해야 한다. 오답으로 ③이 많이 나왔는데 **(A) – (C)**의 순서를 정하는 것이 문제 풀이의 성패를 가르는 요인이었음을 알 수 있다.

▶ 문제 해결 방법은?
주어진 문장에서 예시로 넘어가는 **(B)**가 가장 먼저 나온 뒤, **Researchers**를 **They**로 받는 **(A)**가 일단 이어져서 '사고의 수'와 '운전자의 문신 수'가 서로 인과관계로 연결된 요인으로 보기는 어렵다는 이야기가 나와야 'A third variable'을 추가하는 느낌의 **(C)**가 자연스럽게 이어진다. 또한 **(C)**의 첫 문장에 나오는 **both**는 **(A)**에서 언급한 **motorcycle accidenter**와 **tattoo**를 가리킨다. **(C)**부터 배치하면 **(A)**의 **They**가 '연구자'라는 단어와 한참 멀어져서 오히려 **(C)**에 나온 복수 명사 **chances**로 읽힐 수 있는데, 이 경우 맥락이 부자연스럽다.

---

01 ④	02 ③	03 ③	04 ②	05 ④
06 ⑤	07 ②	08 ③	09 ②	10 ⑤
11 ⑤	12 ④			

DAY 16

01 탄수화물의 종류
정답률 57% | 정답 ④

글의 흐름으로 보아, 주어진 문장이 들어가기에 가장 적절한 곳을 고르시오.

All carbohydrates are basically sugars.
모든 탄수화물은 기본적으로 당이다.
① Complex carbohydrates are the good carbohydrates for your body.
복합 탄수화물은 몸에 좋은 탄수화물이다.
② These complex sugar compounds / are very difficult to break down / and can trap other nutrients / like vitamins and minerals / in their chains.
이러한 복당류 화합물은 / 분해하기 매우 어렵고 / 다른 영양소를 가두어 둘 수 있다. / 비타민과 미네랄 같은 / 그것의 사슬 안에
③ As they slowly break down, / the other nutrients are also released into your body, / and can provide you with fuel for a number of hours.
그것들이 천천히 분해되면서, / 다른 영양소도 여러분의 몸으로 방출되고, / 많은 시간 동안 여러분에게 연료를 공급할 수 있다.
✔ Bad carbohydrates, / on the other hand, / are simple sugars.
나쁜 탄수화물은 / 반면에 / 단당류이다.
Because their structure is not complex, / they are easy to break down / and hold few nutrients for your body / other than the sugars from which they are made.
그것의 구조는 복잡하지 않기 때문에 / 그것은 분해되기 쉬우며, / 몸을 위한 영양소를 거의 가지고 있지 않다. / 그것을 구성하는 당 말고는
⑤ Your body breaks down these carbohydrates rather quickly / and what it cannot use / is converted to fat and stored in the body.
여러분의 몸은 이러한 탄수화물을 상당히 빨리 분해하며, / 몸이 사용하지 못하는 것은 / 지방으로 바뀌어 몸에 저장된다.

모든 탄수화물은 기본적으로 당이다. ① 복합 탄수화물은 몸에 좋은 탄수화물이다. ② 이러한 복당류 화합물은 분해하기 매우 어렵고, 비타민과 미네랄 같은 다른 영양소를 그것의 사슬 안에 가두어 둘 수 있다. ③ 그것들이 천천히 분해되면서, 다른 영양소도 여러분의 몸으로 방출되고, 많은 시간 동안 여러분에게 연료를 공급할 수 있다. ④ 반면에 나쁜 탄수화물은 단당류이다. 그것의 구조는 복잡하지 않기 때문에 분해되기 쉬우며, 그것을 구성하는 당 말고는 몸을 위한 영양소를 거의 가지고 있지 않다. ⑤ 여러분의 몸은 이러한 탄수화물을 상당히 빨리 분해하며, 몸이 사용하지 못하는 것은 지방으로 바뀌어 몸에 저장된다.

Why? 왜 정답일까?

복합 탄수화물과 단당류의 차이점을 설명하는 글이다. ④ 앞은 복합당의 경우 구조가 복잡하기 때문에 분해 시간이 느리고 오랜 시간 몸에 연료를 공급한다는 내용이다. 한편 주어진 문장은 '나쁜 탄수화물'인 단당류를 언급하고, ④ 뒤에서는 이 단당류를 they로 받아 이것이 분해되기 쉽고 당 외에는 다른 영양소를 가지고 있지도 않아서 몸에서 다 쓰지 못하면 지방이 되어 쌓인다는 설명을 이어 간다. 따라서 주어진 문장이 들어가기에 가장 적절한 곳은 ④이다.

- **carbohydrate** ⓝ 탄수화물
- **break down** 분해하다
- **release** ⓥ 방출하다
- **a number of** 많은
- **be made from** ~로 구성되다
- **basically** ⓐⓓ 기본적으로
- **nutrient** ⓝ 영양소
- **provide A with B** A에게 B를 공급하다
- **structure** ⓝ 구조
- **convert** ⓥ 바꾸다

구문 풀이

부사적 용법(~하기에)
5행 These complex sugar compounds are very difficult to break
보어(형용사구)
down and can trap other nutrients like vitamins and minerals in their
chains.

02 소리가 들리는 원리
정답률 59% | 정답 ③

글의 흐름으로 보아, 주어진 문장이 들어가기에 가장 적절한 곳을 고르시오.

Sound and light travel in waves.
소리와 빛은 파장으로 이동한다.

An analogy often given for sound / is that of throwing a small stone / onto the surface of a still pond.
소리 현상에 대해 자주 언급되는 비유는 / 작은 돌멩이를 던지는 것이다. / 고요한 연못 표면에

Waves radiate outwards from the point of impact, / just as sound waves radiate from the sound source.
파장이 충격 지점으로부터 바깥으로 퍼져나간다. / 음파가 음원으로부터 사방으로 퍼지는 것처럼

① This is due to a disturbance / in the air around us.
이것은 교란 작용 때문이다. / 우리 주변 공기 중의

② If you bang two sticks together, / you will get a sound.
만약에 당신이 막대기 두 개를 함께 꽝 친다면 / 당신은 소리를 듣게 될 것이다.

✔ As the sticks approach each other, / the air immediately in front of them / is compressed / and energy builds up.
막대기들이 서로 가까워질 때, / 막대들 바로 앞에 있는 공기가 / 압축되고 / 에너지는 축적된다.

When the point of impact occurs, / this energy is released as sound waves.
충돌점이 발생하면 / 이 에너지는 음파로 퍼져나간다.

④ If you try the same experiment with two heavy stones, / exactly the same thing occurs, / but you get a different sound / due to the density and surface of the stones, / and as they have likely displaced more air, / a louder sound.
당신이 두 개의 무거운 돌을 가지고 같은 실험을 해보면 / 똑같은 일이 일어나지만, / 당신은 다른 소리를 듣게 된다. / 돌의 밀도와 표면 때문에 / 그리고 그 돌이 아마 더 많은 공기를 바꿔 놓았기 때문에 / 더 큰 소리를

⑤ And so, / a physical disturbance in the atmosphere around us / will produce a sound.
따라서 / 우리 주변의 대기 중에서 일어나는 물리적 교란 작용이 / 소리를 만든다.

소리와 빛은 파장으로 이동한다. 소리 현상에 대해 자주 언급되는 비유는 작은 돌멩이를 고요한 연못 표면에 던지는 것이다. 음파가 음원으로부터 사방으로 퍼지는 것처럼 파장이 충격 지점으로부터 바깥으로 퍼져나간다. ① 이것은 우리 주변 공기 중의 교란 작용 때문이다. ② 만약에 당신이 막대기 두 개를 함께 꽝 친다면 소리를 듣게 될 것이다. ③ 막대기들이 서로 가까워질 때, 막대들 바로 앞에 있는 공기가 압축되고 에너지는 축적된다. 충돌점이 발생하면 이 에너지는 음파로 퍼져나간다. ④ 두 개의 무거운 돌을 가지고 같은 실험을 해보면 똑같은 일이 일어나지만, 돌의 밀도와 표면 때문에 당신은 다른 소리를 듣게 되고, 그 돌이 아마 더 많은 공기를 바꿔 놓았기 때문에 당신은 더 큰 소리를 듣게 된다. ⑤ 따라서 우리 주변의 대기 중에서 일어나는 물리적 교란 작용이 소리를 만든다.

Why? 왜 정답일까?

소리를 듣게 되는 원리를 설명한 글로, ③ 앞의 문장에서 막대기 두 개를 함께 쳐서 소리를 듣는 상황을 예로 들고 있다. 주어진 문장은 두 막대기(the sticks)가 서로 가까워질 때 막대 바로 앞의 공기가 압축되고 에너지가 모인다고 설명한다. ③ 뒤의 문장은 그러다 충돌점이 발생하면 모였던 에너지(this energy)가 음파 형태로 퍼져나간다고 언급한다. 따라서 주어진 문장이 들어가기에 가장 적절한 곳은 ③이다.

- compress ⓥ 압축하다
- surface ⓝ 표면
- disturbance ⓝ 교란, 방해
- density ⓝ 밀도
- build up 축적되다
- impact ⓝ 충격, 여파
- release ⓥ 방출하다
- displace ⓥ 대체하다, 옮겨 놓다

구문 풀이

3행 An analogy often given for sound is that of throwing a small
주어   과거분사   동사   → 지시대명사(= analogy)
stone onto the surface of a still pond.

03 성별에 관한 연구에서 개인차를 고려할 필요성   정답률 46% | 정답 ③

글의 흐름으로 보아, 주어진 문장이 들어가기에 가장 적절한 곳을 고르시오.

Gender research shows / a complex relationship between gender and conflict styles.
성별에 관한 연구는 보여준다. / 성별과 갈등 유형 사이의 복잡한 관계를

① Some research suggests / that women from Western cultures tend to be more caring than men.
몇몇 연구는 시사한다. / 서양 문화권에서 여성이 남성보다 더 주변을 돌보는 경향이 있다는 것을

② This tendency may result from socialization processes / in which women are encouraged to care for their families / and men are encouraged to be successful / in competitive work environments.
이런 경향은 사회화 과정의 결과물일지 모른다. / 여성은 가족을 돌보도록 권장 받고, / 남성은 성공하도록 권장 받는 / 경쟁적인 직업 환경에서

✔ However, / we live in a society / where gender roles and boundaries / are not as strict as in prior generations.
그러나, / 우리는 사회에 살고 있다. / 성 역할과 경계가 / 이전 세대만큼 엄격하지 않은

There is significant variability / in assertiveness and cooperation among women, / as well as among men.
상당한 정도의 차이가 있다. / 여성들 사이에서도 단호함과 협동에는 / 남성들 사이에서뿐 아니라

④ Although conflict resolution experts should be able to recognize cultural and gender differences, / they should also be aware / of within-group variations and the risks of stereotyping.
갈등 해결 전문가는 문화적 차이와 성별의 차이를 인지할 수 있어야 하지만, / 그들은 또한 알고 있어야 한다. / 그룹 내의 차이와 유형화의 위험성도

⑤ Culture and gender may affect the way / people perceive, interpret, and respond to conflict; / however, / we must be careful / to avoid overgeneralizations / and to consider individual differences.
문화와 성별은 방식에 영향을 미칠 수도 있다. / 사람들이 갈등을 인식하고 해석하고 갈등에 반응하는 / 하지만, / 우리는 주의해야 한다. / 과잉일반화를 피하고 / 개인적인 차이를 고려하도록

성별에 관한 연구는 성별과 갈등 유형 사이의 복잡한 관계를 보여준다. ① 몇몇 연구는 서양 문화권에서 여성이 남성보다 더 주변을 돌보는 경향이 있다고 시사한다. ② 이런 경향은 여성은 가족을 돌보도록 권장 받고, 남성은 경쟁적인 직업 환경에서 성공하도록 권장 받는 사회화 과정의 결과물일지 모른다. ③ 그러나 우리는 성 역할과 경계가 이전 세대만큼 엄격하지 않은 사회에 살고 있다. 남성들 사이에서뿐 아니라 여성들 사이에서도 단호함과 협동에는 상당한 정도의 차이가 있다. ④ 갈등 해결 전문가는 문화적 차이와 성별의 차이를 인지할 수 있어야 하지만, 그들은 또한 그룹 내의 차이와 유형화의 위험성도 알고 있어야 한다. ⑤ 문화와 성별은 사람들이 갈등을 인식하고 해석하고 갈등에 반응하는 방식에 영향을 미칠 수도 있지만, 우리는 과잉 일반화를 피하고 개인적인 차이를 고려하도록 주의해야 한다.

Why? 왜 정답일까?

③ 앞에서 성별과 갈등 유형을 서로 연관시켜 분석하는 것은 남성과 여성이 전통적으로 서로 다른 역할을 맡는다고 여겨져 온 것의 결과물일 수 있다고 언급한 데 이어, 주어진 문장은 However로 흐름을 반전시키며 오늘날에는 성 역할에 대한 경계가 무너져 가고 있음을 지적한다. ③ 뒤에서는 그리하여 남녀 각 집단에서도 개인에 따라 단호함과 협동이 나타나는 정도가 다르다는 내용을 제시하며 개인차의 중요성을 환기하고 있다. 따라서 주어진 문장이 들어가기에 가장 적절한 곳은 ③이다.

- strict ⓐ 엄격한
- socialization ⓝ 사회화
- significant ⓐ 상당한, 유의미한
- assertiveness ⓝ 단호함, 자기 주장
- stereotyping ⓝ 유형화
- overgeneralization ⓝ 과잉 일반화
- generation ⓝ 세대
- competitive ⓐ 경쟁적인
- variability ⓝ 가변성
- resolution ⓝ 해결
- interpret ⓥ 해석하다

구문 풀이

6행 This tendency may result from socialization processes
            ~에서 기인하다   선행사
[in which women are encouraged to care for their families and men
「전치사＋관·대」 주어1   동사1   보어1   주어2
are encouraged to be successful in competitive work environments].
동사2   보어2

04 계획을 실천할 때 동기를 쉽게 잃게 되는 이유   정답률 53% | 정답 ②

글의 흐름으로 보아, 주어진 문장이 들어가기에 가장 적절한 곳을 고르시오.

When we set a plan, / we are very excited about it.
우리가 목표를 세울 때, / 우리는 매우 신이 난다.

① In this stage, / we can even imagine ourselves / victoriously dancing on the top of that mountain, / feeling successful and ultimately happy.
이 단계에서 / 우리는 우리 자신을 상상하기까지 한다. / 산의 정상 위에서 의기양양하게 춤추고 있는 / 성공감과 궁극적으로는 행복을 느끼며

✔ However, when you start putting the plan into practice / to achieve your goal, / the happiness, excitement, and a lot of fuel / suddenly disappear.
하지만, 여러분이 계획을 실천하기 시작하면서, / 여러분의 목표를 성취하기 위해 / 그 행복감, 즐거움, 많은 에너지원은 / 갑자기 사라진다.

That is because the road to your goal, the implementation of the plan / is not as appealing as the plan.
그것은 여러분의 목표로 향하는 길인 계획의 이행이 / 그 계획만큼 매력적이지 않기 때문이다.

③ You can easily lose motivation / when you face the plain reality of the road to success.
여러분은 쉽게 동기를 잃을 수 있다. / 여러분이 성공으로 가는 길의 명백한 현실에 직면했을 때

④ The road is paved with grey stones / and offers less intense emotions / than those imagined at the beginning.
그 길은 회색 돌로 포장되어 있고, / 덜 강렬한 감정을 제공한다. / 시작할 때 상상했던 것보다

⑤ When you reach the end / and look back at the road, however, / you'll realize how much more valuable, colorful, and meaningful it was / than you anticipated it to be in the moment.
하지만 여러분이 마지막 지점에 도달해서 / 그 길을 되돌아봤을 때, / 여러분은 그것이 얼마나 더 많이 가치 있고, 다채롭고, 의미가 있었는지를 깨달을 것이다. / 여러분이 그 순간에 그럴 것이라고 예상했던 것보다

우리가 목표를 세울 때, 우리는 매우 신이 난다. ① 이 단계에서 우리는 성공감과 궁극적으로는 행복을 느끼며, 산의 정상 위에서 의기양양하게 춤추고 있는 우리 자신을 상상하기까지 한다. ② 하지만, 여러분의 목표를 성취하기 위해 계획을 실천하기 시작하면서, 그 행복감, 즐거움, 많은 에너지원은 갑자기 사라진다. 그것은 여러분의 목표로 향하는 길인 계획의 이행이 그 계획만큼 매력적이지 않기 때문이다. ③ 여러분이 성공으로 가는 길의 명백한 현실에 직면했을 때 여러분은 쉽게 동기를 잃을 수 있다. ④ 그 길은 회색 돌로 포장되어 있고, 시작할 때 상상했던 것보다 덜 강렬한 감정을 제공한다. ⑤ 하지만 여러분이 마지막 지점에 도달해서 그 길을 되돌아봤을 때, 여러분은 그것이 그 순간에 그럴 것이라고 예상했던 것보다 얼마나 더 많이 가치 있고, 다채롭고, 의미가 있었는지를 깨달을 것이다.

Why? 왜 정답일까?

② 앞의 문장에서 우리는 목표와 계획을 세울 때 행복감을 느낀다고 말하는데, 주어진 문장은 However로 이 흐름을 반전시키며 막상 계획을 실천할 때에는 그런 행복감이나 즐거움 등은 사라지고 만다는 내용을 제시한다. ② 뒤의 문장에서는 'That is because ~' 표현을 통해 그 이유를 제시한다. 따라서 주어진 문장이 들어가기에 가장 적절한 곳은 ②이다.

- put into practice ~을 실천하다
- ultimately ad 궁극적으로
- appealing a 매력적인
- intense a 강렬한
- victoriously ad 의기양양하게
- implementation n 실행, 시행
- be paved with ~로 포장되다
- anticipate v 예상하다, 기대하다

구문 풀이

1행 However, when you start putting the plan into practice
시간 접속사(~할 때) ~하기 시작하다
to achieve your goal, / {the happiness, excitement, and a lot of fuel}
~하기 위해 { } : 주어
suddenly disappear.
자동사(사라지다)

---

05 할 수 없는 일에 대해 말하는 기술   정답률 50% | 정답 ④

글의 흐름으로 보아, 주어진 문장이 들어가기에 가장 적절한 곳을 고르시오. [3점]

Whenever you say what you can't do, / say what you can do.
여러분이 할 수 없는 것을 말할 때마다, / 여러분이 할 수 있는 것을 말하라.

This ends a sentence on a positive note / and has a much lower tendency / to cause someone to challenge it.
이것은 긍정적인 어조로 문장을 마무리하는 것이고 / 경향을 훨씬 더 낮춘다. / 누군가의 이의 제기를 불러일으킬

① Consider this situation / — a colleague comes up to you / and asks you to look over some figures with them / before a meeting they are having tomorrow.
이 상황을 생각해 보아라. / 한 동료가 여러분에게 다가와서 / 자신들과 일부 수치를 검토해 보자고 요청하는 / 내일 회의를 하기 전에

② You simply say, / 'No, I can't deal with this now.'
여러분은 그저 말한다. / '안 돼요, 지금은 이 일을 할 수 없어요.'라고

③ This may then lead to them insisting / how important your input is, / increasing the pressure on you / to give in.
이것은 그들에게 주장하게 만들 수도 있어서, / 여러분의 참여가 얼마나 중요한지를 / 여러분에 대한 압박을 증가시킨다. / (여러분이) 양보하도록(그 요청을 들어줄 수밖에 없도록)

✔ Instead of that, say to them, / 'I can't deal with that now / but what I can do is / I can ask Brian to give you a hand / and he should be able to explain them.'
그 대신, 그들에게 말해보라. / '저는 지금 그 일을 할 수 없지만 / 제가 할 수 있는 것은 / Brain에게 당신을 도와주라고 부탁하는 것이고 / 그러면 그가 그 수치를 설명해 줄 수 있을 것 같아요.'라고

Or, 'I can't deal with that now / but I can find you in about half an hour / when I have finished.'
혹은, '저는 지금 그 일을 할 수 없지만 / 약 30분 뒤에 당신을 찾아 갈게요. / 제 일이 끝나면'

⑤ Either of these types of responses / are better than ending it with a negative.
이런 형태의 대답들 중 어느 것이라도 / 부정적인 어조로 그 상황을 끝내는 것보다 더 낫다.

여러분이 할 수 없는 것을 말할 때마다, 여러분이 할 수 있는 것을 말하라. 이것은 긍정적인 어조로 문장을 마무리하는 것이고 누군가의 이의 제기를 불러일으킬

일으킬 경향을 훨씬 더 낮춘다. ① 한 동료가 여러분에게 다가와서 내일 회의를 하기 전에 일부 수치를 검토해 보자고 요청하는 상황의 대화를 생각해 보아라. ② 여러분은 그저 '안 돼요, 지금은 이 일을 할 수 없어요.'라고 말한다. ③ 이것은 그들에게 여러분의 참여가 얼마나 중요한지를 주장하게 만들 수도 있어서, 여러분이 그 요청을 들어줄 수밖에 없도록 압박을 증가시킨다. ④ 그 대신, '저는 지금 그 일을 할 수 없지만 Brain에게 당신을 도와주라고 부탁할 수는 있고 그러면 그가 그 수치를 설명해 줄 수 있을 것 같아요.'라고 그들에게 말해보라. 혹은, '저는 지금 그 일을 할 수 없지만 약 30분 뒤에 제 일이 끝나면 당신을 찾아 갈게요.' ⑤ 이런 형태의 대답들 중 어느 것이라도 부정적인 어조로 그 상황을 끝내는 것보다 더 낫다.

Why? 왜 정답일까?

④ 앞의 두 문장은 동료가 어떤 일을 부탁할 때 그저 할 수 없다고만 말하면 도리어 동료로 하여금 일을 도와줄 필요성이 있음을 더 피력하게 만들어 결국에는 부탁을 들어줄 수밖에 없는 상황에 처할 수 있음을 언급하고 있다. 이에 대한 조언으로서 Instead of that으로 시작하는 주어진 문장은 무엇을 해줄 수 있는지를 언급할 것을 제안하고, ④ 뒤의 문장은 '혹은' 지금은 아니더라도 나중에 다시 찾아가겠다는 여지를 남길 것을 제안하고 있다. 따라서 주어진 문장이 들어가기에 가장 적절한 곳은 ④이다.

- instead of ~ 대신에
- explain v 설명하다
- note n 어조
- challenge v 이의를 제기하다, 도전하다
- figure n 수치
- input n 참여, 투입
- pressure n 압박, 압력
- give a hand 도와주다
- sentence n 문장
- tendency n 성향, 경향
- colleague n 동료
- insist v 주장하다, 고집하다
- increase v 상승시키다

구문 풀이

5행 This ends a sentence on a positive note and has a much
동사1   동사2
lower tendency to cause someone to challenge it.
형용사적 용법 「cause + 목적어 + to부정사 : ~이 …하도록 야기하다」

---

06 과학에서의 제도화   정답률 46% | 정답 ⑤

글의 흐름으로 보아, 주어진 문장이 들어가기에 가장 적절한 곳을 고르시오.

As particular practices are repeated over time / and become more widely shared, / the values that they embody / are reinforced and reproduced / and we speak of them as becoming 'institutionalized'.
특정 관행이 오랜 기간 반복되고 / 더 널리 공유되면서 / 그 관행이 구현하는 가치는 / 강화되고 재생산되며, / 우리는 이것이 '제도화된' 것이라고 말한다.

① In some cases, / this institutionalization has a formal face to it, / with rules and protocols written down, / and specialized roles created / to ensure that procedures are followed correctly.
어떤 경우, / 이러한 제도화는 공식적인 면모를 갖추기도 하는데, / 규칙과 프로토콜이 문서화되고 / 전문화된 역할이 만들어진다. / 절차가 올바르게 지켜지도록 확실히 하기 위해

② The main institutions of state / — parliament, courts, police and so on — / along with certain of the professions, / exhibit this formal character.
국가의 주요 기관이 / 의회, 법원, 경찰 등 / 일부 전문직과 더불어 / 이러한 공식적 성격을 보여준다.

③ Other social institutions, / perhaps the majority, / are not like this; / science is an example.
다른 사회 기관들, / 아마도 대다수는 / 이와 같지 않을 것인데, / 과학이 그 예이다.

④ Although scientists are trained in the substantive content of their discipline, / they are not formally instructed / in 'how to be a good scientist'.
과학자들은 자기 학문의 실질적인 내용에 대해서는 훈련받겠지만, / 그들은 공식적으로 교육받지 않는다. / '좋은 과학자가 되는 방법'에 대해서는

✔ Instead, / much like the young child learning how to play 'nicely', / the apprentice scientist gains his or her understanding of the moral values / inherent in the role / by absorption from their colleagues / — socialization.
대신, / 마치 '착하게' 노는 법을 배우는 어린아이처럼 / 도제 과학자는 도덕적 가치에 대한 이해를 얻는다. / 그 역할에 내재한 / 동료들로부터의 흡수를 통해 / 즉 사회화

We think / that these values, / along with the values that inform many of the professions, / are under threat, / just as the value of the professions themselves / is under threat.
우리는 생각한다. / 이러한 가치가 / 그 전문직에 관한 많은 것을 알려주는 가치와 더불어, / 위협받고 있다고 / 마치 그 전문직 자체의 가치가 / 위협받고 있는 것과 마찬가지로

특정 관행이 오랜 기간 반복되고 더 널리 공유되면서 그 관행이 구현하는 가치는 강화되고 재생산되며, 우리는 이것이 '제도화된' 것이라고 말한다. ① 어떤 경우, 이러한 제도화는 공식적인 면모를 갖추기도 하는데, 규칙과 프로토콜이 문서화되고 절차가 올바르게 지켜지도록 확실히 하기 위해 전문화된 역할이

DAY 16

만들어진다. ② 의회, 법원, 경찰 등 국가의 주요 기관이 일부 전문직과 더불어 이러한 공식적 성격을 보여준다. ③ 다른 사회 기관들, 아마도 대다수는 이와 같지 않을 것인데, 과학이 그 예이다. ④ 과학자들은 자기 학문의 실질적인 내용에 대해서는 훈련받겠지만, '좋은 과학자가 되는 방법'에 대해서는 공식적으로 교육받지 않는다. ⑤ 대신, 마치 '착하게' 노는 법을 배우는 어린아이처럼 도제 과학자는 동료들로부터의 흡수, 즉 사회화를 통해 그 역할에 내재한 도덕적 가치에 대한 이해를 얻는다. 우리는 이러한 가치가 그 전문직에 관한 많은 것을 알려주는 가치와 더불어, 그 전문직 자체의 가치가 위협받고 있는 것과 마찬가지로 위협받고 있다고 생각한다.

Why? 왜 정답일까?

⑤ 앞에서 과학자는 학문의 실질적 내용은 배워도, '좋은 과학자가 되는 법'에 관해서는 교육받지 못한다고 언급하는데, ⑤ 뒤에서는 갑자기 '이러한 가치'를 언급한다. 즉 앞에서 언급되지 않은 내용을 가까운 대명사(these values)로 받아 흐름이 끊기는 상황이다. 이때 주어진 문장을 보면 the moral values가 언급된다. ⑤ 뒤의 these values는 바로 이 '도덕적 가치'를 가리키는 것이므로, 주어진 문장이 들어가기에 가장 적절한 곳은 ⑤이다.

- apprentice ⓝ 도제, 견습
- absorption ⓝ 흡수, 받아들임
- repeat ⓥ 반복하다
- reinforce ⓥ 강화하다
- institutionalize ⓥ 제도화하다
- protocol ⓝ 프로토콜, 규약
- procedure ⓝ 절차
- parliament ⓝ 의회
- profession ⓝ 전문직
- under threat 위협받고 있는
- inherent ⓐ 내재된
- socialization ⓝ 사회화
- embody ⓥ 구현하다
- reproduce ⓥ 재생산하다, 복제하다
- institutionalization ⓝ 제도화
- ensure ⓥ 보장하다, 반드시 ~하다
- state ⓝ 국가
- court ⓝ 법원
- substantive ⓐ 실질적인

구문 풀이

8행 In some cases, this institutionalization has a formal face to it, with rules and protocols written down, and specialized roles created
「with + 명사구1 + 과거분사1 + and + 명사구2 + 과거분사2 : 부대상황 분사구문(~이 …된 채로)」
to ensure that procedures are followed correctly.

★★★ 1등급 대비 고난도 2점 문제

07 느리게라도 계속 진행되는 변화 | 정답률 39% | 정답 ②

글의 흐름으로 보아, 주어진 문장이 들어가기에 가장 적절한 곳을 고르시오.

Sometimes the pace of change is far slower.
때때로 변화의 속도는 훨씬 더 느리다.
① The face you saw / reflected in your mirror this morning / probably appeared no different / from the face you saw the day before / — or a week or a month ago.
당신이 본 얼굴은 / 오늘 아침 거울에 비춰진 / 아마도 다르지 않게 보였을 것이다. / 당신이 그 전날에 본 얼굴과 / 또는 일주일이나 한 달 전에
✔ Yet we know / that the face that stares back at us from the glass / is not the same, / cannot be the same, / as it was 10 minutes ago.
그러나 우리는 안다. / 거울에서 우리를 마주보는 얼굴이 / 같지 않고, 같을 수 없다는 것을 / 10분 전과
The proof is in your photo album: / Look at a photograph / taken of yourself 5 or 10 years ago / and you see clear differences / between the face in the snapshot / and the face in your mirror.
증거는 당신의 사진 앨범에 있다. / 사진을 보라 / 5년 또는 10년 전에 당신을 찍은 / 그러면 당신은 명확한 차이를 보게 될 것이다. / 스냅사진 속의 얼굴과 / 거울 속 얼굴 사이의
③ If you lived in a world without mirrors for a year / and then saw your reflection, / you might be surprised by the change.
만약 당신이 일 년간 거울이 없는 세상에 살고 / 그 이후 (거울에) 비친 당신의 모습을 본다면, / 당신은 그 변화 때문에 깜짝 놀랄지도 모른다.
④ After an interval of 10 years / without seeing yourself, / you might not at first recognize the person / peering from the mirror.
10년의 기간이 지난 후, / 스스로를 보지 않고 / 당신은 그 사람을 처음에는 알아보지 못할지도 모른다. / 거울에서 쳐다보고 있는
⑤ Even something as basic as our own face / changes from moment to moment.
심지어 우리 자신의 얼굴같이 아주 기본적인 것조차도 / 순간순간 변한다.

때때로 변화의 속도는 훨씬 더 느리다. ① 오늘 아침 당신이 거울에 비춰진 것을 본 얼굴은 아마도 당신이 그 전날 또는 일주일이나 한 달 전에 본 얼굴과 다르지 않게 보였을 것이다. ② 그러나 우리는 거울에서 우리를 마주보는 얼굴이 10분 전과 같지 않고, 같을 수 없다는 것을 안다. 증거는 당신의 사진 앨범에 있다. 5년 또는 10년 전에 찍은 당신의 사진을 보면 당신은 스냅사진 속의 얼

굴과 거울 속 얼굴 사이의 명확한 차이를 보게 될 것이다. ③ 만약 당신이 일 년간 거울이 없는 세상에 살고 그 이후 (거울에) 비친 당신의 모습을 본다면, 당신은 그 변화 때문에 깜짝 놀랄지도 모른다. ④ 스스로를 보지 않고 10년의 기간이 지난 후, 당신은 거울에서 쳐다보고 있는 사람을 처음에는 알아보지 못할지도 모른다. ⑤ 심지어 우리 자신의 얼굴같이 아주 기본적인 것조차도 순간순간 변한다.

Why? 왜 정답일까?

② 앞은 오늘 아침 거울로 본 얼굴이 전날, 일주일 전, 또는 한 달 전에 본 얼굴과 다르지 않았을 것이라는 내용인데, ② 뒤는 얼굴이 명확히 '달라졌다'는 것을 알 수 있는 증거에 관한 내용이다. 즉 ② 앞뒤로 상반된 내용이 제시되어 흐름이 어색하게 끊기므로, 주어진 문장이 들어가기에 가장 적절한 곳은 ②이다.

- reflect ⓥ 반사하다
- snapshot ⓝ 스냅사진, 짧은 묘사
- surprised ⓐ 놀란
- peer ⓥ 응시하다
- clear ⓐ 명확한
- reflection ⓝ (물이나 거울에 비친) 그림자
- interval ⓝ 간격
- from moment to moment 시시각각

구문 풀이

16행 Even something as basic as our own face changes from moment to moment.
「as + 원급 + as : ~만큼 …한」

★★ 문제 해결 꿀~팁 ★★

▶ 많이 틀린 이유는?
가장 헷갈리는 ③ 앞을 보면, 우리가 5~10년 전 찍은 사진을 보면 지금 거울로 보는 얼굴과 다르다는 것을 알 수 있다는 내용이며, 주어진 문장 또한 우리 얼굴이 단 10분 사이에도 '달라진다'는 내용이다. 하지만 주어진 문장은 Yet(그럼에도 불구하고)으로 시작하므로, 이 앞에는 '다르지 않다'라는 반대되는 내용이 나와야 한다. 따라서 주어진 문장 내용과 똑같은 내용이 앞에 나오는 ③ 자리에 주어진 문장을 넣을 수는 없다.

▶ 문제 해결 방법은?
② 앞뒤로 발생하는 논리적 공백에 주목하자. ②는 거울로 보는 우리 얼굴이 '별 차이가 없어보인다'는 내용인데, ②는 사진 앨범 속 우리 얼굴이 '명확한 차이'를 보인다는 내용이다. 즉 ② 앞뒤의 의미가 '다르지 않다 ↔ 다르다'로 상반되는 상황인데, 이 경우 반드시 역접 연결어(주어진 문장의 Yet)가 있어야만 한다.

★★★ 1등급 대비 고난도 2점 문제

08 생체 시계를 다시 설정하는 데 이용되는 신호들 | 정답률 40% | 정답 ③

글의 흐름으로 보아, 주어진 문장이 들어가기에 가장 적절한 곳을 고르시오.

Daylight isn't the only signal / that the brain can use / for the purpose of biological clock resetting, / though it is the principal and preferential signal, / when present.
햇빛은 유일한 신호는 아니다. / 뇌가 사용할 수 있는 / 생체 시계 재설정을 목적으로 / 비록 그것이 중요하고 우선시되는 신호지만, / 있을 때
① So long as they are reliably repeating, / the brain can also use other external cues, / such as food, exercise, and even regularly timed social interaction.
그것들이 확실하게 반복되는 한, / 뇌는 다른 외부적인 신호들도 사용할 수 있다. / 음식과 운동과 심지어는 정기적인 사회적 상호 작용과 같은
② All of these events / have the ability to reset the biological clock, / allowing it to strike a precise twenty-four-hour note.
이 모든 경우는 / 생체 시계를 재설정하는 능력이 있어 / 정확한 24시간 음을 치도록 한다.
✔ It is the reason / that individuals with certain forms of blindness / do not entirely lose their circadian rhythm.
그것이 이유이다. / 어떤 유형의 시력 상실이 있는 개인도 / 24시간 주기의 리듬을 완전히 잃지 않는
Despite not receiving light cues / due to their blindness, / other phenomena act as their resetting triggers.
빛 신호를 받지 않음에도 불구하고, / 그들의 시력 상실 때문에 / 다른 현상들이 재설정의 유인 역할을 한다.
④ Any signal / that the brain uses for the purpose of clock resetting / is termed a zeitgeber, / from the German "time giver" or "synchronizer."
모든 신호는 / 뇌가 시계 재설정을 목적으로 이용하는 / 차이트게버(자연 시계)라고 불린다. / '시간 제공자' 또는 '동기화 장치'라는 독일어에서 유래한
⑤ Thus, / while light is the most reliable and thus the primary zeitgeber, / there are many factors / that can be used in addition to, or in the absence of, daylight.
따라서, / 빛이 가장 신뢰할 수 있어서 주된 자연 시계인 반면, / 많은 요인이 있다. / 햇빛과 함께 혹은 햇빛이 없을 때 사용될 수 있는

햇빛은 비록 있을 때는 중요하고 우선시되는 신호지만 뇌가 생체 시계 재설정을 목적으로 사용할 수 있는 유일한 신호는 아니다. ① 확실하게 반복되는 한, 뇌는 음식과 운동과 심지어는 정기적인 사회적 상호 작용과 같은 다른 외부적인 신호들도 사용할 수 있다. ② 이 모든 경우는 생체 시계를 재설정하는 능력이 있어 정확한 24시간 음을 치도록 한다(24시간을 정확히 알게 한다). ③ 이러한 이유로 어떤 유형의 시력 상실이 있는 개인도 24시간 주기의 리듬을 완전히 잃지 않는다. 그들의 시력 상실 때문에 빛 신호를 받지 않음에도 불구하고, 다른 현상들이 재설정의 유인 역할을 한다. ④ 뇌가 시계 재설정을 목적으로 이용하는 모든 신호는 '시간 제공자' 또는 '동기화 장치'라는 독일어에서 유래한 차이트게버(자연 시계)라고 불린다. ⑤ 따라서, 빛이 가장 신뢰할 수 있어서 주된 자연 시계인 반면, 햇빛과 함께 혹은 햇빛이 없을 때 사용될 수 있는 많은 요인이 있다.

Why? 왜 정답일까?

③ 앞의 두 문장에서 뇌는 햇빛뿐 아니라 음식, 운동, 정기적인 상호 작용 등 다양한 외부 신호를 이용하여 생체 시계를 재설정할 수 있기에 우리 몸이 정확히 24시간의 주기를 알 수 있다고 설명하고 있다. 여기에 이어 주어진 문장은 '이러한 이유로' 시력 상실을 경험하고 있는 개인일지라도 생체 리듬을 잃지 않는다는 내용을 제시한다. ③ 뒤의 문장은 주어진 문장에서 언급한 'individuals with certain forms of blindness'을 'their blindness'로 다시 언급하며, 시력 상실을 겪고 있는 사람들은 비록 빛을 볼 수 없지만 다른 현상을 통해 생체 시계를 맞춰나갈 수 있다고 설명한다. 따라서 주어진 문장이 들어가기에 가장 적절한 곳은 ③이다.

- **entirely** [ad] 완전히, 전적으로
- **reliably** [ad] 확실하게, 믿을 수 있게
- **strike** [v] 치다, 부딪치다
- **note** [n] (음악의) 음
- **trigger** [n] 계기, 유인
- **in the absence of** ~의 부재 시에
- **preferential** [a] 우선시되는, 특혜의
- **external** [a] 외부적인
- **precise** [a] 정확한
- **phenomenon** [n] 현상 (pl. phenomena)
- **synchronizer** [n] 동기화 장치

구문 풀이

[3행] Daylight isn't the only signal [that the brain can use for the
선행사   목적격 관계대명사
purpose of biological clock resetting], though it is the principal and
접속사(~일지라도)
preferential signal, when (it is) present.
접속사 생략 형용사 보어

★★ 문제 해결 꿀~팁 ★★

▶ 많이 틀린 이유는?
생체 시계 재설정이라는 생소한 소재에 관한 글이다. 최다 오답인 ④ 앞에서 햇빛 외에도 다른 현상들이 생체 시계를 다시 설정하도록 유인하는 역할을 할 수 있다고 설명한 데 이어, ④ 뒤의 문장에서는 이렇듯 시간 재설정에 기여할 수 있는 모든 신호를 '차이트게버'라는 용어로 부를 수 있다고 언급하고 있다. 즉 ④ 앞까지 다룬 내용을 ④ 뒤에서 용어와 함께 정리해주며 맥락이 자연스럽게 연결되므로 주어진 문장을 ④에 넣으면 안 된다.

▶ 문제 해결 방법은?
③ 뒤의 문장에서 '시력 상실을 경험하고 있는 사람'을 대명사인 their로 지칭하고 있다. 즉 이 문장 바로 앞에 시력 상실을 경험하고 있는 사람들(individuals with certain forms of blindness)에 관한 언급이 있어야 한다.

★★★ 1등급 대비 고난도 2점 문제

09 작은 발전으로 이루는 큰 변화   정답률 36% | 정답 ②

글의 흐름으로 보아, 주어진 문장이 들어가기에 가장 적절한 곳을 고르시오.

It is so easy / to overestimate the importance of one defining moment / and underestimate the value of making small improvements on a daily basis.
매우 쉽다. / 결정적인 한순간의 중요성을 과대평가하고 / 매일 작은 발전을 이루는 것의 가치를 과소평가하기는
Too often, / we convince ourselves / that massive success requires massive action.
너무 자주 / 우리는 스스로를 납득시킨다. / 거대한 성공에는 거대한 행동이 필요하다고
① Whether it is losing weight, / winning a championship, / or achieving any other goal, / we put pressure on ourselves / to make some earthshaking improvement / that everyone will talk about.
그것이 체중을 줄이는 것이든, / 결승전에서 이기는 것이든, / 혹은 어떤 다른 목표를 달성하는 것이든 간에, / 우리는 우리 스스로에게 압력을 가한다. / 지축을 흔들 만한 발전을 이루도록 / 모두가 이야기하게 될
✔Meanwhile, / improving by 1 percent isn't particularly notable, / but it can be far more meaningful in the long run.

The difference / this tiny improvement can make over time / is surprising.
변화는 / 시간이 지남에 따라 이 작은 발전이 이룰 수 있는 / 놀랍다.
③ Here's how the math works out: / if you can get 1 percent better each day for one year, / you'll end up thirty-seven times better / by the time you're done.
다음과 같이 계산이 이루어지는데, / 만일 여러분이 1년 동안 매일 1퍼센트씩 더 나아질 수 있다면, / 여러분은 결국 37배 더 나아질 것이다. / 여러분이 끝마칠 때 즈음
④ Conversely, if you get 1 percent worse each day for one year, / you'll decline nearly down to zero.
역으로, 여러분이 1년 동안 매일 1퍼센트씩 나빠지면 / 여러분은 거의 0까지 떨어질 것이다.
⑤ What starts as a small win or a minor failure / adds up to something much more.
작은 승리나 사소한 패배로 시작한 것은 / 쌓여서 훨씬 더 큰 무언가가 된다.

결정적인 한순간의 중요성을 과대평가하고 매일 작은 발전을 이루는 것의 가치를 과소평가하기는 매우 쉽다. 너무 자주 우리는 거대한 성공에는 거대한 행동이 필요하다고 스스로를 납득시킨다. ① 체중을 줄이는 것이든, 결승전에서 이기는 것이든, 혹은 어떤 다른 목표를 달성하는 것이든 간에, 우리는 모두가 이야기하게 될 지축을 흔들 만한 발전을 이루도록 우리 스스로에게 압력을 가한다. ② 한편, 1퍼센트 발전하는 것은 특별히 눈에 띄지는 않지만, 장기적으로는 훨씬 더 의미가 있을 수 있다. 시간이 지남에 따라 이 작은 발전이 이룰 수 있는 변화는 놀랍다. ③ 다음과 같이 계산이 이루어지는데, 만일 여러분이 1년 동안 매일 1퍼센트씩 더 나아질 수 있다면, 끝마칠 때 즈음 여러분은 결국 37배 더 나아질 것이다. ④ 역으로, 1년 동안 매일 1퍼센트씩 나빠지면 여러분은 거의 0까지 떨어질 것이다. ⑤ 작은 승리나 사소한 패배로 시작한 것은 쌓여서 훨씬 더 큰 무언가가 된다.

Why? 왜 정답일까?

② 앞에서는 우리가 작은 변화의 가치를 과소평가하고 거대한 발전에 맞는 거대한 행동을 해나가도록 스스로를 압박한다는 내용이 주를 이룬다. 이에 이어 주어진 문장은 Meanwhile로 흐름을 전환하며 '1퍼센트만큼' 작게 발전하는 것이 당장은 눈에 띄지 않아도 장기적으로는 큰 의미를 가질 수 있다고 설명한다. ② 뒤의 문장은 주어진 문장에서 언급한 '1퍼센트의 발전'을 this tiny improvement라는 말로 바꾸어 '작은 발전'으로 인한 변화가 시간이 지난 후에는 놀라울 수 있음을 환기시킨다. 따라서 주어진 문장이 들어가기에 가장 적절한 곳은 ②이다.

- **meanwhile** [ad] 한편
- **in the long run** 장기적으로
- **underestimate** [v] 과소평가하다
- **convince** [v] 납득시키다, 설득하다
- **put pressure on** ~에 압박을 가하다
- **tiny** [a] 극히 작은
- **decline** [v] 떨어지다, 감소하다
- **notable** [a] 눈에 띄는, 두드러지는
- **overestimate** [v] 과대평가하다
- **on a daily basis** 매일
- **massive** [a] 거대한
- **earthshaking** [a] 세상을 떠들썩하게 하는
- **conversely** [ad] 역으로

구문 풀이

[8행] (Whether it is losing weight, winning a championship, or
       주어↑동사 동명사 보어1   동명사 보어2
achieving any other goal), we put pressure on ourselves to make
동명사 보어3 ( ): 부사절(~이든 ···이든)
some earthshaking improvement [that everyone will talk about].
선행사   목적격 관계대명사

★★ 문제 해결 꿀~팁 ★★

▶ 많이 틀린 이유는?
최다 오답인 ④ 앞뒤는 Conversely를 기점으로 매일 조금씩 1년 동안 발전하는 경우와 나빠지는 경우가 적절히 대비를 이루는 맥락이다. 따라서 ④에 주어진 문장을 넣기에는 부적절하다.

▶ 문제 해결 방법은?
② 앞에서는 거창한 결과를 이룩하려면 거창한 행동이 필요하다고 생각한다는 내용이 주를 이루는데, ② 뒤에서는 '이 작은 발전(this tiny improvement)'에 관해 언급한다. 즉 ② 앞뒤 내용이 서로 상충하므로 Meanwhile(한편)으로 시작하며 흐름을 반전하는 주어진 문장이 ②에 들어가야 한다.

★★★ 1등급 대비 고난도 2점 문제

10 성향과 책임감이 학습 방식에 미치는 영향   정답률 41% | 정답 ⑤

글의 흐름으로 보아, 주어진 문장이 들어가기에 가장 적절한 곳을 고르시오.

Your personality and sense of responsibility affect / not only your relationships with others, your job, and your hobbies, / but also your learning abilities and style.
여러분의 성향과 책임감은 영향을 끼친다. / 다른 사람과 여러분의 관계, 직업, 그리고 취미는 물론 / 학습 능력과 방식에도

① Some people are very self-driven.
어떤 사람들은 매우 자기 주도적이다.

② They are more likely to be lifelong learners.
그들은 평생 학습자가 될 가능성이 더 크다.

③ Many tend to be independent learners / and do not require structured classes / with instructors to guide them.
많은 사람들은 독립적인 학습자인 경향이 있고 / 구조화된 수업을 필요로 하지 않는다. / 자신을 가르칠 선생님이 있는

④ Other individuals are peer-oriented / and often follow the lead of another in unfamiliar situations.
다른 사람들은 동료 지향적이며 / 익숙하지 않은 상황에서 자주 다른 사람의 지도를 따른다.

✔ They are more likely to benefit / from the assistance of a formal teaching environment.
그들은 혜택을 받을 가능성이 더 크다. / 형식적인 교육 환경의 도움에서

They may be less likely to pursue learning throughout life / without direct access to formal learning scenarios / or the influence of a friend or spouse.
그들은 평생 학습을 추구할 가능성이 더 낮을 수도 있다. / 형식적인 학습 계획을 직접 접하지 않거나 / 친구 혹은 배우자의 영향이 없으면

여러분의 성향과 책임감은 다른 사람과 여러분의 관계, 직업, 그리고 취미는 물론 학습 능력과 방식에도 영향을 끼친다. ① 어떤 사람들은 매우 자기 주도적이다. ② 그들은 평생 학습자가 될 가능성이 더 크다. ③ 많은 사람들은 독립적인 학습자인 경향이 있고 자신을 가르칠 선생님이 있는 구조화된 수업을 필요로 하지 않는다. ④ 다른 사람들은 동료 지향적이며 익숙하지 않은 상황에서 자주 다른 사람의 지도를 따른다. ⑤ 그들은 형식적인 교육 환경의 도움에서 혜택을 받을 가능성이 더 크다. 그들은 형식적인 학습 계획을 직접 접하지 않거나 친구 혹은 배우자의 영향이 없으면 평생 학습을 추구할 가능성이 더 낮을 수도 있다.

Why? 왜 정답일까?

우리의 성향과 책임감은 학습 능력과 방식에 영향을 미친다는 내용을 설명하는 지문이다. 주어진 문장은 형식적인 교육 환경의 도움에서 혜택을 받을 가능성이 더 크다고 하므로 앞이나 뒤에 형식적인 교육과 관련한 내용이 있는 부분을 찾으면 된다. 따라서 주어진 문장이 들어가기에 가장 적절한 것은 ⑤이다.

- be likely to ~할 것 같다
- formal ⓐ 형식적인, 정규적인
- self-driven 자기 주도적인
- structured ⓐ 구조화된
- peer-oriented 동료 지향적인
- pursue ⓥ 추구하다, 애쓰다, 따라가다
- influence ⓥ ~에 영향을 주다 ⓝ 영향
- assistance ⓝ 도움, 원조, 지원
- affect ⓥ 영향을 주다
- require ⓥ 요구하다, ~을 필요로 하다
- individual ⓐ 개인의, 독특한
- unfamiliar ⓐ 익숙하지 않은
- access ⓝ 접근 ⓥ ~에 접근하다
- spouse ⓝ 배우자, 남편, 아내

구문 풀이

3행 Your personality and sense of responsibility <u>affect</u>
                              (주어)   (동사)
not only [your relationships with others, your job, and your hobbies],
not only+[A]+
but also [your learning abilities and style].
but also+[B] : A뿐만 아니라 B도

★★ 문제 해결 꿀~팁 ★★

▶ 많이 틀린 이유는?
오답으로 ④가 많이 나왔는데 이는 많은 수험생들이 '형식적인 교육 환경'이 '교사의 구조화된 수업'과 같은 말임을 이해하기 어려워했음을 시사한다.

▶ 문제 해결 방법은?
'자기 주도적 학습자: 선생님, 수업 ×' vs. '동료 지향적 학습자: 선생님, 수업 ○(형식적 교육 환경), 동료 영향 ○'의 대조 관계를 이해한다.

★★★ 1등급 대비 고난도 3점 문제

| 11 | 운동 에너지와 위치 에너지 | 정답률 35% \| 정답 ⑤ |

글의 흐름으로 보아, 주어진 문장이 들어가기에 가장 적절한 곳을 고르시오. [3점]

In general, / kinetic energy is the energy associated with motion, / while

---

potential energy represents the energy / which is "stored" in a physical system.
일반적으로 / 운동 에너지는 운동과 관련 있는 에너지이며 / 반면에 위치 에너지는 에너지를 나타낸다. / 물리계에 '저장되는'

Moreover, the total energy is always conserved.
게다가 총 에너지는 항상 보존된다.

① But while the total energy remains unchanged, / the kinetic and potential parts of the total energy / can change all the time.
그러나 총 에너지가 변하지 않는 채로 있는 반면 / 총 에너지의 운동과 위치 에너지 비율은 / 항상 변할 수 있다.

② Imagine, for example, a pendulum / which swings back and forth.
예를 들어 추를 상상해 보자. / 앞뒤로 흔들리는

③ When it swings, / it sweeps out an arc / and then slows down / as it comes closer to its highest point, / where the pendulum does not move at all.
그것이 흔들릴 때 / 그것은 호 모양으로 쓸어내리듯 움직이다 / 그리고 나서 속도가 줄어드는데, / 그것이 최고점에 가까워지면서 / 이 지점에서 추는 더 이상 움직이지 않는다.

④ So at this point, / the energy is completely given in terms of potential energy.
그래서 이 지점에서, / 에너지는 완전히 위치 에너지로 주어지게 된다.

✔ But after this brief moment of rest, / the pendulum swings back again / and therefore part of the total energy is then given / in the form of kinetic energy.
하지만 이 짧은 순간의 멈춤 이후에 / 그 추는 다시 뒤로 흔들리게 되며 / 따라서 총 에너지의 일부가 그때 주어진다. / 운동 에너지의 형태로

So as the pendulum swings, / kinetic and potential energy / constantly change into each other.
그래서 그 추가 흔들리면서 / 운동과 위치 에너지는 / 끊임없이 서로 바뀐다.

일반적으로 운동 에너지는 운동과 관련 있는 에너지인 반면에, 위치 에너지는 물리계에 '저장되는' 에너지를 나타낸다. 게다가 총 에너지는 항상 보존된다. ① 그러나 총 에너지가 변하지 않는 채로 있는 반면 총 에너지의 운동과 위치 에너지 비율은 항상 변할 수 있다. ② 예를 들어 앞뒤로 흔들리는 추를 상상해 보자. ③ 그것은 흔들릴 때 호 모양으로 쓸어내리듯 움직이다가, 그리고 나서 최고점에 가까워지면서 속도가 줄어드는데, 이 지점에서 추는 더 이상 움직이지 않는다. ④ 그래서 이 지점에서 에너지는 완전히 위치 에너지로 주어지게 된다. ⑤ 하지만 이 짧은 순간의 멈춤 이후에 그 추는 다시 뒤로 흔들리게 되며, 따라서 총 에너지의 일부가 그때 운동 에너지의 형태로 주어진다. 그래서 그 추가 흔들리면서 운동과 위치 에너지는 끊임없이 서로 바뀐다.

Why? 왜 정답일까?

위치 에너지와 운동 에너지는 같은 에너지 총량 안에서 계속 서로 바뀐다는 내용의 글로, ② 뒤의 문장부터 흔들리는 추를 예로 들어 이 변화를 설명하고 있다. ⑤ 앞의 두 문장에서 추의 높이가 최고점에 이르면 추는 더 이상 움직이지 않고, 모든 에너지가 위치 에너지로 바뀐다고 언급한다. 주어진 문장은 But으로 흐름을 전환하며, 이 짧은 멈춤(this brief moment of rest) 이후로 다시 추가 뒤로 흔들리면서 일부 에너지가 다시 운동 에너지로 바뀐다고 설명한다. ⑤ 뒤의 문장은 그리하여 운동 에너지와 위치 에너지는 서로 끊임없이 교환되는 관계라는 결론을 제시한다. 따라서 주어진 문장이 들어가기에 가장 적절한 곳은 ⑤이다.

- brief ⓐ 짧은
- kinetic energy 운동 에너지
- conserve ⓥ 보존하다
- sweep out 쓸어내리다
- constantly ⓐⓓ 지속적으로, 끊임없이
- pendulum ⓝ (시계의) 추
- potential energy 위치 에너지
- swing back and forth 앞뒤로 흔들리다
- arc ⓝ 호(弧)

구문 풀이

11행 When it swings, it sweeps out an arc and then <u>slows down</u>
                                        (동사1)   (동사2)
as it comes closer to its highest point, where the pendulum does not
접속사(~하면서, ~함에 따라)   (선행사)   관계부사(계속적 용법)
move at all.

★★ 문제 해결 꿀~팁 ★★

▶ 많이 틀린 이유는?
④ 앞의 does not move가 바로 주어진 문장의 this brief moment of rest로 연결되는 것처럼 보일 수 있지만, 사실 이 does not move는 ④ 뒤의 at this point로 연결된다. 이 '움직이지 않는' 지점에서 에너지는 모두 위치에너지로 전환되었음을 알 수 있다는 것이다.

▶ 문제 해결 방법은?
⑤ 앞뒤 문장에 모두 결론의 So가 나오므로, 이 So가 어느 내용에 이어져야 하는지에 주목하며 읽는다.

★★★ 1등급 대비 고난도 3점 문제

12 개인의 행동에 영향을 미치는 사회구조적 요인   정답률 41% | 정답 ④

글의 흐름으로 보아, 주어진 문장이 들어가기에 가장 적절한 곳을 고르시오. [3점]

Have you heard someone say, / "He has no one to blame but himself" / for some problem?
당신은 누군가 말하는 것을 들어본 적이 있는가? / "그는 자신 외에 다른 누구도 탓할 수 없다"고 / 어떤 문제에 대해
In everyday life we often blame people / for "creating" their own problems.
매일의 삶에서 우리는 사람들을 종종 비난한다. / 자신의 문제를 '만들어'내는 것을
① Although individual behavior can contribute to social problems, / our individual experiences are often largely beyond our own control.
비록 개인의 행동이 사회적 문제의 원인이 되기도 하지만, / 우리의 개인적 경험은 종종 우리의 통제 범위를 넘어선다.
② They are determined by society as a whole / — by its historical development and its organization.
그것들은 사회 전반에 의해 결정된다. / 즉 사회의 역사적 발달과 구조에 의해
③ If a person sinks into debt / because of overspending or credit card abuse, / other people often consider the problem / to be the result of the individual's personal failings.
만약 한 사람이 빚을 진다면 / 과도한 지출이나 신용카드 남용 때문에 / 다른 이들은 종종 그 문제를 간주한다. / 개인적 실패의 결과라고
✔ However, thinking about it this way / overlooks debt among people in low-income brackets / who have no other way than debt / to acquire basic necessities of life.
하지만, 그것을 이런 식으로 생각하는 것은 / 저소득 계층 사람들의 빚을 간과한다. / 빚을 지는 것 외에 다른 방법이 없는 / 기초적 생활필수품을 획득하기 위해
By contrast, at middle- and upper-income levels, / overspending takes on a variety of meanings / typically influenced / by what people think of as essential for their well-being / and associated with the so-called "good life" / that is so heavily marketed.
대조적으로 중간 또는 상위 소득 계층에서 / 과도한 지출은 여러 다양한 의미를 가지는데, / (그 의미는) 주로 영향을 받고, / 사람들이 자신의 복지를 위해 필수적이라고 생각하는 것에 / 이른바 '좋은 삶'과 관련된다. / 그토록 집중적으로 마케팅의 대상이 된
⑤ But across income and wealth levels, / larger-scale economic and social problems / may affect the person's ability to pay / for consumer goods and services.
하지만 소득과 부의 수준을 넘어, / 큰 규모의 경제적·사회적 문제들은 / 개인의 지불 능력에 영향을 미칠 수 있다. / 소비자 재화와 서비스에 대한

당신은 어떤 문제에 대해 "그는 자신 외에 다른 누구도 탓할 수 없다"고 누군가 말하는 것을 들어본 적이 있는가? 매일의 삶에서 우리는 사람들이 자신의 문제를 '만들어'내는 것을 종종 비난한다. ① 비록 개인의 행동이 사회적 문제의 원인이 되기도 하지만, 우리의 개인적 경험은 종종 우리의 통제 범위를 넘어선다. ② 그것들은 사회 전반, 즉 사회의 역사적 발달과 구조에 의해 결정된다. ③ 만약 한 사람이 과도한 지출이나 신용카드 남용 때문에 빚을 진다면 다른 이들은 종종 그 문제가 개인적 실패의 결과라고 간주한다. ④ 하지만, 그것을 이런 식으로 생각하는 것은 기초적 생활필수품을 획득하기 위해 빚을 지는 것 외에 다른 방법이 없는 저소득 계층 사람들의 빚을 간과한다. 대조적으로 중간 또는 상위 소득 계층에서 과도한 지출은 여러 다양한 의미를 가지는데, 그 의미는 주로 사람들이 자신의 복지를 위해 필수적이라고 생각하는 것에 영향을 받고, 그토록 집중적으로 마케팅의 대상이 된 이른바 '좋은 삶'과 관련된다. ⑤ 하지만 소득과 부의 수준을 넘어, 큰 규모의 경제적·사회적 문제들은 소비자 재화아 서비스에 대한 개인의 지불 능력(개인이 수비자 재화와 서비스의 대가를 지불하는 능력)에 영향을 미칠 수 있다.

Why? 왜 정답일까?

흔히 개인의 행동이나 문제에 대해서 개인에 탓을 돌리기 쉽지만 사실은 사회구조적 요인이 배후에서 관여할 수 있다는 내용을 다룬 글이다. ④ 앞에서 개인이 빚을 지면 이는 개인적 실패의 결과로 여겨진다는 예를 제시한 데 이어, 주어진 문장은 However로 흐름을 반전시키며 기초적인 생활을 영위하기 위해 빚을 질 수밖에 없는 '계층'의 문제가 있을 수 있음을 지적한다. ④ 뒤의 문장에서는 중간 및 상위 소득 계층의 지출 문제가 이와는 다른 의미를 지닌다는 내용을 언급한다. 따라서 주어진 문장이 들어가기에 가장 적절한 곳은 ④이다.

- **overlook** ⓥ 간과하다, 넘어가다
- **bracket** ⓝ 계층
- **basic necessities** 기본적 필수품
- **organization** ⓝ 구조, 조직
- **overspending** ⓝ 과도한 지출, 낭비, 탕진
- **typically** ⓐⓓ 주로, 전형적으로
- **affect** ⓥ 영향을 미치다
- **debt** ⓝ 빚, 부채
- **acquire** ⓥ 획득하다, 습득하다
- **individual** ⓝ (집단의 일원으로서의) 개인
- **sink into** ~에 빠지다
- **abuse** ⓝ 남용
- **associated with** ~에 관련된, 연관된

구문 풀이

1행 However, thinking about it this way overlooks debt among
명사구 주어 / 동사(단수) / 목적어
people in low-income brackets [who have no other way than debt
선행사 ↵ ~ 외에 다른 방법이 없다
to acquire basic necessities of life].

★★ 문제 해결 꿀~팁 ★★

▶ **많이 틀린 이유는?**
③ 앞까지 개인의 경험은 개인 스스로의 행동뿐 아니라 사회적 요인에도 영향을 받는다는 일반론을 제시하고 ③ 뒤에서 예시를 드는 글이다. 길고 까다로운 구문이 많은 데다 전통적으로 오답이 많이 나오는 경제학적 사례를 들고 있어 난이도가 높은 지문이다.

▶ **문제 해결 방법은?**
④ 뒤의 문장에 있는 역접의 연결어 By contrast에 주목한다. 이 뒤에서 '중간 또는 상위계층'의 소비 문제를 언급한다는 것은 앞에서 이와 대조되는 대상(저소득 계층)에 대한 언급이 이미 있어야 한다는 뜻이다.

DAY 16

DAY 17 — 문장 삽입 02

01 ⑤	02 ③	03 ②	04 ③	05 ③
06 ④	07 ②	08 ④	09 ③	10 ①
11 ⑤	12 ③			

---

01 보완재의 개념　　정답률 50% | 정답 ⑤

글의 흐름으로 보아, 주어진 문장이 들어가기에 가장 적절한 곳을 고르시오.

A "complementary good" is a product / that is often consumed alongside another product.
'보완재'는 제품이다. / 종종 또 다른 제품과 함께 소비되는

① For example, / popcorn is a complementary good to a movie, / while a travel pillow is a complementary good / for a long plane journey.
예를 들어, / 팝콘은 영화에 대한 보완재인 한편, / 여행 베개는 보완재이다. / 긴 비행기 여행에 대한

② When the popularity of one product increases, / the sales of its complementary good / also increase.
한 제품의 인기가 높아지면 / 그것의 보완재 판매량도 / 또한 늘어난다.

③ By producing goods / that complement other products / that are already (or about to be) popular, / you can ensure a steady stream of demand for your product.
제품을 생산해서 / 다른 제품을 보완하는 / 이미 인기가 있는 (또는 곧 있을) / 여러분은 여러분의 제품에 대한 꾸준한 수요 흐름을 보장할 수 있다.

④ Some products enjoy perfect complementary status / — they *have* to be consumed together, / such as a lamp and a lightbulb.
일부 제품들은 완벽한 보완적 상태를 누리고 있고, / 그것들은 함께 소비되*어야* 한다. / 램프와 전구와 같이

✔However, / do not assume / that a product is perfectly complementary, / as customers may not be completely locked in to the product.
그러나 / 가정하지 말라. / 어떤 제품이 완벽하게 보완적이라고 / 고객들이 그 제품에 완전히 고정되어 있지 않을 수 있으므로

For example, / although motorists may seem required to purchase gasoline / to run their cars, / they can switch to electric cars.
예를 들어, / 비록 운전자들이 휘발유를 구매할 필요가 있는 것처럼 보이기는 해도, / 차를 운전하기 위해 / 이들이 전기 자동차로 바꿀 수도 있다.

'보완재'는 종종 또 다른 제품과 함께 소비되는 제품이다. ① 예를 들어, 팝콘은 영화에 대한 보완재인 한편, 여행 베개는 긴 비행기 여행에 대한 보완재이다. ② 한 제품의 인기가 높아지면 그것의 보완재 판매량도 늘어난다. ③ 여러분은 이미 인기가 있는 (또는 곧 있을) 다른 제품을 보완하는 제품을 생산해서 여러분의 제품에 대한 꾸준한 수요 흐름을 보장할 수 있다. ④ 일부 제품들은 완벽한 보완적 상태를 누리고 있고, 그것들은 램프와 전구와 같이 함께 소비되*어야* 한다. ⑤ 그러나 고객들이 그 제품에 완전히 고정되어 있지 않을 수 있으므로, 어떤 제품이 완벽하게 보완적이라고 가정하지 말라. 예를 들어, 비록 운전자들이 차를 운전하기 위해 휘발유를 구매할 필요가 있는 것처럼 보이기는 해도, 이들이 전기 자동차로 바꿀 수도 있다.

Why? 왜 정답일까?

보완재에 관해 설명하는 글이다. ⑤ 앞에서 일부 제품은 램프 – 전구의 예시처럼 완벽히 서로 보완 관계에 있다고 하는데, ⑤ 뒤에서는 자동차 – 기름의 예시를 들며, 운전자들이 전기 차로 넘어갈 수도 있기 때문에 둘을 완벽한 보완 관계로 볼 수 없다고 한다. 즉, ⑤ 앞뒤로 내용이 서로 반대된다. 이때 주어진 문장은 '보완재인 두 재화가 항상 보완 관계에 있을 거라고 가정하지 말라'는 내용으로, However가 있어 흐름 전환을 적절히 유도한다. 따라서 주어진 문장이 들어가기에 가장 적절한 곳은 ⑤이다.

- assume ⓥ 가정하다
- locked in 갇힌, 고정된
- journey ⓝ 여정
- ensure ⓥ 확실히 하다, 보장하다
- status ⓝ 지위, 입지
- motorist ⓝ 운전자
- switch to ~로 바꾸다
- complementary ⓐ 보완하는
- alongside prep ~와 함께
- complement ⓥ 보완하다, 보충하다
- stream ⓝ 흐름
- lightbulb ⓝ 전구
- gasoline ⓝ 휘발유
- electric ⓐ 전기의

구문 풀이

15행 For example, although motorists may seem required to
　　　　　접속사(~에도 불구하고)　　　2형식 동사　주격 보어
purchase gasoline to run their cars, they can switch to electric cars.
　　　　　~하기 위해

---

02 무대에서 관객을 집중시키는 방법　　정답률 58% | 정답 ③

글의 흐름으로 보아, 주어진 문장이 들어가기에 가장 적절한 곳을 고르시오.

Achieving focus in a movie is easy.
영화에서 (관객의) 집중을 얻는 쉽다.

Directors can simply point the camera / at whatever they want the audience to look at.
감독은 단지 카메라를 향하게 하면 된다. / 자신이 관객으로 하여금 바라보기를 원하는 어떤 것에든

① Close-ups and slow camera shots / can emphasize a killer's hand / or a character's brief glance of guilt.
근접 촬영과 느린 카메라 촬영이 / 살인자의 손을 강조할 수 있다. / 또는 등장인물의 짧은 죄책감의 눈짓

② On stage, focus is much more difficult / because the audience is free to look / wherever they like.
무대 위에서는 (관객의) 집중이 훨씬 더 어려운 일이다. / 관객이 자유롭게 볼 수 있기 때문에 / 자신이 원하는 어느 곳이든

✔The stage director must gain the audience's attention / and direct their eyes to a particular spot or actor.
무대 감독은 관객의 주의를 얻고 / 그들의 시선을 특정한 장소나 배우로 향하게 해야만 한다.

This can be done / through lighting, costumes, scenery, voice, and movements.
이것은 이루어질 수 있다. / 조명, 의상, 배경, 목소리, 움직임을 통해

④ Focus can be gained / by simply putting a spotlight on one actor, / by having one actor in red and everyone else in gray, / or by having one actor move / while the others remain still.
(관객의) 집중은 얻어질 수 있다. / 단지 한 명의 배우에게 스포트라이트를 비추거나, / 한 명의 배우는 빨간색으로 입히고 다른 모든 배우들은 회색으로 입히거나, / 한 명의 배우는 움직이게 함으로써 / 다른 배우들이 가만히 있는 동안

⑤ All these techniques / will quickly draw the audience's attention to the actor / whom the director wants to be in focus.
이러한 모든 기법들은 / 관객의 주의를 배우 쪽으로 빠르게 끌 것이다. / 감독이 (관객의) 집중 안에 들기를 원하는

영화에서 (관객의) 집중을 얻는 쉽다. 감독은 자신이 관객으로 하여금 바라보기를 원하는 어떤 것에든 단지 카메라를 향하게 하면 된다. ① 근접 촬영과 느린 카메라 촬영이 살인자의 손이나 등장인물의 짧은 죄책감의 눈짓을 강조할 수 있다. ② 무대 위에서는 관객이 자신이 원하는 어느 곳이든 자유롭게 볼 수 있기 때문에 (관객의) 집중이 훨씬 더 어려운 일이다. ③ 무대 감독은 관객의 주의를 얻고 그들의 시선을 특정한 장소나 배우로 향하게 해야만 한다. 이것은 조명, 의상, 배경, 목소리, 움직임을 통해 이루어질 수 있다. ④ (관객의) 집중은 단지 한 명의 배우에게 스포트라이트를 비추거나, 한 명의 배우는 빨간색으로 입히고 다른 모든 배우들은 회색으로 입히거나, 다른 배우들이 가만히 있는 동안 한 명의 배우는 움직이게 함으로써 얻어질 수 있다. ⑤ 이러한 모든 기법들은 감독이 (관객의) 집중 안에 들기를 원하는 배우 쪽으로 관객의 주의를 빠르게 끌 것이다.

Why? 왜 정답일까?

③ 앞에서 무대 위에서는 관객을 집중시키기가 더 어렵다고 언급한 데 이어, 주어진 문장은 '무대 감독'이 관객의 주의를 끌어 특정한 방향으로 시선을 향하게 해야 한다고 설명한다. ③ 뒤의 문장은 주어진 문장의 내용을 This로 가리키며, 관객의 주의를 얻기 위해서는 조명, 의상, 배경, 목소리, 움직임 등이 동원될 수 있다고 한다. 따라서 주어진 문장이 들어가기에 가장 적절한 곳은 ③이다.

- emphasize ⓥ 강조하다
- guilt ⓝ 죄책감
- draw A's attention to B ⓥ A의 관심을 B로 돌리다
- glance ⓝ 흘긋 봄

구문 풀이

3행 Directors can simply point the camera at whatever they
　　　　　　　　　　　　　　　　　　　　복합관계대명사(= anything that)
want the audience to look at.
「want+목적어+to부정사 : ~이 …하기를 원하다」

---

03 업무에 대한 비금전적 보상과 그 영향　　정답률 53% | 정답 ②

글의 흐름으로 보아, 주어진 문장이 들어가기에 가장 적절한 곳을 고르시오.

Rewarding business success / doesn't always have to be done in a material way.
일의 성공을 보상하는 것은 / 항상 물질적인 방식으로 되어야 하는 것은 아니다.

① A software company I once worked for / had a great way of recognizing sales success.
내가 예전에 근무했던 한 소프트웨어 회사는 / 판매 성공을 인정해주는 멋진 방법을 가지고 있었다.

✔The sales director kept an air horn outside his office / and would come out and blow the horn / every time a salesperson settled a deal.
영업부장은 자기 사무실 밖에 경적을 두고 / 나와서 경적을 불곤 했다. / 영업직원이 거래를 성사할 때마다
The noise, of course, / interrupted anything and everything / happening in the office / because it was unbelievably loud.
물론, 그 소리는 / 무슨 일이든 방해했다. / 사무실에서 생기는 / 그것이 믿을 수 없이 시끄러웠기 때문에
③ However, / it had an amazingly positive impact on everyone.
그러나 / 그것은 모두에게 놀랄 만큼 긍정적인 영향을 주었다.
④ Sometimes rewarding success can be as easy as that, / especially when peer recognition is important.
때때로 성공을 보상하는 것은 그처럼 쉬울 수 있는데, / 특히 동료의 인정이 중요할 때 그렇다.
⑤ You should have seen the way / the rest of the sales team wanted / the air horn blown for them.
당신은 그 방식을 봤어야 했다. / 그 영업부서의 나머지 사람들이 바라는 / 자신을 위해 경적이 불리기를

일의 성공을 보상하는 것은 항상 물질적인 방식으로 되어야 하는 것은 아니다. ① 내가 예전에 근무했던 한 소프트웨어 회사는 판매 성공을 인정해주는 멋진 방법을 가지고 있었다. ② 영업부장은 자기 사무실 밖에 경적을 두었고 영업직원이 거래를 성사할 때마다 나와서 경적을 불곤 했다. 물론, 그 소리는 믿을 수 없이 시끄러웠기 때문에 사무실에서 생기는 무슨 일이든 방해했다. ③ 그러나 그것은 모두에게 놀랄 만큼 긍정적인 영향을 주었다. ④ 때때로 성공을 보상하는 것은 그처럼 쉬울 수 있는데, 특히 동료의 인정이 중요할 때 그렇다. ⑤ 당신은 그 영업부서의 나머지 사람들이 자신을 위해 경적이 불리기를 바라는 그 방식을 봤어야 했다.

Why? 왜 정답일까?
② 앞에서 필자는 자신이 다녔던 소프트웨어 회사에 업무 성과를 보상해주는 멋진 방법이 있었다고 언급하는데, 주어진 문장은 그 방법의 구체적 내용을 제시한다. 즉 영업부장이 자기 사무실 밖에 경적을 두고 거래가 성사될 때마다 그 경적을 불어주었다는 것인데, ② 뒤의 문장은 그 경적 소리(The noise)에 관해 언급한다. 따라서 주어진 문장이 들어가기에 가장 적절한 곳은 ②이다.

- sales director 영업부장
- rewarding ⓐ 보람 있는
- interrupt ⓥ 방해하다
- unbelievably [ad] 믿을 수 없을 정도로
- amazingly [ad] 놀랄 만큼
- settle a deal 거래를 성사시키다
- material ⓐ 물질적인
- anything and everything 무슨 일이든
- have an impact on ~에 영향을 미치다
- peer ⓝ 동료, 또래, 동배

구문 풀이
13행 You should have seen the way [the rest of the sales team
「should have p.p. : ~했어야 했다」 선행사
wanted the air horn blown for them].
동사 목적어 목적격 보어

04 기회를 알아차릴 수 없는 이유 정답률 72% | 정답 ③

글의 흐름으로 보아, 주어진 문장이 들어가기에 가장 적절한 곳을 고르시오.

George Orwell wrote: / "To see what is in front of your nose / needs constant struggle."
George Orwell은 썼다. / "코앞에 있는 것을 보는 것은 / 끊임없는 노력을 필요로 한다."라고
We are surrounded by opportunities, / but often we do not even see them.
우리는 기회에 둘러싸여 있지만, / 자주 이를 알아보지 못한다.
① Professor Richard Wiseman / did a dramatic and extreme test of this.
Richard Wiseman 교수는 / 이것에 대한 인상적이면서 극단적인 실험을 했다.
② He asked a group of volunteers / to count the number of times / a basketball team passed the ball.
그는 한 그룹의 자원자들에게 부탁했다. / 횟수를 세어 달라고 / 농구팀이 공을 패스한
✔As they passed the ball, / a man in a gorilla suit / walked into the middle of the group, / thumped his chest a bit / and then walked off.
그들이 공을 패스하는 동안, / 고릴라 옷을 입은 사람이 / 그 그룹 사이로 걸어 들어가, / 가슴을 몇 번 두드리고 나서 / 걸어 나갔다.
Quite a few volunteers counted correctly, / but only 5 out of over 20 volunteers / noticed the gorilla.
상당수의 자원자들은 정확히 숫자를 셌지만, / 20명이 넘는 자원자 중 5명만 / 그 고릴라를 알아차렸다.
④ The same applies to our professional lives.
동일한 것이 직업 생활에 적용된다.
⑤ We are so focused / on keeping score and managing day to day / that we do not notice the endless opportunities / that are in front of our noses.
우리는 너무 집중하느라 / 점수를 기록하고 그날그날 살아가는 데 / 우리는 무한한 기회를 알아차리지 못한다. / 우리 코앞에 있는

George Orwell은 "코앞에 있는 것을 보려면 끊임없는 노력이 필요하다."라고 썼다. 우리는 기회에 둘러싸여 있지만, 자주 이를 알아보지 못한다. ① Richard Wiseman 교수는 이것에 대한 인상적이면서 극단적인 실험을 했다. ② 그는 한 그룹의 자원자들에게 농구팀이 공을 패스한 횟수를 세어 달라고 부탁했다. ③ 그들이 공을 패스하는 동안, 고릴라 옷을 입은 사람이 그 그룹 사이로 걸어 들어가, 가슴을 몇 번 두드리고 나서 걸어 나갔다. 상당수의 자원자들은 정확하게 숫자를 셌지만, 20명이 넘는 자원자 중 5명만 그 고릴라를 알아차렸다. ④ 동일한 것이 직업 생활에 적용된다. ⑤ 우리는 점수를 기록하고 그날그날 살아가는 데 너무 집중하느라 코앞에 있는 무한한 기회를 알아차리지 못한다.

Why? 왜 정답일까?
주어진 문장에 공을 패스했다는 내용이 있으므로 앞에 공을 패스한 것과 관련한 내용이 있어야 한다. 따라서 주어진 문장이 들어가기에 가장 적절한 곳은 ③이다.

- constant ⓐ 끊임없는
- be surrounded by ~에 둘러싸이다
- quite a few 상당수의
- manage day to day 그날그날 살아가다
- struggle ⓝ 노력, 투쟁
- extreme ⓐ 극단적인
- apply ⓥ 적용되다, 쓰다, 신청하다

구문 풀이
1행 As they passed the ball, / a man in a gorilla suit [walked]
접속사(~할 때)   [ ]: 병렬 구조
into the middle of the group, [thumped] his chest a bit and then [walked off].

05 문제 해결로서의 언어 학습 정답률 51% | 정답 ③

글의 흐름으로 보아, 주어진 문장이 들어가기에 가장 적절한 곳을 고르시오. [3점]

Our brains are constantly solving problems.
우리의 뇌는 끊임없이 문제를 해결하고 있다.
① Every time we learn, or remember, or make sense of something, / we solve a problem.
우리가 무언가를 배우거나, 기억하거나, 이해할 때마다, / 우리는 문제를 해결한다.
② Some psychologists / have characterized all infant language-learning as problem-solving, / extending to children / such scientific procedures as "learning by experiment," or "hypothesis-testing."
일부 심리학자들은 / 모든 유아 언어 학습을 문제 해결이라고 특정지었고, / 이를 어린이에게 확장하여 / 그러한 과학적 절차들을 '실험을 통한 학습' 혹은 '가설 검증'으로 보았다.
✔Grown-ups rarely explain the meaning of new words to children, / let alone how grammatical rules work.
어른들은 아이들에게 새로운 단어의 의미를 거의 설명하지 않는다. / 문법적인 규칙이 어떻게 작용하는지는 말할 것도 없고
Instead they use the words or the rules in conversation / and leave it to children / to figure out what is going on.
대신에 그들은 대화에서 단어나 규칙을 사용하고, / 아이들에게 맡긴다. / 무슨 일이 일어나고 있는지 알아내는 일을
④ In order to learn language, / an infant must make sense of the contexts / in which language occurs; / problems must be solved.
언어를 배우기 위해서는, / 유아는 맥락을 파악해야 하는데, / 언어를 사용하는 / 즉 문제는 반드시 해결돼야 한다는 것이다.
⑤ We have all been solving problems of this kind since childhood, / usually without awareness of what we are doing.
우리 모두는 어린 시절부터 이런 종류의 문제들을 해결해왔다. / 우리가 무엇을 하고 있는지 대체로 인식하지 못한 채

우리의 뇌는 끊임없이 문제를 해결하고 있다. ① 우리가 무언가를 배우거나, 기억하거나, 이해할 때마다, 우리는 문제를 해결한다. ② 일부 심리학자들은 모든 유아 언어 학습을 문제 해결이라고 특정지었고, 이를 어린이에게 확장하여 그러한 과학적 절차들을 '실험을 통한 학습' 혹은 '가설 검증'으로 보았다. ③ 어른들은 아이들에게 문법적인 규칙이 어떻게 작용하는지는 말할 것도 없고, 새로운 단어의 의미를 거의 설명하지 않는다. 대신에 그들은 대화에서 단어나 규칙을 사용하고, 무슨 상황인지 알아내는 일을 아이들에게 맡긴다. ④ 언어를 배우기 위해서는, 유아는 언어를 사용하는 맥락을 파악해야 하는데, 즉 문제는 반드시 해결돼야 한다는 것이다. ⑤ 우리 모두는 우리가 무엇을 하고 있는지 인식하지 못한 채 이 어린 시절부터 이런 종류의 문제들을 해결해왔다.

Why? 왜 정답일까?
③ 앞에서 일부 심리학자들은 유아 언어 학습을 문제 해결로 규정하였다고 언급한 후, ③ 뒤의 문장에 they가 나오는데, 이 they는 앞에 이어서 Some psychologists를 가리키지 않는다. 즉 심리학자들이 언어 학습을 문제 해결의 과정으로 보았다는 내용 뒤

로, 실제로 어른들이 언어를 배우는 아이들에게 문법 규칙이나 단어에 관해 설명하는 경우는 드물다는 주어진 문장이 연결된 후, '대신에' 이 어른들은 아이들이 스스로 파악하고 해결할 수 있도록 내버려둔다는 설명이 이어지는 맥락인 것이다. 따라서 주어진 문장이 들어가기에 가장 적절한 곳은 ③이다.

- let alone ~은 말할 것도 없고
- constantly [ad] 끊임없이
- characterize ⓥ ~의 특징을 기술하다
- extend ⓥ 확장시키다
- hypothesis ⓝ 가설
- grammatical ⓐ 문법적인
- make sense of ⓥ ~을 이해하다
- infant ⓝ 유아
- procedure ⓝ 절차
- awareness ⓝ 인식, 앎

구문 풀이

11행 In order to learn language, an infant must make sense of
목적(~하기 위해)
the contexts [in which language occurs]; problems must be solved.
선행사　　 = where　　　　　　　 조동사 수동태

---

06 물질 이용의 확장　　　　정답률 46% | 정답 ④

글의 흐름으로 보아, 주어진 문장이 들어가기에 가장 적절한 곳을 고르시오.

The earliest humans had access / to only a very limited number of materials, / those that occur naturally: / stone, wood, clay, skins, and so on.
초기 인류는 접근했다. / 매우 제한된 수의 물질에만 / 즉 자연적으로 존재하는 것들 / 돌, 나무, 찰흙, 가죽 등
① With time, / they discovered techniques for producing materials / that had properties / superior to those of the natural ones; / these new materials included pottery and various metals.
시간이 흐르면서 / 그들은 물질을 만들어 내는 기술을 발견했는데, / 특성을 가진 / 자연적인 특성의 물질보다 더 우수한 / 이 새로운 물질에는 도자기와 다양한 금속이 포함되었다.
② Furthermore, / it was discovered / that the properties of a material could be altered / by heat treatments / and by the addition of other substances.
게다가, / 발견되었다. / 물질의 특성이 바뀔 수 있다는 것이 / 열처리로 인해 / 그리고 여타 다른 물질의 첨가로 인해
③ At this point, / materials utilization was totally a selection process / that involved deciding / from a given, rather limited set of materials, / the one best suited for an application / based on its characteristics.
이 시기에, / 물질 이용은 전적으로 선택의 과정이었다. / 결정하는 것을 수반하는, / 상당히 제한된 특정 물질 집합 중에서 / 용도에 가장 적합한 물질을 / 물질의 특성에 근거하여
✔It was not until relatively recent times / that scientists came to understand the relationships / between the structural elements of materials and their properties.
비교적 최근에 이르러서였다. / 과학자들이 비로소 관계를 이해하게 된 것은 / 물질의 구조적 요소와 물질 특성 사이의
This knowledge, / acquired over approximately the past 100 years, / has empowered them / to fashion, to a large degree, the characteristics of materials.
이 지식은 / 대략 지난 100년 동안 습득된 / 그들에게 힘을 주었다. / 상당한 정도로 물질의 특성을 형성할
⑤ Thus, / tens of thousands of different materials / have evolved / with rather specialized characteristics / that meet the needs of our modern and complex society, / including metals, plastics, glasses, and fibers.
따라서 / 수만 가지의 다양한 물질이 / 발전해 왔다. / 상당히 특화된 특성을 가진 / 복잡한 우리 현대 사회의 요구를 충족하는 / 금속, 플라스틱, 유리, 섬유를 포함하여

초기 인류는 매우 제한된 수의 물질, 즉 돌, 나무, 찰흙, 가죽 등 자연적으로 존재하는 물질에만 접근할 수 있었다. ① 시간이 흐르면서 그들은 자연적인 특성의 물질보다 더 우수한 특성을 가진 물질을 만들어 내는 기술을 발견했는데, 이 새로운 물질에는 도자기와 다양한 금속이 포함되었다. ② 게다가, 물질의 특성이 열처리와 여타 다른 물질의 첨가로 인해 바뀔 수 있다는 것이 발견되었다. ③ 이 시기에, 물질 이용은 상당히 제한된 특정 물질 집합 중에서 물질의 특성에 근거하여 용도에 가장 적합한 물질을 결정하는 것을 수반하는, 전적으로 선택의 과정이었다. ④ 과학자들이 물질의 구조적 요소와 물질 특성의 관계를 비로소 이해하게 된 것은 비교적 최근에 이르러서였다. 대략 지난 100년 동안 습득된 이 지식으로 그들은 상당한 정도로 물질의 특성을 형성할 수 있게 되었다. ⑤ 따라서 금속, 플라스틱, 유리, 섬유를 포함하여, 복잡한 우리 현대 사회의 요구를 충족하는 상당히 특화된 특성을 가진 수만 가지의 다양한 물질이 발전해왔다.

Why? 왜 정답일까?

인류가 이용하는 물질 범위가 확장된 과정에 관해 설명하는 글이다. ④ 앞까지 초기 인류는 자연적으로 존재하는 물질만 이용하다가, 열처리 등을 통해 물질 특성을 변화시킬 수 있다는 것을 알게 되면서 물질을 만들어낼 수 있게 되었는데, 이때 생성 가능한 물질 범

위는 크게 제한되어 있었다는 내용이 전개된다. 여기에 이어 주어진 문장은 비교적 최근에 이르러서야 과학자들이 물질의 구조적 요소와 특성 사이의 관계를 알게 되었다고 언급한다. ④ 뒤의 문장은 이 관계에 관한 이해를 This knowledge로 받으며, 이를 바탕으로 많은 물질이 생성 가능해졌다는 내용을 제시한다. 따라서 주어진 문장이 들어가기에 가장 적절한 곳은 ④이다.

- relatively [ad] 비교적
- property ⓝ 특성, 속성
- superior to ~보다 우수한
- utilization ⓝ 이용, 활용
- characteristic ⓝ 특징
- structural ⓐ 구조적인
- have access to ~에 접근하다
- substance ⓝ 물질
- suited for ~에 적합한
- empower ⓥ 권한을 주다

구문 풀이

1행 It was not until relatively recent times that scientists came
「it is[was] not until ~ that …: ~하고 나서야 비로소 …하다」
to understand the relationships between the structural elements of materials and their properties.

★★★ 1등급 대비 고난도 2점 문제

07 우리 생활의 다방면에 연관된 밤하늘　　정답률 34% | 정답 ②

글의 흐름으로 보아, 주어진 문장이 들어가기에 가장 적절한 곳을 고르시오.

We are connected to the night sky in many ways.
우리는 많은 방식으로 밤하늘과 연결되어 있다.
① It has always inspired people / to wonder and to imagine.
그것은 항상 사람들에게 영감을 주었다, / 궁금해하고 상상하도록
✔Since the dawn of civilization, / our ancestors created myths / and told legendary stories / about the night sky.
문명의 시작부터, / 우리 선조들은 신화를 만들었고 / 전설적 이야기를 했다, / 밤하늘에 대해
Elements of those narratives became embedded / in the social and cultural identities of many generations.
그러한 이야기들의 요소들은 깊이 새겨졌다. / 여러 세대의 사회·문화적 정체성에
③ On a practical level, / the night sky helped past generations / to keep track of time and create calendars / — essential to developing societies / as aids to farming and seasonal gathering.
실용적인 수준에서, / 밤하늘은 과거 세대들이 ~하도록 도왔다 / 시간을 기록하고 달력을 만들도록 / 이는 사회를 발전시키는 데 필수적이었다 / 농업과 계절에 따른 수확의 보조 도구로서
④ For many centuries, / it also provided a useful navigation tool, / vital for commerce and for exploring new worlds.
수 세기 동안, / 그것은 또한 유용한 항해 도구를 제공하였다. / 무역과 새로운 세계를 탐험하는 데 필수적인
⑤ Even in modern times, / many people in remote areas of the planet / observe the night sky / for such practical purposes.
심지어 현대에도, / 지구의 외딴 지역에 있는 많은 사람이 / 밤하늘을 관찰한다. / 그러한 실용적인 목적을 위해

우리는 많은 방식으로 밤하늘과 연결되어 있다. ① 그것은 항상 사람들이 궁금해하고 상상하도록 영감을 주었다. ② 문명의 시작부터, 우리 선조들은 밤하늘에 대해 신화를 만들었고 전설적 이야기를 했다. 그러한 이야기들의 요소들은 여러 세대의 사회·문화적 정체성에 깊이 새겨졌다. ③ 실용적인 수준에서, 밤하늘은 과거 세대들이 시간을 기록하고 달력을 만들도록 도왔고 이는 농업과 계절에 따른 수확의 보조 도구로서 사회를 발전시키는 데 필수적이었다. ④ 수 세기 동안, 그것은 또한 무역과 새로운 세계를 탐험하는 데 필수적인 유용한 항해 도구를 제공하였다. ⑤ 심지어 현대에도, 지구의 외딴 지역에 있는 많은 사람이 그러한 실용적인 목적을 위해 밤하늘을 관찰한다.

Why? 왜 정답일까?

② 앞에서 인류는 밤하늘을 궁금해했다고 언급한 후, 주어진 문장은 인류가 거의 문명이 시작되던 시기부터 밤하늘에 대한 다양한 전설과 신화를 만들어냈다고 설명한다. 그리고 ② 뒤의 문장은 주어진 문장의 myths and legendary stories를 those narratives로 가리킨다. 따라서 주어진 문장이 들어가기에 가장 적절한 곳은 ②이다.

- civilization ⓝ 문명
- legendary ⓐ 전설의
- inspire ⓥ 영감을 주다
- element ⓝ 요소
- embed ⓥ ~을 깊이 새겨 두다
- practical ⓐ 실용적인
- calendar ⓝ 달력
- farming ⓝ 농업
- gathering ⓝ 수집, 수확
- commerce ⓝ 무역, 상업
- ancestor ⓝ 선조
- connect ⓥ 연결되다
- wonder ⓥ 궁금하다
- narrative ⓝ 이야기
- identity ⓝ 정체성
- keep track of ~을 기록하다
- aid ⓝ 보조 도구
- seasonal ⓐ 계절에 따른
- navigation ⓝ 항해
- planet ⓝ 지구

★★ 문제 해결 꿀~팁 ★★

▶ 많이 틀린 이유는?
③ 앞에서 밤하늘에 대한 이야기는 '사회문화적 정체성에 깊이 새겨졌다'고 하는데, ③ 뒤에서는 '실용적으로 살펴보면' 밤하늘 연구가 달력 제작 등에 영향을 미쳤다고 한다. 즉 On a practical level 앞뒤로 일반적 논의에서 더 구체적 논의로 나아가는 내용이 자연스럽게 연결된다.

▶ 문제 해결 방법은?
② 앞에서는 '이야기'로 볼 만한 내용이 없는데, ② 뒤에서는 갑자기 those narratives를 언급하므로 논리적 공백이 발생한다. 이때 주어진 문장을 보면 myths와 legendary stories가 있으므로, 이것을 ② 뒤에서 those narratives로 연결했다는 것을 알 수 있다.

★★★ 1등급 대비 고난도 2점 문제

08 그리스 시대의 주인 – 손님 관계 　　정답률 43% | 정답 ④

글의 흐름으로 보아, 주어진 문장이 들어가기에 가장 적절한 곳을 고르시오.

Geography influenced human relationships in Greece.
지리는 그리스의 인간관계에 영향을 미쳤다.

Because the land made travel so difficult, / the guest-host relationship was valued.
땅 때문에 이동이 매우 어려웠기에, / 주인과 손님 간의 관계가 중시되었다.

① If a stranger, even a poor man, appeared at your door, / it was your duty / to be a good host, / to give him a shelter / and share your food with him.
심지어 가난한 사람일지라도 낯선 사람이 문앞에 나타나면, / 당신의 의무였다. / 좋은 주인이 되어 / 그에게 쉴 곳을 주고 / 그와 음식을 나누는 것이

② "We do not sit at a table only to eat, / but to eat together," / said the Greek author Plutarch.
"우리는 단지 먹으려고 식탁에 앉는 것이 아니라, / 함께 먹으려고 앉는 것이다."라고 / 그리스의 작가인 Plutarch는 말했다.

③ Dining was a sign of the human community / and differentiated men from beasts.
식사는 인간 사회의 표식이었고 / 인간을 짐승과 구별지었다.

☑ In return, the guest had duties to his host.
답례로 손님은 주인에 대한 의무가 있었다.

These included not abusing his host's hospitality / by staying too long, / usually not more than three days.
여기에는 주인의 환대를 악용하지 않는 것이 포함되었는데, / 너무 오래 머무르는 것으로 / 보통 사흘 이상을 넘지 않는 것을 가리켰다.

⑤ A violation of this relationship by either side / brought human and divine anger.
양쪽 중 어느 쪽에 의한 것이든 이러한 관계의 위반은 / 인간과 신의 분노를 불러왔다.

지리는 그리스의 인간관계에 영향을 미쳤다. 땅 때문에 이동이 매우 어려웠기에, 주인과 손님 간의 관계가 중시되었다 ① 심지어 가난한 사람일지라도 낯선 사람이 문앞에 나타나면 좋은 주인이 되어 그에게 쉴 곳을 주고 음식을 나누는 것이 의무였다. ② "우리는 단지 먹으려고 식탁에 앉는 것이 아니라, 함께 먹으려고 앉는 것이다."라고 그리스의 작가인 Plutarch는 말했다. ③ 식사는 인간 사회의 표식이었고 인간을 짐승과 구별지었다. ④ 답례로 손님은 주인에 대한 의무가 있었다. 여기에는 너무 오래 머물러서, 보통 사흘 이상을 넘지 않는 것을 가리켰는데, 주인의 환대를 악용하지 않는 것이 포함되었다. ⑤ 양쪽 중 어느 쪽에서든 이러한 관계를 위반하면 인간과 신의 분노를 불러왔다.

Why? 왜 정답일까?

지리적 특성으로 인해 고대 그리스 사회에서는 주인 – 손님간의 관계가 중시되었고 둘은 각자의 의무를 지녔다는 것을 설명한 글이다. ④ 앞의 문장에서는 '주인'의 의무에 초점을 두어 손님에게 음식을 나누어 주고 '함께 식사'할 수 있도록 준비해주는 것이 중요했다는 내용을 말하고 있다. 주어진 문장은 In return이라는 부사로 흐름을 뒤집으며 '손님'의 의무가 뒤에 제시될 것을 암시하는데, 이에 이어 ④ 뒤의 문장에서는 너무 오래 머물러서 주인의 환대를 악용하지 않는 것이 손님의 할 일이었다는 점을 언급한다. 따라서 주어진 문장이 들어가기에 가장 적절한 곳은 ④이다.

- in return 답례로, 대신에
- geography ⓝ 지리, 지리학
- appear ⓥ 나타나다
- differentiate ⓥ 구별짓다, 차별화하다
- abuse ⓥ 악용하다, 남용하다
- duty ⓝ 의무, 직무
- influence ⓥ 영향을 미치다
- author ⓝ 작가, 저자
- beast ⓝ 짐승
- violation ⓝ 위반

★★ 문제 해결 꿀~팁 ★★

▶ 많이 틀린 이유는?
주어진 문장에 흐름 전환의 연결사인 'In return'이 있으므로 앞뒤 흐름이 서로 달라지는 지점에 주어진 문장을 넣어야 한다. 최다 오답인 ②의 앞뒤는 공통적으로 '주인'의 도리를 설명하고 있으므로 흐름을 반전시키는 주어진 문장이 들어갈 자리로 보기 어렵다.

▶ 문제 해결 방법은?
주어진 문장 넣기 유형에서 큰 힌트로 작용하는 것 중 하나가 대명사이다. 여기서도 ④ 뒤의 문장에 'These'가 나오는데 여기에 ④ 앞의 문장에 나온 'beasts'를 넣어 해석하면 부자연스럽다. 이는 곧 ④ 앞뒤 문장 간의 논리적 공백을 암시하므로 ④에 주어진 문장을 넣어 해석하고 자연스러운지 여부를 확인한다.

★★★ 1등급 대비 고난도 2점 문제

09 읽기와 스키 타기의 유사성 　　정답률 47% | 정답 ③

글의 흐름으로 보아, 주어진 문장이 들어가기에 가장 적절한 곳을 고르시오.

Reading is like skiing.
읽는 것은 스키를 타는 것과 같다.

When done well, when done by an expert, / both reading and skiing / are graceful, harmonious activities.
잘되었을 때, 즉 전문가에 의해 이뤄졌을 때 / 읽기와 스키 타기는 / 모두 우아하고 조화로운 활동이다.

When done by a beginner, / both are awkward, frustrating, and slow.
초보자가 수행하면, / 둘 다 어색하고 좌절감을 주며 느린 활동이다.

① Learning to ski / is one of the most embarrassing experiences / an adult can undergo.
스키 타기를 배우는 것은 / 가장 당혹스러운 경험들 중 하나이다. / 성인이 겪을 수 있는

② After all, an adult has been walking for a long time; / he knows where his feet are; / he knows how to put one foot in front of the other / in order to get somewhere.
어쨌든, 성인은 오랫동안 걸어 다녔고, / 자기 발이 어디 있는지 알며, / 한 발을 다른 발 앞에 어떻게 놓을지를 안다, / 어딘가로 가기 위해서

☑ But as soon as he puts skis on his feet, / it is as though he had to learn to walk all over again.
하지만 발에 스키를 신자마자, / 이는 마치 걷는 법을 처음부터 다시 배워야만 하는 것과 같다.

He slips and slides, / falls down, / has trouble getting up, / and generally looks — and feels — like a fool.
그는 발을 헛디뎌 미끄러지고, / 넘어지고, / 일어나기가 어려우며, / 대체로 바보처럼 보이고 느껴지기도 한다.

④ It is the same with reading.
읽기도 마찬가지이다.

⑤ Probably you have been reading for a long time, too, / and starting to learn all over again / would be humiliating.
아마 여러분도 역시 오랫동안 읽기를 해 왔으므로, / 처음부터 다시 배우기를 시작하는 것은 / 창피할 수 있다.

읽는 것은 스키를 타는 것과 같다. 잘되었을 때, 즉 전문가에 의해 이뤄졌을 때 읽기와 스키 타기는 모두 우아하고 조화로운 활동이다. 초보자가 수행하면, 둘 다 어색하고 좌절감을 주며 느린 활동이다. ① 스키 타기를 배우는 것은 성인이 겪을 수 있는 가장 당혹스러운 경험들 중 하나이다. ② 어쨌든, 성인은 오랫동안 걸어 다녔고, 자기 발이 어디 있는지 알며, 어딘가로 가기 위해서 한 발을 다른 발 앞에 어떻게 놓을지를 안다. ③ 하지만 발에 스키를 신자마자, 이는 마치 걷는 법을 처음부터 다시 배워야만 하는 것과 같다. 발을 헛디뎌 미끄러지고, 넘어지고, 일어나기가 어려우며, 대체로 바보처럼 보이고 느껴지기도 한다. ④ 읽기도 마찬가지이다. ⑤ 아마 여러분도 역시 오랫동안 읽기를 해 왔으므로, 처음부터 다시 배우기를 시작하는 것은 창피할 수 있다.

Why? 왜 정답일까?

③ 앞의 문장에서 성인은 어찌되었든 오랜 세월 걸어 다녀서 걸어 다니는 법을 잘 알고

있다고 말한 데 이어, 주어진 문장은 그렇다 하더라도 스키를 발에 신으면 다시 처음부터 걷는 법을 배워야 하는 것과 다름이 없다는 내용을 제시한다. ③ 뒤의 문장에서는 미끄러지고 넘어지며 '다시 걷는 법을 배우는' 이런 과정이 매우 '바보 같고' '당혹스럽다'고 여겨질 수 있음을 지적한다. 따라서 주어진 문장이 들어가기에 가장 적절한 곳은 ③이다.

- **as soon as** ~하자마자
- **expert** ⓝ 전문가
- **harmonious** ⓐ 조화로운
- **frustrating** ⓐ 좌절감을 주는
- **undergo** ⓥ 겪다
- **humiliating** ⓐ 창피한, 굴욕적인
- **as though** 마치 ~처럼
- **graceful** ⓐ 우아한
- **awkward** ⓐ 어색한, 불편한
- **embarrassing** ⓐ 당혹스러운
- **slip** ⓥ (어떤 위치나 손을 벗어나) 미끄러지다

구문 풀이

> **3행** When done well, when done by an expert, both reading and skiing are graceful, harmonious activities.
> (they are 생략) (they are 생략)
> 접속사(~할 때) 접속사(~할 때) 「both A and B : A와 B 둘 다」
> 동사(복수)

★★ 문제 해결 꿀~팁 ★★

▶ **많이 틀린 이유는?**
주어진 문장에 But이 있으므로 흐름 반전의 포인트를 찾아야 하는데, 최다 오답인 ④는 '스키 타기 → 독서'로 소재가 바뀌어서 얼핏 볼 때 흐름상 가장 큰 전환이 일어나는 부분이다. 이렇게 함정이 있는 문장 위치 찾기 문항은 비교적 세부적인 흐름까지 체크하며 꼼꼼히 독해해야 실수 없이 정답을 고를 수 있다.

▶ **문제 해결 방법은?**
주어진 문장은 '스키 신발을 신은 직후' 상황에 대해 이야기하는데, ③ 앞의 문장은 '평소'의 상황, ③ 뒤의 문장은 '스키를 신고 걸을 때'의 상황을 말하고 있다. 따라서 '평소에는 멀쩡히 걷지만 → 스키를 신으면 처음부터 걷기를 배우는 기분이고 → 실제로 무척 넘어지며 배운다'는 흐름이 되도록 ③에 주어진 문장을 넣는 것이 가장 적절하다.

★★★ 1등급 대비 고난도 2점 문제

10 오늘날 이야기의 특징인 열린 결말 　　정답률 30% | 정답 ①

글의 흐름으로 보아, 주어진 문장이 들어가기에 가장 적절한 곳을 고르시오.

In the classical fairy tale / the conflict is often permanently resolved.
고전 동화에서 / 갈등은 흔히 영구적으로 해결된다.

Without exception, / the hero and heroine live happily ever after.
예외 없이 / 남자 주인공과 여자 주인공은 영원히 행복하게 산다.

☑ By contrast, / many present-day stories have a less definitive ending.
이와 대조적으로, / 많은 오늘날의 이야기들은 덜 확정적인 결말을 가진다.

Often the conflict in those stories / is only partly resolved, / or a new conflict appears / making the audience think further.
흔히 이러한 이야기 속의 갈등은 / 부분적으로만 해결되거나, / 새로운 갈등이 등장하여 / 관객들을 더 생각하도록 이끈다.

② This is particularly true of thriller and horror genres, / where audiences are kept on the edge of their seats throughout.
이것은 스릴러와 공포물 장르에서 특히 그런데, / 이런 장르에서 관객들은 내내 (이야기에) 매료된다.

③ Consider Henrik Ibsen's play, A Doll's House, / where, in the end, Nora leaves her family and marriage.
Henrik Ibsen의 희곡 A Doll's House를 생각해 보라, / 그 작품에서는 결국 Nora가 가정과 결혼 생활을 떠난다.

④ Nora disappears out of the front door / and we are left with many unanswered questions / such as "Where did Nora go?" / and "What will happen to her?"
Nora가 현관 밖으로 사라지고, / 답을 얻지 못한 많은 질문들이 우리에게 남는다. / "Nora는 어디로 갔을까?", / "그녀에게 무슨 일이 일어날까?"와 같이

⑤ An open ending is a powerful tool, / providing food for thought / that forces the audience to think / about what might happen next.
열린 결말은 강력한 도구인데, / 사고의 양식을 제공한다. / 관객에게 생각해보게 만드는 / 다음에 무슨 일이 일어날지

흔히 고전 동화에서 갈등은 영구적으로 해결된다. 예외 없이 남자 주인공과 여자 주인공은 영원히 행복하게 산다. ① 이와 대조적으로, 많은 오늘날의 이야기들은 덜 확정적인 결말을 가진다. 흔히 이러한 이야기 속의 갈등은 부분적으로만 해결되거나, 새로운 갈등이 등장하여 관객들을 더 생각하도록 이끈다. ② 이것은 스릴러와 공포물 장르에서 특히 그런데, 이런 장르에서 관객들은 내내 (이야기에) 매료된다. ③ Henrik Ibsen의 희곡 A Doll's House를 생각해 보라, 그 작품에서는 결국 Nora가 가정과 결혼 생활을 떠난다. ④ Nora가 현관 밖으로 사

라지고, "Nora는 어디로 갔을까?", "그녀에게 무슨 일이 일어날까?"와 같이 답을 얻지 못한 많은 질문들이 우리에게 남는다. ⑤ 열린 결말은 강력한 도구인데, 관객에게 다음에 무슨 일이 일어날지 생각해보게 만드는 사고의 양식을 제공한다.

Why? 왜 정답일까?

① 앞의 문장에서 확정적인 결말 형태가 많은 고전 동화를 언급한 데 이어, 주어진 문장은 비교적 덜 확정적인 결말 형태(a less definitive ending)를 갖는 오늘날의 이야기들을 언급한다. ① 뒤의 문장에서는 결말이 덜 확정적인 경우의 예로서 갈등이 부분적으로만 해결되거나 새로운 갈등이 등장하는 경우 등을 열거한다. 따라서 주어진 문장이 들어가기에 가장 적절한 곳은 ①이다.

- **fairy tale** 동화, 옛날이야기
- **permanently** ⓐ 영구적으로
- **exception** ⓝ 예외, 이례
- **audience** ⓝ 관객
- **be true of** ~에 해당하다
- **audience** ⓝ 청중
- **throughout** prep 내내
- **food for thought** 생각할 거리
- **conflict** ⓝ 갈등
- **resolve** ⓥ 해결하다
- **definitive** ⓐ 확정적인
- **particularly** ⓐ 특히
- **genre** ⓝ 장르
- **on the edge of one's seat** 매료되어
- **disappear** ⓥ 사라지다

구문 풀이

> **12행** Nora disappears out of the front door / and we are left with many unanswered questions / such as "Where did Nora go?" and "What will happen to her?"
> 자동사(사라지다) ~와 함께 남겨지다
> 과거분사 ~와 같은(예시)

★★ 문제 해결 꿀~팁 ★★

▶ **많이 틀린 이유는?**
① 뒤의 'those stories'가 가리키는 바를 잘못 파악하면 오답을 고르기 쉬운 문제이다. ① 앞에서 'the classic fairy tale'이 단수로 제시되므로, ① 뒤에서 이를 복수대명사로 나타낼 수 없다는 데 유의한다.

▶ **문제 해결 방법은?**
고전 동화와 오늘날의 이야기 전개를 대조하는 글이므로, '오늘날 이야기'로 소재가 전환되는 부분을 파악하는 데 중점을 둔다.

★★★ 1등급 대비 고난도 3점 문제

11 나이가 들면서 호기심이 줄어드는 까닭 　　정답률 31% | 정답 ⑤

글의 흐름으로 보아, 주어진 문장이 들어가기에 가장 적절한 곳을 고르시오. [3점]

According to educational psychologist Susan Engel, / curiosity begins to decrease / as young as four years old.
교육 심리학자 Susan Engel에 따르면, / 호기심은 줄어들기 시작한다. / 네 살 정도라는 어린 나이에

By the time we are adults, / we have fewer questions and more default settings.
우리가 어른이 될 무렵, / 질문은 더 적어지고 기본값은 더 많아진다.

As Henry James put it, / "Disinterested curiosity is past, / the mental grooves and channels set."
Henry James가 말했듯이, / '무관심한 호기심은 없어지고, / 정신의 고랑과 경로가 자리잡는다.'

① The decline in curiosity / can be traced / in the development of the brain through childhood.
호기심의 감소는 / 원인을 찾을 수 있다. / 유년 시절 동안의 뇌의 발달에서

② Though smaller than the adult brain, / the infant brain contains millions more neural connections.
비록 성인의 뇌보다 작지만, / 유아의 뇌는 수백만 개 더 많은 신경 연결을 가지고 있다.

③ The wiring, however, is a mess; / the lines of communication between infant neurons / are far less efficient / than between those in the adult brain.
그러나 연결 상태는 엉망인데, / 유아의 뉴런 간의 전달은 / 훨씬 덜 효율적이다. / 성인 뇌 속 뉴런끼리의 전달보다

④ The baby's perception of the world / is consequently both intensely rich and wildly disordered.
세상에 대한 아기의 인식은 / 결과적으로 매우 풍부하면서도 상당히 무질서하다.

☑ As children absorb more evidence / from the world around them, / certain possibilities become much more likely and more useful / and harden into knowledge or beliefs.
아이들이 더 많은 증거를 흡수함에 따라, / 그들 주변의 세상으로부터 / 특정한 가능성들이 훨씬 더 커지게 되고 더 유용하게 되어 / 지식이나 믿음으로 굳어진다.

The neural pathways / that enable those beliefs / become faster and more

automatic, / while the ones / that the child doesn't use regularly / are pruned away.
신경 경로는 / 그러한 믿음을 가능하게 하는 / 더 빠르고 자동적으로 이루어지게 되고, / 반면에 경로는 / 아이가 주기적으로 사용하지 않는 / 제거된다.

교육 심리학자 Susan Engel에 따르면, 호기심은 네 살 정도라는 어린 나이에 줄어들기 시작한다. 우리가 어른이 될 무렵, 질문은 더 적어지고 기본값은 더 많아진다. Henry James가 말했듯이, '무관심한 호기심은 없어지고, 정신의 고랑과 경로가 자리잡는다.' ① 호기심의 감소는 유년 시절 동안의 뇌의 발달에서 원인을 찾을 수 있다. ② 비록 성인의 뇌보다 작지만, 유아의 뇌는 수백만 개 더 많은 신경 연결을 가지고 있다. ③ 그러나 연결 상태는 엉망인데, 유아의 뉴런 간의 전달은 성인 뇌 속 뉴런끼리의 전달보다 훨씬 덜 효율적이다. ④ 결과적으로 세상에 대한 아기의 인식은 매우 풍부하면서도 상당히 무질서하다. ⑤ 아이들이 그들 주변의 세상으로부터 더 많은 증거를 흡수함에 따라, 특정한 가능성들이 훨씬 더 커지게 되고 더 유용하게 되며 지식이나 믿음으로 굳어진다. 그러한 믿음을 가능하게 하는 신경 경로는 더 빠르고 자동적으로 이루어지게 되고, 반면에 아이가 주기적으로 사용하지 않는 경로는 제거된다.

Why? 왜 정답일까?

⑤ 앞은 아기의 인식이 성인에 비해 무질서하다는 내용인데, ⑤ 뒤에서는 갑자기 '믿음'을 언급하며, 신경 경로의 자동화와 제거를 설명한다. 이때 주어진 문장을 보면, 아이들이 주변 세상에서 더 많은 근거를 얻고 더 유용한 가능성들을 취하면서 '믿음'이 굳어지기 시작한다고 한다. 이 '믿음'이 ⑤ 뒤와 연결되는 것이므로, 주어진 문장이 들어가기에 가장 적절한 곳은 ⑤이다.

- absorb ⓥ (정보를) 받아들이다
- educational ⓐ 교육의
- decrease ⓥ 감소하다
- disinterested ⓐ 무관심한
- channel ⓝ 경로
- childhood ⓝ 어린 시절
- neural ⓐ 신경의
- perception ⓝ 지각, 인식
- intensely ⓐ 대단히, 강렬하게
- pathway ⓝ 경로
- prune ⓥ 가지치기하다
- harden ⓥ 굳어지다
- curiosity ⓝ 호기심
- default setting 기본값
- groove ⓝ 고랑
- development ⓝ 발달
- infant ⓝ 유아
- mess ⓝ 엉망
- consequently ⓐ 그 결과
- disordered ⓐ 무질서한
- automatic ⓐ 자동적인

구문 풀이

1행 As children absorb more evidence from the world around
접속사(~함에 따라)
them, certain possibilities become much more likely and more useful
=children   동사1   주격 보어(비교급 형용사)
and harden into knowledge or beliefs.
동사2

★★ 문제 해결 꿀~팁 ★★

▶ 많이 틀린 이유는?
① 뒤의 문장 이후, ②~⑤ 사이의 내용은 모두 부연 설명이다. 호기심이 감소하는 까닭은 뇌 발달에 있다는 일반적인 내용 뒤로, 아이들의 뇌가 성인의 뇌보다 작지만 연결고리가 훨씬 더 많다는 설명, 그렇지만 그 연결고리가 엉망이라는 설명, 그렇기에 아이의 세상 인식은 어른보다 풍부할지언정 무질서하다는 설명이 모두 자연스럽게 이어지고 있다. 주어진 문장은 이 모든 설명이 마무리된 후 '어쩌다' 호기심이 떨어지는 것인지 마침내 언급하는 문장이다.

▶ 문제 해결 방법은?
연결어 힌트가 없어서 난해하게 느껴질 수 있지만, 지시어 힌트를 활용하면 아주 쉽다. ⑤ 뒤에는 '그러한 믿음(those beliefs)'이라는 표현이 나오는데, 이는 앞에서 '믿음'을 언급했어야만 쓸 수 있는 표현이다. 하지만 ⑤ 앞까지는 beliefs가 전혀 등장하지 않고, 오로지 주어진 문장에만 knowledge or beliefs가 등장한다.

★★★ 1등급 대비 고난도 3점 문제

12 호혜주의가 침팬지 무리 서열 결정에 끼친 결과   정답률 28% | 정답 ③

글의 흐름으로 보아, 주어진 문장이 들어가기에 가장 적절한 곳을 고르시오. [3점]

Reciprocity can be explored in captivity / by handing one chimpanzee a large amount of food, / such as a watermelon or leafy branch, / and then observing what follows.
호혜주의는 포획된 상황에서 탐구될 수 있다. / 침팬지 한 마리에게 많은 양의 먹이를 건네주고 / 수박이나 잎이 많은 나뭇가지처럼 / 뒤이어 일어나는 것을 관찰함으로써

① The owner will be center stage, / with a group of others around him or her, / soon to be followed by newly formed groups / around those who obtained a sizable share, / until all food has been distributed.
먹이 소유자가 중심에 있게 되고, / 자기 주위의 다른 침팬지들에 둘러싸여 / 새로이 형성된 무리들이 곧 뒤따르게 된다. / 꽤 큰 몫을 얻은 침팬지들 주변으로 / 모든 먹이가 다 분배될 때까지

② Beggars may complain and cry, / but aggressive conflicts are rare.
먹이를 구걸하는 침팬지들은 불평하고 울부짖을 수도 있지만 / 호전적인 충돌은 드물다.

✔ The few times that they do occur, / it is the possessor / who tries to make someone leave the circle.
간혹 그러한 일이 정말 일어날 때, / 먹이 소유자다. / 누군가를 무리에서 떠나게 하려는 것은
She will hit them over their head with her branch / or bark at them in a high-pitched voice / until they leave her alone.
먹이 소유자는 그들의 머리를 나뭇가지로 때리거나 / 그들에게 고음으로 울부짖는다. / 그들이 자신을 귀찮게 하지 않을 때까지

④ Whatever their rank, / possessors control the food flow.
그들의 서열이 무엇이든 간에, / 먹이 소유자가 먹이의 흐름을 제어한다.

⑤ Once chimpanzees enter reciprocity mode, / their social rank no longer matters.
침팬지들이 호혜주의 상태에 접어들게 되면, / 사회적 서열은 더 이상 중요한 것이 아니다.

호혜주의는 포획된 상황에서 침팬지 한 마리에게 수박이나 잎이 많은 가지처럼 많은 양의 먹이를 건네주고 뒤이어 일어나는 것을 관찰함으로써 탐구될 수 있다. ① 먹이 소유자가 주위의 다른 침팬지들에 둘러싸여 중심에 있게 되고, 모든 먹이가 다 분배될 때까지 꽤 큰 몫을 얻은 침팬지들 주변으로 새로이 형성된 무리들이 곧 뒤따르게 된다. ② 먹이를 구걸하는 침팬지들은 불평하고 울부짖을 수도 있지만 호전적인 충돌은 드물다. ③ 간혹 그러한 일이 정말 일어날 때, 누군가를 무리에서 떠나게 하려는 것은 먹이 소유자다. 먹이 소유자는 그들이 자신을 귀찮게 하지 않을 때까지 그들의 머리를 나뭇가지로 때리거나 그들에게 고음으로 울부짖는다. ④ 그들의 서열이 무엇이든 간에, 먹이 소유자가 먹이의 흐름을 제어한다. ⑤ 침팬지들이 호혜주의 상태에 접어들게 되면, 사회적 서열은 더 이상 중요한 것이 아니다.

Why? 왜 정답일까?

침팬지들이 호혜주의에 접어들면 서열보다도 먹이 소유자인지 아닌지가 중요해진다는 내용의 글이다. ③ 앞의 문장은 먹이 소유자에게 먹이를 구걸하는 침팬지들이 불평은 할 수 있지만 충돌은 피한다는 내용을 제시하는데, 주어진 문장은 '그런 상황', 즉 충돌의 상황이 빚어질 때 이를 통제하는 것이 먹이 소유자임을 언급한다. ③ 뒤의 문장은 먹이 소유자가 갈등 상황에서 취하는 행동을 열거한다. 따라서 주어진 문장이 들어가기에 가장 적절한 곳은 ③이다.

- possessor ⓝ 소유자
- leafy ⓐ 잎이 많은
- sizable ⓐ 상당한
- distribute ⓥ 분배하다
- high-pitched ⓐ 고음의
- captivity ⓝ 포획, 감금
- obtain ⓥ 얻다
- share ⓝ 몫 ⓥ 나누다
- aggressive ⓐ 공격적인
- leave ~ alone ⓥ ~을 그대로 내버려 두다

구문 풀이

1행 The few times [that they do occur], it is the possessor who
선행사   동사 강조   「it is ~ who[that] … : 강조 구문
tries to make someone leave the circle.
(…한 것은 바로 ~이다)

★★ 문제 해결 꿀~팁 ★★

▶ 많이 틀린 이유는?
④ 앞의 문장에서 먹이 소유자가 다른 구성원들을 '때리며' 상황에 대한 자신의 의사를 표현할 수 있다고 언급한 것을 근거로, ④ 뒤에서는 서열보다도 먹이 소유자인지 아닌지가 먹이 흐름을 제어할 권한을 준다는 결론을 정리하고 있다. 따라서 ④ 앞뒤에는 논리적 공백이 없다.

▶ 문제 해결 방법은?
③ 앞뒤의 논리적 공백에 주목한다. ③ 앞에서 갈등은 '드물다'고 언급했는데 ③ 뒤에서는 갑자기 She, 즉 먹이 소유자가 구성원들을 때리며 불편함을 나타내는 상황이 제시된다. 이는 '드물게도 갈등이 일어났을 때' 먹이 소유자가 취할 행동으로 볼 수 있으므로, '갈등이 일어났을 때'라는 말로 시작하는 주어진 문장은 ③에 들어가야 한다.

[문제편 p.114]

DAY 18 　　　문장 삽입 03

01 ③	02 ④	03 ③	04 ③	05 ④
06 ④	07 ⑤	08 ②	09 ④	10 ④
11 ⑤	12 ③			

01　온도와 화학적 성질이 다른 물잔 섞기　　정답률 48% | 정답 ③

글의 흐름으로 보아, 주어진 문장이 들어가기에 가장 적절한 곳을 고르시오.

Take two glasses of water.
물 두 잔을 가져오라.

Put a little bit of orange juice into one / and a little bit of lemon juice into the other.
하나의 잔에는 약간의 오렌지주스를 넣고, / 다른 잔에는 약간의 레몬주스를 넣으라.

① What you have / are essentially two glasses of water / but with a completely different chemical makeup.
여러분이 가지고 있는 것은 / 본질적으로 물 두 잔이다. / 완전히 다른 화학적 성질을 지닌

② If we take the glass containing orange juice / and heat it, / we will still have two different glasses of water / with different chemical makeups, / but now they will also have different temperatures.
만약 우리가 오렌지주스가 든 잔을 가져와서 / 그것을 가열한다면, / 우리는 여전히 서로 다른 물 두 잔을 가지고 있을 것이지만, / 다른 화학적 성질을 지닌 / 이제 그것들은 또한 다른 온도를 가질 것이다.

✔ If we could magically remove the glasses, / we would find / the two water bodies would not mix well.
만약 우리가 마법처럼 그 유리잔들을 없앨 수 있다면, / 우리는 알게 될 것이다. / 두 액체가 잘 섞이지 않는다는 것을

Perhaps they would mix a little / where they met; / however, / they would remain separate / because of their different chemical makeups and temperatures.
어쩌면 그것들은 조금 섞일 것이다. / 그것들이 접한 부분에서 / 하지만, / 이것들은 분리된 상태로 남아 있을 것이다. / 다른 화학적 성질과 온도로 인해

④ The warmer water would float / on the surface of the cold water / because of its lighter weight.
더 따뜻한 물은 떠 있을 것이다. / 찬물의 표면에 / 그것의 무게가 더 가볍기 때문에

⑤ In the ocean we have bodies of water / that differ in temperature and salt content; / for this reason, / they do not mix.
바다에는 수역(물줄기)들이 있다. / 온도와 염분 함량이 다른 / 이러한 이유로, / 그것들은 섞이지 않는다.

물 두 잔을 가져오라. 하나의 잔에는 약간의 오렌지주스를 넣고, 다른 잔에는 약간의 레몬주스를 넣으라. ① 여러분이 가지고 있는 것은 본질적으로 물 두 잔이지만 둘은 완전히 다른 화학적 성질을 지녔다. ② 만약 우리가 오렌지주스가 든 잔을 가져와서 가열한다면, 우리는 여전히 다른 화학적 성질을 지닌 서로 다른 물 두 잔을 가지고 있을 것이지만, 이제 그것들은 또한 다른 온도를 가질 것이다. ③ 만약 우리가 마법처럼 그 유리잔들을 없앨 수 있다면, 우리는 두 액체가 잘 섞이지 않는다는 것을 알게 될 것이다. 어쩌면 그것들은 서로 접한 부분에서 조금 섞일 것이다. 하지만, 이것들은 다른 화학적 성질과 온도로 인해 분리된 상태로 남아 있을 것이다. ④ 더 따뜻한 물은 무게가 더 가볍기 때문에 찬물의 표면에 떠 있을 것이다. ⑤ 바다에는 온도와 염분이 다른 수역(물줄기)들이 있다. 이러한 이유로, 그것들은 섞이지 않는다.

Why?　왜 정답일까?

③ 앞까지는 물 두 잔에 각각 오렌지주스와 레몬주스를 섞어 성질을 달리하고, 한쪽에만 약간의 열을 더해 온도 또한 달리하는 과정을 설명한다. 여기에 이어 주어진 문장은 만일 이 상황에서 유리잔을 제거해보면 두 액체가 서로 잘 섞이지 않는다는 사실을 알게 된다고 설명한다. ③ 뒤는 주어진 문장에 이어 두 액체가 서로 화학적 성질과 온도가 달라 섞이지 않는다고 설명한다. 따라서 주어진 문장이 들어가기에 가장 적절한 곳은 ③이다. 글은 원칙적으로 일반적 진술에서 구체적 진술로 나아가므로, ③에서 주어진 문장이 '두 액체가 안 섞인다'는 일반적 사실을 제시해야 ③ 뒤에서 '왜 안 섞이는지'에 대한 구체적 진술이 자연스럽게 이어질 수 있음을 유념해 둔다.

- **magically** [ad] 희한하게, 마법처럼
- **essentially** [ad] 본질적으로
- **makeup** [n] 구성
- **temperature** [n] 온도
- **because of** ~로 인해
- **surface** [n] 표면
- **remove** [v] 제거하다
- **completely** [ad] 완전히
- **contain** [v] 포함하다
- **separate** [a] 분리된
- **float** [v] 뜨다
- **content** [n] 함량

구문 풀이

1행 If we could magically remove the glasses, we would find the
「if + 주어 + 과거 동사 ~　　　　　주어 + 조동사 과거 + 동사원형 : 가정법 과거」
two water bodies would not mix well.

02　우주 연구가 무인선에 의해 이루어지는 이유　　정답률 45% | 정답 ④

글의 흐름으로 보아, 주어진 문장이 들어가기에 가장 적절한 곳을 고르시오.

Currently, we cannot send humans to other planets.
현재, 우리는 인간을 다른 행성으로 보낼 수 없다.

One obstacle is / that such a trip would take years.
한 가지 장애물은 / 그러한 여행이 수 년이 걸릴 것이라는 점이다.

① A spacecraft would need to carry enough air, water, and other supplies / needed for survival on the long journey.
우주선은 충분한 공기, 물, 그리고 다른 물자를 운반할 필요가 있을 것이다. / 긴 여행 중 생존에 필요한

② Another obstacle is the harsh conditions on other planets, / such as extreme heat and cold.
또 다른 장애물은 다른 행성들의 혹독한 기상 조건이다. / 극심한 열과 추위 같은

③ Some planets do not even have surfaces to land on.
어떤 행성들은 착륙할 표면조차 가지고 있지 않다.

✔ Because of these obstacles, / most research missions in space / are accomplished through the use of spacecraft / without crews aboard.
이러한 장애물들 때문에, / 우주에서의 대부분의 연구 임무는 / 우주선을 사용해서 이루어진다. / 승무원이 탑승하지 않은

These explorations pose no risk to human life / and are less expensive than ones involving astronauts.
이런 탐험들은 인간의 생명에 아무런 위험도 주지 않으며 / 우주 비행사들을 포함하는 탐험보다 비용이 덜 든다.

⑤ The spacecraft carry instruments / that test the compositions and characteristics of planets.
이 우주선은 기구들을 운반한다. / 행성의 구성 성분과 특성을 실험하는

현재, 우리는 인간을 다른 행성으로 보낼 수 없다. 한 가지 장애물은 그러한 여행이 수 년이 걸릴 것이라는 점이다. ① 우주선은 긴 여행 중 생존에 필요한 충분한 공기, 물, 그리고 다른 물자를 운반할 필요가 있을 것이다. ② 또 다른 장애물은 극심한 열과 추위 같은, 다른 행성들의 혹독한 기상 조건이다. ③ 어떤 행성들은 착륙할 표면조차 가지고 있지 않다. ④ 이러한 장애물들 때문에, 우주에서의 대부분의 연구 임무는 승무원이 탑승하지 않은 우주선을 사용해서 이루어진다. 이런 탐험들은 인간의 생명에 아무런 위험도 주지 않으며 우주 비행사들을 포함하는 탐험보다 비용이 덜 든다. ⑤ 이 우주선은 행성의 구성 성분과 특성을 실험하는 기구들을 운반한다.

Why?　왜 정답일까?

우주 탐사가 주로 무인 우주선에 의해 이루어지는 이유를 설명한 글이다. ④ 앞에서는 우주 여행이 너무 오래 걸리고, 다른 행성이 착륙이나 생존에 적합한 조건을 갖추고 있는 것도 아니라는 이유를 제시한다. 주어진 문장은 앞에 열거된 이유를 these obstacles로 나타내며 '그리하여' 우주 연구에 무인 우주선이 동원된다는 점을 언급한다. ④ 뒤의 문장은 무인 우주선에 의한 탐사를 These explorations로 지칭한다. 따라서 주어진 문장이 들어가기에 가장 적절한 곳은 ④이다.

- **obstacle** [n] 장애물
- **crew** [n] 승무원
- **currently** [ad] 현재, 지금
- **send** [v] 보내다
- **survival** [n] 생존
- **supplies** [n] 물자, 보급품
- **condition** [n] 조건
- **land on** ~에 착륙하다
- **pose a risk** 위험을 끼치다
- **instrument** [n] 기구
- **spacecraft** [n] 우주선
- **aboard** [ad] 탑승하여
- **planet** [n] 행성
- **carry** [v] 운반하다
- **journey** [n] (특히 멀리 가는) 여행
- **harsh** [a] 혹독한
- **extreme** [a] 극심한
- **exploration** [n] 탐험, 탐사
- **astronaut** [n] 우주 비행사

구문 풀이

11행 These explorations pose no risk to human life and are
　　　　　　　　　　　　　　　동사1　　　　　　　　　　　　　동사2
less expensive than ones involving astronauts.
「less + 원급 : 덜 ~한」　　　= explorations

03　리허설 후 피드백 기록하기　　정답률 45% | 정답 ③

글의 흐름으로 보아, 주어진 문장이 들어가기에 가장 적절한 곳을 고르시오.

110 영어 독해 [빈칸·순서·삽입] – 기본

After the technical rehearsal, / the theater company will meet / with the director, technical managers, and stage manager / to review the rehearsal.
테크니컬 리허설 후에, / 극단은 만나서 / 총감독, 기술 감독들, 그리고 무대 감독을 / 리허설을 검토할 것이다.

Usually there will be comments / about all the good things about the performance.
보통은 의견이 있을 것이다. / 공연에 대한 온갖 좋은 것들에 관한

① Individuals should make mental and written notes / on the positive comments / about their own personal contributions / as well as those directed / toward the crew and the entire company.
개인은 마음에 새기고 글로 적어놓아야 한다. / 긍정적인 의견을 / 그들의 개인적인 기여에 대한 / 긍정적인 의견 뿐만 아니라, / 단원들과 극단 전체에 관해 주어지는

② Building on positive accomplishments / can reduce nervousness.
긍정적인 성과를 바탕으로 하면 / 긴장감을 줄일 수 있다.

✔ In addition to positive comments, / the director and manager / will undoubtedly have comments / about what still needs work.
긍정적인 의견 이외에, / 총감독과 부감독은 / 분명히 의견도 가지고 있을 것이다. / 여전히 노력이 필요한 부분에 대한

Sometimes, these negative comments / can seem overwhelming and stressful.
때로, 이러한 부정적인 의견은 / 괴롭고 스트레스를 주는 것처럼 보일 수 있다.

④ Time pressures to make these last-minute changes / can be a source of stress.
이러한 막판 수정을 하는 데 대한 시간 압박은 / 스트레스의 원인이 될 수 있다.

⑤ Take each suggestion with good humor and enthusiasm / and tackle each task one by one.
각 제안을 좋은 기분으로 열정을 가지고 받아들이고 / 각 과제를 하나씩 해결해 나가라.

테크니컬 리허설(기술 연습) 후에, 극단은 총감독, 기술 감독들, 그리고 무대 감독을 만나서 리허설을 검토할 것이다. 보통은 공연에 대한 온갖 좋은 것들에 관한 의견이 있을 것이다. ① 개인은 단원들과 극단 전체에 관해 주어지는 긍정적인 의견뿐만 아니라, 그들의 개인적인 기여에 대한 긍정적인 의견도 마음에 새기고 글로 적어놓아야 한다. ② 긍정적인 성과를 바탕으로 하면 긴장감을 줄일 수 있다. ③ 긍정적인 의견 이외에, 총감독과 부감독은 분명히 여전히 노력이 필요한 부분에 대한 의견도 가지고 있을 것이다. 때로, 이러한 부정적인 의견은 괴롭고 스트레스를 주는 것처럼 보일 수 있다. ④ 이러한 막판 수정을 하는 데 대한 시간 압박은 스트레스의 원인이 될 수 있다. ⑤ 각 제안을 좋은 기분으로 열정을 가지고 받아들이고 각 과제를 하나씩 해결해 나가라.

Why? 왜 정답일까?

테크니컬 리허설 후 피드백을 기록해두었다가 문제 해결에 참고하라는 내용을 다룬 글이다. ③ 앞의 두 문장에서 긍정적인 피드백을 마음에 새기고 기록해 둘 것을 언급한 이후, 주어진 문장에서는 여전히 노력이 필요한 부분, 즉 부족한 부분에 대한 의견이 또한 있을 것임을 환기한다. ③ 뒤에서는 이러한 부정적 의견이 괴롭고 스트레스의 원인처럼 여겨질 수 있지만 기분 좋게 받아들이고 남은 과제를 해결하는 데 활용하라는 조언을 이어가고 있다. 따라서 주어진 문장이 들어가기에 가장 적절한 곳은 ③이다.

- in addition to ~ 이외에, ~에 더하여
- undoubtedly [ad] 분명히, 의심의 여지없이
- contribution ⓝ 기여
- nervousness ⓝ 긴장감
- enthusiasm ⓝ 열정
- theater company 극단
- performance ⓝ 공연
- crew ⓝ (전체) 단원들
- overwhelm ⓥ 괴롭히다, 압도하다
- tackle ⓥ 해결하다

구문 풀이

8행 Individuals should make mental and written notes on the
　　　　　　　　주어　　　　　　　동사
positive comments about their own personal contributions as well as
　　　　　　　　　　　　　　　　　　　　「A + as well as + B : A뿐만 아니라 B도」
those [directed toward the crew and the entire company].

---

04 중국의 통합과 유럽의 분열 대조　　정답률 46% | 정답 ③

글의 흐름으로 보아, 주어진 문장이 들어가기에 가장 적절한 곳을 고르시오.

China's frequent times of unity / and Europe's constant disunity / both have a long history.
중국의 빈번한 통합과 / 유럽의 지속적인 분열은 / 둘 다 역사가 오래되었다.

① The most productive areas of modern China / were politically joined for the first time in 221 BC, / and have remained so for most of the time since then.
현대 중국에서 가장 생산성이 높은 지역들은 / 기원전 221년에 처음 정치적으로 통합되었고, / 그때 이후로 대부분의 시간을 그렇게 유지해 왔다.

② It has had only a single writing system from the beginning, / a single

---

principal language for a long time, / and solid cultural unity for two thousand years.
중국은 처음부터 단 하나의 문자 체계를 지니고 있었다. / 오래도록 하나의 표준어를, / 그리고 2천 년 동안 견고한 문화적인 단일성을

✔ In contrast, / Europe has never come close to political unification.
이와 반대로, / 유럽은 정치적 통합에 가까이 가본 일이 없었다.

It was divided into 500 states in AD 1500, / got down to a minimum of 25 states in the 1980s, / and is now up again to over 40.
유럽은 서기 1500년에 500개 나라로 쪼개졌고, / 1980년대에는 최소 25개로 줄어들었다가, / 현재 다시 40개 이상으로 늘어났다.

④ It still has 45 languages, / and even greater cultural diversity.
유럽에는 아직도 45개 언어가 있으며, / 그것보다 훨씬 더 큰 문화적 다양성이 있다.

⑤ The current disagreements / about the issue of unifying Europe / are typical of Europe's disunity.
현재의 의견 차이가 / 유럽 통합의 문제에 대한 / 유럽 분열의 대표적이다.

중국의 빈번한 통합과 유럽의 지속적인 분열은 둘 다 역사가 오래되었다. ① 현대 중국에서 가장 생산성이 높은 지역들은 기원전 221년에 처음 정치적으로 통합되었고, 그때 이후로 대부분의 시간을 그렇게 (통합된 상태로) 유지해 왔다. ② 중국은 처음부터 단 하나의 문자 체계를, 오래도록 하나의 표준어를, 2천 년 동안 견고한 문화적인 단일성을 지니고 있었다. ③ 이와 반대로, 유럽은 정치적 통합에 가까이 가본 일이 없었다. 유럽은 서기 1500년에 500개 나라로 쪼개졌고, 1980년대에는 최소 25개로 줄어들었다가, 현재 다시 40개 이상으로 늘어났다. ④ 유럽에는 아직도 45개 언어가 있으며, 그것보다 훨씬 더 큰 문화적 다양성이 있다. ⑤ 유럽 통합의 문제에 대한 현재의 의견 차이가 유럽 분열의 대표적이다.

Why? 왜 정답일까?

③ 앞에서는 중국이 오랜 통합의 역사를 지니고 있으며 하나의 언어와 견고한 문화적 단일성을 지니고 있음을 이야기하는데, 주어진 문장은 In contrast로 이 흐름을 뒤집으며 유럽의 역사는 통합과 거리가 멀었다는 점을 언급한다. 이에 이어 ③ 뒤의 문장에서는 유럽이 수백, 수십 개 국가로 나뉘어 분열을 거듭하였다는 내용을 구체적으로 말한다. ③ 뒤의 문장에서 주어인 It이 ③ 앞에 이어 China를 가리키지 않고 주어진 문장에 이어 Europe을 가리키고 있음을 참고한다. 따라서 주어진 문장이 들어가기에 가장 적절한 곳은 ③이다.

- political ⓐ 정치적인, 정치의
- frequent ⓐ 빈번한
- constant ⓐ 지속적인
- productive ⓐ 생산성이 높은, 생산적인
- writing system 문자 체계
- solid ⓐ 견고한, 단단한
- diversity ⓝ 다양성
- unification ⓝ 통합, 통일
- unity ⓝ 통합, 일치, 결속
- disunity ⓝ 분열
- remain ⓥ 계속 ~이다
- principal ⓐ 주된, 주요한
- state ⓝ 나라, 국가
- disagreement ⓝ 불일치, 의견 차이

구문 풀이

5행 The most productive areas of modern China
　　　　　　　　　　　　주어
were politically joined for the first time in 221 BC, and have remained
　　동사1(과거)　　　　　　　　　　　　　　　　　　　동사2(현재완료)
so for most of the time since then.
　　「for + 기간 표현 : ~동안」　~이후로(현재완료와 호응)

---

05 생물 다양성으로 인한 이득　　정답률 52% | 정답 ④

글의 흐름으로 보아, 주어진 문장이 들어가기에 가장 적절한 곳을 고르시오. [3점]

When an ecosystem is biodiverse, / wildlife have more opportunities / to obtain food and shelter.
생태계에 생물 종이 다양할 때, / 야생 생물들은 더 많은 기회를 얻는다. / 먹이와 서식지를 얻을

Different species react and respond / to changes in their environment / differently.
다양한 종들은 작용하고 반응한다. / 그들의 환경 변화에 / 다르게

① For example, / imagine a forest with only one type of plant in it, / which is the only source of food and habitat / for the entire forest food web.
예를 들어, / 단 한 종류의 식물만 있는 숲을 상상해 보라 / 그 식물은 유일한 먹이원이자 서식지이다. / 숲의 먹이 그물 전체에게 있어

② Now, / there is a sudden dry season / and this plant dies.
이제, / 갑작스러운 건기가 오고 / 이 식물이 죽는다.

③ Plant-eating animals / completely lose their food source and die out, / and so do the animals / that prey upon them.
초식 동물은 / 그들의 먹이원을 완전히 잃고 죽게 되고, / 동물들도 그렇게 된다. / 그들을 먹이로 삼는

✔ But, when there is biodiversity, / the effects of a sudden change / are not so dramatic.
하지만 종 다양성이 있을 때, / 갑작스러운 변화의 영향은 / 그렇게 극적이지 않다.

Different species of plants / respond to the drought differently, / and many can survive a dry season.
다양한 종의 식물들이 / 가뭄에 다르게 반응하고, / 많은 식물이 건기에 살아남을 수 있다.
⑤ Many animals have a variety of food sources / and don't just rely on one plant; / now our forest ecosystem is no longer at the death!
많은 동물은 다양한 먹이원을 가지고 있으며 / 그저 한 식물에 의존하지는 않는다. / 그래서 이제 우리의 숲 생태계는 더는 종말에 처해 있지 않다!

생태계에 생물 종이 다양할 때, 야생 생물들은 먹이와 서식지를 얻을 더 많은 기회를 얻는다. 다양한 종들은 그들의 환경 변화에 다르게 작용하고 반응한다. ① 예를 들어, 단 한 종류의 식물만 있는 숲을 상상해 보면, 그 식물은 숲의 먹이 그물 전체의 유일한 먹이원이자 서식지이다. ② 이제, 갑작스러운 건기가 오고 이 식물이 죽는다. ③ 초식 동물은 그들의 먹이원을 완전히 잃고 죽게 되고, 그들을 먹이로 삼는 동물들도 그렇게 된다. ④ 하지만 종 다양성이 있을 때, 갑작스러운 변화의 영향은 그렇게 극적이지 않다. 다양한 종의 식물들이 가뭄에 다르게 반응하고, 많은 식물이 건기에 살아남을 수 있다. ⑤ 많은 동물은 다양한 먹이원을 가지고 있으며 한 식물에만 의존하지 않기에, 이제 우리의 숲 생태계는 더는 종말에 처해 있지 않다!

Why? 왜 정답일까?

생물 다양성이 보장되면 환경 변화에 대처하기가 더 좋다는 내용의 글로, ④ 앞에서는 식물이 한 종류만 있는 숲의 예를 들어 이 경우 갑작스러운 건기라도 찾아와 식물이 죽으면 숲 전체 생태계가 망가진다는 내용을 제시한다. 한편 주어진 문장은 But으로 흐름을 반전시키며 생물 다양성이 있으면 상황이 다르다는 것을 언급한다. ④ 뒤에서는 '다양한 식물 종'을 언급하며, 이것들이 건기에 대처하는 방식이 모두 다르기에 많은 수가 살아남아 생태계가 유지될 수 있음을 설명한다. 따라서 주어진 문장이 들어가기에 가장 적절한 곳은 ④이다.

● ecosystem ⓝ 생태계
● die out 멸종되다, 자취를 감추다
● food web 먹이 그물, 먹이 사슬 체계
● prey upon ～을 잡아먹다, 괴롭히다

구문 풀이

6행 For example, imagine a forest with only one type of plant in
　　　　　　　　　　　　　　　　　　　　선행사
it, which is the only source of food and habitat for the entire forest
　　　계속적 용법
food web.

06　커피의 기원에 관한 전설　　정답률 57% | 정답 ④

글의 흐름으로 보아, 주어진 문장이 들어가기에 가장 적절한 곳을 고르시오.

Although humans have been drinking coffee for centuries, / it is not clear just where coffee originated / or who first discovered it.
수 세기 동안 사람들은 커피를 마셔왔지만, / 단지 어디서 커피가 유래했는지는 분명하지 않다. / 혹은 누가 그것을 처음 발견했는지는
① However, the predominant legend has it / that a goatherd discovered coffee in the Ethiopian highlands.
그러나, 유력한 전설에 따르면 / 한 염소지기가 에티오피아 고산지에서 커피를 발견했다.
② Various dates for this legend / include 900 BC, 300 AD, and 800 AD.
이 전설에 대한 다양한 시기는 / 기원전 900년, 기원후 300년, 기원후 800년을 포함한다.
③ Regardless of the actual date, / it is said that Kaldi, the goatherd, / noticed that his goats did not sleep at night / after eating berries / from what would later be known as a coffee tree.
실제 시기와 상관없이, / 염소지기인 Kaldi가 / 그의 염소들이 밤에 잠을 자지 않았다는 것을 발견했다고 한다. / 열매를 먹은 후 / 후에 커피나무라고 알려진 나무로부터
✔ When Kaldi reported his observation to the local monastery, / the abbot became the first person / to brew a pot of coffee / and note its flavor and alerting effect / when he drank it.
Kaldi가 그 지역 수도원에 그의 관찰 내용을 보고했을 때, / 수도원장은 최초의 사람이 되었다. / 한 주전자의 커피를 우려내고 / 그것의 풍미와 각성 효과를 알아차린 / 그가 그것을 마셨을 때
Word of the awakening effects and the pleasant taste / of this new beverage / soon spread beyond the monastery.
각성 효과와 좋은 풍미에 대한 소문은 / 이 새로운 음료의 / 이내 수도원 너머로 널리 퍼졌다.
⑤ The story of Kaldi might be more fable than fact, / but at least some historical evidence indicates / that coffee did originate in the Ethiopian highlands.
Kaldi의 이야기는 사실이라기보다 꾸며낸 이야기일지도 모르지만, / 적어도 몇몇 역사적 증거는 보여준다. / 커피가 정말 에티오피아 고산지에서 유래했다는 것을

수 세기 동안 사람들은 커피를 마셔왔지만, 단지 어디서 커피가 유래했는지 혹은 누가 그것을 처음 발견했는지는 분명하지 않다. ① 그러나, 유력한 전설에

따르면 한 염소지기가 에티오피아 고산지에서 커피를 발견했다. ② 이 전설에 대한 다양한 시기는 기원전 900년, 기원후 300년, 기원후 800년을 포함한다. ③ 실제 시기와 상관없이, 염소지기인 Kaldi가 그의 염소들이 후에 커피나무라고 알려진 나무로부터 열매를 먹은 후 밤에 잠을 자지 않았다는 것을 발견했다고 한다. ④ Kaldi가 그 지역 수도원에 그의 관찰 내용을 보고했을 때, 수도원장은 한 주전자의 커피를 우려내어 마시고 그것의 풍미와 각성 효과를 알아차린 최초의 사람이 되었다. 이 새로운 음료의 각성 효과와 좋은 풍미에 대한 소문은 이내 수도원 너머로 널리 퍼졌다. ⑤ Kaldi의 이야기는 사실이라기보다 꾸며낸 이야기일지도 모르지만, 적어도 몇몇 역사적 증거는 커피가 정말 에티오피아 고산지에서 유래했다는 것을 보여준다.

Why? 왜 정답일까?

이 글은 커피의 기원과 관련한 전설을 다루고 있다. ④ 앞의 문장에서 염소지기인 Kaldi가 자신의 염소들이 커피나무의 열매를 먹고 잠들지 않았다는 것을 발견했다는 내용이 나온 뒤, 주어진 문장에서는 이를 보고 받은 수도원장이 커피를 우려내어 마셔본 최초의 사람이 되었다는 이야기를 이어 간다. ④ 뒤의 문장에서는 이후 수도원 밖으로 커피에 대한 소문이 퍼졌음을 이야기하고 있다. 따라서 주어진 문장이 들어가기에 가장 적절한 곳은 ④이다.

● observation ⓝ 관찰, 관측
● abbot ⓝ 수도원장
● flavor ⓝ 풍미, 맛, 향
● goatherd ⓝ 염소지기, 염소 돌보는 사람
● pleasant ⓐ 좋은, 즐거운, 쾌적한, 유쾌한
● spread ⓥ 퍼지다, 퍼뜨리다
● indicate ⓥ (사실임을) 나타내다, 보여주다
● monastery ⓝ 수도원
● brew ⓥ (차 등을) 끓이다
● predominant ⓐ 유력한, 우세한, 지배적인
● regardless of ～에 상관없이
● beverage ⓝ 음료
● historical ⓐ 역사적인

구문 풀이

1행 When Kaldi reported his observation to the local monastery,
　　　시간 접속사(～할 때)
/ the abbot became the first person [to brew a pot of coffee / and
　　　　　　　　　　　　　　　　　　　　　to부정사1
(to) note its flavor and alerting effect when he drank it].
to부정사2

★★★ 1등급 대비 고난도 2점 문제

07　선천적 시각장애인의 세상 이해　　정답률 46% | 정답 ⑤

글의 흐름으로 보아, 주어진 문장이 들어가기에 가장 적절한 곳을 고르시오.

Humans born without sight / are not able to collect visual experiences, / so they understand the world / entirely through their other senses.
선천적으로 시각장애가 있는 사람은 / 시각적 경험을 수집할 수 없어서, / 그들은 세상을 이해한다. / 전적으로 다른 감각을 통해
① As a result, / people with blindness at birth / develop an amazing ability / to understand the world / through the collection of experiences and memories / that come from these non-visual senses.
그 결과, / 선천적으로 시각장애가 있는 사람들은 / 놀라운 능력을 발달시킨다. / 세상을 이해하는 / 경험과 기억의 수집을 통해 / 이러한 비시각적 감각에서 오는
② The dreams of a person / who has been without sight since birth / can be just as vivid and imaginative / as those of someone with normal vision.
사람이 꾸는 꿈은 / 선천적으로 시각장애가 있는 / 생생하고 상상력이 풍부할 수 있다. / 정상 시력을 가진 사람의 꿈처럼
③ They are unique, however, / because their dreams are constructed / from the non-visual experiences and memories / they have collected.
그러나 그들은 특별하다. / 그들의 꿈은 구성되기 때문에 / 비시각적 경험과 기억으로부터 / 그들이 수집한
④ A person with normal vision / will dream about a familiar friend / using visual memories of shape, lighting, and colour.
정상적인 시력을 가진 사람들은 / 친숙한 친구에 대해 꿈을 꿀 것이다. / 형태, 빛 그리고 색의 시각적 기억을 사용하여
✔ But, / a blind person will associate the same friend / with a unique combination of experiences / from their non-visual senses / that act to represent that friend.
하지만, / 시각장애인은 그 친구를 연상할 것이다. / 독특한 조합의 경험으로 / 비시각적 감각에서 나온 / 그 친구를 구현하는 데 작용하는
In other words, / people blind at birth / have similar overall dreaming experiences / even though they do not dream in pictures.
다시 말해, / 선천적 시각장애인은 / 전반적으로 비슷한 꿈을 경험한다. / 그들이 시각적인 꿈을 꾸지는 않지만

선천적으로 시각장애가 있는 사람은 시각적 경험을 수집할 수 없어서, 전적으로 다른 감각을 통해 세상을 이해한다. ① 그 결과, 선천적으로 시각장애가 있

는 사람들은 이러한 비시각적 감각에서 오는 경험과 기억의 수집을 통해 세상을 이해하는 놀라운 능력을 발달시킨다. ② 선천적으로 시각장애가 있는 사람이 꾸는 꿈은 정상 시력을 가진 사람의 꿈처럼 생생하고 상상력이 풍부할 수 있다. ③ 그러나 그들의 꿈은 그들이 수집한 비시각적 경험과 기억으로부터 구성되기 때문에 특별하다. ④ 정상적인 시력을 가진 사람들은 형태, 빛 그리고 색의 시각적 기억을 사용하여 친숙한 친구에 대해 꿈을 꿀 것이다. ⑤ <u>하지만, 시각장애인은 그 친구를 구현하는 데 작용하는 자신의 비시각적 감각에서 나온 독특한 조합의 경험으로 바로 그 친구를 연상할 것이다.</u> 다시 말해, 선천적 시각장애인들은 시각적인 꿈을 꾸지는 않지만, 전반적으로 비슷한 꿈을 경험한다.

Why? 왜 정답일까?

선천적 시각장애인은 시각적 경험이 없지만 비시각적 경험과 기억을 통해 세상을 이해하는 특별한 방법을 구성해 나간다는 내용의 글로, ② 이후로 시각장애인이 꿈꾸는 방식을 예로 들고 있다. ⑤ 앞의 문장에서 비시각장애인은 시각적 경험을 이용해 친구에 관한 꿈을 꾼다고 언급하는데, 주어진 문장은 But으로 흐름을 뒤집으며 선천적 시각장애인은 비시각적 감각 경험을 토대로 친구를 연상한다고 설명한다. In other words로 시작하는 ⑤ 뒤의 문장은 주어진 문장의 의미를 풀어볼 때 시각장애인도 결국 꿈을 비슷하게 경험한다는 것을 알 수 있다고 결론 짓는다. 따라서 주어진 문장이 들어가기에 가장 적절한 곳은 ⑤이다.

- **associate A with B** A와 B를 연결 짓다, 연상하다
- **experience** ⓝ 경험
- **sense** ⓝ 감각
- **collect** ⓥ 모으다, 수집하다
- **entirely** ⓐⓓ 전적으로
- **amazing** ⓐ 놀라운
- **collection** ⓝ 수집
- **vivid** ⓐ 생생한
- **normal** ⓐ 정상적인
- **familiar** ⓐ 익숙한, 친숙한
- **in other words** 다시 말해서
- **non-visual** 비시각적
- **sight** ⓝ 시력
- **understand** ⓥ 이해하다
- **result** ⓝ 결과
- **ability** ⓝ 능력
- **dream** ⓝ 꿈
- **imaginative** ⓐ 상상력이 풍부한
- **vision** ⓝ 시력
- **shape** ⓝ 모양, 형태
- **similar** ⓐ 비슷한, 유사한

구문 풀이

[10행] The dreams of a person [who has been without sight since birth] can be just as vivid and imaginative as those of someone with normal vision.

주어(복수) / 주격 관·대(a person 수식) / 전치사(~ 이후로) / 동사 / 「as + 원급 + as : ~만큼 …한」 / 대명사(= the dreams)

★★ 문제 해결 꿀~팁 ★★

▶ 많이 틀린 이유는?
가장 헷갈리는 ③ 앞을 보면, 선천적 시각 장애인의 꿈도 비장애인의 꿈과 마찬가지로 생생하고 상상력이 풍부하다는 내용이다. 이어서 ③ 뒤에서는 however와 함께, '그런데' 이들의 꿈은 비시각적 경험과 기억에 바탕을 두기 때문에 '특별하다'는 내용을 추가하고 있다. 즉, ③ 앞뒤는 역접어 however를 기점으로 '우리와 다르지 않다 → 특별하다'로 자연스럽게 전환되는 흐름인 것이다.

▶ 문제 해결 방법은?
⑤ 앞에서 언급된 a familiar friend가 주어진 문장의 the same friend, that friend로 이어진다. 또한, In other words로 시작하는 ⑤ 뒤의 문장은 주어진 문장을 일반화한 내용이다.

★★★ 1등급 대비 고난도 2점 문제

| 08 | 팀 구성원의 다양성 | 정답률 38% | 정답 ② |

글의 흐름으로 보아, 주어진 문장이 들어가기에 가장 적절한 곳을 고르시오.

Most of us have hired many people / based on human resources criteria / along with some technical and personal information / that the boss thought was important.
우리 대부분은 많은 사람을 고용해 왔다. / 인적 자원 기준에 근거하여 / 어떤 전문적인 정보 및 개인 정보와 더불어 / 사장이 생각하기에 중요한

① I have found / that most people like to hire / people just like themselves.
나는 알게 되었다. / 대부분의 사람이 고용하고 싶어 한다는 것을 / 자신과 똑 닮은 사람을

✔ This may have worked in the past, / but today, with interconnected team processes, / we don't want all people who are the same.
이것이 과거에는 효과가 있었을지도 모르지만, / 오늘날에는 상호 연결된 팀의 업무 과정으로 인해 / 우리는 전원이 똑같은 사람이기를 원치 않는다.

In a team, / some need to be leaders, / some need to be doers, / some need to

provide creative strengths, / some need to be inspirers, / some need to provide imagination, and so on.
팀 내에서 / 어떤 사람은 지도자일 필요가 있고, / 어떤 사람은 실행가일 필요가 있으며, / 어떤 사람은 창의적인 역량을 제공할 필요가 있고, / 어떤 사람은 사기를 불어넣는 사람일 필요가 있으며, / 어떤 사람은 상상력을 제공할 필요가 있다는 것 등이다.

③ In other words, / we are looking for a diversified team / where members complement one another.
달리 말하자면, / 우리는 다양화된 팀을 찾고 있다. / 구성원들이 서로를 보완해 주는

④ When putting together a new team / or hiring team members, / we need to look at each individual / and how he or she fits into the whole of our team objective.
새로운 팀을 짜거나 / 팀 구성원을 고용할 때 / 우리는 각 개인을 보고 / 그 사람이 어떻게 우리의 팀 목적 전반에 어울리는지 살펴볼 필요가 있다.

⑤ The bigger the team, / the more possibilities exist for diversity.
팀이 크면 클수록 / 다양해질 가능성이 더욱 더 많이 존재한다.

우리 대부분은 사장이 생각하기에 중요한 어떤 전문적인 정보 및 개인 정보와 더불어 인적 자원 기준에 근거하여 많은 사람을 고용해 왔다. ① 나는 대부분의 사람이 자신과 똑 닮은 사람을 고용하고 싶어 한다는 것을 알게 되었다. ② 이것이 과거에는 효과가 있었을지도 모르지만, 오늘날에는 상호 연결된 팀의 업무 과정으로 인해 우리는 전원이 똑같은 사람이기를 원치 않는다. 팀 내에서 어떤 사람은 지도자일 필요가 있고, 어떤 사람은 실행가일 필요가 있으며, 어떤 사람은 창의적인 역량을 제공할 필요가 있고, 어떤 사람은 사기를 불어넣는 사람일 필요가 있으며, 어떤 사람은 상상력을 제공할 필요가 있다는 것 등이다. ③ 달리 말하자면, 우리는 구성원들이 서로를 보완해 주는 다양화된 팀을 찾고 있다. ④ 새로운 팀을 짜거나 팀 구성원을 고용할 때 우리는 각 개인을 보고 그 사람이 어떻게 우리의 팀 목적 전반에 어울리는지 살펴볼 필요가 있다. ⑤ 팀이 크면 클수록 다양해질 가능성이 더욱더 많이 존재한다.

Why? 왜 정답일까?

팀의 구성원은 서로 똑같기보다 다양할 필요가 있다는 내용을 다룬 글이다. ② 앞의 문장에서 사람들 대부분은 자신과 비슷한 사람을 고용하고 싶어 한다는 내용을 말한 데 이어, 주어진 문장은 이 내용을 This로 받으며 과거에는 괜찮았지만 오늘날에는 우리가 팀 내 모든 사람들이 서로 똑같기를 원하지 않는다고 설명한다. ② 뒤의 문장에서는 한 팀 내에서 구성원들이 각기 다른 역할을 수행할 필요가 있음을 언급한다. 따라서 주어진 문장이 들어가기에 가장 적절한 곳은 ②이다.

- **interconnected** ⓐ 상호 연결된
- **human resource** 인적 자원, 인력
- **doer** ⓝ 실행가, 행동하는 사람
- **inspirer** ⓝ 격려하는 사람
- **complement** ⓥ 보완하다, 보충하다
- **fit into** ~에 꼭 들어맞다, 적응하다
- **exist** ⓥ 존재하다, 있다
- **process** ⓝ 과정
- **technical** ⓐ 전문적인, 기술적인
- **strength** ⓝ 힘, 기운
- **diversified** ⓐ 다양화된, 가지각색의
- **individual** ⓐ 각각의
- **objective** ⓝ 목표, 목적

구문 풀이

[14행] When putting together a new team or hiring team members,
분사구문1(~할 때) / 분사구문2
/ we need to look at each individual and {how he or she fits into the whole of our team objective}.
동사 / 목적어1 / { } : 목적어2(간접의문문)

★★ 문제 해결 꿀~팁 ★★

▶ 많이 틀린 이유는?
논리적 공백을 세밀하게 포착해야 올바른 답을 고를 수 있는 문제이다. 최다 오답인 ③ 앞뒤는 In other words로 연결되어, '한 팀 내에 각각 다른 역할을 하는 사람들이 있어야 한다 → 즉, 서로 보완하며 다양화된 팀이 되기를 추구한다'는 내용이 자연스럽게 이어진다.

▶ 문제 해결 방법은?
주어진 문장의 This가 가리키는 바를 정확히 이해해야 올바른 답을 낼 수 있다. 이 This는 '과거에는 통했지만 지금은 통하지 않는' 관행을 가리킨다. 따라서 '비슷한 사람들을 채용하고자 한다 vs. 구성원끼리 역할이 다를 필요가 있다'는 내용이 앞뒤로 대조되는 ②에 주어진 문장이 들어가야 한다.

★★★ 1등급 대비 고난도 2점 문제

| 09 | 심정지와 사망 선고 | 정답률 50% | 정답 ④ |

글의 흐름으로 보아, 주어진 문장이 들어가기에 가장 적절한 곳을 고르시오.

Traditionally, people were declared dead / when their hearts stopped beating, / their blood stopped circulating / and they stopped breathing.
전통적으로 사람들은 사망한 것으로 선고되었다. / 그들의 심장이 뛰는 것을 멈추고, / 혈액 순환이 멈추고, / 호흡이 멈출 때

① So doctors would listen for a heartbeat, / or occasionally conduct the famous mirror test / to see if there were any signs of moisture / from the potential deceased's breath.
그래서 의사들은 심장박동을 듣거나, / 이따금씩 유명한 거울검사를 실시하곤 했다. / 습기의 흔적이 있는지를 보기 위해 / 잠정적 사망자의 호흡에

② It is commonly known / that when people's hearts stop and they breathe their last, / they are dead.
흔히 알려져 있다. / 사람들은 심장이 멈추거나 마지막 호흡을 할 때 / 죽은 것이라는 사실은

③ But in the last half-century, / doctors have proved time and time again / that they can revive many patients / whose hearts have stopped beating / by various techniques such as cardiopulmonary resuscitation.
하지만 지난 반세기 동안 / 의사들은 거듭하여 입증해 왔다. / 많은 환자들을 소생시킬 수 있다는 것을 / 심장이 멎은 / 심폐소생술과 같은 여러 기술들로

✔ So a patient whose heart has stopped / can no longer be regarded as dead.
그래서 심장이 멎은 환자는 / 더 이상 사망한 것으로 간주될 수 없다.

Instead, the patient is said to be 'clinically dead'.
대신에 그 환자는 '임상적으로 사망한' 것으로 일컬어진다.

⑤ Someone who is only clinically dead / can often be brought back to life.
임상적으로 사망한 사람은 / 종종 소생될 수 있다.

전통적으로 사람들은 심장이 뛰는 것을 멈추고, 혈액 순환이 멈추고, 호흡이 멈출 때, 사망한 것으로 선고되었다. ① 그래서 의사들은 심장박동을 듣거나, 잠정적 사망자의 호흡에 습기의 흔적이 있는지를 보기 위해 이따금씩 유명한 거울검사를 실시하곤 했다. ② 사람들은 심장이 멈추거나 마지막 호흡을 할 때 죽은 것이라는 사실은 흔히 알려져 있다. ③ 하지만 지난 반세기 동안 의사들은 심폐소생술과 같은 여러 기술들로 심장이 멎은 많은 환자들을 소생시킬 수 있다는 것을 거듭하여 입증해 왔다. ④ 그래서 심장이 멎은 환자는 더 이상 사망한 것으로 간주될 수 없다. 대신에 그 환자는 '임상적으로 사망한' 것으로 일컬어진다. ⑤ 임상적으로 사망한 사람은 종종 소생될 수 있다.

Why? 왜 정답일까?

전통적으로 심정지는 사망 선고의 시점과 연관되었지만 의술이 발달한 오늘날 심정지는 '임상적 사망'의 근거가 된다 하더라도 완전한 사망과 동일시되지 않는다는 내용을 다룬 글이다. ④ 앞의 문장에서 의사들은 심장이 멎은 환자들도 여러 기술로 살려낼 수 있게 되었다는 내용을 다룬 데 이어, 주어진 문장은 '그래서' 심정지 환자들이 사망자로 간주될 수 없다는 내용을 제시하고 있다. ④ 뒤에서는 '대신에' 심정지 환자들이 종종 소생할 가능성이 있는 임상적 사망자로 여겨진다는 내용을 이어간다. 따라서 주어진 문장이 들어가기에 가장 적절한 곳은 ④이다.

- regard ⓥ 간주하다, 여기다
- declare ⓥ 선언하다
- occasionally ⓐⓓ 이따금씩, 종종
- clinically ⓐⓓ 임상적으로
- traditionally ⓐⓓ 전통적으로
- circulate ⓥ 순환하다, 돌다
- deceased ⓐ 사망한, 죽은, 돌아가신
- bring back to life 소생시키다, 되살리다

구문 풀이

5행 So doctors would listen for a heartbeat, or occasionally
~하곤 했다 └동사원형1 →~인지 아닌지
conduct the famous mirror test / to see if there were any signs of
동사원형2 ~하기 위해 동사(복수) 주어
moisture from the potential deceased's breath.

★★ 문제 해결 꿀~팁 ★★

▶ 많이 틀린 이유는?
최다 오답인 ③은 앞뒤로 '과거: 심정지 = 사망 vs. 오늘날: 심정지 ≠ 완전한 사망'의 내용이 서로 대조되는데 이 사이에 So로 시작하는 주어진 문장이 들어가기는 부적절하다.

▶ 문제 해결 방법은?
So는 크게 보아 역접이 아닌 순접의 연결어이므로, 주어진 문장 앞은 주어진 문장과 마찬가지로 심정지가 곧 완전한 사망으로 이어지는 것이 아니라는 내용을 언급하고 있어야 한다.

★★★ 1등급 대비 고난도 2점 문제

| 10 | 이상 사회를 설명해주는 캠핑 여행의 비유 | 정답률 31% | 정답 ④ |

글의 흐름으로 보아, 주어진 문장이 들어가기에 가장 적절한 곳을 고르시오.

The philosopher G. A. Cohen / provides an example of a camping trip / as a metaphor for the ideal society.
철학자 G. A. Cohen은 / 캠핑 여행을 예로 제시한다. / 이상적인 사회에 대한 비유로

① On a camping trip, / he argues, / it is unimaginable / that someone would say something like, / "I cooked the dinner / and therefore you can't eat it / unless you pay me for my superior cooking skills."
캠핑 여행에서, / 그는 주장한다. / 상상할 수 없다고 / 어떤 사람이 말하는 것은 / "내가 저녁 식사를 준비했으니 / 저녁을 먹을 수 없어, / 나의 뛰어난 요리 솜씨에 대해 네가 나에게 돈을 지불하지 않으면"이라고

② Rather, one person cooks dinner, / another sets up the tent, / another purifies the water, and so on, / each in accordance with his or her abilities.
오히려, 한 사람은 저녁 식사를 준비하고, / 다른 사람은 텐트를 치고, / 또 다른 사람은 물을 정화하는 등, / 각자는 자신의 능력에 맞추어 일한다.

③ All these goods are shared / and a spirit of community makes all participants happier.
이 모든 재화들은 공유되며, / 공동체 의식은 모든 참여자들을 더 행복하게 만든다.

✔ A camping trip / where each person attempted to gain the maximum rewards / from the other campers / in exchange for the use of his or her talents / would quickly end in disaster and unhappiness.
캠핑 여행은 / 각자 최대의 보상을 얻으려고 하는 / 다른 야영객으로부터 / 자신의 재능을 사용하는 대가로 / 곧 재앙과 불행으로 끝날 것이다.

Moreover, the experience would be ruined / if people were to behave in such a way.
게다가 캠핑 경험은 망쳐질 것이다. / 사람들이 그런 식으로 행동한다면

⑤ So, we would have a better life / in a more equal and cooperative society.
그래서 우리는 더 나은 삶을 살게 될 것이다. / 더 평등하고 협력하는 사회에서

철학자 G. A. Cohen은 이상적인 사회에 대한 비유로 캠핑 여행을 예로 제시한다. ① 그는 캠핑 여행에서, 어떤 사람이 "내가 저녁 식사를 준비했으니 나의 뛰어난 요리 솜씨에 대해 네가 나에게 돈을 지불하지 않으면 저녁을 먹을 수 없어."라고 말하는 것은 상상할 수 없다고 주장한다. ② 오히려, 한 사람은 저녁 식사를 준비하고, 다른 사람은 텐트를 치고, 또 다른 사람은 물을 정화하는 등, 각자는 자신의 능력에 맞추어 일한다. ③ 이 모든 재화들은 공유되며, 공동체 의식은 모든 참여자들을 더 행복하게 만든다. ④ 각자 자신의 재능을 사용하는 대가로 다른 야영객으로부터 최대의 보상을 얻으려고 하는 캠핑 여행은 곧 재앙과 불행으로 끝날 것이다. 게다가 사람들이 그런 식으로 행동한다면 캠핑 경험은 망쳐질 것이다. ⑤ 그래서 더 평등하고 협력하는 사회에서 우리는 더 나은 삶을 살게 될 것이다.

Why? 왜 정답일까?

모두가 각기 능력에 맞는 역할을 맡아 조화롭게 일하고 자원을 공유하는 캠핑 여행의 예를 들어 협력적인 이상 사회의 모습을 설명한 글이다. ④ 앞의 문장에서 모든 사람들의 공동 재화 및 공동체 의식은 행복한 캠핑을 만든다고 언급한 데 이어, 주어진 문장에서는 만일 여기에 '대가'를 바라는 마음이 끼어든다면 캠핑이 재앙과 불행으로 끝나게 되리라는 점을 지적하고 있다. ④ 뒤에서는 주어진 문장에 이어 '그러한' 경우 캠핑이 망쳐질 수 있다고 이야기한다. 따라서 주어진 문장이 들어가기에 가장 적절한 곳은 ④이다.

- attempt ⓥ 시도하다, 애써 해보다
- philosopher ⓝ 철학자
- unimaginable ⓐ 상상할 수 없는
- rather ⓐⓓ 오히려
- in accordance with ~에 맞추어
- participant ⓝ 참여자, 참가자
- ruin ⓥ 망치다
- in exchange for ~의 대가로
- ideal ⓐ 이상적인
- superior ⓐ 뛰어난
- purify ⓥ 정화하다
- a spirit of community 공동체 의식
- experience ⓝ 경험
- behave ⓥ 행동하다

구문 풀이

1행 A camping trip [where each person attempted to gain the
주어 관계부사 ~하려고 시도하다
maximum rewards from the other campers in exchange for the use
~의 대가로
of his or her talents] would quickly end in disaster and unhappiness.
동사구(~로 끝나다)

★★ 문제 해결 꿀~팁 ★★

▶ 많이 틀린 이유는?
캠핑과 협력적인 이상 사회라는, 겉으로 보기에는 무관해 보이는 두 개념을 연결시킨 추상적인 글이다. 최다 오답은 ②였는데, 여기에 주어진 문장을 넣어 앞뒤 맥락을 읽어보면 '서로에게 대가를 기대하면 캠핑이 불행해진다 → 각자는 능력에 맞게 일한다'는 연결이 부자연스럽다.

▶ 문제 해결 방법은?
주어진 문장은 주로 흐름이 반전되는 포인트에 위치한다. 여기서도 정답인 ④ 앞뒤로

주어진 문장 없이 내용을 읽어보면 '협력 = 행복한 캠핑 vs. 대가를 기대하는 마음 = 불행한 캠핑'과 같이 상반되는 내용이 전개된다.

3행 Boundaries between work and home are blurring as portable digital technology makes it increasingly possible to work anywhere, anytime.
(가목적어 / 접속사(~ 때문에) / 5형식 동사 / 목적격 보어 / 진목적어)

★★★ 1등급 대비 고난도 3점 문제

11 일과 가정의 경계 　　　　정답률 26% | 정답 ⑤

글의 흐름으로 보아, 주어진 문장이 들어가기에 가장 적절한 곳을 고르시오. [3점]

Boundaries between work and home / are blurring / as portable digital technology makes it increasingly possible / to work anywhere, anytime.
직장과 가정의 경계가 / 흐릿해지고 있다. / 휴대용 디지털 기술이 점차 가능하게 하면서, / 언제 어디서든 작업하는 것을

Individuals differ / in how they like to manage their time / to meet work and outside responsibilities.
사람들은 서로 다르다. / 자기 시간을 관리하기를 바라는 방식에 있어서 / 직장과 외부의 책임을 수행하기 위해

① Some people prefer to separate or segment roles / so that boundary crossings are minimized.
어떤 사람들은 역할을 분리하거나 분할하기를 선호한다. / 경계 교차 지점이 최소화되도록

② For example, / these people might keep separate email accounts / for work and family / and try to conduct work at the workplace / and take care of family matters / only during breaks and non-work time.
예를 들어, / 이러한 사람들은 별개의 이메일 계정을 유지하고 / 직장과 가정을 위한 / 직장에서 일하려고 하며, / 집안일을 처리하려고 할지도 모른다 / 쉴 때나 일하지 않는 시간 중에만

③ We've even noticed / more of these "segmenters" / carrying two phones / — one for work and one for personal use.
우리는 심지어 알게 되었다. / 더 많은 이러한 '분할자들'이 / 전화기 두 대를 가지고 다니고 있음을 / 하나는 업무용이고 다른 하나는 개인용인

④ Flexible schedules work well for these individuals / because they enable greater distinction / between time at work and time in other roles.
유연근무제는 이런 사람들에게 잘 적용되는데, / 이것은 더 큰 구별을 가능하게 하기 때문이다. / 직장에서의 시간과 다른 역할에서의 시간 간에

✔ Other individuals prefer / integrating work and family roles all day long.
다른 사람들은 선호한다. / 하루 종일 직장과 가정의 역할을 통합하기를

This might entail / constantly trading text messages with children from the office, / or monitoring emails at home and on vacation, / rather than returning to work to find hundreds of messages in their inbox.
이것은 수반할 수도 있다. / 사무실에서 아이들과 문자 메시지를 계속 주고받는 것을 / 혹은 집에 있을 때나 휴가 중에 이메일을 체크하는 것을 / 직장으로 돌아가서 받은 편지함에서 수백 개의 메시지를 발견하는 대신

휴대용 디지털 기술이 언제 어디서든 작업하는 것을 점차 가능하게 하면서, 직장과 가정의 경계가 흐릿해지고 있다. 사람들은 직장과 외부의 책임을 수행하기 위해 자기 시간을 관리하기를 바라는 방식이 서로 다르다. ① 어떤 사람들은 경계 교차 지점이 최소화되도록 역할을 분리하거나 분할하기를 선호한다. ② 예를 들어, 이러한 사람들은 직장과 가정을 위한 별개의 이메일 계정을 유지하고 직장에서 일하려고 하며, 쉴 때나 일하지 않는 시간 중에만 집안일을 처리하려고 할지도 모른다. ③ 우리는 더 많은 이러한 '분할자들'이 하나는 업무용이고 다른 하나는 개인용인 전화기 두 대를 가지고 다니고 있음을 심지어 알게 되었다. ④ 유연근무제는 이런 사람들에게 잘 적용되는데, 직장에서의 시간과 다른 역할에서의 시간 간에 더 큰 구별을 가능하게 하기 때문이다. ⑤ 다른 사람들은 하루 종일 직장과 가정의 역할을 통합하기를 선호한다. 이것은 직장으로 돌아가서 받은 편지함에서 수백 개의 메시지를 발견하는 대신, 사무실에서 아이들과 문자 메시지를 계속 주고받거나, 집에 있을 때나 휴가 중에 이메일을 체크하는 것을 수반할 수도 있다.

Why? 왜 정답일까?

⑤ 앞까지 일과 가정을 '분리하는' 사람들을 언급하는데, ⑤ 뒤에는 직장에서도 가족들과 연락하고, 집에 있을 때도 업무 처리를 하는 등 둘을 '통합하는' 사람들을 언급하고 있다. 따라서 '통합자들'에 관한 화제로 처음 넘어가는 주어진 문장이 들어가기에 가장 적절한 곳은 ⑤이다.

- integrate ⓥ 통합하다
- boundary ⓝ 경계
- outside ⓐ 외부의
- separate ⓥ 분리하다 ⓐ 분리된, 개별의
- minimize ⓥ 최소화하다
- conduct ⓥ 수행하다
- carry ⓥ 들고 다니다
- distinction ⓝ 구별
- constantly 〔ad〕 계속
- on vacation 휴가 중인

- all day long 하루 종일
- portable ⓐ 휴대용의
- responsibility ⓝ 책무, 책임
- segment ⓥ 분할하다, 나누다
- account ⓝ 계정
- workplace ⓝ 직장
- flexible schedule 유연근무제
- entail ⓥ 수반하다
- monitor ⓥ 확인하다, 감독하다, 점검하다
- inbox ⓝ 수신함

★★ 문제 해결 꿀~팁 ★★

▶ 많이 틀린 이유는?
주어진 문장이 Other로 시작하므로, 앞에 Some이 있는 ②를 고르기 쉽다. 「Some ~ Other …」의 대구가 자연스러워 보이기 때문이다. 하지만 ② 뒤의 these people이 문맥상 앞의 Some people이므로, 주어진 문장을 ②에 넣어 대명사의 흐름을 끊으면 안 된다. 또한 뒤에 갑자기 '유연근무제'라는 새로운 소재가 등장하는 ④도 정답처럼 보이기 쉽지만, ④ 앞뒤가 여전히 '일과 가정을 분리하는' 사람들에 대해서 설명하고 있어서 흐름이 끊기지 않기 때문에 다른 문장이 필요하지 않다.

▶ 문제 해결 방법은?
⑤ 뒤의 'trading ~ or monitoring ~'이 주어진 문장의 'integrating ~'에 대한 예시임을 파악해야 한다.

★★★ 1등급 대비 고난도 3점 문제

12 농업 체제의 변화 　　　　정답률 43% | 정답 ③

글의 흐름으로 보아, 주어진 문장이 들어가기에 가장 적절한 곳을 고르시오. [3점]

Earlier agricultural systems / were integrated with and co-evolved with technologies, beliefs, myths and traditions / as part of an integrated social system.
초기의 농업 시스템은 / 기술, 신념, 신화 그리고 전통과 통합되고 함께 발전했다. / 통합된 사회 시스템의 일부로서

① Generally, / people planted a variety of crops in different areas, / in the hope of obtaining a reasonably stable food supply.
일반적으로 / 사람들은 여러 지역에 다양한 작물을 심었다. / 상당히 안정적인 식량 공급을 얻기를 기대하며

② These systems could only be maintained at low population levels, / and were relatively non-destructive (but not always).
이 시스템은 낮은 인구 수준에서만 유지될 수 있었고, / 비교적 파괴적이지 않았다(항상 그런 것은 아니지만).

✔ More recently, / agriculture has in many places lost its local character, / and has become incorporated into the global economy.
더 최근에는 / 농업이 많은 곳에서 그 지역적 특성을 잃고 / 세계 경제에 통합되어 왔다.

This has led to increased pressure on agricultural land / for exchange commodities and export goods.
이로 인해 농경지에 대한 압력이 증가하게 되었다. / 교환 상품과 수출 상품을 위한

④ More land is being diverted / from local food production / to "cash crops" / for export and exchange; / fewer types of crops are raised, / and each crop is raised in much greater quantities than before.
더 많은 땅이 전환되고 있는데, / 지역 식량 생산에서 / '환금 작물'로 / 수출과 교환을 위한 / 더 적은 종류의 작물이 재배되고, / 각 작물은 이전보다 훨씬 더 많은 양으로 재배된다.

⑤ Thus, / ever more land is converted from forest (and other natural systems) / for agriculture for export, / rather than using land for subsistence crops.
따라서 / 어느 때보다 더 많은 토지가 산림(그리고 다른 자연 시스템)으로부터 전환된다. / 수출을 위한 농업을 위해 / 자급자족용 작물을 위해 땅을 사용하기보다는

초기의 농업 시스템은 통합된 사회 시스템의 일부로서 기술, 신념, 신화 그리고 전통과 통합되고 함께 발전했다. ① 일반적으로 사람들은 상당히 안정적인 식량 공급을 얻기를 기대하며 여러 지역에 다양한 작물을 심었다. ② 이 시스템은 낮은 인구 수준에서만 유지될 수 있었고, 비교적 파괴적이지 않았다(항상 그런 것은 아니지만). ③ 더 최근에는 농업이 많은 곳에서 그 지역적 특성을 잃고 세계 경제에 통합되어 왔다. 이로 인해 교환 상품과 수출 상품을 위한 농경지에 대한 압력이 증가하게 되었다. ④ 더 많은 땅이 지역 식량 생산에서 수출과 교환을 위한 '환금 작물'로 전환되고 있는데, 더 적은 종류의 작물이 재배되고, 각 작물은 이전보다 훨씬 더 많은 양으로 재배된다. ⑤ 따라서 자급자족용 작물을 위해 땅을 사용하기보다는, 수출을 위한 농업을 위해 어느 때보다 더 많은 토지가 산림(그리고 다른 자연 시스템)으로부터 전환된다.

Why? 왜 정답일까?

③ 앞에서 초기의 농업 시스템은 사회 시스템의 일부로 여러 다른 체계와 통합되어 발전하면서 식량 공급을 주 목적으로 했고 파괴성이 덜했다고 설명한다. 이어서 More recently로 시작하는 주어진 문장은 '더 최근'의 시점으로 넘어와 농업은 지역적 특성을

잃고 세계 경제에 통합되어 왔다는 사실을 제시한다. ③ 뒤에서는 주어진 문장과 같은 상황이 되었기 때문에 교환 상품이나 수출 상품을 재배할 농경지가 더 많이 필요해졌고, 재배되는 작물의 종류는 줄어들었으며, 환금 작물 중심의 농업이 이루어지고 있다는 내용이 이어진다. 따라서 주어진 문장이 들어가기에 가장 적절한 곳은 ③이다.

- agriculture ⓝ 농업
- integrate ⓥ 통합하다
- stable ⓐ 안정적인
- commodity ⓝ 상품
- convert ⓥ 전환하다, 개조하다
- incorporate A into B A를 B에 통합시키다
- in the hope of ~라는 희망으로
- non-destructive ⓐ 파괴적이지 않은
- divert ⓥ 전환시키다, 다른 데로 돌리다

구문 풀이

14행 More land is being diverted from local food production to
주어 / 동사(현재진행 수동태) / 「from+A+to+B : A에서 B로」
"cash crops" for export and exchange; fewer types of crops are raised,
and each crop is raised in much greater quantities than before.
주어2 / 동사2 / 비교급 수식 부사 / 주어1 / 동사1 / 비교급 형용사

★★ 문제 해결 꿀~팁 ★★

▶ **많이 틀린 이유는?**
농경 변천에 관한 글로, 흐름을 잘 파악해야 한다. 최다 오답인 ④ 앞에서 교환 및 수출 작물용 농경지에 대한 압박이 커졌다고 하는데, ④ 뒤에서는 이를 '환금 작물'이라는 용어로 바꾸며 식량보다는 무역 수익을 위한 농경이 많이 이루어지는 상황임을 설명하고 있다. 즉 ④ 앞뒤로 흐름 전환이나 논리적 공백이 발생하지 않으므로 ④에 주어진 문장을 넣을 필요가 없다.

▶ **문제 해결 방법은?**
③ 앞에서 초기 농업은 안정적 식량 확보를 주된 목적으로 했다고 설명하는데, ③ 뒤에서는 '이로 인해' 교환 작물 또는 수출 작물을 키워야 한다는 압력이 커진다고 언급한다. 두 내용은 서로 상충하므로, ③에 '최근의 농업' 이야기로 흐름을 전환하는 문장이 들어가야 함을 알 수 있다.

DAY 19 문장 삽입 04

01 ④	02 ⑤	03 ③	04 ④	05 ⑤
06 ③	07 ⑤	08 ④	09 ②	10 ②
11 ⑤	12 ④			

01 마찰력의 특징 　　　정답률 73% | 정답 ④

글의 흐름으로 보아, 주어진 문장이 들어가기에 가장 적절한 곳을 고르시오.

Friction is a force / between two surfaces / that are sliding, or trying to slide, / across each other.
마찰력은 힘이다. / 두 표면 사이에 작용하는 / 미끄러지거나 미끄러지려고 하는 / 서로 엇갈리게

For example, / when you try to push a book along the floor, / friction makes this difficult.
예를 들어, / 당신이 바닥 위 책을 밀려고 할 때, / 마찰이 이를 어렵게 만든다.

Friction always works in the direction / opposite to the direction / in which the object is moving, or trying to move.
마찰은 항상 방향으로 작용한다. / 방향과 반대인 / 물체가 움직이거나 움직이려고 하는

So, friction always slows a moving object down.
그래서 마찰은 항상 움직이는 물체를 느리게 만든다.

① The amount of friction depends on the surface materials.
마찰의 양은 표면 물질에 따라 달라진다.

② The rougher the surface is, / the more friction is produced.
표면이 거칠수록 / 더 많은 마찰력이 발생한다.

③ Friction also produces heat.
마찰은 또한 열을 발생시킨다.

✔ For example, / if you rub your hands together quickly, / they will get warmer.
예를 들어, / 만약 당신이 손을 빠르게 비비면, / 손이 더 따뜻해질 것이다.

Friction can be a useful force / because it prevents our shoes slipping on the floor / when we walk / and stops car tires skidding on the road.
마찰력은 유용한 힘으로 작용할 수 있다. / 그것이 신발이 바닥에서 미끄러지는 것을 방지하고 / 우리가 걸을 때 / 자동차 타이어가 도로에서 미끄러지는 것을 막아주므로

⑤ When you walk, / friction is caused / between the tread on your shoes and the ground, / acting to grip the ground and prevent sliding.
당신이 걸을 때, / 마찰은 발생하며, / 당신의 신발 접지면과 바닥 사이에 / 땅을 붙잡아 미끄러지는 것을 방지하는 역할을 한다.

마찰력은 서로 엇갈리게 미끄러지거나 미끄러지려고 하는 두 표면 사이에 작용하는 힘이다. 예를 들어, 당신이 바닥 위 책을 밀려고 할 때, 마찰이 이를 어렵게 만든다. 마찰은 항상 물체가 움직이거나 움직이려고 하는 방향과 반대 방향으로 작용한다. 그래서 마찰은 항상 움직이는 물체를 느려지게 만든다. ① 마찰의 양은 표면 물질에 따라 달라진다. ② 표면이 거칠수록 더 많은 마찰력이 발생한다. ③ 마찰은 또한 열을 발생시킨다. ④ 예를 들어, 만약 당신이 손을 빠르게 비비면, 손이 더 따뜻해질 것이다. 마찰력은 우리가 걸을 때 신발이 바닥에서 미끄러지는 것을 방지하고 자동차 타이어가 도로에서 미끄러지는 것을 막아주므로 유용한 힘이 될 수 있다. ⑤ 걸을 때, 마찰은 당신의 신발 접지면과 바닥 사이에 발생하여 땅을 붙잡아 미끄러지는 것을 방지하는 역할을 한다.

Why? 왜 정답일까?

주어진 문장은 마찰과 열을 관련지어 설명하고 있으므로, 앞에 열에 관한 내용이 언급된 후 예시(For example)로 이어질 수 있다. 글에서 열에 관해 언급하는 문장은 ④ 앞의 문장이므로, 주어진 문장이 들어가기에 가장 적절한 곳은 ④이다.

- rub ⓥ 문지르다
- surface ⓝ 표면
- slow down ~을 느려지게 하다
- slip ⓥ 미끄러지다
- friction ⓝ 마찰
- opposite ⓐ 반대의
- rough ⓐ 거친
- grip ⓥ 붙잡다

구문 풀이

10행 The rougher the surface is, the more friction is produced.
「the+비교급 ~, the+비교급 … : ~할수록 더 …하다」

02 첫인상의 중요성 　　　정답률 39% | 정답 ⑤

글의 흐름으로 보아, 주어진 문장이 들어가기에 가장 적절한 곳을 고르시오.

You've probably heard the expression, / "first impressions matter a lot".
여러분은 아마도 표현을 들어본 적이 있을 것이다. / '첫인상이 매우 중요하다'라는
① Life really doesn't give many people a second chance / to make a good first impression.
삶은 실제로 많은 사람들에게 두 번째 기회를 주지 않는다. / 좋은 첫인상을 만들
② It has been determined / that it takes only a few seconds / for anyone to assess another individual.
밝혀져 왔다. / 단지 몇 초만 걸린다는 것이 / 누군가가 또 다른 개인을 평가하는 데
③ This is very noticeable in recruitment processes, / where top recruiters can predict the direction / of their eventual decision on any candidate / within a few seconds of introducing themselves.
이것은 채용 과정에서 매우 두드러지는데, / 최고의 모집자는 방향을 예측할 수 있다. / 어떤 지원자에 대한 자신의 최종 결정의 / 그들이 자신을 소개하는 몇 초 안에
④ So, a candidate's CV may 'speak' knowledge and competence, / but their appearance and introduction / may tell of a lack of coordination, fear, and poor interpersonal skills.
따라서 후보자의 이력서가 지식과 능력을 '진술'할지도 모르지만, / 그들의 외모와 소개는 / 신체 조정 능력의 부족, 불안, 그리고 형편없는 대인 관계 기술을 알려줄지도 모른다.
✔ In this way, / quick judgements are not only relevant in employment matters; / they are equally applicable / in love and relationship matters too.
이런 식으로 / 빠른 판단들이 단지 채용 문제에만 관련된 것은 아니며 / 이것들은 똑같이 적용된다. / 또한 사랑과 관계 문제에도
On a date with a wonderful somebody / who you've painstakingly tracked down for months, / subtle things like bad breath or wrinkled clothes / may spoil your noble efforts.
멋진 누군가와의 데이트에서, / 여러분이 몇 달간 공들여 쫓아다닌 / 입 냄새 또는 구겨진 옷과 같은 미묘한 것들이 / 여러분의 숭고한 노력을 망칠지도 모른다.

여러분은 아마도 '첫인상이 매우 중요하다'라는 표현을 들어본 적이 있을 것이다. ① 삶은 실제로 많은 사람들에게 좋은 첫인상을 만들 두 번째 기회를 주지 않는다. ② 누군가가 또 다른 개인을 평가하는 데 단지 몇 초만 걸린다는 것이 밝혀져 왔다. ③ 이것은 채용 과정에서 매우 두드러지는데, 채용 과정에서 최고의 모집자는 (지원자가) 자신을 소개하는 몇 초 안에 지원자에 대한 자신의 최종 결정의 방향을 예측할 수 있다. ④ 따라서 후보자의 이력서가 지식과 능력을 '진술'할지도 모르지만, 그들의 외모와 소개는 신체 조정 능력의 부족, 불안, 그리고 형편없는 대인 관계 기술을 알려줄지도 모른다. ⑤ 이런 식으로 빠른 판단들은 단지 채용 문제에만 관련된 것은 아니며 또한 사랑과 관계 문제에도 똑같이 적용된다. 여러분이 몇 달간 공들여 쫓아다닌 멋진 누군가와의 데이트에서, 입 냄새 또는 구겨진 옷과 같은 미묘한 것들이 여러분의 숭고한 노력을 망칠지도 모른다.

Why? 왜 정답일까?

⑤ 앞에서 채용 과정을 예로 들어 첫인상의 중요성을 주로 설명한 데 이어, 주어진 문장은 첫인상의 문제가 사랑이나 관계 문제에도 마찬가지로 적용될 수 있다고 한다. ⑤ 뒤의 문장은 데이트 상황에서 첫인상을 망치게 되면 몇 달간의 노력이 허사가 될 수도 있다는 설명으로 주어진 문장의 내용을 보충한다. 따라서 주어진 문장이 들어가기에 가장 적절한 곳은 ⑤이다.

- relevant ⓐ 관련 있는, 적절한
- assess ⓥ 평가하다
- recruitment ⓝ 채용, 모집
- eventual ⓐ 최종의, 궁극적인
- competence ⓝ 능력, 역량
- coordination ⓝ (신체 동작의) 조정력
- painstakingly ⓐⓓ 공들여, 힘들여
- spoil ⓥ 망치다
- applicable ⓐ 적용 가능한
- noticeable ⓐ 두드러지는, 눈에 띄는
- predict ⓥ 예측하다
- candidate ⓝ 지원자, 후보자
- tell of ⓥ ~을 알려주다
- interpersonal ⓐ 대인 관계의
- subtle ⓐ 미묘한, 감지하기 힘든

구문 풀이

16행 On a date with a wonderful somebody [who(m) you've
　　　　　　　　　　선행사　　　　　　　목적격 관계대명사
painstakingly tracked down for months], subtle things like bad breath
　　　　　　　　　　　　　　　　　　　　　　　　　주어
or wrinkled clothes may spoil your noble efforts.
　　　　　　　　　　　동사

---

03 수면을 대체할 수 없는 카페인　　　정답률 66% | 정답 ③

글의 흐름으로 보아, 주어진 문장이 들어가기에 가장 적절한 곳을 고르시오.

Studies have consistently shown / caffeine to be effective / when used together with a pain reliever / to treat headaches.
연구는 지속적으로 밝혀왔다. / 카페인이 효과가 있다는 것을 / 진통제와 함께 사용할 때 / 두통 치료 목적으로

---

① The positive correlation / between caffeine intake / and staying alert throughout the day / has also been well established.
양의 상관관계가 / 카페인 섭취와 / 하루 종일 각성 상태를 유지하는 것 사이에는 / 또한 잘 확립되어 있다.
② As little as 60 mg / (the amount typically in one cup of tea) / can lead to a faster reaction time.
60mg만큼의 적은 양으로도 / (일반적으로 차 한 잔에 들어 있는 양) / 반응 시간이 빨라질 수 있다.
✔ However, / using caffeine to improve alertness and mental performance / doesn't replace getting a good night's sleep.
하지만, / 각성과 정신적 수행능력을 향상시키기 위해 카페인을 사용하는 것은 / 숙면을 취하는 것을 대체하지 못한다.
One study from 2018 showed / that coffee improved reaction times / in those with or without poor sleep, / but caffeine seemed to increase errors / in the group with little sleep.
2018년 한 연구는 보여주었다. / 커피는 반응 시간은 개선시켰지만, / 수면이 부족한 사람이나 부족하지 않은 사람에게나 / 카페인은 오류를 증가시키는 듯 하다는 것을 / 수면이 부족한 집단 내에서는
④ Additionally, / this study showed / that even with caffeine, / the group with little sleep did not score as well / as those with adequate sleep.
게다가, / 이 연구는 보여주었다. / 카페인을 섭취하더라도, / 수면이 부족한 그룹은 점수를 잘 받지 못했다는 것을 / 충분한 수면을 취한 집단만큼
⑤ It suggests / that caffeine does not fully make up for inadequate sleep.
이는 보여준다. / 카페인이 불충분한 수면을 충분히 보충하지 못한다는 것을

연구에서 지속적으로 밝히기로는 카페인을 두통 치료 목적으로 진통제와 함께 사용할 때 효과가 있다. ① 또한 카페인 섭취와 하루 종일 각성 상태를 유지하는 것 사이에는 양의 상관관계가 잘 확립되어 있다. ② 60mg(일반적으로 차 한 잔에 들어 있는 양)만큼의 적은 양으로도 반응 시간이 빨라질 수 있다. ③ 하지만, 각성과 정신적 수행능력을 향상시키기 위해 카페인을 사용하는 것은 숙면을 취하는 것을 대체하지 못한다. 2018년 한 연구가 밝히기로 커피는 수면이 부족한 사람이나 부족하지 않은 사람에게나 반응 시간은 개선시켰지만, 카페인은 수면이 부족한 집단 내에서는 오류를 증가시키는 듯 하다. ④ 게다가, 이 연구는 카페인을 섭취하더라도, 수면이 부족한 그룹은 충분한 수면을 취한 집단만큼 점수를 잘 받지 못했다는 것을 보여주었다. ⑤ 이는 카페인이 불충분한 수면을 충분히 보충하지 못한다는 것을 보여준다.

Why? 왜 정답일까?

③ 앞뒤로 글의 흐름이 반전되고 있다. ③ 앞에서 카페인 섭취와 각성 상태 사이에는 양의 상관관계가 있으며, 차 한 잔에 들어있는 양만큼 마셔도 우리의 반응 시간이 빨라진다는 내용이 제시된다. 하지만 ③ 뒤에는 수면이 부족한 집단에 카페인을 주었을 때 오류가 증가되는 것 같다고 한다. 이러한 맥락으로 보아, However로 시작하여 흐름을 반전시킬 수 있는 주어진 문장이 들어가기에 가장 적절한 곳은 ③이다.

- improve ⓥ 향상시키다, 개선하다
- get a good night's sleep 숙면하다
- pain reliever 진통제
- additionally ⓐⓓ 게다가
- inadequate ⓐ 불충분한
- alertness ⓝ 각성 상태, 기민함
- consistently ⓐⓓ 지속적으로, 일관되게
- established ⓐ 확립된
- make up for ~을 보상하다

구문 풀이

3행 Studies have consistently shown caffeine to be effective
　　　　　　　　　　　　　　동사　　　　　　목적어　　목적격 보어
when (it is) used together with a pain reliever to treat headaches.
접속사　생략　과거분사　　　　　　　　　　　　　　　　　부사적 용법(목적)

---

04 공룡과 용의 중요한 차이　　　정답률 61% | 정답 ④

글의 흐름으로 보아, 주어진 문장이 들어가기에 가장 적절한 곳을 고르시오.

When I was very young, / I had a difficulty telling the difference / between dinosaurs and dragons.
내가 아주 어렸을 때 / 나는 차이를 구별하는 데 어려움이 있었다. / 공룡과 용의
① But there is a significant difference between them.
그러나 그들 사이에는 중요한 차이가 있다.
② Dragons appear in Greek myths, / legends about England's King Arthur, / Chinese New Year parades, / and in many tales throughout human history.
용은 그리스 신화에 등장한다. / 영국 Arthur 왕의 전설, / 중국의 새해 행렬, / 그리고 인류 역사에 걸친 많은 이야기에
③ But even if they feature in stories created today, / they have always been the products of the human imagination / and never existed.
그러나 비록 그들이 오늘날 만들어진 이야기에서 중요한 역할을 한다 해도, / 그들은 항상 인간 상상의 산물이었으며 / 결코 존재하지 않았다.
✔ Dinosaurs, however, did once live.
하지만 공룡은 한때 실제로 살았다.

They walked the earth for a very long time, / even if human beings never saw them.
그들은 오랫동안 지구에 살았다. / 비록 인간이 그들을 보지는 못했지만

⑤ They existed around 200 million years ago, / and we know about them / because their bones have been preserved as fossils.
그들은 2억 년 쯤 전에 존재했고 / 우리는 그들에 대해 알고 있다 / 그 뼈가 화석으로 보존되어 있기 때문에

나는 아주 어렸을 때 공룡과 용의 차이를 구별하는 데 어려움이 있었다. ① 그러나 그들 사이에는 중요한 차이가 있다. ② 용은 그리스 신화, 영국 Arthur 왕의 전설, 중국의 새해 행렬, 그리고 인류 역사에 걸친 많은 이야기에 등장한다. ③ 그러나 그들은 비록 오늘날 만들어진 이야기에서 중요한 역할을 한다 해도, 항상 인간 상상의 산물이었으며 결코 존재하지 않았다. ④ 하지만 공룡은 한때 실제로 살았다. 비록 인간이 그들을 보지는 못했지만, 그들은 오랫동안 지구에 살았다. ⑤ 그들은 2억 년 쯤 전에 존재했고 그 뼈가 화석으로 보존되어 있기 때문에 우리는 그들에 대해 알고 있다.

Why? 왜 정답일까?
공룡과 용의 차이를 설명한 글이다. ④ 앞의 문장에서 비록 용은 많은 인간의 이야기에 등장했지만 실재한 적은 없다고 말한 데 이어, 주어진 문장에서는 '이와는 반대로' 공룡의 경우에는 실제로 존재한 적이 있음을 언급한다. ④ 뒤에서는 인간이 비록 공룡을 본 적이 없다 하더라도 그들이 실재했다는 것은 사실임을 부연하고 있다. 따라서 주어진 문장이 들어가기에 가장 적절한 곳은 ④이다.

- **tell the difference** 차이를 구별하다
- **significant** ⓐ 중요한, 상당한, 유의미한
- **tale** ⓝ 이야기, 소설
- **feature** ⓥ (주연으로) 나오다, 출연시키다
- **exist** ⓥ 존재하다, 있다
- **fossil** ⓝ 화석
- **dinosaur** ⓝ 공룡
- **appear** ⓥ 등장하다, 나오다
- **throughout** prep ~에 걸쳐, ~ 내내
- **imagination** ⓝ 상상력
- **preserve** ⓥ 보존하다, 지키다

구문 풀이
7행 But even if they feature in stories [created today], / they
비록 ~일지라도 (주연으로) 출연하다, 나오다 과거분사
have always been the products of the human imagination and never
현재완료1
existed.
현재완료2(have에 연결)

05 초기 정보와 기대의 영향　　정답률 48% | 정답 ⑤

글의 흐름으로 보아, 주어진 문장이 들어가기에 가장 적절한 곳을 고르시오. [3점]

People commonly make the mistaken assumption / that because a person has one type of characteristic, / then they automatically have other characteristics / which go with it.
흔히 사람들은 잘못된 가정을 한다. / 어떤 사람이 어떤 특성 하나를 가지고 있으므로 / 그러면 그들은 자동으로 다른 특성을 지니고 있다 / 그것과 어울리는

① In one study, / university students were given descriptions of a guest lecturer / before he spoke to the group.
한 연구에서, / 대학생들은 어떤 초청 강사에 대한 설명을 들었다. / 그가 그들 집단 앞에서 강연하기 전

② Half the students received a description / containing the word 'warm', / the other half were told / the speaker was 'cold'.
학생들 절반은 설명을 들었고, / '따뜻하다'라는 단어가 포함된 / 나머지 절반은 들었다. / 그 강사가 '차갑다'는 말을

③ The guest lecturer then led a discussion, / after which the students were asked / to give their impressions of him.
그러고 나서 그 초청 강사가 토론을 이끌었고, / 이후 학생들은 요청받았다. / 강사에 대한 인상을 말해 달라고

④ As expected, / there were large differences / between the impressions formed by the students, / depending upon their original information of the lecturer.
예상한 대로, / 큰 차이가 있었다. / 학생들에 의해 형성된 인상 간에는 / 그 강사에 대한 학생들의 최초 정보에 따라

✔ It was also found / that those students / who expected the lecturer to be warm / tended to interact with him more.
또한 밝혀졌다. / 그런 학생들은 / 그 강사가 따뜻할 거라고 기대했던 / 그와 더 많이 소통하는 경향이 있었다는 것이

This shows / that different expectations / not only affect the impressions we form / but also our behaviour and the relationship which is formed.
이것은 보여준다. / 서로 다른 기대가 / 우리가 형성하는 인상뿐만 아니라 (~에도) 영향을 미친다는 것을 / 우리의 행동 및 형성되는 관계에도

흔히 사람들은 어떤 사람이 어떤 특성 하나를 가지고 있으면 자동으로 그것과 어울리는 다른 특성을 지니고 있다는 잘못된 가정을 한다. ① 한 연구에서, 대

학생들은 어떤 초청 강사가 그들 집단 앞에서 강연하기 전 그 강사에 대한 설명을 들었다. ② 학생들 절반은 '따뜻하다'라는 단어가 포함된 설명을 들었고, 나머지 절반은 그 강사가 '차갑다'는 말을 들었다. ③ 그러고 나서 그 초청 강사가 토론을 이끌었고, 이후 학생들은 강사에 대한 인상을 말해 달라고 요청받았다. ④ 예상한 대로, 학생들에 의해 형성된 인상 간에는 그 강사에 대한 학생들의 최초 정보에 따라 큰 차이가 있었다. ⑤ 또한, 그 강사가 따뜻할 거라고 기대했던 학생들은 그와 더 많이 소통하는 경향이 있었다는 것이 밝혀졌다. 이것은 서로 다른 기대가 우리가 형성하는 인상뿐만 아니라 우리의 행동 및 형성되는 관계에도 영향을 미친다는 것을 보여준다.

Why? 왜 정답일까?
대학생들 집단을 대상으로 초기 정보의 영향력을 연구한 실험을 소개하는 글이다. ① 이후 ⑤ 앞까지 대학생들 두 집단이 똑같은 강사에 관해 상반된 정보를 들었고, 이에 따라 동일한 사람에 대해 서로 다른 인상을 갖게 되었다는 실험 내용이 소개된다. 이어서 주어진 문장은 추가적인 결과(was also found)로 각 집단에 따라 강사와 소통하는 정도에도 영향이 있었다는 내용을 제시한다. 마지막으로 ⑤ 뒤에서는 서로 다른 초기 정보와 기대로 인해 강사에 대한 인상뿐 아니라 관계 맺음에도 차이가 생겼다는 최종적 결론을 제시한다. 따라서 주어진 문장이 들어가기에 가장 적절한 곳은 ⑤이다.

- **lecturer** ⓝ 강사, 강연자
- **commonly** ad 흔히
- **assumption** ⓝ 가정, 추정
- **description** ⓝ 설명
- **be told** ~을 듣다
- **impression** ⓝ 인상
- **original** ⓐ 최초의, 원래의
- **relationship** ⓝ 관계
- **interact with** ~와 상호작용하다
- **mistaken** ⓐ 잘못된, 틀린
- **automatically** ad 자동으로, 저절로
- **contain** ⓥ 포함하다, (~이) 들어 있다
- **discussion** ⓝ 토론, 논의
- **as expected** 예상된 대로
- **expectation** ⓝ 기대, 예상

06 사회 과학에 대한 비판에 반박하기　　정답률 41% | 정답 ③

글의 흐름으로 보아, 주어진 문장이 들어가기에 가장 적절한 곳을 고르시오. [3점]

Some people believe / that the social sciences are falling behind the natural sciences.
어떤 사람들은 믿는다. / 사회 과학이 자연 과학에 뒤처지고 있다고

① They maintain / that not only does social science have no exact laws, / but it also has failed to eliminate great social evils / such as racial discrimination, crime, poverty, and war.
그들은 주장한다. / 사회 과학이 정확한 법칙을 가지고 있지 않을 뿐만 아니라 / 거대한 사회악을 제거하는 데에도 실패했다고 / 인종 차별, 범죄, 가난, 그리고 전쟁과 같은

② They suggest / that social scientists have failed to accomplish / what might reasonably have been expected of them.
그들은 주장한다. / 사회 과학자들이 달성하는 데 실패했다고 / 그들에게 마땅히 기대되어졌을지도 모르는 것을

✔ Such critics are usually unaware / of the real nature of social science / and of its special problems and basic limitations.
그러한 비판자들은 대체로 알지 못하고 있다. / 사회 과학의 진정한 본질과 / 그것의 특수한 문제 그리고 기본적인 한계를

For example, / they forget / that the solution to a social problem requires / not only knowledge / but also the ability to influence people.
예를 들어 / 그들은 잊는다. / 사회 문제에 대한 해결책은 필요로 한다는 사실을 / 지식뿐만 아니라 / 사람들에게 영향력을 행사할 수 있는 능력도

④ Even if social scientists discover the procedures / that could reasonably be followed to achieve social improvement, / they are seldom in a position / to control social action.
비록 사회 과학자들이 절차를 발견한다 할지라도 / 사회적 발전을 이루기 위해 마땅히 따라야 할 / 그들은 좀처럼 위치에 있지 않다. / 사회적 행동을 통제할

⑤ For that matter, / even dictators find / that there are limits to their power / to change society.
그 점에서는 / 심지어 독재자들도 알게 된다. / 자신들의 권력에 한계가 있다는 것을 / 사회를 변화시키는

어떤 사람들은 사회 과학이 자연 과학에 뒤처지고 있다고 믿는다. ① 그들은 사회 과학이 정확한 법칙을 가지고 있지 않을 뿐만 아니라 인종 차별, 범죄, 가난, 그리고 전쟁과 같은 거대한 사회악을 제거하는 데에도 실패했다고 주장한다. ② 그들은 사회 과학자들이 그들에게 마땅히 기대되었을지도 모르는 것을 달성하는 데 실패했다고 주장한다. ③ 그러한 비판자들은 대체로 사회 과학의 진정한 본질과 그것의 특수한 문제 그리고 기본적인 한계를 알지 못하고 있다. 예를 들어 그들은 사회 문제에 대한 해결책은 지식뿐만 아니라 사람들에게 영향력을 행사할 수 있는 능력도 필요로 한다는 사실을 잊는다. ④ 비록 사회 과학자들이 사회적 발전을 이루기 위해 마땅히 따를 수 있는 절차를 발견한다 할지라도 그들은 좀처럼 사회적 행동을 통제할 위치에 있지 않다. ⑤ 그 점에서

는 심지어 독재자들도 사회를 변화시키는 자신들의 권력에 한계가 있다는 것을 알게 된다.

Why? 왜 정답일까?

③ 앞에서 사회 과학에 대해 비판을 하는 사람들이 있다고 말한 데 이어, 주어진 문장은 '그러한 비판자들'이 사회 과학의 본질과 특유의 문제 및 한계를 인식하지 못하고 있음을 지적한다. ③ 뒤에서는 비판자들의 한계를 보여주는 구체적인 예를 제시한다. 따라서 주어진 문장이 들어가기에 가장 적절한 곳은 ③이다.

- **fall behind** 뒤처지다, 낙오하다
- **social evil** 사회악
- **discrimination** ⓝ 차별
- **accomplish** ⓥ 달성하다, 성취하다
- **influence** ⓥ 영향을 미치다 ⓝ 영향
- **improvement** ⓝ 향상, 개선
- **eliminate** ⓥ 제거하다, 없애다
- **racial** ⓐ 인종의
- **poverty** ⓝ 가난
- **reasonably** ⓐⓓ 마땅히, 합리적으로
- **procedure** ⓝ 절차
- **dictator** ⓝ 독재자

구문 풀이

[14행] Even if social scientists discover the procedures [that could
양보 접속사(비록 ~일지라도)   주격 관계대명사
reasonably be followed to achieve social improvement], / they are
~하기 위해
seldom in a position to control social action.
좀처럼 ~않다   형용사적 용법

---

07 자연과 도시의 관계를 반영해 조성되는 공원   정답률 48% | 정답 ⑤

글의 흐름으로 보아, 주어진 문장이 들어가기에 가장 적절한 곳을 고르시오.

Parks take the shape / demanded by the cultural concerns of their time.
공원은 형태를 취한다. / 그것이 속한 시대의 문화적 관심사가 요구하는

Once parks are in place, / they are no inert stage / — their purposes and meanings are made and remade / by planners and by park users.
일단 공원이 마련되면, / 그것은 비활성화된 단계가 아니다. / 그것의 목적과 의미는 만들어지고 또 만들어진다. / 계획자와 공원 이용자에 의해

Moments of park creation are particularly telling, / however, / for they reveal and actualize ideas / about nature and its relationship to urban society.
공원을 조성하는 순간들은 특히 의미가 있는데, / 그러나 / 그것들이 생각을 드러내고 실현하기 때문이다. / 자연 그리고 자연과 도시 사회의 관계에 관한 (생각)

① Indeed, / what distinguishes a park from the broader category of public space / is the representation of nature / that parks are meant to embody.
실제로 / 공원을 더 넓은 범주의 공공 공간과 구별하는 것은 / 자연의 표현이다 / 공원이 구현하려는

② Public spaces include parks, concrete plazas, sidewalks, even indoor atriums.
공공 공간에는 포함된다 / 공원, 콘크리트 광장, 보도, 심지어 실내 아트리움도

③ Parks typically have trees, grass, and other plants / as their central features.
일반적으로 공원에는 나무, 풀, 그리고 다른 식물들이 있다 / 그들의 중심적인 특색으로

④ When entering a city park, / people often imagine a sharp separation / from streets, cars, and buildings.
도시 공원에 들어갈 때, / 사람들은 흔히 뚜렷한 분리를 상상한다. / 거리, 자동차, 그리고 건물과의

✔There's a reason for that: / traditionally, / park designers attempted to create such a feeling / by planting tall trees at park boundaries, / building stone walls, / and constructing other means of partition.
거기에는 이유가 있는데, / 전통적으로 / 공원 설계자들은 그런 느낌을 만들어 내려고 했다. / 공원 경계에 키 큰 나무를 심고, / 돌담을 쌓고, / 다른 칸막이 수단을 세워

What's behind this idea is / not only landscape architects' desire / to design aesthetically suggestive park spaces, / but a much longer history of Western thought / that envisions cities and nature as antithetical spaces and oppositional forces.
이 생각의 배후에는 있다. / 조경가의 욕망뿐만 아니라 / 미적인 암시가 있는 공원 공간을 설계하려는 / 훨씬 더 오래된 서구 사상의 역사가 / 도시와 자연을 대조적인 공간과 반대 세력으로 상상하는

공원은 그것이 속한 시대의 문화적 관심사가 요구하는 형태를 취한다. 일단 공원이 마련되면, 그것은 비활성화된 단계가 아니다. 그것의 목적과 의미는 계획자와 공원 이용자에 의해 만들어지고 또 만들어진다. 그러나 공원을 조성하는 순간들은 특히 의미가 있는데, 자연 그리고 자연과 도시 사회의 관계에 관한 생각이 드러나고 실현되기 때문이다. ① 실제로 공원을 더 넓은 범주의 공공 공간과 구별하는 것은 공원이 구현하려는 자연의 표현이다. ② 공공 공간에는 공원, 콘크리트 광장, 보도, 심지어 실내 아트리움도 포함된다. ③ 일반적으로 공원에는 그들의 중심적인 특색으로 나무, 풀, 그리고 다른 식물들이 있다. ④ 도시 공원에 들어갈 때, 사람들은 흔히 거리, 자동차, 그리고 건물과의 뚜렷한 분리를 상상한다. ⑤ 거기에는 이유가 있는데, 전통적으로 공원 설계자들은 공원 경계에 키 큰 나무를 심고, 돌담을 쌓고, 다른 칸막이 수단을 세워 그런 느낌을

만들어 내려고 했다. 이 생각의 배후에는 미적인 암시가 있는 공원 공간을 설계하려는 조경가의 욕망뿐만 아니라 도시와 자연을 대조적인 공간과 반대 세력으로 상상하는 훨씬 더 오래된 서구 사상의 역사가 있다.

Why? 왜 정답일까?

⑤ 앞에서 도시 사람들은 공원에 들어갈 때 (도시의) 거리, 자동차, 건물 등과 뚜렷하게 분리되는 것을 상상한다고 언급한 데 이어, 주어진 문장에서는 그런 상상에 '이유'가 있다고 설명한다. ⑤ 뒤의 this idea는 주어진 문장에서 설명한 이유, 즉 '공원 설계자들이 공원 경계에 나무나 칸막이를 두어서 분리의 느낌을 내고자 했다'는 관념을 지칭하는 것이다. 따라서 주어진 문장이 들어가기에 가장 적절한 곳은 ⑤이다.

- **traditionally** ⓐⓓ 전통적으로
- **plant** ⓥ 심다
- **demand** ⓥ 요구하다
- **in place** 제자리에 있는, 준비가 되어 있는
- **telling** ⓐ 효과적인, 현저한, 보여주는
- **actualize** ⓥ 실현하다
- **distinguish A from B** A와 B를 구별하다
- **be meant to** ~하기로 되어 있다
- **sidewalk** ⓝ 인도
- **feature** ⓝ 특색, 특징, 기능
- **landscape** ⓝ 조경
- **suggestive** ⓐ 암시하는
- **antithetical** ⓐ 대조적인
- **attempt to** ~하려고 시도하다, 노력하다
- **boundary** ⓝ 경계
- **concern** ⓝ 관심사
- **inert** ⓐ 비활성의
- **reveal** ⓥ 드러내다
- **relationship** ⓝ 관계
- **representation** ⓝ 표현
- **embody** ⓥ 구현하다
- **atrium** ⓝ 아트리움
- **separation** ⓝ 분리
- **aesthetically** ⓐⓓ 미적으로
- **envision** ⓥ 상상하다, 머릿속에 그리다
- **oppositional** ⓐ 반대의

구문 풀이

[17행] When entering a city park, people often imagine a sharp
접속사 + 현재분사(~할 때)
separation from streets, cars, and buildings.

★★★ 1등급 대비 고난도 2점 문제

08 사회적 활동 시간을 줄이는 텔레비전   정답률 47% | 정답 ④

글의 흐름으로 보아, 주어진 문장이 들어가기에 가장 적절한 곳을 고르시오.

Television is the number one leisure activity / in the United States and Europe, / consuming more than half of our free time.
텔레비전은 제1의 여가활동으로, / 미국과 유럽에서 / 우리의 자유 시간 중 절반 이상을 소비한다.

① We generally think of television / as a way to relax, tune out, and escape from our troubles / for a bit each day.
일반적으로 우리는 텔레비전을 취급한다. / 휴식하고, 관심을 끄고, 우리의 문제로부터 탈출하는 한 가지 방법으로서 / 매일 잠시나마

② While this is true, / there is increasing evidence / that we are more motivated / to tune in to our favorite shows and characters / when we are feeling lonely / or have a greater need for social connection.
이것이 사실이긴 하지만, / 증거가 늘어나고 있다. / 우리가 동기가 더 부여된다는 / 우리가 좋아하는 쇼들과 등장인물들을 보려는 / 우리가 외롭다고 느끼고 있거나 / 사회적 관계를 위한 더 큰 욕구를 가질 때

③ Television watching does satisfy these social needs / to some extent, / at least in the short run.
텔레비전을 보는 것이 이러한 사회적인 욕구를 정말로 만족시킨다. / 어느 정도까지는 / 적어도 단기적으로는

✔Unfortunately, / it is also likely to "crowd out" other activities / that produce more sustainable social contributions to our social well-being.
불행히도, / 그것은 또한 다른 활동들을 '몰아내기' 쉽다. / 우리의 사회적 행복에 더 지속적인 사회적 기여를 만들어 내는

The more television we watch, / the less likely we are / to volunteer our time / or to spend time with people / in our social networks.
텔레비전을 더 많이 볼수록, / 우리는 가능성이 더 적다. / 우리의 시간을 기꺼이 할애하거나 / 사람들과 함께 시간을 보낼 / 사회적 관계망 속에서

⑤ In other words, / the more time we make for *Friends*, / the less time we have for friends in real life.
다시 말해서, / 우리가 *Friends*를 위해 더 많은 시간을 낼수록, / 우리는 실제 친구들을 위한 시간은 덜 갖게 된다.

텔레비전은 미국과 유럽에서 제1의 여가활동으로, 우리의 자유시간 중 절반 이상을 소비한다. ① 일반적으로 우리는 휴식하고, 관심을 끄고, 매일 잠시나마 우리의 문제로부터 탈출하는 한 가지 방법으로서 텔레비전을 취급한다. ② 이것이 사실이긴 하지만, 우리가 외롭다고 느끼고 있거나 사회적 관계를 위한 더 큰 욕구를 가질 때 우리가 좋아하는 쇼들과 등장인물들을 보려는 동기가 더 부여된다는 증거가 늘어나고 있다. ③ 적어도 단기적으로는, 텔레비전을 보는 것이 이러한 사회적인 욕구를 어느 정도까지는 정말로 만족시킨다. ④ 불행히도, 그것은 또한 우리의 사회적 행복에 더 지속적인 사회적 기여를 만들어 내는 다른 활동들을 '몰아내기' 쉽다. 텔레비전을 더 많이 볼수록, 우리는 사회적 관계망 속에서 우리의 시간을 기꺼이 할애하거나 사람들과 함께 시간을 보

DAY 19

낼 가능성이 더 적다. ⑤ 다시 말해서, 우리가 *Friends*를 위해 더 많은 시간을 낼수록, 실제 친구들을 위한 시간은 덜 갖게 된다.

Why? 왜 정답일까?

주어진 문장에 역접어인 **Unfortunately**가 있으므로, 글의 흐름이 갑자기 반전되는 지점에 주어진 문장이 들어갈 것이다. ④ 앞에서 텔레비전은 어느 정도 사회적 욕구 충족에 도움이 된다고 하는데, ④ 뒤에서는 갑자기 텔레비전을 볼수록 사회적 활동 시간이 줄어든다고 한다. 즉 ④ 앞뒤로 글의 논리적 흐름이 단절되는 것으로 보아, 주어진 문장이 들어가기에 가장 적절한 곳은 ④이다.

- **crowd out** 몰아내다
- **leisure** ⓝ 여가, 레저
- **escape from** ~로부터 도망치다
- **satisfy** ⓥ 만족시키다, 충족하다
- **sustainable** ⓐ 지속 가능한
- **tune out** 주의를 돌리다, 관심을 끄다
- **tune in to** ~에 채널을 맞추다
- **in the short run** 단기적으로

구문 풀이

6행 We generally think of television as a way to relax, tune out,
「think of + A + as + B : A를 B로 여기다」 형용사적 용법(a way 수식)
and escape from our troubles for a bit each day.

★★ 문제 해결 꿀~팁 ★★

▶ **많이 틀린 이유는?**
가장 헷갈리는 ③ 앞뒤를 보면, 먼저 ③ 앞에서 우리가 사회적 욕구를 충족하고 싶을 때 TV를 보고 싶어 한다고 언급한 후, ③ 뒤는 실제로 TV 시청이 '어느 정도는' 사회적 욕구 충족에 도움이 된다고 설명하고 있다. 즉 ③ 앞에 제시된 내용을 ③ 뒤에서 일부 긍정하는 흐름이므로, '일반적 사실 – 보충 설명'의 흐름이 적절하게 연결된다.

▶ **문제 해결 방법은?**
정답인 ④ 앞은 TV가 사회적 욕구 충족에 적어도 단기적으로 도움을 준다는 내용인데, ④ 뒤의 두 문장은 모두 TV 시청을 하다 보면 실생활에서 친구를 사귀려는 노력이 덜해진다는 내용이다. 즉, ④ 앞뒤로 서로 반대되는 내용이 제시되지만 역접어가 등장하지 않는데, 주어진 문장을 보면 이 논리적 공백을 메꿔줄 역접어(Unfortunately)가 있다.

기자들에게 말했다. ⑤ 그는 그렇게 했던 이유 중 하나를 덧붙여 말했다. "저는 거짓말쟁이가 되고 싶지 않았어요."

Why? 왜 정답일까?

② 앞에서 철자 대회에 참가한 소년이 답을 잘못 말했음에도 불구하고 심판이 이를 잘못 듣고 그를 다음 단계로 진출시켰다는 이야기가 나오는데, 주어진 문장에서는 그 소년이 자신이 틀렸다는 것을 알았을 때 심판에게 가서 이를 털어놓았다는 내용을 이어서 언급한다. ② 뒤에서는 그리하여 소년이 결국 탈락했다는 내용이 이어진다. 따라서 주어진 문장이 들어가기에 가장 적절한 곳은 ②이다.

- **misspell** ⓥ 철자를 잘못 말하다
- **tendency** ⓝ 경향
- **mishear** ⓥ 잘못 듣다
- **eliminate** ⓥ 탈락시키다, 제거하다
- **headline** ⓝ 표제
- **honesty** ⓝ 정직, 솔직함
- **judge** ⓝ 심판, 심사위원
- **repeat** ⓥ 반복하다
- **advance** ⓥ 진출하다, 나아가다
- **competition** ⓝ 경쟁
- **appear** ⓥ 발간되다
- **motive** ⓝ 동기

구문 풀이

6행 Although he misspelled the word, / the judges misheard
양보 접속사(비록 ~일지라도) 동사1
him, told him (that) he had spelled the word right, and allowed him
동사2 생략(접속사) 동사3
to advance.
목적격 보어(~하도록)

★★ 문제 해결 꿀~팁 ★★

▶ **많이 틀린 이유는?**
문장 삽입 문제는 논리적 공백 찾기에 주력해야 한다. 최다 오답인 ① 앞뒤는 '철자 경연 대회에 나간 소년이 제시어를 받고 → 철자를 잘못 말했는데 심판이 제대로 듣지 못하고 통과시켰다'는 내용이므로 서로 자연스럽게 이어진다.

▶ **문제 해결 방법은?**
만일 ②에 주어진 문장이 들어가지 않으면 ② 앞뒤는 '심판이 통과시켰다 → 그래서 소년은 탈락했다'는 뜻이 되므로, 중간에 논리적 공백이 발생한다.

★★★ **1등급 대비 고난도 2점 문제**

09 철자 맞히기 대회에서 정직함을 보여준 한 소년   정답률 44% | 정답 ②

글의 흐름으로 보아, 주어진 문장이 들어가기에 가장 적절한 곳을 고르시오.

Some years ago / at the national spelling bee in Washington, D.C., / a thirteen-year-old boy was asked to spell *echolalia*, / a word that means a tendency / to repeat whatever one hears.
몇 년 전 / Washington D.C.에서 있었던 전국 단어 철자 맞히기 대회에서, / 한 13세 소년이 *echolalia*의 철자를 말하도록 요구받았다. / '경향'을 의미하는 단어인 / '들은 것은 무엇이든 반복하는'

① Although he misspelled the word, / the judges misheard him, / told him he had spelled the word right, / and allowed him to advance.
그는 철자를 잘못 말했지만 / 심판은 잘못 듣고 / 그에게 철자를 맞혔다고 말했고 / 그가 (다음 단계로) 진출하도록 허락했다.

☑ When the boy learned / that he had misspelled the word, / he went to the judges and told them.
그 소년이 알았을 때 / 자신이 단어 철자를 잘못 말했다는 것을 / 그는 심판에게 가서 말했다.

So he was eliminated from the competition after all.
그래서 그는 결국 대회에서 탈락했다.

③ Newspaper headlines the next day / called the honest young man a "spelling bee hero," / and his photo appeared in *The New York Times*.
다음 날 신문기사 헤드라인이 / 그 정직한 소년을 "단어 철자 맞히기 대회 영웅"으로 알렸고, / 그의 사진이 *The New York Times*에 실렸다.

④ "The judges said I had a lot of honesty," / the boy told reporters.
"심판은 내가 아주 정직하다고 말했어요."라고 / 그 소년은 기자들에게 말했다.

⑤ He added / that part of his motive was, / "I didn't want to feel like a liar."
그는 덧붙여 말했다, / 그렇게 했던 이유 중 하나를 / "저는 거짓말쟁이가 되고 싶지 않았어요."

몇 년 전 Washington D.C.에서 있었던 전국 단어 철자 맞히기 대회에서, 한 13세 소년이 '들은 것은 무엇이든 반복하는 경향'을 의미하는 단어인 echolalia의 철자를 말하도록 요구받았다. ① 그는 철자를 잘못 말했지만 심판은 잘못 듣고 철자를 맞혔다고 말했고 그가 (다음 단계로) 진출하도록 허락했다. 그 소년은 자신이 단어 철자를 잘못 말했다는 것을 알았을 때 심판에게 가서 말했다. ② 그래서 그는 결국 대회에서 탈락했다. ③ 다음 날 신문기사 헤드라인이 그 정직한 소년을 "단어 철자 맞히기 대회 영웅"으로 알렸고, 그의 사진이 *The New York Times*에 실렸다. ④ "심판은 내가 아주 정직하다고 말했어요."라고 그 소년은 기자들에게 말했다. ⑤ 그는 덧붙여 말했다, 그렇게 했던 이유 중 하나를 "저는 거짓말쟁이가 되고 싶지 않았어요."

★★★ **1등급 대비 고난도 2점 문제**

10 어린 시절의 친구가 주는 이점   정답률 41% | 정답 ②

글의 흐름으로 보아, 주어진 문장이 들어가기에 가장 적절한 곳을 고르시오.

Childhood friends — friends you've known forever — / are really special.
당신이 평생 동안 알아왔던 어린 시절의 친구는 / 정말로 특별하다.

① They know everything about you, / and you've shared lots of firsts.
그들은 당신에 대해서 모든 것을 알고, / 당신은 그들과 많은 것들을 처음으로 함께 했다.

☑ When you hit puberty, however, / sometimes these forever-friendships go through growing pains.
하지만 사춘기가 되면, / 때때로 이런 영원한 우정은 성장통을 겪는다.

You find / that you have less in common than you used to.
당신은 알게 된다. / 과거보다 공유하는 것이 적다는 것을

③ Maybe you're into rap and she's into pop, / or you go to different schools / and have different groups of friends.
아마 당신은 랩을 좋아하는데 친구는 팝을 좋아한다거나, / 학교가 달라지고 / 서로 다른 친구 무리와 어울리게 될 수 있다.

④ Change can be scary, but remember:
변화는 무서울 수 있지만, 기억하라.

Friends, even best friends, / don't have to be exactly alike.
심지어 가장 친한 친구더라도 친구들이 / 완전히 똑같을 필요는 없다.

⑤ Having friends with other interests / keeps life interesting / — just think of what you can learn from each other.
다른 관심사를 가진 친구를 두는 것은 / 삶을 흥미롭게 만들 수 있다. / 그저 서로에게 무엇을 배울 수 있겠는지 생각해 보라.

당신이 평생 동안 알아왔던 어린 시절의 친구는 정말로 특별하다. ① 그들은 당신에 대해서 모든 것을 알고, 당신은 그들과 많은 것들을 처음으로 함께 했다. ② 하지만 사춘기가 되면, 때때로 이런 영원한 우정은 성장통을 겪는다. 당신은 과거보다 공유하는 것이 적다는 것을 알게 된다. ③ 아마 당신은 랩을 좋아하는데 친구는 팝을 좋아한다거나, 학교가 달라지고 서로 다른 친구 무리와 어울리게 될 수 있다. ④ 변화는 무서울 수 있지만, 기억하라. 심지어 가장 친한 친구더라도 친구들이 완전히 똑같을 필요는 없다. ⑤ 다른 관심사를 가진 친구를 두는 것은 삶을 흥미롭게 만들 수 있다. 그저 서로에게 무엇을 배울 수 있겠는지 생각해 보라.

② 그러나 현대 인지 과학은 언어가 인간에게 매우 중요한 사고의 한 측면일 뿐 모든 종류의 사고에 근본적이지는 않다고 당연히 판단한다. ③ 수많은 종의 동물들이 인간의 사고 속에 대체로 보존된 두뇌의 메커니즘을 통해 언어를 사용하지 않고 세계를 항해하고, 문제를 해결하고, 학습해낸다. ④ 언어가 정신 작용의 기본이라고 가정할 이유는 없다. ⑤ 그럼에도 불구하고, 언어는 인간의 삶에서 매우 중요하며 세계를 다루는 데 있어서 서로 협력하는 우리의 능력에 상당히 기여한다. 우리 종족인 호모 *사피엔스*는 놀라운 성공을 거두어 왔는데, 이것은 처음에는 협력적인 문제 해결에 효과적인 기여 요소로서, 그리고 훨씬 나중에는 글로 쓰인 기록을 통한 집단 기억으로서의 언어에 부분적으로 의존했다.

Why? 왜 정답일까?

② 앞의 문장에서는 어린 시절의 친구가 모든 것을 서로 공유하고 많은 처음을 함께 나눈 '특별한 사이'임을 말하는데, 주어진 문장은 이를 however로 뒤집으며 사춘기가 되면 이러한 우정에 '성장통'이 찾아온다는 내용을 제시한다. ② 뒤의 문장에서는 주어진 문장에 이어 사춘기 이후에 사람들은 어린 시절의 친구와 서로 공유하는 것이 적어지고 관심사가 달라지게 될 수 있다는 내용을 제시한다. 따라서 주어진 문장이 들어가기에 가장 적절한 곳은 ②이다.

- puberty ⓝ 사춘기
- scary ⓐ 무서운, 겁나는
- alike ⓐ (아주) 비슷한
- go through ～을 겪다
- exactly [ad] 정확히
- interest ⓝ 관심사, 흥미

구문 풀이

```
11행  Having friends with other interests keeps│life interesting /
      주어(동명사)                              동사(단수)  목적격 보어(현재분사)
— just think of what you can learn from each other.
              의문사(무엇)
```

★★ 문제 해결 꿀~팁 ★★

▶ 많이 틀린 이유는?
주어진 문장에 however라는 역접의 연결어가 있으므로 본문에서 앞뒤가 서로 다른 말을 하는 지점에 주어진 문장을 넣어야 한다. 최다 오답은 ④인데 ④의 앞뒤 모두 '어린 시절의 친구가 시간이 지나서 서로 안 맞게 될 수 있지만 괜찮다'는 내용으로 요약될 수 있으므로 ④를 흐름 반전의 지점으로 보기는 어렵다.

▶ 문제 해결 방법은?
주어진 문장 넣기 유형에서 주어진 문장은 보통 흐름 반전의 연결사를 포함하고 있기 마련이다. 본문을 읽을 때 각 번호 앞뒤 문장이 요약했을 때 서로 같은 말인지 다른 말인지를 계속 비교해 보면 오답을 피할 수 있다.

Why? 왜 정답일까?

언어가 먼저인지 사고가 먼저인지 논하는 글로, 분석 철학과 현대 인지 과학의 시각이 대비되고 있다. ⑤ 앞까지는 주로 현대 인지 과학의 관점에서 언어가 중요하기는 해도 근간은 사고력에 있다는 내용이 제시된다. 하지만 주어진 문장은 언어가 매우 중요함을 강조하며 특히 인간의 협동 능력에 크게 기여한다는 내용으로 흐름의 반전을 이끈다. 이어서 ⑤ 뒤의 문장은 주어진 문장에서 언급한 '협력'과 관련하여 언어가 중요했다는 내용을 다시금 설명한다. 따라서 주어진 문장이 들어가기에 가장 적절한 곳은 ⑤이다.

- enormously [ad] 대단히, 거대하게
- deal with ～을 다루다, ～에 대처하다
- philosophy ⓝ 철학
- make sense 이치에 맞다
- fundamental ⓐ 근본적인
- navigate ⓥ 항해하다
- contribute to ～에 기여하다
- analytic ⓐ 분석적인
- historically [ad] 역사적으로
- appreciate ⓥ 제대로 인식하다
- countless ⓐ 무수히 많은
- astonishingly [ad] 놀랍도록

구문 풀이

```
16행  There is no reason to assume [that language is fundamental
to mental operations].  [ ] : to assume의 목적어
```

★★ 문제 해결 꿀~팁 ★★

▶ 많이 틀린 이유는?
④ 앞뒤로 논리적 공백이 발생하는지 점검해 보면, 먼저 ④ 앞은 언어가 없는 동물도 세계를 항해하고 문제를 해결하는 데 문제가 없다는 내용이다. 한편 ④ 뒤는 그렇기에 언어가 정신 작용의 근간이라고 추정할 근거가 없다는 내용이다. 즉 ④ 앞을 근거로 ④ 뒤와 같은 결론을 내릴 수 있는 것이므로, ④의 위치에서 논리적 공백은 발생하지 않는다.

▶ 문제 해결 방법은?
⑤ 앞은 언어가 정신 작용에 근본적이라고 추정할 필요는 없다는 내용인데, ⑤ 뒤는 호모 사피엔스의 성공에 언어가 부분적으로는 중요한 기여를 했다는 내용이다. 즉 ⑤ 앞뒤가 서로 반대되는 내용이므로, 사이에 적절한 역접어(Nevertheless)가 있어야 흐름이 자연스러워진다.

★★★ 1등급 대비 고난도 3점 문제

| 11 | 언어와 사고의 관계 | 정답률 42% \| 정답 ⑤ |

글의 흐름으로 보아, 주어진 문장이 들어가기에 가장 적절한 곳을 고르시오. [3점]

Should we use language to understand mind / or mind to understand language?
우리는 사고를 이해하기 위해 언어를 사용해야 할까, / 아니면 언어를 이해하기 위해 사고를 사용해야 할까?

① Analytic philosophy historically assumes / that language is basic / and that mind would make sense / if proper use of language was appreciated.
분석 철학은 역사적으로 가정한다. / 언어가 기본이고 / 그 사고가 이치에 맞을 것이라고 / 적절한 언어 사용이 제대로 인식된다면

② Modern cognitive science, / however, / rightly judges / that language is just one aspect of mind / of great importance in human beings / but not fundamental to all kinds of thinking.
현대 인지 과학은 / 그러나 / 당연히 판단한다. / 언어가 사고의 한 측면일 뿐 / 인간에게 매우 중요한 / 하지만 모든 종류의 사고에 근본적이지는 않다고

③ Countless species of animals / manage to navigate the world, / solve problems, / and learn / without using language, / through brain mechanisms / that are largely preserved in the minds of humans.
수많은 종의 동물들이 / 세계를 항해하고, / 문제를 해결하고, / 학습해낸다 / 언어를 사용하지 않고 / 두뇌의 메커니즘을 통해 / 인간의 사고 속에 대체로 보존된

④ There is no reason to assume / that language is fundamental to mental operations.
가정할 이유는 없다. / 언어가 정신 작용의 기본이라고

✔ Nevertheless, / language is enormously important in human life / and contributes largely to our ability / to cooperate with each other / in dealing with the world.
그럼에도 불구하고, / 언어는 인간의 삶에서 매우 중요하며 / 우리의 능력에 상당히 기여한다. / 서로 협력하는 / 세계를 다루는 데 있어서

Our species *homo sapiens* / has been astonishingly successful, / which depended in part on language, / first as an effective contributor / to collaborative problem solving / and much later, as collective memory / through written records.
우리 종족인 호모 *사피엔스*는 / 놀라운 성공을 거두어 왔는데, / 이것은 언어에 부분적으로 의존했다. / 처음에는 효과적인 기여 요소로서, / 협력적인 문제 해결에 / 그리고 훨씬 나중에는 집단 기억으로서 / 글로 쓰인 기록을 통한

우리는 사고를 이해하기 위해 언어를 사용해야 할까, 아니면 언어를 이해하기 위해 사고를 사 용해야 할까? ① 분석 철학은 언어가 기본이고 적절한 언어 사용이 제대로 인식된다면 그 사고가 이치에 맞을 것이라고 역사적으로 가정한다.

★★★ 1등급 대비 고난도 3점 문제

| 12 | Amondawa 부족의 독특한 시간 관념 | 정답률 38% \| 정답 ④ |

글의 흐름으로 보아, 주어진 문장이 들어가기에 가장 적절한 곳을 고르시오. [3점]

There are some cultures / that can be referred to as "people who live outside of time."
어떤 문화가 있다. / '시간 밖에서 사는 사람들'이라고 부를 수 있는

The Amondawa tribe, living in Brazil, / does not have a concept of time / that can be measured or counted.
브라질에 사는 Amondawa 부족에게는 / 시간이라는 개념이 없다. / 측정되거나 셀 수 있는

① Rather they live in a world of serial events, / rather than seeing events as being rooted in time.
오히려 그들은 연속되는 사건의 세상에서 산다. / 사건이 시간에 뿌리를 두고 있다고 간주하기보다는

② Researchers also found that no one had an age.
연구자들은 또한 나이가 있는 사람이 아무도 없다는 것을 알아냈다.

③ Instead, they change their names / to reflect their stage of life and position within their society, / so a little child will give up their name to a newborn sibling / and take on a new one.
대신에 그들은 이름을 바꾼다. / 자신들의 생애 단계와 사회 내 위치를 반영하기 위해 / 그래서 어린아이는 자신의 이름을 갓 태어난 형제자매에게 넘겨주고 / 새로운 이름을 갖는다.

✔ In the U.S. we have so many metaphors for time and its passing / that we think of time as "a thing," / that is "the weekend is almost gone," or "I haven't got the time."

미국에는 시간과 시간의 흐름에 관한 매우 많은 은유가 있어서 / 우리는 시간을 '물건'으로 간주하는데, / 즉 "주말이 거의 다 지나갔다."라거나 "나는 시간이 없다."라는 식이다.

We think such statements are objective, / but they aren't.
우리는 그러한 말들이 객관적이라고 생각하지만, / 그것들은 그렇지 않다.

⑤ We create these metaphors, / but the Amondawa don't talk or think in metaphors for time.
우리는 이런 은유를 만들어 내지만, / Amondawa 사람들은 시간을 은유적으로 말하거나 생각하지 않는다.

'시간 밖에서 사는 사람들'이라고 부를 수 있는 어떤 문화가 있다. 브라질에 사는 Amondawa 부족에게는 측정되거나 셀 수 있는 시간이라는 개념이 없다. ① 오히려 그들은 사건이 시간에 뿌리를 두고 있다고 간주하기보다는 연속되는 사건의 세상에서 산다. ② 연구자들은 또한 나이가 있는 사람이 아무도 없다는 것을 알아냈다. ③ 대신에 그들은 자신들의 생애 단계와 사회 내 위치를 반영하기 위해 이름을 바꾸어서 어린아이는 자신의 이름을 갓 태어난 형제자매에게 넘겨주고 새로운 이름을 갖는다. ④ 미국에는 시간과 시간의 흐름에 관한 매우 많은 은유가 있어서 우리는 시간을 '물건'으로 간주하는데, 즉 "주말이 거의 다 지나갔다."라거나 "나는 시간이 없다."라는 식이다. 우리는 그러한 말들이 객관적이라고 생각하지만, 그렇지 않다. ⑤ 우리는 이런 은유를 만들어 내지만, Amondawa 사람들은 시간을 은유적으로 말하거나 생각하지 않는다.

Why? 왜 정답일까?

Amondawa 부족의 독특한 시간 관념을 소개한 글이다. ④ 앞에서는 이들이 사건을 시간별로 파악하기보다는 그저 연속된 사건 속에 살며 나이도 세지 않는다는 내용을 제시한다. 반면 주어진 문장은 미국의 예를 들어 시간과 시간의 흐름을 물건처럼 느끼게 하는 많은 은유가 있다고 언급하는데, ④ 뒤에서는 '이러한 은유적인 말들'이 객관적으로 보이더라도 Amondawa 부족의 관점에는 적용될 수 없다는 이야기임을 덧붙이고 있다. 따라서 주어진 문장이 들어가기에 가장 적절한 곳은 ④이다.

- passing ⓝ (시간의) 흐름, 경과
- refer to A as B ⓥ A를 B라고 부르다
- measure ⓥ 측정하다
- reflect ⓥ 반영하다
- objective ⓐ 객관적인
- think of A as B ⓥ A를 B라고 간주하다
- tribe ⓝ 부족
- rooted in ~에 뿌리를 둔
- statement ⓝ 말, 진술

구문 풀이

1행 In the U.S. we have so many metaphors for time and its
「so ~ that … : 너무 ~해서 …하다」
passing that we think of time as "a thing," that is "the weekend is
「think of + A + as + B : A를 B라고 간주하다」 └→ 즉, 다시 말해
almost gone," or "I haven't got the time."

★★ 문제 해결 꿀~팁 ★★

▶ 많이 틀린 이유는?
⑤의 these metaphors가 주어진 문장의 따옴표 구절과 이어진다고 보면 ⑤를 답으로 고르기 쉽지만, 앞에 나오는 such statements 또한 가리키는 바가 불분명함을 염두에 두어야 한다.

▶ 문제 해결 방법은?
④ 뒤의 such statements가 가리키는 바에 주목해야 한다. 앞에서 '진술'로 받을 만한 말이 따로 나오지 않았는데 바로 '이러한 진술'이라는 언급을 이어가기는 부적절하며, 마침 주어진 문장이 따옴표로 다양한 구절을 제시하고 있는 것으로 볼 때, such statement 앞에 주어진 문장이 나와야 함을 알 수 있다.

DAY 20 문장 삽입 05

01 ④	02 ④	03 ⑤	04 ⑤	05 ③
06 ④	07 ⑤	08 ⑤	09 ④	10 ⑤
11 ⑤	12 ④			

01 보충제를 통한 영양소 섭취　　정답률 58% | 정답 ④

글의 흐름으로 보아, 주어진 문장이 들어가기에 가장 적절한 곳을 고르시오.

According to top nutrition experts, / most nutrients are better absorbed and used by the body / when consumed from a whole food / instead of a supplement.
최고의 영양 전문가들에 의하면 / 많은 영양소가 신체에 의해 더 잘 흡수되고 사용된다. / 자연식품으로부터 섭취되었을 때 / 보충제 대신에

① However, / many people feel the need / to take pills, powders, and supplements / in an attempt to obtain nutrients / and fill the gaps in their diets.
그러나 / 많은 사람들이 필요성을 느낀다. / 알약, 분말 그리고 보충제를 섭취할 / 영양소를 얻기 위한 시도로 / 그리고 자신의 식단에 있어 부족한 부분을 채우기 위한

② We hope / these will give us more energy, / prevent us from catching a cold in the winter, / or improve our skin and hair.
우리는 바란다. / 이것들이 우리에게 더 많은 에너지를 주고, / 우리가 겨울에 감기에 걸리는 것을 막아 주거나 / 혹은 우리의 피부와 모발을 개선해 주기를

③ But in reality, / the large majority of supplements are artificial / and may not even be completely absorbed by your body.
그러나 실제로는 / 대다수의 보충제가 인위적이고 / 여러분의 신체에 의해 완전히 흡수조차 되지 않을 수도 있다.

✔Worse, / some are contaminated with other substances / and contain ingredients not listed on the label.
더 심각한 것은, / 어떤 것들은 다른 물질로 오염되어 있으며 / 라벨에 실려 있지 않은 성분을 포함한다.

For example, / a recent investigative report found heavy metals / in 40 percent of 134 brands of protein powders on the market.
예를 들어 / 최근 한 조사 보고는 중금속을 발견했다. / 시장에 있는 단백질 분말 134개 브랜드 중 40퍼센트에서

⑤ With little control and regulation, / taking supplements is a gamble and often costly.
단속과 규제가 거의 없다면 / 보충제를 섭취하는 것은 도박이며 종종 대가가 크다.

최고의 영양 전문가들에 의하면 많은 영양소가 보충제 대신에 자연식품으로부터 섭취되었을 때 신체에서 더 잘 흡수되고 사용된다. ① 그러나 많은 사람들이 영양소를 얻고 식단에 있어 부족한 부분을 채우기 위한 시도로 알약, 분말 그리고 보충제를 섭취할 필요성을 느낀다. ② 우리는 이것들이 우리에게 더 많은 에너지를 주거나, 겨울에 감기에 걸리는 것을 막아 주거나 우리의 피부와 모발을 개선해 주기를 바란다. ③ 그러나 실제로는 대다수의 보충제가 인위적이고 여러분의 신체에서 완전히 흡수조차 되지 않을 수도 있다. ④ 더 심각한 것은, 어떤 것들은 다른 물질로 오염되어 있으며 라벨에 실려 있지 않은 성분을 포함한다. 예를 들어 최근 한 조사 보고는 시장에 있는 단백질 분말 134개 브랜드 중 40퍼센트에서 중금속을 발견했다. ⑤ 단속과 규제가 거의 없다면 보충제를 섭취하는 것은 도박이며 종종 대가가 크다.

Why? 왜 정답일까?

보충제를 통해 영양소를 섭취하는 것은 생각보다 효과가 없거나 위험할 수 있다는 내용의 글이다. ④ 앞의 문장에서 대다수의 보충제가 실제로 우리 몸에서 잘 흡수되지 않는다고 설명한 후, 주어진 문장은 이것보다 더 심각한 문제(Worse)로 보충제가 다른 물질로 오염되어 있거나 라벨에 없는 성분을 포함하기도 한다고 지적한다. ④ 뒤의 문장은 주어진 문장에 대한 예시로 시중 단백질 분말 브랜드의 40%가 중금속으로 오염되어 있다는 내용을 언급한다. 따라서 주어진 문장이 들어가기에 가장 적절한 곳은 ④이다.

- whole food 자연식품
- nutrition ⓝ 영양
- fill the gap 부족한 부분을 채우다
- regulation ⓝ 규제
- substance ⓝ 물질
- absorb ⓥ 흡수하다
- artificial ⓐ 인위적인

구문 풀이

9행 We hope (that) these will give us more energy, prevent us
생략　　　　동사1　　　　동사2(prevent + A +
from catching a cold in the winter, or improve our skin and hair.
from + B : A가 B하지 못하게 막다)　　　　동사3

02 다른 사람의 감정 파악하기
정답률 60% | 정답 ④

글의 흐름으로 보아, 주어진 문장이 들어가기에 가장 적절한 곳을 고르시오.

Have you ever thought / about how you can tell / what somebody else is feeling?
당신은 생각해본 적이 있는가? / 당신이 어떻게 알 수 있는지 / 다른 누군가가 어떤 기분인지를

① Sometimes, friends might tell you / that they are feeling happy or sad / but, even if they do not tell you, / I am sure that you would be able to make a good guess / about what kind of mood they are in.
때때로, 친구들이 당신에게 말할지도 모르지만, / 그들이 행복하거나 슬프다고 / 당신에게 말하지 않는다고 해도, / 나는 당신이 추측을 잘 할 수 있을 것이라고 확신한다. / 그들이 어떤 기분인지에 대해

② You might get a clue / from the tone of voice that they use.
당신은 단서를 얻을지도 모른다. / 그들이 사용하는 목소리의 어조로부터

③ For example, / they may raise their voice if they are angry / or talk in a shaky way if they are scared.
예를 들어, / 그들이 화가 나 있다면 그들은 목소리를 높일 것이고, / 그들이 두려워하고 있다면 떠는 식으로 말할 것이다.

✔The other main clue you might use / to tell what a friend is feeling / would be to look at his or her facial expression.
당신이 사용할지도 모르는 다른 주요한 단서는 / 친구가 어떤 감정인지를 알기 위해 / 그 사람의 얼굴 표정을 보는 것일 것이다.

We have lots of muscles in our faces / which enable us to move our face / into lots of different positions.
우리는 얼굴에 많은 근육들이 있는데 / 이는 우리의 얼굴을 움직일 수 있게 한다. / 많은 다른 위치로

⑤ This happens spontaneously / when we feel a particular emotion.
이것은 자동적으로 일어난다. / 우리가 특정한 감정을 느낄 때

당신은 다른 누군가가 어떤 기분인지를 당신이 어떻게 알 수 있는지 생각해본 적이 있는가? ① 때때로, 친구들이 당신에게 그들이 행복하거나 슬프다고 말할지도 모르지만, 당신에게 말하지 않는다고 해도, 나는 당신이 그들이 어떤 기분인지에 대해 추측을 잘 할 수 있을 것이라고 확신한다. ② 당신은 그들이 사용하는 목소리의 어조로부터 단서를 얻을지도 모른다. ③ 예를 들어, 그들이 화가 나 있다면 그들은 목소리를 높일 것이고, 그들이 두려워하고 있다면 떠는 식으로 말할 것이다. ④ 친구가 어떤 감정인지를 알기 위해 당신이 사용할지도 모르는 다른 주요한 단서는 그 사람의 얼굴 표정을 보는 것일 것이다. 우리는 얼굴에 많은 근육들이 있는데 이는 우리의 얼굴을 많은 다른 위치로 움직일 수 있게 한다. ⑤ 이것은 우리가 특정한 감정을 느낄 때 자동적으로 일어난다.

Why? 왜 정답일까?

다른 사람의 감정을 파악하는 방법에 관해 설명한 글이다. ④ 앞의 두 문장에서 타인의 어조를 통해 그 사람의 감정에 대한 단서를 얻을 수 있다고 언급한 이후, 주어진 문장은 다른 주요한 단서(The other main clue)로서 표정을 언급한다. ④ 뒤의 두 문장은 우리 얼굴에 많은 근육이 있어 감정에 따라 다양한 위치로 움직일 수 있다는 설명을 덧붙인다. 따라서 주어진 문장이 들어가기에 가장 적절한 곳은 ④이다.

- facial expression 얼굴 표정
- clue ⓝ 실마리, 힌트
- spontaneously [ad] 자동적으로
- make a guess 추측하다
- shaky ⓐ 떨리는
- particular ⓐ 특정한, 특별한

구문 풀이

1행 The other main clue [(that) you might use / to tell what a
　　　　　　　　주어　　목적격 관계대명사(생략)　　　～하기 위해
friend is feeling] would be to look at his or her facial expression.
　　　　　　　　　　　동사　　주격 보어(~것)

03 학교 도서관 내 소음 관리
정답률 45% | 정답 ⑤

글의 흐름으로 보아, 주어진 문장이 들어가기에 가장 적절한 곳을 고르시오.

Acoustic concerns in school libraries / are much more important and complex today / than they were in the past.
학교 도서관에서 소리에 대한 염려는 / 오늘날 훨씬 더 중요하고 복잡하다. / 과거보다

① Years ago, / before electronic resources were such a vital part / of the library environment, / we had only to deal with noise / produced by people.
오래 전, / 전자 장비들이 아주 중요한 일부가 되기 전에는 / 도서관 환경의 / 우리는 소음을 처리하기만 하면 되었다. / 사람들이 만들어 내는

② Today, the widespread use of computers, printers, and other equipment / has added machine noise.
오늘날에는, 컴퓨터, 프린터 그리고 다른 장비들의 폭넓은 사용이 / 기계 소음을 더했다.

③ People noise has also increased, / because group work and instruction / are essential parts of the learning process.

사람의 소음도 또한 증가했다. / 집단 활동과 교사의 설명이 / 학습 과정의 필수적인 부분이기 때문에

④ So, the modern school library / is no longer the quiet zone / it once was.
그래서 현대의 학교 도서관은 / 더는 조용한 구역이 아니다. / 예전에 그것이 그랬던 것처럼

✔Yet libraries must still provide quietness / for study and reading, / because many of our students want a quiet study environment.
그러나 도서관은 여전히 조용함을 제공해야 한다. / 공부와 독서를 위해 / 많은 학생들이 조용한 학습 환경을 원하기 때문에

Considering this need for library surroundings, / it is important to design spaces / where unwanted noise can be eliminated / or at least kept to a minimum.
도서관 환경에 대한 이러한 요구를 고려해 볼 때, / 공간을 만드는 것이 중요하다. / 원치 않는 소음이 제거되거나 / 적어도 최소한으로 유지될 수 있는

학교 도서관에서 소리에 대한 염려는 과거보다 오늘날 훨씬 더 중요하고 복잡하다. ① 오래 전, 전자 장비들이 도서관 환경의 아주 중요한 일부가 되기 전에는 사람들이 만들어 내는 소음을 처리하기만 하면 되었다. ② 오늘날에는, 컴퓨터, 프린터 그리고 다른 장비들의 폭넓은 사용이 기계 소음을 더했다. ③ 집단 활동과 교사의 설명이 학습 과정의 필수적인 부분이기 때문에, 사람의 소음도 또한 증가했다. ④ 그래서 현대의 학교 도서관은 더는 예전처럼 조용한 구역이 아니다. ⑤ 그러나 많은 학생들이 조용한 학습 환경을 원하기 때문에, 도서관은 공부와 독서를 위해 여전히 조용함을 제공해야 한다. 도서관 환경에 대한 이러한 요구를 고려해 볼 때, 원치 않는 소음이 제거되거나 적어도 최소한으로 유지될 수 있는 공간을 만드는 것이 중요하다.

Why? 왜 정답일까?

학교 도서관의 환경적인 변화에 관해 설명한 글이다. Today 이하로 ⑤ 앞의 문장까지는 각종 장비가 도서관에 들어오고 집단 활동이나 교사의 설명까지도 도서관에서 이루어지게 되면서, 과거에 비해 도서관이 조용한 공간만일 수는 없음을 이야기한 반면, 주어진 문장에서는 '그럼에도 불구하고' 도서관이 여전히 조용함을 제공할 필요가 있음을 말하고 있다. ⑤ 뒤의 문장은 주어진 문장에 이어 도서관 내 소음을 최소로 유지하려는 노력이 필요함을 이야기한다. 따라서 주어진 문장이 들어가기에 가장 적절한 곳은 ⑤이다.

- quietness ⓝ 조용함
- acoustic ⓐ 소리의, 음향의, 청각의
- electronic ⓐ 전자의
- deal with ~을 처리하다, 다루다
- equipment ⓝ 장비, 용품, 설비
- essential ⓐ 필수적인, 본질적인
- surroundings ⓝ 환경, 주변
- keep to a minimum ~을 최소로 유지하다
- environment ⓝ (주변·자연) 환경
- complex ⓐ 복잡한
- vital ⓐ 필수적인
- widespread ⓐ 폭넓은 광범위한
- instruction ⓝ 설명, 가르침
- no longer 더 이상 ~않다
- unwanted ⓐ 원치 않는, 반갑지 않은

구문 풀이

14행 Considering this need for library surroundings, / it is important
　　　　 ～을 고려할 때　　　～에 대한 요구, 필요　　　　　가주어
to design spaces [where unwanted noise can be eliminated or at least
진주어　　　　　　　　　관계부사　　　　　　　　　　　과거분사1
kept to a minimum].
과거분사2

04 머리카락과 세포가 사후에 자라지 않는 이유
정답률 53% | 정답 ⑤

글의 흐름으로 보아, 주어진 문장이 들어가기에 가장 적절한 곳을 고르시오.

Do hair and fingernails continue to grow / after a person dies?
머리카락과 손톱은 계속해서 자랄까? / 사람이 죽은 뒤에

The short answer is no, / though it may not seem that way to the casual observer.
간단한 대답은 '아니다'이다. / 무심코 보는 사람에게는 그렇게 보이지 않을 수도 있지만

① That's because after death, / the human body dehydrates, / causing the skin to shrink, or become smaller.
이것은 사후에 / 인간 몸은 수분이 빠지는데, / 이는 피부가 수축되게, 즉 더 작아지게 만들기 때문이다.

② This shrinking exposes the parts of the nails and hair / that were once under the skin, / causing them to appear longer than before.
이러한 수축은 손톱과 머리카락의 일부를 노출시켜 / 한때 피부 밑에 있었던 / 이전보다 길어 보이게 만든다.

③ Typically, fingernails grow about 0.1 millimeters a day, / but in order to grow, / they need glucose / — a simple sugar that helps to power the body.
일반적으로, 손톱은 하루에 약 0.1mm씩 자라지만 / 손톱이 자라기 위해서는 / 그들은 글루코오스가 필요하다. / 신체가 작동하도록 도와주는 단당인

④ Once the body dies, / there's no more glucose.
일단 몸이 죽으면 / 더 이상 글루코오스는 없다.

✔So skin cells, hair cells, and nail cells / no longer produce new cells.
따라서 피부 세포, 머리카락 세포, 손톱 세포는 / 더 이상 새로운 세포를 만들어 내지 않는다.

Moreover, / a complex hormonal regulation / directs the growth of hair and nails, / none of which is possible / once a person dies.

더욱이, / 복잡한 호르몬 조절 시스템은 / 머리카락과 손톱의 성장을 지휘하지만 / 그 어떤 것도 가능하지 않다. / 일단 사람이 죽게 되면

사람이 죽은 뒤에 머리카락과 손톱은 계속해서 자랄까? 무심코 보는 사람에게는 그렇게 보이지 않을 수도 있지만, 간단한 대답은 '아니다'이다. ① 사후에 인간 몸은 수분이 빠지는데, 이는 피부가 수축되게, 즉 더 작아지게 만들기 때문이다. ② 이러한 수축은 한때 피부 밑에 있었던 손톱과 머리카락의 일부를 노출시켜 이전보다 길어 보이게 만든다. ③ 일반적으로, 손톱은 하루에 약 0.1mm씩 자라지만 손톱이 자라기 위해서는 신체가 작동하도록 도와주는 단당 글루코오스가 필요하다. ④ 일단 몸이 죽으면 더 이상 글루코오스는 없다. ⑤ 따라서 피부 세포, 머리카락 세포, 손톱 세포는 더 이상 새로운 세포를 만들어 내지 않는다. 더욱이, 복잡한 호르몬 조절 시스템은 머리카락과 손톱의 성장을 지휘하지만 일단 사람이 죽게 되면 그 어떤 것도 가능하지 않다.

Why? 왜 정답일까?

⑤ 앞의 두 문장에서 본래 손톱과 머리카락이 자라려면 글루코오스가 필요한데 사람이 죽고 나면 더 이상의 글루코오스는 없게 된다고 설명한 데 이어, 주어진 문장은 '그렇기 때문에' 피부 세포, 머리카락 세포, 손톱 세포가 새로운 세포를 만드는 것이 불가능해진다는 내용을 제시한다. ⑤ 뒤에서는 사람이 죽고 나면 호르몬 조절 시스템도 일절 작용할 수 없다는 점을 추가로 언급하며 머리카락의 손톱의 성장이 불가능하다는 내용을 다시 한 번 말한다. 따라서 주어진 문장이 들어가기에 가장 적절한 곳은 ⑤이다.

- no longer 더 이상 ~않다
- dehydrate ⓥ 수분이 빠지다, 탈수하다
- expose ⓥ 노출시키다, 드러내다
- typically ⓐ𝖽 일반적으로, 대개
- regulation ⓝ 조절, 통제
- casual ⓐ 대충 하는, 건성의, 일상의
- shrink ⓥ 수축시키다
- appear ⓥ ~하게 보이다, ~인 것 같다
- hormonal ⓐ 호르몬의

구문 풀이

14행 Moreover, a complex hormonal regulation directs the growth
　　　　　　　　　　　　　　　　　　　　　　　　　선행사
of hair and nails, none of which is possible / once a person dies.
　　　　　　　　　　계속적 용법　　　　　　　접속사(일단 ~하면)

05　그림을 나아지게 할 방법　　정답률 54% | 정답 ③

글의 흐름으로 보아, 주어진 문장이 들어가기에 가장 적절한 곳을 고르시오. [3점]

Imagine in your mind / one of your favorite paintings, drawings, cartoon characters / or something equally complex.
마음속으로 그려 보라, / 좋아하는 회화, 소묘, 만화의 등장인물이나 / 그 정도로 복잡한 어떤 것 중 하나를

① Now, / with that picture in your mind, / try to draw what your mind sees.
이제 / 그 그림을 염두에 두고 / 마음이 본 것을 그려 보라.

② Unless you are unusually gifted, / your drawing will look completely different / from what you are seeing / with your mind's eye.
특별하게 재능이 있는 게 아니라면 / 여러분이 그린 그림은 완전히 다르게 보일 것이다. / 여러분이 보고 있는 것과 / 마음의 눈으로

✔However, / if you tried to copy the original / rather than your imaginary drawing, / you might find / your drawing now was a little better.
하지만 / 원본을 베끼려고 애쓴다면 / 마음속에 존재하는 그림보다 / 알게 될 것이다. / 여러분의 그림은 이제 조금 더 나아졌다는 것을

Furthermore, / if you copied the picture many times, / you would find / that each time your drawing would get a little better, / a little more accurate.
게다가 / 그 그림을 여러 번 베낀다면 / 알게 될 것이다. / 매번 여러분의 그림이 조금 더 나아지고 / 조금 더 정확해질 거라는 것을

④ Practice makes perfect.
연습하면 완전해진다.

⑤ This is because you are developing the skills / of coordinating what your mind perceives / with the movement of your body parts.
이것은 능력이 발달되고 있기 때문이다. / 마음이 인식한 것을 조화시키는 / 신체 부위의 움직임과

좋아하는 회화, 소묘, 만화의 등장인물이나 그 정도로 복잡한 어떤 것 중 하나를 마음속으로 그려 보라. ① 이제 그 그림을 염두에 두고 마음이 보는 것을 그리려고 애써 보라. ② 특별하게 재능이 있는 게 아니라면 여러분이 그린 그림은 여러분이 마음의 눈으로 보고 있는 것과 완전히 다르게 보일 것이다. ③ 하지만 상상 속 그림보다 원본을 베끼려고 애쓴다면 여러분은 그림이 이제 조금 더 나아졌다는 것을 알게 될 것이다. 게다가 그 그림을 여러 번 베낀다면 매번 여러분의 그림이 조금 더 나아지고 조금 더 정확해질 거라는 것을 알게 될 것이다. ④ 연습하면 완전해진다. ⑤ 이것은 마음이 인식한 것을 신체 부위의 움직임과 조화시키는 능력이 발달되고 있기 때문이다.

Why? 왜 정답일까?

어떤 원본을 마음으로 상상하며 재현하려 하기보다 실제로 두고 따라 그리는 연습을 할 때 그림이 좋아질 수 있다는 내용을 다룬 글이다. ③ 앞의 문장에서 원본을 마음으로 생각하고 그리면 실제 그림은 원본과 달라진다는 내용을 말한 데 이어, However로 시작하는 주어진 문장은 실제 원본을 놓고 베끼려고 애쓴다면 그림이 나아진다는 반전된 내용을 제시한다. ③ 뒤에서는 보고 그리기를 여러 번 반복할수록 그림이 더 정확해질 것이라는 내용을 이어 간다. 따라서 주어진 문장이 들어가기에 가장 적절한 곳은 ③이다.

- copy ⓥ 베끼다
- drawing ⓝ (색칠을 하지 않은) 그림, 데생
- complex ⓐ 복잡한
- unusually ⓐ𝖽 특별하게
- completely ⓐ𝖽 완전히
- practice ⓝ 연습
- imaginary ⓐ 상상의, 가상적인
- equally ⓐ𝖽 똑같이
- unless ⓒ𝗈𝗇𝗃 ~하지 않는 한
- gifted ⓐ 재능 있는
- accurate ⓐ 정확한
- perceive ⓥ 인지하다, 인식하다

구문 풀이

　　　　　　　　┌ 조건 접속사(~하지 않으면)
7행 Unless you are unusually gifted, your drawing will look
　　　　　현재시제　　　　　　　　　　　　　주어　　　　　　미래시제
completely different from what you are seeing with your mind's eye.
　　형용사 보어　　　　관계대명사(~것)

06　먹이 사슬의 특징　　정답률 58% | 정답 ④

글의 흐름으로 보아, 주어진 문장이 들어가기에 가장 적절한 곳을 고르시오. [3점]

Food chain means the transfer of food energy / from the source in plants / through a series of organisms / with the repeated process of eating and being eaten.
먹이 사슬은 식품 에너지가 이동하는 것을 의미한다. / 식물 안에 있는 에너지원으로부터 / 일련의 유기체를 통해 / 먹고 먹히는 반복되는 과정 속에서

① In a grassland, / grass is eaten by rabbits / while rabbits in turn are eaten by foxes.
초원에서 / 풀은 토끼에게 먹히지만 / 토끼는 이윽고 여우에게 먹힌다.

② This is an example of a simple food chain.
이것은 단순한 먹이 사슬의 예이다.

③ This food chain implies the sequence / in which food energy is transferred / from producer to consumer or higher trophic level.
이 먹이 사슬은 연쇄를 의미한다. / 식품 에너지가 전달되는 / 생산자로부터 소비자 또는 더 높은 영양 수준으로

✔It has been observed / that at each level of transfer, / a large proportion, 80 − 90 percent, of the potential energy / is lost as heat.
관찰되어 왔다. / 각 이동 단계에서 / 잠재적 에너지의 상당한 부분이 80~90%가 / 열로 손실되는 것으로

Hence / the number of steps or links in a sequence / is restricted, / usually to four or five.
그래서 / 하나의 사슬 안에 있는 단계나 연결의 수는 / 제한된다. / 보통 4~5개로

⑤ The shorter the food chain / or the nearer the organism is to the beginning of the chain, / the greater the available energy intake is.
먹이 사슬이 짧을수록 / 또는 유기체가 사슬의 시작 단계에 가까울수록 / 이용 가능한 에너지 섭취량이 더 커진다.

먹이 사슬은 식물 안에 있는 에너지원으로부터 먹고 먹히는 반복되는 과정 속에서 일련의 유기체를 통해 식품 에너지가 이동하는 것을 의미한다. ① 초원에서 풀은 토끼에게 먹히지만 토끼는 이윽고 여우에게 먹힌다. ② 이것은 단순한 먹이 사슬의 예이다. ③ 이 먹이 사슬은 식품 에너지가 생산자로부터 소비자 또는 더 높은 영양 수준으로 전달되는 연쇄를 의미한다. ④ 각 이동 단계에서 잠재적 에너지의 상당한 부분인 80~90%가 열로 손실되는 것으로 관찰되어 왔다. 그래서 하나의 사슬 안에 있는 단계나 연결의 수는 보통 4~5개로 제한된다. ⑤ 먹이 사슬이 짧을수록 또는 유기체가 사슬의 시작 단계(하위 영양 단계)에 가까울수록 이용 가능한 에너지 섭취량이 더 커진다.

Why? 왜 정답일까?

④ 앞의 문장에서 먹이 사슬은 식품 에너지가 생산자에서 소비자로, 즉 더 높은 영양 수준으로 이동하는 연쇄적 과정을 의미하는 것이라고 한다. 이어서 주어진 문장은 먹이 사슬의 각 이동 단계(each level of transfer)에서 에너지의 80~90%가 열로 손실되어 버린다는 사실을 언급한다. ④ 뒤의 문장은 주어진 문장에서 언급된 이유로(Hence) 한 먹이 사슬 안의 단계 수가 4~5개로 제한된다고 설명한다. 따라서 주어진 문장이 들어가기에 가장 적절한 곳은 ④이다.

- transfer ⓝ 이동
- in turn 이윽고, 차례로
- restrict ⓥ 제한하다
- proportion ⓝ 비율
- imply ⓥ 암시하다
- intake ⓝ 섭취량

- **glow** ⓥ 빛나다 ⓝ 빛
- **disgusting** ⓐ 역겨운
- **prey** ⓝ 먹잇감
- **immature** ⓐ 미숙한
- **trait** ⓝ 특성
- **throw up** ⓥ 토하다
- **act as** ⓥ ~의 역할을 하다

구문 풀이

13행 The shorter the food chain or the nearer the organism is to
「the+비교급1 ~
the beginning of the chain, the greater the available energy intake is.
the+비교급2 ~」
「the+비교 … : ~하거나 ~할수록 더 …하다」

---

07   반딧불이가 빛을 내는 이유
정답률 43% | 정답 ⑤

글의 흐름으로 보아, 주어진 문장이 들어가기에 가장 적절한 곳을 고르시오.

Fireflies don't just light up their behinds / to attract mates, / they also glow to tell bats not to eat them.
반딧불이는 단지 꽁무니에 불을 밝히는 것이 아니라, / 짝의 주의를 끌기 위해서 / 박쥐에게 자기들을 먹지 말라고 말하기 위해 빛을 내기도 한다.

This twist in the tale of the trait / that gives fireflies their name / was discovered by Jesse Barber and his colleagues.
특성에 대한 이야기의 이 반전은 / 반딧불이의 이름을 지어주는 / Jesse Barber와 그의 동료들에 의해 발견되었다.

The glow's warning role benefits both fireflies and bats, / because these insects taste disgusting to the mammals.
빛이 하는 경고 역할은 반딧불이와 박쥐 모두에게 유익한데, / 왜냐하면 이 곤충이 그 포유동물(박쥐)에게는 역겨운 맛이 나기 때문이다.

① When swallowed, / chemicals released by fireflies / cause bats to throw them back up.
(반딧불이가) 삼켜지면, / 반딧불이가 배출하는 화학 물질은 / 박쥐가 그것을 다시 토해내게 만든다.

② The team placed eight bats in a dark room / with three or four fireflies / plus three times as many tasty insects, / including beetles and moths, / for four days.
연구팀은 여덟 마리의 박쥐를 어두운 방에 두었다. / 서너 마리의 반딧불이와, / 그보다 수가 세 배가 많은 맛 좋은 곤충들과 함께 / 딱정벌레와 나방을 포함해서 / 나흘 동안

③ During the first night, / all the bats captured at least one firefly.
첫날 밤 동안에, / 모든 박쥐는 적어도 한 마리의 반딧불이를 잡았다.

④ But by the fourth night, / most bats had learned to avoid fireflies / and catch all the other prey instead.
그러나 네 번째 밤에 이르러서는, / 대부분의 박쥐는 반딧불이를 피하고 / 대신 다른 모든 먹이를 잡는 법을 배웠다.

✔ When the team painted fireflies' light organs dark, / a new set of bats took twice / as long to learn to avoid them.
그 팀이 반딧불이에서 빛이 나는 기관을 어둡게 칠했을 때, / 새로운 한 무리의 박쥐는 두 배의 시간이 걸렸다. / 그것들을 피하는 법을 배우는 데

It had long been thought / that firefly bioluminescence mainly acted as a mating signal, / but the new finding explains / why firefly larvae also glow / despite being immature for mating.
오랫동안 생각되었지만, / 반딧불이의 생물 발광(發光)은 주로 짝짓기 신호의 역할을 한다고 / 새로운 연구 결과는 설명해 준다. / 반딧불이 애벌레 역시 빛을 내는 이유를 / 짝짓기를 하기에 미숙함에도 불구하고

반딧불이는 단지 짝의 주의를 끌기 위해서 꽁무니에 불을 밝히는 것이 아니라, 박쥐에게 자기들을 먹지 말라고 말하기 위해 빛을 내기도 한다. 반딧불이의 이름을 지어주는 특성에 대한 이야기의 이 반전은 Jesse Barber와 그의 동료들에 의해 발견되었다. 빛이 하는 경고 역할은 반딧불이와 박쥐 모두에게 유익한데, 왜냐하면 이 곤충이 그 포유동물(박쥐)에게는 역겨운 맛이 나기 때문이다. ① 반딧불이를 삼키면, 반딧불이가 배출하는 화학 물질 때문에 박쥐가 그것을 다시 토해내게 된다. ② 연구팀은 여덟 마리의 박쥐를 서너 마리의 반딧불이와, 딱정벌레와 나방을 포함해서 그보다 수가 세 배가 많은 맛 좋은 곤충들과 함께 어두운 방에 나흘 동안 두었다. ③ 첫날 밤 동안에, 모든 박쥐는 적어도 한 마리의 반딧불이를 잡았다. ④ 그러나 네 번째 밤에 이르러서는, 대부분의 박쥐는 반딧불이를 피하고 대신 다른 모든 먹이를 잡는 법을 배웠다. ⑤ 그 팀이 반딧불이에서 빛이 나는 기관을 어둡게 칠했을 때, 새로운 한 무리의 박쥐는 그것들을 피하는 법을 배우는 데 두 배의 시간이 걸렸다. 오랫동안 반딧불이의 생물 발광(發光)은 주로 짝짓기 신호의 역할을 한다고 생각되었지만, 새로운 연구 결과는 짝짓기를 하기에 미숙함에도 불구하고 반딧불이 애벌레 역시 빛을 내는 이유를 설명해 준다.

Why? 왜 정답일까?

반딧불이가 박쥐에게 먹히지 않기 위해 빛을 낸다는 사실을 실험의 예로 설명하고 있는 글이다. ⑤ 앞에서 실험이 시작된 후 나흘째 밤이 되자 박쥐가 반딧불이를 피하고 다른 먹이만을 잡았다고 언급하는데, 주어진 문장에서는 이어서 연구자들이 반딧불이의 몸에서 빛이 나는 기관을 까맣게 칠하자 박쥐가 반딧불이를 피하기까지 두 배의 시간이 들었다고 서술한다. ⑤ 뒤에서는 주어진 문장까지의 내용을 바탕으로 반딧불이가 짝짓기 목적만이 아닌, 추가적인 이유로 빛을 내는 것이라는 결론을 도출한다. 따라서 주어진 문장이 들어가기에 가장 적절한 곳은 ⑤이다.

구문 풀이

10행 When swallowed, chemicals released by fireflies cause bats
접속사   분사구문   주어   과거분사   「cause+목적어+
to throw them back up.
to부정사 : ~이 …하게 야기하다」

★★★ 1등급 대비 고난도 2점 문제

08   공동체 형성 방식으로서의 토론
정답률 24% | 정답 ⑤

글의 흐름으로 보아, 주어진 문장이 들어가기에 가장 적절한 곳을 고르시오.

The way we communicate / influences our ability / to build strong and healthy communities.
우리가 의사소통하는 방식은 / 우리의 능력에 영향을 미친다. / 강하고 건강한 공동체를 만드는

Traditional ways of building communities / have emphasized debate and argument.
공동체를 만드는 전통적인 방식은 / 토론과 논쟁을 강조해왔다.

① For example, / the United States has a strong tradition / of using town hall meetings / to deliberate important issues within communities.
예를 들어, / 미국은 확고한 전통을 갖고 있다. / 타운홀 미팅을 활용하는 / 공동체 내의 중요한 쟁점들을 숙고하기 위해

② In these settings, / advocates for each side of the issue / present arguments for their positions, / and public issues have been discussed / in such public forums.
이러한 환경에서 / 쟁점의 각 입장에 있는 옹호자들이 / 자신의 입장에 대한 논거들을 제시하고, / 공공의 쟁점들이 논의되었다. / 그러한 공개적인 토론회에서

③ Yet for debate and argument to work well, / people need to come to such forums / with similar assumptions and values.
그러나 토론과 논쟁이 효력을 잘 발휘하기 위해서는 / 사람들이 그러한 토론회에 올 필요가 있다. / 비슷한 가정과 가치를 가지고

④ The shared assumptions and values / serve as a foundation for the discussion.
공유된 가정과 가치가 / 논의를 위한 기반의 역할을 한다.

✔ However, / as society becomes more diverse, / the likelihood / that people share assumptions and values / diminishes.
하지만 / 사회가 더욱 다양해짐에 따라, / 가능성은 / 사람들이 가정과 가치를 공유할 / 줄어든다.

As a result, / forms of communication / such as argument and debate / become polarized, / which may drive communities apart / as opposed to bringing them together.
결과적으로, / 의사소통의 형태는 / 논쟁과 토론 같은 / 양극화되고, / 이것은 멀어지도록 몰아갈 수 있다. / 공동체를 결합하는 것이 아니라

우리가 의사소통하는 방식은 강하고 건강한 공동체를 만드는 우리의 능력에 영향을 미친다. 공동체를 만드는 전통적인 방식은 토론과 논쟁을 강조해왔다. ① 예를 들어, 미국은 공동체 내의 중요한 쟁점들을 숙고하기 위해 타운홀 미팅을 활용하는 확고한 전통을 갖고 있다. ② 이러한 환경에서 쟁점의 각 입장에 있는 옹호자들이 자신의 입장에 대한 논거들을 제시하고, 공공의 쟁점들이 그러한 공개적인 토론회에서 논의되었다. ③ 그러나 토론과 논쟁이 효력을 잘 발휘하기 위해서는 사람들이 비슷한 가정과 가치를 가지고 그러한 토론회에 올 필요가 있다. ④ 공유된 가정과 가치가 논의를 위한 기반의 역할을 한다. ⑤ 하지만 사회가 더욱 다양해짐에 따라, 사람들이 가정과 가치를 공유할 가능성은 줄어든다. 결과적으로 논쟁과 토론 같은 의사소통의 형태는 양극화되고, 이것은 공동체를 결합하는 것이 아니라 멀어지도록 몰아갈 수 있다.

Why? 왜 정답일까?

공동체를 형성하는 방식으로서 토론과 논쟁의 역할에 대해 설명한 글로, ⑤ 앞에서는 공유된 가정과 가치가 그 기반을 이룰 때 토론이 제대로 기능할 수 있다는 점을 언급하는데 ⑤ 뒤에서는 이로 인해 의사소통이 양극화된 형태로 나타날 수 있다는 내용이 나온다. **However**로 시작하는 주어진 문장은 사회의 다양화로 공유된 가치나 가정을 가질 가능성이 줄어든다는 내용이므로 흐름이 반전되는 ⑤에 들어가는 것이 자연스럽다. 따라서 주어진 문장이 들어가기에 가장 적절한 곳은 ⑤이다.

- **diverse** ⓐ 다양한
- **assumption** ⓝ 가정, 추정
- **emphasize** ⓥ 강조하다
- **advocate** ⓝ 옹호자
- **polarize** ⓥ 양극화를 초래하다, 양극화되다
- **as opposed to** ~이 아니라, ~와는 대조적으로
- **likelihood** ⓝ 가능성
- **diminish** ⓥ 줄어들다, 감소하다
- **deliberate** ⓥ 숙고하다, 신중히 생각하다
- **serve as** ~의 역할을 하다, ~로 기능하다
- **drive apart** ~을 멀어지게 하다

구문 풀이

16행 As a result, forms of communication such as argument and
　　　　　　주어(복수)
debate become polarized, which may drive communities apart
　동사　　주격 보어　계속적 용법(앞의 절)　~을 멀어지게 하다
as opposed to bringing them together.
「as opposed to+동명사 : ~이 아니라」

★★ 문제 해결 꿀~팁 ★★

▶ 많이 틀린 이유는?

토론의 공동체 형성 기능을 다룬 추상적인 지문으로, 논리적 공백에 주목하지 않으면 오답을 고르기 쉽다. 최다 오답인 ④ 앞뒤의 문장은 '비슷한 가정과 가치관'을 공통된 소재로 다루며, 서로 가정과 가치관이 공유되어야 이것이 건전한 토론의 기반 역할을 할 수 있다는 일관된 내용을 전개하고 있다. 즉 ④는 논리적 공백이 발생하는 지점이 아니므로 주어진 문장이 들어가기에 적절하지 않다.

▶ 문제 해결 방법은?

문장 삽입 문제에서는 항상 주어진 문장을 먼저 읽고 글의 흐름을 예상하도록 한다. 주어진 문장에 However가 있으므로, 앞에는 공유된 가치나 가치관이 비교적 정립된 경우가 언급될 것이고, 뒤에는 이 정립이 잘 이루어지지 않아 공동체 의사소통이 원활하지 않다는 내용이 연결될 것이다.

★★★ 1등급 대비 고난도 2점 문제

09 어린이와 함께 음악을 즐기는 것 　　　 정답률 40% | 정답 ④

> 글의 흐름으로 보아, 주어진 문장이 들어가기에 가장 적절한 곳을 고르시오.

Music appeals powerfully to young children.
음악은 어린 아이들에게 강력하게 어필한다.

① Watch preschoolers' faces and bodies / when they hear rhythm and sound / — they light up and move eagerly and enthusiastically.
미취학 어린이들의 얼굴과 몸을 살펴보아라. / 그들이 리듬과 소리를 들을 때 / 그들은 밝아지고 열렬히 열정적으로 움직인다.

② They communicate comfortably, / express themselves creatively, / and let out all sorts of thoughts and emotions / as they interact with music.
그들은 편안하게 의사소통하고, / 창의적으로 자신을 표현하고, / 모든 생각과 감정을 분출해 낸다. / 그들이 음악과 상호작용하면서

③ In a word, / young children think / music is a lot of fun, / so do all you can / to make the most of the situation.
한마디로, / 어린 아이들은 생각하므로, / 음악이 아주 재미있다고 / 당신이 할 수 있는 모든 것을 하라. / 이 상황을 최대로 활용하기 위해

✔ Throw away your own hesitation / and forget all your concerns / about whether you are musically talented / or whether you can sing or play an instrument.
망설임을 버리고 / 걱정을 모두 잊어라. / 당신이 음악적으로 재능이 있는가 / 혹은 노래를 하거나 악기를 연주할 수 있는가에 대한

They don't matter / when you are enjoying music with your child.
그것들은 중요하지 않다. / 당신이 아이와 함께 음악을 즐길 때

⑤ Just follow his or her lead, / have fun, / sing songs together, / listen to different kinds of music, / move, dance, and enjoy.
그저 아이의 리드를 따라가며, / 즐기고, / 함께 노래하고, / 다양한 종류의 음악을 들으며, / 움직이고 춤추고 즐겨라.

음악은 어린 아이들에게 강력하게 어필한다. ① 미취학 어린이들이 리듬과 소리를 들을 때 그들의 얼굴과 몸을 살펴보아라. 밝아지고 열렬히 열정적으로 움직인다. ② 음악과 상호작용하면서 그들은 편안하게 의사소통하고, 창의적으로 자신을 표현하고, 모든 생각과 감정을 분출해 낸다. ③ 한마디로, 어린 아이들은 음악이 아주 재미있다고 생각하므로, 이 상황을 최대로 활용하기 위해 당신이 할 수 있는 모든 것을 하라. ④ 망설임을 버리고 당신이 음악적으로 재능이 있는가 혹은 노래를 하거나 악기를 연주할 수 있는가에 대한 걱정을 모두 잊어라. 그것들은 당신이 아이와 함께 음악을 즐길 때 중요하지 않다. ⑤ 그저 아이의 리드를 따라가며, 즐기고, 함께 노래하고, 다양한 종류의 음악을 들으며, 움직이고 춤추고 즐겨라.

Why? 왜 정답일까?

④ 앞의 문장에서 언급한 'all you can'에 대한 예시가 주어진 문장에서 제시되고 있다. 또한 ④ 뒤의 문장에서는 주어진 문장에서 예로 든 다양한 '걱정'을 They로 받으며 이것들이 아이들과 음악을 즐길 때 그다지 중요하지 않다는 점을 언급한다. 따라서 주어진 문장이 들어가기에 가장 적절한 곳은 ④이다.

어휘

- hesitation ⓝ 망설임, 주저함
- appeal to ~에 어필하다, ~에 호소하다
- light up (안색이) 밝아지다
- enthusiastically ⓐ 열정적으로
- comfortably ⓐ 편안하게
- creatively ⓐ 창의적으로
- make the most of ~을 최대한 활용하다
- talented ⓐ 재능이 있는
- preschooler ⓝ 미취학 아동
- eagerly ⓐ 열렬히
- communicate ⓥ 의사소통하다
- express ⓥ 나타내다, 표현하다
- interact with ~와 상호작용하다
- matter ⓥ (사건, 일 등이) 중요하다

구문 풀이

11행 In a word, / young children think music is a lot of fun, / so do
　　　　　한 마디로(요약)　　　　　　(접속사 that 생략)┘ 　　　명령문
all you can to make the most of the situation.
　목적어　　　　부사적 용법(~하기 위해)

★★ 문제 해결 꿀~팁 ★★

▶ 많이 틀린 이유는?

대명사의 쓰임에 유의하지 않으면 자칫 오답을 고르기 쉬운 문제였다. ④에 주어진 문장을 넣지 않는다면 ④ 뒤의 They는 'young children'일 수밖에 없는데, 이렇게 되면 '어린 아이들은 당신이 아이와 함께 음악을 즐길 때 중요하지 않다'라는 의미상 모순이 생기고 만다. 문법적으로도 matter는 주로 사물 주어를 취하여 '(어떤 일이나 사안이) 중요하다'라는 뜻으로 쓰인다는 점을 기억해 둔다.

▶ 문제 해결 방법은?

주어진 문장에 역접의 연결사가 있으면 본문 중 흐름 반전의 포인트를 잡아 주어진 문장을 넣으면 되지만, 이 문제에서 본문은 하나의 논지만을 일관되게 말하고 있다. 이 경우는 대명사가 풀이에 절대적 힌트를 제공하므로, '단수 명사 – 단수 대명사, 복수 명사 – 복수 대명사'의 연결고리를 하나씩 체크하며 꼼꼼하게 독해하도록 한다.

★★★ 1등급 대비 고난도 2점 문제

10 각종 동식물에 대한 태도 차이 　　 정답률 39% | 정답 ⑤

> 글의 흐름으로 보아, 주어진 문장이 들어가기에 가장 적절한 곳을 고르시오.

The natural world provides a rich source of symbols / used in art and literature.
자연계는 상징의 풍부한 원천을 제공한다. / 예술과 문학에서 사용되는

① Plants and animals are central / to mythology, dance, song, poetry, rituals, festivals, and holidays around the world.
식물과 동물은 중심에 있다. / 전 세계의 신화, 춤, 노래, 시, 의식, 축제 그리고 기념일의

② Different cultures can exhibit opposite attitudes / toward a given species.
각기 다른 문화는 상반되는 태도를 보일 수 있다. / 주어진 종에 대해

③ Snakes, for example, / are honored by some cultures / and hated by others.
예를 들어, 뱀은 / 일부 문화에서는 존경의 대상이고 / 다른 문화에서는 증오를 받는다.

④ Rats are considered pests in much of Europe and North America / and greatly respected in some parts of India.
쥐는 유럽과 북아메리카의 많은 지역에서 유해 동물로 여겨지고, / 인도의 일부 지역에서는 매우 중시된다.

✔ Of course, within cultures / individual attitudes can vary dramatically.
물론 (같은) 문화 내에서 / 개인의 태도는 극적으로 다를 수 있다.

For instance, in Britain many people dislike rodents, / and yet there are several associations / devoted to breeding them, / including the National Mouse Club and the National Fancy Rat Club.
예를 들어, 영국에서는 많은 사람들이 설치류를 싫어하지만, / 여러 협회들이 있다. / 그들을 기르는 데 전념하는 / National Mouse Club과 National Fancy Rat Club을 포함해서

자연계는 예술과 문학에서 사용되는 상징의 풍부한 원천을 제공한다. ① 식물과 동물은 전 세계의 신화, 춤, 노래, 시, 의식, 축제 그리고 기념일의 중심에 있다. ② 각기 다른 문화는 주어진 종에 대해 상반되는 태도를 보일 수 있다. ③ 예를 들어, 뱀은 일부 문화에서는 존경의 대상이고 다른 문화에서는 증오를 받는다. ④ 쥐는 유럽과 북아메리카의 많은 지역에서 유해 동물로 여겨지고, 인도의 일부 지역에서는 매우 중시된다. ⑤ 물론 (같은) 문화 내에서 개인의 태도는 극적으로 다를 수 있다. 예를 들어, 영국에서는 많은 사람들이 설치류를 싫어하지만, National Mouse Club과 National Fancy Rat Club을 포함해서 설치류를 기르는 데 전념하는 여러 협회들이 있다.

Why? 왜 정답일까?

각종 자연물에 대한 태도 차이를 설명한 글로, ⑤ 앞의 문장에서는 쥐가 유럽과 북미 등지에서는 유해한 동물로, 인도 일부 지역에서는 매우 귀중한 동물로 여겨진다는 점을 대조하여 설명하고 있다. 주어진 문장은 이에 추가적으로 같은 문화권 내에서 개인의 태도 또한 다를 수 있다는 점을 언급하고, ⑤ 뒤에서는 영국의 예를 들어 많은 사람들이 설치

류를 싫어하지만 설치류를 기르기 위해 전념하는 여러 협회들이 또한 있다는 내용을 부연한다. 따라서 주어진 문장이 들어가기에 가장 적절한 곳은 ⑤이다.

- **dramatically** ad 극적으로
- **mythology** n 신화
- **exhibit** v 보여주다, 전시하다
- **given** a (이미)정해진; 특정한
- **association** n 협회, 연관
- **literature** n 문학
- **ritual** n 의식
- **opposite** a 정반대의
- **honor** v 존경하다
- **breed** v 기르다, 낳다

구문 풀이

10행 Rats are considered pests in much of Europe and North
「A+be considered+B : A가 B로 간주되다」
America and (are) greatly respected in some parts of India.
생략

★★ 문제 해결 꿀~팁 ★★

▶ 많이 틀린 이유는?
② 앞의 두 문장은 자연계의 대상들이 세계 각지의 예술과 문학에 핵심적인 역할을 했다는 넓은 내용을, ② 뒤의 문장은 특히 한 자연물에 대해서도 문화권마다 시각이 다르다는 좁은 내용을 제시한다. ③ 뒤의 문장은 이 좁혀진 내용에 대한 예를 제시하므로, ②와 ③ 앞뒤는 흐름이 자연스럽게 이어진다.

▶ 문제 해결 방법은?
Of course로 시작하는 주어진 문장은 '물론 한 문화권 내에서도' 사람따라 반응이 다르다는 내용을 이어 가고 있다. 따라서 앞에서 각 문화권의 시각 차이에 대한 언급이 마무리되고, 한 나라 안에서도 같은 대상에 대한 서로 다른 입장이 존재한다는 예로 넘어가는 ⑤에 주어진 문장이 들어가야 한다.

★★★ 1등급 대비 고난도 3점 문제

11 정확한 온도 측정 정답률 42% | 정답 ⑤

글의 흐름으로 보아, 주어진 문장이 들어가기에 가장 적절한 곳을 고르시오. [3점]

We often associate the concept of temperature / with how hot or cold an object feels / when we touch it.
우리는 흔히 온도 개념을 연관 짓는다. / 얼마나 뜨겁게 또는 차갑게 느껴지는지와 / 우리가 물건을 만졌을 때
In this way, / our senses provide us / with a qualitative indication of temperature.
이런 식으로, / 우리의 감각은 우리에게 제공한다. / 온도의 정성적 지표를
① Our senses, / however, / are unreliable / and often mislead us.
우리의 감각은 / 그러나, / 신뢰할 수 없으며 / 종종 우리를 잘못 인도한다.
② For example, / if you stand in bare feet / with one foot on carpet / and the other on a tile floor, / the tile feels colder than the carpet *even though both are at the same temperature.*
예를 들어, / 여러분이 맨발로 서 있다면, / 한쪽 발은 카펫 위에, / 다른 한쪽 발은 타일 바닥 위에 놓고 / 카펫보다 타일이 더 차갑게 느껴질 것이다. / 둘 다 같은 온도임에도 불구하고
③ The two objects feel different / because tile transfers energy by heat / at a higher rate than carpet does.
그 두 물체는 다르게 느껴진다. / 타일이 에너지를 열의 형태로 전달하기 때문에 / 카펫보다 더 높은 비율로
④ Your skin "measures" the rate of energy transfer by heat / rather than the actual temperature.
여러분의 피부는 열에너지 전도율을 '측정한다'. / 실제 온도보다는
✔ What we need / is a reliable and reproducible method / for measuring the relative hotness or coldness of objects / rather than the rate of energy transfer.
우리가 필요로 하는 것은 / 신뢰할 수 있고 재현 가능한 수단이다. / 물체의 상대적인 뜨거움과 차가움을 측정하기 위한 / 에너지 전도율보다는
Scientists have developed a variety of thermometers / for making such quantitative measurements.
과학자들은 다양한 온도계를 개발해 왔다. / 그런 정량적인 측정을 하기 위해

우리는 흔히 물건을 만졌을 때 얼마나 뜨겁게 또는 차갑게 느껴지는지를 온도 개념과 연관 짓는다. 이런 식으로, 우리의 감각은 우리에게 온도의 정성적 지표를 제공한다. ① 그러나, 우리의 감각은 신뢰할 수 없으며 종종 우리를 잘못 인도한다. ② 예를 들어, 여러분이 맨발로 한쪽 발은 카펫 위에, 다른 한쪽 발은 타일 바닥 위에 놓고 서 있다면, 둘 다 같은 온도임에도 불구하고 카펫보다 타일이 더 차갑게 느껴질 것이다. ③ 타일이 카펫보다 더 높은 비율로 에너지를 열의 형태로 전달하기 때문에 그 두 물체는 다르게 느껴진다. ④ 여러분의 피부는 실제 온도보다는 열에너지 전도율을 '측정한다'. ⑤ 우리가 필요로 하는 것은 에너지 전도율보다는 물체의 상대적인 뜨거움과 차가움을 측정하기 위한 신뢰할 수 있고 재현 가능한 수단이다. 과학자들은 그런 정량적인 측정을 하기 위해 다양한 온도계를 개발해 왔다.

우리의 감각은 온도에 대한 정성적 지표를 제공하기는 하지만 완전히 정확한 정보를 주지는 못한다는 내용의 글로, ⑤ 앞의 문장은 이것이 피부가 실제 온도보다는 열에너지 전도율을 측정하기 때문이라고 설명한다. 한편 주어진 문장에서는 이 상황에서 우리에게 필요한 것이 상대적 온도를 신뢰도 높게 측정할 수 있는 도구라고 언급하고, ⑤ 뒤에서는 이 도구가 바로 정량적 측정이 가능한 온도계라고 밝힌다. 따라서 주어진 문장이 들어가기에 가장 적절한 곳은 ⑤이다.

- **reproducible** a 재현 가능한
- **qualitative** a 정성적인, 질적인
- **bare** a 맨, 벌거벗은
- **energy transfer** 에너지 전도
- **mislead** v 잘못 이끌다
- **quantitative** a 성냥석인

구문 풀이

13행 The two objects feel different because tile transfers energy
감각동사 형용사 보어
by heat at a higher rate than carpet does.
대동사(= transfers)

★★ 문제 해결 꿀~팁 ★★

▶ 많이 틀린 이유는?
③, ④가 헷갈리므로 하나씩 살펴보자. 먼저 ③ 앞은 서로 온도가 같은 타일과 카펫이 '다르게' 느껴진다는 예를 드는데, ③ 뒤는 그것이 '열에너지 전도율의 차이' 때문이라고 설명한다. 이어서 ④ 뒤도 우리 피부가 실제 온도보다는 '열에너지 전도율'에 집중한다고 한다. 즉, ③~④ 앞뒤 문장들은 지시어나 연결어의 공백 없이 모두 자연스럽게 연결된다.

▶ 문제 해결 방법은?
⑤ 앞에서 우리가 측정하는 것이 '열에너지 전도율'이라고 언급한 데 이어서, 주어진 문장은 '이것 말고 우리에게 실제 필요한 것'이 무엇인지 언급하고 있다. 그것이 바로 주어진 문장에서 언급한, '물체의 상대적 온도를 신뢰성 있게 측정할 수 있는 수단'인데, ⑤ 뒤에서는 '그래서' 온도계가 개발되었다는 결론을 제시하고 있다.

★★★ 1등급 대비 고난도 3점 문제

12 현지 환경을 미리 조사하고 대비하기 정답률 54% | 정답 ④

글의 흐름으로 보아, 주어진 문장이 들어가기에 가장 적절한 곳을 고르시오. [3점]

The continued survival of the human race / can be explained / by our ability to adapt to our environment.
인류의 지속적인 생존은 / 설명될 수 있을 것이다. / 환경에 적응하는 우리의 능력으로
① While we may have lost some of our ancient ancestors' survival skills, / we have learned new skills / as they have become necessary.
우리가 고대 조상들의 생존 기술 중 일부를 잃어버렸을지도 모르지만, / 우리는 새로운 기술을 배웠다. / 새로운 기술이 필요해지면서
② Today, / the gap / between the skills we once had / and the skills we now have / grows ever wider / as we rely more heavily on modern technology.
오늘날 / 한때 우리가 가졌던 기술과 / 현재 우리가 가진 기술 사이의 / 어느 때보다 더 커졌다. / 우리가 현대 기술에 더 크게 의존함에 따라
③ Therefore, / when you head off into the wilderness, / it is important / to fully prepare for the environment.
그러므로, / 여러분이 미지의 땅으로 향할 때에는 / 중요하다. / 그 환경에 대해 충분히 준비하는 것이
✔ Before a trip, / research / how the native inhabitants dress, work, and eat.
떠나기 전에, / 조사하라. / 토착 주민들이 어떻게 옷을 입고 일하고 먹는지를
How they have adapted to their way of life / will help you to understand the environment / and allow you to select the best gear / and learn the correct skills.
그들이 어떻게 자신들의 생활 방식에 적응했는가는 / 여러분이 그 환경을 이해하도록 도울 것이고, / 여러분이 최선의 장비를 선별하도록 해 줄 것이다. / 그리고 적절한 기술을 배우도록
⑤ This is crucial / because most survival situations arise / as a result of a series of events / that could have been avoided.
이것은 중요하다. / 생존이 걸린 대부분의 상황이 발생하기 때문에 / 일련의 사건의 결과로 / 피할 수도 있었던

인류의 지속적인 생존은 환경에 적응하는 우리의 능력으로 설명될 수 있을 것이다. ① 우리가 고대 조상들의 생존 기술 중 일부를 잃어버렸을지도 모르지만, 새로운 기술이 필요해지면서 우리는 새로운 기술을 배웠다. ② 오늘날 우리가 현대 기술에 더 크게 의존함에 따라 한때 우리가 가졌던 기술과 현재 우리가 가진 기술 사이의 간극이 어느 때보다 더 커졌다. ③ 그러므로, 미지의 땅으로 향할 때에는 그 환경에 대해 충분히 준비하는 것이 중요하다. ④ 떠나기 전에, 토착 주민들이 어떻게 옷을 입고 일하고 먹는지를 조사하라. 그들이 어떻게 자신들의 생활 방식에 적응했는가는 여러분이 그 환경을 이해하도록 도

[문제편 p.131]

올 것이고, 여러분이 최선의 장비를 선별하고 적절한 기술을 배우도록 해 줄 것이다. ⑤ 생존이 걸린 대부분의 상황이 피할 수도 있었던 일련의 사건의 결과로 발생하기 때문에 이것은 중요하다.

Why? 왜 정답일까?

④ 앞의 두 문장에서 현대 기술에 대한 우리의 의존도가 높아짐에 따라 과거의 기술과 오늘날의 기술 간에 격차가 더 벌어졌으므로 잘 모르는 곳에 갈 때에는 그 환경에 대한 충분한 준비가 필요하다고 언급한다. 이에 대한 구체적인 조언으로서 주어진 문장은 떠나기 전 '토착 주민'의 옷, 음식, 일하는 문화 등을 조사하라고 언급한다. ④ 뒤의 문장은 주어진 문장의 '토착 주민'을 they로 언급하며 이들이 나름의 삶의 방식에 어떻게 적응해 있는지를 파악하면 그 환경을 이해하는 데 도움이 될 것이라고 설명한다. 따라서 주어진 문장이 들어가기에 가장 적절한 곳은 ④이다.

- adapt to ~에 적응하다
- rely on ~에 의존하다
- wilderness ⓝ 황무지
- arise ⓥ 발생하다, 일어나다
- ancestor ⓝ 조상
- heavily ⓐⓓ 심하게, 많이
- crucial ⓐ 매우 중요한
- as a result of ~의 결과로

구문 풀이

12행 How they have adapted to their way of life will help you
주어(간접의문문 : 어떻게 ~하는지)   「help + 목적어 +
to understand the environment and allow you to select the best gear
to부정사 : ~이 …하는 데 도움이 되다」
and (to) learn the correct skills.
└───→「allow + 목적어 + to부정사 : ~이 …하게 하다」

★★ 문제 해결 꿀~팁 ★★

▶ 많이 틀린 이유는?
인간은 환경에 맞추어 계속 적응하고 변하는데, 오늘날 인간은 기술에 대한 의존도가 커서 과거와의 간극이 더욱 벌어졌기에 미지의 땅으로 나아갈 때에는 항상 환경에 대한 대비와 조사가 필요하다는 내용의 글이다. 특히 최다 오답인 ③ 앞뒤로 '과거 기술과 현대 기술의 간극이 커져서 → 새로운 땅으로 갈 때 환경을 잘 알아봐야 한다'라는 내용이 적절한 인과 관계로 연결되어 있다. 따라서 주어진 문장을 ③에 넣는 것은 부적절하다.

▶ 문제 해결 방법은?
④ 뒤의 문장에 they가 나오므로 앞에서 they로 받을 만한 복수 명사가 언급되어야 한다. ④ 앞의 문장에는 적절한 복수 명사가 없는 반면, 주어진 문장에는 the native inhabitants가 있다. 따라서 이 they에 '토착 주민'을 넣어서 읽어 보고 맥락이 자연스러운지 확인해 보면 답을 찾을 수 있다.

수능 내신 1등급 대비 전국연합 학력평가

20일 완성 영어독해

기본

The Real series ipsifly provide
questions in previous real test and you can
practice as real college scholastic ability test.

하루 20분! 20일 완성!

영어 독해
빈칸·순서·삽입
기본

영어 독해
빈칸·순서·삽입
완성

영어 독해
빈칸·순서·삽입
실전

**Believe in
yourself and
show us what
you can do!**

자신을 믿고 자신의 능력을 당당히 보여주자.

리얼 오리지널 하루 20분 20일 완성 | 영어 독해 | 빈칸·순서·삽입 [기본]

발행처 수능 모의고사 전문 출판 입시플라이 **발행일** 2024년 6월 1일 **등록번호** 제 2017-22호
홈페이지 www.ipsifly.com **대표전화** 02-433-9979 **구입문의** 02-433-9975 **팩스** 02-6305-9907
발행인 조용규 **편집책임** 양창열 김유 이혜민 임명선 김선영 **물류관리** 김소희 이혜리 **주소** 서울특별시 중랑구 용마산로 615 정민빌딩 3층

※ 페이지가 누락되었거나 파손된 교재는 구입하신 곳에서 교환해 드립니다. ※ 발간 이후 발견되는 오류는 입시플라이 홈페이지 정오표를 통해서 알려드립니다.